THE BEST PLAYS OF 1980–1981

THE
BURNS MANTLE
YEARBOOK

THE
BEST PLAYS
OF 1980-1981

EDITED BY OTIS L. GUERNSEY JR.

*Illustrated with photographs and
with drawings by* HIRSCHFELD

DODD, MEAD & COMPANY
NEW YORK • TORONTO

"Chekhov in Yalta (Featuring a Rare and Delightful Visit by the Moscow Art Theartre)": by John Driver and Jeffrey Haddow. Copyright ©1978 by John Driver and Jeffrey Haddow. Reprinted by permission of the authors. See CAUTION notice below. All inquiries should be addressed to the author's agent: William Craver, Helen Merrill Agency, 337 West 22nd Street, New York, N.Y. 10011.

"A Life": by Hugh Leonard. Copyright ©1980 by Hugh Leonard. Reprinted by permission of Atheneum Publishers, Inc. See CAUTION notice below. All inquiries concerning publication rights should be addressed to: Atheneum Publishers, Inc., 597 Fifth Avenue, New York, N.Y. 10017. All other inquiries should be addressed to: William Morris Agency, Inc., 1350 Avenue of the Americas, New York, N.Y. 10019.

"Lunch Hour": by Jean Kerr. Copyright ©1981 by Collin Productions, Inc., Jean Kerr, President. Reprinted by permission of Doubleday & Company, Inc. See CAUTION notice below. All inquiries should be addressed to: Doubleday & Company, Inc., 245 Park Avenue, New York, N.Y. 10017.

"A Lesson From Aloes": by Athol Fugard. Copyright ©1981 by Athol Fugard. Reprinted by permission of Random House, Inc. See CAUTION notice below. All inquiries concerning publication rights should be addressed to: Random House, Inc., 201 East 50th Street, New York, N.Y. 10022. All other inquiries should be addressed to the author's representative: Esther Sherman, William Morris Agency, Inc., 1350 Avenue of the Americas, New York, N.Y. 10019.

"Zooman and the Sign": by Charles Fuller. Copyright ©1979, 1981 by Charles Fuller. Reprinted by permission of the author. See CAUTION notice below. All inquiries concerning stock and amateur production rights should be addressed to: Samuel French, Inc., 25 West 45th Street, New York, N.Y. 10036. All other inquiries should be addressed to the author's representative: Esther Sherman, William Morris Agency, Inc., 1350 Avenue of the Americas, New York, N.Y. 10019.

"Amadeus": by Peter Shaffer. Copyright ©1980, 1981 by Peter L. Shaffer. Reprinted by permission of Harper and Row, Publishers, Inc. See CAUTION notice below. All inquiries concerning publication rights should be addressed to: Harper and Row, Publishers, Inc., 10 East 53rd Street, New York, N.Y. 10022. All other inquiries should be addressed to the author's agent: The Lantz Office, Inc., 888 Seventh Avenue, New York, N.Y. 10019.

"Crimes of the Heart": by Beth Henley. Copyright ©1981 by Beth Henley. Reprinted by permission of the author. See CAUTION notice below. Publisher of the complete play: Viking Penguin, Inc., 625 Madison Avenue, New York, N.Y. 10022. All inquiries should be addressed to the author's representative: William Morris Agency, Inc., 1350 Avenue of the Americas, New York, N.Y. 10019.

"Translations": by Brian Friel. Copyright ©1980 by Brian Friel. Reprinted by permission of International Creative Management. See CAUTION notice below. Inquiries concerning stock and amateur production rights in the United States and Canada should be addressed to: Samuel French, Inc., 25 West 45th Street, New York, N.Y. 10036. All other inquiries should be addressed to the author's representative: Bridget Aschenberg, International Creative Management, 40 West 57th Street, New York, N.Y. 10019.

EDITOR'S NOTE

WE ARE PROUD OF OUR TRADITIONAL EMBELLISHMENTS in this, the 62nd volume in the *Best Plays* series; embellishments like the synopses of the Best Plays themselves; Al Hirschfeld's drawings of the main events of the theater year, which grace and enliven these pages; the examples of outstanding costume and scenic design; the wide-ranging photographs; the statistical data; the reports on plays in New York and around the country. Most of all, though, we're proud of the *completeness* of our listing of 1980–81 productions on Broadway, off Broadway, off off Broadway and in regional theater. Our *Best Plays* listings are complete where completeness is possible; and where it is not, owing to conflicts and uncertainties of definition, they are as comprehensive a reference as any anywhere. This is admirably true, for example, of Camille Croce's list of plays produced off off Broadway, an area whose very great importance to the whole theater scene was emphasized this year when an OOB play, Beth Henley's *Crimes of the Heart*, was awarded both the Pulitzer Prize and the Critics Award for best American play.

The cross-country theater is again covered in full breadth by Ella A. Malin's listing of theater programs in LORT theaters, and in depth with the assistance of the American Theater Critics Association committee, chaired by Dan Sullivan of the Los Angeles *Times*, which covers the professional production of new plays from coast to coast and provides brief reviews of the standouts. The ATCA committee also selects one of these to be fully synopsized in the manner of the New York Best Plays. This year the critics' choice is *Chekhov in Yalta* by John Driver and Jeffrey Haddow.

Major New York cast replacements and touring leads come under the scrutiny of Stanley Green for his annual listing in these volumes, while Rue Canvin assembles the necrology, publication and other data, and William Schelble supplies the Tony Awards information. The present editor, the fifth in the line of those who have overseen this series of theater yearbooks, reports on the Broadway and off-Broadway scene, selects the Best Plays and prepares their synopses, assembles the facts of New York production with the painstaking support of a willing wife, and in general plans and executes this many-faceted enterprise under the effective guidance of Jonathan Dodd of Dodd, Mead and Company, publishers of this Best Plays series since its inception following the season of 1919–20.

The point is, *The Best Plays of 1980–81* is a group enterprise, deeply indebted to the many who create both its completeness and its embellishments. These include Robert Fletcher, Patricia McGourty and Tony Walton, who have permitted us to reproduce samples of their stage designs for the record here. On behalf of our readers, we also express our thanks for services rendered by Jeffrey Sweet, Hobe Morrison of *Variety*, Ralph Newman of the Drama Book Shop, Henry Hewes, Alan Hewitt and Thomas T. Foose. We thank the scores of press agents and others in the production offices, without whose patient assistance no *Best Plays* volume would be possible. Likewise we thank the photographers who have caught the look of theater everywhere for the reader's perusal here: Martha

Swope and Bert Andrews, Susan Cook, Peter Cunningham, Zoe Dominic, Kenn Duncan, Michael Eastman, Lisa Ebright, Marvin Einhorn, Richard Feldman, George Gammon, Chip Goebert, Gerry Goodstein, Bruce Goldstein, Roger Greenawalt, Joe B. Mann, Cliff Moore, Inge Morath, Lanny Nagler, James D. Radiches, Stephanie Saia, Donna Svennevik, David S. Talbott and Jay Thompson.

And as always, it is the dramatists and other artists who are the real founders of the feast of American theater, whose mere menu occupies these hundreds of pages annually. Our admiration and enjoyment of their work constitute our thanks; and this yearly record of their deeds, compiled with care and affection by many people, is our applause.

OTIS L. GUERNSEY Jr.

July 1, 1981

CONTENTS

Drawings by HIRSCHFELD

SUMMARIES
OF THE
SEASONS

"WE'RE IN THE MONEY!"—Lee Roy Reams and ensemble in a Gower Champion number in the musical *42nd Street*, produced by David Merrick

THE SEASON IN NEW YORK

By Otis L. Guernsey Jr.

FOR SOME MYSTERIOUS REASON, the New York theater took its first steps into the new decade in uncertain stride and with a ragged profile in the large and small playhouses alike. Did the inflationary surge in the price of theater tickets alter the mix of the audience? Did the damming-up of a creative tributary, off off Broadway, by playwrights' resistance to Equity's enforcement of a showcase code, result in a drying-up of the mainstream? Did a coincidence of mediocrity suddenly enervate a significant proportion of authors old and young, producers angeled and unangeled? Were any or all of these the underlying reason why the 1980–81 theater season in New York was one in which vigor was remarkably scarce and experience no warranty of success? We can only guess, but we know for certain that in 1980–81 some climatic influence was altering the very personality of the New York stage, and not for the better.

To consider these factors one at a time, the price of a top ticket to a Broadway show broke the double sawbuck barrier in 1980 and did not even pause respectfully at the $25 mark in 1981 on its way to the $35 top ($50 for house seats) at David Merrick's musical *42nd Street* and $30 at the straight play *Amadeus*—both Best Plays, to be sure. Inflation kept flooding the box office at every level, as Broadway attracted an all-time record week's gross of $4,886,970 on a 244,323 attendance the week of Jan. 3. By the end of the season, there was no ongoing new 1980–81 Broadway production that *wasn't* asking at least $25 for third row center on Saturday night. $30 was no longer unusual, *Woman of the Year* was venturing to join *42nd Street* up there at $35, and the *average* price of a Broadway ticket had risen from $15.49 in 1979–80 to $19.72 in 1980–81 according to *Variety's* estimate—about 27.5 per cent.

At those prices, a holdover like *Deathtrap* was a real bargain at a $17.50 top; and at those prices, it's not surprising that *Variety's* annual estimate of the total twelve-month Broadway gross soared to an unbelievable $194,481,091 for 1980–81, dwarfing last year's all-time record high of $143 million and wiping out of memory the seasons not so long ago when $50 million seemed an impossible dream. An additional 1980–81 road gross of almost $219 million brought the year's total income of Broadway productions to more than $413 million. At the same time, playing weeks (if ten shows play ten weeks, that's 100 playing weeks) climbed to a record 1,545, just topping last year's 1,541, and 1,472 the year before, with an additional 1,343 (almost the same as last year) on the road. What's importantly more, *Variety* estimated that Broadway attendance took a healthy jump this year to 10,822,324 from about 9.4 million and 9.1 million in the past two seasons, sharply reinforcing the upward trend.

3

There were slightly fewer new shows to attract these paying customers (see the one-page summary accompanying the next chapter of this report). Not counting specialties, there were 51 new Broadway productions in 1980–81, as compared with 58 last year. These included 14 revivals, so that the total number of new plays, musicals and revues amounted to 37 (including two return engagements and two transfers), as compared with 47 and 37 in the past two seasons. In the strange circumstances, a running show developed irresistable momentum, so that of the 14 longest-running Broadway shows as of June 1, 1980, 12 were still going a year later. And six of the holdovers—a very large number compared to recent seasons—achieved hit status and began making a profit during the twelve-month period.

$194 million gross . . . $50 top . . . to some extent this is mere numerology, not the prosperity it might appear to be. At these prices, a large part of the New York theater audience is transformed from theater-lovers to occasion-seekers. This makes a difference, affecting the kind of material that can be profitably produced. The splashy musical (*42nd Street*), the big star vehicle (*Woman of the Year* or *The Little Foxes*), the out-and-out comedy (*Lunch Hour*), the trumpeted revival (*The Pirates of Penzance*), the vaunted prizewinner (*Amadeus*) provide an *occasion* along with an evening of theater. They manage to attract celebrants and thrill-seekers at any price, while a finely-tuned instrument like *A Life,* written, acted and directed to perfection, dies of neglect where a few seasons ago it might have flourished, because mere theater-lovers can no longer afford often to attend a Broadway show unless they manage to arrive there by the reduced-price route of the TKTS booth in Duffy Square (and a good many of those near-capacity throngs at the $27.50 shows are there thanks to TKTS and other twofer arrangements).

Equity's attempt to establish and enforce an actor-favoring policy for showcase productions in New York and around the country (for which neither the actor nor the dramatist receives any pay) was inhibiting dramatists from offering their works for production off off Broadway because of conditions which might be placed upon their scripts in future, larger productions. The status of this confrontation as of season's end is outlined in the Offstage chapter of this report. We mention it here because it seems to have affected materially the quality of the whole theater season, like a plant whose roots are parched. We cannot of course point to any specific group of scripts witheld in 1980 or 1981 from experimental production because of the showcase code and which otherwise would have enhanced the season with their presence. We know, however, that many scripts *have* been withheld by their authors, inhibiting the creative flow at its source and most certainly affecting the quality of theater seeping up through the production levels toward Broadway.

Paradoxically, Beth Henley's *Crimes of the Heart,* a play about three sisters in a small Mississippi town, which made its New York entrance at the off-off-Broadway level, carried off two of the season's major awards—the Pulitzer Prize and the Critics Award as best American play. *Crimes of the Heart* was produced at the OOB level by Manhattan Theater Club, an exception that stood out even farther from the crowd in this stunted season than it otherwise might have. We have included it among the Best Plays in this volume, though as an OOB produc-

BROADWAY LADIES—*Above, Lena Horne: The Lady and Her Music; below left,* Elizabeth Taylor in *The Little Foxes; below right,* Glenda Jackson in *Rose*

tion we consider it a work-in-progress not formally eligible for Best Play citation. Our inclusion of it here does not signal a change in our policy either now or in the future, however. As we have stated in other *Best Plays* volumes, we will sometimes include a multiple major prizewinner in our Best Plays list for journalistic reasons alone, whatever (in our view) its qualifications or lack of them, because the prizes themselves convey an historical identity apart from any other considerations. We would have preferred to "wait till next year" when *Crimes of the Heart* is scheduled to reappear in New York with script certainly "frozen" in a full-scale Broadway production. Because of the 1980–81 OOB production's prizewinning ways, however, waiting would be awkward journalistically, and so we include it now.

Established dramatists experienced less competition from the upstarts than usual this season, but for the most part they appeared only at their second best, with all too many of them suffering the fate of the mighty Casey in *his* moment of greatest opportunity. An exception was Peter Shaffer with the first-rate play *Amadeus,* a drama of envy, imported from the London stage, very much the best play of the 1980–81 season. Hugh Leonard was also at the top of his form with *A Life,* a warm and winning elaboration of the character of Drumm, the Irish civil servant introduced in the previous Leonard Best Play *Da*. Others who kept the faith were Athol Fugard with a study of South African interracial friendship, *A Lesson from Aloes;* Jean Kerr with a merry marital whimsy, *Lunch Hour;* Brian Friel with yet another sensitive and mournful study of Irish character and endurance in *Translations;* and Woody Allen with Brooklyn variations on the theme of a domineering mother in *The Floating Light Bulb.* Charles Fuller's closeup of a killer punk in *Zooman and the Sign* and Caryl Churchill's sex-identity farce *Cloud 9* complete this year's list of Best Plays with *42nd Street* and *Crimes of the Heart.* Other major contributions to the season were provided by Stephen Poliakoff in *American Days,* about the high-pressure record business; Lanford Wilson with a Broadway revision of his opening play in the Talley trilogy, *Fifth of July* (ineligible for Best Play consideration because it was already named a Best Play in its off-Broadway incarnation as *The 5th of July* in 1978); and Romulus Linney with *The Captivity of Pixie Shedman* and *Childe Byron,* Christopher Durang with *Beyond Therapy* and Gus Edwards with *Weep Not for Me.*

While these authors did not fail us, many of them did not surprise us with their best, either. There were plenty of surprises at the other end of the scale among so-called "established" dramatists. High hopes for Arthur Miller's *The American Clock,* Edward Albee's *Lolita* and Neil Simon's *Fools* were unfulfilled, while elsewhere there was a succession of indifferent offerings by the otherwise promising likes of Albert Innaurato, Steve Tesich, Sidney Michaels, Joanna M. Glass, Sam Shepard, Samm-Art Williams and Simon Gray.

Much the same was true of the musical side of New York production which took on momentum in August with David Merrick's admittedly fabulous *42nd Street,* adapted by Michael Stewart and Mark Bramble from the same source as the famous 1933 movie. At season's end it was still leading the parade, easily the best musical of 1980–81 and of course a Best Play selection. Especially disappointing was the failure of Michael Stewart's second effort, *Bring Back Birdie,* in collaboration with the distinguished Messrs. Lee Adams and Charles

Strouse (the latter suffering the double jeopardy of the score for the short-lived *Charlie and Algernon*). *Woman of the Year,* the Lauren Bacall vehicle based by Peter Stone on the 1942 Katharine Hepburn-Spencer Tracy movie, with a John Kander-Fred Ebb score, was a creditable effort with some good results. Off Broadway, Stephen Sondheim's trunk songs were collected with distinction in *Marry Me a Little,* and James Lapine's ardent direction almost managed to make something resembling a silk purse out of the emotional postures in *March of the Falsettos.* With Broadway's two shiniest new musicals based on old movies, and with heavy reliance on hit revivals like *Camelot* and *The Pirates of Penzance,* the adventurous spirit was in notably short supply on the musical scene, even while money poured into some of the box offices.

So the profile of the 1980–81 ten Best Plays list bulged for only one musical in the midst of nine straight plays. It contained five foreign plays (*Amadeus, A Life, A Lesson from Aloes, Translations, Cloud 9*) and five American; two comedies (*Lunch Hour* and *Cloud 9*), two dramas (*A Lesson from Aloes* and *Zooman and the Sign*), and the others a mix; six Broadway productions, three off-Broadway (*Translations, Zooman and the Sign, Cloud 9*) and one off-off-Broadway (*Crimes of the Heart*), which was also the only one of the American Best Plays to reach New York following production in regional theater. Of the other four, three (*42nd Street, Lunch Hour* and *The Floating Light Bulb*) were devised directly for Broadway and *Zooman and the Sign* was developed off Broadway by The Negro Ensemble Company.

Whatever it is that the theater lacks today, it doesn't seem to be backing. $2 million no longer sounded exorbitant for the production cost of a musical star vehicle like *Woman of the Year* or *Camelot*, nor did David Merrick balk at spending $2.5 million (*Variety* reported) to mount his nonesuch. A straight play in 1980–81 could easily cost more than $800,000 to put on, and the lavishly electrical production of *Frankenstein* failed to electrify the audience and closed after its opening night performance which reportedly cost its backers $2 million. While we're on the subject of costs, we should note that off Broadway too was raising its sights materially. It cost a hefty $175,000 to get *Cloud 9* on at the Theater de Lys, and as spring turned into summer it was playing there at an $18.50 top, a level achieved at the same time by the Al Pacino revival of *American Buffalo.*

Ongoing success stories kept backers interested in the New York theater, however. For example, according to *Variety* estimate, *Sugar Babies* had gilded its angels' haloes in the amount of $1–2 million and was earning a steady $70,000 a week on Broadway (but its road company dropped $1 million while folding in Boston). *Annie*'s various companies topped $100 million total gross (once an impossible dream for an entire Broadway season) and the show has paid a profit of going on $10 million on an $800,000 investment. *Deathtrap* has earned 355 per cent profit ($1,340,000 on $200,000), *They're Playing Our Song* $3.6 million on $800,000, *Children of a Lesser God* $865,000 on $400,000. The revival of *The Pirates of Penzance* was earning back its $1.3 million cost at the rate of $50,000 a week (and the movie rights to this conception of the golden Gilbert & Sullivan oldie were sold for $1.5 million).

Remember the 1967 off-Broadway musical *You're a Good Man Charlie*

John Heffernan and Derek Jacobi in *The Suicide,* a Russian comedy

Brown? It has paid its backers $58 for every dollar invested, and still counting. Such sensational statistics provide a glossy facade for the theater's economic structure; but behind them, shows of quality struggle to survive. For example, the operating loss of the Broadway *Fifth of July* stood at $135,000 at season's end, and the two productions of the recent *Whose Life Is It Anyway?* totaled a $132,000 Broadway loss.

If 1980–81 had been an exceptionally effective season, the producers would claim credit (as they do in the Tony ceremonies, trooping up onto the podium to collect the best-play and best-musical awards). They must therefore share with the playwrights a portion of whatever shortcomings 1980–81 has evidenced. Most frequently billed above the title on Broadway were James M. Nederlander (producer of three musical revivals, the two one-performance comets *Franken-stein* and *Broadway Follies,* along with *Woman of the Year,* Lena Horne's one-woman show and a musical that closed in previews); The Shubert Organization (a partner in *Division Street, Brigadoon, Piaf* and *Rose* as well as *Amadeus*); Elizabeth I. McCann and Nelle Nugent *(Amadeus, Piaf* and *Rose);* Richmond Crinkley (with several institutional offerings for Lincoln Center and ANTA); Emanuel Azenberg *(Division Street* and *Fools);* Kennedy Center *(Charlie and Algernon* and *Mixed Couples);* and Mike Merrick and Don Gregory winning one with *Camelot* and losing one with *Copperfield.* This is hardly a record of bold or sensitive production judgment. Distinction alit like Noah's dove upon the shoulder of David Merrick in August, but it eluded him in a production of Oliver Hailey's *I Won't Dance* in May. In passing, it should dip its wings in honor of the 1980–81 good taste of Lester Osterman *(A Life),* Roger Berlind *(Amadeus* and *Sophisticated Ladies,* Robert Whitehead *(Lunch*

Hour) and even Warner Theater Productions (led by Claire Nichtern), a partner in *Fifth of July*, *The American Clock* and *Woman of the Year*.

Off Broadway, it was much the same story—half a loaf at the Public Theater, Circle Repertory and American Place, limited excitement elsewhere. The exception was Lynne Meadow's and Barry Grove's Manhattan Theater Club, which provided in its DownStage Theater a schedule of foreign plays that was without exception interesting and exceptionally so in the cases of the Best Play *Translations* and *American Days;* and in its UpStage Theater introduced to New York audience the OOB prizewinner *Crimes of the Heart.* The rule of lacklustre was also broken by Douglas Turner Ward's Negro Ensemble Company, notably with *Zooman and the Sign*, and in independent production by Michel Stuart, Harvey J. Klaris et al with *Cloud 9.*

The directors made something of a mark in 1980–81 when they found scripts worthy of their mettle. The late Gower Champion's *42nd Street*, Peter Hall's *Amadeus* and Peter Coe's *A Life* on Broadway and Tommy Tune's *Cloud 9*, James Lapine's *March of the Falsettos* and Joe Dowling's *Translations* off Broadway were conspicuous standouts. Also carrying out their assignments to more than average effect were Marshall W. Mason (restaging *Fifth of July*), Robert Moore (*Woman of the Year*), Ellis Rabb (*The Philadelphia Story*), Ulu Grosbard (*The Floating Light Bulb*) and Robert Drivas (*It Had to Be You*). And add the name of Graciela Daniele to that of Gower Champion as the distinguished choreographers of 1980–81, she for *The Pirates of Penzance*, *Alice in Concert* and *Girls, Girls, Girls*.

Among designers, the busiest were John Lee Beatty with the scenery for at least half a dozen shows on and off Broadway, Jennifer Von Mayrhauser with the costumes for seven, Theoni V. Aldredge with the costumes for four (including *42nd Street* and *Woman of the Year),* Jane Greenwood with four off Broadway and Santo Loquasto with two on Broadway and one in Brooklyn. Conspicuous single achievements in the design field included the scenery for Robert Fletcher's multi-level *A Life*, John Bury's *Amadeus,* Robin Wagner's *42nd Street* and Tony Walton's *Woman of the Year;* and the costumes by Patricia McGourty for *The Pirates of Penzance,* Patricia Zipprodt for *Fools* and John Bury for *Amadeus.*

It is the actors, however, who by the extrovert nature of their art are conspicuous even in unfavorable circumstances (like George C. Scott, David Dukes, Geraldine Page, Rip Torn, Julie Harris, Donald O'Connor, Donald Sutherland, Ian Richardson, George S. Irving, John Rubinstein and Meryl Streep this season) or find the means in their vehicle and/or themselves to leave an indelible mark on the audience's memory. Such were Ian McKellen with Tim Curry and Nicholas Kepros as Salieri, Mozart and Emperor Joseph in *Amadeus* . . . Roy Dotrice mirrored by Adam Redfield and supported by Pat Hingle in *A Life* . . . Jane Lapotaire's Piaf, Glenda Jackson's severe Rose . . . The return of Richard Burton in *Camelot* and Nicol Williamson in *Inadmissible Evidence* . . . Lauren Bacall and Harry Guardino propelling *Woman of the Year* and Marilyn Cooper stopping it cold with her bit as a frumpy housewife . . . Edward Herrmann and Blythe Danner in *The Philadelphia Story* . . . The memorable ensembles of *The Pirates of Penzance, Translations, Long Day's Journey Into*

Robert Fletcher's sketch for his outstanding scene design of *A Life*

Night, Cloud 9 . . . Beatrice Arthur the eager-beaver mother, Jack Weston the gentleman caller, Brian Backer the terrified youth in *The Floating Light Bulb* . . . Elizabeth Taylor in a blazing stage debut in *The Little Foxes,* with Maureen Stapleton as Birdie . . . Gilda Radner's scatterbrain in *Lunch Hour* and Eva Le Gallienne's grandmother in *To Grandmother's House We Go* . . . Jerry Orbach and Gregory Hines leading their hit musicals . . . Derek Jacobi and John Heffernan as pawns of the state in *The Suicide* . . . Harris Yulin and James Earl Jones making interracial connections in *A Lesson from Aloes* . . . Pippa Pearthree as a would-be rock star in *American Days* and Giancarlo Esposito as a murderous animal in *Zooman and the Sign* . . . The colorful support by Paxton Whitehead as King Pellinore in *Camelot,* Jessica Tandy as a sympathetic mother in *Rose,* Helen Stenborg and Aideen O'Kelly as the wives in *A Life,* Wanda Richert as the enchanted chorus girl of *42nd Street,* Swoosie Kurtz as a friend of the young Talleys in *Fifth of July.*

The ultimate insignia of New York professional theater achievement (we insist) are the Best Play citations in these volumes, designations which are 16 years older than the Critics Awards and only three years younger than the Pulitzer Prizes. Each Best Play selection is made by the present editor with the script itself as the first consideration, for the reason (as we've stated in previous volumes) that the script is the spirit of the theater's physical body. The script is not only the quintessence of the present, it is most of what endures into the future. So the Best Plays are the best scripts, with as little weight as humanly possible given to comparative production values. The choice is made without any regard whatever to a play's type—musical, comedy or drama—or origin on or off Broadway, or popularity at the box office, or lack of same.

We don't take the scripts of other eras into consideration for Best Play citation in this one, whatever their technical status as American or New York "premieres" which don't happen to have had a previous New York production of record. We draw a line between adaptations and revivals, the former eligible for Best Play selection but the latter not, on a case-by-case basis. We likewise consider the eligibility of borderline examples of limited-engagement and showcase production one at a time, ascertaining that they are "frozen" in final script version, and no longer changeable works-in-progress, before they are considered for Best Play citation (and in the case of a late-season arrival the final decision may await a determination the following year).

If a script of above-average quality influences the very character of a season, or by some function of consensus wins the Critics, Pulitzer or Tony Awards, we take into account its future historical as well as present esthetic importance to the season as a whole (*Crimes of the Heart* is an example). This is the only special consideration we give, and we don't always tilt in its direction, as the record shows.

The ten Best Plays of 1980–81 are listed here for visual convenience in the order in which they opened in New York (a plus sign + with the performance number signifies that the play was still running after May 31, 1981).

42nd Street
  (Broadway; 320+ perfs)

A Life
  (Broadway; 72 perfs.)

Lunch Hour
  (Broadway; 231+ perfs.)

A Lesson from Aloes
  (Broadway; 96 perfs.)

Zooman and the Sign
  (Off Broadway; 33 perfs.)

Amadeus
  (Broadway; 189+ perfs.

Crimes of the Heart
  (Off off Broadway; 35 perfs.)

Translations
  (Off Broadway; 48 perfs.)

The Floating Light Bulb
  (Broadway; 41+ perfs.)

Cloud 9
  (Off Broadway; 16+ perfs.)

Swoosie Kurtz, Joyce Reehling, Christopher Reeve and Jonathan Hogan (*at top*) in the Broadway version of Lanford Wilson's *Fifth of July,* about the Talleys

Broadway

The 1980–81 Broadway season caught its full stride in the summer weeks with David Merrick's musical comedy event, *42nd Street* (reviewed in detail in the Best Plays section of this volume), which was certainly never rivaled during the rest of the musical season. In fact, it was alone in its glory until the end of March, when *Woman of the Year* arrived to keep it company in the line of musicals. Like *42nd Street, Woman of the Year* tells a tale previously told on film (in the 1942 Katharine Hepburn-Spencer Tracy comedy of the same title, written by Ring Lardner Jr. and Michael Kanin), thoroughly modernized in a book by Peter Stone (instead of a sports writer and a quiz-show whiz, the ill-matched couple in the stage version are a cartoonist and a TV talk-show hostess) and embellished with an attractive score by John Kander and Fred Ebb. Lauren Bacall is not a singer, but she *is* a Star with a capital S, and in the title role she commanded the stage with every gesture, while Harry Guardino played the cartoonist as a mere mortal wooing the intellectual lady in congenial fashion. Roderick Cook was a suitably self-possessed male secretary, while Marilyn Cooper made the most of her only scene as a kitchen-bound housewife with hair in curlers, standing up to her glamorous house guest, Miss Bacall, in the number "The Grass Is Always

Greener." Robert Moore's direction and the designs by Tony Walton and Theoni V. Aldredge served the purposes of this prototypical Broadway musical.

Vinnette Carroll's Gospel musical *Your Arms Too Short to Box with God* payed Broadway a return visit for 149 summer performances, while Micki Grant's early-June effort to celebrate a city neighborhood in song, *It's So Nice to Be Civilized,* came a fast cropper. Then there were the Franks, Fearless and Perfectly: *Fearless Frank,* a short-lived attempt to set the life and loves of Frank Harris in a musical context, and *Perfectly Frank,* a vehicle strained to carry its collection of more than 60 numbers by the late, great Frank Loesser. A Charles Strouse score was the principal ingredient of *Charlie and Algernon*, based on the novel about a medical experiment on a brain-damaged subject which was also the basis for the movie *Charly,* but it could not carry the day. Much more disappointing because it aroused higher expectations was Strouse's second 1980–81 effort, *Bring Back Birdie,* a two-decades-later sequel to *Bye Bye Birdie,* starring Donald O'Connor in a Michael Stewart book (speaking of second efforts) and with Lee Adams lyrics, surviving for only 4 performances in the cruel world of the modern musical theater. The latter was also inhospitable to two other major efforts with 19th century scenes: *Onward Victoria,* about the feminist Victoria Woodhull, closing after its opening performance; and *Copperfield,* with George S. Irving as Mr. Micawber, in a musicalization of the Dickens novel.

The musical theater season was greatly enhanced in the revue section by *Sophisticated Ladies,* with Gregory Hines leading the cast through a selection of Duke Ellington songs in one of his uniquely and inimitably energetic song-and-dance performances under the direction and with the choreography of Michael Smuin and Donald McKayle. In this revue category, it was perplexing that *Tintypes,* a show that proved itself inimitable in its own Gay-Nineties-turn-of-the-century way off Broadway last season, couldn't attract an audience to sustain a run of more than 93 performances in transfer. In effect, nostalgia seemed to be a thread running through the few popular new musical offerings of the season— *42nd Street*, *Woman of the Year* and *Sophisticated Ladies*—and among the musical revivals *Camelot* and *The Pirates of Penzance* (of which more in a later section of this report)—but it was no absolute guarantee of popularity.

There can seldom have been a New York theater season in which foreign plays dominated the scene as they did in this one. On Broadway, each and every one of the half-dozen foreign scripts showed some credentials of craft and vision, in marked comparison to the halting American efforts, three times as numerous and less than a third as effective. Far and away the year's best play was Peter Shaffer's *Amadeus*, an import from the National Theater which set Broadway aflame with the warmth of its dramatization of the nature of genius—its overwhelming superiority to mere talent. Shaffer himself is a genius at summoning up in his plays a sort of Platonic ideal looming behind the reality of his subject: the ideal of Horse in *Equus*, the very spirit of Music in *Amadeus*. *Amadeus* is told in monologue, to an even greater extent than *Equus*, by the character upon whom the events of the play are having the most profound intellectual as well as emotional impact: in *Equus* not the frantic boy but his doctor, in *Amadeus* not the genius Mozart but his jealous rival Salieri. The latter, played in high style by Ian McKellen, recalled all too well in aching detail how it was when brash,

The 1980–81 Season on Broadway

PLAYS (18)

Passione
Division Street
Fifth of July
  (return engagement)
Tricks of the Trade
LUNCH HOUR
The American Clock
Mixed Couples
Frankenstein
To Grandmother's House
  We Go
Heartland
The Survivor
Lolita
Fools
Animals
*THE FLOATING LIGHT
  BULB*
Inacent Black
I Won't Dance
It Had To Be You

MUSICALS (11)

Your Arms Too Short to
  Box With God
  (return engagement)
It's So Nice To Be Civilized
Fearless Frank
42ND STREET
Charlie and Algernon
Perfectly Frank
Onward Victoria
Bring Back Birdie
Woman of the Year
Copperfield
The Moony Shapiro
  Songbook

REVUES (2)

Tintypes (transfer)
Sophisticated Ladies

FOREIGN PLAYS IN
ENGLISH (6)

The Suicide
A LIFE
A LESSON FROM ALOES
AMADEUS
Piaf
Rose

REVIVALS (14)

The Music Man
Circle in Square 1980:
  The Man Who Came to
  Dinner
Camelot
Circle in Square 1981:
  The Bacchae
John Gabriel Borkman
The Father
Brigadoon
Lincoln Center:
  The Philadelphia Story
Macbeth
The Pirates of Penzance
  (transfer)
The Five O'Clock Girl
Jacques Brel
Can-Can
The Little Foxes

SPECIALTIES (12)

Radio City Music Hall:
  Manhattan Showboat
  America
Insideoutandallaround
  Shelley Berman
Banjo Dancing
Quick Change
Emlyn Williams as Charles
  Dickens
  (return engagement)
Shakespeare's Cabaret
  (transfer)
Broadway Follies
Aaah Oui Genty!
Passionate Ladies
Lena Horne
St. Mark's Gospel

HOLDOVERS WHICH
BECAME HITS IN
1980–81

Barnum
Children of a Lesser God
A Day in Hollywood/A
  Night in the Ukraine
Evita
I Ought To Be in Pictures
Peter Pan

Categorized above are all the new productions listed in the Plays Produced on Broadway section of this volume.
Plays listed in CAPITAL LETTERS have been designated Best Plays of 1980-81.
Plays listed in *italics* were still running after May 31, 1981.
Plays listed in **bold face type** were classified as hits in *Variety*'s annual estimate published June 3, 1981.

uncouth, ill-mannered but gloriously gifted young Mozart (Tim Curry) arrived at the Austrian court, where Salieri was the Emperor's musical mentor, but where Mozart proceeded to overshadow the older man with his heart-stopping concert and opera works.

In his own youth, Salieri had made a bargain with God, a vow of a lifetime of service and obeisance in exchange for the talent to become renowned in the world of music. God seemed to have kept his bargain with Salieri until "Amadeus" intruded upon the scene—Wolfgang Amadeus Mozart who is apparently heedless of God's will but is so entirely, unfairly beloved of God that the divine harmonies pouring out of him (Mozart doesn't find it necessary even to rewrite his scores) expose the most intense musical efforts of all others, including Salieri's, as earthbound mechanical compositions. Salieri's resentment of God's unfairness finally grows out of control; emotions darken while the music becomes more sublime. The play's grand design was most sensitively realized in Peter Hall's direction of Shaffer's brilliant script, in the manipulation of the musical background, in the tastefully gilded John Bury sets and costumes and in the supporting performances including Nicholas Kepros's philistine Emperor Joseph. *Amadeus* would be a peak of dramatic accomplishment in any season; in this one, rising from the valley floor, its presence was immense.

The Irish play *A Life* by Hugh Leonard, a sort of companion piece to his popular *Da,* was the year's chief rival to its English competitor in every department except audience response. For reasons suggested earlier in this report, Leonard's fine play couldn't find acceptance on Broadway, where it remained for a scant 72 performances but left glowing embers of warmth in the memory of theatergoers who were lucky enough to have seen it. In *Da*, the crusty Irish civil servant Drumm was a colorful minor character; *A Life* moved in for a closeup of this intellectually dominant but emotionally forbidding fellow. The rich characterization takes Drumm from ambitious youth to disillusioned age, from half-realized love to half-appreciated wedlock, in a dual performance by Roy Dotrice as Old Drumm and Adam Redfield as Young Drumm, as these two actors uncannily reflected each other's mannerisms and even general appearance. The supporting performances by Pat Hingle (Drumm's pal), Helen Stenborg (Drumm's wife) and Aideen O'Kelly (Drumm's youthful infatuation), the Peter Coe direction and the ingenious Robert Fletcher multilevel setting were all worthy of a script that ranked among the very best the theater had to offer this season.

The inbred ability of the aloe to flourish and bloom in a desert climate became a metaphor of the human spirit in the searing sociological climate of South Africa, in yet another distinguished 1980–81 script from abroad. Athol Fugard's *A Lesson from Aloes* celebrated the friendship between two South Africans, one white and the other black, just as it is coming to an end because the black has decided, after a prison term for a political offense, that he's had enough of trying to survive in this forbidding environment and is taking himself and his family away to resettle in England. Like other notable Fugard works (*The Blood Knot*, *Boesman and Lena*, *Sizwe Banzi Is Dead*, *The Island*), this one was a cry of despair echoed by hope for his beloved country. Harris Yulin as the doggedly enduring white Afrikaner, the "aloe;" Maria Tucci as his wife, who has already broken down once and is probably not going to be able to stay the course; and James Earl Jones as the black friend

were directed by the author as the work was written, in steady and determined progress through somber measures. In the consensus voting of the New York Drama Critics Circle, *A Lesson from Aloes* was cited as the best-of-bests for 1980-81, an award to which it certainly does honor.

Two other British plays provided platforms for outstanding performances by their leading ladies: *Piaf* by Pam Gems, with Jane Lapotaire recreating the entertainment style and the street-wise, doomed personality of the famous French singer Edith Piaf, in a Tony Award-winning performance; and *Rose* by Andrew Davies, a less flamboyant but more complex portrait of an enlightened Midlands school teacher trying achingly hard to reshape both her humdrum marriage and the inadequate education system into more satisfactory form. As played by Glenda Jackson, with Jessica Tandy as her mother and confidante, Rose was a raw-boned, close-cropped mass of contradictions: masculine and feminine, arrogant and vulnerable, repellant and appealing, in one of the year's strongest performances.

Also on the distinguished visitors list was *The Suicide*, a 1920s Russian play

WOMAN OF THE YEAR—Two of Tony Walton's models for his scene designs are pictured on the opposite page (Tess's apartment *above left*, the Inkpot restaurant *below left*). *Above,* Lauren Bacall is the center of attention at the Inkpot in the musical number "One of the Boys"

by Nikolai Erdman satirizing the drawbacks of collectivism, denied production in Russia and now rescued from oblivion in translation, first in England in 1979 and then in a regional theater production here in 1980. The play considers in comedic terms the plight of an unemployed worker brushed off by his closest neighbors as well as by the state until he attracts attention by announcing that he is going to shoot himself. This production was stretched well beyond the limits of its content by excesses of style, but the show did boast an engaging performance in the leading role by the British actor Derek Jacobi, and by John Heffernan in support as a tatterdemalion intellectual.

Easily the best American play on Broadway this season was Jean Kerr's effervescent *Lunch Hour*, about wife-swapping in the Hamptons, staged by Mike Nichols, with one member of the quartet (a marriage counselor played by Sam Waterston) at the extreme of sophistication in these matters, another (the wide-eyed Gilda Radner, dangerously innocent) at the opposite extreme, and with their spouses caught and manipulated in the middle. The point of *Lunch Hour* isn't that it explored profound truths, but that like all other Jean Kerr plays it was a lark. Her very stylishly constructed comedy found its laughter in fellow-feeling for the characters rather than in jokes at their expense—and with any luck there may after all be something like a profound truth lurking there among the witticisms.

Woody Allen's *The Floating Light Bulb*, another American Best Play on Broadway this season, sets a *Glass Menagerie*-type mother upon her achingly shy son (Brian Backer), whose favorite magic trick gives the play its title. In the indomitable person of Beatrice Arthur, the mother pushes the boy into auditioning for a theatrical manager (Jack Weston), the equivalent of a gentleman caller in these variations on a theme similar to Tennessee Williams's, with a similar resolution: Williams's crippled girl will never find a suitor, and Allen's terrified youth will never make it in public as a magician. In the latter case, the caller is perceived as both a professional opportunity for the son and a romantic refuge for the mother, in a touching encounter (delicately performed under Ulu Grosbard's direction) between two people who are long past their prime and almost past hoping for the best, but still in possession of courage and self-respect.

The equal of this year's best in any category was Lanford Wilson's *Fifth of July*, which was named a Best Play in its off-Broadway production at Circle Rep three years ago. This was the first of Wilson's Talley family plays, but a generation later in time than *Talley's Folly*, with a widowed Aunt Sally watching a new Talley generation trying to get over the aftereffects of Vietnam shock. This new Broadway production could not be called a "transfer" from off-Broadway (though Jeff Daniels as Ken Talley's loving attendant, Jonathan Hogan as his friend, Joyce Reehling as his sister and Amy Wright as her daughter remain from the original cast), nor a "revival" (directed by Marshall W. Mason, like the original), nor a "new play" (though somewhat rewritten), and of course we cannot re-include it in the Best Plays list, where it would certainly belong had it not appeared there previously. For want of a better term we've classified this as a "return engagement," certainly an illustrious one, in which both Christopher Reeve and his successor, Richard Thomas, made an impression in the role of Ken Talley.

Here and there among the other new American offerings on Broadway was a script which, though falling short of success this first time around, seems likely to find a new life elsewhere. The romantic adventures of Renee Taylor as a TV actress and Joseph Bologna as a producer of TV commercials in their *It Had To Be You* worked up quite a comic froth under Robert Drivas's direction and should prove to be a cheerful and durable item on the road. Edward Albee's *Lolita* succumbed quickly to critical overkill, but among its admittedly sometimes offensive clutter there lurked sequences of intensely powerful theater. In this dramatization of Vladimir Nabokov's sardonic tale of the professor (Donald Sutherland), his nymphet and his nemesis (Clive Revill in a weirdly colorful performance), emotional electricity went out of control, but this is not to say that this project is forever impossible—nor was it, like so much else on this year's schedule, narrow in vision or weak in effect.

We also have to believe that Neil Simon may some day find a way to twist the controls of *Fools* and get it going as a properly stylized farce of the intellect, in its tale of a Russian village mysteriously cursed with stupidity; that Arthur Miller will finally get his feelings about the Depression across to the audience in some future version of his *The American Clock*; that Albert Innaurato will write another play about an Italian family, possibly including a segment of this year's *Passione*; that Steve Tesich's *Division Street*, about the mellowing of 1960s radi-

Jane Lapotaire as Edith Piaf and Zoe Wanamaker as her friend in *Piaf*

cals, will have a life after its mere 21 Broadway performances, as it did before them at Mark Taper Forum in this Gordon Davidson-directed production; that James Prideaux (*Mixed Couples*, about wife-swappers meeting 25 years later) and Joanna M. Glass (*To Grandmother's House We Go*, with Eva Le Gallienne as the matriarch of a troubled family) will be heard from more eloquently in future, and the sooner the better.

Other short-lived American scripts, whose very existence on Broadway was proof that some producers considered them sufficiently vibrant to make a go of it in the biggest time of all, included *Heartland* about homicidal mania, *The Survivor* about Nazi persecution in the Warsaw ghetto and *Inacent Black*, the name of an angel (Melba Moore) who comes down to earth to help out with the problems of an upper middle class black family in Westbury, L.I. Certainly no work considered deserving of Broadway production deserves to feel the hook after only one performance, but this debacle happens more often than it should, this season to *Frankenstein*, *Onward Victoria*, *Broadway Follies* and to Sidney Michaels's spy melodrama *Tricks of the Trade* and the trio of short comedies entitled *Animals*. The only import to suffer this fate this season was *The Moony Shapiro Songbook*, a British musical satirizing anthology shows of famous composers' works, which opened and closed after only one Broadway performance—and was nominated for a Tony in the best-book category. David Merrick, who began the season with the fireworks display of *42nd Street* made another kind of spectacle as he withdrew Oliver Hailey's *I Won't Dance*, a dark and violent play about the emotions of a paraplegic in a wheelchair, after only one Sunday afternoon performance, thus running the gamut of production experience in a single season. He made his entrance, after a long absence, onto the Broadway scene both with his shield and on it, in the highest triumph and the most attenuated defeat.

Specialty productions were both numerous and conspicuous in the Broadway environs this season. Lena Horne knocked them dead in a one-woman show as musically enthralling as the star herself. Radio City Music Hall launched two of its extravaganzas—*Manhattan Showboat* and *America*, a salute to all the 50 states —in which the Rockettes were and always will be the prime attraction. At the other end of the scale, the theater district is scheduled to lose the little Bijou Theater on 45th Street if the developers have their way, at a time when its importance to the area has never been more apparent. Its intimate proportions provided a comfortable fit for one-performer shows by Shelley Berman, Michael McGiveney (portraying 30 different characters in *Quick Change*) and Barbara Perry (playing five specially chosen *Passionate Ladies*), as well as for the French marionette show *Aaah Oui Genty!* and the revue *Shakespeare's Cabaret*, transferred from the Colonnades and setting many of the Bard's songs, poems and lyrical passages to music by Lance Mulcahy. In other parts of the specialty forest were *Banjo Dancing*, a one-man instrumental concert by Stephen Wade; Emlyn Williams returning in his memorable stage portrait of Charles Dickens; Alec McCowen also returning in his rendition of the Gospel according to St. Mark; and *Broadway Follies,* a comeback of vaudeville to the big time—but only for one performance.

Here's where we list the *Best Plays* choices for the top individual achievements of the season. In the acting categories, clear distinctions among "starring," "featured" or "supporting" players can't be made on the basis of official billing, which is sometimes set by contractual rather than esthetic considerations. Here in these volumes we divide acting into "primary" and "secondary" roles, a primary role being one which carries a major responsibility for the show; a role which might some day cause a star to inspire a revival in order to appear in that character. All others, be they vivid as Mercutio, are classed as secondary.

Furthermore, our list of individual bests makes room for more than a single choice in some categories. We believe that no useful purpose is served by forcing ourselves into the arbitrary selection of a single best when we come upon multiple examples of comparable quality. In that case we include them all in our list.

Here, then, are the *Best Plays* bests of 1980–81:

PLAYS

BEST PLAY: *Amadeus* by Peter Shaffer

BEST AMERICAN PLAY: *Lunch Hour* by Jean Kerr

BEST REVIVAL: *The Philadelphia Story* by Philip Barry, directed by Ellis Rabb

Gregory Hines and Judith Jamison in Duke Ellington's *Sophisticated Ladies*

BEST ACTOR IN A PRIMARY ROLE: Roy Dotrice as Drumm in *A Life*; Ian McKellen as Antonio Salieri in *Amadeus*

BEST ACTRESS IN A PRIMARY ROLE: Beatrice Arthur as Enid Pollack in *The Floating Light Bulb*; Glenda Jackson as Rose in *Rose*

BEST ACTOR IN A SECONDARY ROLE: Brian Backer and Jack Weston in *The Floating Light Bulb*

BEST ACTRESS IN A SECONDARY ROLE: Pippa Pearthree as Lorraine in *American Days*

BEST DIRECTOR: Peter Hall for *Amadeus*; Tommy Tune for *Cloud 9*

BEST SCENERY: Robert Fletcher for *A Life*

BEST COSTUMES: John Bury for *Amadeus*

MUSICALS

BEST MUSICAL: *42nd Street*

BEST BOOK: *42nd Street* by Michael Stewart and Mark Bramble

BEST SCORE: *Woman of the Year* by John Kander and Fred Ebb

BEST REVIVAL: *The Pirates of Penzance* by W.S. Gilbert and Arthur Sullivan, directed by Wilford Leach

BEST ACTOR IN A PRIMARY ROLE: Gregory Hines in *Sophisticated Ladies*

BEST ACTRESS IN A PRIMARY ROLE: Lauren Bacall as Tess Harding in *Woman of the Year*

BEST ACTOR IN A SECONDARY ROLE: Paxton Whitehead as King Pellinore in *Camelot*

BEST ACTRESS IN A SECONDARY ROLE: Wanda Richert as Peggy Sawyer in *42nd Street*

BEST DIRECTOR: Gower Champion for *42nd Street*

BEST CHOREOGRAPHER: Gower Champion for *42nd Street*

BEST SCENERY: Robin Wagner for *42nd Street*; Tony Walton for *Woman of the Year*

BEST COSTUMES: Theoni V. Aldredge for *42nd Street*; Patricia McGourty for *The Pirates of Penzance*

Off Broadway

In the smaller playhouses, the tail wagged the dog. The plays arousing the most enthusiasm among New York theatergoers came from that area called "off off Broadway," or OOB—paradoxically, in a season which starved OOB for new scripts because of the dispute between Equity and the dramatists over showcase commitments. Only one American play in full-fledged off-Broadway production (*Zooman and the Sign*) and two scripts from abroad (*Translations* and *Cloud 9*) rivaled the mighty OOB mites who stole the passing show: *How I Got That Story, Crimes of the Heart* (the Pulitzer and Critics Award winner and a Best Play) and *March of the Falsettos*, which moved up to full off-Broadway status after first appearing as an OOB offering. Certainly all three of them will continue to make ever-widening circles, with plans afoot to present them in expanded productions.

We have no intention of drawing indelible lines across the off-Broadway programming to divide it absolutely into professional and experimental categories; but we must make some distinction between what is possibly a work-in-progress and what is probably a "frozen" script ready to face the world as a completed work in publication or production. Only the latter is regularly considered for Best Play designation, so that we must make some attempt to identify what we mean by the term "off Broadway." Off-Broadway plays and musicals are eligible for Best Play selection on the same terms as those listed under the Broadway heading, whereas works-in-progress are not.

By the lights of these *Best Plays* volumes, an off-Broadway production is one a) with an Equity cast b) giving 8 performances a week c) in an off-Broadway theater d) after inviting public comment by critics on an opening night or nights. And according to Paul Libin, president of the League of Off-Broadway Theaters, an off-Broadway theater is a house seating 499 or fewer and situated in Manhattan *outside* the area bounded by Fifth and Ninth Avenues between 34th and 56th Streets, and by Fifth Avenue and the Hudson River between 56th and 72d Streets.

Obviously there are exceptions to each of these rules; no dimension of "off Broadway" or "off off Broadway" can be applied exactly. In each *Best Plays* volume we stretch these definitions somewhat in the direction of inclusion—never of exclusion. For example, the word "Manhattan" means what we want it to mean when we include the Brooklyn Academy of Music programs. Casts are often only part-Equity, and schedules are sometimes limited to 7 performances a week.

The point is that off Broadway isn't an exact location either geographically or esthetically. It's a state of the art (generally advanced but heavily weighted with revivals), a structure of production costs (once manageable but now rising dramatically), a level of expertise and commitment. We must keep emphasizing as the seasons pass that the borderline between professional (off Broadway) and semi- or non-professional (off off Broadway) has all but disappeared. OOB groups often use part-Equity casts under special showcase and mini-contract arrangements, while off-Broadway groups don't always maintain all the technical off-Broadway standards in all their productions. Most other publications have stopped trying to categorize these areas. We'll continue doing so, however, as long as it seems useful for the record, while reminding those who read these lines that formal distinctions are no longer as clear as they were, and we tend to include rather than exclude—and that elsewhere in this volume we publish the most comprehensive list of 1980–81 OOB productions anywhere.

This said, let us note that 1980–81 production of new scripts off Broadway dwindled somewhat for the third straight year: 55 productions including 33 American straight plays, 14 musicals and 8 foreign plays in English, as compared with 58 (39-7-12) last year and 64 (38-15-11) the previous season. The number of revues dropped dramatically from 11 last year to only one this year (see the one-page summary accompanying this report), while the revival total held at 44 for the second straight season.

Foreign playwrights stole the show off Broadway as they did on, leading the long parade with the exceptionally effective works produced by Lynne Meadow and Barry Grove at Manhattan Theater Club. Brian Friel's *Translations* was a shade the best of the entire off-Broadway year, with an affectionate, caring dramatization of an 1833 episode in the English-Irish struggle of character and policy. Friel's Best Play recalls a time when there was a formidable language as well as an emotional barrier between the two factions, with Barnard Hughes as the principal of a one-room "Hedge School" teaching all subjects including Latin and Greek to Gaelic-speaking country folk. The British presence is symbolized by Army personnel come to occupy, map and Anglicize the country. Daniel Gerroll as a young lieutenant who falls in love with Irish ways and an Irish lass, Jarlath Conroy as a bilingual Irish intellectual, Stephen Burleigh as one inclined to collaboration and Jake Dengel as a boozy old classicist led the skillful ensemble through these measures, directed by Joe Dowling. The play was sometimes irresolute but never unfeeling, squeezing out every drop of compassion for both sides of the conflict.

Another very bright spot on the MTC program was Stephen Poliakoff's *American Days*, a brash and kookie treatment of the rock music scene, previously produced in London. Its aspiring performers slaver for the limelight, as they try to attract the attention of a bored record publisher with eccentricities of dress and behavior reminiscent of TV quiz show contestants. Pippa Pearthree gave a stunning performance as the least likely but finally most successful of the aspirants, in a play that was remarkable for both intensity and style under Jacques Levy's direction. The MTC's exceptionally distinguished 1980–81 schedule also included *Close of Play*, an enigmatic rummaging among family frictions by the British playwright Simon Gray, and Steve Metcalfe's *Vikings*, about craftsmen coping with this era of mass production—not to mention MTC's program of productions in the OOB category in its UpStage Theater (see the Plays Produced off off Broadway section of this volume), which included Beth Henley's Best Play *Crimes of the Heart*, winner of the Pulitzer Prize and the Critics Award for best American play.

In independent off-Broadway production, a British playwright, Caryl Churchill, carried off top honors with a farce of sexual identity and preference, *Cloud 9*, masterfully staged by Tommy Tune. Its characters—father, mother, son, daughter, servant, family friends—were seen first as an assemblage of 1880

Michael Rupert, Alison Fraser, James Kushner, Chip Zien and Stephen Bogardus in William Finn's *March of the Falsettos,* directed by James Lapine

The 1980–81 Season Off Broadway

PLAYS (33)

American Place 1980:
Killings on the Last Line
Knitters in the Sun
Circle Rep 1980:
The Woolgatherer
Public Theater 1980:
FOB
Cassatt
A Sleepless Night With an Honest Man
An Act of Kindness
Transcendental Love
Album
Richie
Circle Rep 1981:
The Diviners
Childe Byron
In Connecticut
Negro Ensemble:
The Sixteenth Round
ZOOMAN AND THE SIGN
Weep Not for Me
In an Upstate Motel
Home (return engagement)
Vikings
Judgement
Bohemian Heaven
Moma
Coming Attractions
The One Act Play Festival

Last Summer at Bluefish Cove
Public Theater 1981:
True West
Phoenix:
Beyond Therapy
The Captivity of Pixie Shedman
Memory of Whiteness
The Legendary Stardust Boys
Marching to Georgia
Black Elk Lives
The Buddy System

SPECIALTIES (8)

Macready
American Place 1981:
The Impossible H.L Mencken
The Amazin' Casey Stengel
Public Theater 1981:
Dead End Kids
Penguin Touquet
The Haggadah (return engagement)
Truman Capote at Lincoln Center
It's Me, Sylvia

MUSICALS (14)

Chase a Rainbow
Billy Bishop Goes to War (transfer)
A Matter of Opinion
Public Theater 1981:
Girls, Girls, Girls
Alice in Concert
Really Rosie
Frimbo
Ka-Boom!
Trixie True, Teen Detective
Hijinks
An Evening with Joan Crawford
Marry Me a Little
I Can't Keep Running in Place
March of the Falsettos

REVUE (1)

Ah, Men

FOREIGN PLAYS IN ENGLISH (8)

Phoenix:
Bonjour, Là, Bonjour
Meetings
Manhattan Theater Club:
American Days
Close of Play
TRANSLATIONS
We Won't Pay! We Won't Pay!
Glasshouse
CLOUD 9

REVIVALS (44)

The Cocktail Party
Roundabout 1980:
Look Back in Anger
Fallen Angels
To Bury a Cousin
LOOM:
Trial by Jury, The Zoo and Cox & Box
The Desert Song
(11 operettas in running repertory)
Public Theater 1981:
The Pirates of Penzance
The Sea Gull
Mary Stuart
Long Day's Journey Into Night

Circle Rep:
Twelfth Night
The Beaver Coat
Roundabout 1981:
The Winslow Boy
Don Juan in Hell
Inadmissible Evidence
A Taste of Honey
Hedda Gabler
CSC:
Oedipus Rex
Oedipus at Colonus
Antigone
Gilles de Rais
Woyzeck and Leonce and Lena
The Chekhov Sketchbook
Naomi Court
BAM
A Midsummer Night's Dream
The Recruiting Officer
The Wild Duck
Jungle of Cities
Oedipus the King
Veronica's Room
Acting Company:
Il Campiello
Waiting for Godot
A Midsummer Night's Dream

Categorized above are all the new productions listed in the Plays Produced off Broadway section of this volume.
Plays listed in CAPITAL LETTERS have been designated Best Plays of 1980–81.
Plays listed in *italics* were still running after May 31, 1981.

Empire Victorians in Africa. Under their facade of decorum, their sexual activity covers just about the whole spectrum of possibility—and then some, because the characters are cast transsexually. It was the author's fancy that some of this group appear 100 years later (but only 25 years older) in the second act, in sexually liberated 1980, with a whole new set of preferences and personae. It was never entirely clear who was doing what to whom in *Cloud 9*, and it scarcely ever mattered; as in a Feydeau farce, it is the contest and not the order of finish that provides the hilarity, with a cast who gave a new meaning to the term "ensemble." Pitfalls of vulgarity which gape on either side of an enterprise like this weren't even visible from the perspective of *Cloud 9*, styled, paced and performed as it was to outlandish perfection under Tommy Tune's adventurous guidance.

T. Edward Hambleton's Phoenix Theater, too, offered a 1980–81 schedule of scripts consistent in superior quality, among them the world premiere of the Trinidadian dramatist Mustapha Matura's *Meetings*, with a gleaming but foodless kitchen symbolizing the flaws of upward mobility among its Trinidadian characters. The Phoenix also offered a translation of French Canadian playwright Michel Tremblay's *Bonjour, Là, Bonjour*, about a troubled family, as well as new works by two of our accomplished younger dramatists: *Beyond Therapy* by Christopher Durang, a stirred mixture of sex and psychiatry, and *The Captivity of Pixie Shedman* by Romulus Linney, a Southerner's evocation of his past. Linney himself had a two-play season off Broadway, as his *Childe Byron* examined the relationship between the poet and his daughter in strong performances by Lindsay Crouse and William Hurt, the outstanding 1980–81 production at Circle Repertory.

Along with the Phoenix and MTC offerings of foreign scripts, there were three in independent production: Dario Fo's comedy of Italians coping with inflation, *We Won't Pay! We Won't Pay!*, which managed a respectable 120 off-Broadway performances; Fatima Dike's short-lived *Glasshouse*, about an interracial friendship; and the aforementioned *Cloud 9*.

Among American scripts produced off Broadway this season, Charles Fuller's Best Play *Zooman and the Sign* at The Negro Ensemble Company was the standout. Under Douglas Turner Ward's direction, it brought into sharply antipathetic focus a teen-aged punk whose criminal violence causes the death of a child in a black Philadelphia neighborhood. The child's father (Ray Aranha) becomes a nonviolent nemesis of this "Zooman" (played by Giancarlo Esposito in a repusively telling performance) when he sees that his neighbors in the community want no part of testifying against the killer or helping in any way to bring him to justice. Fuller's play points the finger at everybody and has some compassion for everybody—Zooman included. Other subjects dramatized in works put on by the NEC this season were the plight of a has-been prize fighter hiding from gangsters (*The Sixteenth Round* by Samm-Art Williams, whose 1980 Best Play *Home* was brought back on this year's NEC schedule), multiple murder in the black ghetto (*Weep Not for Me* by Gus Edwards) and big-city violence in which victim is also perpetrator (*In an Upstate Motel* by Larry Neal).

In other 1980–81 institutional production, Joseph Papp's busy (with musicals, revivals and guest productions) New York Shakespeare Festival Public Theater came up with only one new play in its 1981 season: *True West*, Sam She-

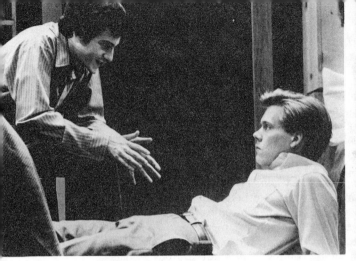

ALBUM—Keth Gordon, Kevin Bacon *(above)* and Jenny Wright *(right)* in the David Rimmer play

pard's latest, not a Western but a clash of siblings, one of whom is a screen writer and the other a vagrant ne'er-do-well—symbolizing, as in other Shepard plays, the decay of American life and spirit. The Public's finest hours took place in June 1980 with *FOB*, a play by David Henry Hwang about the difficulties of Chinese immigrants adjusting to America, directed by Mako; and, much later in the season, as it gave over its stage to the Mabou Mines anti-nuclear diatribe *Dead End Kids*, an inventive company led by JoAnne Akalaitis in acting out warnings by famous scientists re the perils of unleashed radiation. Richard Foreman's Ontological-Hysteric Theater production of *Penguin Touquet*, a kaleidoscope of stage imagery; Jean-Claude Van Itallie's version of *The Sea Gull* directed by Andrei Serban; Elizabeth Swados's musical rearrangement of Lewis Carroll, *Alice in Concert*, with Joseph Papp directing and Meryl Streep in the title role; the Dodger Theater's *Mary Stuart*; and *Long Day's Journey Into Night* played by an all-black cast under Geraldine Fitzgerald's direction were also on the Public's varied guest and house program this season.

Circle Repertory began with William Mastrosimone's *The Woolgatherer*, a two-character encounter between a truck driver and a salesgirl, which opened in June 1980 and was later joined in repertory by Frank Barrie's impersonation of the famous actor William Charles Macready. Circle Rep then proceeded to the American College Theater Festival winner, *The Diviners* by Jim Leonard Jr., which looked at life in a small Indiana town through the eyes of a child with a gift for dowsing, a retired preacher and other such individuals. After revivals of *Twelfth Night* and Gerhart Hauptmann's 1893 German comedy *The Beaver Coat*, Circle Rep came up with *Childe Byron*, followed by *In Connecticut* by Roy London, a play developed in Circle Rep workshop and in production at GeVa in Rochester, N.Y., about the tribulations of moving from the suburbs to a New York apartment. As the 1980–81 season ended, this group was aiming toward a June production of Lanford Wilson's *A Tale Told*, the third in its author's series of plays about the Talley family, the subject of his previous *Fifth of July* and *Talley's Folly*.

American Place had little luck this year, either with its presentations of single characters onstage (*The Impossible H.L. Mencken* with John Rothman and *The*

Amazin' Casey Stengel with Paul Dooley) or with its more extensive dramatizations *Memory of Whiteness*, a family conflict play by Richard Hamburger, or, just across the border in June 1981, *The Fuehrer Bunker*, a dramatization by W.D. Snodgrass of the last days of the Hitler gang, with music by Richard Peaslee. Lincoln Center made an effort to launch its small Newhouse Theater as an off-Broadway showcase with a personal appearance during the Christmas holidays by Truman Capote reading from his own works, and later with a program of one-acters by Jeffrey Sweet, John Guare and Percy Granger. The arrangement by which Edward Albee served as artistic director of this enterprise, produced by Richmond Crinkley, probably will not continue, nor is there an ongoing program for the Newhouse firmed up at this writing.

Within the broad pipeline of independent play production off Broadway, there was scarcely a trickle of real interest. David Rimmer's *Album* was one noteworthy arrival, with the mid-1960s growing pains of a quartet of teen-agers intimately dramatized, directed (by Joan Micklin Silver) and performed. This script emerged from a previous OOB production at the WPA Theater and is perhaps a measure of what might have been had not this year's flow been somewhat stemmed by the Equity showcase controversy. Also emergent from OOB

April Lerman, Joe La Benz IV, B.J. Barie, Tisha Campbell and Wade Raley in the musical *Really Rosie* by Maurice Sendak and Carole King

in The Glines production was Jane Chambers's *Last Summer at Bluefish Cove*, a strong script about the summer loves of single women, who happen in this case to be lesbians. Other subjects raised in the new scripts in their numbers were the painters Mary Cassatt and Degas (*Cassatt*), Benedict Arnold (*A Sleepless Night With an Honest Man*); Ralph Waldo Emerson (*Transcendental Love*), cannibalism (*Judgement*), economics (*Bohemian Heaven*), Vietnam (*Moma*), the Sioux (*Black Elk Lives*) and an array of domestic and marital conflicts, forgettable as speedily as their departure from the scene after very short runs.

The production of book musicals off Broadway doubled from 7 in 1980 to 14 in 1981, and they were generally more substantial than the straight plays. Playwrights Horizons established a presence off Broadway this season with upward-mobile OOB productions: *Coming Attractions* (a Ted Tally melodrama about a terrorist and the media), and much more firmly with *March of the Falsettos*, a musical by William Finn describing the emotional stresses of husband, wife and child when the former takes off with a homosexual lover and the family psychiatrist takes his place in the bed. The show had no spoken dialogue but was made up of 20 songs, without intermission. James Lapine's direction was an irresistible driving force adding voltage to the material and propelling an energetic cast headed by Michael Rupert as the father torn between passion and parenthood.

Another of the off-Broadway year's musical attractions was *Marry Me a Little*, a bundle of Stephen Sondheim trunk songs (written for shows but dropped in production, often for reasons other than quality) and numbers from *Saturday Night*, which never reached the New York stage. Two young performers— Suzanne Henry and Craig Lucas (who collaborated with the director Norman René on the development of the show itself)—acted out a love story implied by the succession of Sondheim lyrics, previously unheard but now, fortunately, embedded in the record of the New York stage. That a leading composer's trunk songs are not necessarily, or even probably, inferior work was proven again in *Marry Me a Little*. There was nothing second-rate about the Sondheim numbers or the show.

The multi-character Canadian musical *Billy Bishop Goes to War* by and with Eric Peterson and John Gray reversed the usual flow of traffic by moving down from Broadway to off-Broadway for an extended summer visit. Maurice Sendak's *Really Rosie*, with music by Carole King, setting forth the adventures of the Nutshell Kids and their alligator friend, made it past indifferent reviews and cheered up the off-Broadway season in a long run. Unhappily, *Frimbo*, a musical adaptation of *New Yorker* stories about an avid railroad buff, lasted for only one performance, even though staged in the ultra-realistic setting of Tracks 39 to 42 at Grand Central Terminal, where the coming and going of a real railroad train was no problem for the technical crew.

The title of *Ka-boom!* said it all, or almost all, in a musical comedy fantasy about what it might be like, after a nuclear holocaust, to put on a show. *Trixie True, Teen Detective*, with book, music and lyrics by Kelly Hamilton, parodied its genre of detective adventure to some effect, in a tale of a novelist (Gene Lindsey) trying to kill off his popular, but by him unwanted, teen-aged detective heroine. The Chelsea Theater Center's *Hijinks!*, a musical adaptation by Robert

John Shea and Pippa Pearthree in *American Days* at Manhattan Theater Club

Kalfin, Steve Brown and John McKinney of *Captain Jinks of the Horse Marines*, was a highlight of the off-Broadway season, though it didn't develop an audience to keep it on for any length of time—or to encourage the Chelsea group, which had decided to call it quits after this year, to try for another season of off-Broadway production.

Barbara Schottenfeld's *I Can't Keep Running in Place*, with Marcia Rodd as a psychiatrist in workshop sessions with the sextet of woman patients, and with a decidedly feminist orientation, advanced its cause ardently in a musical context. In the revue catgory, *Ah, Men*, a series of reflections on "the male experience," was assembled by Paul Shyre from the works of a couple of dozen savants from Jean-Jacques Rousseau to Groucho Marx, with songs by Will Holt—a tingling entertainment. It very likely signifies nothing but coincidence that only this one revue appeared off Broadway this year as compared with 11 in 1980. A corresponding rise in the production of book shows in 1981 almost balanced out the shortfall.

The ebb and flow of indifferent material off Broadway this season cannot demean its accomplishments: the three Best Plays *Translations*, *Cloud 9* and

Zooman and the Sign, the best moments of its musicals, the stimulating revivals which are considered in the next chapter. If its vision narrowed and its creativity attenuated in 1981, off Broadway shared those failings with the whole expanse of New York theater. It could not escape the widespread epidemic of mediocrity for which there is no cure except a new and better season and renewed resolve.

Revivals on and off Broadway

This was the year that Joseph Papp pulled a rabbit out of his hat and made the Messrs. Gilbert and Sullivan hit musical authors of 1981 with a smashing revival of *The Pirates of Penzance*. In athletic style under the direction of Wilford Leach; in rock-star magnetism with the presence of Linda Ronstadt as Mabel and Rex Smith as Frederic; in show-biz flair with the casting of Kevin Kline as the Pirate King and Patricia Routledge (and later Estelle Parsons) as Ruth; in ineffable G & S humor with George Rose as a very model of a Major-General; in design, melody and general allure, this was a first-rate entertainment, removed from the shelf of 19th century theater and brought first to Central Park and then to Broadway without a speck of dust upon its silvery surface. Joseph Papp waved some kind of wand over these pirates and general's daughters and brought forth the revival of the New York theater year.

Much newer, and still shining brightly in reproduction, was *Camelot*, with Richard Burton recreating his role of King Arthur in the Lerner-Loewe musical theater adaptation of this folk tale as told by T.H. White in *The Once and Future King*. Burton commanded the stage so completely it was hard to believe that Guenevere would look elsewhere for excitement; nevertheless this production regenerated the original's emotional and melodic appeal. This wasn't true of other full-scale Broadway musical revivals this year. Shows that came and went without attracting the new audience to whom it had been presumed they would appeal were *Brigadoon*, *The Music Man* with Dick Van Dyke, Cole Porter's *Can-can* (revised by Abe Burrows) with Zizi Jeanmaire, a Goodspeed Opera House revamping of *The Five O'clock Girl* and the Jacques Brel musical on a visit to Broadway. On the other hand, Light Opera of Manhattan (LOOM) demonstrated its usual staying power, going its tuneful way through a 52-week season in its small East Side theater with its extensive Gilbert and Sullivan repertory, plus the operetta likes of *The Desert Song*, *The Vagabond King*, *The Student Prince* and *The Merry Widow*.

Among straight-play revivals it was no contest for the limelight, as Elizabeth Taylor and company swept New York's audiences (if not its drama critics) off their feet in *The Little Foxes*. It was the glittering international movie star's stage debut they came to see, not so much Lillian Hellman's acerbic play about greed and family abrasions. Miss Taylor gave them a vivid presence as Regina, leaving to other members of the cast—most notably Maureen Stapleton as Birdie—to fill in the subtler tones. Miss Taylor's effort was so conspicuously whole-hearted, holding nothing back that she had to offer, that it overshadowed any minor shortcomings in the esthetics of the enterprise.

Uniformly the best of Broadway's 1980–81 straight play revivals was Philip Barry's *The Philadelphia Story* as staged by Ellis Rabb, with Blythe Danner as Tracy, Edward Herrmann as Mike and Frank Converse as Dexter. The enduring charm of this comedy of Main Line manners was brought to full flower in all departments of the show, which reopened the Vivian Beaumont Theater at Lincoln Center under Richmond Crinkley's production supervision, following the dark seasons since its abandonment by Joseph Papp. After this attractive begin-

ning, the Beaumont survived a difficult *Macbeth* staged by opera impresario Sarah Caldwell and went on to a new work of Best Play dimensions, Woody Allen's *The Floating Light Bulb*. Mr. Crinkley and his colleagues have of course not yet charted the Beaumont's destiny, but at least they made their presence felt after they turned the lights back on.

Another major function of a New York revival season, apart from dusting off classics or remounting hits for a new audience, is the second look at a contemporary script, perhaps from an angle somewhat different from the original. A success in this category this season was the off-Broadway revival of Ira Levin's *Veronica's Room*, a thriller of impersonation and its consequences which first played Broadway in 1973 and was reshaped somewhat in a 1978 Hasty Pudding production in Boston, the blueprint for this one. Similar efforts to try again with Gus Weill's *To Bury a Cousin* and Michael Sawyer's *Naomi Court* met with little acceptance; but in one of the OOB byways, the Richard Allen Center for Culture

THE PIRATES OF PENZANCE—*Above* are reproduced Patricia McGourty's sketches of her costume designs for the Pirate King and the Major General in the Broadway revival of the Gilbert and Sullivan operetta. *On opposite page,* the Pirate King (Kevin Kline) and his pirates in a scene from the operetta

and Art, Eugene O'Neill's *Long Day's Journey Into Night* was put on by a distinguished all-black cast under the direction of Geraldine Fitzgerald, in an experiment so felicitous that it was soon invited into Joseph Papp's Public Theater to settle down for an extended run.

After closing its 1980 schedule in summer with the Kaufman-Hart comedy *The Man Who Came to Dinner* starring Ellis Rabb, Theodore Mann's and Paul Libin's Circle in the Square moved through reported financial problems into its 30th anniversary season. It was one of sturdy classical selections: Euripides's *The Bacchae*, Ibsen's *John Gabriel Borkman* and Strindberg's *The Father*. Off Broadway, the Classic Stage Company (CSC) followed Sophocles's *Oedipus Rex, Oedipus at Colonus* and *Antigone* (in repertory, but including 4 marathon performances of the three-play cycle) with the first English-language presentation of Roger Planchon's play about Bluebeard, *Gilles de Rais*, plus adaptations by and with the company's artistic director, Christopher Martin, of Büchner's *Woyzeck* and *Leonce and Lena*.

John Houseman's Acting Company was invited by Joseph Papp to the Public Theater for 10 guest performances of plays by Goldoni, Beckett and Shakespeare. Over in Brooklyn, the BAM Theater Company put on a repertory of five revivals: yet another version of Sophocles's *Oedipus*, plus works of Shakespeare, George Farquhar, Ibsen and Brecht. After this formidably eclectic season, BAM announced that it would cease to function after this, its second year at the Brooklyn Academy of Music. The demise of any theater organization as professionally accomplished as BAM is regrettable, but hope springs eternal that another way may be found to use the Academy for the continuing benefit of New York legitimate theater audiences.

Of all the revival producing organizations, Gene Feist's and Michael Fried's Roundabout Theater Company seems to have the surest sense of theater on its two stages, usually selecting fairly modern works ready to be seen again, like last summer's *Look Back in Anger* or, later in the season, *The Winslow Boy* and *A Taste of Honey*, the latter following the path beaten by Joseph Papp and Circle Rep by transferring to Broadway after its run at the Roundabout. This group often casts its shows aggressively, as with Arlene Francis, Paul Sparer and Philip Bosco in *Don Juan in Hell* or Nicol Williamson in his original role in *Inadmissible Evidence* or Susannah York as *Hedda Gabler*, always producing with care and insight. The Roundabout is a perennial star of the huge New York revival show, which is surely a precious and unique cultural asset, covering as it always does the whole spectrum of theater from the starkest nightmare of the ancient Greeks to the frothiest operetta of the mauve decade. As the song says, "That's entertainment . . . It could be *Oedipus Rex*/Where a chap kills his father/And causes a lot of bother." On the 1980-81 New York revival scene, it actually was—twice.

Edward Herrmann, Michael Gross and Blythe Danner in a scene from the Lincoln Center revival of Philip Barry's *The Philadelphia Story*

Offstage

Occupying a major portion of the New York theater's offstage attention this season were the feast-or-famine economy and the Equity showcase controversy, both rooted in the past and carrying over into the seemingly ever-more-problematical future. The rising cost of everything from production costs at one end to theater tickets at the other was resulting in outlandish grosses at the Broadway hits and severe penury elsewhere. Inflation was a contributing cause of the demise of two important off-Broadway producing groups, Chelsea Theater Center and BAM Theater Company (whose expenses this season exceeded its $1 million income and $700,000 subsidy by about $1 million, according to *Variety* estimate). A 1980s economy in which a $200,000 off-Broadway production cost no longer seemed impossible, and an $18.50 ticket had become a reality, would very likely stifle the activity of other groups before very long.

Meanwhile, in the governmental part of the forest, Little Red Riding Hood arrived at Grandmother's door hoping for a warm welcome and a goodly $175 million from the National Endowment on the Arts, only to be confronted by wolfish teeth and a proposed 50 per cent slash in the 1982 Federal arts subsidy penciled in by the previous administration. This severe reduction at a time when the partially subsidized sector was already hurting moved Joseph Papp (whose New York Shakespeare Festival receives subsidies but is also heavily self-endowed with a share of the Broadway profits from *A Chorus Line* and now *The Pirates of Penzance*) to declare publicly that the National Endowment should be abolished, thereby saving $10 million in administration expenses, and any Federal arts allotment be distributed directly to the state arts councils. "I do not believe that an agency for the arts needs to exist in Washington," Papp stated, "I don't think it's proper for people in Washington to make decisions about the arts in New York City." They will continue to do so, however, and no doubt there will be a large reduction in the 1982 arts subsidy by the Federal budget-cutters.

The drying-up of adventurous new scripts in the area of off-off-Broadway production because of Equity's insistence on a showcase code of future commitment to participating actors was the second major offstage preoccupation this season. We reported the details of the controversy in the offstage chapter of our report in *The Best Plays of 1979–80* (which see). Little has changed in the past twelve months. The majority of dramatists continued to feel that the conditions of the proposed showcase code would inhibit future productions of their scripts, and therefore they continued reluctant to release them for presentation in showcases, the staple of the OOB diet. Back in June 1980 the Equity Council accepted a recommendation from its members that the proposed code's wording be changed to assure the author that his or her "only obligation, both morally and financially, is to give notice in writing to any future producer and Equity, prior to bonding, that the play was done in showcase" (so that, under certain circumstances, Equity could oblige sponsors of a new production to hire or indemnify actors who contributed their services to the showcase). While this freed the author from personal financial obligation (to indemnify such actors not hired), it did not free his work from the risk of being turned down for possible production because of the albatross of obligation tied round its neck by the terms of the Equity code.

This change in wording had little effect upon the dramatists' determination not to obligate their scripts under this code. Neither did the Equity Council's vote in August not to renew the contract of Executive Secretary Donald Grody, one of the chief proponents of the code. Michael Weller and other authors brought a suit against Equity in Federal court in October charging the actors' union with violating sections of the Sherman Antitrust Act and the National Labor Relations Act, after Equity had ordered its actors to cease performing in Weller's OOB production *Split* when Weller refused to sign the code. The complaint, as quoted in *Variety,* also alleges that "a provision of Equity's contract with the League of Resident Theaters requiring LORT managements to hire or compensate earlier showcase casts is also illegal and should be nullified." As of June 1981 no resolution of this case had been announced.

Meanwhile, as bargaining agent for the actors, Equity won from the League of Off-Broadway Theaters a 10.6 per cent pay increase for performers in off-Broadway productions, in a new contract to remain in effect until October 1984. New weekly minimums for the five categories of off-Broadway shows range from $169 to $351. And Equity members contributing their services in showcase productions are to receive three weeks' salary in lieu of an offer to repeat the role, if the show moves to the off-Broadway level from OOB.

In June 1980 a New York Federal Court agreed that The Shubert Organization could manage the National Theater in Washington, under a waiver of a 1956 "consent decree" in a Justice Department antitrust action prohibiting the Shuberts from acquiring more theaters. Then, in midwinter, The Shubert Organization filed a motion to overturn this decree, under which they have been operating for a quarter of a century. They now seek court permission to expand, asking that the consent decree be terminated by 1985. In May the Justice Department recommended to the court that The Shubert Organization be freed from the consent decree's ban against new theater acquisitions by the Shuberts in New York and on the road, and a decision in the case was still pending at season's end.

The threatened demolition of the Morosco, Helen Hayes and Bijou Theaters to make way for the proposed quarter-billion-dollar Portman Hotel complex loomed over the theater district all year, while the little Bijou continued to prove its value to the Broadway scene as a home for miniature legitimate stage concepts like one-man and one-woman shows and revues. Protests against this demolition by outraged groups of theater folk and others also continued and were heard in the press and in court, but the outcries seemed to be growing weaker with the passage of time. On a more positive note, the New York State and City development and planning agencies opened discussions of a large-scale scheme to renovate the Broadway-Eighth Avenue block of 42nd Street, reconverting some of its now-sleazy film houses to stage use. And an $8 million gift from the Fan Fox and Leslie R. Samuels Foundation was earmarked for renovation of the New York State and Vivian Beaumont Theaters at Lincoln Center, including improvement of acoustics.

An important change in the personnel of New York theater critics took place in September with the New York *Times's* announcement that Frank Rich would

LONG DAY'S JOURNEY INTO NIGHT—This revival of the O'Neill play began OOB at Richard Allen Center, performed by Gloria Foster and Samantha McCoy (pictured *above*), plus Al Freeman Jr., Earle Hyman and Peter Francis-James

replace Walter Kerr in the daily reviewing spot, with Kerr returning to that role of unhurried observer of the passing theater scene in the Sunday paper which he prefers. Rich, 31, a native of Washington, D.C., served his reviewing apprenticeship on the Harvard *Crimson, Time* and other publications before joining the *Times* in April 1980. Rich called theater "a dominant passion" from his early childhood, "*before* I made the discovery of movies and TV." In his first season of reviewing he proved to be neither a crowd follower nor an iconoclast, calling them as he saw them but without often raising his voice, with sensitivities that seemed more personal than Olympian. In another post, Katie Kelly replaced Chauncey Howell as WNBC-TV's theater commentator. And at the Dramatists Guild, leadership of that organization of playwrights, composers, lyricists and librettists passed to a new president, Peter Stone, after Past President Stephen Sondheim declined to run for a fifth two-year term. And at Equity a ten-month search for an executive secretary to fill the post formerly held by Donald Grody ended with the selection of a Washington labor lawyer, Alan D. Eisenberg.

The ceremony of announcing and presenting the Tony Awards for Broadway's bests has become an annual TV fiesta. This year it certainly symbolized the twelve months of New York theater which it was trying to celebrate. Three of its four nominees for best play were foreign scripts, the other a return engagement from a previous off-Broadway season. All of its musicals were retreads of old material. One of its best-book nominees had survived for only one performance. Three of its best-score nominees had been palpable flops. The number of producers who nowadays huddle in groups to put on a single show was so large that it defeated the efforts of an admittedly slow reader, Elizabeth Taylor, to handle all their names in the cumbersome list of nominees. And yet . . . and yet there were the shining individual achievements of a Gower Champion, a Peter Shaffer. There was even one producer who was able to put on a show all by himself, David Merrick, who, as he accepted the best-musical award, posed the rhetorical question, "What would the musical season have been without *42nd Street*?" We shudder to think what this or any other theater season would have been without those special inspirations for which the theater of any time is remembered. We are more than usually grateful for the very few which brightened the 1980–81 season in New York and hope for a brighter cluster in the year to come.

THE SEASON
AROUND THE UNITED STATES

with

A DIRECTORY OF PROFESSIONAL
REGIONAL THEATER

Including casts and credits of new plays, selected Canadian programs and children's programs

and

OUTSTANDING NEW PLAYS
CITED BY
AMERICAN THEATER CRITICS
ASSOCIATION

THE American Theater Critics Association (ATCA) is the organization of more than 125 leading drama critics of all media in all sections of the United States. One of this group's stated purposes is "To increase public awareness of the theater as a *national* resource" (italics ours). To this end, ATCA has cited a number of outstanding new plays produced this season across the country, to be listed and briefly described in this volume; and has designated one of them for us to offer

41

as an introduction to our coverage of "The Season Around the United States" in the form of a synopsis with excerpts, in much the same manner as Best Plays of the New York season.

The critics made their citations, including their principal one of *Chekhov in Yalta* by John Driver and Jeffrey Haddow, in the following manner: member critics everywhere were asked to call the attention of an ATCA committee—chaired by Dan Sullivan, drama critic of the Los Angeles *Times*—to outstanding new work in their areas. Scripts of these nominated plays were studied by committee members who made their choices, as the editor of this volume makes his New York Best Plays choice, on the basis of script rather than production. There were no eligibility requirements (such as Equity cast or formal resident-theater status) except that a nominee be the first full professional production of a new work outside New York City within this volume's time frame of June 1, 1980 to May 31, 1981.

The list of other 1980–81 plays nominated by members of ATCA as outstanding presentations in their areas, with descriptions written by the critics who saw and nominated them, follows the synopsis of *Chekhov in Yalta*. The synopsis itself was prepared by the *Best Plays* editor.

Cited by American Theater Critics as an Outstanding New Play of 1980–81

CHEKHOV IN YALTA

A Play in Two Acts

BY JOHN DRIVER AND JEFFREY HADDOW

Cast and credits appear on page 90

JOHN DRIVER was born in Erie, Pa. on Jan. 16, 1947, the son of a research and electrical engineer. He received his B.S. in speech and theater from Northwestern in 1968 and his M.F.A. from Smith College in 1970. His first work in New York was off off Broadway with the Shirtsleeve Theater, which in December 1976 produced Scrambled Feet, *a revue written by Driver and Jeffrey Haddow, which Driver also directed. That same season, in March, he supplied the conception and direction of the musical* Children of Adam *at Shirtsleeve, also produced off Broadway for 69 performances that summer. The following season at Shirtsleeve, Driver directed a revival of* Dear Liar. *In August 1978 the Driver Haddow-revue* Scrambled Feet *was presented at St. Nicholas Theater in Chicago as a special event; and almost a year later, on June 11, 1979, it was produced off Broadway with Driver both performing and directing, in a run that had reached 823 performances as this season ended.*

Chekhov in Yalta, *whose subtitle is* Featuring a Rare and Delightful Visit by the Moscow Art Theater, *the second major Driver-Haddow collaboration for the theater, was designated an outstanding 1980–81 play by the American Theater Critics Association on the basis of its production at the Mark Taper Forum in Los Angeles. Driver is married, with two children, and lives in New York City.*

JEFFREY HADDOW, *a Long Islander born in 1947, met John Driver while they were both students at Northwestern and began his playwriting career in collaboration with Driver on* Scrambled Feet *in 1976 (see above). Haddow was a staff writer on the Chicago TV show "The Screaming Yellow Theater" and collaborated with Dick Orkin on a Chicago radio series. Haddow is also the co-author, with Driver, of TV pilots for NBC, CBS and a Home Box Office comedy special, plus a Warner Brothers feature motion picture. He is married and lives in New York City.*

Time: April 1900

Place: Anton Chekhov's villa in Yalta

ACT I

Scene 1

SYNOPSIS: Fyokla the maid *("an unselfconsciously voluptuous creature in her early 20s")* is setting up tea on the terrace of Anton Chekhov's villa overlooking the sea at Yalta on an April afternoon. There are two entrances into the three-story house in the background and a path leading off toward the water. Chekhov —a doctor as well as a writer—enters carrying his medical bag *("he is 40 but looks much older")* and sinks into a wicker chair, tired after having attended all night to a patient. He tells Fyokla, "You know, I saw a curious thing on the way back here. A drunken ice merchant had run his cart into a ditch. He was sitting on a block of ice, sobbing and tearing his hair out." Chekhov decides to turn this tableau into a story about an ice man named Semyon. "In his youth he marries an abrasive, domineering woman. She's nagging, gluttonous . . ."

Fyokla leaves to go to market, and Chekhov finishes the story alone: 20 years later, more terrible than ever, Semyon's wife chokes to death on a piece of bread. Racing home, Semyon runs his cart into a ditch and sits there, not knowing whether to laugh or cry at losing his wife.

Maxim Gorky, 30 *("tall, dark, with Tartar features, flowing black hair and full moustache, dressed in peasant blouse, breeches and riding boots"),* living in Yalta to treat his consumption, and Ivan Alexeivich Bunin, 31, a popular writer, *"elegant, aristocratic,"* are in the midst of a political argument as they join Chekhov on his terrace. Gorky points out to Chekhov that two men posing as gravediggers in the cemetery on the other side of the wall are probably secret police, watching Gorky because of leaflets he's been writing. Chekhov cautions Gorky about his political activities.

CHEKHOV: Maxim, you're too impatient. Change and growth will only come when the season is right and the ground has been carefully prepared.

GORKY: Yes, but the ground must be scorched, cleansed by fire then plowed under. Ground covered with ashes is fertile ground.

CHEKHOV: But to burn, to tear down. No, give the people books, teach them to read, make them healthy . . .

GORKY: I want to see it in my lifetime. The solution is quick and simple. Cut off the head of the Imperial eagle.

CHEKHOV: For God's sake, Gorky, keep your voice down.

BUNIN: You look tired, Anton. You really should rest for awhile.

CHEKHOV: I was at Tolstoy's all night.

BUNIN: Oho. That's enough to exhaust a plow horse. Take a nap. We'll come back later.

CHEKHOV: No, no, don't go. His wife was ill. You won't believe what Tolstoy came up with this time. He said he couldn't tolerate Shakespeare's plays.

BUNIN: What conceit!

GORKY: Only Tolstoy could get away with that.

CHEKHOV: Then he said my plays were even worse. *(Imitating Tolstoy.)* "Nothing happens in your plays, Anton." *(Silence.)* He must have seen Stanislavski's production of *Seagull.* All those pauses.

Pause.

I almost fell asleep myself. I know many people consider Stanislavski a genius, but the things he did to my play. Granted, it was supposed to be night, but the lights were so dim the audience could hardly see the stage. And that constant cacophany of nightingales, hoofbeats, creaking gates, rustling leaves, strange noises in the forest. And his brilliant idea of a plague of imaginary insects. All through the first act the players kept slapping themselves so loudly you couldn't hear what they were saying. In the next play I write, I'll have someone make an entrance in every scene just to say, "What a marvelous place! There are no mosquitoes."

BUNIN: Anton, you must admit, the acting at the Moscow Art is more real than at other theaters. Sometimes Stanislavski's off the mark but he's bold. He's an experimenter.

CHEKHOV: My plays are not laboratory animals.

Stanislavsky and the Moscow Art Theater troupe are to arrive in Yalta from Sebastopol tomorrow, and Chekhov is preparing a reception for them here at the villa. After some reference to recent affairs with actresses, Chekhov goes on to esthetics: "Why does the Moscow Art insist on doing my plays the same way they do Ibsen's? I write comedies." The three writers philosophize about the sea; Chekhov claims he once wrote a perfect description of the sea—"The sea is huge"—and keeps it with him as a reminder to write simply.

Masha, Chekhov's sister, joins the group. She is 34, *"a plain, matronly woman who has devoted much of her life to looking after her brother's welfare."* She is accompanied by Olga Knipper, 36, *"vibrant, strong-willed leading lady of the Moscow Art."* The troupe has arrived in Yalta early, including Vladimir Nemirovich-Danchenko, its director, who also joins the group on the terrace. Chekhov makes the introductions while Masha goes off to see to the preparations for the reception. Gorky realizes that the acting company must have been in Moscow during recent disturbances.

GORKY:. . . . .The students must have marched right down your street.

NEMIROVICH: Yes, we were in the midst of a rehearsal when we heard singing. We watched the whole bloody fiasco crouched at the front windows of the theater.

CHEKHOV: What are you talking about?

NEMIROVICH: You didn't hear about it? People were killed. Students and Cossacks fighting in the streets. The gutters ran with blood.

CHEKHOV: There was no mention of it in the newspapers.

GORKY (*contemptuously*): The newspapers.

NEMIROVICH: A large group of students were demonstrating about something or other, and the Cossacks wouldn't let them pass.

GORKY: The bastards!

NEMIROVICH: At first everyone just stopped and looked at each other. Then, one student began shouting slogans, and the rest of them lost their heads. Anton, they charged a brigade of mounted Cossacks.

OLGA: I felt as if I were in a dream. Just outside the entrance of the theater, a blonde boy wearing glasses and a blue scarf tried to pull a Cossack from his horse. The officer was grinning when he cut off the boy's hand.

NEMIROVICH: Several students were trampled to death.

OLGA: It made us sick but what could we do?

　　　Masha enters.

GORKY: They'll pay for this. For each one killed, a thousand will rise up to take his place.

BUNIN: I can't believe there are that many suicidal fools, even in Russia.

MASHA: At the station we saw them loading coffins onto the mail train.

GORKY: Wait till the workers start joining the students.

MASHA: God help us.

Masha has brought oysters from Moscow, on ice, and they all proceed to eat them. Chekhov has a bad coughing fit but protests that he is all right. Masha insists on taking him into the house. Chekhov, like everybody else in Yalta, has consumption. Nemirovich thinks he looks badly and fears that he might become too ill to write, which would be a disaster for their theater: "If we don't have a financial success this season, and that means a new Chekhov play, the doors of the Moscow Art will close forever. Why do you think we're here?" To get a new play from Chekhov, of course.

Olga chides Nemirovich for paying too much attention to Stanislavski's wife Lilina. Lilina knows what she's doing, Nemirovich asserts, and asks Olga whether Chekhov is in love with her (she's not sure). If he were, she could exert her influence in favor of a play for the troupe.

Masha comes in and declares that she's worried about her brother—his consumption seems to be getting worse. Masha is in love with Bunin, wishes he would pay her more attention and that Olga could help her. Olga will try—but in return she asks Masha for information about her brother (he has recently entertained another actress whom he calls affectionately his "Russian Duse," Olga learns). The two women are weeping for each other's romantic yearnings, as Chekhov enters, declaring that as a doctor he knows he is "healthy as a bull." He demands his cigars. Angrily, Masha goes off.

Alone with Olga, Chekhov calles her his "little Russian Bernhardt." ("Why not Duse?" Olga wants to know. "Duse is a tragic figure," Chekhov replies.) Fyokla comes in bringing Chekhov his cigars—locked in a humidor to which Masha holds the key. Chekhov goes at the lock with a hairpin, to no effect, in the meantime encouraging Olga with the information that he's written a good part for her into his new play, *Three Sisters*. What Chekhov needs now, Olga maintains, is to stop smoking and concentrate on a cure for his consumption. He tells her that his doctor, Altshuler, has prescribed an amorous actress in residence in his beach house as a desirable part of the cure. Olga indicates that she will hold out for a more lasting relationship than "just another finger on your glove." Nemirovich comes in to take her away, leaving Chekhov alone to think things over.

> *Chekhov extracts notebook and pencil from his pocket and begins to write.* Pauses.

CHEKHOV: Semyon the ice man. Where was I?

> *Slaps the notebook shut.*

Why do I bother with this inconsequential tripe? Vanity. How long do I really expect my work to outlive me? Twenty years? Twenty-five years? Oh, let's be honest, seven. No, seven and a half.

> *Goes back to work on the humidor lock.*

Damn! Olga makes me nervous. Even when she's not here she invades my privacy. I can't get any work done. . . . .Oh, Knipper, we could share beautiful evenings in the beach house but you want more than that. You deserve more. How can I let you betroth yourself to my misery? It will catch up with me. I haven't the breath to outrun it. It's coming as surely as the tide. . . . .I'll sleep all day, my face will be flushed and bloated, my clothes will hang on my emaciated body and flap in the wind, my hands won't have the strength to hold even a pencil. I'll have to be bathed. Me! Who can't even bear to be seen without a tie.

> *The lock springs open. Chekhov takes out a cigar and lights it.*

No, no wife. I have work to do.

> *Coughs. Lights fade. Curtain.*

Scene 2

The following night, Chekhov's friends and members of the Moscow Art Theater are heard singing offstage, while a group comes onto the terrace, dancing and carrying wine and vodka: Olga, Bunin, Gorky, Nemirovich, Masha and Fyokla, plus Luzhki (*"a fat, sentimental actor"*), Moskvin (*"a young, acrobatic character man"*) and Lilina (*"the delicately beautiful wife of Stanislavski"*). The party is in full swing, with the guests milling about in search of wine, food and flirtation.

Lilina complains to Olga that her husband's passion for the theater is coming between them: "His mind never leaves the stage." The riots in Moscow are getting on her nerves, too: "The ground is moving under our feet." Lilina admits she's tempted by Nemirovich's obvious passion for her. When he comes back to ask her to dance, Lilina goes off with him.

Olga sends for Bunin, who joins her on the terrace. She tells Bunin a tale about a friend (meaning Masha) who is in love with a writer (meaning Bunin) but too shy to tell him so. Bunin, however, assumes Olga is talking about herself and Chekhov, and to her chagrin, he observes: "If Anton marries you, he'll be committing suicide. . . . .You know how sick he is. In his condition, he's an easy mark for a beautiful woman like you. If he tries to keep up with your hyperactive Moscow social life, he'll be dead before the honeymoon's over."

Olga explains that she was speaking of Masha, not herself, but before she can go any further the conversation is interrupted by other guests, coming onto the terrace with Chekhov and discussing tonight's performance of *Uncle Vanya*. The actors believe the play is moving, but Chekhov explains that it is "practically a vaudeville. How could you misinterpret it so? It's all there in the text. I wrote it all down."

At this moment the co-director of the Moscow Art Theater, Konstantine Sergeivich Stanislavski (who that evening substituted a speech from *Hedda Gabler* for one of Chekhov's *Uncle Vanya* monologues), 37, flamboyant, makes his entrance. The others ignore him until he commands their attention and turns the conversation to that evening's performance. He noticed that Chekhov left early.

CHEKHOV:. . . . .It wasn't my play.

STANISLAVSKI: What do you mean? We did our best to present the reality of your text. We used real food, real tea, we created the atmosphere of a real country dacha with the sounds of birds, cows, crickets.

CHEKHOV: The stage is not a barnyard. The stage is not life. It is the quintessence of life.

STANISLAVSKI: I spoke to a critic after the show. He loved it. I remember his exact words. He said . . . uh . . . well, he was impressed with the, let me see, yes, "the twilight mood of melancholy."

CHEKHOV: What melancholy? There isn't even one death.

STANISLAVSKI: Anton, you seem to be unaware of the depth of your gift.

CHEKHOV: When I write, I know exactly what I'm doing. *Uncle Vanya* is a comedy.

STANISLAVSKI: Certainly it has its comic moments, yes, but on the whole anyone would have to agree, it's a tragedy.

LUZHKI: Why don't we take a vote?

STANISLAVSKI: When I'm wrong, I'm the first to admit it.
      Moskvin whistles.

LUZHKI: How many think *Uncle Vanya* is a comedy?
      Nobody. Then Chekhov, then Masha, then Gorky raise their hands.

GORKY: An artist must always be supported is his own opinions about his work . . . even when he's wrong.

NEMIROVICH: Anton, try to look at it as a practical solution to a creative problem. Most playgoers come to the theater to cry.

CHEKHOV: Sheep. Let them cry at weddings and funerals.

NEMIROVICH: And if they cry, they tell their friends, and their friends buy tickets. No tears, no Moscow Art.

CHEKHOV: But surely they want to laugh, too.

Robin Gammell as Anton Pavlovich Chekhov and Rene Auberjonois as
Konstantin Sergeievich Stanislavski in a scene from *Chekhov in Yalta*

STANISLAVSKI: There's too much truth in your plays.

CHEKHOV: Sometimes the truth is comical. Even ridiculous.

STANISLAVSKI: Then why don't they laugh at it?

CHEKHOV: Because you make them cry.

LUZHKI: It's my fault. It's all my fault.

STANISLAVSKI: Your plays touch people. They move people. They strike a responsive chord, Anton Pavlovich. I remember when we were in rehearsal for our first production of *Seagull.* Quite frankly, I have to admit it, I, Konstantine Stanislavski, did not understand the play. I thought, my God, the audience will be throwing cabbages at us by the end of the first act. It was only the encouragement and prophetic genius of Nemirovich-Danchenko that prevented me from losing all hope. You see, our very survival depended on the reception of this play. The theater had spent its last ruble on the production. Our noble experiment to change the course of theatrical history was in danger of being dashed on the reefs of financial ruin. . . . .

In the midst of rehearsals, Stanislavski recalls, Masha arrived to beg them not to put the play on; if it failed it might be the last straw for Chekhov, already greatly weakened by his illness. But they had gone too far to stop now, and, trembling, they presented *The Seagull* to the opening night audience. When the curtain fell, there was total silence—then, after a few moments, "an explosion of applause! They cheered, they screamed, they stamped their feet. . . . .They shouted again and again for the author. Our theater was saved, and our Anton Chekhov was baptized as Russia's greatest living playwright."

During this account by Stanislavski, Chekhov has slipped away—he cannot bear praise in public. Luzhki borrows some money from Bunin, then the actors and Bunin exit. Stanislavski confides to Nemirovich his real opinion of Chekhov.

STANISLAVSKI:. . . . .You know, I don't think he understands his own plays. With any other director, *Uncle Vanya* would be inaccessible to the public.

NEMIROVICH: It's the best thing you've done.

STANISLAVSKI: Mark my words, Chekhov will not be remembered. Now, Potapenko or Griboyedov—those are names that will echo down the halls of history. He steals from Ibsen.

NEMIROVICH: Oh, Kostya, he doesn't steal.

STANISLAVSKI: He's boring. His characters do nothing but chase each other's wives.

Lilina enters.

LILINA: Kostya, it's late.

STANISLAVSKI: We should make a new policy. From now on, we only do plays by deceased writers. They don't make such a fuss when you improve on their work.

But Stanislavski admits that they need the new play Chekhov is working on now. A drunken Gorky joins them and discloses that he himself is working on a play, which he will let them have if they will perform it admission-free. Others come in and out, posturing and posing each in his own way. Finally, observed only by the maid Fyokla, Stanislavski practices weeping, then tries to show her how an actor assumes an emotion he must imagine he is feeling in order to express it to his audience. He tries to coach Fyokla into doing a scene in which she changes quickly from rapture to deep sorrow. She seems to be a willing but not very promising pupil.

Fyokla goes off to practise acting, and Lilina comes in bringing Stanislavski's makeup kit, at his request. Lilina is tired of make-believe, however, and tries to bring her husband back to the real world.

Stanislavski kneads putty, sets up mirror on bench.
STANISLAVSKI: You must be tired. Go to bed.
LILINA: I want you to come to bed with me, Kostya.
STANISLAVSKI: Are you blind? Can't you see I'm building a nose?
LILINA: Kostya . . .
STANISLAVSKI: Kostya, Kostya, Kostya! Leave me alone.
LILINA: This is important.
STANISLAVSKI: Important? This nose is the single most important external detail of my Dr. Astrov.
Looks for something in kit.
LILINA: I've got to talk to you.
STANISLAVSKI: It's the wrong time to talk now.
LILINA: It's always the wrong time to talk.
STANISLAVSKI: We talk all the time.
LILINA: No, we don't. You talk. I listen.
STANISLAVSKI: You left the top off the clown white again. Details, my dear, details. Attention to detail is everything.
LILINA: I need attention, Kostya. Maybe you don't feel it, but our marriage is falling apart, and I'm afraid.
STANISLAVSKI: Rubbish! It's a phase, like the moon. It'll pass. Lilina, how many times do I have to tell you . . . the spirit gum goes to the right of the brushes, and the face powder should always be set alongside the dry rouge. Is that so difficult to remember?
LILINA: Why, no. I'll rearrange it right now.
She picks up the kit and dashes it to the floor.

Stanislavski carries his mirror and putty off in a huff. Lilina starts to put the kit back together. Nemirovich comes in, helps her, then uses the kit to make up her face and kisses her passionately. She offers only token resistance as he leads her in the direction of the bedrooms.

Olga and Chekhov enter, exchanging endearments (they have obviously been undressed together, because he is wearing her corset). Chekhov suggests they might go off to Italy, but again Olga indicates she wants a more lasting relationship; she offers to give up the theater if he will marry her. Chekhov pleads his ill health, but Olga delivers an ultimatum, "Set a date, Anton, or get another mistress," and goes.

Stanislavski returns from a stroll through the adjacent cemetery and is supplied with a drink, as he supplies Chekhov with a cigar. Stanislavski offers a toast.

STANISLAVSKI: To women.

CHEKHOV: What would we do without them?

STANISLAVSKI: Get some work done.

CHEKHOV: Become extinct.

STANISLAVSKI: Ah, memento mori. Isn't it curious how sex and death are so intimately related?

CHEKHOV: Are they? I think that's perverse.

STANISLAVSKI: How can you say that? The greatest literary minds have made the comparison.

CHEKHOV: And now you.

STANISLAVSKI: What was it Tolstoy said? In death, the individual soul . . .

CHEKHOV: . . . merges ecstatically with the cosmic ocean.

STANISLAVSKI: Yes!

CHEKHOV: So?

STANISLAVSKI: So death becomes the ultimate sexual act.

CHEKHOV: You make it sound like fun.

He pours them another drink.

STANISLAVSKI: When one remembers one's own death, one's life becomes more precious, don't you think?

CHEKHOV *(coughs):* Yes, but Tolstoy is mistaken. Death is the final curtain. Finita la commedia.

STANISLAVSKI: It's getting light.

CHEKHOV: Pretty.

STANISLAVSKI: Ah, the ocean. I was walking on the beach tonight when suddenly I stopped and stood transfixed by the waves. I was struck with an incredible revelation. Anton, the sea is huge.

Chekhov takes out notebook, rips out page, throws it away.

Chekhov pours a nightcap and the two men discuss the institution of marriage. Chekhov fears it would stifle his creative freedom, but Stanislavski assures him that "marriage is poetry itself" and Chekhov might find an idyllic relationship with Olga Knipper. Wives will simply have to understand that men like Chekhov and Stanislavski are preoccupied with making theater history.

STANISLAVSKI: We're firing poison arrows at the old theatrical traditions while we break ground for the twentieth century with our own unique approach to dramatic reality. We are becoming demi-gods of the stage, Anton! True, it's difficult for our personal lives, but Lilina will come to accept it. She'll have to. I'm so glad we're having this little talk. Oh, yes, we've had our differences. I know, sometimes I can be a pompous ass.

CHEKHOV: You're absolutely right.

STANISLAVSKI: No, no, don't be kind. I can, I can be. But I want you to know, I do everything in my power to make your plays work.

CHEKHOV: I know. I appreciate it, but you don't have to go to all that trouble.

STANISLAVSKI: Why, if it weren't for you and *The Wild Duck* . . .

CHEKHOV: *The Seagull.*

STANISLAVSKI: Whoops, wrong bird.
> *Pause.*

We have to work together. After all, if you've got a play but no director, you don't have a play.

CHEKHOV: No play.

STANISLAVSKI: And if you've got a director but no play, you don't have a play.

CHEKHOV: No play.

STANISLAVSKI: We need each other.

CHEKHOV: You're absolutely right.
> *They get up, unsteadily walk toward house. Stanislavski throws his arm around Chekhov.*

STANISLAVSKI: Anton?

CHEKHOV: What?

STANISLAVSKI: Are you wearing a corset?
> *They exit into house. Morning sounds. Lights fade. Curtain.*

ACT II

On Sunday morning a week later, Olga and Fyokla are setting up the terrace for a party. Masha comes in (Luzhki has escorted her to church) and criticizes the arrangements—Olga has put on the best crystal and lace, which will suffer if it should rain. Moskvin and Gorky are keeping Chekhov away on a fishing expedition until after noon, while Stanislavski is preparing a speech. The party is to be some sort of tribute to their host.

Lilina comes in, having slept late—her extra-marital adventure seems to be agreeing with her. On her part, Olga feels she is getting closer to Chekhov, but not close enough yet for wedding plans to materialize.

Stanislavski comes in with Nemirovich, who is warning his co-director not to go too far with jokes at Chekhov's expense, or they might anger him and lose his new play. Lilina sides with Nemirovich. Stanislavski reprimands Lilina for not supporting him in this and orders her into the kitchen with the other women, where he says she belongs. Stubbornly, he insists he's going to handle the affair his way.

STANISLAVSKI: You can't stop me, Vladimir, I'm going to do it.

NEMIROVICH: Fine. You're the one who'll destroy the theater. The responsibility will be on your shoulders.

LILINA: Vladimir and I are lovers.
> *Nemirovich freezes. Stanislavski turns.*

STANISLAVSKI: What?

LILINA: Vladimir and I are lovers.

NEMIROVICH: Oh, Lilina.

STANISLAVSKI: Cuck-cold?

NEMIROVICH: It's not true. Lilina, what a cruel joke!

STANISLAVSKI: I've done nothing to deserve this.

LILINA: What have I done? Oh my God, what have I done?

NEMIROVICH: Why did you tell him?
STANISLAVSKI: Why did you do it?
LILINA: I only wanted to get your attention.
      Lilina exits.

Stanislavski, "stabbed in the back," warns Nemirovich that since their partnership is now obviously severed, the Moscow Art Theater will die. Each in turn deprecates the other's ability to run such a company alone, and the other's contributions to it so far. "Windbag" and "clerk" are names they level at each other. They are obviously coming to blows, but their quarrel is broken off abruptly and completely by the arrival on the scene of Chekhov and the actors carrying a string of fish. They must immediately shout "Surprise!" and make much of Chekhov, who is to be the guest of honor at this celebration of "your invaluable contribution to our theater" by the Moscow Art company. Chekhov promises: "No matter how unbearable the praise becomes, I will try with all my heart to avoid leaving."

Masha brings on champagne. After the others are settled, Nemirovich introduces Stanislavski "with an entertainment entirely of his own devising." Stanislavski enters made up as a parody of Chekhov and proceeds to a description of an imaginary play entitled *Uncle Cuckoo* (to Chekhov's standing applause). It concerns a "well-known writer Pavel Antonovich and his sister Marfa" who are obsessed with matters of planting and animal husbandry on their country estate. "Throughout the entire play all the minor characters are involved in amorous triangles," Stanislavski explains; then, looking at Lilina and Nemirovich, he breaks up and has to remove himself from the scene. The others think it is all acting and admire his ability. Chekhov's comment is, "There you see? I told you I write comedies."

Masha is becoming inebriated. Gorky tells them all of an old squire nearby who ignores change: "His land is being divided and parceled out to creditors, but what does he do? He sits and stares out the window while workmen chop down his trees and plow up his gardens." Change will no doubt benefit Gorky—in the event of revolution, he'll probably be the new Minister of Culture. As for Bunin, he's sure he'll be shot.

Bunin has brought Chekhov a present from Tolstoy: a photo inscribed "Remember, there is no death" and signed. The Moscow Art Theater group also presents a token of their high esteem—a painting of Chekhov done by a famous artist from a photograph loaned by Masha. Chekhov appreciates the gesture, but not the painting (he finds it gloomy). He hands out gifts of his own, lockets inscribed with flattering statements about the individual work of each of his Moscow Art Theater guests.

Finally, the piece de resistance: Chekhov holds up the script of his new play, *Three Sisters,* and offers it to Stanislavski and Nemirovich. Before they can decide which one is to accept it, Gorky staggers in, beaten and bloodied, having picked a fight with the two men who were spying on him. Chekhov attends to Gorky, finds him not seriously injured. All but Nemirovich help Gorky into the house. Nemirovich picks up Chekhov's script, as Stanislavski immediately comes back to the terrace.

STANISLAVSKI (*snatching the script*): You knew it, didn't you?
> *Pause.*

You knew you could do as you liked, and the collaboration would continue.
> *Pause.*

If I am to do this play with you, what kind of man will you think I am?

NEMIROVICH: A smart man. This production will allow the twentieth century's most significant theatrical institution to survive another six months.

STANISLAVSKI: You've never had any difficulty separating business affairs and personal adventures, have you?

NEMIROVICH: None, whatsoever.

STANISLAVSKI: With me, if my dinner doesn't digest well, I become an insufferable martinet at rehearsal.

NEMIROVICH: Why let something so trivial get in the way of your work?

STANISLAVSKI: We're not talking about a slice of tainted veal, are we?

NEMIROVICH: Ah, Kostya, for me, an interlude with a desirable woman is like a game of chance.

STANISLAVSKI: A toss of the dice, a spin of the wheel, a bet on a horse?

NEMIROVICH: Exactly.

STANISLAVSKI: Well, you shouldn't have taken the mare from my stable.

Stanislavski tries to torture himself further by asking Nemirovich how it was with his wife, but Nemirovich refuses to discuss it. Stanislavski is prepared for vengeance; he has brought a pistol which he aims at a terrified Nemirovich and fires. Nemirovich falls, but he is not hurt—the pistol was loaded only with a wad of cotton. As always, Stanislavski was play-acting—and very effectively. He takes the new Chekhov script away with him to read.

Nemirovich and others of his troupe go off to make their preparations for departure from Yalta, leaving the terrace to Masha and Bunin. Masha, still inebriated, throws her arms around Bunin, asking him to marry her. Gently, he explains that he doesn't love her, but she clings to him nevertheless, pulling his boot off and throwing it after him as he makes his escape.

Chekhov enters, smoking a cigar which Masha promptly takes from him. Masha blames Chekhov for the present emptiness of her life, because 14 years ago he successfully opposed her marriage to a certain bank clerk. She has made up her mind to leave Chekhov and go to Moscow.

Olga comes in and returns the locket Chekhov gave her as a symbol of the end of their week-long affair. Chekhov assures Olga that he loves her, but he is gravely ill; he has been fighting consumption for 11 years now, and the disease is gaining on him. Olga suggests a sanatarium or mountain air, but Chekhov thinks that Yalta itself is treatment enough. Only one in a thousand as sick as he is can survive, and Chekhov will not subject Olga to the ordeal of sitting by his bedside watching him die.

CHEKHOV:. . . . .My conscience will not allow you to suffer an experience like that.

OLGA: No matter what your conscience says, Anton, you want me to be with you, don't you?

CHEKHOV: Yes.

OLGA: I'll do anything for you. I'll make love to you, I'll bathe your forehead, I'll walk through hell with you, and if the worst should happen, I'll be with you when you die.

CHEKHOV *(breaking down):* I'm afraid. I'm so afraid.

Olga cradles Chekhov in her arms.

How futile! Now I begin to yearn for a miracle.

He holds up the locket.

I'll have a date engraved on this.

They kiss.

OLGA: Come to Moscow.

CHEKHOV: I can't. Altshuler forbids it, and for once I must concur with his opinion.

OLGA: I could leave the company.

CHEKHOV: I promise you, by the end of summer we'll be together.

Enter Stanislavski and Moskvin.

STANISLAVSKI: At first glance it seems Vershinin is my part, but the play is actually centered around Toozenbach. The fire is exciting, isn't it? But why does it take place offstage? If we put it onstage, now that would be a challenge! *(Notices Chekhov.)* Anton, what would you think of putting the fire onstage?

CHEKHOV: That's an awful idea.

STANISLAVSKI: Just think of it. A packed house of theatergoers confronted with the spectacle of a roaring inferno.

CHEKHOV: Lovely. An entire audience pouring into the streets yelling "Fire!"

STANISLAVSKI: I think we could stage it so it would be quite safe.

CHEKHOV: No. I would rather the play were not produced at all.

STANISLAVSKI: Maybe we could work out a compromise.

CHEKHOV: No.

Chekhov goes off with Olga, while Lilina joins Stanislavski on the terrace. She is apologetic for her behavior; her husband is understanding and forgiving. The other members of the troupe rush about in preparation for leaving, as does Masha. All make their goodbyes to Chekhov, who reminds Moskvin that the part of Toozenbach was written for him. Chekhov embraces Olga, bidding her goodbye with the remark, "I'll envy the rat that lives below the floor of your theater."

Chekhov sits on the terrace bench and fails to notice Fyokla passing by, carrying a suitcase and dressed for travel—even she is on her way to Moscow. Chekhov hears the sound of the carriage leaving.

CHEKHOV: They're gone. Now maybe I can have some peace. Fyokla! Bring my notebook! So, *The Three Sisters* are on their way to Moscow. If I could only go with them. I can see rehearsals. He'll have the whole cast snapping twigs to simulate the sound of the fire. *(Laughs.)* Oh, Knipper, what hast thou wrought? Chekhov married at this point in his life? *(Listens; sea.)* Ah, in a hundred years, all this might be washed into the sea. *(Thunder.)* Maybe sooner. They're gone. The air is so heavy. Fyokla! *(Thunder.)* Let it rain. Anton Chekhov has made a decision! It's life that matters, not vapid stories and silly vaudevilles. *(Thunder.)*

The storm is nothing. The *fear* of the storm is everything. Let it rain! *(He has an attack of coughing.)* . . . . .If I only have time. Why, why now? Why did I wait so long? I'm living my life in reverse. A lovestruck schoolboy at death's door, an optimist with lungs full of blood.

> *He lights a cigar. The rain begins. Big drops hit the ground, and one puts out the cigar. Chekhov starts to house, covers the portrait with the protective cloth, thinks, then uncovers the painting again. He exits into the house)*

Fyokla!

> *Curtain.*

Other Oustanding New Plays Cited

By American Theater Critics Association Members

Eminent Domain by Percy Granger (Princeton, N.J.: McCarter Theater)—*Eminent Domain* is a straightforward account of Holmes Bradford, an eccentric English professor at a Midwest university, who is about to be named to a newly created prestigious position at Boston University. Prof. Bradford is an irreverent, outspoken man, but one who also is deeply and sincerely devoted to his field of study and to his students. He is a funny, acerbic, realistic Mr. Chips. His routine is interrupted by a suavely opportunistic young Harvard graduate who is writing a book about Bradford's 23-year-old son, an emerging poet on the brink of fame. The son is estranged from his parents and does not appear in the play. But he is a major character just the same because so much of the action and the dialogue revolves around him.

Eminent Domain is a substantial contemporary work in which author Percy Granger deals with solid middle-class characters and the professional and professorial world of academe. Their language is literary and witty, and yet they are capable of slyness, as well as being prone to great sadness. Granger's play, which is exceedingly well written and traditional in tone, appears to be especially accessible to theater audiences that heretofore have been reluctant to expose themselves to new works on the grounds that they are too avant garde or offensive.

BETTE SPERO
Newark *Star-Ledger*

Extremities by William Mastrosimone (Actors' Theater of Louisville, Ky.)— Marjorie is home alone in the old farmhouse she shares with two women friends when a stranger, Raul, wanders in. He rips out the phone and assaults her, threatens to smother her unless she makes love to him, tells her he plans to rape her and her friends. Marjorie sprays insecticide in his eyes and manages to tie and blindfold him. He taunts her and threatens to return with a knife once he is set free. She in turn threatens to set him on fire, then to bury him alive. Her friends Terry and Patricia return home and are appalled at her violence and her treatment of Raul. He plays on their sympathies, claiming Marjorie seduced him when he came to use the telephone. She claims the only way they all will be safe is to kill him, as she has no evidence of his attack on her. But she allows Patricia to give him food and lets Terry drive off to the local drugstore for ointment for his eyes. When they examine his injuries they discover a heavy hunting knife strapped to his chest. Raul breaks down, admits that he is the rapist sought by police for beheading his victims and asks for help. The women send for the police.

GLENNE CURRIE
United Press International

The Lady and the Clarinet by Michael Cristofer (Los Angeles: Mark Taper Forum)—Luba, a middle-aged woman who has had many men in her life but has loved—or thinks she has loved—only three of them, is preparing to entertain the one who sticks most persistently in her memory. To underscore the important event, she has hired a clarinet player. Luba talks to him as she goes about planning her intimate dinner party, and he responds only through his music. This nonverbal presence allays her fears and encourages her to reminisce out loud. She stalks the room reliving her encounters with these three very different men she thinks she may have loved.

The first is her first lover—a sweet lummox of a guy barely out of his teens whom she seduced with blunt and unrelenting pleas and tantrums. The second is a very married, very middle class, very neurotic maker of TV commercials who could not decide if he should spend his time with his wife and kids, his girl friend, his commercials or simply in the bathroom. And the third is a man she married —such a model of domestic accommodation that this perfect bliss drove her to divorce. As the play ends, the doorbell rings and Luba stands frozen in the center of the room, unable to answer it.

Superficially speaking, Cristofer is questioning whether love exists at all. But as a playwright seemingly incapable of reducing thought to simplistic expression, he has created a very funny, very biting and often sexually explicit dramatic symphony in three movements. The humor, poignance and ultimate resignation in the text are echoed in Leonard Rosenman's score for the clarinet player. It is a sexual comedy with a musical structure and rhythm, whose deceptively simple throughline is really a series of sweet-sour concentric circles effectively counterpoised by its musical thread.

SYLVIE DRAKE
Los Angeles *Times*

The Lady Cries Murder by John William See (San Diego Repertory Theater)— Admirers of baroque crime fiction will recognize *The Lady Cries Murder* immediately. Fans of formal philosophy will take a bit longer but find more to enjoy. The dedication is to Dashiell Hammett and Raymond Chandler. The former is represented principally by some plot threads lifted from *The Maltese Falcon*. The latter even appears as a character in the story. It is a crowded, dense play, crammed with notions at once confused and intensely theatrical. See has a remarkable feeling for the cadences of tough-guy tales, an impressive awareness of the period's cliches and a flashy deftness in harnessing this knowledge to the service of mischief. What one finds at the bottom of *The Lady Cries Murder* is a very craftsmanlike prank. There is fun in suggesting a genre and there is good experience for a young playwright in messing around with intellectualism on the "what is reality?" level. But this play is mostly showing off; *enjoyable* showing off, not the tedious kind.

WELTON JONES
San Diego *Union*

The Man Who Killed the Buddha by Martin Epstein (Los Angeles: Odyssey Theater)—A young novice, Kenji, goes to the old sage, Misou Roshi, to worship at his feet and learn. Old priest makes a fool of young novice by telling him to clean the bird droppings from the Buddha's nonexistent statue in the courtyard. Afraid to tell the emperor that he has no clothes, Kenji begins to polish the air. A year goes by, then two, then many. Still Kenji fulfills his appointed task, which becomes a daily obsession. American tourists and old acquaintances visit. Among them is Kenshi, the woman Kenji once loved. Still Kenji polishes, but secretly he has begun to wonder if he has made a terrible mistake.

Kenshi returns a widow. She wants Kenji to marry her, but demands first that he spit on the Buddha. Kenji, who wants her for his bride, confesses he has never seen the Buddha or a statue and that, for all these years, he has polished the air. The tourists are outraged. They clamor for their money back and chase old Misou Roshi out of the temple when he refuses to return it. Meanwhile, Kenji tries but finds he cannot spit on the Buddha—even the nonexistent Buddha. Kenshi abandons him and, in his rage, he shoots an arrow in the air which, much to his (and our) surprise, bags him the real live Buddha. Frustrated beyond all bearing, Kenji strangles him.

Epstein's play is a comic fable, a deft conundrum for the human condition, rooted in a fine sense of the ridiculous and dealt to us with a highly original hand. It's charming, with a delicious latitude for laughter and the wisdom to treat a serious subject not too seriously.

SYLVIE DRAKE
Los Angeles *Times*

My Sister in This House by Wendy Kesselman (Actors' Theater of Louisville, Ky.)—Based on a real crime committed years ago in France, the play tells the story of two sisters, Christine and Lea, servant girls whose mutual dependence leads them to become lovers and who, discovered by their employer, murder the woman and her daughter. The play is interesting not for its lurid subject matter but for the growing likeness between Christine and Mme. Danzard, both meticulous about the care of the house, and the implicit sympathy—perhaps even sexual

ACTORS' THEATER OF LOUIS-
VILLE—Anne Pitoniak, Marianne
Owen (standing), Patricia Charbon-
neau and Cristine Rose (kneeling) in
Wendy Kesselman's *My Sister in This
House*

attraction—between Lea and the daughter, each of whom appears trapped by the
stronger figure in her couple. The paucity of language and the emphasis on
physical business of the most ordinary kind give the play an austerity that belies
yet reinforces the passions that inform it.

GERALD WEALES
Philadelphia

A Perfect Gentleman by Herbert Appleman (Missouri Repertory Theater, Kansas City)—Set in 18th century London, *A Perfect Gentleman* depicts the efforts
of the celebrated and now-retired Lord Chesterfield to turn his illegitimate son,
Philip, into a budget version of himself by arranging for the young man to marry
a well-connected widow, buying him a seat in Parliament and bribing the prime
minister to give Philip an ambassadorship to Venice.

Alas, Philip is not a promising specimen. He is, in fact, a thoroughly ordinary
fellow, what his father would call a "booby." Therein lies the play's universal
conflict: the desire to please a parent while being true to oneself. That theme, and

the love that binds generations, is examined by Appleman through superb use of language, a fine sense of irony and a genuine feeling for the parent-child relationship.

ROBERT W. BUTLER
Kansas City *Star*

Swop by Ken Jenkins (Actors' Theater of Louisville, Ky.)—A swop, variant of swap, becomes the encompassing metaphor for a startling series of retaliations toward the end of this colorful and suspenseful vernacular play. Actor-director-playwright Ken Jenkins has designated a choice pair of antagonists and has drawn them in an easy flow of regional dialogue. They represent the clash not only of generations and cultures but of primitive spirituality against meanness and harsh reality.

On the one hand, there's 81-year-old H.E. Rowe who maintains a dusty old store to which no one comes to buy, but through whose sliding window he swops odd items for unlikely objects with a tiny coterie of friends of all ages. Among them is a youngster; an oldtimer, Carver, who sits on the store's porch and whittles; and Kalija, an apparent wooden Indian played by a live actor who moves mysteriously on certain occasions. Rowe, part mystic, part eccentric, wears the masks of coyotes, owls or gorillas, and as a nature lover, believes in talking with trees and dancing with deer in the clearing up on the ridge when the moon is high. A 14-point buck is a favorite friend.

But the old man has it in for young Lannie Pope Wilson. Lannie went out with Rowe's innocent granddaughter, who soon became pregnant. He has since dutifully married her, but his attitude is surly and dissatisfied. His marriage and his job—selling used trucks—are getting nowhere. At nights he swills beer at End of the World Cafe with a couple of cronies, putting off going home. Lannie's neglect of his wife and his bad temper collide with Rowe's simmering distrust. The old man sends Lannie an insult, delivered before his friends in the cafe. Rowe promises him the same shotgun treatment used for "egg-suckin'" dogs. Lannie goes home for his gun, but he has more in mind than killing Rowe. He goes to the woods and slays the great trusting buck and brings the animal's bloody head to the store. The wooden Indian watches, then places an antique rifle across the antlers. He carries the horrendous armful to the ridge where Rowe is dancing with the other deer. Rowe understands. He takes up the rifle, leaves Kalija to continue the moonlight rites, heads for the motel to make his final deadly swop with Lannie.

ANN HOLMES
Houston *Chronicle*.

Winterplay by Adele Edling Shank (San Francisco: Magic Theater)—This is the second in a series of what Shank calls "hyperreal" comedies, focused on the same ill-at-ease California family visited in last season's *Sunset/Sunrise*. "Hyperreal" means candid, unedited—as if a video camera were to record everything that had gone on in a given space over a given few hours. Actually, Shank edits the events of her plays as carefully as a documentary film maker, but the impression of an uncritical mix of trivial moments and important ones is there. Perhaps Chekhov's plays struck early audiences as "hyperreal" too.

Sunset/Sunrise studied the family at a backyard barbecue. *Winterplay* sees them through a long Christmas afternoon, and its events include the real basting of a real Christmas turkey. It is the best-smelling play in some seasons. Well-fed as its characters are, however, they still seem to be looking for something solid on which to base their lives. Even the father, an established lawyer, seems to be asking himself what he will do when he grows up.

One thing they are agreed on: it's embarrassing that the older brother has brought the young man he lives with home to dinner, for they are clearly more than friends. Still, he *is* a nice guy. *Winterplay* catches what Europeans call the innocence of Americans, without judging whether it's culpable. Comical, yes.

DAN SULLIVAN
Los Angeles *Times*

A DIRECTORY OF PROFESSIONAL REGIONAL THEATER

Compiled by Ella A. Malin

Professional 1980–81 programs and repertory productions by leading resident companies around the United States, plus selected Canadian programs and major Shakespeare festivals including that of Stratford, Ontario (Canada), are grouped in alphabetical order of their locations and listed in date order from May, 1980 to June, 1981. This list does not include Broadway, off-Broadway or touring New York shows (unless the local company took some special part), summer theaters, single productions by commercial producers or college or other non-professional productions. The Directory was compiled by Ella A. Malin for *The Best Plays of 1980–81* from information provided by the resident producing organizations at Miss Malin's request. First productions of new plays—American or world premieres—in regional theaters are listed with full cast and credits, as available. Figures in parentheses following title give number of performances and date given is opening date, included whenever a record of these facts was obtainable from the producing managements.

Summary

This Directory lists 637 productions of 517 plays (including one-acters, workshops, staged readings, plays-in-progress productions) presented by 60 groups in 113 theaters in 53 cities (48 in the United States, 5 in Canada) during the 1980–81 season. Of these, 320 were American plays in 250 regular productions and 72 workshop productions. 83 were world premieres, 11 American premieres, 4 professional premieres. In addition, 21 groups presented 45 children's and youth theater productions of 43 plays, and 18 groups presented 18 productions of *A Christmas Carol* (by various adapters). Some groups presented selected plays from their regular repertory for special matiness for high school and college students. Guest productions listed in the Directory were not included in this summary, unless the host theater was directly involved in the production or was the first point of origin. Producing organizations continued community outreach programs for special audiences, some of which are noted in the Directory. Many theaters have installed special facilities, and sometimes performances, for the physically handicapped.

Frequency of productions of individual scripts was as follows.

1 play received 18 productions *(A Christmas Carol)*.
1 play received 11 productions *(On Golden Pond)*

1 play received 6 productions *(Talley's Folly)*
2 plays received 5 productions *(Agnes of God; Betrayal)*
5 plays received 4 productions *(Ah, Wilderness!; The Elephant Man; Romeo and Juliet; Terra Nova; Wings)*
20 plays received 3 productions *(American Buffalo; Artichoke; Custer; Cyrano de Bergerac; The Comedy of Errors; Da; For Colored Girls Who Have Considered Suicide/When The Rainbow Is Enuf; How I Got That Story; Love's Labour's Lost; Lone Star; Laundry and Bourbon; Macbeth; Much Ado About Nothing; A Midsummer Night's Dream; Sea Marks; The Suicide; Starting Here, Starting Now; Strider; Twelfth Night; Tintypes)*
47 plays received 2 productions
439 plays received 1 production

Listed below are the playwrights who received the greatest number of productions. The first figure is the number of productions; the second figure (in parentheses) is the number of plays produced, including one-acts.

Shakespeare	48	(26)	Fennario	3	(3)
Tennessee Williams	13	(12)	Netzel	3	(3)
Thompson	12	(2)	Weller	3	(3)
O'Neill	11	(6)	Davis	3	(2)
Pinter	9	(5)	Gelbart	3	(2)
Brecht	7	(5)	Hart	3	(2)
Amlin Gray	7	(4)	Ibsen	3	(2)
Lanford Wilson	7	(2)	Leonard	3	(2)
Shepard	6	(5)	McLure	3	(2)
Mamet	6	(3)	Orlock	3	(2)
Pielmeier	6	(2)	Wheeler	3	(2)
Shaw	5	(5)	Erdman	3	(1)
Coward	5	(4)	Ingham	3	(1)
Fugard	5	(4)	Kalfin-Brown	3	(1)
Hellman	5	(3)	Kyte-Marvin-Pearle	3	(1)
Sheridan	5	(3)	McKay	3	(1)
Tally	5	(2)	Ayckbourn	2	(2)
Pomerance	5	(1)	Barry	2	(2)
Beckett	4	(4)	Barrie	2	(2)
Kaufman	4	(3)	Babe	2	(2)
Sondheim	4	(3)	Cristofer	2	(2)
Glass	4	(2)	Feiffer	2	(2)
Maltby	4	(2)	Field	2	(2)
Miller	4	(2)	Goldoni	2	(2)
Kopit	4	(1)	Giardina	2	(2)
Anouilh	3	(3)	Gelbart	2	(2)
Chekhov	3	(3)	Hample	2	(2)
Christie	3	(3)	Inge	2	(2)
Friel	3	(3)	Jenkins	2	(2)

Litz	2	(2)	Norman	2	(2)
Leib	2	(2)	Parnell	2	(2)
Molière	2	(2)	Strindberg	2	(2)
Mastrosimone	2	(2)	Glenn Allen Smith	2	(2)

ABINGDON, VA.

Barter Theater: Mainstage

(Producing director, Rex Partington)

THE ROYAL FAMILY (32). By George S. Kaufman and Edna Ferber. June 11, 1980. Director, Patricia Carmichael. With Leta Bonynge, Russell Gold, Cleo Holladay, Roger Kozol.

AH, WILDERNESS! (27). By Eugene O'Neill. June 18, 1980. Director, Jeff Meredith. With Bruce McPherson, Carol Ann Runion, Cleo Holladay, Luke Sickle.

THE DESPERATE HOURS (25). By Joseph Hayes. July 9, 1980. Director, Rex Partington. With Rebecca Taylor, Paul Merrill, Cynthia Parva.

THE HEIRESS (23). By Ruth and Augustus Goetz; from *Washington Square* by Henry James. September 3, 1980. Director, John

Olon. With Rex Partington, Eunice Anderson, Piper Smith, Joseph Colliton.

BLITHE SPIRIT (23). By Noel Coward. September 24, 1980. Director, Jeff Meredith. With Olivia Negron, Piper Smith, Ralph Redpath, Joleen Fodor, Cleo Holladay.

THE FANTASTICKS (15). By Tom Jones and Harvey Schmidt; based on Edmond Rostand's *Les Romantiques.* April 17, 1981. Director, Byron Grant; musical director, Marvin Jones. With Lessie Burnaum, Tony Partington, Kenton Benedict, Donald Norris, Jeff Burchfield.

HOME OF THE BRAVE (16). By Arthur Laurents. May 15, 1981. Director, George Touliatos. With Gerald Walling, Ray Hill, Mike Champagne, Daniel Oreskes, Richard Tabor, Con Roche.

Barter Theater: Playhouse

BERLIN TO BROADWAY WITH KURT WEILL (31). Music by Kurt Weill; text and format, Gene Lerner; lyrics by Maxwell Anderson, Marc Blitzstein, Bertolt Brecht, Jacques Deval, Michael Feingold, Ira Gershwin, Paul Green, Langston Hughes, Alan Jay Lerner, Ogden Nash, George Tabori, Arnold Weinstein. June 4, 1980. Director, Pamela Hunt; musical director, Marvin Jones. With Allan Marks, Deborah Moldow, Barbara Niles, Curt Williams.

RIVERWIND (31). Book, music, lyrics by John Jennings. July 2, 1980. Director, James Kirkland; musical director, Marvin Jones. With Gregory Colan, Deborah Moldow, Barbara Niles, Roger Fawcett, Patty O'Brien, Marion Hunter, David Vogel.

STARTING HERE, STARTING NOW (31). By Richard Maltby Jr. and David Shire. July 30, 1980. Director, Jeff Meredith; musical director, Marvin Jones. With Deborah Moldow, Barbara Niles, Jean-Paul Richard.

Designers: scenery, Bennet Averyt, Rex Partington, Haynes Tuell, C. L. Hundley, Galen M. Logsdon; lighting, Bennet Averyt, Tony Partington, Christopher Shaw, Karen Wenderoff; costumes, Rachel Kurland, Nancy Atkinson, Carol Blevins, Judith Dolan, Sigrid Insull, C. L. Hundley, Galen M. Logsdon.

Barter Theater: Children's Theater—Playhouse

TWO KIDS AND A WITCH (20). By Glenn Allen Smith; adapted from *Hansel and Gretel.* June 25, 1980 (world premiere). Director, Owen Phillips; designer, Sally Murphy.
Hansel...................... Glenn McCoy
Gretel .... Mary Blake Doubles

Mother .... Connie Bonner
The Witch .... Nancy Kay Hunt
Her Gnome .... Katherine Henry
Woodsman............. Jerry A. Bowyer Jr.
Gypsys ... Lee Ann Weems, Michael Grasselli
    One intermission.

Note: Barter Theater's production of *Misalliance* by George Bernard Shaw, directed by John Going, toured 18 cities and towns in Virginia, February 25–March 29, 1981. Barter Players production of *The Odyssey,* adapted by Gregory A. Falls and Kurt Beattie, played at schools in sixteen

Virginia localities April 21–May 15, 1981; director, Allen Schoer; designers, Shelley Henze Schermer, Rachel Kurland, with the Players Company.

ANCHORAGE, ALASKA

Alaska Repertory Theater: Sydney Laurence Auditorium

(Artistic director, Robert J. Farley; producing director, Paul V. Brown)

WILL ROGERS' U.S.A. (16). By Paul Shyre, adapted from Rogers' writings, statements and lectures. January 22, 1981. Director, Robert J. Farley. With Sid Conrad.

ON GOLDEN POND (16). By Ernest Thompson. February 19, 1981. Director, Clayton Corzatte. With William Swetland, Shirley Bryan, Mitchell Edmonds, Tanny McDonald, Michael Johnson, Michael Santo.

THE ELEPHANT MAN (16). By Bernard

Pomerance. March 19, 1981. Director, Robert J. Farley. With Jeffrey Prather, Edwin J. McDonough, Kermit Brown, John Clarkson.

A MIDSUMMER NIGHT'S DREAM (16). By William Shakespeare. April 16, 1981. Director, Walton Jones; musical director, Richard Stillman. With Ralph Redpath, Diane Salinger, Joan Shangold, Kathleen Melvin, Ann McDonough, E. E. Norris, John Pielmeier, Pirie MacDonald.

Designers: scenery, Timothy Ames, Karen Gjelsteen, Robert W. Zentis, Kathleen Armstrong; lighting, Hugh Hall, Michael Stauffer, Robert W. Zentis, James D. Sale; costumes, Timothy Ames, Nanrose Buchman, Michael Olich, William Ivey Long.

Note: The Anchorage production of *A Midsummer Night's Dream* played 10 performances in Fairbanks beginning May 8, 1981, at the University of Alaska Fine Arts Theater.

ASHLAND, ORE.

Oregon Shakespearean Festival: Elizabethan Stage (Outdoors)

(Founder, Angus L. Bowmer; producing director, Jerry Turner; general manager, William W. Patton)

THE MERRY WIVES OF WINDSOR (43). By William Shakespeare. June 13, 1980. Director, Jon Cranney. With Cal Winn, Phyllis Courtney, Margaret Rubin, Michael T. Folie, Richard Elmore, Annette Helde, Jeffrey Woolf.

RICHARD II (30). By William Shakespeare. June 14, 1980. Director, Jerry Turner. With

James Edmondson, Stuart Duckworth, Maureen Kilmurry.

LOVE'S LABOUR'S LOST (31). By William Shakespeare. June 15, 1980. Director, Dennis Bigelow. With Philip Davidson, Barry Kraft, James Edmondson, Joan Stuart-Morris, Linda Alper, Sally Smythe, Patricia Slover.

Oregon Shakespearean Festival: Angus Bowmer Theater (Indoors)

THE PHILADELPHIA STORY (26). By Philip Barry. June 4, 1980. Director, James Moll. With Linda Alper, Stephen J. Godwin, Philip Davidson, Stuart Duckworth.

CORIALANUS (34). By William Shakespeare. June 5, 1980. Director, Jerry Turner. With Denis Arndt, Cal Winn, Sally Smythe, Mimi Carr.

JUNO AND THE PAYCOCK (35). By Sean O'Casey. August 2, 1980. Director, Michael

Kevin. With Richard Riehle, Mimi Carr, Traber Burns, Jeanne Paulsen.

OF MICE AND MEN (25). By John Steinbeck. September 2, 1980. Director, Pat Patton. With James Edmondson, John Norwalk, Richard Riehle, John Shepard, Joan Stuart-Morris.

WILD OATS (30). By John O'Keeffe. February 27, 1981. Director, Jerry Turner. With Richard

Riehle, Annette Helde, Stuart Duckworth, Wayne Ballantyne, Shirley Patton.

TWELFTH NIGHT (31). By William Shakespeare. February 28, 1981 (matinee). Director, Pat Patton. With Richard Elmore, Joan Stuart-Morris, Linda Alper, Wayne Ballantyne, Lawrence Paulsen, Larry Friedlander, Annette Helde, Bruce T. Gooch.

DEATH OF A SALESMAN (30). By Arthur Miller. February 28, 1981. Director, Robert Loper. With James Edmondson, Anne Krill, Richard Elmore, Bruce T. Gooch, Paul Duke.

'TIS PITY SHE'S A WHORE (6). By John Ford. May 15, 1981. Director, Jerry Turner. With Joan Stuart-Morris, Kathy Brady, Stuart Duckworth, Wayne Ballantyne.

Oregon Shakespearean Festival: Black Swan Theater

SIZWE BANZI IS DEAD (53). By Athol Fugard, John Kani, Winston Ntshona. June 4, 1980. Director, Luther James. With J. Esley Huston, James Avery.

LONE STAR and LAUNDRY AND BOURBON (67). By James McLure. July 5, 1980. Director, Pat Patton. With Richard Elmore, Joe Carpenter, Robert M. Reid, Linda Alper, Joan Stuart-Morris, Patricia Slover.

ARTICHOKE (54). By Joanna M. Glass. March 1, 1981. Director, Joy Carlin. With Jeanne Paulsen, Patricia Slover, Philip Davidson, Joe Vincent.

THE BIRTHDAY PARTY (16). By Harold Pinter. April 4, 1981. Director, Andrew J. Traister. With Jeffrey Woolf, Phyllis Courtney, Bill Geisslinger, Joan Stuart-Morris, Cal Winn, James Carpenter.

Designers: scenery, William Bloodgood, Richard L. Hay, Jesse Hollis; lighting, Richard Riddell, Robert Peterson, Christopher Sackett; costumes, Jeannie Davidson, Deborah Dryden, Toni M. Lovaglia, Richard V. Parks.

ATLANTA

Alliance Theater Company: Mainstage

(Managing director, Bernard Havard; artistic director, Fred Chappell; associate director, Charles Abbott)

A HISTORY OF THE AMERICAN FILM (28). By Christopher Durang; music by Mel Marvin. October 15, 1980. Director, Fred Chappell. With Ivar Brogger, Nancy Clay, Jack Hoffmann, Judy Langford.

THE KING AND I (33). Music by Richard Rodgers; book and lyrics by Oscar Hammerstein II, based on Margaret Landon's novel Anna and the King of Siam. November 26, 1980. Director, Charles Abbott; choreographer, Dennis Grimaldi. With David Pendleton, Linda Stephen, Edward Ball, Terry Beaver.

ON GOLDEN POND (29). By Ernest Thompson. January 7, 1981. Director, Fred Chappell. With Harry Ellerbe, Mary Nell Santacroce, Spencer Cox, Bea Swanson, Al Hamacher, Anthony Sabon.

DR. JEKYLL AND MR. HYDE (27). By Jim Marvin, based on Robert Louis Stevenson's novel. February 11, 1981 (world premiere). Director, Fred Chappell; scenery, Michael Stauffer; lighting, Michael Orris Watson; costumes, Thom Coates.

Gabriel John Utterson . . . . Terry Beaver
Dr. Henry Hyde . . . . Anthony Newfield
Edward Hyde . . . . Jack Hoffmann
  Voice #1; Mother; Greta; Deamus; Landlady
  —Anne Gartlan, Voice #2; Poole; Sir Danvers
  Carew; Keeper—Chris Curran, Voice #3; Mary
  Ann; Dory; Maid; Kerny—Chondra Wolle,
  Voice #4; Neighbor; Sara; Mrs. Weston; Old
  Woman—Betsy Banks Harper, Voice #5; Dr.
  Haste Lanyon; Father; Inspector, Newcomen;
  Balloon Man—Al Hamacher.
  Time: 1885. Place: London. One intermission.

SLY FOX (28). By Larry Gelbart; based on Ben Jonson's Volpone. March 18, 1981. Director, Charles Abbott. With William Hutt, Hal Bennett, Nancy Jane Clay, Anne Garlan, Charlie Hensley, Woody Romoff.

ANTONY AND CLEOPATRA (39). By William Shakespeare. April 22, 1981. Director, Fred Chappell. With Jane Alexander, Edward Moore, Donzaleigh A. Abernathy, James Eckhouse.

Designers: scenery, John Doepp, Philipp Jung, Mark Morton, Michael Stauffer, W. Joseph Stell; lighting, John Doepp, William B. Duncan, Michael Orris Watson; costumes, Thom Coates, David Robinson.

Alliance Theater Company—Studio Theater

HONEY (12). By Jim Peck. January 27, 1981 (world premiere). Director, Robert A. Wright; scenery, David Stover; lighting, William B. Duncan; costumes, Fannie Schubert.

Honey	George Ellis
Crony #1	Charlie Gonzalez
Crony #2	Lynn Mitchell
Vince	Larry Larson
Shorty	Marshall Rosenblum
Victor	David Head
Brenda	Judy Langford

THE SEA HORSE (12). By Edward J. Moore. March 3, 1981. Director, Charles Hensley. With David Head, Roberta Illg.

THE ACTORS (12). By Lezley Havard. April 7, 1981 (world premiere). Director, Gordon B. Smith; scenery, Dorset Noble; lighting, William B. Duncan; costumes, Fannie Schubert; musical consultant, Charlie Otte.

Terry Farr	Charles Abbott
Jean Paul	David Wasman

Place: The main room of a small apartment in an old building. One intermission.

BENT (24). By Martin Sherman. May 26, 1981, Director, Charles Abbott. With David Head, Jeroy Hannah, David McCann, Anthony Newfield, Gordon Paddison.

Designers: scenery, Michelle Bellavance, Dale Brubaker; lighting, David O. Traylor, Fred Fonner; costumes, Vicki Cox, Fannie Schubert.

Alliance Theater: Atlanta Children's Theater

THE LEGEND OF SLEEPY HOLLOW (68). By Sandra Deer, based on Washington Irving's story. September 29, 1980. Director, Charles Abbott; musical director, Joe Collins.

THE FORGOTTEN DOOR (38). By Gregory A. Falls, based on Alexander Key's novel. January 19, 1981. Director, Laurence Carr.

Acting Company: Kevin Barrows, Allison Biggers, Jim Caden, Nancy Clay, Joe Collins, Adrian Elder, Travis Fine, Jesse Friedlander, Will Hall, David Head, Ellen Heard, Roberta Illg, Irene Knowles, Judy Langford, David McCann, Jan McMillan, Kelly Moore, Kathryn Sterling, Wanda Strange, Robert C. Torri, Jack Wieland.

Designers: scenery, W. Joseph Stell, Philipp Jung, Mark Morton; lighting, Michael Orris Watson, William B. Duncan; costumes, Thom Coates, Fannie Schubert.

NOT JUST KID STUFF (63). Conceived and adapted by Liza Nelson and Charles Abbott from the poems and stories of Georgia school children. March 9, 1981 (world premiere). Directors and choreographers, Charles Abbott, Fred Chappell; music composed and directed by Michael Fauss; lyrics and additional dialogue by Charles Abbott; scenery, Mark Morton; lighting, William B. Duncan; costumes, Fannie Schubert.

Ms. Popular	Nancy Farrar
Quiet One	Jeroy Hannah
Brainy	Pat Hardin
Clumsy	Jan Maris
Sport	Dan Spalding
Street-wise	James Stovall

Orchestra and Adults: Joe Collins, Charlie Gonzalez, David Rifkin.

Musical Numbers: "Cleaning Out an Ol' Locker," "The Regular Life," "Song of the Sinuses," "Uglier Than Me," "If I Were a Boy/-Girl," "Angry," "What About Black?", "I Need a Friend," "What a Bummer!", "Sometimes I Like To Be Alone," "Not Just Kid Stuff."

Alliance Theater: New Works Programs

IN PRAISE OF CAMBRIC TEA by Richard Harris; THE MURDER OF EINSTEIN by Robert Eisele; CROSSING THE CRAB NEBULA by Lewis Black (4). July 23, 1980. THROWING SMOKE by Keith Reddin; TALL STORIES FROM THE BUTCHER'S BLOCK by Mark Berman Berger (4). July 24, 1980. BY

BABYLON'S WATERS by William Stancil (4). July 25, 1980. Directed and performed by the Acting Program (workshop premieres).

THE HALF CIRCLE by Bob Tabaka, directed by Sandra Holden; DOWN BY THE GRAVOIS (UNDER THE ANHEUSER BUSCH) by

James Nicholson, directed by Bea Swanson; THE LAST OF THE CIVIL WAR ORPHANS by Tom McHaney, directed by Charles Otte; LADIES FIRST by Rob Gerlach and Jim McDonald, directed by Sandra Holden; LIFE AFTER DEATH by Sybil Rosen, directed by Charles Hensley. 1980–81 season. Performed by the Acting Program (workshop premieres).

Note: Alliance Theater Company presented *For Colored Girls Who Have Considered Suicide/When The Rainbow Is Enuf* (40) by Ntozake Shangé; directed by Walter Dallas; choreographer, Barbara Sullivan; with Handspike Sullivan, Denise Burse-Mickelbury, Sharlene Ross, Paulette Stevens, Rita D. Byrd, Donzaleigh A. Abernathy, Bernardine Mitchell, culminating in performances at the Opportunities Industrialization Center Theater in Atlanta, March 10–15, 1981.

BALTIMORE

Center Stage: Mainstage

(Artistic director, Stan Wojewodski Jr.; managing director, Peter W. Culman)

THE FRONT PAGE (50). By Ben Hecht and Charles MacArthur. September 19, 1980. Director, Stan Wojewodski Jr. With Terrance O'Quinn, Richard Kneeland, John Pielmeier, Patricia Kalember, Diana Stagner.

AGNES OF GOD (50). By John Pielmeier. October 31, 1980. Director, Stan Wojewodski Jr. With Jo Henderson, Anne Pitoniak, Tania Myren.

THE DUENNA (50). By Richard Brinsley Sheridan; adapted and composed by Lance Mulcahy. December 12, 1980. Director, Garland Wright; scenery and costumes, Desmond Heeley; lighting, Frances Aronson; musical director and arranger, Michael Ward; choreographer, Randolyn Zinn. With Lu Leonard, Gordon Connell, Betsy Beard, Mary Elizabeth Mastrantonio, Lance Davis.

A MAN FOR ALL SEASONS (50). By Robert Bolt. January 20, 1981. Director, Geoffrey Sherman. With Robert Burr, Patrick Cronin, Wil Love, Michael Thompson, Sylvia Short, Denise Koch.

SALLY'S GONE, SHE LEFT HER NAME (50). By Russell Davis. March 20, 1981 (world premiere). Director, Stan Wojewodski Jr.; scenery, Hugh Landwehr; lighting, Bonnie Ann Brown; costumes, Linda Fisher.

Cynthia	Elizabeth Franz
Sally	Talia Balsam
Henry	Frederick Coffin
Christopher	Paul McCrane
Ruth	Peggy Cosgrave.

One intermission.

INHERIT THE WIND (50). By Jerome Lawrence and Robert E. Lee. May 8, 1981. Director, Jackson Phippin. With Robert Burr, Hilmar Sallee, Robert Gerringer, Patricia Falkenhain, Robert Pastene.

Center Stage: First Stage

(Three groups of staged readings, 5 performances each. WSP indicates the play is a workshop premiere)

HOME AGAIN, KATHLEEN (WSP) by Thomas Babe, directed by Robert Allan Ackerman; SACRED PLACES (WSP) by Kermit Frazier, directed by Stan Wojewodski Jr; BACK TO BACK (WSP) by Al Brown and SALLY'S GONE, SHE LEFT HER NAME by Russell Davis, directed by Jackson Phippin. January 22, 1981.

CAPTIVE RITES (WSP) by Irene Oppenheim, directed by Donald Hicken; THE STUDY by Sophy Burnham, directed by Peter W. Culman; THE WIND-UP TOYS (WSP) by Sylvia Regan, directed by Jackson Phippin; THE FURTHER ADVENTURES OF SALLY (WSP) by Russell Davis, directed by Tony Giordano. March 12, 1981.

THE WOODS by David Mamet and THE WOOLGATHERER by William Mastrosimone, directed by Stan Wojewodski Jr. April 30, 1981.

Acting Company: Laurinda Barrett, Graham Beckel, Dennis Boutsikaris, Frederick Coffin, Lance Davis, Rick Duet, William Duff-Griffin, Jay Fernandez, David Marshall Grant, Rosemary Knower, Denise Koch, Pat Karpen, Edie Karpen, Carol Jean Lewis, Anne Lynn, Paul McCrane, James McDonnell, Kathy McKenna, John McMartin, Paula Marmon, Ben Masters, Peg Murray, Terrance O'Quinn, Cristine Rose, Hansford Rowe, Susan Sharkey, Suzanne Stone, Katherine Squire, Michael Thompson, Brenda Wehle.

Designers: scenery, Barry Robison, Hugh Landwehr, Desmond Heeley; lighting, Bonnie Ann Brown, Spencer Mosse, Frances Aronson; costumes, Lesley Skannal, Dona Granata, Desmond Heeley.

Note: Center Stage's Young Peoples Theater toured the schools during 1980–81 with two productions: *The Odyssey* by Homer, adapted by Jackson Phippin, and *The Dream King* by Kermit Frazier, adapted from T. H. White's *The Sword in the Stone.* Lenore Blank directed the plays; designers were Rick Goodwin, Lesley Skannal, Julie Taymor. YPT Company: Peter Alexander, Denise Boston, Judith Daniel, Timothy Green, Charlie Halden, Teresa Tabron.

BERKELEY, CALIF.

Berkeley Repertory Theater

(Producing director, Michael W. Leibert; general manager, Mitzi K. Sales)

GALILEO (33). By Bertolt Brecht; translated by Ralph Manheim and Wolfgang Sauerlander. September 25, 1980. Director, Michael W. Leibert. With Brian Thompson, Barbara Oliver, Roberta Callahan, David Booth, Vincent Barnett, Don West.

FALLEN ANGELS (33). By Noel Coward. November 4, 1980. Director, Dennis Bigelow. With Roberta Callahan, Paul Laramore, David Booth, Kimberly King, Don West.

MY HEART'S IN THE HIGHLANDS (33). By William Saroyan. December 9, 1980. Director, Michael W. Leibert. With Tony Amendola, McGurrin Leibert, Mary Gerber, Brian Thompson, Kristin Hass.

PYGMALION (33). By George Bernard Shaw. January 20, 1981. Director, Peter Layton. With Brian Thompson, Judith Marx, Robert Haswell, Shirley Jac Wagner.

MEASURE FOR MEASURE (33). By William Shakespeare. February 24, 1981. Directors, Michael W. Leibert, Jeffrey Hirsch. With David Booth, Stephen J. Godwin, Kimberly King, Roberta Callahan, Vincent Barnett.

THE SHADOW BOX (33). By Michael Cristofer. March 31, 1981. Director, Dennis Bigelow. With Charles Dean, Bob Babish, David Booth, Richard Rossi, Mary Turner, Barbara Oliver.

A LIFE IN THE THEATER (33). By David Mamet. May 5, 1981. Director, William I. Oliver. With Michael W. Leibert, Stephen J. Godwin.

Designers: scenery, Richard L. Hay, Jesse Hollis, William Bloodgood, Ralph Funicello, Andrew DeShong; lighting, S. Leonard Auerbach, Robert Peterson, Dirk Epperson, Greg Sullivan, John Chapot; costumes, Deborah Dryden, Cathleen Edwards, Warren Travis, Diana L. Smith.

BUFFALO

Studio Arena Theater

(Artistic director, David Frank; managing director, Barry Hoffman)

LADY OF THE DIAMOND (39). By Mark Berman. September 26, 1980 (world premiere). Director, Jack O'Brien; scenery and costumes, Robert Morgan; lighting, John McLain.

Connie Weaver	Christine Baranski
Vendor	Robert Spencer
Hap "Coach" Farrell	Robert Darnell
Moose Katrina	Victor Arnold

AMERICAN REPERTORY THEA-
TER, CAMBRIDGE, MASS.—Bob
Dishy and Cheryl Giannini in Jules
Feiffer's *Grownups*

Bomber....................John Goodman
Benton ....Terry Alexander
Willie ....Joel Polis
Mom (Clara Kocinski)........ Lynn Cohen
Sportscaster .... Timothy Meyers
Sammy (Batboy) .... Mark Missert
Hedley Wooster............... Carl Schurr
Groundskeepers........... Philip Knoerzer,
                            Brian DeMarco
   Time: Baseball Season. Place: The Major
Leagues. Act I: Fun and games. Act II: Winning
games. Act III: End of the game. Two intermis-
sions.

ONE FLEW OVER THE CUCKOO'S
NEST (41). By Dale Wasserman; adapted from
Ken Kesey's novel. October 31, 1980. Director,
Davey Marlin-Jones. With Robert Darnell, Mar-
garet Winn, Darrell Sandeen, Terry Alex-
ander.

WRITE ME A MURDER (46). By Frederick
Knott. December 5, 1980. Director, David
Frank. With Robin Chadwick, Joan Croydon,
Cara Duff-MacCormick, David Lamb, Timothy
Meyers, Robert Schenkkan.

THE CURSE OF THE STARVING CLASS
(39). By Sam Shepard. January 9, 1981. Director,
Lawrence Kornfeld. With Robert Darnell, Eddie
Jones, Stephen Lang, Timothy Meyers, Angela
Patton, Carl Schurr, Gretchen West.

AH, WILDERNESS! (39). By Eugene
O'Neill. February 13, 1981. Director, Davey
Marlin-Jones. With Robert Darnell, Joan
Matthiessen, David Noll, Elise Pearlman.

LOOT (39). By Joe Orton. March 20, 1981. Director, David Frank. With Robert Darnell, Carl Schurr, Timothy Meyers, Richard Seer, Gordon Thomson, Linda Thorson.

TALLEY'S FOLLY (39). By Lanford Wilson. April 24, 1981. Director, Lawrence Kornfeld. With Christine Baranski, Robert Darnell.

Designers: scenery, Paul Wonsek, Mischa Petrow, Hal Tiné, John Arnone; lighting, Paul Wonsek, Mischa Petrow, James H. Gage, Robby Monk, Joe Pacitti, Frances Aronson; costumes, Lewis D. Rampino, Mischa Petrow, Sayurie N. Pinckard, Robert Morgan.

Note: Studio Arena presented *A Christmas Carol* (8), by Charles Dickens; adapted and directed by Geoffrey Sherman, December 10–14, 1980; designed by John T. Baun, James H. Gage, Sayurie N. Pinckard and performed by Robert Spencer, Robert Darnell, Edward Abell, Beth Dixon, Wil Love, Wyman Pendleton, Ron Randell. The same production was presented at the American Shakespeare Theater (Conn.) December 26–30, 1980.

CAMBRIDGE, MASS.

American Repertory Theater: Wilbur Theater

(Artistic director, Robert Brustein; managing director, Robert J. Orchard)

A MIDSUMMER NIGHT'S DREAM (27). By William Shakespeare; music by Henry Purcell. November 1, 1980. Director, Alvin Epstein; music director, Daniel Stepner; choreographer, Carmen de Lavallade. With Cynthia Darlow, Stephen Rowe, Eric Elice, Cherry Jones, John Bottoms, Kenneth Ryan, Carmen de Lavallade.

American Repertory Theater: Loeb Drama Center

AS YOU LIKE IT (36). By William Shakespeare. September 11, 1980. Director, Andrei Belgrader. With Jeremy Geidt, Thomas Derrah, Tony Shalhoub, Stephen Rowe, Gerry Bamman, Cherry Jones, Karen MacDonald.

THE SEVEN DEADLY SINS (35). By Bertolt Brecht and Kurt Weill; translated by Michael Feingold. November 23, 1980. Director, Alvin Epstein; music director, Gary Fagin; choreographic associate, Carmen de Lavallade. With Ellen Greene, Carmen de Lavallade, Kim Scown, David Ripley, Harry Murphy, Eric Allice.

LULU (38). By Frank Wedekind; adapted by Michael Feingold from *Earth-Spirit* and *Pandora's Box*. December 11, 1980. Director, Lee Breuer. With Catherine Slade, Frederick Neumann, Eric Elice, Richard Spore, Kenneth Ryan, Jeremy Geidt.

HAS "WASHINGTON" LEGS? (34). By Charles Wood. January 24, 1981 (American premiere). Director, Michael Kustow; "Washington" sequence director, Midge McKenzie; scenery, Michael H. Yeargan; lighting, James F. Ingalls; costumes, Nancy Thun; sound collages, Tim Mukherjee.

The Americans:

Joe Veriato	Stephen Rowe
Wesley	Tony Shalhoub
Sy Hoelmersbagger	Richard Spore
Daniel Rashur	Eric Elice
Carl Dorf	Kenneth Ryan
Mickey Boorman; Actor	Thomas Derrah
Pat Sligo	William McGlinn
John Bean	Frederick Neumann
Mary Jane Pendejo	Karen MacDonald

The British:

Sir Flute Parsons	Jeremy Geidt
Gaffer	Harry S. Murphy

Waiter; Soundman;

Lord Howe	Michael Atwell
Bernie the Volt	Kenneth Ryan
Focus Puller	Richard Spore
Camera Operator	William McGlinn
Heinrich Guttmeir	Eric Elice

Grips, Minuteman: David Frutkoff, Peter Stein, John Gunnison-Wiseman. Redcoats: Gary Kirby, Kevin Fennessey, Leonard Sullivan. Film Crew, Technicians, assistants: Michael Harrington, Helena Blaker, Laura Eliasoph, Maggie Topkis

Act I: The Savoy Hotel, London, circa 1976. Act II: Location in Ireland for Bunker Hill sequence of "Washington," circa 1976. One intermission.

THE MARRIAGE OF FIGARO (35). By Pierre-Augustin Caron de Beaumarchais; translated and adapted by Mark Leib. May 7, 1981. Director, Alvin Epstein; composer and director, Stephen Drury. With Harry S. Murphy, Cheryl Giannini, Tony Shalhoub, Karen MacDonald, Barbara Orson, Linda Atkinson, George Martin.

GROWNUPS (35). By Jules Feiffer. May 24, 1981 (world premiere). Director, John Madden; scenery, Andrew Jackness; lighting, James F. Ingalls; costumes, Dunya Ramicova.

Helen .... Barbara Orson
Jack....................... George Martin
Marilyn................. Karen MacDonald
Jake.......................... Bob Dishy
Louise................... Cheryl Giannini
Edie .... Jennifer Dundas

Scene 1: The present, Marilyn's kitchen in New Rochelle. Scene 2: One year later, Jake and Louise's apartment in New York. Scene 3: The following Sunday, Jake and Louise's apartment. One intermission.

Designers: scenery, Tony Straiges, Michael H. Yeargan, Adrianne Lobel, Kate Edmunds, Tom Lynch; lighting, Paul Gallo, James F. Ingalls, William Armstrong; costumes, Zack Brown, Dunya Ramicova, Rita Ryack, Nancy Thun, Adrianne Lobel.

Note: American Repertory Theater is a year-round theater. April 3, 1980, the world premiere of Mark Leib's *Terry By Terry* (38) was presented; *Happy End* (28) by Bertolt Brecht and Kurt Weill opened April 26, 1980, and *The Inspector General* (28) by Gogol, adapted by Sam Guckenheimer and Peter Sellars, opened May 22, 1980. ART sponsors Art Mondays, special events and staged readings of new plays with members of the regular company. *Paley's Woman, Landesman's Lyrics,* from short stories by Grace Paley and jazz lyrics by Fran Landesman, was presented January 5, 1981; directors, Michael Kustow and Joann Green. *Company* by Samuel Beckett, an American premiere, was given February 16 and 23, 1981, directed by Joann Green. The third event was an American premiere reading of *Family Voices* (3) by Harold Pinter, June 8, 15 and 22, 1981, with Tom Derrah, Jeremy Geidt, Bronia Stefan. ART's Loeb Cabaret presented *There Are Bad Times Just Around the Corner* (6), a revue featuring Harold Arlen and Noel Coward songs, on two weekends from May 14, 1981; and *Dreck/Vile* (12+) by Steve Lawson and Gary Fagin, from June 4, 1981.

CHICAGO

Goodman Theater: Mainstage

(Artistic director, Gregory Mosher; managing director, Roche Schuler)

THE SUICIDE (33). By Nikolai Erdman; adapted by Richard Nelson from a translation by Zenia Youhn. October 9, 1980. Director, Gregory Mosher. With Seth Allen, Audrie J. Neenan, Eugene Troobnick.

A CHRISTMAS CAROL (50). By Charles Dickens; adapted by Barbara Field. November 25, 1980. Directors, Tony Mockus, Sandra Grand, William J. Norris. With William J. Norris, Tim Halligan, Aaron Kramer, Del Close.

BETRAYAL (35). By Harold Pinter. January 22, 1981. Director, Andre Ernotte. With Caroline Kava/Lissa Bell, Munson Hicks, Sean Griffin, David Mink.

PLENTY (35). By David Hare. March 5, 1981. Director, Gregory Mosher. With Caitlin Clarke, Alan Coates, Pippa Pearthree, John Wardwell.

PLAY MAS (40). By Mustapha Matura. April 10, 1981 (American premiere). Director, Derek Walcott; scenery and costumes, Adrianne Lobel; lighting, Robert Christen.

Randolph Gookool .... Shelly Desai
Samuel .... Arthur French
Miss Gookool .... Bina Sharif
Frank .... Kim Sullivan
Mr. McKay .... G. John Walsh
Doctor .... James Spinks
Woman Bishop; Mrs. Banks . Celestine Heard
Undertakers .... Phillip East, Azid Farid
Sergeant .... Ernest Perry Jr.
Mrs. Samuel................... Pat Bowie
Chuck Reynolds .... Dan Conway

Act I: Pre-Independance Trinidad, 1962. Scene 1: A tailor shop. Scene 2: The same, some weeks later. Act II: Some years later in post-Independence Trinidad. Scene 1: Samuel's office. Scene 2: Some weeks later. Scene 3: Some weeks later, Carnival Day.

DWARFMAN: MASTER OF A MILLION SHAPES (35). By Michael Weller. May 22, 1981 (world premiere). Director, Emily Mann; scenery, Adrianne Lobel; lighting, Robert Christen; costumes, Rita Ryack.

Libby Landower	Jody Naymik
Dwarfman	Ian Trigger
Elektra	Marilyn Hamlin
Dr. Azabov	J. Pat Miller

Stanley Dorman	Stephen Pearlman
Leon Dorfman	Pierre Epstein
Sobol; Dr. Sobolow	James Eichling
Bettina-Mae Alfieri	Elizabeth McGovern
Roach King; Dr. Prince	Gerry Bamman
Naomi Dorfman	Kathryn Grody
Stanley's father	Rudy Bond

Act I: Dorfman's mind and studio. Act II: Dorfman's mind and cabin.

Designers: scenery, Michael Merritt; Joseph Nieminski, Tom Lynch; lighting, Arden Fingerhut, Robert Christen, Paul Gallo; lighting, Christa Scholtz, James Edmund Brady, Tom Lynch.

Goodman Theater: Studio Theater

In repertory, September 23–October 19, 1980:
ENDGAME and KRAPP'S LAST TAPE (29). By Samuel Beckett. Rick Cluchy and the San Quentin Drama Workshop.

STILL LIFE (12). Written and directed by Emily Mann. October 23, 1980. With John Spencer, Mary McDonnell, Timothy Near.

A PERFECT ANALYSIS GIVEN BY A PARROT; THE FROSTED GLASS COFFIN; and SOME PROBLEMS FOR THE MOOSE LODGE (world premiere). By Tennessee Williams. November 11, 1980 (15). Director, Gary Tucker. With Marji Bank, Nathan Davis, Scott Jaeck, Cynthia Baker Johnson, Leonard J. Kraft, Muriel Moore, Les Podewell, Rachel Stevens.

KUKLA AND OLLIE LIVE (24). By Burr Tillstrom. December 3, 1980. With the Kuklapolitans.

A HOUSE NOT MEANT TO STAND (12). An expanded version of *Some Problems for the*

Moose Lodge by Tennessee Williams. April 1, 1981. Director, Gary Tucker; scenery, Joseph Nieminski; lighting, Robert Christen; costumes, Ellen Ryba.

Bella	Marji Bank
Cornelius	George Womack
Charlie	Scott Jaeck
Emerson	Les Podewell
Stacey	Bonnie Sue Arp
Jessie	Rachel Stephens
Dr. Crane	Leonard J. Kraft
Police Officer	Brooks Gardner

Place: Pascagoula, Mississippi. Act I: Midnight a few days after Christmas, 1980. Act II, Scene 1: A few moments later. Scene 2: A few moments later.

Songs: "A House of Papier Mache," written and performed by Schuyler Wyatt; "One More Ride on the Merry-Go-Round," by Sadaka and Greenfield.

AVNER THE ECCENTRIC (32). Conceived and performed by Avner Eisenberg. May 29, 1981.

St. Nicholas Theater Company: Ivanhoe Theater—Mainstage

(Artistic Director, Cynthia Sherman; managing director, Bill Conner)

CELIMARE, THE GOOD FRIEND (42). By Eugene Labiche and Delacour. July 16, 1980. Director, George Sherman. With Michael Pace, Rhonda Aldrich, Sheila Keenan, Richard Sallenberger.

TABLE SETTINGS (56). Written and directed by James Lapine. October 1, 1980. With Paul Sparer, Bernard Beck, Ellen Crawford, Fredric Stone, Patti Wilkus.

A SORROW BEYOND DREAMS (56). By Peter Handke; translated by Ralph Manheim. February 18, 1981. Director, Robert Falls. With John Malkovich.

NASTY RUMORS AND FINAL REMARKS (56). By Susan Miller. April 29, 1981. Director, Elinor Renfield; scenery, Joseph Nieminski; lighting, Dan Kobayashi; costumes, Jordan Ross; composer, Louis Rosen.

Nicholas	Mike Genovese
Raleigh	Kit Flanagan
Doctor	Terry Bozeman
Fran	Virginia Morris
Max	Lissa Bell
T.K.	Peter Wittrock
Woman	Jayne Alexander

Time: The present. One intermission

GOODMAN THEATER, CHICAGO—Marji Bank and Rachel
Stephens in *A House Not Meant to Stand* by Tennessee Williams

St. Nicholas Theater: Performance Group

TWENTY-SEVEN WAGONS FULL OF
COTTON; HELLO FROM BERTHA; I
CAN'T IMAGINE TOMORROW; A CASE
OF CRUSHED PETUNIAS (8). By Tennessee
Williams. June 2, 1980. Directors, Steven
Schachter, Louis Hall.

HOOTERS (8). By Ted Tally. January 5, 1981.

Director Jan Holby. LIVING AT HOME (8).
By Tony Giardina. May 25, 1981. Director, Stephen Scott.
Company: Byron Jones, Moira McMahon,
Michael Shapiro, Shawna Tucker, John Slank-
ard, Dawn Arnemann, Margaret Lawrence, Edward Henzel.

St. Nicholas: Theater for Young Audiences

THE PRINCE, THE DWARF AND THE
BLACKSMITH'S DAUGHTER (30). Adapted
and directed by Tom Mula from John Gardner's *In the Suicide Mountains;* music by Les
Stahl. October 20, 1980 (world premiere).

Chudu.....................John Mahoney
Armida...................Jodean Culbert
Prince Christopher ....Peter Syversten
  Others: Dale Calendra, Jim Murphy, Greg
Vinkler, Puppets

Designers: scenery, David Emmons, Michael Philippi, Jeremy Conway, Gary Baugh, Nancy McCarty; lighting, Rita Pietraszek, Michael Philippi, Gary Heitz, Dan Kobayashi; costumes, Jessica Hahn, Cookie Gluck, Doug Koertage, Emily Erickson.

Note: St. Nicholas Theater presented a series of staged readings: *Under the Rose* by David Ives, director, David Michael Weiss, October 6, 1980; *Autobiography of a Pearl Diver* by Martin Epstein, director, Brian Kaufman, October 26, 1980; *The Fine Art of Suffering* by Bruce Jones, director, Judy Fogt-Gilmore, October 21, 1980; *Christie in Love* by Howard Brenton, director, James McCutchen, January 10, 1981; *The Painters* by Heinrich Henkel, director, Joe Sutton, February 8, 1981. With members of the Performance Company.

CINCINNATI

Cincinnati Playhouse in the Park: Robert S. Marx Theater

(Producing director, Michael Murray; managing director, Robert W. Tolan)

COMPULSION (35). By Meyer Levin. October 7, 1980. Director, Michael Murray. With Neil Sims, Richard Hayes, John Wylie, Michael M. Ryan, Eileen Letchworth.

THE MAN WHO CAME TO DINNER (35). By Moss Hart and George S, Kaufman. November 25, 1980. Director, Edward Berkeley. With John High, Monica Merryman, Leslie Meeker, Kip Baker, Suzanne Granfield.

LOOSE ENDS (35). By Michael Weller. January 6, 1981. Director, Amy Saltz. With Sandy Faison, J. Courtlandt Miller, Pat Karpen, Jay Patterson.

THE SCHOOL FOR SCANDAL (35). By Richard Brinsley Sheridan. February 24, 1981. Director, Jacques Cartier. With Robertson Dean, J. Courtlandt Miller, Paul C. Thomas, Jana Robbins, Gwendolyn Lewis, Thomas Carson.

A VIEW FROM THE BRIDGE (35). By Arthur Miller. April 7, 1981. Director, Michael Murray. With Alan Ansara, Yolanda Delgado, Tom Mardirosian, Diane Martella.

TINTYPES (35). Conceived by Mary Kyte with Mel Marvin and Gary Pearle. May 26, 1981. Director, John Going; musical director, Boyd Staplin; choreographer, David Holdgreiwe; orchestrator and vocal arranger, John McKinne. With Tom Flagg, Beth Fowler, David Green, Mary Louise, Tanny McDonald.

Cincinnati Playhouse in the Park: Thompson Shelterhouse Theater

BURIED CHILD (24). By Sam Shepard. November 6, 1980. Director, Michael Hankins. With John Wylie, Eileen Letchworth, Michael M. Ryan, Jay Patterson.

SERENADING LOUIE (24). By Lanford Wilson. February 5, 1981. Director, Michael Murray. With Jill O'Hara, Jim De Marse, Lynn Ritchie, Edmond Genest.

THE GIN GAME (24). By D. L. Coburn. May 7, 1981. Director, Michael Hankins. With John Wylie, Anne Pitoniak.

Designers: scenery, Neil Peter Jampolis, Joseph A. Varga, Patricia Woodbridge, Karl Eigsti, David Jenkins, William Schroeder, Karen Schulz, Jonathan Arkin; lighting, Neil Peter Jampolis, Spencer Mosse, Jay Depenbrock, F. Mitchell Dana; costumes, Jennifer Von Mayrhauser, Caley Summers, Ann Firestone, Elizabeth Palmer, Jeanne Button, William Schroeder, Rebecca Senske.

Note: Following its run at the Shelterhouse Theater, *The Gin Game* played an additional two weeks at another theater in the city.

CLEVELAND

The Cleveland Play House: Euclid—77th Street Theater

(Director, Richard Oberlin; managing director, Janet Wade)

FILUMENA (26). By Eduardo de Filippo; adapted by Willis Hall and Keith Waterhouse. October 31, 1980. Director, Michael Maggio. With Evie McElroy, Domenico Soriano, Jim Richards, Si Osborne, Paul Floriano.

BEDROOM FARCE (45). By Alan Ayckbourn. December 5, 1980. Director, Paul Lee. With Richard Halverson, June Gibbons, Si Osborne, Judy Nevits, David O. Frazier, Carolyn Reed, Kenneth Albers, Mary Adams-Smith.

CHILDREN OF DARKNESS (26). By Edwin Justus Mayer. February 6, 1981. Director, Peter Sander. With Richard Halverson, John Buck Jr., Carolyn Reed.

ON GOLDEN POND (36). By Ernest Thompson. March 20, 1981. Director, Kenneth Albers. With Paul Lee, Evie McElroy, Allan Byrne.

The Cleveland Play House: Drury Theater

WATCH ON THE RHINE (33). By Lillian Hellman. October 10, 1980. Director, Paul Lee. With Katherine Squire, Carolyn Reed, Kenneth Albers, Joe D. Lauck, Richard Halverson, Sharon Bicknell.

A CHRISTMAS CAROL (31). By Charles Dickens; adapted by Doris Baizley. November 28, 1980. Director, William Rhys. With Wayne S. Turney and the Cleveland Play House Company.

STRIDER: THE STORY OF A HORSE (33). Adapted from Leo Tolstoy's story by Mark Rozovsky; English version by Robert Kalfin and Steve Brown; based on a translation by Tamara Bering Sunguroff; music by Mark Rozovsky and

S. Vetkin; adapted with additional music by Norman L. Berman; new English lyrics by Steve Brown; original Russian lyrics by Uri Riashentsev. January 23, 1981. Director, Larry Tarrant. With William Rhys, James P. Kisicki, Morgan Lund, Sharon Bicknell, Wayne S. Turney.

A FUNNY THING HAPPENED ON THE WAY TO THE FORUM (31). Book by Burt Shevelove and Larry Gelbart; music and lyrics by Stephen Sondheim. March 27, 1981. Director, Michael Maggio; music director, David Gooding; choreographer, Susan Epstein Irwin. With James P. Kisicki, Joe D. Lauck, Sharon Bicknell, Norman L. Berman, Harper Jane McAdoo, Wayne S. Turney.

The Cleveland Play House: Brooks Theater

INDULGENCES IN THE LOUISVILLE HAREM (18). By John Orlock. October 17, 1980. Director, William Rhys. With Harper Jane McAdoo, Catherine Albers, Allan Leatherman, Wayne S. Turney.

EMIGRES (23). By Slawomir Mrozek; tran-

slated by Peter Sander. December 19, 1980. Director, Evie McElroy. With James P. Kisicki, James Richards.

HOW I GOT THAT STORY (18). By Amlin Gray. April 10, 1981. Director, Peter Sander. With Kenneth Albers, Si Osborne.

Designers: scenery, Paul Rodgers, Wayne Merritt, Richard Gould, Charles Berliner, James Irwin, Gary Eckhart; lighting, Paul Rodgers, Wayne Merritt, Richard Gould, James Irwin; costumes, Richard Gould, Estelle Painter, Charles Berliner, Larry Bauman.

The Cleveland Play House: Chautauqua Season—Summer 1980

A HISTORY OF THE AMERICAN FILM (3). Book and lyrics by Christopher Durang; music, Mel Marvin. June 26, 1980.

CUSTER (2). By Robert E. Ingham. July 3, 1980.

WUTHERING HEIGHTS (2). Adapted by Paul Lee from Emily Bronte's novel. July 10, 1980.

A MIDSUMMER NIGHT'S DREAM (2). By William Shakespeare. July 17, 1980.

CATSPLAY (2). By Istvan Orkeny; translated by Clara Gyorgyey. July 24, 1980.

PRESENT LAUGHTER (2). By Noel Coward. July 31, 1980.

WINGS (2). By Arthur Kopit. August 7, 1980.

DA (3). By Hugh Leonard. August 14, 1980.

Directors, Richard Halverson, Paul Lee, Evie McElroy, William Rhys, Larry Tarrant.

Note: Pat Carroll appeared in *Gertrude Stein, Gertrude Stein, Gertrude Stein* (7), by Marty Martin, March 17, 1981 at the Drury. Cleveland Play House presented two Youth Theater productions: *Aesop's Fabulous Fable Factory* (4), book by Joseph Robinette, music by Thomas Tierney, December 31, 1980; and *Androcles and the Lion* (2), by Aurand Harris, directors Kerro Knox III and Elizabeth Farwell, April 25, 1981.

COCONUT GROVE, FLA.

Players State Theater

(Artistic and producing director, David Robert Kanter; managing director, G. David Black)

GEMINI (28). By Albert Innaurato. October 17, 1980. Director, David Robert Kanter. With Peter Ivanov, Robert Reisel, Roz Simmons.

HAMLET (28). By William Shakespeare. November 14, 1980. Director, David Robert Kanter. With Craig Dudley, J. Cameron, William Metzo, Isa Thomas, Miller Lide.

A CHRISTMAS CAROL (21). By Charles Dickens; adapted by David Robert Kanter. December 12, 1980. Director, Michael Montel. With Harold Bergman, Adam Finkle, Lamont Johnson, Miller Lide.

GETTING OUT (28). By Marsha Norman. January 9, 1981. Director, David Robert Kanter. With J. Cameron, Anne Gilliam, Max Howard, Megan McTavish.

1959 PINK THUNDERBIRD: LAUNDRY AND BOURBON; LONE STAR (28). By James McLure. February 6, 1981. Director, David Robert Kanter. With Ann Crumb, Gregory Grove, Max Howard, Margo Martindale, Susan Pitts, Steve Vande Griek.

AGNES OF GOD (28). By John Pielmeier. March 6, 1981. Director, David Robert Kanter. With Barbara Bradshaw, J. Cameron, Anne Gilliam.

GO BACK FOR MURDER (28). By Agatha Christie. April 3, 1981 (American premiere). Director, Michael Montel; scenery, Kenneth N. Kurtz; lighting, Jean E. Shorrock; costumes, Barbara A. Bell.

Justin Ford	Stephen Temperley
Turnball	Ronald Shelley
Carla; Caroline Crale	Barbara Bradshaw
Jeff Rogers	Ralph Wakefield
Philip Blake	Wil..m Meisle
Meredith Blake	Tom McDermott
Lady Melksham	Brenda Curtis
Miss Williams	Anne Gilliam
Angela Warren	J. Cameron
Amyas Crale	Peter Brandon

Designers: scenery, Paul H. Mazer, Lyle Baskin, Kenneth N. Kurtz; lighting, Andrea Wilson, Michael Martin, Jean E. Shorrock, Paul H. Mazer, Kenneth N. Kurtz, Maria Marrero.

Note: Players State toured two bilingual productions to elementary and secondary schools, Feb. 23–March 28, 1981; *Tales and Remembrances,* book by Barry M. Colfelt, music and lyrics by Tom Spivey, Spanish translation by Antolin Garcia Carbonell, director, Alan Yaffe, music director, Tom Spivey, choreographer, Marilyn Laudadio; and *Tails of Two Cities* by Rafael V. Blanco, director, Fernando Fonseca. Company: Lillian Graff, Stefan Klum, Ana Margarita, Alex Mustelier, Ruben Robasa; designers, Paul Wonsek, Barbara A. Bell, Katherine Williams.

COSTA MESA, CALIF.

South Coast Repertory Theater: Mainstage

(Artistic directors, David Emmes, Martin Benson)

HOTEL PARADISO (40). By Georges Feydeau and Maurice Desvallieres; translated by Peter Glenville. September 23, 1980. Director, David Emmes. With Jeffrey Tambor, Martha McFarland, Caroline Smith, John-David Keller, Christopher Metas, Anni Long, James Gallery.

THE GLASS MENAGERIE (41). By Tennessee Williams. November 6, 1980. Director, Lee Shallat. With Kristoffer Tabori, Patricia Fraser, Sara Rush, James Staley.

A CHRISTMAS CAROL (16). By Charles Dickens; adapted by Jerry Patch. December 16, 1980. Director, John-David Keller. With Hal Landon Jr., John Ellington, Mary Beth Evans, Don Tuche, Oliver Wright.

THE ELEPHANT MAN (40). By Bernard Pomerance. January 13, 1981. Director, Martin Benson. With Jonathan McMurtry, Ron Boussom, John-David Keller, Penelope Windust, Wayne Grace.

THE MERCHANT OF VENICE (40). By William Shakespeare. March 3, 1981. Director, John Going. With William Needles, John Wylie, Katharine Houghton, Anni Long.

CHILDE BYRON (40). By Romulus Linney. April 14, 1981. Director, Martin Benson. With John de Lancie, Megan Cole.

ANYTHING GOES (48). Music and lyrics by Cole Porter; book by Guy Bolton, P. G. Wodehouse, Howard Lindsay, Russel Crouse.

May 26, 1981. Director, John-David Keller; musical director, Jerry Frohmader, choreographer, Keith Clifton. With Steve DeNaut, Don Tuche, Patti Appel, Ellen Travolta, Art Koustik, Richard Doyle.

South Coast Repertory Theater: Second Stage

AMERICAN BUFFALO (21). By David Mamet. October 29, 1980. Director, Martin Benson. With Art Koustik, Hal Landon Jr., Jim Staskel.

BOSOMS AND NEGLECT (20). By John Guare. January 7, 1981. Director, David Ostwald. With Richard Doyle, Karen Hensel, Sylvia Meredith.

SCREWBALL (20). By L. J. Scheiderman. February 18, 1981 (world premiere). Director, David Emmes; scenery, Susan Tuohy; lighting, Mary Martin; costumes, Dwight Richard Odle.
Glynn . . . . Candice Copeland
Dr. Hager. . . . . Clarke Gordon
P.J. . . . . Arye Gross
Jessica. . . . . Patti Johns

Shooby . . . . Hal Landon Jr.
Miss Cahill. . . . . Nomi Mitty
Time: The present. Place: Berkshire House, a private institution for developmentally disabled youths.

ASHES (20). By David Rudkin. April 8, 1981. Director, Lee Shallat, With Dean Santoro, Marnie Mosiman, Don Tuche, Irene Roseen.

CHEVALIERE (20). By David Trainer. May 20, 1981 (world premiere). Director, David Emmes; scenery, Cliff Faulkner; lighting, Cameron Harvey.
Chevalier d'Eon. . . . . R. W. Boussom
Caron de Beaumarchais . . . . George McDaniel
Time: 1775. Place: London, the chambers of Caron de Beaumarchais and the Chevalier d'Eon. One intermission.

Designers: scenery, Michael Devine, Cliff Faulkner, Susan Tuohy, Mark Donnelly; lighting, Susan Tuohy, Tom Ruzika, Donna Ruzika, Cameron Harvey; costumes, Cliff Faulkner, Dwight Richard Odle, Merrily Ann Murray, William Schroeder.

Note: South Coast Repertory's 1980–81 educational touring production was *The Communication Show: Signs, Lines and Waves;* book by Doris Baizley; music and lyrics by Robin Frederick; director, John-David Keller; choreographer, Diane dePriest; company, Candice Copeland, Chris Graham, Tricia Matthews, Tom Shelton.

DALLAS

Dallas Theater Center: Kalita Humphreys Theater

(Managing director, Paul Baker)

DA (38). By Hugh Leonard. June 24, 1980. Director, Judith Kelly Davis. With Randolph Tallman, C.P. Hendrie, Jacque Thomas.

CYRANO DE BERGERAC (42). By Edmond Rostand, translated by Brian Hooker. October 7, 1980. Director, Anton Rodgers with Candy Buckley and Paul Munger. With Randy Moore, Pamela Hurst, Randolph Tallman, Kenneth Hill.

ON GOLDEN POND (35). By Ernest Thompson. December 2, 1980. Director, Joan Vail Thorne, with Carol Miles. With Mary Sue Jones, Ryland Merkey, Randy Bonifay, John Figlmiller, Robyn Flatt.

THE FRENCH HAVE A WORD FOR IT (32).

By Georges Feydeau, translated from *Le Dindon* by Barnett Shaw. February 10, 1981. Director, Derek Goldby with Bryant J. Reynolds. With Mary Rohde, Jeffrey Kinghorn, Christopher Pennywitt, John Figlmiller.

THE INCREDIBLE MURDER OF CARDINAL TOSCA (38). By Alden Nowlan and Walter Learning. March 31, 1981. Director, Judith Davis with Hanna Cusick. With Randy Moore, Russell Henderson, John Figlmiller, Norma Moore, John Henson.

CHILDREN OF A LESSER GOD (38). Written and directed by Mark Medoff. May 19, 1981. Interpreter, sign language coordinator and coach, Ruth Aleskovsky. With Philip Reeves, Bobbie Beth Scoggins.

Dallas Theater Center: Down Center Stage

LAND OF FIRE (20). By Glenn Allen Smith. October 28, 1980 (world premiere). Director, John Logan; scenery, John Henson; costumes, Sally Dorothy Bailey.

Irene .... Jacque Thomas
Bill .... Christopher Pennywitt

GOYA (20). By Henry Beissel. January 6, 1981 (world premiere). Director, Peter Lynch; scenery, Yoichi Aoki; lighting, Robert Duffy; costumes, Yoichi Aoki, Renee Le Cuyer; music, Russ Hoffman.

Goya.................... Russell Henderson
Leocadia Weiss; Josefa .. Susan McDaniel Hill
Canon Juan de Llorente ...... George Speer
Duchess of Alba .... Eleanor Lindsay
King Carlos IV .... John S. Davies
Queen Luisa Maria Teresa.... Stella McCord
Crown Prince Ferdinand; Javier . Ken Hudson
Francois Bayeu; Majo........ Kenneth Hill
General Manuel de Godoy;
  Hidalgo................... Lee Wheatley
Maja .... Sally Dorothy Bailey
Maja; Bar Maid............ Annette Bishop

GRANDMA DUCK IS DEAD by Larry Shue; director, Paul Munger; and STAGG AND STELLA (world premiere) by Fred Getchell; director, Michael Scudday (20). Feb-

ruary 24, 1981.
Stagg and Stella
Amos Alonzo Stagg .... Tim Green
Stella Stagg .... Synthia Rogers
Barney; Harold Iverson ...... Lee Lowrimore
Ruth Stagg.................. Pamela Hurst
Nurse .... Linda LeNoir
  No intermission.

THE CHRONICLE OF QUEEN JANE (20). By Florence Stevenson. April 14, 1981 (world premiere). Director, Jeffrey Kinghorn; scenery, Zak Herring; lighting, Robert Duffy; costumes, Mary Lou Hoyle.

Lady Jane Grey............... Carol Miles
Ellen.................... H. Byron Ballard
Henry Grey .... John Logan
Frances Grey............... Cheryl Denson
Lady Dudley .... Ronni Lopez
Guildford Dudley .... Jim Marvin
John Dudley .... Michael Scudday
Earl of Arundel............. John S. Davies
Bess Tylney .... Susan McDaniel Hill
Earl of Pembroke .... John Brook
Mary Tudor................ Mary McClure
Priest .... Garry Beveridge
  Time: Spring of 1553 to late winter of 1554. Place: England. One intermission.

Designers: scenery, Peter Lynch, Cheryl Denson, Virgil Beavers, John Henson, Robert Duffy, Zak Herring, Allen Hibbard; lighting, Robert Duffy, Allen Hibbard, Michael Scudday, Randy Moore, Martin L. Sachs, Carol Miles; costumes, Tim Haynes, Peter Lynch, Zak Herring, Cheryl Denson, Sally Askins, Carol Miles, Mary Lou Hoyle, Jeff Storer.

Dallas Theater Center: Magic Turtle Children's Theater

BEAUTY AND THE BEAST (5). By Sally Netzel; director, Eleanor Lindsay. October 18, 1980.

WINNIE-THE-POOH (7). By A.A. Milne, adapted by Kristen Sergel; director, Mary Lou Hoyle. December 13, 1980.

THE WANDERER'S STONE (5). Book, music and lyrics by Martha Goodman. February 21, 1981 (world premiere). Director, Hanna Cusick; scenery, Raynard Harper, Barbara Sanderson; lighting, Stella McCord; costumes, Gregory Schwab; musical director, Alan Hoffman.
King Agamyth.............. Royal Brantley
Queen Ariel Asphodel .... Ann Fischer
Noland .... John Wright

Meggen...................... Lisa Marsh
Witch Maire................. Byron Ballard
The Wizard .... David Edwards
Hooter .... Tim Reischauer
Web Weavers.............. Trudy Wheeler,
                          Susan Engbrecht
Magic Turtle .... Sally Smith-Petersen
  Place: The enchanted kingdom of Aroundell. Act I. The Wizard's dwelling. Act II, Scene 1: A place in the forest. Scene 2: A secret place in the forest. Scene 3: Skullscap, an evil place in the forest. One intermission.

THE STONECUTTER by Ruth Cantrell and PETER AND THE WOLF by Prokofieff (5). April 11, 1981. Director, Robyn Flatt.

Acting Company: Annette Bishop, Royal Brantley, Lisa Brown, Felicia Denney, Nancy Lewis Edwards, David Edwards, Martha Goodman, Zak Herring, Robert Hess, Kenneth Hill, Pamela

Hurst, Lee Lowrimore, Shelley McClure, Lisa Marsh, Lynne Moon, Sam Patterson, Spencer Prokop, Tim Reischauer, Greg Schulte, Gregory Schwab, Marie Hanes Smithers, Sally Smith-Petersen, Octavio Solis, Paula Unrau, Dennis Vincent, Gary Whitehead.

Designers: scenery, Stella McCord; lighting, Raynard Harper, Gregory Schwab, Scott L. Hammar; costumes, Nancy Wilkins, Doug Jackson.

Dallas Theater Center: Eugene McKinney New Play Readings

(Workshop premieres)

DRIVE TIME by James Weslowski; director, Dennis W. Vincent. October 20, 1980.
SNOWBOUND by Deborah A. Allen; director, Jeffrey Kinghorn. November 10 and 17, 1980.
MORRISEY VS. SEACAMP by Charles E. Beachley, III; director, Andrew Gaupp. December 8, 1980.

FIRE ON THE MOUNTAIN (2). By George Speer; director, John Logan. February 23, 1981.
THE LOVECHILD AND THE RAINBOW MAN by Jelly Fielding; director, Paul Baker. April 6, 1981.

Note: DTC's mime troupe, MimeAct, presented *Alice in Wonderland* and *Androcles and the Lion* (26) in 15 city parks, June-July 1980. *To Kill a Mockingbird* and *Alice in Wonderland* toured schools and community centers in 22 Texas towns and cities, spring 1981, sponsored by the Texas Commission on the Arts and the NEA. *A Christmas Carol* (13) by Charles Dickens; adapted by John Figlmiller and Sally Netzel, played in the Kalita Humphreys Theater, December 18–27, 1980. The Dallas Theater Center's affiliation with the M.F.A. degree graduate study program of Trinity University in San Antonio provided the staff of the theater arts program from the professional company and gave students in the program an opportunity to work with the company on the season's productions.

EVANSTON, ILL.

North Light Repertory

(Artistic director, Eric Steiner; producing director, Gregory Kandel)

LIGHT UP THE SKY (38). By Moss Hart. September 25, 1980. Director, Michael Maggio. With Gerry Becker, Susan Dafoe, Ron Parady, Sheila Keenan, Norm Tobin.

FAMILY BUSINESS (38). By Dick Goldberg, November 20, 1980. Director, Joe Sturniolo. With members of the company.

ON GOLDEN POND (38). By Ernest Thompson. January 22, 1981. Director, Montgomery Davis. With Bob Thompson, Jean Sincere, Jodean Culbert, Mark Christopher Maranto.

THE INCREDIBLE MURDER OF CARDINAL TOSCA (38). By Alden Nowlan and Walter Learning. March 19, 1981. Director, Mark Milliken. With Ron Parady, James Deuter, John Mohrlein, Sheila Keenan, Michael Tezla.

HOW I GOT THAT STORY (38). By Amlin Gray. May 14, 1981. Director, Sharon Ott. With Tim Halligan, Jack McLaughlin-Gray.

Designers: scenery, Maher Ahmad, Jeremy Conway, Joseph C. Nieminski; lighting, Maher Ahmad, Mark Mongold, Rita Pietraszek, Robert Shook; costumes, Julie Jackson, Kate Bergh, Colleen Muscha, Kaye Nottbusch.

HARTFORD

Hartford Stage Company: John W. Huntington Theater

(Artistic director, Mark Lamos; managing director, William Stewart)

THE BEAUX' STRATAGEM (44). By George Farquhar. September 26, 1980. Director, Mark Lamos. With Bernard Frawley, Kathleen Doyle, Alan Coates, Tom Donaldson, Linda Thorson, Meg Wynn Owen, William Andrews, Timothy Landfield.

EINSTEIN AND THE POLAR BEAR (44). By Tom Griffin. November 14, 1980 (world premiere). Director, J. Ranelli, scenery and costumes, Fred Voelpel; lighting, Arden Fingerhut.

Andrew Allenson	John Wardwell
Charlie Milton	Robert Nichols
Diane Ashe	Pamela Blair
Bill Allenson	Terrance O'Quinn
Helen Bullins	Marjorie Lovett
Bobby Bullins	David Strathairn

Time: February. Place: Spider Lake, a small New England town, during a raging blizzard. Act I: Friday evening. Act II: The next morning.

CYMBELINE (44). By William Shakespeare. January 2, 1981. Director, Mark Lamos. With Richard Mathews, Barbara Bryne, Mary Layne, Bernard Frawley.

UNDISCOVERED COUNTRY (44). By Arthur Schnitzler; version by Tom Stoppard. February 20, 1981 (American premiere). Director, Mark Lamos; scenery, David Jenkins; lighting, Pat Collins; costumes, Lowell Detweiler; wigs, Paul Huntley.

Genia Hofreiter	Jennifer Harmon
Kathi	Pan Riley
Mrs. Wahl	Ruby Holbrook
Erna Wahl	Mary Layne
Otto von Aigner	James Phipps
Franz Mauer	Davis Hall
Friedrich Hofreiter	Keith Baxter
Paul Kreindl	Mark Capri
Adele Natter	Carol Fox Prescott
Demeter Stanzides	Nafe Katter
Mr. Natter	William Wright
Mrs. Meinhold von Aigner	Barbara Bryne
Rosenstock	David Murphy
Hikers	Stephen Rust, Ted McAdams
Mr. Serknitz	Bernard Frawley
Dr. von Aigner	Stefan Schnabel

Spanish Girl	Joan Parrish
Albertus Rhon	Jerry Allan Jones
Italian Girl	Diane MacDonald
Penn	Ian Drosdova
Gustl Wahl	Peter Davies
Mrs. Rhon	Mary Munger
French Girl	Meg Young
Headwaiter	Mark Nelson
Bellboy	Sean Kellner
Natter Children	Adam Joseph Dexter, Christine Kluntz
French Nanny	Hannah Shapiro

Time: 1911, summer. Place: Austria.

Act I: The Hofreiter villa in Baden, near Vienna, late afternoon. Act II: Same, two weeks later, morning. Act III: The Lake Vols Hotel in the Dolomites, late afternoon a week later. Act IV: Hofreiter Villa, afternoon, some weeks later. Act V: The same, next morning. One intermission.

IS THERE LIFE AFTER HIGH SCHOOL? (44). Book by Jeffrey Kindley; music and lyrics by Craig Carnelia; suggested by Ralph Keyes's book. April 10, 1981 (world premiere). Director, Melvin Bernhardt; scenery, John Lee Beatty; lighting, Spencer Mosse; costumes, Jess Goldstein; musical director and orchestrator, Bruce Coughlin; choreographer, Nora Peterson. With Raymond Baker, Susan Bigelow, Roger Chapman, Joel Colodner, David Patrick Kelly, Elizabeth Lathram, Michael McCormick, Maureen Silliman.

Musical Numbers—Act I: "The Kid Inside," "Things I Learned in High School," "Second Thoughts," "Nothing Really Happened," "Beer," "For Them," "Shove It," "Diary of a Homecoming Queen." Act II: "Thousands of Trumpets," "I'm Glad You Didn't Know Me," "Reunion," "The School Song."

I, JAMES McNEILL WHISTLER (44). By Lawrence and Maggie Williams, based on Lawrence Williams's novel. May 22, 1981 (world premiere). Director, Jerome Kilty; designer, David Gropman; lighting, William Armstrong. With John Cullum as Whistler.

Designers: Scenery and costumes, Lowell Detweiler, John Conklin; lighting, Spenser Mosse, Pat Collins.

HARTFORD STAGE COMPANY—Terrance O'Quinn and David Strathairn in *Einstein and the Polar Bear* by Tom Griffin

HOUSTON

The Nina Vance Alley Theater: Large Stage

(Artistic director, Pat Brown; managing director, Iris Siff)

TO GRANDMOTHER'S HOUSE WE GO (38). By Joanna M. Glass. October 16, 1980 (world premiere). Director, Clifford Williams; scenery, Matthew Grant; lighting, Jonathan Duff; costumes, Jane Greenwood.

Grandie .... Eva Le Gallienne
Harriet .... Kim Hunter
Jared................. Shepperd Strudwick
Clementine.................. Ruth Nelson
Muffy .... Pamela Brook
Paul .... David Snell
Twyla .... Leslie Denniston
Beatrice .... Anne Twomey
Time: Thanksgiving Eve. Place: Grandie's home in Connecticut.

THE THREEPENNY OPERA (64). By Bertolt Brecht and Kurt Weill, adapted by Marc Blitzstein. November 27, 1980. Director, Pat Brown; musical director, Sterling Tinsley. With Joe Barrett, Richard Erdman, Patricia Kilgarriff, Roxann Parker, Nathan Adler, Mary Ayres, Tommy Hollis.

FATHERS AND SONS (38). By Thomas Babe. January 22, 1981. Director, Louis Criss. With Alan Feinstein, Barbara Anderson, Alan Stack.

ON GOLDEN POND (38). By Ernest Thompson. March 5, 1981. Director, Pat Brown.. With Wiley Harker, Lynn Wood, Lillian Evans, Philip Fisher, Mike Hartman, David Wurst.

ROMEO AND JULIET (38). By William Shakespeare. April 16, 1981. Director, Louis Criss. With Scott Wentworth, Patrizia Narcia, Neil Flanagan, Jeannette Clift, John Sanford.

TEN LITTLE INDIANS (38). By Agatha Christie. May 28, 1981. Director, Robert Symonds. With Bernard Frawley, Ivar Barry, James Ray, Holly Villaire.

The Nina Vance Alley Theater: Arena Stage

STRIDER: THE STORY OF A HORSE (32). Adapted from Leo Tolstoy's story by Mark Rozovsky; English version by Robert Kalfin and Steve Brown; based on a translation by Tamara Bering Sunguroff; music by Mark Rozovsky and S. Vetkin; adapted with additional music by Norman L. Berman; new English lyrics by Steve Brown; original Russian lyrics by Uri Riashentsev. December 11, 1980. Director, Beth Sanford; musical director, Jan Cole; choreogra-

pher, Chesley Santoro. With Robert Donley, Joan Dunham, Neil Flanagan, Richard Loder.

BETRAYAL (38). By Harold Pinter. March 12, 1981. Director, Beth Sanford. With Michael Fletcher, Barbara Anderson, Robert Phalen.

DA (38). By Hugh Leonard. April 30, 1981. Director, Beth Sanford. With Dale Helward, Robert Donley, Helen Halsey, Bettye Fitzpatrick.

Children's Theater: Arena Stage

THE ADVENTURES OF TOM SAWYER (53). Adapted by Timothy Mason, from Mark Twain's novel. November 8, 1980 (world premiere). Director, John Vreeke; scenery, John Bos; lighting Albert Oster; costumes, Tom McKinley.

Tom	Dustye Winniford
Aunt Polly	Sharon Jarvis
Becky Thatcher	Lisa Cook
Muff Potter	Paris Peet
Injun Joe	Wyn Warren
Amy Lawrence	Emily Riddle
Miss Dobbins	Darcey Ferrer
Doc Robinson	Milton Blankenship
Judge Thatcher	Mark Volland
Mrs. Harper	Robin Bludworth
Susan Harper	Celia Nolte
Ben Rogers	Fritz Dickman
Narrator	Helen Halsey

New Play Readings: Arena Stage

PARADISE by Philip Halamon. December 15, 1980. Director, John Vreeke; designer, Jack Stewart. With Bettye Fitzpatrick, J. Shane McClure, Emily Riddle, Nathan Adler, Linda Callahan.

THINK OF AFRICA by Gordon Dryland. February 16, 1981. Director, John Vreeke; designers, James Middleton, Albert Oster. With Bettye Fitzpatrick, Michael LaGue, Gale Fury Childs, Michael Cunningham, Philip Schuster, Helen Halsey.

Designers: scenery, Matthew Grant, William Trotman, John Bos; lighting, Jonathan Duff, Matthew Grant; costumes, Michael J. Cesario, Tom McKinley, Ariel Baliff.

Note: The tradition of presenting the Merry-Go-Round production of *The Yellow Brick Road,* Iris Siff's musical adaptation of The *Wizard of Oz,* was continued. Two performances were given on January 31, 1981, directed by Bob Feingold, music by George Morgenstern. Three performances of *Gertrude Stein, Gertrude Stein, Gertrude Stein* by Marty Martin, with Pat Carroll, were presented on the Large Stage, February 24–25, 1981.

INDIANAPOLIS

Indiana Repertory Theater: Indiana Theater—Mainstage

(Artistic director, Tom Haas; producing director, Benjamin Mordecai)

HOAGY, BIX AND WOLFGANG BEETHOVEN BUNKHAUS (27). By Adrian Mitchell, a jazz play based on the music of Hoagy Carmichael. October 24, 1980 (American premiere). Director, Tom Haas; scenery and costumes, Steven Rubin; lighting, Jeff Davis; music director, Richard M. Sudhalter; choreographer, Lynette Schisla.

Hoagy Carmichael	Jamey Sheridan
Bix Beiderbecke	Armin Shimerman
Wolfgang Beethoven Bunkhaus	Gregory Salata
Betty	Linda Daugherty
Coed	Phyllis Somerville
Paul Whiteman	Frank Kopyc
Pete Costas	Bernard Kates

Music from Carmichael's repertory of songs, including "Stardust," "Georgia on My Mind,"

"Up a Lazy River," "Ole Buttermilk Sky," "Rockin' Chair".

A CHRISTMAS CAROL (31). By Charles Dickens; adapted and directed by Tom Haas. November 28, 1980. With Win Atkins, Robert Boyle, David Adamson, Tom Bade, Jack Couch, Judith Elaine.

ROCKET TO THE MOON (26). By Clifford Odets. January 9, 1981. Director, Eric Steiner. With Kevin O'Connor, Katie Grant, Carole Monferdini, Bernard Kates, Scott Wentworth, Steve Mendillo, Zeke Zaccaro.

TREATS (24). By Christopher Hampton. February 13, 1981. Director, William Peters. With Priscilla Lindsay, William Perley, Scott Wentworth.

THE FAILURE TO ZIGZAG (28). By John B. Ferzacca. March 17, 1981 (world premiere). Director, Tom Haas; scenery, Kate Edmunds; lighting, Jeff Davis; costumes, Leon Brauner.

Second Officer	Stan Birnbaum
Crewman	John Daggan
Capt. Charles McVay III	Richard Council

Prosecution	Bernard Kates
Defense	Victor Arnold
First Witness	Gregory Chase
Rear Admiral	Richard Voigts
Operations Officer	Edward Cannan
Survivor One	Joel Swetow
Survivor Two	Michael Margulis
Survivor Three	Larry Welch
Survivor Four	Dallas Greer
Survivor Five	Christopher McCann
Survivor Six	Andrew Davis
Mochitsura Hashimoto	Ernest Abuba
Capt. Donaho	Steve Pudenz

Others: Jon R. Bailey, Tony Cerola, Craig Gaylor, John K. Hedges, Donald Lang, Steven Laughn, Joseph Hayes Lilley, Rockey Mitchell, Kurt. S. Owens, Gregor Paslawsky.

Time and Place: December, 1945, the Navy Yard, Washington, D.C.; July, 1945, somewhere in the South Pacific; July, 1980, Indianapolis.

AH, WILDERNESS! (25). By Eugene O'Neill. April 24, 1981. Director, David Rotenberg. With John Carpenter, Bette Henritze, Stephen Preuss, Maxine Taylor-Morris, Cynthia Judge, Bernard Kates.

Indiana Repertory Theater: Upper Stage

OEDIPUS AT THE HOLY PLACE (19). By Robert Montgomery; adapted from *Oedipus at Colonus* by Sophocles. January 23, 1981. Director, Tom Haas. With David Little, Linda Selman, Dan Desmond, Marci Rigsby, William Verderber, Arthur Hanket.

LIVE TONIGHT: EMMA GOLDMAN (19). By Michael Bigelow Dixon. February 27, 1981 (world premiere). Director, Lynne Gould-Guerra; scenery, Bob Barnett; lighting, Rachel Budin; costumes, Skip Gindhart.

Emma Goldman	Lynn Cohen

Frank Heiner	Ralph Elias

COMING OF AGE (19). By Barbara Field. April 3, 1981 (world premiere). Director, Leonard Peters; scenery, Russell Metheny; lighting, William Armstrong; costumes, Carol Oditz.

Jake Millar	Norman Parker
Zoe Millar	Julie Garfield
Parker	David Chandler
Ben	Scott McKay

Time: The present and four hours later. Place: A beach cottage on the south New Jersey coast.

Designers: scenery, Karen Schulz, David Potts, Heidi Landesman, Steven Rubin, Bob Barnett; lighting, Jeff Davis, William Armstrong, Rachel Budin; costumes, Susan Hilferty, Rachel Kurland, Nan Cibula, Rita Ryack, Skip Gindhart.

Indiana Repertory Theater: Cabaret Theater

MURDER IN THE CABARET (51). Written and directed by Tom Haas. May 12, 1981 (world premiere). Musical director, James Kowal; cabaret designer, Bob Barnett.

Harry	Don Ruddy

Cherry	Margaret McCall-Carmichael
Chuck	Scott F. Bylund
Flossie	Bernadette Galanti

One intermission.

Note: IRT presented a state-wide tour of *Musical Mirage Express '81* (58), created and directed by John Abajian; music by A. Paul Johnson; designer, Bob Barnett; costumes, Dana Harnish Tinsley. Touring company: Vickie D. Chappell, Jeffrey Dreisbach, Rae Randall, John Scalzi, Jeffrey V. Thompson, Teresa Metzger.

KANSAS CITY, MO.

Missouri Repertory Theater: University of Missouri at Kansas City—Helen F. Spencer Theater Center

(Producing director, Patricia McIlrath)

MEDEA (19). By Robinson Jeffers; from *Medea* by Euripides. July 10, 1980. Director, Erik Vos. With Juliet Randall, Ronetta Wallman, Robert Lewis Karlin, William Metzo, David Coxwell.

WHAT EVERY WOMAN KNOWS (18). By J. M. Barrie. July 17, 1980. Director, Francis J. Cullinan. With Kathryn C. Sparer, Gerard A. Burke, Richard Gustin, Edith Owen, Cynthia Dozier.

THE LEARNED LADIES (17). By Molière; translated by Richard Wilbur. July 31, 1980. Director, Norman Ayrton. With Gerard A. Burke, Edith Owen, Doris Martin, Cynthia Dozier, David Coxwell, Francis Peter.

CATSPLAY (18) By Istvan Orkeny; translated by Clara Gyorgyey. August 7, 1980. Director, James Assad. With Francis Peter, Edith Owen, William Metzo, Robert Lewis Karlin.

Missouri Repertory Theater: Winter Repertory

LADY AUDLEY'S SECRET (18). Adapted and directed by Francis J. Cullinan from the novel by Mary Elizabeth Braddon and William Suter's play. January 29, 1981. With Jim Birdsall, Richard Gustin, Cynthia Dozier, Nancy Nichols, Mark Robbins.

THE NIGHT OF THE IGUANA (19). By Tennessee Williams. February 5, 1981. Director, George Hamlin. With Ronetta Wallman, William Metzo, Carolgene Burd, Jerome Collamore.

WINGS (18). By Arthur Kopit. February 19, 1981. Director, James Assad. With Peg Small, Cynthia Dozier, Jim Birdsall, Robert Lewis Karlin, Ronetta Wallman.

A PERFECT GENTLEMAN (19). By Herbert Appleman. February 26, 1981 (professional premiere). Director, John Reich; scenery, James Leonard Joy; lighting, Joseph Appelt; costumes,

Vincent Scassellati.

Solomon Dayrolles	Jim Birdsall
Lord Chesterfield	Donald Woods
Lady Chesterfield	Robin Humphrey
John	Joseph Collamore
Philip Stanhope	Richard Gustin
Walter Harte	Robert Lewis Karlin
Duke of Newcastle	William Metzo
Lady Cynthia Harrington	Barbara Houston
Eugenia Peters	Nancy Nichols

Time: Spring of 1755. Place: London. Act I, Scene 1: The library of Chesterfield House, morning. Scene 2: Same, an afternoon three weeks later. Scene 3: Same, the following morning. Act II, Scene 1: Private sitting room in a London inn, an hour later. Scene 2: Library of Chesterfield House, early the following evening. Scene 3: Same, an afternoon a month later. One intermission (see synopsis in introduction to this section).

Designers: scenery, Richard Hay, John Ezell, Carolyn L. Ross, James Leonard Joy, Franco Colavecchia; lighting, Joseph Appelt, Ruth Ludwick, Arden Fingerhut; costumes, Douglas Russell, Baker S. Smith, Vincent Scassellati, Michele Bechtold.

Missouri Repertory Theater: Showcase Theater—Studio Theater

(Director, James Assad. New Plays-in-Progress)

CLEARVIEW HEIGHTS (3). By Penny Weiner. August 25, 1980.
THE FALL OF TROY (3). By Larry Martin. September 8, 1980.

CHOICES (3). By Jess Lynn. September 15, 1980
With Apprentice/Intern Company.

Note: MRT toured to 20 communities in Missouri, Kansas and Oklahoma, September 24–November 2, 1980 with *What Every Woman Knows* and *The Learned Ladies.*

LAKEWOOD, OHIO

Great Lakes Shakespeare Festival

(Artistic director, Vincent Dowling; general manager, Mary Bill)

HENRY IV, PART 1 (10). By William Shakespeare. July 10, 1980. Director, Donald MacKechnie. With Bernard Kates, Emery Battis, Thomas Waites/Daniel Tamm, Nancy Roykin, Patricia Doyle, Clayton Corbin.

CHARLEY'S AUNT (13). By Brandon Thomas. July 17, 1980. Director, Vincent Dowling. With Daniel Tamm, Thomas Waites, John Q. Bruce, Nancy Boykin, Madylon Branstetter, Sarah Nall.

MY LADY LUCK (4). By James A. Brown; based on the life and works of Robert W. Service. July 24, 1980 (world premiere). Director, Michael Egan. With Vincent Dowling.

HUGHIE by Eugene O'Neill and THE BOOR by Anton Chekhov (6). August 7, 1980. Director, Edward Stern. With Festival Acting Company.

THE COMEDY OF ERRORS (10). By William Shakespeare. August 14, 1980. Director, Robert Ellenstein. With Bruce Matley, John Q. Bruce, Robert Elliott, Bairbre Dowling.

TITUS ANDRONICUS (6). By William Shakespeare. August 28, 1980. Director, Vincent Dowling. With Emery Battis, Robert Elliott, Sarah Nall, Madylon Branstetter/Bairbre Dowling.

Designers: scenery, John Ezell, Robert Schmidt; lighting, Jonathan Duff, Kirk Bookman; costumes, Richard Donnelly, Linda Vigdor.

LOS ANGELES

Center Theater Group: Ahmanson Theater

(Managing director, Robert Fryer)

HOLIDAY (51). By Philip Barry. October 3, 1980. Director, Robert Allan Ackerman. With Sally Kellerman, Kevin Kline, Marisa Berenson, Maurice Evans.

THE CRUCIFER OF BLOOD (51). Written and directed by Paul Giovanni. December 5, 1980. With Charlton Heston, Jeremy Brett, Suzanne Lederer.

THE WEST SIDE WALTZ (58). By Ernest Thompson. January 21, 1981 (world premiere). Director, Noel Willman; scenery, Ben Edwards; lighting, Thomas Skelton; costumes, Jane Greenwood; music supervisor and arranger, David Krane.
Cara Varnum . . . . Dorothy Loudon
Serge Barrescu . . . . David Margulies
Margaret Mary
  Elderdice . . . . Katharine Hepburn

Robin Bird . . . . Regina Baff
Glen Dabrinsky . . . . Don Howard
    Place: The living room of a West Side New York apartment. Act 1, Scene 1: Winter. "Du Und Du" (Johann Strauss). Scene 2: Spring. "Gelaufigkeit" (Carl Czerny). Scene 3: Summer. "Playing Together Is Fun" (Saul Minsch and Wolfgang Mozart). Act II, Scene 1: Winter. "The Little Dog Waltz" (Frederic Chopin). Scene 2: Spring: "Wein, Weib, und Gasang" (Johann Strauss). Scene 3: Fall. "One More Waltz" (Dorothy Fields and Jimmy McHugh). One intermission.

MARY STUART (51). By Friedrich Schiller; translated and adapted by Joe McClinton. April 10, 1981. Director, Jack O'Brien. With Marsha Mason, Michael Learned, Robert Foxworth, Stephen McHattie, William Schallert.

Designers: scenery, John Lee Beatty, John Wulp, Sam Kirkpatrick; lighting, Arden Fingerhut, David Hersey, John McLain; costumes, Robert Wojewodski, Noel Taylor, Sam Kirkpatrick.

Center Theater Group: Mark Taper Forum—Mainstage

(Artistic director, Gordon Davidson)

THE LADY AND THE CLARINET (54). By Michael Cristofer; music by Leonard Rosenman; lyric by Alan and Marilyn Bergman. August 14, 1980 (world premiere). Director, Gordon Davidson; scenery, John Lee Beatty; lighting, John Gleason; costumes, Carrie F. Robbins.

Luba	Rose Gregorio
Paul	Kevin Geer
Jack	David Spielberg
George	Josef Sommer
The Clarinet	Bill Lamden

One intermission (see synopsis in introduction to this section).

BILLY BISHOP GOES TO WAR (54). By John Gray and Eric Peterson. October 16, 1980. Director, John Gray. With Eric Peterson.

HOAGY, BIX AND WOLFANG BEETHOVEN BUNKHAUS (54). By Adrian Mitchell; based on *The Stardust Road* by Hoagy Carmichael. January 15, 1981. Director, Steven Robman; musical director and arranger, Richard M. Sudhalter. With Larry Cedar, Harry Groener, Philip Baker Hall, Bruce French.

TINTYPES (54). Conceived by Mary Kyte with Mel Marvin and Gary Pearle. March 19, 1981. Director, Gary Pearle; musical staging, Mary Kyte; musical and vocal arranger, Mel Marvin; orchestrator, John McKinney. With Carolyn Mignini, Lynne Thigpen, Trey Wilson, Mary Catherine Wright, Jerry Zaks.

CHEKHOV IN YALTA (35). By John Driver and Jeffrey Haddow. May 24, 1981 (world premiere). Directors, Ellis Rabb, Gordon Davidson; scenery, Douglas W. Schmidt; lighting, Martin Aronstein; costumes, John Conklin.

Fyokla	Louis Foraker
Anton Pavlovich Chekhov	Robin Gammell
Maxim Gorky	Keene Curtis
Ivan Alexeivich Bunin	James R. Winker
Masha Chekhov	Marian Mercer
Olga Leonardova Knipper	Penny Fuller
Vladimir Nemirovich-Danchenko	Dana Elcar
Lilina Stanislavski	Andra Akers
Luzhki	Michael Monk
Moskvin	Jeffrey Combs
Konstantin Sergeievich Stanislavski	Rene Auberjonois

Time: April 1900. Place: Anton Chekhov's villa in Yalta. Act I, Scene 1: A spring morning. Scene 2: The next evening. Act II: Sunday morning, one week later (see synopsis in introduction to this section).

Designers: scenery, Tony Walton, David Gropman, Tom Lynch, Douglas W. Schmidt; lighting, Tharon Musser, Jennifer Tipton, Paul Gallo, Martin Aronstein; costumes, Jess Goldstein, John Conklin, Dona Granata.

Center Theater Group: Mark Taper Forum—Improvisational Theater Project

A CHRISTMAS CAROL (24). By Charles Dickens; adapted by Doris Baizley. December 7, 1980. Director, Frank Condon. With Bruce French, Socorro Valdez, Ralph Steadman and the ITP Company.

Center Theater Group: Mark Taper Forum—Forum Lab

(Play developmant program)

TONGUES and SAVAGE/LOVE (16). By Sam Shepard, Joseph Chaikin; music by Sam Shepard, Skip LaPlante, Harry Mann. October 21, 1980. Director, Robert Woodruff. Performed by Joseph Chaikin and musicians, Skip LaPlante, Harry Mann.

THE LAST YIDDISH POET (15). Created by A Traveling Jewish Theater; written by Naomi Newman Pollack, Albert Greenberg, Corey Fischer. November 12, 1980. Director, Naomi Newman Pollack. With Corey Fischer, Albert Greenberg. Additional texts by Peretz Markish, Rochl Korn, Jacob Glatstein, Itzik Manger, Mordechai Gebirtik.

APEWATCH (15). By Elaine Osio. January 14, 1981. Director, G. W. Bailey. With Carol Williard, Dean Santoro, Linda Carlson, Andy Wood.

MARK TAPER FORUM, LOS ANGELES—Bill Lamden and Rose
Gregorio in *The Lady and the Clarinet* by Michael Cristofer

STARS IN YOUR EYES (12). Conceived by Oz
Scott, Ron Abel; music and lyrics by Ron
Abel with Bob Garrett. March 10, 1981. Direc-
tor, Oz Scott; musical staging and choreography,
Murphy Cross, Newton Winters; arranger, Gary
Bristol. With Ron Abel (piano), Nathan
Cook, Nedra Dixon, Kara Grannum, Elizabeth
Lamers, Jaison Walker. Additional lyrics by
Robin Blair, Warren Ham, Marilyn Pasekoff.

Designers: scenery, Charles Berliner, Tom Clover, Keith Gonzales; lighting, Tom Ruzika, Beverly
Emmons, Tom Clover, Brian Gale, Greg Sullivan; costumes, Charles Berliner, Mary Brecht, Sherry
Thompson, Betty Gage.

LOUISVILLE

Actors' Theater of Louisville: Pamela Brown Auditorium

(Producing director, Jon Jory)

TERRA NOVA (27). By Ted Tally. October 2,
1980. Director, Michael Hankins. With William
Cain, Andy Backer, Katharine Houghton, William McNulty.

CYRANO DE BERGERAC (27). By Edmond Rostand; translated by Brian Hooker. October 29, 1980. Director, Jon Jory. With Ken Jenkins, Lee Anne Fahey, Richard Bowne, Jean Barker, Michael Kevin, Andy Backer.

A CHRISTMAS CAROL (24). By Charles Dickens; adapted by Barbara Field. December 5, 1980. Director, Frazier Marsh. With Ray Fry, Michael Kevin, Doc Manning, William McNulty, Dierk Toporzysek.

SLY FOX (27). By Larry Gelbart; based on Ben Jonson's *Volpone* as adapted by Stefan Zweig. January 1, 1981. Director, Jon Jory. With Ken Jenkins, William McNulty, Adale O'Brien, Cecelia Riddett, Brian Rose.

ON GOLDEN POND (28). By Ernest Thompson. January 29, 1981. Director, Victor Jory. With Ray Fry, Anne Pitoniak, William McNulty, Adale O'Brien, Shannon Ragland, Michael Kevin.

SWOP (12). By Ken Jenkins. February 26, 1981 (world premiere). Director, Jon Jory; scenery and lighting, Paul Owen; costumes, Kurt Wilhelm.

Kalija	Michael Sokoloff
H. E. Rowe	Ken Jenkins
J. R. Carver	Andy Backer
Timothy	Burt Adams
Ruth Ann	Cristine Rose
Carlisle	Dierk Toporzysek
Lanny	Robert Schenkkan
Delores	Susan Kingsley
Bud	Brian Rose

Time: The present. Place: A small town in South Central Kentucky. One intermission (see synopsis in introduction to this section).

A FULL LENGTH PORTRAIT OF AMERICA (10). By Paul D'Andrea. March 1, 1981 (world premiere). Director, Ken Jenkins; scenery and lighting, Paul Owen; costumes, Kurt Wilhelm.

Emma	Frances Foster
Harold	Robert Judd
Tibbett	Brian Rose
Tuli Latum	Susan Kingsley
Wilbur Tibury	Dierk Toporzysek
Lieutenant	Robert Schenkkan

Time: The Present. Place: Preservation Hall, New Orleans. Two intermissions.

MY SISTER IN THIS HOUSE (11). By Wendy Kesselman. March 6, 1981 (world premiere). Director, Jon Jory. Scenery and lighting, Paul Owen; costumes, Kurt Wilhelm.

Christine	Cristine Rose
Lea	Patricia Charbonneau
Madame Cottin	Eloise Terry
Mlle. Isabelle Danzard	Marianne Owen

Recorded Voices: Chief Justice—Ken Jenkins, Priest—Tom McPaul, Judge—Michael Kevin, Policeman—David Jaffe:

Time: 1925 through 1933. Place: Different houses, in and around the town of Le Mans, France (see synopsis in introduction to this section).

BLACK COFFEE (27). By Agatha Christie. April 2, 1981. Director, Ray Fry. With William McNulty, Michael Kevin, Charles Kissinger, Laura Hicks, Adale O'Brien, Brian Rose.

ARTICHOKE (27). By Joanna M. Glass. April 30, 1981. Director, Adale O'Brien. With Beth Dixon, Patricia Charbonneau, Ray Fry, Michael Kevin, William McNulty.

Actors Theater of Louisville: Victor Jory Theater

SEA MARKS (18). By Gardner McKay. September 24, 1980. Director, B. J. Whiting. With Michael Kevin, Laura Hicks.

SEMI-PRECIOUS THINGS by Terri Wagener, director, Marsha Norman; FINAL PLACEMENT by Ara Watson, and CHOCOLATE CAKE by Mary Gallagher, director, Amy Saltz (8). December 2, 1980 (world premieres). With Laura Hicks, Robert Blackburn, Susan Kingsley, Kathy Bates.

JUST HORRIBLE by Nicholas Kazan, director, Larry Deckel; MORNING CALL by Alan Gross, director, Adale O'Brien; PROPINQUITY by Claudia Johnson, director, Radha

Delamarter (7). December 4, 1980 (world premieres). With Adale O'Brien, Susan Cash, Andy Backer, Peter M. Sgro, Brian Keeler, Timothy Busfield, Cecelia Riddett, George Kimmel, Jane Kinsey, Stephen Daley.

CHUG by Ken Jenkins, directed by Jon Jory and Ken Jenkins; THE MOST TRUSTED MAN IN AMERICA by Stuart Hample; LET'S US by Vaughn McBride, directed by Elizabeth Ives (7). December 6, 1980 (world premieres). With Ken Jenkins, Andy Backer, Adale O'Brien, Hal Tenney, Robert Blackburn, Stephen Daley.

FUTURE TENSE: two plays by David Kranes. PARK CITY: MIDNIGHT directed by

Jon Jory and AFTER COMMENCEMENT directed by Frazier Marsh (9). February 18, 1981 (world premieres).

Park City: Midnight

Theodore Long . . . . Timothy Busfield
Andrew Chalmers . . . . Christopher W. Cooper
Debra Lund . . . . Susan Cash
Julie Forester . . . . Laura Hicks
Thomas Forester . . . . Kent Broadhurst
    Time: After midnight. Place: A rented condominium in Park City, Utah.

After Commencement

Howie . . . . Brian Keeler
Andrew . . . . Christopher W. Cooper
Friday . . . . Lisa Goodman
    Time: Early afternoon, the day after graduation. Place: A small college in New England.

EARLY TIMES (10): A Dramatic Anthology. February 20, 1981 (world premieres). Including: PROPINQUITY by Claudia Johnson, directed by Radha Delamarter. With Timothy Busfield (Dale), Christopher W. Cooper (Roo), Laura Hicks (Alexis), Brian Keeler (Marshall). QUADRANGLE, written and directed by Jon Jory. With Sally Fay Reit (Danielle), Christopher W. Cooper (Sam). CHAPTER TWELVE—THE FROG by John Pielmeier, directed by Larry Deckel. With Susan Cash (Carol), Lisa Goodman (Judy). SPADES by Jim Beaver, directed by Larry Deckel. With Timothy Busfield (Rob), Brian Keeler (Jack), Kent Broadhurst (Young Marine).

TWIRLER by Anonymous, directed by Radha Delamarter. With Lisa Goodman (April). THE A**HOLE MURDER CASE by Stuart Hample, directed by Radha Delamarter. With Timothy Busfield (Nelson), Greg Alexander (Seymour), Sally Fay Reit (Emily), Kent Broadhurst (Mr. Epstein). WATERMELON BOATS by Wendy MacLaughlin, directed by Larry Deckel. With Laura Hicks (Kate), Susan Cash (Kitty)

THE AUTOBIOGRAPHY OF A PEARL DIVER (8). By Martin Epstein. February 25, 1981 (world premiere). Director, Michael Hankins.

P.H. . . . . Ray Fry
Joyce . . . . Adale O'Brien
Bingo Karp . . . . Michael Kevin
Bill . . . . William McNulty
    Time: The recent past. Place: A residential neighborhood.

EXTREMITIES (8). By William Mastrosimone. March 3, 1981 (world premiere). Director, John Bettenbender.

Marge . . . . Ellen Barber
Raul . . . . Danton Stone
Terry . . . . Peggity Price
Patricia . . . . Kathy Bates
    Time: The present, sometime in September. Place: An old farmhouse a few miles from Trenton, N.J. (see synopsis in introduction to this section).

Designers: scenery, Karen Schulz, Paul Owen, James A. Varga, Hugh Landwehr, Hal Tiné; lighting, Geoffrey T. Cunningham, Paul Owen, Jeff Hill; costumes, Kurt Wilhelm.

Note: Actors' Theater of Louisville presented two children's theater productions, *Gallymander Stew* (13), a potful of American folk tales, directed by Radha Delamarter, October 11, 1980 and *Mother Goose* (8), directed by Larry Deckel, January 17, 1981; designed by Kurt Wilhelm, Karl Haas, Thomas B. Dean, in the Pamela Brown Auditorium. *Generations* (2), a dramatic anthology by Stuart Hample, Rebecca Jernigan, Lee Johnsohn, Jon Jory, Bob Manning, Judy Romberger, L. S. Rowland, Craig Volk, directed by Richard Cunningham, Larry Deckel, Radha Delamarter, Jon Jory, December 18, 1980, and *Stages* by Paula Cizmar, Burton Cohen, Jon Jory, Jane Martin, Vaughn McBride, Daniel Meltzer, Robert Schenkkan, Jeffrey Sweet, William Tyler (4), directed by Larry Deckel and Radha Delamarter, were presented May 19–23, 1981 with the 1980–81 apprentice Intern Company; designed by David S. S. Davis, Kurt Wilhelm, Karl Haas. The two programs consisted of 19 workshop productions of new playlets. This theater's production of Marsha Norman's *Getting Out* toured three international festivals in Yugoslavia, Israel and Eire, September–October, 1980. In May, 1981 *Twirler, Chug, Final Placement* and *Chocolate Cake,* four one-acters of the 1980–81 season were presented at the Toronto Festival, and *Extremities* represented the U. S. at the Baltimore International Festival.

MADISON, N.J.

New Jersey Shakespeare Festival: Drew University

(Artistic director, Paul Barry; producing director, Ellen Barry)

THE COMEDY OF ERRORS (32). By William Shakespeare. June 24, 1980. Director, Paul Barry. With Davis Hall, William Pitts, William Perley, Dana Mills, Callan White, Susanne Marley.

MACBETH (33). By William Shakespeare. July 8, 1980. Director, Paul Barry. With Paul Barry, Callan White, Dana Mills, Ron Coralian, Richard Graham, Davis Hall.

VOLPONE (29). By Ben Jonson. August 5, 1980, Director, Paul Barry. With Ron Coralian, Bill Roberts, Jane Newton Staub, Phillip Pruneau, Richard Graham, William Preston, Susanne Marley.

THE CARETAKER (29). By Harold Pinter. September 23, 1980. Director, Paul Barry. With Phillip Pruneau, Davis Hall, William Perley.

THE WALTZ OF THE TOREADORS (29). By Jean Anouilh. October 21, 1980. Director, Samuel Maupin. With David Howard, Victoria Boothby, Catherine Byers.

KNOCK, KNOCK (29). By Jules Feiffer. November 18, 1980. Director, Dan Held. With Ellen Barry, David S. Howard, David Tabor, William Pitts.

A CHRISTMAS CAROL (16). By Charles Dickens; adapted by Paul Barry. December 16, 1980. Director, Paul Barry. With Don Perkins, Geddeth Smith, William Pitts, David Tabor, Margery Shaw, Elizabeth Horowitz.

Designers; scenery, Peter Harrison; lighting, Richard Dorfman, David Bosboom; costumes, Kathleen Blake, Alice S. Hughes.

Note: The N.J. Shakespeare Festival presented a series of twelve Monday Night Specials, July-September, 1980, including: *The Man Without a Country*, adapted by Paul Barry from Edward Everett Hale's novel, July 28; Michael A. Del Medico as Maxim Gorky in *The Festival of Liberation*, August 18; the Richard Morse Mime Theater, August 11; *African Folk Tales* and *Silent Comedy* from PART Children's Theater, July 21.

MILWAUKEE

Milwaukee Repertory Theater: Pabst Theater

(Artistic director, John Dillon; managing director, Sara O'Connor)

CYRANO DE BERGERAC (30). By Edmond Rostand. September 12, 1980. Director, Richard Cottrell. With William Leach, Anne Kerry, Alan Brooks.

Milwaukee Repertory Theater: Todd Wehr Theater—Mainstage

MOTHER COURAGE AND HER CHILDREN (46). By Bertolt Brecht. October 17, 1980. Director, Sharon Ott. With Rose Pickering, C.C.H. Pounder, Larry Shue, Jack Wallace, Ellen Dolan, Leland Crooks, Gregory Daniel.

CHILDREN OF A LESSER GOD (46). By Mark Medoff. November 28, 1980. Director, John Dillon. With Daniel Mooney, Ella Mae Lentz.

JULIUS CAESAR (46). By William Shakespeare. January 16, 1981. Director, John Dillon. With Victor Raider-Wexler, Henry Strozier, Peggy Cowles, William Leach, James Pickering.

A STREETCAR NAMED DESIRE (46). By Tennessee Williams. February 27, 1981. Director, Sharon Ott. With Peggy Cowles, Tom Berenger, Janni Brinn, Henry Strozier.

THE NERD (46). By Larry Shue. April 10, 1981 (world premiere). Director, John Dillon; scenery, Hugh Landwehr; lighting, Dawn Chiang; costumes, Colleen Muscha.

William Cubbert .... Larry Shue
Tansy McGinnis .... Maggie Thatcher
Axel Hammond .... Daniel Mooney

Warnock Waldgrave .... Henry Strozier
Clelia Waldgrave .... Rose Pickering
Thor Waldgrave .... Matthew Knuth
Rick Steadman .... James Pickering
    Time: November. Place: Terre Haute, Indiana. Act I: November 4. Act II; Scene 1; Six days later. Scene 2: The following day.

Designers: scenery, William Eckart, Laura Maurer, Karl Eigsti, Hugh Landwehr; lighting, Spencer Mosse, Rachel Budin, Arden Fingerhut, Dawn Chiang; costumes, Susan Tsu, Colleen Muscha, Jo Peters.

Milwaukee Repertory Theater: Court Street Theater

(Staged readings, workshop premieres, 3 performances each)

THE CHRISTMAS EVE MURDER by Daniel Stein, February 27, 1981.
GIANTS IN THE EARTH by Amlin Gray; adapted from O. E. Rolvaag's novel, March 6, 1981.
FRIDAYS by Andrew Johns, March 13, 1981.
THE OUTLANDERS and THE DOUBLE by Amlin Gray, March 20, 1981.

THE YEARS OF THE WHIRLWIND by Daniel Stein, April 3, 1981.
    Directors; John Dillon, Sharon Ott, Rob Goodman, Bruce Cornwell, Eric Hill, Nick Faust. Designers: Laura Maurer, Tim Thomas, Varney Knapp, Colleen Muscha. With the MRT. Acting Company.

Note: MRT's production of *A Streetcar Named Desire* toured Tokyo, Yokohama, Odaka, Nagoya, Kyota, at the invitation of Japan's Institute of Dramatic Arts, May 19–June 14, 1981.

MINNEAPOLIS

The Cricket Theater: Hennepin Center for the Arts—Mainstage

(Artistic director, Lou Salerni; managing director, Cynthia Mayeda)

BLUES (17). By Kirk Ristau. October 24, 1980 (world premiere). Director, Lou Salerni; composer and musical director, Hal Atkinson; scenery and costumes, Vera Polovko-Mednikov; lighting, Michael Vennerstrom.

Woody .... Naomi Hatfield
Jessie....................... Tia Mann
Mecca................... Amy Buchwald
Odie .... Denise Ellis
Arnie .... Robert Mailand
    Time: 1940, just prior to America's entry into World War II. Place: A rooming house in Omaha. No intermission.

SIGHTLINES (21). By Mark Eisman. November 28, 1980. Director, Howard Dallin. With Robert Breuler, Allison Giglio.

TACTICS FOR NON-MILITARY BODIES (21). By John Orlock. January 2, 1981 (world premiere). Director, Lou Salerni.

Sparky .... Robert Mailand
Willis Lister............... Robert Breuler
Apricot Bismark .... Barbara Reid

Sandra Finletter........... Camille Gifford
Douglas Bismark............. James Martin
    Time: 1955. Place: In and around the Bismark household in Altoona, Pa. One intermission.

NORTHERN LIGHTS (21). By Erik Brogger. February 6, 1981 (world premiere). Director, Howard Dallin; scenery, James Guenther; lighting, Michael Vennerstrom; costumes, Gregory Lee Robbins.

Jack Bryant .... John Lewin
Sonny Bryant............. Robert Mailand
Boomer Bradley.............. David Wohl
David Bryant.............. Clive Rosengren
Celeste .... Binky Wood
Sarah Bryant .... Barbara Reid
Oral Whitehead.............. James Harris
Allison Murry .... Chris Forth
    Place: The house and part of the station belonging to Jack Bryant of "Jack's Super America," in Hunter, Minn., a fictitious "northern community" you've probably driven past on your way to Winnipeg. One intermission.

THE DARK AT THE TOP OF THE STAIRS (21). By William Inge. March 13, 1981. Director, Lou Salerni. With Camille Gifford, Robert Mailand, Chris Forth, John Lewin, Shirley Venard Diercks.

SIDE BY SIDE BY SONDHEIM (21). Lyrics by Stephen Sondheim; music by Leonard Bernstein, Mary Rodgers, Richard Rodgers, Jule Styne and Stephen Sondheim; continuity by Ned Sherrin, John Orlock, Lou Salerni, Dave Moore. May 22, 1981. Director, Lou Salerni; musical director, Jimmy Martin; choreographer, Lewis Whitlock. With Richard K. Allison, Susan Long, Dolores Noah, Dave Moore.

Designers: scenery and costumes, Vera Polovko-Mednikov; lighting, Michael Vennerstrom, Lisa Johnson.

Cricket Theater: Works-in-Progress Series

(Artistic director, Sean Michael Dowse; one performance each; workshop premieres)

SISTERS OF THE SACRED HEART by K. J. Austin. November 11, 1980. Director, Sean Michael Dowse. Prologue and 16 scenes.
THE BRIXTON RECOVERY by Jack Gilhooley. December 8, 1980. Director, S. M. Dowse. Time: Mid-1970s. Place: Shirley's flat in the Brixton section of London. Four scenes.

SNOW IN THE VIRGIN ISLANDS by Marisha Chamberlain. December 16, 1980. Director, S. M. Dowse. Place: A small Midwestern city. One intermission.
ALPHA WAVES by Robert Spira. January 20, 1981. Director, John Orlock.

Company: Don Amendolia, Amy Buchwald, Camille Clifford, James Craven, Stephen D'Ambrose, Denise Ellis, Allison Giglio, Naomi Hatfield, Betsy Husting, Michael Kinghorn, Michael Laskin, Lorraine LeBlanc, Jack McLaughlin-Gray, Robert Mailand, Dolores Noah, Barbara Reid, Stephen Yoskam.

The Guthrie Theater Company

(Artistic director, Liviu Ciulei; associate artistic director, Garland Wright; managing director, Donald Schoenbaum)

In repertory, June 12–August 16, 1980:
WILD OATS by John O'Keeffe. June 12, 1980. Director, Kenneth Frankel. With Jeffrey Alan Chandler, Ray Fry, Michael Goodwin, Katherine McGrath.
CAMILLE, adapted by Barbara Field from the novel by Alexandre Dumas *fils.* June 14, 1980. Director, Garland Wright. With Margaret Whitton, William Converse Roberts, Barbara Bryne, Richard Russell Ramos.

In repertory August 21–November 22, 1980:
THE TAVERN by George M. Cohan. August 21, 1980. Director, Stephen Kanee. With Adrian Sparks, Oliver Cliff, Richard M. Davidson, Karen Landry.
DESIRE UNDER THE ELMS by Eugene O'Neill. August 23, 1980. Director, George Keathley. With Tony Mockus, Katherine McGrath, Richard McWilliams.

MARY STUART by Friedrich von Schiller; translated by Joseph Mellish. October 8, 1980. Director, Garland Wright. With Katherine McGrath, Barbara Bryne, Robert Scogin, Oliver Cliff, Michael Goodwin.

A CHRISTMAS CAROL (44). By Charles Dickens; adapted by Barbara Field. November 26, 1980. Director, Tony Mockus. With Richard Hilger, Oliver Cliff, Adrian Sparks, T. R. Knight.

ARMS AND THE MAN (38). By George Bernard Shaw. January 7, 1981. Director, Michael Langham. With Helen Carey, Paul Collins, Michael Goodwin, Kristine Nielsen, Roy Brocksmith, Avril Gentles, Yusef Bulos.

MACBETH (42). By William Shakespeare. February 11, 1981. Director, Edward Hastings. With Paul Shenar, Deborah May, John Noah Hertzler, Timothy Landfield, Julie A. Numbers, Bo Smith.

Designers: scenery Jack Barkla, Joseph Guenther, Desmond Heeley, Sam Kirkpatrick; lighting, John McLain, Craig Miller, Paul Scharfenberger, Duane Schuler; costumes, Lewis Brown, Jack Edwards, Virgil Johnson, Jane Greenwood, Desmond Heeley, Robert Fletcher.

GUTHRIE THEATER, MINNEAPOLIS—Katherine McGrath as Mary Stuart and Barbara Bryne as Elizabeth I in Friedrich von Schiller's *Mary Stuart*

Note: The Guthrie Theater toured two productions to the community during 1980–81 season: *A Midsummer Night's Dream* by William Shakespeare and *Soldiering* by Stephen Willems, both directed by Stephen Willems.

NEW HAVEN

Long Wharf Theater: Mainstage

(Artistic director, Arvin Brown; executive director, M. Edgar Rosenblum)

AMERICAN BUFFALO (50). By David Mamet. October 2, 1980. Director, Arvin Brown. With Clifton James, Al Pacino, Tom Waites.

WAITING FOR GODOT (50). By Samuel Beckett. November 13, 1980. Director and de-

signer, Donald Hawarth. With John Kani, Winston Ntshona, Bill Flynn, Peter Piccolo, Silamour Philander. Baxter Theater of Cape Town (South Africa) Production.

THE ADMIRABLE CRICHTON (50). By James M. Barrie. February 8, 1981. Director,

Kenneth Frankel. With John McMartin, Emery Battis, Lisa Banes, Nancy Boykin, Robin Groves.

ROMEO AND JULIET (50). By William Shakespeare. February 12, 1981. Director, Barry Davis. With Thomas Hulce, Mary Beth Hurt, Emery Battis, Aideen O'Kelly.

BODIES (50). By James Saunders. March 26, 1981 (American premiere). Director, Kenneth Frankel; scenery, Karl Eigsti; lighting, Judy Rasmuson; costumes, Rachel Kurland.

Anne.................... Carolyn Seymour
Helen .... Meg Wynn Owen
David .... Roger Newman
Mervyn.................... Kenneth Haigh
  Time: The present. Place: London. Act I: The living rooms of Anne and Mervyn, and of Helen and David. Act II: Anne and Mervyn's living room, Saturday evening.

A LIFE (50). By Hugh Leonard. May 7, 1981. Director, Bill Ludel. With Emery Battis, William Swetland.

Long Wharf Theater: Stage II

SOLOMON'S CHILD (120). By Tom Dulack. October 21, 1980 (world premiere). Director, John Tillinger; scenery, Marjorie Kellogg; lighting, Ronald Wallace; costumes, Bill Walker.
Allan Solomon.............. Steven Gilborn
Vera Solomon .... Rochelle Oliver
Joe....................... Ellis Williams
Sam....................... Tom Nardini
Shelley Solomon .... Michael O'Keefe
Balthazar .... Peter Michael Goetz
Naomi................... Deborah Hedwall
Liz .... Joyce Ebert
State Trooper.............. James Seymour
  Place: The Solomons' vacation home in the Catskills. Act I: A morning in late June. Act II: Sixteen hours later.

CLOSE TIES (112). By Elizabeth Diggs. February 3, 1981 (professional premiere). Director, Arvin Brown; scenery, Hugh Landwehr; lighting, Ronald Wallace; costumes, Bill Walker.
Josephine Whitaker........ Margaret Barker
Watson Frye .... Donald Symington
Bess Whitaker Frye............. Joyce Ebert
Connie .... Laralu Smith
Anna.................... Alexandra Borrie
Evelyn.................... Deborah Hedwall
Thayer....................... Jeff Rohde
Ira Bienstock .... Mark Blum
  Place: The Fryes' summer home in the Berkshires. Act 1, Scene 1: A Saturday, early in August, midmorning. Scene 2: Several hours later. Scene 3: Late evening. Act II, Scene 1: The next day, morning. Scene 2: late afternoon.

Long Wharf Theater: New Play Readings: Stage II

(John Tillinger, literary manager; workshop premieres, 1 performance)

TOTAL RECALL by Martin Halpern; SPLENDID REBELS by Ernest Joselovitz; JOHNNY BULL by Kathleen Betsko; DEROS ON THE FUNNY FARM by Michael Shannon; ALTERATIONS by Leigh Curran; TEN CENTS ON THE DOLLAR by Elizabeth Karp. Directors, John Tillinger, Emery Battis, Kenneth Frankel. May 26–31, 1981.

Designers: scenery, Marjorie Kellogg, Steven Rubin, Hugh Landwehr; lighting, Ronald Wallace; costumes, Bill Walker.

Note: Long Wharf Theater presented *The Lion in Winter* by James Goldman, director, Kenneth Frankel; *Private Lives* by Noel Coward, director, Bill Ludel, September 1980–May, 1981, on a coast-to-coast tour of the United States. Long Wharf was invited to present *American Buffalo* at the Jerusalem Festival, May, 1981 and at the Festival of Two Worlds (Spoleto, Italy), July, 1981; *Close Ties* at the Dublin Festival in September, 1981.

Yale Repertory Theater

(Artistic director, Lloyd Richards; managing director, Edward A. Martenson)

BOESMAN AND LENA (18). By Athol Fugard. October 10, 1980. Director, Walton Jones. With Novella Nelson, Joe Seneca, Zakes Mokae.

THE SUICIDE (18). By Nikolai Erdman. November 7, 1980. Director, John Madden. With Joe Grifasi, Jane Kaczmarek, Merle Louise, Sasha von Scherler, Jerome Dempsey.

TWELFTH NIGHT (18). By William Shakespeare. December 5, 1980. Director, Bill Ludel. With members of the company.

HEDDA GABLER (18). By Henrik Ibsen. March 3, 1981. Director, Lloyd Richards. With Dianne Wiest, James Earl Jones, Jean-Pierre Stewart, John Glover, Sylvia O'Brien, Katherine Borowitz.

THE MAGNIFICENT CUCKOLD (18). By Fernand Crommelynck; translated by Marnix Gijen. April 3, 1981 (American premiere). Director, Jonas Jurasas; scenery Steve Saklad; lighting, Rick Butler; costumes, Martha Kelly.
Stella...................... Jana Schneider
Cornelia .... Becky London
Romanie.................... Laurel Cronin
Florence .... Eve Gordon
Cowhand .... Earl Hindman
The Count .... Richard Levine
Young Man .... Vytautas Ruginis
Bruno .... Richard Jenkins
Estrugo.................... Yusef Bulos
Mayor.................... William Mesnik
Petrus.................... Bern Sundstedt
Florence's husband ...... Steven Hendrickson
    Two intermissions.

In repertory:
DOMESTIC ISSUES (11). By Corinne Jacker. January 10, 1981 (world premiere). Director, Barnet Kellman.
Steve Porter .... Nicolas Surovy
Nancy Graham .... Gina Franz
Larry Porter................ Daniel Gold
Susan Porter .... Marcia Jean Kurtz
Ellen Porter .... Ellen Parker

George Allison................ Dann Florek
    Time: September, 1979. Place: Highland Park, Ill. One intermission.
ROCOCO (12). By Harry Kondoleon. January 14, 1981 (world premiere). Director, Dana B. Westberg.
Aunt Aphrodite.......... Madeleine le Roux
Adrienne................... Jayne Haynes
Crystal .... Eve Gordon
Cynthia............... Frances McDormand
Dale .... Gary Basaraba
Raymond .... Jeff Ginsberg
    One intermission.
SALLY AND MARSHA (10). By Sybille Pearson. January 17, 1981 (world premiere). Director, Robert Allan Ackerman.
Sally .... Frances Conroy
Marsha.................... Robin Bartlett
    Time: The present. Place: A West Side apartment. One intermission.
THE RESURRECTION OF LADY LESTER (11). By Oyamo. January 21, 1981 (world premiere). Director, James A. Simpson; composer and arranger, Dwight Andrews.
Lester Young.............. Darryl Croxton
Boo-Boo; Slump; Tweek;
    Sergeant .... David Alan Grier
Dr. T.; Manager; Major;
    Proselytizer .... Clarence Felder
Lincoln; Pooky .... Reg E. Cathey
Sarah; Tuta; Agatha .. Zakia Barksdale Hakim
Miss Lady; Lady Day......... Isabell Monk
White Marie;
    Woman in Black........... Cecilia Rubino
Swoop; Grand Marshall;
    Bohannon; Mouse .... Scott Rickey Wheeler
    Time: The night Lester Young died. Place: A room. One intermission.

Yale Repertory Theater: University Theater

AN ATTEMPT AT FLYING (18). By Yordan Radichkov; translated by Bogdan B. Athanassov. May 1, 1981 (American premiere). Director, Mladen Kiselov; scenery, Michael H. Yeargan; lighting, William B. Warfel; costumes, Dunya Ramicova; composer, Vasil Kazandgiev.
Master Kiro............... Kurt Knudson
Iliyko .... Michael Morgan
Hadji Avram .... Clement Fowler
Cockeye .... David Alan Grier
Matthew Nothing ..... Jeffrey Alan Chandler

Avram Shuttle.............. Stephen Rowe
Igo .... David Sabin
Peter................. Mitchell Lichtenstein
Paul .... Jeff Natter
Sweet Basil................. Zakes Mokae
Young Avram .... Steven Hendrickson
Sgt. Major .... Paul Espel
Policemen..... John Harnagel, Matt Sussman
    Time: World War II. Place: The Avramovo Hamlets, scattered along the ridge of the Balkan Mountains. One intermission.

Designers: scenery, Michael H. Yeargan, Raymond Klaga, Steve Saklad, Kevin Rupnik; lighting, William B. Warfel, David Noking, Rick Butler, Michael H. Baumgarten; costumes, Dunya Ramicova, Steve Saklad, Martha Kelly, Doug Stein.

Note: Yale Repertory sponsored the Cabaret, which presented a variety of experimental works. The Yale School of Drama gave *The Bakkhai*, translated from Euripides by Robert Bagg, and Calderon de la Barca's *Life Is a Dream* in the fall term and in the spring of 1981, two Molière plays, *Tartuffe* and *The Learned Ladies*, directed by Walt Jones. All other plays were directed, designed and acted by Drama School students.

PHILADELPHIA

Philadelphia Drama Guild: Zellerbach Theater at Annenberg Center

(Artistic director, Irene Lewis; managing director, Gregory Poggi)

WATCH ON THE RHINE (21). By Lillian Hellman. October 17, 1980. Director, Irene Lewis. With Carmen Mathews, Joseph Hindy, Jennifer Harmon, George Morfogen, Tana Hicken.

A DAY IN THE DEATH OF JOE EGG (21). By Peter Nichols. November 28, 1980. Director, Irene Lewis. With Munson Hicks, Tana Hicken, Dale Hodges, Beverly May, Daniel Szelag.

PHILADELPHIA, HERE I COME! (21). By Brian Friel. January 9, 1981. Director, John Going. With Boyd Gaines, John Christopher Jones, Thomas Barbour, Julia Curry, Hank deLuca.

THE FRONT PAGE (21). By Ben Hecht and Charles MacArthur. March 5, 1981. Director, Irene Lewis. With Geoffrey Pierson, Milton Seltzer, Jeff Brooks, Jack Bittner, Tana Hicken, Carolyn Hurlburt.

OLD WORLD (21). By Aleksei Arbuzov. April 23, 1981. Director, Tony Giordano, With Helen Burns, Donald Davis.

Designers: scenery, Hugh Landwehr, Peter Wingate, Karen Schulz; lighting, Pat Collins, Neil Peter Jampolis, Arden Fingerhut, Paul Gallo; costumes, Linda Fisher, Dona Granata, Jess Goldstein, David Murin.

PITTSBURGH

Pittsburgh Public Theater: Allegheny Theater-Mainstage

(Artistic director, Ben Shaktman; executive director, Howard Millman).

I'M GETTING MY ACT TOGETHER AND TAKING IT ON THE ROAD (39) Book and lyrics by Gretchen Cryer; music by Nancy Ford. September 17, 1980. Director, Amy Saltz; musical director, John Franceschina; choreographer, Helen Kent. With Louisa Flaningam, Allan Carlsen, Linda Langford, Louise Robinson, Ian Cohen.

DEATH OF A SALESMAN (28). By Arthur Miller. November 12, 1980. Director, Ben Shaktman. With John Carpenter, Dorothy Stinnette, David Stocker, James Hunt.

TERRA NOVA (50). By Ted Tally. January 7, 1981. Director, Peter Wexler. With Jack Ryland, Berkeley Harris, Shaine Marinson, Steven Sutherland.

TANGLES (46). By Robert Litz. March 4, 1981 (world premiere). Director, Ben Shaktman; scenery, David Emmons; lighting, Ron Wallace; costumes, David Toser.

Charlene	Dawn Davis
Phil	Terry Layman
Lynn	Monica Merryman
Dehlia	Amy Van Nostrand
Stan	Stephan Mark Weyte

THE TWO GENTLEMEN OF VERONA (40). By William Shakespeare. April 29, 1981. Director, Stephen Kanee. With Kevin O'Rourke, Jack Honor, Michele Seyler, Julia Mackenzie, Robert Blackburn.

Pittsburgh Public Theater: "Plus 6" Series

CAMPAIGN RELIEF (7). Company-developed; based on American election campaign songs and slogans from Thomas Jefferson to the 1980 campaign. October 28, 1980 (workshop premiere). Director and choreographer, Judith Haskell; music director and arranger, John Franceschina. With Louisa Flaningam, Allan Carlsen, Linda Langford, Louise Robinson and the Liberated Man's Band.

O. HENRY'S CHRISTMAS (6). Developed by Thomas Edward West, from five of O. Henry's stories. December 20, 1980 (workshop premiere). Director, Eberle Thomas. With Thomas Carson as O. Henry, and James Hindy, James Hunt, Katherine Knowles, Gregory Lehane, Dan Peters, John Perkins, Sherry Skinker, Rhonda Aldrich, Joe Bays.

APPEAR AND SHOW CAUSE (7). By Stephen Taylor, based on the Lt. Col. Frank Harrow landmark case, story by Taylor and Leon H. Gilden. February 17, 1981 (workshop premiere). Director, Woodie King Jr.

Lt. Col. Harrow	Gordon Heath
Rep. Noah Lincoln Keyes	Graham Brown
Maj. Evans Chandler	Jack Ryland
Capt. Phillip Bresnick	John C. Vennema
Col. Harlan Phillips	Berkeley Harris
Col. Wheldon Kearns	Edward Seamon
Sgt. Andrew Smith	Mark Chamberlin
Sgt. Hugh Connor	John Amplas
Lt. Joshua Harrow	Lamont Arnold
Army Colonels	Kenneth Melchick, Gregory Charles

STREETSONGS (7). Conceived by Geraldine Fitzgerald and Richard Maltby Jr. April 14, 1980. Director, Richard Maltby Jr.; musical director, Stanley Wietrzchowski; vocal director, Andy Thomas Anselmo. With Geraldine Fitzgerald.

Designers: Patricia Woodbridge, Peter Wexler, William Schroder; lighting, Pat Simmons, Bernard J. Brannigan, Ron Wallace; costumes, Mark Pennywell, David Toser, William Schroder.

PORTLAND, ME.

Portland Stage Company

(Artistic director, Charles Towers; managing director, Richard Ostreicher)

SORROWS OF STEPHEN (22). By Peter Parnell. October 18, 1980. Director, Charles Towers. With Michael Garfield, Ellen Parks, Joseph Wilkins, Jock MacDonald.

FAITH HEALER (21). By Brian Friel. November 15, 1980. Director, Jamie Brown. With William Knight, Mary Fogarty, Lium O'Begley.

A CHILD'S CHRISTMAS (19). Company-developed. December 13, 1980. Director, Charles Towers. With Jock MacDonald, Dana Hardwick, Tom Anderson, Richard Greene, Stacie Harvey.

OLD TIMES (27). By Harold Pinter. January 14, 1981. Director, Charles Towers. With David A. Penhale, Natalie Hurst, Jan Granger.

TALLEY'S FOLLY (36). By Lanford Wilson. February 14, 1981. Director, David A. Penhale. With David Rosenbaum, Laura Copland.

ISLAND (36). Music and lyrics by Peter Link; book by Joe Bravaco and Larry Rosler; conceived and developed by Brent Nicholson. March 21, 1981. Director, Evadne Giannini; musical staging, Peter Link; musical director, Alan Smallwood; choreographer, Allan Sobek. With Christopher Wells, Cass Morgan, Terry Burrell, Byron Utley.

SEA MARKS (22). By Gardner McKay. April 25, 1981. Director, John Stix. With John Getz, Kate Kelley.

Designers: scenery, John Doepp, Lisa Devlin, Charles Kading, A. Christina Giannini, Ken Foy; lighting, John Doepp, Steven J. Sysko Jr., Robert Strohmeier, Charles Towers; costumes, Lynda L. Salsbury, A. Christina Giannini.

PORTSMOUTH, N.H.

Theater by the Sea

(Producing director, Jon Kimbell; managing director, William Michael Maher).

A LITTLE NIGHT MUSIC (40). Music and lyrics by Stephen Sondheim; book by Hugh Wheeler. September 26, 1980. Director, Jack Allison; musical director, Bruce W. Coyle. With D'Jamin Bartlett, Michael Davis, Rowena Rollins, Jason Graae, Maureen McNamara.

ON THE MARRY-GO-WRONG (40). By Georges Feydeau and Maurice Desvallieres; adapted by Norman R. Shapiro. October 31, 1980. Director, Philip Minor. With Tom Celli, Louis Beachner, Peter Johnson, Marcia Korb, Carol Gustafason.

SCROOGE AND MARLEY (30). By Israel Horovitz; adapted from Charles Dickens's *A Christmas Carol*. December 5, 1980. Director, Jon Kimbell. With Tom Celli, Roger Curtis, Peter Johnson, Eric Levin.

EMIGRES (40). By Slawomir Mrozek. January 2, 1981. Director, Ben Levit. With John Tormey, William Brenner.

DEATH OF A SALESMAN (40). By Arthur Miller. February 6, 1981. Director, Kent Paul. With Dan Frazer, Anna Minot, Dave

Florek, Allan Carlsen, Michael Norman.

TALLEY'S FOLLY (40). By Lanford Wilson. March 13, 1981. Director, Jon Kimbell. With Robert Silver, Catherine Burns.

NIGHT RIDERS (40). Book by Allan Albert; music by John Lewis; lyrics by Josh Rubins. April 17, 1981 (professional premiere). Director, Jack Allison; scenery, Jack Allison, John Becker; lighting, Paul Sullivan; costumes, J. J. Vak; musical director, Janet Hood.

Dave	David Blue
Eric	Eric Hansen
Ginny	Ginny Russell
John	John Jellison
Kim	Kim Criswell
Jeff	Jeff McCarthy

Musical Numbers—Act I: "Night Riders," "Behind the Wheel," "Waiting Duet," "Nice Talkin' to Ya," "Music and Motion," "Night Lights." Act II: "There's Hardly Room Enough," "The Flashing Neon Roadside TV Screen," "Speed Demon," "Hi, I Miss You," "The Dawn Song."

Designers: scenery, Fred Kolouch, John Wright Stevens, Bob Phillips, Larry Fulton, Quentin Thomas, Joan Brancale; lighting, Fred Kolouch, Tyrone E. Sanders, Donald Soule; costumes, Fred Kolouch, Marcia Dixcy, Kathie Iannicelli, Ann Carnaby.

PRINCETON, N.J.

McCarter Theater Company: McCarter Theater—Mainstage

(Artistic director, Nagle Jackson; managing director, Alison Harris).

In repertory:
THE TAMING OF THE SHREW (16). By William Shakespeare. October 3, 1980. Director, Nagle Jackson. With Leslie Geraci, John Mansfield, Karl Light.
MOBY DICK REHEARSED (16). By Orson Welles; adapted from Herman Melville's novel. October 10, 1980. Director, William Woodman. With Richard Risso, Gary Roberts, Hubert Kelly, John Mansfield.

A CHRISTMAS CAROL (16). By Charles Dickens; adapted and directed by Nagle Jackson. November 28, 1980. Choreographer, Jane

Miller Gifford. With G. Wood, Jay Doyle.

EMINENT DOMAIN (16). By Percy Granger. January 20, 1981 (professional premiere). Director, Paul Austin; scenery, Michael Miller; lighting, Lowell Achziger; costumes, Elizabeth Covey.

Holmes Bradford	MacIntyre Dixon
Victor Salt	Stephen Stout
Katie Bradford	Betty Miller
Stoddard Oates	Thomas Nahrwold
John Ramsey	Barry Boys

Time: February, 1975. Place: A university town in the Midwest. One intermission (see syn-

McCARTER THEATER, PRINCETON—MacIntyre Dixon and
Betty Miller in a scene from *Eminent Domain* by Percy Granger

opsis in introduction to this section).

CUSTER (16). By Robert E. Ingham. March 3, 1981. Director, Nagle Jackson. With Barry Boys, Richard Risso, Katherine McGrath, John Mansfield.

THE PLAY'S THE THING (16). By Ferenc Molnar; adapted by P. G. Wodehouse. March 31, 1981. Director, Nagle Jackson. With Jay Doyle, Gary Roberts, Katherine McGrath, Robert Lanchester.

McCarter Theater Company: Stage II

PUTTING ON THE DOG (12). By Deloss Brown. January 22, 1981 (world premiere). Director, Robert Lanchester; scenery, Karen Eisler; lighting, Don Ehman; costumes, Robin Hirsch.
Sharik . . . . Richard Risso
Svetlana . . . . Derry Light

Prof. Preobrazhensky . . . . Jay Doyle
Zina . . . . Susan Jonas
Dr. Bormenthal . . . . Gary Roberts
Col. Lobchenkov; Josef . . . . G. Wood
Shvonder . . . . Greg Thornton
  Time: 1925–26. Place: Moscow, mostly inside the Professor's apartment. One intermission.

Designers: scenery, Daniel Boylen, Brian Martin, John Jensen; lighting, Frances Aronson, Sean Murphy, Marc B. Weiss; costumes, Elizabeth Covey, Rosemary Ingham, Robert Morgan.

Note: Playwrights at McCarter (project director, Robert Lanchester) gave three new play readings at the Princeton Inn College Theater: *The Moment of the Wandering Jew* by David Cole, October 20, 1980; *My Sister in This House* by Wendy Kesselman, October 27, 1980; *Judevine* by David Budhill, November 3, 1980. The Mainstage production of *Moby Dick Rehearsed* toured for ten weeks, March 20–June 7, 1981, to schools, colleges, civic groups, arts organizations.

PROVIDENCE, R. I.

Trinity Square Repertory Company: Summer Rep

(Director, Adrian Hall)

EL GRANDE DE COCA-COLA (35). By Ron House, John Neville-Andrews, Alan Shearman, Diz White and Sally Willis; from an idea by Ron House and Diz White. June 3, 1980. Director, James Howard Laurence. With Richard Kneeland, Amy Van Nostrand, J.H. Laurence, Gary de Lena, Myra Turley.

AN ALMOST PERFECT PERSON (28). By Judith Ross. July 8, 1980. Director, Melanie Jones. With Margo Skinner, Daniel Von Bargen, Peter Gerety.

DEATHTRAP (33). By Ira Levin. August 5, 1980. Director, William Radka. With Timothy Crowe, Mina Manente, Dan Butler, Margo Skinner, Daniel Von Bargen.

Trinity Square Repertory Company: Upstairs Theater

ARSENIC AND OLD LACE (38). By Joseph Kesselring. October 21, 1980. Director, George Martin. With Lenka Peterson, Bettie Endrizzi, Tom Griffin, Ford Rainey, Bradford Gottlin.

A CHRISTMAS CAROL (51). By Charles Dickens; adapted by Adrian Hall and Richard Cumming. December 2, 1980. Director, Melanie Jones. With George Martin, Ed Hall, Richard Kavanaugh, David C. Jones, Barbara Orson.

THE ICEMAN COMETH (36). By Eugene O'Neill. February 3, 1981. Director, Philip Minor. With Richard Jenkins, George Martin,

David C. Jones, Barbara Orson, Anne Scurria, Susan Payne.

INHERIT THE WIND (36). By Jerome Lawrence and Robert E. Lee. March 24, 1981. Director, Adrian Hall. With Richard Kneeland, George Martin, Ed Hall, David C. Jones, Howard London.

WHOSE LIFE IS IT ANYWAY? (37). By Brian Clark. May 5, 1981. Director, Richard Kneeland. With Richard Kavanaugh, Richard Kneeland, Melanie Jones, Richard Jenkins, Ed Hall.

Trinity Square Repertory Company—Downstairs Theater

BETRAYAL (47). By Harold Pinter. September 30, 1980. Director, Larry Arrick. With Richard Jenkins, April Shawhan, Timothy Crowe.

ON GOLDEN POND (58). By Ernest Thompson. December 9, 1980. Directors, Adrian Hall, Peter Gerety. Wih Ford Rainey, Lenka Peterson, Richard Jenkins, April Shawhan, Daniel Von Bargen, Arthur Roberts.

THE WHALES OF AUGUST (44). By David Berry. February 17, 1981. Director, Adrian Hall. With Sylvia Davis, Ruth Maynard, Hilmar Sallee, Vivienne Shub, Daniel Nagrin.

HOW I GOT THAT STORY (43). By Amlin Gray. April 7, 1981. Director, Larry Arrick. With Peter Gerety, Tim McDonough.

Designers: Scenery, Eugene Lee, Robert D. Soule; lighting, John F. Custer; costumes, William Lane.

Note: Trinity Square Repertory Company continued to present special performances (40) of the regular season's productions to high school students at 10:30 a.m. as part of the schools' curricula.

RICHMOND, VA.

Virginia Museum Theater: Mainstage

(Artistic director, Tom Markus; administrative director, Baylor Landrum)

DEATHTRAP (25). By Ira Levin. September 26, 1980. Director, Tom Markus. With Michael

Lipton, Michael Scott, Jean Sincere, Nicola Sheara, Edward Stevlingson.

GODSPELL (25). Conceived and adapted by John-Michael Tebelak; music and lyrics by Stephen Schwartz. October 24, 1980. Director, Darwin Knight; music director, Harrison Fisher. With Jeff Johnson, Lynn Stafford, Carl Blackwell Lester.

THE FOURPOSTER (25). By Jan de Hartog. November 28, 1980. Director, Terry Burgler. With Kathleen Bishop, James Secrest.

A MIDSUMMER NIGHT'S DREAM (25). By William Shakespeare. January 23, 1981. Director, Tom Markus. With Robert Walsh, Maury Erickson, Jane Cromi, Yolanda Del-

gado, Robert Jackson, Yolande Bavan, Jeff Brooks.

GHOSTS (25). By Henrik Ibsen; translated by Rolf Fjelde. February 20, 1981. Director, Tom Markus. With Betty Leighton, Laurence Hugo, William Denis, Mary Lowry, Michael McKenzie.

SOMETHING'S AFOOT (25). By James McDonald, David Vos, Robert Gerlach. March 27, 1981. Director, Russel Treyz; musical director, Robert J. Bruyr. With Lu Leonard, John High, Una Harrison, William Dennis.

Virginia Museum Theater: Studio Theater

SIZWE BANZI IS DEAD (6). By Athol Fugard, John Kani, Winston Ntshona. November 18, 1980. Director, Tom Markus. With Lou Ferguson, William Jay.

THE SEA HORSE (6). By Edward J. Moore.

January 13, 1981. Director, Terry Burgler. With Judith Drake, David Gale.

HAPPY DAYS (6). By Samuel Beckett. March 17, 1981. Directors, Tom Markus, Jane Page. With Anne Sheldon, James W. Parker.

Designers: scenery, Charles Caldwell, Howard Cummings, Dan Bishop; lighting, Richard Moore, Lynn Hartman; costumes, Richard Hieronymous, Andrew B. Marlay, Linda Bradley, Moppy Vogely.

ROCHESTER, MICH.

Oakland University Professional Theater Program: Meadow Brook Theater

(General director, Terence Kilburn)

THIEVES' CARNIVAL (29). By Jean Anouilh; translated by Lucienne Hill. October 2, 1980. Director, Terence Kilburn. With Barbara Berge, Harry Ellerbe, Terence Marinan, Melanie Resnick, Polly Rowles, Allan Stevens.

OUR TOWN (29). By Thornton Wilder. November 6, 1980. Director, Edward Kay-Martin. With Peter Brandon, Ron Seka, Jeanne Arnold, Fiona Hale, Stanley Flood, Judythe McIntyre.

THE IMAGINARY INVALID (29). By Molière. December 4, 1980. Director, Terence Kilburn. With Donald Ewer, Mary Pat Gleason, Henson Keys, David Kroll, Ray Lonergan, Lynn Mansbach, Marianne Muellerleile.

DON JUAN IN HELL (29). By George Bernard Shaw. January 1, 1981. Director, Charles Nolte. With Barbara Berge, Donald Ewer, George Gitto, Michael Lipton.

ARSENIC AND OLD LACE (29). By Joseph Kesselring. January 29, 1981. Director, Cash Baxter. With Jeanne Arnold, Jean Barker, Kathryn Greech, Carleton Carpenter, Jonathan Freeman, David Green.

ANOTHER PART OF THE FOREST (29). By Lillian Hellman. February 26, 1981. Director, Terence Kilburn. With Jean Ashley, J. Douglas James, Phillip Locker, Cynthia Parva, Michael M. Ryan.

BUS STOP (29). By William Inge. March 26, 1981. Director, Terence Kilburn. With Cyd Quilling, Mark Margolis, Michael Patterson, Faye Haun.

STARTING HERE, STARTING NOW (29). Lyrics by Richard Maltby Jr.; music by David Shire. April 23, 1981. Director, Cash Baxter; music director, Robert McNamee; choreographer, Chris Ze Van. With Mary Gutzi, Barbara Heuman, Michael Scott.

Designers: scenery, Peter-William Hicks, Charles Beal, Barry Griffith; lighting, Barry Griffith, Reid G. Johnson, Larry A. Reed, Daniel Jaffe; costumes, Mary Lynn Bonell.

Note: Meadow Brook toured *The Romance of Shakespeare* (scenes from *The Taming of the Shrew, Richard III, Romeo and Juliet, A Midsummer Night's Dream*), beginning April 24, 1981 for high school students in Michigan communities of Saginaw, Bay City, Houghton Lake, Alma; directed by Jonathan Alper, played by the Satellite Company: Michael Cullen, Deborah Eckols, Patricia Reilly.

ROCHESTER, N.Y.

GeVa Theater

(Artistic director, Gideon Y. Schein)

TERRA NOVA (25). By Ted Tally. November 1, 1980. Director, Ben Levit. With William Brenner, Rand Bridges, David Gale, Jeanne Ruskin.

HAY FEVER (25). By Noel Coward. November 29, 1980. Director, Mark Harrison. With Terry Arundel, Jane Cronin, Zeljko Ivanek, Kristen Lowman, Jonathan Moore.

SEA MARKS (25). By Gardner McKay. January 3, 1981. Director, Gideon Y. Schein. With Richard Zobel, Janni Brenn.

AGNES OF GOD (25). By John Pielmeier. January 31, 1981. Director, Beth Dixon. With Charlotte Booker, Bette Henritze, Brenda Wehle.

KEYSTONE (25). Book by John McKeller; lyrics, John McKeller and Dion McGregor; music, Lance Mulcahy. March 4, 1981 (world premiere). Director, Gideon Y. Schein; music director, Rick Jensen; choreographer, Gretchen Glover; scenery, Desmond Heeley; lighting, Dennis Parichy; costumes, Pamela Scofield.

Mack Sennett	Scott Bakula
Pearl; Others	Valerie Beaman
Charlie Chaplin	Lance Davis
Maisie; Others	Susie Fenner
Ford Sterling	Jason Graae
Mabel Normand	Ann Morrison
Roscoe Arbuckle	Thomas Sinclair
Ben Turpin	Douglas Walker
Others	Caroline Kaiser, Linda Page Neelly

IN CONNECTICUT (25). By Roy London. April 1, 1981 (world premiere). Directors, Marshall W. Mason, Daniel Irvine; scenery, David Potts; lighting, Dennis Parichy; costumes, Joan E. Weiss.

Giannina DiPinto	Henrietta Michelson-Bagley
Federico DiPinto	Shelby Buford Jr.
Maxie	Nicholas Dunn
Irene	Lisa Emery
Andrew	Robert LuPone
Valerie	Sharon Madden
Louis	Jeff McCracken
Candy	Rosemary Prinz

Designers; scenery, Daniel P. Boylen, Barry Robison, Sharon Perlmutter, Susan Hilferty; lighting, John Gisondi, Frances Aronson, Robert Jared, Annie Wrightson; costumes, Pamel Scofield.

ST. LOUIS

Repertory Theater of St. Louis: Mainstage

(Artistic director, Wallace K. Chappell; managing director, Michael P. Pitek III)

EVE (33). By Larry Fineberg; based on *The Book of Eve* by Constance Beresford-Howe. September 5, 1980. Director, Craig Anderson. With Jan Miner, Hansford Rowe, Dan Desmond, Louis Zorich, Susie Bradley.

SWEET PRINCE (35). By A. E. Hotchner. October 10, 1980 (world premiere). Director, Wallace K. Chappell; scenery, Carolyn L. Ross; lighting, Peter E. Sargent; costumes, John Carver Sullivan.

Judd Leland	James Luisi
J. C. Finster	Gavin Reed
Deedie	Elizabeth Burr
Schultz	Brian Worley

REPERTORY THEATER OF ST. LOUIS—Gavin Reed and
James Luisi in a scene from *Sweet Prince* by A.E. Hotchner

Place: The basement of a Broadway theater.
One intermission.

A CHRISTMAS CAROL (39). By Charles
Dickens; adapted by Addie Walsh. November
29, 1980. Director, Michael P. Pitek III; music
by Terrence Sherman. With Michael Geno-
vese, Dana Mills, Joneal Joplin, Christopher
Nickel.

HAPPY LANDING (35). By Dennis de
Brito. December 31, 1980 (world premiere). Di-
rector, Clyde Ventura; scenery, Carolyn L.
Ross; lighting, Glenn Dunn; costumes, Dorothy
Marshall.

Ira Peters	Hal England
Calvin Johnson	Paul Winfield
Carrie	Beth Baur
Beth Burlington	Brett Somers

Ryan Forrester	Don Keefer
Barbara Harnett	Leigh Hamilton
Isabel Edwards	Gertrude Jeannette
Leu Browne	Faye Butler

Time: The present. Act I, Scene 1: The stage
of an off-Broadway theater, midday on a winter
Friday. Scene 2: A house in Yonkers, 8 P.M. the
following Friday. Act II: The house in Yonkers,
immediately following.

RICHARD III (39). By William Shakespeare.
February 4, 1981. Director, Wallace Chappell.
With Philip Kerr, Joneal Joplin, Alan Clarey,
Jon Westholm, Brendan Burke, Julia Jona-
than, Kristin Linklater, Marie Chambers.

TALLEY'S FOLLY (35). By Lanford Wilson.
March 11, 1981. Director, Michael P. Pitek
III. With Lloyd Battista, Donna Davis.

Repertory Theater of St. Louis: Studio Theater

THE ISLAND (30). By Athol Fugard, John
Kani, Winston Ntshona. November 1, 1980. Director, Jim O'Connor. With John Cothran Jr.,

Stephen McKinley Henderson.

AMERICAN SOAP (30). By Ron Mark. January 17, 1981 (world premiere). Director, Wallace

K. Chappell; scenery, John Roslevich Jr.; lighting, Peter E. Sargent; costumes, Jeffrey Ross Struckman.

Joe..................... Jonathan Gillard
Amy .... Susan Maloy Wall
Act I, Scene 1: You First, Me First 1942. Scene 2: Mairzy Doats 1948. Scene 3: Humorous Bones 1953. Scene 4: Don't Touch Me 1959. Scene 5: Show the Way, Love 1963. Scene 6: Ills and

Fever 1968. Scene 7: Bust 'Em Up, Joe 1971. Act II, Scene 1: Return of Superchock 1972. Scene 2: I'll Kill You for This 1972. Scene 3: Memory and 20/20 Vision 2020. Scene 4: Sew Buttons.

A LIFE IN THE THEATER (30). By David Mamet. March 28, 1981. Director, Steven Woolf. With Brendan Burke, Stephan Cowan.

Designers: scenery, Karen Connolly, Steven Rubin, Carolyn Ross, Tim Jozwick, John Roslevich Jr.; lighting, Max de Valder, Peter E. Sargent, Beverly Emmons, Steven G. Rosen; costumes, Carolyn Ross, Dorothy L. Marshall, John Carver Sullivan, Bill Walker, Alison Todd.

Note: The Imaginary Theater Company, Repertory of St. Louis's touring group for young audiences, gave a total of 91 performances of *Windies and Whoppers; The Show-Me Show; The Firebird and Other Stories* at schools in Missouri and Illinois.

ST. PAUL

Actors Theater of St. Paul

(Founder/artistic director, Michael Andrew Miner; managing director, Jan Miner).

FIGHTING BOB (18). By Tom Cole. October 23, 1980. Director, Michael Andrew Miner. With Barbara Kingsley, Mark McGovern, James Cada, Alan Woodward, John P. Connolly.

HOW THE OTHER HALF LOVES (18). By Alan Ayckbourn. November 20, 1980. Director, Jeff Steitzer. With Dianne Benjamin Hill, Barbara Kingsley, James Cada, James Harris, Spencer Beckwith, Louise Goetz.

GIFT OF THE MAGI (18). Book and lyrics by John Olive; music by Libby Larsen; based on O. Henry's short story. December 18, 1980 (world premiere). Director, Scott M. Rubsam; scenery, Chris Johnson; lighting, Michael Vennerstrom; costumes, Michael L. Hansen.
Della .... Dianne Benjamin Hill
Jim .... John P. Connolly
Thelma; Others .... Louise Goetz
Nicky; Others .... Spencer Beckwith
Monsieur Sophronie; Others. ..... James Cada
Time: Turn of the Century. Place: Lower East Side of Manhattan. One intermission.
Musical Numbers—Act I: "Apples, Chestnuts," "Christmas in the City," "Hold Me," "Summer Love," "The Work Song," "Snowfall." Act II: "What Do They Want?", "Thirty Dollars!", "Merry Christmas!".

SPOKESONG (18). By Stewart Parker. January 15, 1981. Director, Michael Andrew Miner. With Jon Cavenaugh, John P. Connolly, Dianne Benjamin Hill, James Cada, Barbara Kingsley, Spencer Beckwith, John D. Blondell (piano).

THE OUTLANDERS (18). By Amlin Gray; based on characters from Strindberg's novel *The Scapegoat*. February 12, 1981 (world premiere). Director, Kristin Overn.
Askanlus..................... James Cada
Karin .... Barbara Kingsley
Apothecary.................... Jim Baron
Ekerot................... Spencer Beckwith
and MISS JULIE by August Strindberg; translated by Michael Meyer. Director, Louis Rackoff. With Mari Rovang, Michael Andrew Miner.

RING ROUND THE MOON (15). By Jean Anouilh; translated by Christopher Fry. March 12, 1981. Director, George C. White. With Gary Rayppy, Alan Woodward, Barbara Kingsley, Jeanne Blake.

VIKINGS (18). By Steve Metcalfe. April 9, 1981. Director, Michael Andrew Miner. With Alan Woodward, James Cada, Spencer Beckwith, Barbara Kingsley.

Designers: scenery, Paul Peloquin, Dick Leerhoff, Chris Johnson, James Guenther; lighting, Bob Bye, Michael Vennerstrom, Paul Scharfenberger, Chris Johnson; costumes, Michael L. Hansen, Ann Ruben, Nan Zabriskie.

SAN DIEGO

Old Globe Theater: San Diego National Shakespeare Festival—Festival Stage

(Producing director, Craig Noel; general manager, Robert E. McGlade)

ROMEO AND JULIET (35). By William Shakespeare. June 10, 1980. With Benjamin Hendrickson, Tovah Feldshuh, Eric Christmas, James R. Winker, Rob Zimmerman.

THE TWO GENTLEMEN OF VERONA (35). By William Shakespeare. June 13, 1980. Director, Craig Noel. With Lane Davies, Lillian Garrett-Bonner, Tom Stechschulte, Richard Dix, Tandy Cronyn.

LOVE'S LABOUR'S LOST (23). By William Shakespeare. July 11, 1980. Director, Jerome Kilty. With Jerry Allan Jones, James R. Winker, Harvey Solin, Eric Christmas, Tandy Cronyn, Jill Tanner.

Old Globe Theater: Edison Center—California Theater

ON GOLDEN POND (29). By Ernest Thompson. November 4, 1980. Director, Craig Noel. With Wiley Harker, Jane Wenman, Anne Archer Krill.

NIGHT MUST FALL (29). By Emlyn Williams. January 6, 1981. Director, Craig Noel. With Katherine Faulconer, Laura Ganz, Jeffrey Combs.

RELATIVELY SPEAKING (29). By Alan Ayckbourn. February 17, 1981. Director, James Tripp. With Buzz Noe, Sherrie Lessard, Hal Chidnoff, Susan Shepard.

ORPHEUS DESCENDING (29). By Tennessee Williams. March 31, 1981. Director, William R. Bruce. With Trina Ciuffo, Melody Rae, Shirley McLaughlin, Peter Smith.

Old Globe Theater: Edison Center—Cassius Carter Center Stage

LONE STAR and LAUNDRY AND BOURBON (36). By James McLure. November 18, 1980. Director, David McClendon. With Nancy Thorsnes, JoAnn Reeves, Catherine O'Connell, Kim Bennett, Michael Lueders, Jonathan Miller.

A MOON FOR THE MISBEGOTTEN (36). By Eugene O'Neill. January 20, 1981. Director, Sandy McCallum. With Lura Lee Landis, Gregory Linus Weiss, Sandy McCallum, Will Bryant, Al Smith.

WHO'S HAPPY NOW? (36). By Oliver Hailey. March 3, 1981. Director, David McClendon; music, Dion McGregor; lyrics, Michael Barr. With Jay T. Loudenback, Bob Ramsey, Kathleen Thompson, Bill Dunnam, Debbi Bush.

FULL CIRCLE (36). By Erich Maria Remarque; adapted by Peter Stone. April 21, 1981. Director, William Roesch. With D'Ann Paton Peace, Laura Larkin, F. Scott Kirton, Malcolm Young.

Designers: scenery, Robert Morgan, Kent Dorsey, Steve Lavino, Nick Reid, Alan Okazaki; lighting, Sean Murphy, Kent Dorsey, William Morse, John Forbes, Steve Peterson; costumes, Robert Morgan, Peggy Kellner, Deborah Dryden, Merrily Murray, Dianne Holly, Susan Muick, Mary Gibson.

Note: Old Globe's Play Disovery Project (coordinator, Diane Sinor) presented staged readings for 1 performance each: *Lone Star* by James McLure and *The Coal Diamond* by Shirley Lauro, director, David McClendon, August 11, 1980; *Scooter Thomas Makes It to the Top of the World* by Peter Parnell, director, Peter Hackett, August 25, 1980; *The Bride of Lammermoor* by Walter Scott, adapted and directed by Karl W. Hesser, September 25, 1980. *Mobile Hymn* by Robert Litz, director, Diane Shea, October 20, 1980; *Right of Way* by Richard Lees, director, James Bush, November 24, 1980. *Agnes of God* by John Pielmeier, director, Giles Colahan, January 26, 1981; *Traces* by Ralph Meyering, director, Kim McCallum, February 16, 1981; *Mixed Quartet* by P. T. Coste, director, Diane Sinor, April 4, 1981; *Sundancers* by Craig Volk, director, Kim McCallum, and *Hear No Evil* by Farrell Foreman, director, Tom Humphrey, April 27, 1981.

A Moon for the Misbegotten was given 25 performance during March 1981 throughout California.

The Globe Educational Tour of *Do Me a Favorite* by Vincent Dowling and *King Midas and His Golden Touch* (141) played public and private schools, handicapped and correctional institutions throughout San Diego City and County, and Imperial County, October 1980–March 1981; director, William Roesch; company, Kim McCallum, Peter Michel, Sharon Silverglate, JoAnn Reeves; designers, Alan Okazaki, Stacey Sutton.

SAN FRANCISCO

American Conservatory Theater: Geary Theater

(General director, William Ball)

THE ELEPHANT MAN (47). By Bernard Pomerance. June 4, 1980. Director, Jack Hofsiss. With Philip Anglim, Penny Fuller, Ken Ruta.

MUCH ADO ABOUT NOTHING (31). By William Shakespeare. October 11, 1980. Director, Jerry Turner. With Sydney Walker, Julia Fletcher, Lawrence Hecht, John Hutton, William Patterson.

GHOSTS (26). By Henrik Ibsen; English translation and direction, Allen Fletcher. October 14, 1980. With Anne Lawder, Thomas Oglesby, Dana Elcar, Raye Birk, Jill Hill.

HAY FEVER (11). By Noel Coward. October 28, 1980. Director, Nagle Jackson. With Marrian Walters, William Patterson, Mark Murphey, Julia Fletcher.

THE TROJAN WAR WILL NOT TAKE PLACE (30). By Jean Giraudoux. November 25, 1980. Directors, Jack O'Brien, James Haire. With Jill Hill, Mark Harelik, Byron Jennings, Michael Winters, DeAnn Mears.

A CHRISTMAS CAROL (22). By Charles Dickens; adapted by Laird Williamson and Dennis Powers. December 4, 1980. Director, Laird Williamson. With Sydney Walker/Raye Birk, Lawrence Hecht/Michael Winters, Todd Kinsey.

NIGHT AND DAY (26). By Tom Stoppard. January 20, 1981. Directors, Elizabeth Huddle and Janice Garcia. With DeAnn Mears, William Patterson, Isaiah Whitlock Jr., Garland J. Simpson.

ANOTHER PART OF THE FOREST (26). By Lillian Hellman. February 10, 1981. Director, Allen Fletcher. With Ray Reinhardt, Anne Lawder, Bruce Williams, Mark Murphey.

THE RIVALS (26). By Richard Brinsley Sheridan. March 10, 1981. Directors, David Hammond, John C. Fletcher. With Marrian Walters, William Patterson, Byron Jennings, Jill Hill, Sydney Walker, Thomas Oglesby.

THE THREE SISTERS (25). By Anton Chekhov. March 31, 1981. Directors, Tom Moore, Larry Russell. With DeAnn Mears, Elizabeth Huddle, Barbara Dirickson, Peter Donat, Ray Reinhardt, Dakin Matthews, Sally Smythe, Raye Birk.

THE LITTLE FOXES (8). By Lillian Hellman. April 21, 1981. Directors, Tom Moore, Eugene Barcone. With Elizabeth Huddle, Peter Donat, Michael Winters, William McKereghan, Joy Carlin.

American Conservatory Theater: The Playroom

(Plays-In-Progress; directors, Raye Birke, John Kauffman. Workshop premieres)

THE COLLABORATORS (7). By Tom Rickman. February 9, 1981. Director, Raye Birk. With Lawrence Hecht, Frank Ottiwell, Joseph Bird, Matt McKenzie, Nicholas Kaledin.

A LITTLE LOVE AND AFFECTION (7). By Raymond Carver. March 18, 1981. Director, John Kauffman. With Lauren R. Klein, Julia Fletcher, Stacy Ray, John Hutton.

STRICTLY A FORMALITY (7). By Thomas F. Silver and Roy Conboy Jr. May 1, 1981. Director, Lawrence Hecht. With Mark Murphey, Lawrence Hecht.

THE LAST ACT: AN ANNOTATED HISTORY OF THE 20th CENTURY (7). By Gunilla Mallory Jones. May 5, 1981. Director, Allen Fletcher. With members of the ACT Company.

Designers: scenery, Richard Seger, David Jenkins, Ralph Funicello, Richard L. Hay, William Bloodgood; lighting, Dirk Epperson, Beverly Emmons, F. Mitchell Dana, Duane Schuler, Richard Devin; costumes, Michael Olich, Julie Weiss, Robert Morgan, Robert Fletcher, Martha Burke, Carrie F. Robbins.

Note: ACT guest productions at the Marines Memorial Theater included: The Pickle Family Circus in *Three High* (4 weeks), January 19, 1981; *Footlight Frenzy* by Ron House, Diz White, Alan Shearman, Bud Slocum, March, 1981; Magic Theater's premiere production of Sam Shepard's *True West* (6 weeks), April 14, 1981. *Night and Day* and *The Little Foxes* toured Hawaii, June 2, 1981. "Voices In The Wilderness", a program of staged readings, included *The Boys in Autumn* and *Moscow Lights* by Bernard Sabath.

SARASOTA

Asolo State Theater Company: Ringling Museums' Court Playhouse

(Artistic director, Robert Strane; managing director, David S. Levenson; executive director/founder, Richard G. Fallon)

MAN AND SUPERMAN (25). By George Bernard Shaw. June 5, 1980. Director, William Woodman. With Bradford Wallace, Peter Burnell, Robert Murch, Deborah Fezelle.

IDIOT'S DELIGHT (24). By Robert E. Sherwood. June 13, 1980. Director, Neal Kenyon; musical director, John Franceschina; Choreographer, Jim Hoskins. With Bernerd Engel, Isa Thomas, David S. Howard, Denise Koch.

THE WARRENS OF VIRGINIA (22). By William C. DeMille. June 20, 1980. Director, Eberle Thomas. With Peter Burnell, Theodore May, Monique Morgan, Bette Oliver, Robert Strane, Robert Murch.

TRANSCENDENTAL LOVE (18). By Daryl Boylan. July 18, 1980 (world premiere). Director, Robert Strane; scenery, Bennet Averyt; lighting, Martin Petlock; costumes, Catherine King.
Ralph Waldo Emerson . . . . Robert Murch
Lydia Emerson . . . . Deborah Fezelle
Margaret Fuller . . . . Monique Morgan
Horace Greeley . . . . Bradford Wallace
Act I, Scene 1: Cambridge, Mass., 1840. 3 p.m., Ralph Waldo Emerson's study. Scene 2: His study, four months later. Scene 3: His study, six months later. Scene 4: Same, 2:30 p.m. Act II: Emerson's study, a few weeks later, 2 p.m.

STAND-OFF AT BEAVER AND PINE (15).

By Sally Netzel. July 24, 1980. Director, Eberle Thomas. With David S. Howard, Bette Oliver, Isa Thomas, Bernerd Engel.

ON GOLDEN POND (46). By Ernest Thompson. February 19, 1981. Director, Isa Thomas. With Edward Stevlingson, Bette Oliver, Cynthia Wells, Miles Larsen.

THE BEGGAR'S OPERA (38). By John Gay. February 27, 1981. Directors, Robert Strane, Jim Hoskins; musical director and orchestrator, John Franceschina. With Lawrence Gallegos, Ruth Kidder, Bradford Wallace, Isa Thomas, Cynthia Wells.

TERRA NOVA (39). By Ted Tally. March 6, 1981. Director, Gene Lesser. With Robert Murch, Ronald Wendschuh, Douglas R. Nielsen, Ruth Kidder.

THE SONG IS KERN (35). Conceived and directed by Neal Kenyon; based on Jerome Kern's music. May 22, 1981 (world premiere). Musical director and arranger, John Franceschina; choreographer, Jim Hoskins. Lyricists: Jerome Kern, Otto Harbach, Edward Laska, Herbert Reynolds, John E. Hazzard, Schuyler Green, P.G. Wodehouse, B.G. DeSylva, Dorothy Fields, Jimmy McHugh, Johnny Mercer, Leo Robin, Ira Gershwin, E.Y. Harburg, Anne Caldwell. With Paula Dewey, Michelle Franks, Davis Gaines, Mark Jacoby, Patricia Masters.

Designers: scenery, Sandro LaFerla, Holmes Easley, Bennet Averyt, John Ezell, Robert Darling, Franco Colavecchia; lighting, Martin Petlock; costumes, Catherine King, Flozanne John, Sally A. Kos.

Note: Asolo's touring theater presented *The Men's Cottage* by Moses Goldberg; *Aladdin*, developed by the company; *Rashomon* by Fay and Michael Kanin, October 1980–May 1981; directors, Eberle Thomas, Maggi Guran, Sharon Ferguson, with the ATT Company.

SEATTLE

A Contemporary Theater

(Founder/artistic director, Gregory A. Falls)

FOR COLORED GIRLS WHO HAVE CONSIDERED SUICIDE/WHEN THE RAINBOW IS ENUF (24). By Ntozake Shangé. May 8, 1980. Director and choreographer, Tawnya Pettiford. With Conni Marie Brazelton, Roxanne Reese, Diane E. Bivens, Juanita Mahone, Arlene E. Quiyou, Demetra Pittman.

CATHOLICS (25). By Brian Moore; adapted from his novel. June 5, 1980 (world premiere). Director, Gregory A. Falls; scenery, Shelley Henze Schermer; lighting, Phil Schermer; costumes, Sally Richardson.

Abbot Thomas O'Malley	David White
Father James Kinsella	John Procaccino
Brother Kevin	Tony Amendola
Father Walter	John Aylward
Brother Seamus	Rod Pilloud
Brother Martin	Richard Marlin Tutor
Father Matthew	Maury Cooper
Father Manus	Bernard Frawley
Father Donald	Peter Kelley
Brother Paul	Glen Mazen

Time: The present. Place: A monastery on an isolated island off the West Coast of Ireland.

ARTICHOKE (25). By Joanna M. Glass. July 3, 1980. Director, M. Burke Walker. With Lynda Myles, Ted D'Arms, Clayton Corzatte, Joan Shangold.

WINGS (25). By Arthur Kopit. July 31, 1980. Director, John Dillon. With Eve Roberts, Katherine Ferrand, Tony Amendola, Calliandra Austin, Marjorie Nelson.

BURIED CHILD (24). By Sam Shepard. August 28, 1980. Director, Robert Loper. With Ted D'Arms, Mark Jenkins, Marjorie Nelson, Clive Rosengren.

STARTING HERE, STARTING NOW (24). Lyrics by Richard Maltby Jr.; music by David Shire. September 25, 1980. Director and choreographer, Judith Haskell; musical director, Stan Keen. With Gwen Arment, Nancy Callman, Robert Manzari.

A CHRISTMAS CAROL (42). By Charles Dickens; adapted by Gregory A. Falls; music by Robert MacDougall. December 5, 1980. Director, Eileen MacRae. With John Gilbert/Michael Santo, R. A. Farrell, Amy Stelz.

Designers: scenery, Karen Gjelsteen, Scott Weldin, Bill Raoul, Shelley Henze Schermer, William Forrester; lighting, Jody Briggs, Frank Simons, Phil Schermer, Donna Grout, Paul W. Bryan; costumes, Laura Crow, Susan Tsu, Julie James, Sally Richardson.

Note: ACT-Seattle, in association with the Bush School, presented *Doors* by Suzan Zeder, a play-in-progress, from February 4–7, 1981, director, Jim Hancock. Beginning February 7–March 14, 1981, Seattle's Young ACT Company, toured Washington State with *The Pushcart War*, adapted and directed by Gregory A. Falls, from Jean Merrill's novel. 11 performances were given in the Seattle area.

Seattle Repertory Theater: Bagley Wright Theater

(Producing director, Peter Donnelley; consulting artistic director, John Hirsch; artistic director, Daniel Sullivan)

STRIDER: THE STORY OF A HORSE (38). Adapted from Leo Tolstoy's story by Mark Rozovsky; English version by Robert Kalfin and Steve Brown; based on a translation by Tamara Bering Sunguroff; adapted with additional music by Norman L. Berman; new English lyrics by Steve Brown; original music by Mark Rozovsky and S. Vetkin; original Russian lyrics by Uri Riashentsev. October 22, 1980. Directors, John Hirsch, John Kauffman. Musical director, Stan

Keen. With Biff McGuire, George Sperdakos, Jeffrey L. Prather, John Procaccino, Robert Loper, Katherine Ferrand.

THE GRAND HUNT (31). By Gyula Hernady; translated by Suzanne Grossman. November 26, 1980. Director, John Hirsch. With Jan Triska, Carole Shelley, Roland Hewgill.

AH, WILDERNESS! (32). By Eugene O'Neill. December 31, 1980. Director, Daniel Sullivan. With Biff McGuire, Anne Gerety, L. Michael Craig, Susan Greenhill, Constance Dix, Thomas Hill.

BORN YESTERDAY (33). By Garson

Kanin. February 4, 1981. Director, M. Burke Walker. With Nora McLellan, John Procaccino, Ric Mancini, Glen Mazen, Susan Ludlow.

THE DANCE OF DEATH (33). By August Strindberg; adapted by Suzanne Grossman. March 18, 1981. Director, Daniel Sullivan. With Robert Lansing, Eve Roberts, Leon Russom.

TINTYPES (33). Conceived by Mary Kyte with Mel Marvin and Gary Pearle. April 22, 1981. Director, Judith Haskell; musical director, Stan Keen. With Stephen Berger, Marie King, Janet Powell, Faith Prince, David Pursley.

Designers: scenery, Richard Belcher, Cameron Porteous, Robert A. Dahlstrom, James Leonard Joy, Ralph Funicello; lighting, David F. Segal, Jeffrey Dallas, Robert A. Dahlstrom, Richard Devin, Richard Nelson, Robert Scales; costumes, Andrew B. Marlay, Cameron Porteous, Kurt Wilhelm, Laura Crow.

Seattle Repertory Theater: Moose Hall

(New Plays in Process; director, Robert Egan. 1 performance each)

BACK TO BACK by Al Brown; director, Clayton Corzatte; January 5, 1981.
TWENTY-THREE YEARS LATER by Michael Weller; director, Robert Egan; January 19, 1981.
RAGGEDY DICK AND PUSS (3). By Tim Kelly; director, Robert Egan; January 28, 1981.
WILD AIR by Tom Huey; director, Tom Towler; February 2, 1981.
SALVATION NOW by Snoo Wilson; director,

Robert Egan; February 16, 1981.
AMERICAN DREAMS: LOST AND FOUND, an entertainment by Studs Terkel; director, John Hirsch; editor, Alison Harris; musical directors, Stan Keen, Daniel Birnbaum. March 2, 1981.

With members of the regular company. Designers: scenery, Jennifer Lupton, Thomas M. Fichter, Richard Belcher; lighting, James Verdery, Richelle Potter; costumes, Lisa Cerveny.

Note: Seattle Repertory's young ensemble (Mobile Outreach Bunch) toured 50 junior high schools with a production of *Newcomers* by Janet Thomas and the Newcomers Company; director, Daniel Sullivan, January 30–March 6, 1981. Company: Bea Kiyohara, Ruben Sierra, Eloise Cardona, Ed Locke, Jill Chan; designers, Richard Belcher, Lisa Cerveny; sound and music, Daniel Birnbaum.

STAMFORD, CONN.

Hartman Theater Company

(Artistic director, Edwin Sherin; managing director, Roger L. Meeker)

SHOWDOWN AT THE ADOBE MOTEL (23). By Lanny Flaherty. February 11, 1981 (world premiere). Director, Edwin Sherin; scenery, Marjorie Kellogg, lighting, Roger Morgan; costumes, Marianna Elliott.
Robert Clarence "Clyde" Lee . . Henry Fonda
Mae June Baker. . . . . Cecilia Hart
Lank Santee . . . . Arthur E. Lund
Time: The present. Place: An old motel on the outskirts of the city. Act I, Scene 1: Early morn-

ing. Scene 2: Mid to late morning of the following day. Act II, Scene 1: Near dusk of the same day. Scene 2: Early morning of the following day.

MOLIERE IN SPITE OF HIMSELF (23). By David Morgan and Michael Lessac, based on writings by and about Mikhail Bulgakov. March 11, 1981. Director, Michael Lessac. With Richard Kiley, Judith Barcroft, Jacqueline Cassel, Ralph Williams.

HARTMAN THEATER COMPANY, STAMFORD, CONN.—Cecilia Hart and Henry Fonda in *Showdown at the Adobe Motel* by Lanny Flaherty.

MERTON OF THE MOVIES (23). By George S. Kaufman and Marc Connelly. April 15, 1981. Director, James Hammerstein. With Leonard Drum, Harry Groener, Roger Kozol, Tom Bade, Annette Kurek, Linda Kampley.

SEMMELWEISS (23). By Howard Sackler. May 13, 1981. Director, Edwin Sherin. With Mary Lou Rosato, Jeffrey De Munn, Lee Richardson, David Schramm, Roberts Blossom.

Designers: scenery, Robert U. Taylor, John Falabella, Robin Wagner; lighting, Roger Morgan, Marcia Madeira, Andy Phillips; costumes, Dona Granata, Walter Pickette, Jane Greenwood, Ann Roth.

STRATFORD, CONN.

American Shakespeare Festival

(President, Konrad Matthaei)

RICHARD III (35). By William Shakespeare. August 5, 1980. Director, Andre Ernotte; scenery, Bill Stabile; lighting, Marc B. Weiss; costumes, Ann Emonts. With Michael Moriarty, Viveca Lindfors, David Huffman, Michael O'Hare, Geoffrey Horne, Richard Seer, Robin Bartlett, Denise Bessette, Vic Polizos.

SYRACUSE, N.Y.

Syracuse Stage: John D. Archbold Theater

(Producing director, Arthur Storch; managing director, James Clark)

THE COMEDY OF ERRORS (32). By William Shakespeare. November 14, 1980. Director, Arthur Storch. With Marcus Smythe, Kevin M. Shumway, Jerry Beal, David Goldstein, Yolande Bavan, Gerard Moses.

DAMES AT SEA (32). By George Haimsohn and Robin Miller; music by Jim Wise. December 12, 1980. Director, Larry Alford; music director, John Visser; choreographer, Sharon Halley. With Dorothy Stanley, Jan Neuberger, Richard Sabellico, Eydie Alyson.

PARADISE IS CLOSING DOWN (32). By Pieter-Dirk Uys. January 16, 1981 (American premiere). Director, Peter Maloney; scenery, Timothy Galvin; lighting, Paul Mathiesen; costumes, Anne Shanto; slide show, Niles Wheeler.

Molly . . . . Le Clanche du Rand
Mouse. . . . . Valery Daemke
Young Man . . . . Basil Wallace
Anna. . . . . Donna Haley

Place: Molly's kitchen in her cottage in Loader Street, Cape Town, South Aftrica. Act I: Early evening, Saturday. Act II: A half hour later.

GOODNIGHT, GRANDPA (32). By Walter Landau. February 20, 1981. Director, Arthur Storch. With Joe DeSantis, John Carpenter, Maxine Taylor-Morris, Richard Kevlin-Bell, Fyvush Finkel.

FOR COLORED GIRLS WHO HAVE CONSIDERED SUICIDE/WHEN THE RAINBOW IS ENUF (32). By Ntozake Shangé. March 27, 1981. Director, Judith Haskell. With Celestine I. DeSaussure, Sharita Hunt, Venida Evans, Leona Johnson, Denise Washington, Arlene Quiyou, Gwyneth Whyte.

A DOLL'S HOUSE (32). By Henrik Ibsen; translated by Christopher Hampton. May 1, 1981. Director, Terry Schreiber. With Erika Petersen, Kenneth Gray, Andrea Masters, Craig Kuehl, Gerard Moses, Joan Kendall.

Designers: scenery, John Doepp, Hal Tiné, William Schroder; lighting, Judy Rasmuson, Michael Newton-Brown, William Thomas Paton, Todd Lichtenstein; costumes, James Berton Harris, Carr Garnett, David A. Schnirman, Nanzi Adzima.

Note: Syracuse Stage's Theater for Young Audiences presented *Where the Sidewalk Ends* by Shel Silverstein, directed by William S. Morris, to schools throughout Central New York, February–March, 1981.

TUCSON

Arizona Theater Company: Tucson Community Center Theater

(Artistic director, Gary Gisselman; managing director, David Hawkanson)

THE RIVALS (24). By Richard Brinsley Sheridan. November 4, 1980. Director, Gary Gisselman. With Jane Murray, Benjamin Stewart, David March, Richard K. Allison.

CUSTER (32). By Robert E. Ingham. December 2, 1980. Director, Gary Gisselman. With Paul Ballantyne, David M. Kwiat, Penny Metropulos, Benjamin Stewart.

INDULGENCES IN THE LOUISVILLE HAREM (24). By John Orlock. January 6, 1981. Director, Richard Russell Ramos. With Sheri-

dan Thomas, Jane Murray, Tony DeBruno, John Jellison.

THE ELEPHANT MAN (36). By Bernard Pomerance. February 6, 1981. Director, Michael Maggio. With George Lee Andrews, Henry Gardner, Benjamin Stewart, Richard K. Allison, David M. Kwiat, Ann-Sara Matthews.

A LITTLE NIGHT MUSIC (30). Music and lyrics by Stephen Sondheim; book by Hugh Wheeler. March 17, 1981. Director, Gary Gisselman; musical director, Jim Sullivan; choreographer, Lewis Whitlock. With Susan Long, Penny Metropulos, Richard K. Allison, Marti Morris, Kip Wahl, Jane McDonough.

TALLEY'S FOLLY (24). By Lanford Wilson. April 14, 1981. Director, Gary Gisselman. With Tony DeBruno, Jane Murray.

Designers: scenery, Tom Butsch, Jack Barkla, Michael Merritt, Gene Davis Buck; lighting, John B. Forbes, Jared Aswegan; costumes, Jack Edwards, Christopher Beesley, Gene Davis Buck.

WASHINGTON, D. C.

Arena Stage: Arena Theater

(Producing director, Zelda Fichandler; associate producer, Nancy Quinn; associate director, Douglas C. Wager)

GALILEO (33). By Bertolt Brecht; translated by Charles Laughton. October 23, 1980. Director, Martin Fried. With Robert Prosky, Annalee Jeffries, Robert W. Westenberg, Halo Wines, Richard Bauer, Ernest Graves.

THE MAN WHO CAME TO DINNER (33). By Moss Hart and George S. Kaufman. December 4, 1980. Director, Douglas C. Wager. With Mark Hammer, Leslie Cass, Ernest Graves, Annalee Jeffries, Halo Wines, Richard Bauer, Kimberly Farr.

THE SUICIDE (33). By Nikolai Erdman; adapted by Richard Nelson. January 22, 1981. Director, Gene Lesser. With Richard Bauer, Stanley Anderson, Halo Wines, Suzanne Costallos.

KEAN (33). By Jean-Paul Sartre; English version by Frank Hauser, based on the play by Alexandre Dumas. March 26, 1981 (American premiere). Director, Martin Fried; scenery, Marjorie Kellogg; lighting, Hugh Lester; costumes, Nan Cibula.

Elena........................ Halo Wines
Amy...................... Gerry Kasarda
Count de Koefeld .... Joe Palmieri

Prince of Wales............. Richard Bauer
Edmund Kean............ Stanley Anderson
Solomon................... Mark Hammer
Anna Danby .... Annalee Jeffries
Philips. .... Charles K. Bortell
Lord Nevill .... Robert W. Westenberg
Major Domo; Peter Potts;
  Innkeeper;
  Stage Manager....... John Neville-Andrews
Tumbler; Audience, Gidsa ...... Kim Merrill
Sadie; Audience............... Cam Magee
Constable; Footman; Audience .. David Toney
Darius; Footman;
  Assassin; Audience .... John Elko
  Footmen, Assassins, Tumblers, Audience: Michael Hartford, John Prosky, Robert Shampain.

GOD BLESS YOU, MR. ROSEWATER (33). Book and lyrics by Howard Ashman; music by Alan Menken; additional lyrics by Dennis Green; adapted from Kurt Vonnegut's novel. May 14, 1981. Directors, Howard Ashman, Mary Kyte; music director, Eric Stern. With Frederick Coffin, Barbara Andres, Robert W. Westenberg, Robert Prosky, Addison Powell.

Arena Stage: Kreeger Theater

ONE MO' TIME (41). Created and directed by Vernel Bagneris. November 6, 1980. Directors, Lars Edegran, Orange Kellin; choreographer,

Pepsi Beekel. With Peggy Alston, Barbara Montgomery, Ron Wyche, Tom Hull.

In repertory:

DISABILITY: A COMEDY (18). By Ron Whyte. March 4, 1981 (world premiere). Director, Richard Russell Ramos.
Larry .... Charles Janasz
Mom....................... Leslie Cass
Dad.................... William Andrews

Jayne..................... Christina Moore
Time: The present. Place: New York City. One intermission.

THE CHILD (18). By Anthony Giardina. March 6, 1981 (world premiere). Director,

ARENA STAGE, WASHINGTON, D.C.—Christina Moore and Charles Janasz in *Disability: A Comedy* by Ron Whyte

Douglas C. Wager.

Thomas	Michael Butler
Leah	Randy Danson
Anna	Mikel Lambert
Daniel	Gary Lee Blumsack
Caroline	Christina Moore
Child; Orderly	Kevin Donovan
Al Martino	Terrence Currier
Nurse	Katherine Leask

Scene 1: Watching TV. Scene 2: Examining Table. Scene 3: Dinner with Daniel and his English bride. Scene 4: Lunch with my gynecologist. Scene 5: Conversations with my son. Scene 6: In the counting house. Scene 7: The truck. Scene 8: Return to return. Scene 9: Daniel Redux. Scene 10: Newfoundland. One intermission.

COLD STORAGE (20). By Ronald Ribman. March 15, 1981. Director, Ron Lagomarsino. With Terrence Currier, Raquel Valadez, Robert Prosky.

PANTOMIME (20). By Derek Walcott. May 20, 1981 (American premiere). Director, Martin Fried.

Harry Trewe	Richard Bauer
Jackson Phillip	Avery Brooks

Place: A gazebo on the edge of a cliff, part of a guest house on the island of Tobago, West Indies. One intermission.

Arena Stage: Old Vat Room

BANJO DANCING. January 15, 1981. Open ended run to June. With Stephen Wade.

AMERICAN BUFFALO (33). By David

Mamet. May 9, 1981. Director, Robert Prosky. With Mark Hammer, Kevin Donovan, Stanley Anderson.

Designers: scenery, Tony Straiges, Adrianne Lobel, Tom Lynch, Karl Eigsti, Lance Pennington; lighting, Arden Fingerhut, William Mintzer, Hugh Lester, Allen Lee Hughes, Nancy Schertler; costumes, Marjorie Slaiman, JoAnn Clevenger, Sandra Yen Fong, Mary Ann Powell.

Note: Arena Stage presented two pre-season events, the return of The Flying Karamazov Brothers, September 23–November 30, 1980, in the Old Vat Room, and Pat Carroll in *Gertrude Stein, Gertrude Stein, Gertrude Stein* by Marty Martin, in the Kreeger, October 3–18, 1980. The Living Stage Theater Company, founded at the Arena by Robert Alexander as an improvisation theater for children and youth and expanded to bring theater to the disabled, the elderly and the incarcerated, presented its concept in workshops and seminars in Milwaukee, (February 8–14), Myrtle Beach, S. C. (May 2–10) and Hawaii at Maui (May 23–24) and Oahu (May 30–31) during the 1980–81 season.

Folger Theater Group: Folger Theater

(Producer/director, Louis W. Scheeder)

MEASURE FOR MEASURE (54). By William Shakespeare. October 6, 1980. Director, Roger Hendricks Simon. With Brenda Curtis, Justin Deas, Janice Fuller, David Little.

THE RIVALS (54). By Richard Brinsley Sheridan. December 8, 1980. Director, Mikel Lambert. With June Hansen, Glynis Bell, Leonardo Cimino, Moultrie Patten, Mark Basile.

CROSSING NIAGARA (40). By Alonson Alegria; translated from the Spanish by the author. February 9, 1981 (American premiere). Director, Louis W. Scheeder; scenery and lighting, Hugh Lester; costumes, Bary Allen Odom.
Blondin................. Michael Tolaydo
Carlo..................... Tobias Haller

Time: Summer of 1859. Place: Niagara Falls. Scene 1: Late at night. Scene 2: Early the following morning. Scene 3: Two days later. Scene 4: Three weeks later. Scene 5: One week later, evening. Scene 6: The following afternoon. One intermission.

LOVE'S LABOUR'S LOST (64). By William Shakespeare. March 30, 1981. Director, Louis W. Scheeder. With Glynis Bell, Leonardo Cimino, Al Corbin, Ralph Cosham, Earle Edgerton, Marion Lines, Michael Tolaydo.

ROMEO AND JULIET (64). By William Shakespeare. June 8, 1981. Director, Michael Tolaydo. With Robert L. Burns, Margaret Whitton, Glynis Bell, David Cromwell, David Chandler, Kenneth Meseroll.

Folger Theater Group: Terrace Theater—Kennedy Center

MUSEUM (27). By Tina Howe. October 25, 1980. Director, Leonard Peters. With Kathleen Helmer, Ralph Cosham, John Gillis, Ruby Holbrook.

HOW I GOT THAT STORY (27). By Amlin Gray. May 23, 1981. Director, Carole Rothman. With Richard Kline, Don Scardino.

Designers: scenery, Ursula Belden, Russell Metheny, Hugh Lester, John Hodges, Patricia Woodbridge; lighting, Hugh Lester, Allen Lee Hughes; costumes, Bary Allen Odom, Julie Weiss, Susan Denison.

John F. Kennedy Center: Eisenhower Theater

(Chairman, Roger L. Stevens; artistic director, Marta Istomin)

A PARTRIDGE IN A PEAR TREE (40). By Leslie Stevens. December 23, 1980 (world pre-

miere). Director, Philip Abbott; designer, Robert Randolph.

Sir Frederick Chasleton .... James Mason
Nora Kimble .... Clarissa Kaye
Edward Hare .... Ivor Barry
Thomas Broxton .... Dan Draper
Sgt. Finch................. Gerald S. Peters
Matron .... Martha McFarland
Marion Chasleton ... Charles Knox Robinson
Cynthia Linwood............. June Barrett
Charles G. Hensley.......... Robert Nadder

Time: The present. Place: London. Act I: High
Court of Justice, Criminal Courts of Assize, Old
Bailey. Act II: Judge's Chambers.

EARLY DAYS (30). By David Storey. May 26,
1981. Director, Lindsay Anderson. With Ralph
Richardson, Sheila Ballantine, Michael Ban-
gerter.

John F. Kennedy Center: Opera House

WILLIE STARK (24). Music and libretto by
Carlisle Floyd; based on Robert Penn Warren's
novel *All the King's Men.* May 9, 1981 (world
premiere). Director, Harold Prince; scenery, Eu-
gene Lee; lighting, Ken Billington; costumes,
Judith Dolan; conductors, John DeMain, Hal
France; choreographer, Frances Patrelle.
Radio Commentator .... Lowell Thomas
Willie Stark .... Timothy Nolen
Reporter..................... Harry Torno
Jack Burden..................... Alan Kays
"Tiny" Duffy.............. David Vosburgh
Sugar Boy................. Robert Moulson
Sadie Burke .... Jan Curtis
Judge Burden................ Don Garrard
George William............. Joseph Pearson
Anne Stanton................ Julia Conwell
Lucy Stark .... Dana Matles

Mrs. Stark .... Lynn Griebling
Hugh and Jeff .... Robert W. Ousley,
                              Robert Williamson
Mayor..................... Donald Bess.
   Act I, Scene 1: A city street adjacent to the
state capitol grounds, and the Governor's office
inside the capitol building. Scene 2: The terrace
of Judge Burden's home, early evening of the
same day. Scene 3: Steps and yard of the court-
house in Mason City. Act II, Scene 1: The Governor's offices. Scene 2: Living room of Willie's
mother's house. Scene 3: Library of the Governor's Mansion and street outside. Act III, Scene
1: Living room and library of Judge Burden's
home. Scene 2: Sadie's office and reception room
of Governor's office. Scene 3: State capitol and
grounds.

Note: The Kennedy Center Eisenhower Theater and Opera House also housed numerous pre-
Broadway and touring shows, including *Lunch Hour, 42nd Street, Mixed Couples* and *Sophisticated
Ladies.* Its Terrace Theater housed other programs including the Black Touring Circuit production
of Ntozake Shangé's *Boogie Woogie Landscapes* and the Acting Company repertory. Kennedy Center
also hosted American College Theater Festival III, March 30–April 18, 1981.

WATERFORD, CONN.

Eugene O'Neill Theater Center: National Playwright's Conference

(President, George C. White; artistic director, Lloyd Richards. Staged readings of new works-in-
progress; 2 performances each)

July 6 to August 3, 1980:

THE SUMMER GARDEN by Terry Curtis
Fox; director, Walt Jones.
SECONDS by Judith GeBauer; director, Barnet
Kellman.
EINSTEIN AND THE POLAR BEAR by Tom
Griffin; director, Dennis Scott.
WILLIE by Leslie Lee; director, Dennis
Scott.
SALLY AND MARSHA by Sybille Pearson;
director, Horacena J. Taylor.

THE SNOW ORCHID by Joseph Pintauro; di-
rector, Tony Giordano.
HOLY MARY by John Faro PiRoman; direc-
tor, Dennis Scott.
DETAILS WITHOUT A MAP by Barbara
Schneider; director, Walt Jones.
SUNDANCERS by Craig Volk; director,
Horacena J. Taylor.
LADIES IN WAITING by Terri Wagner; direc-
tor, Bill Ludel.

Company: Ethel Ayler, Margaret Barker, Trazana Beverley, John Braden, Dominic Chianese, Bryan Clark, Lindsay Crouse, Rosemary DeAngelis, Jeffrey De Munn, Mia Dillon, Clarence Felder, Arthur French, Peter Michael Goetz, Keith Gordon, David Marshall Grant, Kathryn Grody, Jo Henderson, Brent Jennings, Swoosie Kurtz, Ben Masters, George Lee Miles, Mary-Joan Negro, Ellen Parker, Francisco Prodo, Arlene Quiyou, Willie Reale, Marcell Rosenblatt, Jay O. Sanders, Eric Schiff, Joe Seneca, John Shea, Anna Deavere Smith, Helen Stenborg, James Sutorius, Kenneth Welsh, Amy Wright, John Wylie.

Dramaturgs: Martin Esslin, Corinne Jacker, Lee Kalcheim, Edith Oliver, Marilyn Stasio.

Designers: Hugh Landwehr, Bil Mikulewicz, Fred Voelpel; lighting, Frances Aronson, Ian Calderon.

WEST SPRINGFIELD, MASS.

StageWest

(Producing director, Stephen E. Hays; managing director, Robert A. Rosenbaum).

THE DIARY OF ANNE FRANK (31). By Frances Goodrich and Albert Hackett; based on the book *Anne Frank: The Diary of a Young Girl.* October 16, 1980. Director, Ted Weiant. With Emily Phillips, Jeremy Gilbert, Joseph Costa, Jean Richards.

ON GOLDEN POND (25). By Ernest Thompson. November 13, 1980. Director, Geoffrey Sherman. Conrad McLaren, Georgia Southcotte, Ron Johnston, Jean Richards, Brad Steinberg, David Hyatt.

DAMES AT SEA (31). Book and lyrics by George Haimsohn and Robin Miller; music by Jim Wise. December 11, 1980. Director and choreographer, Pamela Hunt; musical director, Stephen E. Hays. With Barbara Niles, Suzanne Dawson, Don Bradford, Virginia Seidel, Kevin Daly, Tod Miller, Don Bradford.

AGNES OF GOD (23). By John Pielmeier. January 15, 1981. Director, Richard Gershman. With Tana Hicken, Gloria Cromwell, Monique Fowler.

A MOON FOR THE MISBEGOTTEN (23). By Eugene O'Neill. February 12, 1981. Director, Robert Brewer. With Karen Shallo, Mike Miller, Donald Gantry, Jamie Cass, D. Peter Moore.

OTHELLO (26). By William Shakespeare. March 19, 1981. Director, Harold Scott. With Leon Morenzie, John Martinuzzi, Anne Kerry, Peter Burnell, Margery Shaw.

13 RUE DE L'AMOUR (25). By Georges Feydeau; adapted by Mawby Green and Ed Feilbert. April 6, 1981. Director, Stephen E. Hays. With John Marinuzzi, Karen Shallo, Charles Antalosky, Deborah Stenard, Richard DeFabees, Richard Burnell, Jety Herlick, Gannon McHale.

Designers: scenery, Joseph Long, Thomas Cariello, Joan Ferenchek Brancale, Brian R. Jackins, Frank J. Boros; lighting, Ned Hallick, Robby Monk, Paul J. Horton, Barry Arnold; costumes, Deborah Shaw, Jan Morrison, Anne Thaxter Watson, Elizabeth Covey.

CANADA

CALGARY, ALBERTA

Theater Calgary

(Artistic director, Rick McNair)

JITTERS (25). By David French. September 18, 1980. Director, Kathryn Shaw. With Peter Jobin, Rita Howell, Les Carlson, David Francis, Guy Bannerman.

BETRAYAL (25). By Harold Pinter. October 23, 1981. Director, Brian Rintoul. With Caroline Yeager, David Fox, Les Carlson, Normand Bouchard.

AUTOMATIC PILOT (25). By Erika Ritter. November 27, 1980. Director, Martin Fishman. With Sharon Corder, Michael Bianchin, Jack Ackroyd, Stephen Hair.

MAGGIE AND PIERRE (34). By Linda Griffiths and Paul Thompson. January 8, 1981. Director, Paul Thompson. With Linda Griffiths.

THE TEMPEST (25). By William Shakespeare. February 19, 1981. Director, Guy Sprung. With Robert Koons, Lewis Gordon, Robert Welch, Peter Donaldson, James Kirchner, Kate Trotter, Richard Partington.

HAPPY END (25). By Kurt Weill and Bertolt Brecht; American adaptation and lyrics by Michael Feingold, from the German play by Dorothy Lane. March 26, 1981. Directors, Felix Mirbt and Bill Glassco. With Skai Leja, Charlotte Moore, Judith Orban, Francine Volker; puppeteers Jean McDuff, Tom Miller, Robert More.

THE KITE (40). By W. O. Mitchell. April 30, 1981 (world premiere). Director, Rick McNair; designer, Terry Gunvordahl.

Keith .... Deryk M. Sinotte
Daddy Sherry .... Jack Creley
Helen .... Sharon Bakker
Dr. David Richardson ...... James Kirchner
Mr. Spicer .... David Francis
Harold Motherwell .... Stephen Hair
Harry .... Christopher Gretener
Eric....................... Cary Durrant
Trumpeter .... Paul McNair

Time: Early May, 1976. Place: Shelby, Alberta. Act I: Front Porch of Helen's house. Act II, Scene 1: Inside Helen's house. Scene 2: Same. Scene 3: Shelby Centennial Center. Scene 4: At home.

Designers: scenery, Michael Nemirsky, Douglas McLean, Paul Kelman, Jim Plaxton; lighting, Jeff Herd, Murray Palmer, Jim Plaxton, Robert Thomson; costumes, Shawn Kerwin.

Theater Calgary: Midnight Series

SOLANGE by Jean Barbeau and THE BEARD by Michael McClure (6). January 16, 1981. Directors, Duval Lang, Steven Schipper. JOGGERS (6). By Allan Stratton. February 27, 1981. director, Rick McNair. YEARS OF SORROW, YEARS OF

SHAME (6). By Rick McNair, based on the book by Barry Broadfoot. April 3, 1981. Director, Martin Fieshman. UNSEEN HAND (5). By Sam Shepard. May 8, 1981. Director, Steven Schipper.

HALIFAX, NOVA SCOTIA

Neptune Theater: Mainstage

In repertory, October 24–November 23, 1980:
MUCH ADO ABOUT NOTHING (21); THE TAMING OF THE SHREW (11). By William Shakespeare. Director, Denise Coffey. With John Neville, Susan Wright and members of the company.

THE FOURPOSTER (19). By Jan de Hartog. December 12, 1980. Director, John Neville. With Joan Gregson, David Brown.

THE NIGHT OF THE IGUANA (21). By Tennessee Williams. January 16, 1981. Director, John Neville. With Roland Hewgill, Amanda Wilcox, Nicola Lipman, Wanda Wilkinson.

MEDEA (21). By Stephen McKernan; a jazz rock version based on Euripides. February 20, 1981. Directors, Maurice E. Evans, John Neville; musical director, Rick Fox; choreographer, Jeanne Robinson. With Victoria Snow, Donald Burda, Bill Carr, James Rutten, Cheryl Wagner, Maurice E. Evans, Walter Borden.

THE DIARY OF A SCOUNDREL (21). By Alexander Ostrovsky. March 27, 1981. Director, John Neville. With Tony Randall, Florence Paterson, Faith Ward.

Neptune Theater: DuMaurier Lunchtime Theater

A VILLAGE WOOING (5). By George Bernard Shaw. December 3, 1980. Director, David Schurmann. With Nicola Lipman, David Brown.

THEATER CALGARY—Deryk. M. Sinotte and Jack Creley in *The Kite*

LUNCH WITH TENNESSEE WILLIAMS (5). Compiled by John Neville from Williams's plays, essays, poems, short stories. January 28, 1981. Director, Don Allison. With Nicola Lipman, Bill Carr, Cheryl Wagner, David Bulger.
SALT COD AND PORK SCRAPS (5). Written and directed by Hans Böggild. February 12,

1981. With Nicola Lipman, John Dunsworth, Timothy Webber, Tony Quinn, Debbie Perrott.
WINNERS (5). By Brian Friel. March 18, 1981. Director, Hans Böggild. With Timothy Webber, Cathy O'Connell, John Dunsworth.

Designers: scenery, Phillip Silver, Peter Perina, Arthur Penson; lighting, Peter Perina; costumes, Phillip Silver, Viven Frow.

Note: Young Neptune toured the province of Nova Scotia with *Tomorrow Will Be Better,* devised, adapted and directed by Irene N. Watts from thoughts, memories, stories and poems by Canadian school children, from September 1980–June 1981, with a special company of actors.

MONTREAL, QUEBEC

Centaur Theater Company

(Artistic director, Maurice Podbrey)

In Repertory, September 2–October 5, 1980:
ON THE JOB. By David Fennario. September 2, 1980. Director, Simon Malgobat. With Griffith Brewer, Marc Gelinas, John Bourgeois, Bembo Davies, Robert King, Michael Kramer, Stephen Mendel, Ralph Pettofrezzo.

NOTHING TO LOSE. By David Fennario. September 9, 1980. Director, Jean Archambault. With Miguel Fernandes, Peter MacNeill, Lubomir Mykytiuk, Michael Rudder, Denis Nadon, Jimmy Sorley.

WINGS (55). By Arthur Kopit. November 27,

1980. Director, Scott Swan. With Ann Casson, Merrilyn Gann, Christopher Gaze. Northern Light Theater production.

THE TOMORROW BOX (55). By Anne Chislett. January 8, 1981. Director, Elsa Bolam. With Joyce Campion, Antony Parr, Diane Belshaw, Richard Blackburn, Kate Trotter.

PASSIONATE LADIES (55). Written and performed by Barbara Perry. February 5, 1981. Director, Edmund Balin.

NIGHT AND DAY (55). By Tom Stoppard. March 19, 1981. Director, Maurice Podbrey. With Fiona Reid, Robert Haley, Errol Slue.

EVER LOVING (55). By Margaret Hollingsworth. April 16, 1981. Director, Jane Heyman. With Maja Ardal, Lee J. Campbell, Louisa Martin, Morris Panyet, Linda Sorgini, Michael Rudder.

TALLEY'S FOLLY (55). By Lanford Wilson. May 28, 1981. Director, Michael Mawson. With Mary Ann McDonald, Richard Geshler.

Designers: scenery and costumes, Felix Mirbt, Barbra Matis, Allan Stichbury, Debra Belshaw, Marcel Daughmais, Michael Eagan, Miro Kinch, Debra Hanson; lighting, Peter Smith, Alexander Gazale, Freddie Grimwood, Steven Hawkins.

Note: Centaur Theater Company performs in two theaters, Centaur I and Centaur II. Two of its productions have toured: *A Lesson From Aloes* by Athol Fugard, was presented in Toronto for three weeks from September 2, 1980; *Balconville* by David Fennario was sent to Manitoba, Vancouver, Bath, England, Belfast and the Old Vic in London.

STRATFORD, ONT.

Stratford Festival: Festival Stage

(Artistic director, Robin Phillips; associate director, Peter Moss; founder, Tom Patterson)

TWELFTH NIGHT (34). By William Shakespeare. June 9, 1980. Director, Robin Phillips. With Brian Bedford, Patricia Conolly, Pat Galloway, William Hutt, Richard McMillan, Jim McQueen, Kate Reid.

HENRY V (39). By William Shakespeare. June 10, 1980. Director, Peter Moss. With Richard Monette/Jack Weatherall, Lewis Gordon, Amelia Hall, Diana Leblanc, Barry MacGregor, Douglas Rain.

TITUS ANDRONICUS (13). By William Shakespeare. June 11, 1980. Director, Brian

Bedford. With Pat Galloway, Max Helpmann, William Hutt, Jack Weatherall.

MUCH ADO ABOUT NOTHING (34). By William Shakespeare. June 13, 1980. Director, Robin Phillips. With Brian Bedford, Diana Leblanc, Barry MacGregor, Jim McQueen, Nicholas Pennell, Stephen Russell, Maggie Smith.

THE SEAGULL (17). By Anton Chekhov; new version by John Murrell. August 8, 1980. Directors, Robin Phillips, Urjo Kareda. With Brian Bedford, Pat Galloway, Max Helpmann, William Hutt, Roberta Maxwell, Jennifer Phipps, Maggie Smith, Jack Weatherall.

Stratford Festival: Avon Stage

THE BEGGAR'S OPERA (26). By John Gay. June 9, 1980. Directors, Robin Phillips, Gregory Peterson; musical director, orchestrator and choral arranger, Berthold Carriere. With Graeme Campbell, Edda Gaborek, Jim McQueen, Jennifer Phipps, Mary Savidge, Stratford Youth Choir (Robert Cooper).

VIRGINIA (17) By Edna O'Brien. June 10, 1980 (world premiere). Director, Robin Phillips; scenery, Phillip Silver; costumes, Daphne

Dare; lighting, Michael J. Whitfield.
Virginia (Woolf) . . . . Maggie Smith
Leonard . . . . Nicholas Pennell
Vita . . . . Patricia Conolly

THE SERVANT OF TWO MASTERS (33). By Carlo Goldoni; adapted by Tom Cone. June 11, 1980. Director, Peter Moss. With Rod Beattie, Barbara Budd, Brent Carver, Lewis Gordon, Jennifer Phipps.

THE GIN GAME (19). By D. L. Coburn. June

12, 1980. Director, Mel Shapiro. With Kate Reid, Douglas Rain.

FOXFIRE (22). By Susan Cooper and Hume Cronyn; based on *Foxfire* by Eliot Wiggenton and his students. August 7, 1980 (world premiere). Directors, Robin Phillips, Peter Moss; designer, Daphne Dare; lighting, Michael J. Whitfield; song lyrics by Susan Cooper, Hume Cronyn, Jonathan Holtzman; music by Berthold Carriere, Jonathan Holtzman.

Dillard Nations . . . . Brent Carver
Holly Burrell . . . . Donna Goodhand
Annie Nations . . . . Jessica Tandy
Hector Nations . . . . Hume Cronyn
Prinz Carpenter . . . . Richard Monette
Doctor . . . . Lewis Gordon
Jackson . . . . Joel Kenyon

Stratford Festival: Third Stage

BRIEF LIVES (20). By Patrick Garland; adapted from writings of John Aubrey. July 19, 1980. Director, Martha Henry. With Douglas Rain.

Jake Bryson . . . . Lewis Gordon
Joe; Gudger . . . . Stephen Beamish

BOSOMS AND NEGLECT (13). By John Guare. July 18, 1980. Director, Mel Shapiro. With Kate Reid, Ray Jewers, Mary Charlotte Wilcox.

KING LEAR (16). By William Shakespeare. September 14, 1980. Director, Robin Phillips. With Martha Henry, William Hutt, Jim McQueen, Richard Monette, Nicholas Pennell, Douglas Rain, Peter Ustinov.

LONG DAY'S JOURNEY INTO NIGHT (11). By Eugene O'Neill. October 4, 1980. Director, Robin Phillips. With Jessica Tandy, William Hutt, Graeme Campbell, Brent Carver, Barbara Budd.

HENRY VI (11). By William Shakespeare; adapted and directed by Pam Brighton. August 13, 1980. With Stephen Russell and the Stratford Company.

Designers: scenery, Daphne Dare, Desmond Heeley, Michael Eagan, Phillip Silver, Susan Benson; lighting, Michael J. Whitfield, Gil Wechsler, Harry Frehner; costumes, Ann Curtis, John Pennoyer, Daphne Dare, Desmond Heeley, Robin Fraser Paye, Sue Lepage, Janice Lindsay.

WINNIPEG, MANITOBA

Manitoba Theater Center: Mainstage

(Artistic director, Richard Ouzounian)

BILLY BISHOP GOES TO WAR (23). Written and directed by John Gray with Eric Peterson. October 3, 1980. With Cedric Smith, Ross Douglas. Vancouver East Cultural Center Production.

JITTERS (27). By David French. November 14, 1980. Director, Malcolm Black. With Jennifer Phipps, Eric House, George Merner, Nicholas Rice, James Rankin.

BALCONVILLE (27). By David Fennario. January 9, 1981. Director, Guy Sprung. With Jean Archambault, Marc Gelinas, Peter McNeill. Centaur Theater Production.

GREASE (35). By Jim Jacobs and Warren

Casey. February 13, 1981. Director, Richard Ouzounian; music director, Peter Yakimovich; choreographer, Jacques LeMay. With Danny Zuko, Cheryl MacInnis, Michelle Fisk, Kemble Hall, Edward Ledson.

THE ELEPHANT MAN (27). By Bernard Pomerance. March 20, 1981. Director, Richard Ouzounian. With Lorne Kennedy, David Schurmann, Carolyn Jones, John Innes.

AS YOU LIKE IT (27). By William Shakespeare. April 24, 1981. Director, Richard Ouzounian. With Goldie Semple, John Wojda, John Innes, Lorne Kennedy, Barbara Budd, Brian Paul.

Manitoba Theater Center: Warehouse Theater

BETRAYAL (19). By Harold Pinter. October 22, 1980. Director, Sharon Pollock. With Mi-

chael Ball, John Innes, Leueen Willoughby.

MACBETH (18). By William Shakespeare. November 26, 1980. Director, Richard Ouzounian. With Michael Ball/John Innes, Leueen Willoughby, Guy Bannerman, Lorne Kennedy, Martha Little.

BENT (19). By Martin Sherman. January 28, 1981. Director, David Schurmann. With Lorne Kennedy, John Innes, Benedict Campbell, Harvey Harding, Adam Henderson, Gordon McCall.

1837: THE FARMERS REVOLT (19). By Rick Salutin and Theater Passe Muraille. April 1, 1981. Director, Gordon McCall. With Tom Anniko, Robert Paterson, Brian Paul, Chick Reid.

Designers: scenery, Dennis Gropman, Phillip Silver, Gavin Semple, Laurence Schafer, Arthur Penson, Guido Tondino, Evan Ayotte, William Chesney; lighting, Jennifer Tipton, Candice Dunn, Phillip Silver, Bill Williams, Robert Thomson, Larry Isacoff; costumes, Evan Ayotte, Phillip Clarkson, Guido Tondino, William Chesney.

Manitoba Theater Center: Young People's Theater

ALICE IN WONDERLAND (21). By Clive Endersby; adapted from Lewis Carroll. December 20, 1980. Director David Schurmann. With members of the regular company.

WINDIGO (50 in Manitoba schools). By Dennis Foon; directed by Gordon McCall. January 26–February 28, 1981. With Jonathan Barratt, Paula Schoppert Peter Smith, David Gillies.

THE TEN
BEST PLAYS

Here are details of 1980–81's Best Plays—synopses, biographical sketches of authors and other material. By permission of the publishing companies which own the exclusive rights to publish these scripts in full in the United States, most of our continuities include substantial quotations from crucial/pivotal scenes in order to provide a permanent reference to style and quality as well as theme, structure and story line.

In the case of such quotations, scenes and lines of dialogue, stage directions and descriptions appear *exactly* as in the stage version or published script unless (in a very few instances, for technical reasons) an abridgement is indicated by five dots (. . . . .). The appearance of the three dots (. . .) is the script's own punctuation to denote the timing of a spoken line.

42ND STREET

A Musical in Two Acts

BOOK BY MICHAEL STEWART AND MARK BRAMBLE

SONGS BY HARRY WARREN AND AL DUBIN

BASED ON THE NOVEL BY BRADFORD ROPES

Cast and credits appear on page 346

MICHAEL STEWART (co-author of book) was born in New York City on August 1, 1924. After graduation in 1953 with an MFA from the Yale School of Drama, he wrote sketches and revues at Green Mansions, a New York summer resort, and for various shows including the Shoestring Revues *of 1955 and 1957,* The Littlest Revue *in 1956 and the TV series* Caesar's Hour. *His first Broadway book was for* Bye Bye Birdie *in 1960, which won him a Tony and eventually, in 1981, the dubious privilege of writing a sequel,* Bring Back Birdie, *which lasted only 4 Broadway performances.*

Stewart's subsequent work is a substantial part of the theater history of his time. It consists of the authorship of the librettos for Carnival *(1961, the Critics Award winner),* Hello, Dolly *(1964, a Best Play and the Critics and Tony Award winner),* Mack & Mabel *(1974),* I Love My Wife *(1977, both the book and the lyrics), as well as the straight play* Those That Play the Clowns, *produced on Broadway in in 1966 for 4 performances, and the lyrics for the hit musical* Barnum *(1980); and co-authorship of the librettos for* George M *(1968),* Elizabeth and Essex *(1978, with Mark Bramble, it never reached Broadway) and* The Grand Tour *(1979, also with Mark Bramble).*

42nd Street *is Stewart's fourth collaboration with Bramble (including* Barnum*), second Best Play and was the 1981 Tony Award winner as best musical of the season. He lives in New York City.*

Jerry Orbach as Julian Marsh and Wanda Richert as Peggy Sawyer in *42nd Street*

MARK BRAMBLE (co-author of book) was born Dec. 7, 1950 in Maryland, where his father was in real estate and construction. He attended McDonogh School near Baltimore and Emerson College in Boston and received his B.A. from N.Y.U. in 1975. As a child, Bramble amused himself putting on plays and puppet plays. For one of his later work-study semesters he was accepted by David Merrick as a volunteer general assistant. After college he continued a career with the Merrick office as an assistant to the late Jack Schlissel and then as a member of ATPAM and company manager of several shows.

Bramble's first libretto of record was T*ts D*amond *(asterisks his) produced OOB at the Loft in January 1977. He collaborated with Jerome Chodorov on the adaptation* Pal Joey '78 *produced for 136 performances that year at the Ahmanson Theater in Los Angeles. His first collaboration with Michael Stewart was on the book of* Elizabeth and Essex, *produced for one performance at the Old Globe Theater in San Diego in 1978 and for 25 performances OOB at the Encompass in 1980. For Broadway, Bramble and Stewart wrote the book for* The Grand Tour, *which played for 61 performances in 1979, and the ongoing hit* Barnum, *with Bramble book and Stewart lyrics. They came up with the idea for* 42nd Street *while looking for a suitable project, and Merrick was immediately enthusiastic. Like his collaborator, Bramble lives in New York City.*

HARRY WARREN (composer, co-author of songs) was born in Brooklyn on Dec. 24, 1893, the son of a factory worker and died in Los Angeles in September, 1981 while his new show was running on Broadway. He attended Commercial High School, graduating in 1912, and served in the Navy in World War I. He wrote his first hit tune in 1922 and contributed music to such shows as Sweet and Low *(1930),* The Laugh Parade *(1931),* Crazy Quilt *(1931) and* Shangri-La *(1956), and Maurice Chevalier included Warren's and Johnny Mercer's "You Must Have Been a Beautiful Baby" in his repertory during his solo Broadway visits in the 1960s.*

It was in the movies, however, that Warren and the lyricist of his 42nd Street *songs, Al Dubin, won their greatest musical fame. Warren contributed to 75 films, including* 42nd Street *(based on the same source as the Broadway show) and the* Gold Diggers *series, scoring his last film in 1962. He won Oscars for his songs "Lullaby of Broadway," "You'll Never Know" and "On the Atchison, Topeka and the Santa Fe" and served as a board member of ASCAP and AMPAS and was a member of AGAC.*

AL DUBIN (lyricist, co-author of songs) was born in Switzerland in 1891 and died in New York in 1945. Like Harry Warren, Dubin achieved his principal reputation as a pioneer of music in sound pictures, often as a collaborator of Warren's. Their score for the movie 42nd Street *is heard again in this stage version of the tale, augmented by the addition of other Warren-Dubin numbers. Dubin's work for the New York theater has included lyrics for* White Lights *(1927),* Streets of Paris *(1939) and* Star and Garter *(1942).*

42nd Street *is as much a point of view on the musical theater as a sequence of events. Instead of synopsizing it in the usual manner of a Best Play, we have chosen to represent it by description and illustration in photos by Martha Swope. Its opening night was not merely the presentation of a new hit, it turned out to be an unforgettable moment of theater history, when fact became more poignant than fiction, and the dream of a Broadway show turned into a nightmare that wouldn't go away after the curtain came down. A detailed eyewitness account of this premiere is included with the following review of the show.*

THE OPENING NUMBER of *42nd Street* is called "Audition." As the orchestra came to the end of its overture and the house lights dimmed to black, a sound like tapping feet penetrated the heavy curtain. Tapping feet? . . . Innocent rhythms of the 1930s musical theater? The curtain rose on the lighted stage, and the muffled tapping became the compelling unison beat of 40—count 'em—40 tap dancers "rehearsing" the musical-within-the-musical that is the subject of this book by Michael Stewart and Mark Bramble, subtitled "The Song and Dance Fable of Broadway." The fable began to revolve like a spinning wheel in a fairy tale, and the audience was soon lost in its enchantment.

This Broadway *42nd Street* was based on the same Bradford Ropes novel from which the well-remembered 1933 Dick Powell-Ruby Keeler-Warner Baxter-Beebe Daniels movie was taken, and it spins the same yarn. Producer-director Julian Marsh (Jerry Orbach) is trying to make a much-needed comeback with a show called *Pretty Lady* in New York rehearsal and Philadelphia tryout, aiming toward a big opening night at the "42nd Street Theater." Julian's difficulties are compounded by the economic strictures of the Depression and the temperament of his star Dorothy Brock (Tammy Grimes), who has persuaded an admirer to angel her show. The worst happens: the star breaks her ankle, so that neither she nor the show can go on. Philadelphia is now the graveyard of hopes and dreams: the sets are struck, Julian is broke, all the kids are out of work, the train is headed back to New York—but wait! That little chorus girl Peggy Sawyer (Wanda Richert), who was fired from the cast the other day, knows all the star's numbers. She can dance up a storm and sing back the blue sky, and her looks and personality are as naturally refreshing as a lilac bush in June. Perhaps . . . perhaps Julian can persuade her to come back and take over the leading role ("Come on along and listen to/The lullaby of Broadway"). The show could go one after all—on and on and on, as a new star is born together with a new smash hit.

This oft-told tale developed a kind of gee-whiz show-biz glamor and bravado on the silver screen in 1933, and it stood up to a clever satirical treatment in the 1960s off-Broadway musical *Dames at Sea*. Searching for a niche somewhere in between, *42nd Street* was reported to be in worse trouble during its tryout tour than the troubled show it was about, so that it seemed for a while that not even a Gower Champion (its director-choreographer and certainly its artistic mentor) or a David Merrick (its producer, a comeback story in himself) could find a way to save it. Their persistence paid off, however. The show found its place, not in awe or mockery, but in a dreamland combination of nostalgic affection and spectacular musical comedy technique: Broadway as fable, embellished by masters. It relished every wishful thought of its larger-than-life Broadway, where ambition knows no shame, talent is triumphant and the production numbers overflow the stage.

Above, Wanda Richert (carrying suitcase) and Jerry Orbach (arms folded, *left*) lead the *42nd Street* cast in "Lullaby of Broadway". *Below,* a detail from the same number, choreographed and directed by Gower Champion

From the 40 tap dancers in the opening scene to the "42nd Street" finale, these numbers were a glorious procession of musical comedy entertainment devised by Gower Champion, a choreographic masterpiece of tap, waltz, balletic and good old hoofing action (see the photos accompanying this report), left as a legacy after Champion's untimely death from leukemia on the afternoon of the show's debut. The director-choreographer's airborne cast glided through a shadow waltz, capered on a double staircase, shuffled off to Buffalo in a cutaway railroad car right out of a Busby Berkeley film and tapped on to the crescendo of the "42nd Street" finale, rivalling in imaginative movement just about anything in the modern musical theater including Champion's own *Bye Bye Birdie* and *Hello, Dolly.* Writing in the New York *Times* about what he called Champion's "best choreography," Frank Rich commented, "One happily finds witty homage to such memorable past Champion show-stoppers as the opening telephone number from *Bye Bye Birdie,* 'Put on Your Sunday Clothes' from *Hello, Dolly* and 'When Mabel Comes Into the Room' from *Mack & Mabel.* "

The Harry Warren-Al Dubin score from their movie *42nd Street,* augmented with other notable Warren-Dubin songs, included such golden oldies as "Young and Healthy," "I Know Now," "You're Getting To Be a Habit With Me," "We're in the Money," "Lullaby of Broadway," "Shuffle Off to Buffalo" and the title number. The show was large physically, with scenery by Robin Wagner and costumes by Theoni V. Aldredge, but all elements of this superbly designed unit are in proportion and tune with the whole, with even the star performances obedient to Champion's staging of the piece not as a joke but always in fun in its romantic, nostalgic way. Orbach's Julian was a take-charge guy who wore his gratifications and disappointments on his sleeve, never leaving the audience in doubt about what it should feel. In the performances of the Misses Grimes and Richert, the star's acid and the chorus girl's sugar were diluted to avoid any dominating flavor in the blend of straight musical talents, simplistic drives, engaging harmonies and compelling rhythms.

David Merrick was reported to have put more than $2 million where his judgment was, providing all the backing, much of the persistence when the show didn't seem to be going well out of town and certainly a significant proportion of the good taste to assemble the marvelously achieving group of design and performance talents. Merrick's one-man, one-vision, one-wallet kind of producing has all but vanished from the Broadway theater, where it now can and often does take a mountainous collective of producers to bring forth a one-performance mouse. Certainly Merrick deserves a major share of the credit for the artistic charge of this enterprise, as well as its box office voltage. He knew what he wanted —a rousing, old fashioned (in concept) but stylishly new (in performance) musical comedy, and he knew what he had after the show opened on Broadway and he read reviews like "For Merrick, this is a most formidable triumph. . . . .It's great to have Merrick back—what was the man doing all those years away?" (Clive Barnes, New York *Post*); "Fabulous it is" (John Beaufort, Christian Science *Monitor*); "Mr. Merrick has shown that he has lost none of his flair . . . Mr. Merrick has taken all the things audiences have responded to in recent musicals and put them in the biggest, brightest package yet" (Edwin Wilson, Wall Street *Journal*); "A miracle of Broadway energy. . . . .a Broadway throwback in which

Carole Cook (foreground) in the "Shuffle Off to Buffalo" number

Broadway surges forward with renewed gaiety" (Douglas Watt, New York *Daily News*).

42nd Street was obviously a massive hit, and its producer immediately attacked the existing structure of ticket prices, partly in an effort—he has said—to thwart the scalping of tickets. He discontinued the practise of block allotments and raised his prices to previous unimagineable heights, nevertheless selling out and grossing a steady $375,000-plus-standees weekly. Economically and esthetically, *42nd Street* has made Broadway history. It has become legend, not only because of its success story, which is only beginning, but also because of the deep sadness that descended so ironically upon it in the midst of its triumphant opening night. A young playwright and poet, Leonard Melfi, was present in the audience and wrote an account for the *Dramatists Guild Quarterly,* the stage authors' intercom. We reprint it here with permission*, to echo for our Best Plays record an unforgetta- ble moment in the theater; a reality which was the emotional equal of anything in show business fiction:

When we got to the Winter Garden theater, there were crowds all over the area behind police barricades, huge spotlights panning the sky and thronging first- nighters walking along a glorious bright red carpet that felt like soft velvet and was surely brand-new for the occasion, and which covered every part of the sidewalk in front of the theater.

The inside of the Winter Garden was slowly filling up, and you could just sense it, smell it in the wonderful air: a special sort of feeling—vibrations, or whatever —of anticipated excitement slowly surging up inside every single member of the opening night audience, like thousands of grown-up little kids, all dressed up, all looking marvelous, heading towards their seats, waiting for the magical explosion of their own individual Emerald City in each and every one of their minds of theatrical fantasy.

I have hardly ever gone to Broadway openings, and so I was really extra- impressed, to put it mildly. Being a playwright made it all twice as exciting for me, particularly proud and overwhelmed to be part of it all.

I was sitting next to my agent, Helen Harvey, and just before the curtain went up I whispered in her ear, "Thanks very much for inviting me to be your guest tonight, I'll always remember it, and the show hasn't even begun yet!" And then we squeezed each other's hand, smiling with good luck glances coming from our eyes as the overture finally began. The music starting, the curtain rising, the opening number—the whole audience themselves!—well, there was no way, *no way* any of us could ever be disappointed that night, or ever let down that night; for me, it seemed impossible, and I was perfectly right—it proved to be totally impossible. From the very beginning to the very end, the show was all pure and powerful joy. The whole audience rose to its feet, applauding and cheering wildly: twelve standing ovation curtain calls! It could have gone on and on.

But the producer of the show suddenly appeared onstage. The audience, recog- nizing that it was David Merrick, began to applaud him now, along with flashes of laughter everywhere. But Mr. Merrick looked very sad. He tried to get us to stop our applause. I heard someone remark wryly, "Oh, what's he got up his sleeve now?"

Finally, Mr. Merrick got us all to quiet down.

And we all waited.

DAVID MERRICK *(barely audible):* This is a very tragic moment for me.
AUDIENCE *(lots of sudden laughter again, and lots of sudden applauding again).*
CAST *(most of them in the same mood as the audience).*

*Copyright © 1980 by The Dramatists Guild, Inc.

MERRICK (raising his hands for us to be quiet again).

AUDIENCE (dead silence this time).

CAST (dead silence too).

MERRICK (looks pale and deeply troubled; then quickly, clearly): This is tragic. Gower Champion died this afternoon.

AUDIENCE (one long, gigantic, moaning gasp, all together at once, like a sudden, mammoth, blowing, sighing wind, created without rehearsal by a great throng of human beings, coming automatically, uniformly from every seat in the house, the likes of which will always remain haunting and unforgettable, and especially when thought of in terms of the contrast just a few short moments before).

CAST (crying, shocked, infinitely saddened, some of them reaching out to one another; Tammy Grimes holding one hand to her mouth, the other hand grabbing at Jerry Orbach's hand. Orbach folds his arms with a look of utter disbelief on his shocked-looking face; Wanda Richert's face, first pained, then sobbing. Merrick immediately turns and goes to Wanda Richert, his arms outstretched, tears filling his eyes).

AUDIENCE (mostly silence now, sounds of crying here and there, no words, staring at the stage. I get to feeling numb all over like everybody else; not knowing what to do. I put my hand on Helen's shoulder. She is staring straight ahead, in deep, numb thought, her lips quivering).

JERRY ORBACH (suddenly): Bring it down! (He looks out in the direction of offstage right.) BRING IT DOWN! (The curtain begins to fall slowly. Respectifully, to the audience.) Good night . . . !

The audience does not respond, but I remember automatically saying "Good night" back to him out loud. The curtain is down. The audience doesn't seem to know how to leave the Winter Garden. We had all been standing up during the last few minutes. Many were now falling back down into their seats.

Slowly, they move out; very little talk; Mr. and Mrs. Joshua Logan, nearby, not knowing what to do, looking very sad; Anne Baxter, in front of me, dropping back into her seat and crying; Helen finally just letting the tears take over now too.

I hear my name called; an actress friend of mine is standing behind me; we reach out and hold hands over a row or two of seats. She was a very close friend of Gower Champion's, and she tells me, "I was with him when he died. I was with him all morning. He wanted it this way. He was very happy about the show. He was very proud of it. He told us, right before he died, that we had to be here in the audience tonight, no matter what. It was his opening, and he wanted us to be here, even though he couldn't be here. He told us to be here and go to the parties afterward, too." A pause. "Oh, yes, Leonard, he was really happy about the show. And he really didn't suffer, either." A pause. "As I said to you just before: he wanted it this way."

The Winter Garden is almost empty now. I see Ethel Merman leaving, slowly, sadly, a very different kind of Ethel Merman than what we are all used to.

The curtain is up again. The stage is dark and bare, stripped of everything. There are only two other people left in the orchestra now: Ruth Gordon and Garson Kanin. Mr. Kanin is simply standing, not looking anywhere in particular,

The song "42nd Street" provides a finale, Gower Champion-style, with Lee Roy Reams *(center)* and Wanda Richert *(right of center)*

dazed I believe, standing at his seat. Miss Gordon is sitting; sometimes her head is bowed; sometimes she gazes at the empty and silent stage.

A stagehand comes out. He is carrying the familiar arc light, used when a show is over for the night; that naked, burning bulb attached very simply, plainly, to the top of a thin, long, skeleton-like standard. The stagehand places the burning arc light in the middle of the stage and exits.

I get a strange feeling at first, standing there in the back of the theater staring at the wide-open stage; full of hope. The burning arc light makes me think of the single burning vigil light on the altars of churches when I was growing up (and I was an altar boy once), and how the vigil light always seemed comforting to me. I feel better now, because I am thinking of lasting things . . . eternity, I guess . . . the supreme endlessness of the theater, I suppose. And as I leave the theater I think of Gower Champion and feel comforted.

A LIFE

A Play in Two Acts

BY HUGH LEONARD

Cast and credits appear on page 354

HUGH LEONARD was born in Dublin in 1926. Thirty years later his first long play, The Big Birthday, *was produced at the Abbey Theater. In subsequent decades he won a place among the leading dramatists of the English-speaking stage with more than 20 works including* Mick and Mack, The Patrick Pearse Motel, Madigan's Lock, Some of My Best Friends Are Husbands, Thieves, Summer *and* A Suburb of Babylon, *all produced in Dublin and/or London. The first two Leonard scripts produced in New York both appeared in the same month, September 1967, off Broadway:* The Poker Session *for 16 performances and* Stephen D *(an adaptation of James Joyce's* A Portrait of the Artist as a Young Man *and* Stephen Hero*) for 56 performances. His Broadway productions have been* The Au Pair Man, *a two-character allegory of British-Irish relations produced by Joseph Papp at Lincoln Center for 37 performances in December 1973, and the Best Play* "Da" *which had various American productions from 1973 on, climaxed by the 697-performance Broadway appearance opening May 1, 1978 and winning both the Critics and Tony Awards as the season's best.*

One of the indelible impressions of "Da" *was the character Drumm, a hard-shelled Irish civil servant. Leonard's second Best Play,* A Life, *moves in for a detailed closeup of Drumm and the friends and forces that shaped his life from promising youth to not-quite-fulfilled maturity.* A Life *was first produced at the 1979 Dublin Festival, where it won the Harvey Award for the best play of the year by an Irish writer. In this hemisphere the present production was mounted at the*

Helen Stenborg as Dolly, Roy Dotrice as Drumm, Dana Delany as Dorothy (young Dolly) and Adam Redfield as Desmond (young Drumm) in *A Life*

Citadel Theater, Edmonton, Alberta Sept. 24 prior to its Broadway appearance Nov. 2, 1980 for an all-too-brief run of only 72 performances, no measure of its stature as a work of international theater.

Among Leonard's movie credits are Interlude, Great Catherine *and* Rake's Progress. *His extensive TV writings have included many originals as well as adaptations of Dickens, Emily Bronte, Flaubert, Maugham, Wilkie Collins, Conan Doyle, de Maupassant, James Joyce and Sean O'Faolain. An autobiographical novel,* Home Before Night, *was published recently by Atheneum. He lives near Dublin with his wife, Paule and daughter Daniele and has served as director of the Dublin Theater Festival and as a columnist for* Hibernia.

Time: The present

Place: A small town just south of Dublin

ACT I

SYNOPSIS: An unroofed bandstand supported by pillars commands stage center, with steps leading down to stage level at both left and right. Drumm enters, dressed in a fawn-colored raincoat—he is *"64, retirement age, intellectually snobbish, aloof, sarcastic, scholarly."* In memory, he hears the strains of "The Missouri Waltz," but at this moment he is conducting a handful of tourists (offstage and unseen) on a walking tour of his village, consulting his notes and addressing them as follows: "To conclude. I have chosen to end today's walk at the bandstand in this park which is remarkable for its views of sea and mountains, such as may have inspired Bernard Shaw's observation that whereas Ireland's men are temporal, its hills are eternal. Any child familiar with the rudiments of geology could have told him otherwise, but then even Shaw was not immune to his countrymen's passion for inexactitude."

Drumm continues to inform his unseen listeners that the coming of the railway in 1834 stimulated the growth of the town, Dalkey, whose birthrate, he notes, is "relentless" and whose mortality rate—he notes after slight hesitation—is "consistent with the national average." He dismisses his audience after a light scattering of applause and smokes a cigarette in solitude until his wife, Dolly—*"age 60, natural gaiety under which is a terror of her husband's displeasure; shy, soft-spoken; tender, forgiving, timid, foolish, devoted"*—walks up to meet him. After catching her breath, she inquires about his talk, assuming it must have been a success. Drumm wonders why she bothered to come all this way to meet him, "crawling through the gorse like a decrepit sheep."

DOLLY:. . . . .I'm not a sheep, Dezzie.
DRUMM: Quite so.
DOLLY: Or decrepit, either.
DRUMM: To be sure.

DOLLY: I know it's only your way and you mean nothing by it, but other people don't know that, and it's not very . . .

DRUMM: Could we have done?

DOLLY: . . . very gentlemanly.

Drumm pretends to be concentrating on the view. Dolly knows that he had a talk with his doctor today and asks about the result of his recent x-rays. Drumm tells her that the doctor, Ben Mulhall, diagnosed a duodenal ulcer: "One lives with it, but at least one lives." Tears of relief come to Dolly's eyes.

DOLLY: I was worried sick.

DRUMM: I hadn't noticed.

DOLLY: I wasn't going to let on to you, was I? But let's face it, Dezzie, we're not youngsters, and when you get to be our age—

DRUMM: Don't bracket our ages.

DOLLY: It's just the sort of thing that happens when you think at long last you're grand and clear and have a chance to enjoy life. Do you know what I said? I said: Ah no, God, not now, not when he'll be finished with the office in August and we can have our holiday and a rest and get the little car and—

> *She stops, dismayed that she has said more than she ought. Pause. He waits until she tries to disentangle herself.*

I mean—

DRUMM: What little car?

DOLLY: If you owned up to it, you were as worried as I was.

DRUMM: You said a car.

Dolly is forced to admit she's been longing for a car. Drumm could learn to operate it despite his ulcer, and they could go for drives and visits. Drumm will have a lump sum upon retirement, so they could afford it. Dolly offers to learn to drive if Drumm doesn't want to. Drumm ridicules the whole notion. He sends Dolly home, although she'd hoped they could walk home together; but he has a visit to make.

The lights come up at right in a newly-decorated but modest living room. It is the Kearns home, and Mary Kearns *("age 60; limps slightly from an accident . . . . .spunky; great individuality, very outspoken; more physical than intellectual; good sense of humor")* enters as Drumm comes into the room. Mary is not ready to welcome Drumm until she finds out what brought him here—it seems he hasn't called on or spoken to the Kearnses, once his close friends, for six years.

Drumm takes off his coat and asks after Mary's husband, Lar, who is at the pub. He sees that she has long since recovered from her accident (at which time Drumm had sent Dolly to see Mary) except that she has a slight limp. Mary scoffs at Drumm's compliment on her looks.

MARY: You go past me every day in the town. I might as well be a midge in the air or a pane of glass a body'd look through. If you see me in time, you go across the street, and if you don't, you put that face on you as if there was a dead dog in the road. Making a show of yourself and of me as well.

DRUMM: We were not on speaking terms.

MARY: And don't I know it!

DRUMM: I am not a hypocrite. I will not affect a pretense of good will simply for the benefit of every prying cornerboy and twitching lace curtain in the street.

MARY: A nod wouldn't have killed you.

DRUMM: You prefer me to be dishonest?

MARY: Be whatever you like. You're a bitter old pill, and you always will be.

DRUMM (smiling tolerantly): I have never yet met the member of your sex who did not prefer common abuse to common sense.

MARY: Did you come in here to vex me?

DRUMM: No. No, I did not, and your point is well taken. Whatever bitterness has been between us is in the past.

MARY (ominously): It's where?

DRUMM: I think it's time that we were friends again.

MARY: Is that what brung you?

DRUMM (gently): Brought me.

MARY: Brought you.

DRUMM: At our age, there aren't so many days left that one can afford to squander them in quarrels.

MARY: Life's too short.

DRUMM: Exactly.

MARY: That's the bee in your bonnet, is it. . . . .

Mary decides to offer Drumm a whiskey, which he accepts. Drumm admits that "a passing shower" over the state of his health caused him to realize that life is too short to hold long grudges. He would have regretted his six years of not speaking to the Kearnses if the doctor's verdict had been a grave one.

Mary keeps at him: "You can get on with no one: a cup of cold water would disagree with you." Drumm protests that he is a reasonable man, albeit a man of principle. Mary agrees: "No need to tell me. You won't be ten minutes in heaven before you're not talking to God." Drumm raises a toast to Mary, promising he'll "never again allow you to provoke me."

Mary calls attention to the redecoration of her home; it was too dark and formal before, she says, but Drumm always felt at home here. Mary leads Drumm into the kitchen to show him what she's done there, and as they cross to the kitchen area "lights come up. We are looking at the kitchen area of 40 years ago, with the dresser, the range and cold-water earthenware sink." As "The Missouri Waltz" is heard in the background, the grown-up Desmond Drumm and Mary Kearns are joined by the youthful Desmond and Mary (who was then known as Mibs) of 40 years before. (Drumm admires Mibs, as Mary shows off her new kitchen (the young people are Drumm's memory figures, of whose presence Mary is unaware). The kitchen is now much more functional but at the same time much less homelike, which does not please Drumm. His negative reaction affronts Mary, as the two grownups make their back to the living room, while the play's attention continues to be centered on young Desmond and Mibs in the kitchen.

MIBS *(pushing her book aside):* I can't make head or tail of it.

DESMOND: It's simple.

MIBS: To them with brains.

DESMOND: What is it you don't understand? Show me.

MIBS: This bit. *(Reading.)* "My friends, we will not go again . . ."

DESMOND: ". . . or ape an ancient rage/Or stretch the folly of our youth to be the shame of age."

MIBS: What's it mean?

DESMOND: "Ape an ancient rage." The writer—Chesterton—what he's saying is that it's only natural for young people to be wild and passionate. *(Almost blushing.)* Angry, that is. And no one minds foolishness, because it's too soon yet for them to be wise.

MIBS: But *you* are.

DESMOND: No. I'm intelligent: there's a difference. But an elderly person who behaves as if he were still young: that's . . . well, it's not nice to see.

MIBS: That's what this means?

DESMOND: Mm.

MIBS: Pity he didn't say so, then. No, it's me. I'm thick.

Desmond tries to continue explaining the poem, but what Mibs wants to know is, "Will you love me when I'm old and grey?" Desmond vows that he will. Desmond insists on discussing the poem further, even though Mibs offers to kiss him instead; he wants her to pass her exam, declaring, "You have a good mind. Fine, quick." But Mibs demurs: "You've druv me distracted," between his idealizing of her as someone she is not and the difficulties of Chesterton.

DRUMM: He's easy.

MIBS: I'm sure. For them that had a schoolmaster for a da, yeah.

DESMOND: That has nothing to do with it.

MIBS: Not much, not half. He beat it into you. Lar Kearns told me.

DESMOND: That ignoramus.

MIBS: He says—

DESMOND *(jealous):* When did you see him?

MIBS: He says you were never let out after tea. You were kept in, and your da would take a cane and flay the legs off you. He says the roars of you were so great—

DESMOND: He's a liar.

MIBS: The whole town knew it.

DESMOND: I never roared; *that's* a lie.

Desmond admits that his father was hard on him, punishing him often in class to show the others he was playing no favorites, giving him extra work at home, caning him on the legs (to leave his hands sound for homework), beating an education into him so that he wouldn't have to spend a life at manual labor. Desmond's father was killed in an accident nine years ago, but his work was well done. Desmond is now a most promising young man, clearly destined for a career in the civil service. He'd be a fine catch for a local maiden, Mibs suggests, while warning him, "I'm not going to get married, not to anyone, and least of all to you, so you needn't ask me. . . . .You're too milk-and-watery for me: there's a nun inside of you."

Desmond pretends he's merely amused by this remark but is in fact infuriated. Icily, he makes motions of departure. She stays him with a question: "Why do you pick on me to persecute? We're night and day, chalk and cheese." Desmond tells Mibs she is "a very fine type of person" for all her frivolity and flirting with "cornerboys" like Lar Kearns, and they are a match.

Desmond asks her to favor him before he goes; Mibs closes her eyes and waits for his kiss. It's not a kiss he means to favor her with, however, it's the last lines of Chesterton's poem. She is outraged as he reads the lines, then they are interrupted by a knock on the door and a strange noise outside. The door opens and young Lar Kearns comes into the kitchen, just as the grown-up Kearns joins Mary and Drumm in the living room area, where the attention of the play now shifts.

Kearns (*"contemporary of Drumm; ineffectual, good-humored, physically gone to seed; big man, enjoys pleasure of life; not intelligent; incapable of suspecting ill will in anyone; tender hearted; messes everything up"*) holds out his hand to Drumm in welcome, but Drumm doesn't take it. Nevertheless, Kearns observes that apparently the peace pipe is now alight, and he insists that his long-absent former friend have another drink with him, "So's the occasion won't go by unmarked."

MARY: I 'clare to God, if the cat died he'd drink to the repose of its soul.

KEARNS: Stop growling.

MARY: He's been in Finnegan's since opening time. Well, it won't be the first time his dinner had to be thrun out.

KEARNS (*handing Drumm a drink*): You see what I put up with? It's the price of me for spoiling her.

MARY (*mock anguish*): God forgive him.

KEARNS: I ought to have borrowed a page from your book. Dolly soon found out who the boss was. You used the whip from the first fence on, and now she's afraid to look crossways at you.

DRUMM: Is that meant to be funny?

KEARNS: That's where I slipped up: too much of a softy. Is it what?

DRUMM: That remark is both untrue and impertinent. Dolly has never been afraid of me.

KEARNS (*grinning*): He's a terror.

DRUMM: Not with cause that is. She's timid by nature, highly-strung, I grant you that. But to imply that I bully her—

MARY: Lar is joking.

DRUMM: Is he? I think not. And I'm sorry, but I do take exception. I despise tyrants, domestic or otherwise.

MARY: Sure we know. (*Glaring at Kearns.*) Trust you.

KEARNS: Trust me to what? Where's the harm in telling a man he wears the trousers? (*To Drumm.*) You're as prickly as bedamned: it's like talking to a gorse bush. Listen . . . good health. Delighted to see you.

He swallows most of his own drink with evident enjoyment.

MARY: That's him. A glass in his hand and not a care in the world. You're talking to us again after six years and he's not even inquisitive enough to ask why.

KEARNS: What's there to ask? He's here and he's welcome.

Drumm tells them he retires in August with pension and lump-sum gratuity. Dolly has plans for them to visit their daughter Stella in Canada, but Drumm doesn't want to accompany her. He has no curiosity about Canada; he finds both his daughters, Stella and Una, "too docile," and his grandchildren, who visited him last summer, "like pygmy lumberjacks." Dolly can make the trip alone, and perhaps she'll forget about wanting a motor car and be satisfied with living close to the bus stop. There are places to go and people to visit outside the range of the bus, Kearns argues. Kearns dreams of getting a car himself by landing a job as a sales representative with car supplied. They could have bought a car with the insurance money for Mary's accident, but Kearns generously told her that it was rightfully hers to spend any way she pleased, redoing the house.

Kearns describes the accident: they borrowed a car to drive to a niece's wedding. Mary was standing behind it when Kearns's foot slipped off the worn clutch pedal. The car moved backward, pinning Mary against a gate. "It could happen to a bishop," Kearns comments, but Drumm suggests that Kearns was probably drunk and continues in an accusatory vein: "You maim the woman for life, and then you have the gall, the impudence to put on airs because you magnanimously allow her to spend her own money as she chooses. . . . .As long as I've known you, you've been a millstone around her neck: soft, easy and worthless, an idler whose idea of hard work was having to stoop to pick up his dole money. I would have thought that trying to cripple her spirit would be enough for you, but apparently not: you wanted to break her body as well. I'm not surprised the boy left home."

Kearns is shaken by Drumm's onslaught, but he manages to take it with a laugh, without rancor. He exits, and Mary declares her anger at Drumm for his outburst. She hands him his coat and asks him to leave the house.

MARY: I don't want you back here.

DRUMM: Nonsense.
    His smile disappears as he realizes that she means it.
Or perhaps it isn't. Very well. *(Affronted.)* As you wish.
    He puts his coat on, watching as he does so for a sign that she may relent. Her face is tight with anger.
You know this is foolishness.

MARY: I won't have Lar talked to like that, by you or anyone.

DRUMM: Where is the crime in saying what every inhabitant of this town over the age of reason knows to be true? He is weak, shiftless and irresponsible. It's hardly a secret.

MARY *(wearily):* Will you go away.

DRUMM: I really don't understand you.
    He goes toward the steps and stops.

Would it change matters if . . .

MARY: No.

DRUMM: . . . if I were to tell you—

MARY: I said no.

DRUMM: I don't thank you for this. You force it upon me. If I'm to be forbidden this house it'll be on your conscience, I'll not have that on mine. I don't thank you at all. Ben Mulhall has just given me less than six months to live. Now am I to go?

> *The lights fade slowly. As if in counterpoint, music is heard: a dance version of "The Missouri Waltz."*

The lights come up in the kitchen area to reveal young Desmond and Lar playing a portable wind-up gramophone, Desmond resenting what he considers to be Lar's intrusion. Mibs comes in, warns them not to play music on Holy Thursday, then goes to get her coat. Lar boasts to Desmond of having a "coort" with older girls at "hops" during the slow tunes. Desmond spies a pencil in Lar's pocket and makes a joke of it. Lar admits pleasantly that he "couldn't even write a Christmas card to save me life. Mind, if I could, at least there's people I could send them to."

Mibs comes back and leaves a note for her parents, telling them she's gone for a walk. She hints that Desmond "has to be off home," and Lar signals Desmond to make himself scarce, but Desmond hangs on, suggesting scornfully that they go to a "hop." Lar accepts this challenge by grabbing the gramophone—which belongs to Mibs's mother—and heading for the bandstand.

The lights come up in the living room where Mary is refusing to believe that Drumm's doctor, Ben Mulhall, gave him such direct bad news about his illness. Drumm insists that it is so.

Lights come up on the bandstand where the young people are playing "The Missouri Waltz" on the gramophone. Lar pretends they're at a "hop" and swings his partner Mibs around.

MIBS: It's Holy Week. Do you want us to be read off the altar?

LAR: Who's to hear? They're all at the devotions. All the Holy Marys. Hey . . .

> *This, as Desmond gets to the gramophone and puts the brake on. A moan from the record as it slows down. Lar puts Mibs down.*

Feck off, that's not yours.

DESMOND: Is it yours?

> *A moment of confrontation. Desmond is between Lar and the gramophone. Lar is too easygoing to want to fight.*

LAR: Be a sport.

MIBS: Leave it off, or I'm going home. You loony, trying to get us a bad name. Oh God. There's someone coming. Quick.

LAR: It's all right for yous. Yous have coats, I'm freezin'.

> *Mibs sits on the steps. Desmond makes haste to sit beside her. Lar blows on his hands and comes down to sit on the other side.*

Dead losses the pair of you. Move over in the bed.

The focus shifts to the living room area, where Drumm is warning Mary not to tell Dolly about his illness, to postpone as long as possible the devoted attention Dolly would give him if she knew: "Beating a path between the chemist's and the church. . . . .She'll tell me hourly on the hour how vastly improved I look. She'll go about on tiptoe until my head splits. Her tenderness will saturate me like damp rot."

Mary tells Drumm he should appreciate Dolly's devotion, but Drumm foresees that the eventual attentions of Dolly and his daughters Stella and Una (who will have to be sent for) will render him totally helpless. Drumm suprises on Mary's face the look of pity that he detests. Mary insists that she is going to feel for him and pray for him, too.

DRUMM:. . . . .You know: I've been a Government employee for forty years . . . . .In our Department, when anyone retires, they have a presentation. A hat is passed. They give him a nest of tables or a set of Waterford. In August it'll be my turn, but I doubt if I'll put a strain on their pockets. I've indulged in unnatural practices with my subordinates, such as obliging them to do a day's work. But whatever it is, even if it's only a fountain pen from Woolworth's, I mean to have it. They won't be let off. I'll last that long. *(He looks up at the ceiling.)* Mary . . . our friend upstairs . . .

MARY: Do you mean Lar?

DRUMM: Is he likely to come in?

MARY: What you said to him, he took it to heart. You mightn't think so, but he did: I know him.

DRUMM *(his thoughts elsewhere):* Yes, I'm sure.

MARY: Will I tell him you didn't mean it?

DRUMM: Mary . . .

MARY: Ah, I will.

DRUMM *(there is an intensity in his voice which stops her):* Mary, I have to know what I amount to. Debit and credit, that much I am owed. If the account is to be closed, so be it: I demand an audit. Or show me the figures: I can add and subtract: I can do my own books. A man has rights: if he is solvent, tell him.

He realizes that Mary has not grasped his meaning.
(More calmly.) I have a most impressive new title at the office these days: Keeper of Records. My enemies grow cunning. It takes a rare kind of peasant villainy to inflict injury and promotion with the same stroke of the pen. I have been a thorn in too many sides, so they have given me a room to myself: the storeroom, where I can antagonize the four walls and abuse the dust. In this room there are files: so many, one could grow old counting them. Each file has a name and a number, and if I were God and breathed on them they would become lives. I seem to have access to everyone's life, except my own.

She has been watching rather than listening; sensing rather than under-standing.

DRUMM: Yes, you may tell him I didn't mean it, and then I must go. And Dolly is not to be told.

Mary goes to get Kearns, as Dolly's youthful counterpart, Dorothy *("She wears a home-knitted Tam-o'-Shanter, with a woollen scarf and gloves to match. She is carrying two library books"),* joins the other three young people on the bandstand. Mibs introduces Dorothy to the two boys and assures them Dorothy won't tell anyone they've been playing music on Holy Thursday. Desmond moves over to make room for her to sit next to him.

Mibs informs Desmond that Dorothy is "blue-mouldy with brains," second in her class and now attending "the Tech in Dun Laoghaire." Dorothy pretends she hadn't noticed Desmond before, though he lives near her. She explains to Desmond that her technical studies comprise typing, shorthand, bookkeeping and senior English, Lar tells them all a slightly off-color joke. Desmond looks at the volumes Dorothy is carrying, pronounces one of them trash and the other enjoyable.

MIBS *(suddenly):* Dolly Drumm.
DESMOND: What?
MIBS: I just remembered. It's a sort of game Dolly used to play.
DOROTHY: Mary, you're not to.
MIBS: When we were at school, like. Honestly. Whenever she'd meet a fellow, anyone at all, she'd put her name along with his.
DOROTHY: No, you're mean.
MIBS: To see how it would sound.
DOROTHY: It was for a joke.
MIBS: Trying it out, like.
DOROTHY: I was not.
MIBS: Dolly Drumm. God, that's the worst yet. Brutal.
> *Dorothy looks at the ground in embarrassment. Desmond is aloof, unamused.*
(Laughing, to Desmond.) There's your hash cooked for you.
DOROTHY *(without looking up; a whisper):* Stop it.
LAR: Hey . . .

Lar lightens the mood with a song, and then the attention shifts to the living room area where Mary enters with Kearns. Drumm apologizes somewhat awkwardly: "Mind, I hold to the substance of what I said, but this is your house and I was unmannerly." Kearns accepts it graciously: "Will you go 'long outa that." Drumm continues, "I ought not to have mentioned the lad. . . . .young Sean," and Kearns manages flatly, "Sure you didn't."

Mary insists that Drumm and Dolly make the reconciliation official by coming over for a visit after tea.

DRUMM: About Dolly: I'll give her this much: she's loyal. Our long silence, yours and mine: she had no part in it. So if she stopped coming here . . .
KEARNS *(amused):* If she what?
MARY *(a warning):* Hold your tongue.

DRUMM: . . . That was my doing, not hers. You mustn't be cross with Dolly.

MARY: Cross with Dolly? Ah, have sense.

Kearns exits. Drumm reminds Mary of the time he was trying to teach her Chesterton's poem including the couplet "But walk with clearer eyes and ears this path that wandereth/And see undrugg'd in evening light the decent inn of death." Drumm comments, "It isn't a decent inn, Mary. When you get up close, it's a bordello."

Drumm leaves the house and goes up the steps of the bandstand, where he stops to watch the memory figures of his youth. Dorothy is admitting to Desmond that she *has* noticed him in the town and knows he's in the civil service. Over Mibs's protest, Lar turns on the gramophone and forces her to dance with him.

DESMOND: Kearns, you stop that.
> *Mibs, yielding, begins to dance with Lar. Encouraged, he holds her close. Desmond looks on, consumed with jealousy.*

LAR: That's the girl.

MIBS: I'm going to be murdered.

LAR: Hey, Cough-Bottle, how about this for a coort, wha'?

DESMOND: Kearns!
> *He goes into the bandstand and makes for the gramophone.*

MIBS *(laughing):* God, if someone sees us . . .
> *Desmond stops the gramophone.*

LAR: Ah, will you put it back on.

DESMOND: You were told to stop.

LAR: Quit actin' the maggot. Fair do's now: give Dolly a dance, come on.
> *He takes a step forward.*

DESMOND: I warned you.
> *He takes the record from the turntable.*

LAR: Sure, you did.

DESMOND: I mean it.

LAR: Look, don't be such a—
> *Desmond deliberately smashes the record. Mibs screams. For a moment, Desmond is appalled by his own action, then, as Lar moves forward, he attempts to take the other records from the lid. Lar picks him up and sets him down on the other side of the bandstand.*

DESMOND: You guttersnipe.
> *He rushes at Lar, who holds him off effortlessly. Desmond strikes out at him, but every intended blow falls short.*

LAR: Easy, now. What the hell is the—

DESMOND *(flailing):* Damned cornerboy . . . you leave her alone . . . you lout, you blackguard, I'll kill you.
> *Lar grins at the ease with which he keeps him at bay. Desmond is close to tears.*

DOROTHY: Mary, stop them.

Pat Hingle as Kearns, Roy Dotrice as Drumm, Adam Redfield as Desmond (young Drumm) and David Ferry as Lar (young Kearns) in *A Life*

MIBS: Yes. Desmond . . . Lar, will yous stop it.
>*Drumm enters the bandstand from the rear. He shoulders his way between Desmond and Lar, causing them to fall apart. He looks at them, his eyes filled with his own pain and anger.*
DRUMM: Be damned the lot of you!
>*Drumm leaves the stage. The others remain. A clock strikes two o'clock. Curtain.*

ACT II

On the bandstand later the same day, Dolly is telling Drumm that the Kearns's redecorating cost a great deal; and when Drumm wants to know how Dolly knows about this, she quickly assures him she heard it in the town.

Dorothy moves toward the Kearns's house, but Drumm lingers as "The Missouri Waltz" makes itself heard in the background. Young Desmond appears. Young Dorothy comes in too and listens as Desmond rehearses a speech for a debate on Irish politics. Dorothy has come to tell Desmond that Mary can't go to the debate with him, pleading a necessary visit to the dentist because of a toothache.

DOROTHY: Her father is dragging her there. I know she'd miles rather go and listen to you and suffer.
He looks at her as if suspecting a gibe. Her face is ingenuous.
Really, she's as cross as two sticks. I mean, who wouldn't be? She said to me: "He'll be there, standing his ground against Government ministers and professors out of colleges and such. The whole town will see him except me."
DESMOND: She won't miss much.
DOROTHY: Do you hear him! Anyway, she said all the best.
DESMOND: It's my first time, you know.
DOROTHY: Go on. After this, you won't talk to us.
DESMOND: Far too grand, yes.
DOROTHY: You might be. Wait till you see tomorrow's papers: you'll be a stone's throw from famous. Do you know what my father says? "Young Desmond Drumm? . . . oh, he's a born genius."
DESMOND: Yes, I'm much liked by fathers.
DOROTHY: From this out, there'll be no stopping you. And Mary is going to be very sorry, you'll see.

Desmond suspects that Mibs's tooth problem may be a fabrication to avoid going to the debate with him. She's going out with Lar, he supposes—but Dorothy assures him Lar is going to the debate with a claque to cheer Desmond on. And Dorothy tells Desmond, "I thought I might go as well. . . . .if nobody minded."

Desmond, obviously suffering from stage fright, rechecks his notes, as Drumm and Dolly join Mary and Kearns in the living room area. Kearns pretends he hasn't seen Dolly in "donkey's years" and gives her a knowing wink. In the midst of their small talk, Dolly all but gives herself away (she has been visiting the Kearnses by herself every Friday morning during Drumm's six years of not speaking, and she can't remember to pretend she's seeing the redecoration for the first time).

Mary and Dolly go into the kitchen, as Kearns prepares to serve Drumm whiskey with his tea. Kearns is supposed to stay away from hard liquor but, Kearns believes, Drumm can drink as much of it as he pleases, because Drumm's acid-glutted system neutralizes any harmful effects.

Kearns mentions a recently-deceased friend whose funeral drew a large crowd, and Drumm comments: "I'd expect no less. He worked hard and lived decently, and by now he'll have given his mind back to the Almighty in the same unused condition as he received it. Why shouldn't they pack the church? All his life he ran with the herd and honored the eleventh commandment: Thou shalt not make the rest of us seem inferior."

Drumm pleases Kearns to the point of blushing by commenting that Kearns will have a huge funeral, too, some day; then he makes Kearns uneasy by bringing up the subject of his son Sean, whom Drumm took under his wing. Kearns sometimes gets news of his son in letters from Sean to his mother. Sean is teaching in a school near London; was married but is now separated from his wife.

DRUMM: He had no right to go, not as he did.

KEARNS: Ah, well.

DRUMM: Ah, well what?

KEARNS: That's the way o' the world.

DRUMM: Will you stop mouthing banalities? He had a life here: his people. I'd have thought better of him: it showed a want of feeling.

KEARNS: Sean and me never hit it off. Chalk an' cheese.

DRUMM *(reluctant to seem to care):* Does he ask for me?

KEARNS: Hoh?

DRUMM: In his letters.

KEARNS: Oh, I'm sure he does.

DRUMM: Well, does he or doesn't he?

KEARNS: Yes. Oh, catch him forgettin'. "How's . . . uh, Uncle Dezzie?"
       Drumm glares at him, not convinced.

Dolly and Mary enter from the kitchen (where the Mibs character has been sitting, weeping gently, through the foregoing) bringing the tea.

Mibs calls out for her parents but gets no answer and remains sitting at the kitchen table.

Dolly has told Mary about Drumm's talk to the tourists. They all speak very flatteringly of Drumm's ability, remembering the debate of years ago.

Desmond leaves the bandstand in a state of nervous anticipation of the debate. Dorothy follows him, speaking words of encouragement.

Dolly tries to make Drumm commit himself to the task of writing a book about the town's history. "You have all the time you want now," she reminds him. Mary is quick to change the subject.

Kearns assures Drumm that the morning after the debate "The talk in the town was that you might end up runnin' the country." Drumm remembers the debate differently: Lar and his friends sitting on a window sill gave Desmond a weak cheer when he rose to speak. The crowd began to shout at him, and he lost his nerve: "Whenever I used a word with more than two syllables, they hooted. I skipped to the end, I fled to it." The parish priest restored order, and the debate continued.

The Desmond figure runs onstage *"in flight from the humiliation of his speech,"* stopping by the bandstand and holding onto one of the pillars, retching. In the living room, however, Drumm is pretending to his listeners that after his speech "I was calm, quite unperturbed. You see, I understood. It was a punishment. I had broken the eleventh commandment."

Dolly admits she cried that evening, but Drumm still maintains that the episode amused him: "I had discovered that cleverness was like having a deformed hand. It was tolerated as long as you kept a glove on it."

Dorothy enters in the background looking for Desmond, who runs off, Dorothy following him.

Drumm admits he'd hoped to be admired at the debate, to become "one of our own." Never again did he try to please "the implacable."

Desmond joins Mibs who is still in obvious distress in the kitchen area (representing her home in this scene, not the Kearns's). Mibs confesses to Desmond that she was not taken to the dentist by her father, but to the priest, because of a letter she received from Lar, opened and read by her father. Mibs goes about making tea for Desmond, while telling him that the letter professed Lar's love for Mibs. It described in affectionate detail an incident of their passionate lovemaking on the railway embankment, in which Mibs nevertheless "didn't go all the way with him. . . . .because I haven't the nerve."

Deeply hurt, Desmond suggests that the only thing left for Mibs to do now is marry Lar, thought she clearly hasn't made up her mind that she wants to.

MIBS: He hasn't even a proper job. Give over.

DESMOND: Jobs aren't important. I think you should marry him because I think you're his sort.

MIBS: Yeah, the perfect—*(Her smile dies away as the insult goes home.)*

DESMOND: And you won't need a railway back then, will you, or to be afraid of going all the way with him.

MIBS: Ah, Desmond—

DESMOND: No, you could do worse. I doubt if you'll do better. And you'll be much more your own self at his level than at . . . anyone else's.

> *She realizes that he is determined to tear down their relationship past all chance of repair. She starts to clear the tea things.*

MIBS: Sure. Go on, now: go home.

DESMOND: Mm, it's all hours. I'm sure you'll have a happy life. You'll make a nice home for him perhaps in one of those cottages in the Alley lane. He needs someone like you: you can help him count his dole money.

MIBS *(waiting for him to go):* Yeah, thanks.

DESMOND: Because—

MIBS: I said, go. You done what you wanted: you said what can't be took back.

DESMOND: Taken back.

> *He is unable to leave ill enough alone. He wants to draw blood, needs to be certain that her hurt equals his own.*

I'm very stupid. I mistook you for someone with self-respect. It was my fault. I thought that at least your ambitions went higher than Lar Kearns.

MIBS: Do you mean you?

DESMOND: I was wrong.

MIBS: Yes . . . you do. Well at least Lar is a bit of gas. I can laugh with him. He's glad of me the way I am. I don't need to have a scaffolding put around me brain before I'm fit to be seen with him. He can give a body a coort and a kiss, and they know it's a person, not bones and cold skin. . . . .

Desmond may think well of himself, Mibs adds, but the town thinks differently. They laugh at him and consider the Drumms a bit "cracked."

Desmond leaves as the lights fade in the kitchen and come up on the living room, where Drumm is in a mood of genial reminiscence, joking about a time when a baby bird they found and placed in a nest with others turned out to be a cuckoo. On a more somber note, Drumm remembers the priest coming to the house after Drumm's father was killed taking a short cut through a railroad tunnel. The priest questioned the boy to determine whether his father's seeming accident was in reality a suicide. Drumm has since concluded that "If the poor man, as you call him, did die by accident, it was by the same law of probability as being run down by the Dun Laoghaire mailboat halfway up the Volga."

The other three prefer to think of the schoolmaster's death as an accident, particularly Dolly who can't bear the thought of a suicide's soul in mortal sin. Drumm comments bitterly: "God made him, let God put up with him. At least He knew him: I never did. Whatever was breakable in him, he kept under lock and key, away from vandals. Sooner a shuttered house than a plundered one. You were welcome to what was left, what passed for all there was of him . . . the bones and cold skin. If he ever tried to speak to me, or to anyone, it was in that tunnel. And damn them: they called it an accident, so he said nothing."

Drumm makes a move to depart, but Kearns insists that his guests stay for at least one drink, which he prepares while he reminisces about the days of steam trains (a palpable gaffe which he hurriedly glosses over), nuns in striped bathing suits and other colorful memories of the good old days. Dolly and Mary share a private giggle over something Kearns has said, and soon Dolly has to leave the room to control her laughter.

Kearns presses on to tell them of the best thing that ever happened to him in his whole life. He was flat broke, but he won a couple of shillings playing pitch-and-toss and bought a sweepstakes ticket. He drew a horse, Workman, which won the race and 50 pounds for Kearns: "Fifty quid put into me fist, and I mean fifty quid then, not now. We were landed. . . . .We were in the clear. Everythin' back from the pawn—may I drop down dead, I had to borry a handcart—and the pram and the stuff for the baby bought and paid for." Kearns states his belief that God provided then and God will always provide for those that have faith.

DRUMM: Ah, yes. Don't dig the garden: pray for an earthquake.

KEARNS: Jeer away.

DRUMM: Faith? If either of us, you or I, had a scrap of it, we'd be in a monastery living on black bread and doing atonement. What we have is hope. We call it faith.

KEARNS: Rubbidge.

DRUMM: Mind, I'll concede that as a race we have more to believe in than others. Christians elsewhere worship three Divine Beings: God the Father, God the Son and God the Holy Ghost. We have added a fourth: God the Jockey.

KEARNS: You won't act the hard root when your time comes.

MARY: Now, Lar . . .

KEARNS: Then what'll you do?

DRUMM: Envy your certainty.

KEARNS (crowing): Ah! You've had it too soft, Dezzie. No goin' short, nothin' to pray for. A grand cushy job with a collar an' tie on it, an' a pension in the wind-up.

MARY: Don't row with the man.

KEARNS: What rowin'? Sure more power to him. I'm only sayin' that poor people like ourselves, them that has it hard, we're more in with God, like, than the rest of them.

DRUMM: He's one of your own.

KEARNS *(delighted):* Now you have it. *(Grabbing Drumm's glass.)* Gimme that.

DRUMM: I won't.

KEARNS *(masterful):* I say you will.

DRUMM: A cushy job, you called it. Perhaps it is. But a man who carves penny whistles at least knows his own worth: I don't know mine. If I licked envelopes all day, the pay would be the same. I spend a third of my life in a hot-house of intrigue and skulduggery which would make the court of the Borgias seem like a whist drive, and I do work of doubtful value for a government of doubtful morality. Cogito, ergo sum. I am a cog, therefore I am.

Kearns reminds Drumm that he's "on the home stretch now," with a pension and lump sum for his and Dolly's pleasure. Kearns goes on about what a wonderful girl Dolly is, the perfect one for Drumm, "Only you were slow in findin' out, on account of you had a soft spot for this one." Kearns always was perfectly aware that Desmond was a rival for Mary's affections. "I bested you," Kearns tells Drumm, "But you got Dolly, and she's a credit to you. . . . .a smasher, so she is."

Drumm is somewhat nettled by this line of talk, but he keeps his temper and suggests that Kearns pay his compliments to Dolly directly, in person. "Many's the time" he's done just that, Kearns declares, as recently as last Friday right here in this house. With this, Kearns has let the cat out of the bag about Dolly's visits during the six years Drumm was not on speaking terms. Kearns tries to gloss this over, but to no avail; Drumm has heard and understood. Mary takes a more direct tack.

MARY *(to Drumm):* She came in for a cup of coffee. She'd do her shoppin' and buy the few things for the week, and she'd come and I'd put the kettle on. No harm in that.

Drumm is silent.

Ten minutes the one day in the week. She has her neighbors: who else has she? Do you expect her to live like a statue? I said to her: "Tell him, why can't you?" She said: "I'm afraid to."

Drumm does not react. A faint cough as Dolly comes into the living room.

Now let it lie. You will.

DOLLY: Honestly and truly, I'm weak from laughing. Look at me: I'm a sight for the crows.

Drumm looks toward her.

You're very quiet. Is something up?

Touching her hair.

Is it me?

Lights down in the living room area and up in the kitchen, where Lar is showing off a new suit to Desmond and Mibs. With "The banns called, the new suit bought and the chapel booked," Lar and Mibs are soon to be married. Mibs's father has arranged a job for Lar working on the trams in the yard. Desmond has brought a present, and Lar unwraps it—it is a framed print of a Van Gogh still life (which still hangs in the Kearns living room). Lar takes the gift in stride, but Mibs admires it greatly: "It's like whoever done it . . . got himself inside of it." Because of her sensitive reaction, Desmond almost dares to approach Mibs one more time right here in front of Lar, but she forestalls him: ". . . . .With Lar there'd be a bit of me left over. Not with you: you'd want the lot. The bit of me that's not yours at all: that likes to go to a do or a hop and sing songs on the road home. Or talk too loud and say 'Shag it' and be what you call common. You'd take it all: there'd be nothing left for Lar, not even the bit of harmless likin'. You don't know where halfway is. Lar does: he's glad of what you can give him. He won't begrudge you the bit of me that's yours."

Desmond accepts her verdict, takes his leave stiffly. Lar admits he doesn't think much of the print, but he wouldn't hurt Desmond's feelings by telling him so. Mibs reads the card that came with the gift—another couplet from Chesterton —and comments, "He'd make me finish that bloody poem if it killed him."

Lights fade in the kitchen and come up in the living room, where Dolly is sitting tensely while Mary tries first to cajole and then to bully Drumm into forgiving Dolly what was, after all, a very minor offense. It's not the act itself but the deception that's hard to forgive, Drumm tells them—Dolly's visiting the Kearnses behind his back, no doubt with the whole town knowing and laughing at him. Mary continues on the offensive, broadening her attack.

MARY:. . . . .They made a mock of you because you were out of step, so you got your own back on them. You stopped walkin'. You were going to do the divil and all: yes, you were . . . but no, you might get laughed at. You let on they're not worth passing the time of day with, but they rule you.

DOLLY: Mary, they do not.

DRUMM: Thank you, I can defend myself.

MARY: It's true: they bett you.

DRUMM: Beat me.

MARY: However you say it.

DRUMM: I fear them, yes. I fear their easy freemasonry. But if I failed to do what you call the devil and all, it wasn't on their account. It was because the devil and all wasn't in me. But I'll tell you what is. I've never lied to or about a man. I've never smiled into the face of a knave, or pretended to see virtue where I found none. Or been a loafer or a hanger-on, or a licker of boots. I don't call that a total defeat. I grant you there's a debit side to those accounts. Too much pride, too little charity. And if it makes you happy, the reason I was angry with Dolly is that I can no longer afford to be angry with her. I consider that . . . an impertinence.

> Mary's smile is hard as she turns to Dolly. Inside her, probably to her own surprise, an old wound has been re-opened.

Both Kearns and Mary accept this statement of Drumm's as a sign of forgiveness—or as close to it as Drumm is ever likely to come. Dolly in her turn admits,

"I'm glad Dezzie found out. . . . .because I hate anything that's hole-and-corner."

Both Drumm and Kearns have noticed how aggressively Mary approached this crisis between Drumm and Dolly. Kearns is glad that Mary's interfering between husband and wife didn't have serious consequences. Mary justifies it: "He interfered between *us,*" and the tension mounts again with her accusation. Kearns denies this; Drumm does too, and Dolly warns him, "Dezzie, leave it. She's upset." Drumm obeys and prepares to leave, but Mary holds him, telling him she means to grant his request to be advised of the debits and credits of his life. Drumm was very good to their son Sean (Mary tells Drumm), spending time with him, making sure he got a good education, paying for his Confirmation suit.

MARY:. . . . .It was "Uncle Desmond, Uncle Desmond" . . . That's all we ever heard out of him. Now I'm not saying you meant to do it—

KEARNS: I'm boss here, and I'm telling you No.

MARY: I'm not saying that. But you turned him against Lar.

KEARNS *(at Drumm and Dolly):* Get out, get out.

DRUMM: No. It is untrue.

MARY: Maybe without meaning to . . .

DRUMM: It is untrue.

MARY: His father was good for nothing. He was lazy. He was useless. He smelled of porter. He was ignorant.

KEARNS *(weakly):* I told you. The lad an' me . . . ile an' water.

DRUMM: This is not true.

MARY: You never said a word against Lar: I'll give you that. But you schooled Sean well: he heard you talk to Lar and he seen you look at him. Sean couldn't be in the same room with him. Do you wonder he got the idea into his head?

KEARNS: She's tellin' lies.

DRUMM: Idea? Tell me . . . what idea?

MARY: He said it to us. The time he had the row with Lar and went off to England. It's why you've heard the last of him. The exam he passed that summer and the marks they gave him. Maybe he wondered where he got his brains from.

Drumm and Mary look at each other. A pause.

KEARNS: Dezzie, listen . . .

MARY: Be quite now.

KEARNS: . . . a bee in his bonnet.

MARY *(ignoring him, to Drumm):* So now you can do your adding up.

DRUMM: Are you trying to tell me that the boy left because he thought I was his father?

KEARNS: Not at all. Not at all. *(To Mary.)* All them years gone by, dead an' buried. What the hell did you want to go upsettin' the man for?

MARY: It wasn't to harm him.

DRUMM: I don't accept it. Very well: I took too much upon myself. He was your son: I meddled, I went where I had no business to go. But I'd go there again, because it was to find the boy a place in the world, away from street corners. He was a fine boy: worthwhile . . . he had manners. I cared for him. But to put that idea into his head, to work that kind of mischief: no. Not I.

DOLLY: Dezzie wouldn't, Mary. It's not in him.

DRUMM *(looking at Mary):* Not even without meaning to.

KEARNS: Sure, don't we know, aren't we sayin'? Me oul' comrade, wha'?

DRUMM *(to Kearns):* And you. You've known why the boy went, what he believed, and all these years you've made me welcome in this house.

KEARNS: Why wouldn't I? Aren't we pals, tried an' true, the last o' the oul' stock? Put it there!

Drumm accepts his hand. It is the nearest he has come to liking Kearns.

DRUMM: You really are an impossible man.

KEARNS: And in the heel o' the hunt wasn't it tit for tat? I took your one here offa you. So you took the lad, and aren't we even?

Drumm looks at him in shock. It is as if a blow had been struck.

Kearns starts to offer Drumm another drink, but Drumm goes, followed by Dolly, carrying his coat. The lights go down in the living room and up on the bandstand, where Drumm pauses for breath and where his memory figures of Desmond, Dorothy, Lar and an obviously pregnant Mibs are contemplating an afternoon stroll. Lar offers to show them a bird's nest and leads Dorothy off. Desmond and Mibs follow.

Dolly helps Drumm on with his coat and tells him not to mind what Mary said, she talks that way only because she is jealous: "She missed her chance" at the first prize, "the brainiest boy in the town." But Drumm is now convinced that he has spent his life doing work he hates and accomplishing nothing.

DRUMM:. . . . .Instead of friends, I've had standards, and woe betide those who failed to come up to them. Well, *I* failed. My contempt for the town, for the wink and the easy nod and the easier grin . . . it was cowardice: Mary was right. What I called principles was vanity. What I called friendship was malice.

DOLLY: Will you go 'way. This is because Mary upset you.

DRUMM: Not much to boast of at the end of the day.

DOLLY: The end, how are you.

DRUMM: Well, is it?

DOLLY: You're in the glooms: I'm not going to answer you. And if it was true itself . . .

DRUMM: Well?

DOLLY: And it isn't, not a blessed word of it. You have me as bad as yourself.

DRUMM: Go on. If it were true itself . . .

DOLLY: I was going to say, if it *was* true, it needn't be from now on. I mean, Dezzie, are we alive or aren't we? *(Pause.)* Now don't stand here: come home. Look at the way the evenings are getting a stretch: there's still light in the sky.

DRUMM: I have a question.

DOLLY *(smiling):* More silliness.

DRUMM: If I were to offer you a choice between buying a motor car—

DOLLY *(excited):* Dezzie!

DRUMM: Be quiet. Between that and my writing a book about this place. Which would you choose?

DOLLY *(after a pause):* The motor car.

DRUMM *(a little sadly):* Of course you would.

DOLLY: Because . . . whatever I want, you do the opposite.

DRUMM: You are a most aggravating woman: you get more foolish every day. All right . . . off home with you. Make a start.

> *Dolly starts off. Drumm hears "The Missouri Waltz." A drop of rain hits his cheek. He feels it and holds out his hand to check. He turns the collar of his raincoat up and starts off. Curtain.*

LUNCH HOUR

A Comedy in Two Acts

BY JEAN KERR

Cast and credits appear on page 355

JEAN KERR, nee Jean Collins, was born in Scranton, Pa. July 10, 1923. Possibly she inherited some penchant for the stage, not neccessarily through her father, who was a construction foreman, but on the side of her mother, who was Eugene O'Neill's second cousin. Miss Collins was educated at Mary Wood Seminary and Mary Wood College in Scranton, graduating in 1943. Shortly thereafter, on August 16, 1943, she married the man who was to become America's leading drama critic, Walter Kerr, then a teacher of drama at Catholic University in Washington, D.C., changing both her name and her byline to Jean Kerr.

Mrs. Kerr received her M.A. at Catholic University in 1944. It was while she and her husband were teaching there, in 1946, that they adapted Franz Werfel's novel The Song of Bernadette *into a play which made Broadway for only 3 performances. In 1948 Mrs. Kerr's first comedy,* Jenny Kissed Me, *played on Broadway for 20 performances, and in 1949 Mr. and Mrs. Kerr wrote the revue* Touch and Go, *a 176-performance hit. Mrs. Kerr contributed sketches to* John Murray Anderson's Almanac *in 1953 and followed this up with the comedy (written in collaboration with Eleanor Brooke)* King of Hearts, *directed by her husband and produced in 1954 for 279 performances. The musical* Goldilocks, *with book by the Kerrs and lyrics by the Kerrs and Joan Ford, was produced in 1958 for 161 performances under Walter Kerr's direction.*

In 1961 Mrs. Kerr had her biggest hit to date with the comedy Mary, Mary *which was named a Best Play of its season and became Broadway's all-time sixth longest-running play with 1,572 performances ending in 1964 (in the present era*

of sensationally long runs, it is still in the top 20). Her Poor Richard *followed in
1964 for 118 performances, and then there was* Finishing Touches *in 1973 for 164
performances, a Best Play of its season. This year's comedy* Lunch Hour *is her third
Best Play and tenth Broadway production—none of them, we hasten to add, ever
reviewed publicly by her husband.*

Mrs. Kerr's other writings have included a stage adaptation of Our Hearts Were
Young and Gay *for amateur and stock performance, and many articles and essays
collected into books with titles such as* Please Don't Eat the Daisies, The Snake
Has All the Lines *and* Penny Candy. *Hollywood films have been made of* Daisies
(which also became a TV series), King of Hearts *and* Mary, Mary. *As everyone
who can read must know by now, the Kerrs live in a baronial house they discovered
on the shore of Long Island Sound in Larchmont, and they are the parents of six
children, five sons (including one pair of twins) and a daughter.*

Time: Summertime

Place: A house in the Hamptons, Long Island

ACT I

SYNOPSIS: The living room of the second-floor apartment of a beach house is
entered from the front door at left, gives off into other rooms at right and
overlooks the ocean from a sun deck beyond glass doors upstage. Oliver DeVreck,
36, a psychiatrist, is reading the proofs of his new book. His wife Nora answers
the phone when it rings. She refers the caller to her husband's Manhattan number.

NORA *(to Oliver, as she hangs up):* Obviously, one of your ladies. She sounded
very tense.

OLIVER *(a trace of exasperation):* They are not my ladies, they are my patients.
And why on earth would you offer to give her the New York number? She'd just
get the answering service.

NORA: Because I wanted to sound lovable and cooperative. Not jealous and
suspicious.

OLIVER: Why are you suspicious?

NORA: Because she said her name was Mrs. Amaganset.

OLIVER: And?

NORA: You know there is nowhere, anywhere, a Mrs. Amaganset. There are
no Amagansets.

OLIVER: Wasn't that a tribe? Maybe she's an indian.

NORA: I don't know about indians, but I can tell you that this woman just didn't
want to give her real name.

OLIVER: And you conclude—?

NORA: I don't conclude, I never conclude. I'm over all that.

OLIVER: You're over it? What have you got to be over?

NORA: Let's not, okay? Let's just not. But I do have one question. How come you won't answer the phone?

OLIVER *(back to work):* But you know how come.

NORA: I know you're trying to finish that book. But then you've been trying to finish it for eighteen months. That never kept your great heart from caring about the needy beautiful women.

OLIVER: For God's sake, Nora.

NORA: I'm sorry. Erase that, I never said it.

OLIVER: But you did say it—

NORA: Well, there you are. It's a flareup of my old paranoia. It's like bursitis. You think you're over it, and then suddenly you start getting these damn little twinges.

Oliver remains silent.

Come on, Oliver. I'm declaring a cease-fire.

OLIVER: Okay, okay—

Nora suggests they go swimming, the ocean looks so inviting. Oliver is determined to stick to his proofreading, so Nora leaves to visit her mother a few doors down the beach, but taking the car rather than walking.

The phone rings—it's Oliver's publisher reminding him the book is due at the end of the week. The doorbell rings insistently, and Oliver cuts off his phone conversation to answer it. There on his doorstep is Carrie Sachs, 23, *"pretty and seems somewhat fussed. She is slender, and her clothes are well made but somehow less than chic."* Carrie looks Oliver over, decides she must have the wrong house. But when he closes the door she rings the bell again and this time enters the room, though she won't tell Oliver what her name is. She is the "Mrs. Amaganset" who just phoned, and she expected to see Nora here, not Nora's husband. Now she wants a cab to take her away again.

Oliver calls the cab, urging them to "hurry it up." He offers Carrie a drink while waiting. Carrie settles for water. The phone rings again—this time it's Nora, calling about a minor household problem. Oliver suggests that Carrie can now talk to Nora on the phone, but Carrie refuses to do so, challenging Oliver to ask his wife to put her mother on the phone. Oliver hangs up the phone and asks Carrie, "Why are you so certain that my wife wasn't with her mother?" Carrie replies promptly, "Because she's with my husband."

Oliver makes a joke of this statement. He is amused by his voluble visitor and manages to settle her into a chair and offer her something to eat. But Carrie begins to weep and to unburden herself to Oliver: her husband was a widower with a child (his first wife was charming but promiscuous) and married Carrie because at that time she was greatly overweight.

Carrie makes a move to depart, but when she discovers that Oliver is a psychiatrist who specializes in marriage counseling, her curiosity about him becomes intense. She finds that she has read his book *Settled Out of Court* and comments, "My God, maybe I'll be in your next one, slightly disguised—'Sally, bursting in like a raving maniac, definitely flabby from her recent weight-loss, her body a question mark expressing fear, doubt, pain.'"

Oliver decides that now he definitely needs a drink. There is nothing in the

Gilda Radner as Carrie, Sam Waterston as Oliver and Max Wright as Leo in *Lunch Hour*

house, so he phones his landlord Leo, who lives in an apartment downstairs, to borrow some bourbon. Meanwhile, Carrie goes on.

CARRIE: Do you know what is sad about your book?
OLIVER: Everything, I gather.
CARRIE: I mean sad-wistful. Most of the people who come to you are women. I guess that means that women are more helpless, more desperate.
OLIVER: No, they're just more practical. If the dishwasher breaks, a woman calls a plumber. A man says, "I'll look into it." Five days later he looks into it with a putty knife—and now it needs a whole new unit. Women are quicker to get professional help.
CARRIE: These women that come to you—do they have sexual problems?
OLIVER: Sometimes.
CARRIE: Do you—uh—console them?
OLIVER: What you really mean is do I sleep with them.
CARRIE: I didn't mean that.
OLIVER: Yes you did. And no, I don't. I don't think bartenders should drink.
CARRIE: I don't get it. *(Very slight pause.)* I get it. You think it's unsuitable.

OLIVER: And unethical. And, as a matter of fact, illegal.

CARRIE: Can I ask you one more question?

OLIVER: No.

CARRIE: But this is really important. It's my whole life that's broken down. *(Breaking.)* Peter won't talk to me. We never talk about important things. The thing is, I talk, and he sort of smiles and takes his glasses off and listens to me. I don't understand why he takes his glasses off to listen. And then he chews on the ear-piece, and he can actually talk this way.

> *She demonstrates with a pair of sunglasses from her pocket.*

Why does he do that? There must be some deep psychological reason.

OLIVER: Or did he just recently stop smoking?

CARRIE: As a matter of fact, he did! That's really very perceptive of you. I should take you more seriously.

OLIVER *(leaning forward on the desk and staring at her):* I don't want your cab to come. I think you should stay on for the whole summer. I think we should grow old together.

CARRIE *(hearing the sarcasm):* Oh—

OLIVER: But I'm serious. This is a valuable learning experience. I've never had a nervous breakdown before.

Carrie repeats to Oliver that his wife is "playing around" (he still doesn't take her seriously). Carrie insists over Oliver's protests that they are going to get to know each other better; meanwhile the landlord Leo comes in from the deck area carrying a cup of whiskey. No longer thinking about the drink, Oliver begs Leo to take Carrie out of here and drive her somewhere—anywhere. But Leo and Carrie are now preoccupied with greeting each other. They are old friends. Leo compliments her on her dramatic weight loss, and Carrie compliments him on a recent performance of Benvolio (Leo is an actor). Carrie catches him up on her news: she has married Peter Sachs, who "doesn't exactly do anything. He's rich for a living."

Oliver goes out of the room on an errand, and Carrie immediately wants to know what Oliver's wife is like. Before Leo can tell her, the phone rings and Oliver returns. He gets Leo to answer the phone—it's Nora, on her way home, asking if Oliver wants anything from the deli.

Carrie is reluctant to meet Oliver's wife, and Leo offers her a refuge in his apartment, which is in total disarray at the moment—he exits to go and straighten it up before Carrie comes downstairs. Alone with Oliver, however, Carrie decides she must meet Nora face to face. Oliver suggests she make an appointment to talk to Nora some other time.

CARRIE: . . . . .Mrs. DeVreck wouldn't make an appointment with me!

OLIVER: What makes you so sure of that?

CARRIE: Because if she has any decency at all, she'd feel too guilty. . . . .She has to be a decent person, because otherwise somebody as nice as Peter is— wouldn't like her. *(Starts to cry.)* Like her—he loves her! He told me he loves her. He shouldn't have told me this.

OLIVER *(quietly, seriously):* Look, I am really sorry. Really. And I ask you to believe that I'm not exactly the cold haddock I appear to be. After a while, you find ways to protect yourself. Let's just say that my heart has cried wolf too often.

CARRIE: But do you want her back?

OLIVER: She hasn't gone anywhere.

CARRIE: That's a silly statement! Do they have to fly to Bermuda to make it real for you? You just want this thing to blow over. I want it to *be* over! Don't you?

OLIVER: Yes, yes, all right, yes. But what could you say to her that I couldn't say?

CARRIE: I could explain to her the difference between her situation and my situation. Peter wouldn't tell her. He'd be too loyal. And isn't that crazy? I still think of Peter as loyal.

OLIVER: And what is this difference?

CARRIE: You've only just met me. But can't you tell! My problem first, last and always is that I am a beautiful person. Everybody says so. *(Imitating.)* "Carrie is a beautiful person."

OLIVER: And what does that mean?

CARRIE: First it means that I'm not beautiful. And the rest of it means that I'm quick and reliable and I have a good disposition. Exactly the qualities you'd look for if you were buying a Labrador retriever.

Peter has been the only man in her life, Carrie continues. She likens herself to an air fern—the only way you can tell it ever was alive is when it turns brown and dies. Carrie believes she can make Nora understand that though Peter is replaceable in Nora's life, he isn't in Carrie's.

Perhaps an affair with Leo might make Peter take notice of her, Carrie suggests —fighting fire with fire. Dangerous, Oliver warns. Then Carrie looks at Oliver speculatively, but Oliver backs off. Carrie is about to pursue this ironic possibility, when the phone rings. It's a patient of Oliver's in an emotional crisis. Oliver goes to take the call in the next room. Just as Carrie hangs up the phone in the living room, there is a sound at the front door. Carrie goes to open it and finds Nora standing there, her arms loaded with grocery bags. Nora is taken aback by the sight of a stranger on the inside of her threshold, but she soon understand that this is the mysterious "Mrs. Amaganset" and is startled to discover that she is Carrie Sachs, Peter's wife.

"And you're Peter's girl friend," Carrie declares, putting Nora on the defensive. Nora explains that she and Peter met by chance and had lunch a couple of times, and then "One day we were walking back to the car. And I guess he wanted to know what time it was. Anyway, he reached down and picked up my wrist to look at my watch—he wasn't wearing one. That's all there was to it. He was holding my wrist and we didn't say anything. And I knew what was going to happen, and I'm so very, very sorry."

Carrie, embarrassed, pretends to be preoccupied with preventing the wet grocery bag from leaving a ring on the table. She finally comes to the point.

CARRIE: . . . . .I know all that. Peter told me. Well, not about the wrist watch, but everything else. But that's just half the story. And I can feel in my bones that you don't have a clue about the other half.

NORA: What other half? What are you talking about?

CARRIE: That's what I figured. You don't know. And I don't want to be the one that has to tell you. Though, in all the circumstances, there's no reason why *we* should be embarrassed.

NORA: Can I try to pin this down? *Who* is we?

CARRIE: Me and Oliver.

NORA: You and Oliver what?

CARRIE: The simple answer to that is yes. We are.

NORA (getting the general idea, and totally incredulous): *You* and Oliver?

CARRIE: You're thinking the worst. That's right.

Nora takes it calmly as Carrie informs her that she met Oliver as a patient in his office. Nora scarcely believes her story, but Carrie tries to persuade her that it might be true. Oliver re-enters the room. He sees that something is transpiring between the two women, and he wants no part of it. But Nora insists on explaining to him distinctly that Carrie is claiming to be having an affair with him.

OLIVER (to Nora, exploding): But you didn't believe her—you don't believe her—!

NORA: Of course not.

CARRIE: You would have believed me on the telephone. In real life, I don't make a very good impression. I look like a story in the *News* about unwed mothers.

NORA: Mrs. Sachs, I am not clairvoyant and in ten minutes I don't pretend to have any clear impression of you—

CARRIE: More time wouldn't help.

NORA (ignoring the last remark): But I do, of course, know my husband. And I know him to be incapable of what you are suggesting. It's simply not in him.

CARRIE: Why? He's too ethical?

NORA: With a patient, of course he's too ethical. And with anybody else he's too— (She's groping for the word.)

OLIVER (a bit sharply, interested now): Too what?

NORA: Too repressed. Too rigid. *And,* I would think, too uninterested.

Oliver resents his wife's statement and is challenged by it. Carrie decides that the moment has come for her to leave, but Oliver detains her with a clear signal that he will go along with the deception. "It's out in the open," Oliver declares to Carrie in front of Nora, "There's no need to hide it, anymore." He kisses Carrie and escorts her to the deck, where she exits to Leo's apartment.

Nora still scarcely believes what she is seeing and hearing, much to Oliver's continued annoyance. Nora admits that she has always played the role of the jealous wife in order to make Oliver feel like a sex symbol, which in fact—she implies—he is not. She tries to soften the blow a little: "I think you're sexually desirable. *You* don't," but her efforts to define the reasons for his feelings of insecurity merely annoy him further.

OLIVER: You see, what we have here is a classic case of mistaken identity. Here you were, loyally trying to build up my confidence, and I, all along, I thought your recriminations were part of a smoke screen to cover up your own little affair with Peter Sachs.

NORA: You knew about him?

OLIVER: I didn't always know his name but I have learned that by the time my snoring gets so bad that you have to move into the guest room, it means something—

NORA: Well, if you knew, why the hell didn't you say something? Why didn't you *do* something?

OLIVER: Like what?

NORA: Like anything. Like put your foot down, belt me—walk out!

OLIVER: After all, I knew when I married you that you were the girl who had to dance with everybody.

NORA: Bravo! Noel Coward would applaud. You're so civilized. You're so damned civilized you're practically inert!

They start recriminating about why they got married, who asked whom, (it was Nora who did the proposing), who loved whom and how much. Nora weeps at the sweet memories of their early relationship, when she believed that Oliver needed her. Now (Nora asserts, recovering), Oliver is so preoccupied with other people's emotions that he no longer has any of his own.

NORA: Now you're going to tell me you do feel something for her.

OLIVER: For who?

NORA: For *who?* That's perfect, that's absolutely perfect! Have you forgotten her name, or have you already forgotten her existence?

OLIVER *(a fool, and he knows it):* Oh, oh God—Mrs. Sachs.

NORA: Yes. Oh God, Mrs. Sachs. Mrs. Sachs? Is it possible that you are not on a first-name basis?

OLIVER *(doing his best to square himself for it, moving away from the desk):* All right. You're asking me a direct question. I'll give you an honest answer.

NORA: Please do.

OLIVER: I'm thinking about it. And the truth is yes—I *do* feel something for Carrie.

NORA: You admit it? I'm surprised.

OLIVER *(short pause):* You're not as surprised as I am. *(Wait, then sharply.)* And while we're playing Truth or Consequences, what do *you* feel about Peter Sachs?

NORA: I don't know. I'd like to find out.

OLIVER: Find out! Be my guest!

NORA: I have your permission. That's great. And you have your little teen-ager in her orthopedic sneakers! Well, you won't have me. Fine. I'll go.

OLIVER: What are you doing?

NORA: I'm leaving. I'm clearing out.

OLIVER: You're what?

NORA: I'm going to go and leave the field open for you and your nymphet.

Gilda Radner and Sam Waterston in a scene from *Lunch Hour*

OLIVER: Are you going for the evening, for the night? For the week?

NORA: I'm going for whatever damn well suits me. And you should get right down to that little book of yours. Maybe it's not too late to add a chapter. You've got a hell of a lot of new material.

OLIVER: You keep in touch, hear.

Nora stalks out. Oliver picks up the cigarette lighter Carrie left behind, flicks it absent-mindedly, then settles in to his desk to read the proofs of his book. *"He doesn't notice, as he flips the long corrected galleys over the desk-railing in front of him, that they are slowly descending into the fish-tank just beneath. Curtain."*

ACT II

Scene 1

Early that evening, Oliver is pressing the wet galley proofs with an electric iron, when Leo enters to say that Carrie is getting nervous about waiting. If Oliver wants to see her before she goes, O.K.; afterward Leo will drive her home.

Carrie comes in; she has changed into a borrowed dress after spilling a glass of wine all over her own clothing. Carrie overheard the quarrel between Oliver and Nora. She promises to straighten matters out by confessing to her husband that she made the whole thing up; Peter will then tell Nora.

OLIVER: That's what you will absolutely *not* do.

CARRIE: But why shouldn't I tell him that—

OLIVER (*interrupting quickly*): Because if you pull at just one thread of this idiotic web you've woven—the whole thing will unravel. And we'll both look like fools.

CARRIE: Is that so terrible?

OLIVER: I happen to think so, yes. Besides, you will have stirred up a mess— and accomplished nothing. I guess you still want him back?

CARRIE: Of course I do.

OLIVER: Then you will go home and admit everything.

CARRIE: Wait a minute. Tell him that I had an affair with my marriage counselor! Isn't that awfully tacky?

OLIVER: It's very, *very* tacky! But you should have thought of that sooner.

Oliver tells Carrie to go home and say nothing (Nora will already have told her story to Peter), act as though nothing were out of the ordinary; act like an adult, keep telling herself, "These things happen." This will be to Carrie's advantage, Oliver tells her, because "Even if the whole truth comes out, he'll have to concede that you are far more complicated than he suspected."

Carrie sees his point, but before she goes she wants to get her story straight. She wants to know the location of Oliver's office (Park Avenue near 61st Street) so she can tell Peter a plausible tale about going with Oliver to the nearby French restaurant for lunch and then to a hotel room. Oliver gets into the spirit of invention: "There's a luggage store around the corner. We go there, we buy a suitcase and we dump a couple of phone books in it. Then we go to some classy hotel like the St. Regis. And I say to the room clerk, 'You have a reservation for Professor and Mrs. Roscoe Sommers?' And then, while he's checking, you say out loud, 'Roscoe, did you check the rates? This place seems very expensive to me.' Nobody but a wife would say a dumb thing like that in a hotel lobby. So the clerk will come back and say, 'I can't seem to find the reservation, but we do have a room, Professor.' "

Oliver's regular lunch break is from one to two o'clock, so Carrie would have to arrange for the twelve-to-one o'clock appointment just before that, so that Oliver's secretary won't suspect a prearranged lunch date. Their first lunch will be entirely innocent; but at the second, Carrie says, "You gradually overcome my objections." They rehearse this, using a settee to represent a restaurant booth. He lights her cigarette with the lighter she left behind. He comments on her locket, which she shows him. It contains a picture of her father when he was in the Navy.

OLIVER (*holding onto the locket*): I see.

CARRIE: But you're not looking at it.

OLIVER: Carrie, I didn't want to see your locket. I wanted you to come a little closer.

CARRIE: Oliver, I think maybe I want to stop this.

OLIVER: Why? What are you afraid of?

CARRIE: Don't be silly—I'm not afraid.

OLIVER: But you are. There's a little blue vein right there.

    He touches her neck.

I can see it pulsing. And you're pale. I can see little golden freckles.

CARRIE: I have a lot of freckles. I put stuff on—so you don't notice.

OLIVER: You shouldn't. They're lovely. Have you ever been to Paris?

CARRIE: No, I've never been to anything. I've just been in the United States.

OLIVER: Well, in the Jeu de Paume—that's a small gallery that's a part of the Louvre—there's a Monet painting of a girl with a parasol. She's standing on a little hill. And you can tell from the light that the day is perfect. And you can tell from her expression that she is expecting somebody wonderful. Her happiness is so tangible. I've seen the painting a dozen times, and every time I see it, I have the same feeling: "This is the way life is supposed to be. Whatever happened?" Anyway, you remind me of that girl in the painting—so wide-eyed and so expectant. I just wish that—

CARRIE *(picking up the thread):* You wish that I was happy, like the girl in the painting.

OLIVER: Yes, that's what I wish.

CARRIE: But, see, that's just one moment. We don't know what happened, Maybe she waited and waited. And it started to rain. And then she had to walk down the hill all alone.

OLIVER: Carrie—whatever happens, I really don't want you to have to walk down the hill alone. Do you hear me?

CARRIE *(touching his cheek with her hand):* Oliver, you really are very sweet. Don't worry about me. I'm used to walking down hills alone.

Oliver kisses Carrie two or three times, and now in their fantasy they decide they aren't hungry after all—but Carrie still wouldn't be quite ready to buy that suitcase.

Impulsively, Oliver suggests they go swimming in the moonlight. They are about to do so when Leo shows up, wondering why Carrie has delayed going home. The phone rings, but Oliver and Carrie leave Leo to answer it, as it's probably Nora. Leo picks it up and says in a flat voice, "This—is a recording," as the curtain falls.

Scene 2

Half an hour later, Peter Sachs and Nora come into the apartment to get Nora's belongings (she will need her passport, too, as Peter plans to take her to Venezuela). Peter assures Nora that Carrie is an innocent, and that her story about an affair with Oliver is "crazy." Peter will borrow a friend's jet to go to a friend's ranch in Venezuela—he has that kind of friends. They kiss as Oliver and Carrie enter and carry on an intimate kind of conversation in front of their astonished spouses, who react simultaneously.

PETER: Carrie, are you stoned or   NORA: Is this little duet going to go
something?   on forever?

OLIVER *(putting his hands over his ears)*: Wait, wait, wait! If you'll just speak
one at a time, I'll be happy to answer all questions. *(Judicially, like a school
teacher.)* Now, who was first?

NORA *(icily)*: I would like to know why you are making this elaborate pretense
that Peter and I are not here?

OLIVER: But we knew. You kind of took us by surprise.

CARRIE *(going over to Peter)*: Oh, Peter, you know it's really special to swim
when there's just a slice of moon. Like tonight. When you walk out on the dock,
the water looks so cold and hard—like a great big pan of fudge. But when you
dive into it—it's so soft and warm.

PETER: You're not really going to give me a disquisition on the glories of
moonlight bathing?

CARRIE *(pleased)*: You're irritated with me. Hey, that's a step! You haven't
noticed me in months.

PETER: Carrie, try to make sense.

CARRIE *(going into her prepared speech)*: Don't be upset. These things happen,
like thunderstorms in April. They're sudden and unexpected, but they're not
dangerous, they're over before you know it—

PETER: It's *not* April, there are NO storms. What the hell are you talking
about?

CARRIE: Oliver, did I say that wrong?

OLIVER: No, I think your husband just chooses not to understand.

NORA *(to Oliver)*: And YOU—who will not go swimming in the middle of the
day when the sun is shining—can suddenly find the time and the strength at this
hour—when if *I* ever—

OLIVER *(lifting one hand)*: PLEASE! Before this breaks down into a series of
little squabbles, I'd like to explain our plan.

Oliver recognizes (he tells them) that Nora and Peter want to be together, and
they are welcome to move into this place. Oliver and Carrie want to be together
too: they are bound for the Hotel Meurice in Paris for the month of July (Oliver
phones his secretary to arrange for the tickets). Peter and Nora can scarcely
believe this is taking place; and Peter angers Nora by trying to talk Carrie out
of the adventure. Nora stalks out of the room, with Peter following.

Oliver and Carrie agree that their ruse seems to be having its desired effect on
their spouses, making them sit up and take notice. Carrie goes into the breakfast
nook to change into her borrowed dress. While she's doing this, Oliver tells her
that maybe they have something besides their marriages to think about; Carrie
admits she feels "funny—I can't swallow" and tells Oliver it's up to him to decide
what they do next. Oliver's decision is to ring the bell summoning Leo (and
bringing Nora and Peter back into the room).

Nora feels she is being manipulated, Peter tries to take charge of the situation,
rousing Oliver to anger at his presumption; they started this, and he means to
finish it. Leo gets into the spirit of things by warning Peter that if he is going to
move in here he must take responsibility for the house plants. Peter and Nora are

being overwhelmed by this barrage of arrangements. Leo suggests a lottery to determine who pairs off with whom.

Peter and Oliver quarrel over which of them is the least effectual: Peter is a rich collector who does no useful work, but on the other hand, he reminds Oliver, "When I wanted to get married I was able to propose to my wife which, I understand, is more than you were able to do." Oliver and Peter try to come to blows, but too awkwardly for any punch to be landed. Finally Peter finds himself confessing, and arousing Carrie's sympathy, with "It's very *hard* to do something if you *don't need* . . . the money. It takes a lot of character. I haven't got a lot of character."

Nora decides to deal with the situation abruptly by ordering everyone out of *her* house (the summer lease is in her name). Leo invites everybody downstairs for a farewell drink, angering Nora to the point of tears because he is making a joke of their predicament. Leo turns on the recorded music and cajoles Nora into forgiving him, pulling her to her feet for a dance. Oliver takes Carrie into the dance, and Leo comes over to change partners at once, leaving Nora with Oliver. Eventually Peter cuts in on Leo and Carrie, so that the husbands and wives are now finally dancing with each other.

Carrie turns off the music and suggests that she and Peter go home, confessing that she isn't quite emancipated enough yet for a trip to Paris: "Besides, Peter needs me. He needs me to be dissatisfied with. Otherwise, he'd have nothing to yearn for. And that's important to him."

Peter won't admit the truth of this, but Carrie is determined to enjoy her new-found confidence. Meanwhile, Nora admits to Peter that she panicked as their relationship grew closer, implying that it probably wouldn't have worked, anyway. Carrie thanks Oliver for counseling her so effectively.

CARRIE:. . . . .But I *will* have further adjustments to make, and I think I should continue with therapy. Is there another therapist you could recommend?

OLIVER *(professionally, taking it at face value):* Yes, certainly, I could give you the names of a couple of men who—

CARRIE *(interrupting):* Actually, it would be much simpler to continue with you. But I suppose that's out of the question. Your wife wouldn't hear of it—now that she's been made kind of insecure. Just please write down a name for me.
    Oliver starts to jot down a memo.
NORA *(bristling):* My dear, I would not have you shopping around for a therapist because of my "insecurities." I assure you I'll manage just fine.

CARRIE *(over her shoulder to Peter, who is really looking at Nora):* What about you, Peter? Do *you* think I should find a new therapist?

PETER: I think all therapy is a waste of time. But suit yourself.

CARRIE: *(turning full to Oliver):* Well, then. Can you fit me in next week?

OLIVER *(it's beginning to dawn on him. He reaches for his appointment book):* Well—I'll see. *(Gaining confidence.)* What time of day did you have in mind?

CARRIE: Oh, any afternoon.

OLIVER *(the plunge, as he studies the book):* N-o-o-o, the afternoons seem to be gone. *(As innocently as he can manage.)* What about the hour before lunch?

CARRIE *(pondering):* Twelve to one?

OLIVER *(snapping it* up*):* Twelve to one.
CARRIE: Sure. What day?
OLIVER: Tuesday?
CARRIE: Tuesday. Fine! Well, good night. Come on, Peter
    Carrie and Peter leave.

Nora takes the glasses, etc. into the kitchen and then returns as Leo takes his leave, flicking on the music again as he goes: a sentimental waltz.

OLIVER *(indicating the music):* Our social director is still at work.
NORA: I hear.
OLIVER *(extending his arms for a dance):* I guess it's required.
    Nora slips into his arms more confidently now, and they dance a few bars before she speaks.
NORA: Oliver, when you pretended to call your secretary earlier—to make the plane reservations—what number did you call?
OLIVER: I don't understand.
NORA: Well, you didn't call your secretary. But you dialed *some* number. Was it the weather?
OLIVER *(sagely):* Oh—you figured that out.
NORA *(complacently):* Sure. The whole business was just a big act to keep me here. You can't fool me.
OLIVER *(smiling, dancing):* Nora, I *knew* I couldn't fool you.
    Music up. A taxi driver enters.
TAXI DRIVER: Taxi, Doc.
    Curtain.

A LESSON FROM ALOES

A Play in Two Acts

BY ATHOL FUGARD

Cast and credits appear on page 357

ATHOL FUGARD was born June 11, 1932 in Middelburg in the semi-desert Karoo country of South Africa. His mother was an Afrikaner, his father of Irish and Hugenot descent. He studied motor mechanics at Port Elizabeth Technical College and philosophy at the University of Cape Town and spent three years in the Merchant Marine, mostly in the Far East. He married an actress, Sheila Meiring, and for a time they ran an experimental theater in Cape Town. His first play, No-Good Friday, *was produced in 1959 with an all-black cast. His next was* Nongogo *(1961) which had its American premiere in 1978 for 20 performances at Manhattan Theater Club.*

In 1963 The Blood Knot *won Fugard an international reputation and reached these shores in an off-Broadway production starring James Earl Jones March 1, 1964 for 240 performances (it is about two black half-brothers, one light-skinned and one dark). His next play,* People Are Living There, *was done in Glasgow in 1968 and then in London during the 1971–72 season. His* Hello and Goodbye *appeared off Broadway with Martin Sheen and Colleen Dewhurst Sept. 18, 1969 for 45 performances and was produced in London in the season of 1972–73. Fugard's* Boesman and Lena *was done off Broadway with James Earl Jones, Ruby Dee and Zakes Mokae June 22, 1970 for 205 performances—and was named a Best Play of its season—a year before its subsequent London premiere. Another Fugard work of that period,* Mille Miglia, *was aired on BBC television, as was* The Blood Knot.

James Earl Jones as Steve Daniels, Maria Tucci as Gladys and Harris Yulin as Piet Bezuidenhout in *A Lesson From Aloes* by Athol Fugard

Fugard's second Best Play, The Island, *had strong mimetic as well as literary elements and is credited as a collaboration "devised" by the author and the actors who appeared in it, John Kani and Winston Ntshona. It reversed the direction of the previous Fugard Best Play by stopping in London before coming to New York, appearing under the auspices of the Royal Court Theater on a two-play program with the effective* Sizwe Banzi Is Dead *by the same authors. The two plays then had their American premieres in tandem, first at the Long Wharf Theater in New Haven, Conn. in October 1974 and then in alternating repertory* (Sizwe Banzi *for 159 performances,* The Island *for 52) in November 1974 in mini-Broadway productions at the Edison Theater.*

Fugard's third Best Play, A Lesson From Aloes, *first appeared on this side of the Atlantic in a production at the Centaur Theater in Montreal on Jan. 1, 1980; then was produced at the Long Wharf Theater March 26 and finally on Broadway Nov. 17 for 96 performances (winning the 1981 New York Drama Critics Circle award as the best play of the season), in all three cases under its author's direction. Other recorded instances of production of Fugard's work in this country have included the short play* Statements After an Arrest Under the Immorality Act *for 35 performances at Manhattan Theater Club in November 1978 and* The Drummer *at Actors' Theater of Louisville in the 1979–80 season. His works are revived perennially on off-off-Broadway and regional theater programs.*

Some of Fugard's training for what has turned out to be his triple profession of actor-director-writer was acquired at Rehearsal Room in Johannesburg's Dorkay House (the headquarters of South Africa's Union Artists, the organization that cares for the cultural interests of non-Europeans in the Transvaal). Later, as resident director of Dorkay House, he staged the work of many modern playwrights including Steinbeck and Pinter. Since the mid-1960s he has been closely associated with Serpent Players of New Brighton, Port Elizabeth, a theater workshop for black Africans experimenting in collaborative "play-making" of works dealing with the contemporary South African scene. Rehearsals and performances of Serpent Players are customarily carried on after hours, with black participants sometimes classified technically as "household employees" of their white colleague Athol Fugard, because "artist" is not an accepted employment category for South African blacks.

Fugard now lives near Port Elizabeth with his wife, and they have a daughter, Lisa-Maria. He has often been a focal point of controversy in his politically controversial land and was once denied a passport by his government when he wanted to come to New York for rehearsals of Boesman and Lena *in the spring of 1970.*

The following synopsis of A Lesson From Aloes *was prepared by Jeffrey Sweet.*

Time: 1963

Place: The action of the play moves between two areas representing the backyard and bedroom of a small house in Algoa Park, Port Elizabeth, South Africa

ACT I

Scene 1

SYNOPSIS: Piet Bezuidenhout and his wife, Gladys, are in their backyard this late afternoon. In the evening they are expecting an old friend named Steve and his family to stop by for dinner. To while away the meantime, Piet, *"an Afrikaner in his mid-40s,"* is thumbing through a book in an effort to identify a species of aloe he has found, the aloe being a plant native to South Africa. Aloes hold a fascination for Piet; his backyard is filled with the different species he has found. Piet makes cheery conversation to his wife, who sits apart. Something is clearly awry with her.

PIET: Well, my dear, we have a stranger in our midst. Aloe Anonymous! Because that is what it is until I know it's name. I've been through my book twice, page by page, but there is nothing that looks quite like it. I don't think I can allow myself to believe I've discovered a new species. That would be something! I'd name it after you, my dear. Hail aloe Gladysiensis! Sounds rather good, doesn't it?
> *He reads the other aloes.*

Hail ferox! And you aristata . . . arborescens . . . ciliaris . . . and now Gladysiensis! Welcome to the most noble order of Eastern Cape aloes. An impressive array of names, isn't it? And knowing them is important. It makes me feel that little bit more at home in my world. And yet, as little Juliet once said: "What's in a name? That which we call a rose/By any other name would smell as sweet."
> *These lines, and all his other quotations, although delivered with a heavy Afrikaans accent, are said with a sincere appreciation of the words involved. He thinks about those he has just quoted.*

Alas, it's not as simple as that, is it?
GLADYS: Are you talking to me?
PIET: Who else, my dear?
GLADYS: The aloes . . . or yourself. I'm never sure these days.
PIET: Names are more than just labels.
> *He sits beside her on the bench.*

Petrus Jacobus Bezuidenhout.
> *He gives a little smile.*

"So, would Petrus, were he not Petrus called/Retain that dear perfection which he owns without that title?"

As an Afrikaner, Piet continues, he would never consent to "Deny thy father and refuse thy name." He is Petrus Jacobus Bezuidenhout, an Afrikaner of Algoa Park, Port Elizabeth, in the year 1963—and he accepts all the consequences of this identity.

In response to her frets about the sun ("My skin can't take it," she says), he fetches her sun hat from the bedroom. She doesn't put it on, but, instead, suddenly expressing concern about her diary, she rushes from the yard to the bedroom. She takes the diary from one hiding place and puts it in a new one, under the bed's mattress. She returns to the backyard. "Safe and sound," she says. Piet replies that he would never "interfere" with it. "I know that!" she insists.

Piet shifts his attention back to the aloe. Perhaps he'll wait for it to flower; then it would be easier to identify. He muses on how dependent the plant is on him for its welfare now that he has it potted in a tin. Potting an aloe is rather like caging an animal. "It's the roots that upset me," he explains. "Even with all my care and attention they are still going to crawl around inside this little tin and tie themselves into knots looking for the space creation intended for them."

Gladys is nervous about the impending visit. She is not sure she can cope with Steve and his family. The four children worry her particularly. She predicts that Piet and Steve will go off to discuss politics, leaving her to fend for herself. To distract her, Piet begins to arrange the table for that evening, placing chairs and planning the seating. Gladys protests when he places the boy Pieterjie, Piet's godson, next to her, so he changes the plan.

She tells him not to expect too much by way of a fancy meal. He replies that the cold buffet she has planned sounds fine. "They'll be our first visitors since I've been back," she says. Piet says that this too is cause for celebration. She remarks that for once she will have something substantive to put into her diary—after a long social exile, she and her husband are entertaining.

Piet tries to come up with the proper name for his aloe. Gladys does not care for aloes. They strike her as thorny and disagreeable and not at all attractive. Piet defends them. In their proper setting, in the veld, they have a kind of glory.

PIET: . . . . . And remember, it's a defiant glory, Gladys. That veld is a hard world. They and the thorn trees were just about the only things still alive in it when I finally packed up the old truck and left the farm. Four years of drought, but they were flowering once again. I'm ashamed to say it, but I resented them for that. It's a small soul that resents a flower, but I suppose mine was when I drove away and saw them there in the veld, surviving where I had failed.

GLADYS: Is that the price of survival in this country? Thorns and bitterness.

PIET: For the aloe it is. Maybe there's some sort of lesson for us there.

GLADYS: What do you mean?

PIET: We need survival mechanisms as well.

GLADYS: Speak for yourself, Peter. I'm a human being not a . . . prickly pear.

Piet stares at her, appalled.

What's the matter?

PIET: The prickly pear isn't an aloe, Gladys.

GLADYS: Please, Peter . . . !

PIET: It's not even indigenous, my dear. The jointed cactus is a declared weed.

GLADYS: This conversation is upsetting me, Peter.

PIET: Sorry, my dear. What . . .

> Gladys moves abruptly into the house. She returns a few seconds later with a tablecloth, which she tries, without too much success because of her agitation, to spread over the "festive board."

PIET: Sorry, my dear. What have I said?

GLADYS: We've already had droughts, prickly pears and despair. I suppose we'll be into politics next and the black man's misery. I'm not exaggerating, Peter. That is what a conversation with you has become—a catalogue of South African disasters. And you never stop! You seem to have a perverse need to dwell on what is cruel and ugly about this country. Is there nothing gentle in your world?

PIET: Is it really as bad as that?

GLADYS: Yes, it is. And don't make me feel guilty for saying it. *(She gestures at the aloes.)* Look at them! Is that what you hope for? To be like one of them? That's not the only possibility in life, you know. If that's what your expectations have shrunk to, it's your business, but God has not planted me in a jam tin. He might have cursed you Afrikaners, but not the whole human race. I want to live my life, not just survive it. I know I'm in this backyard with them, but that is not going to happen to me.

PIET: I . . . *(He makes a helpless gesture.)* . . . what can I say? I'm sorry you don't like them.

GLADYS: Don't like them! It's worse than that, Peter. *(He looks at her.)* I'm going to be very honest with you. They frighten me. Yes, thorns and bitterness? I'm afraid there's more than that to them. They're turgid with violence, like everything else in this country. And they're trying to pass it on to me.

PIET *(carefully):* What do you mean, my dear?

GLADYS: Don't worry. I won't let it happen. I won't!

> She pauses.

PIET *(trying to break the mood)* Well. *(Looks at his wrist watch.)* Time to get ready. They'll be here soon.

GLADYS *(looking fearful):* Who?

PIET: Steve and Mavis.

> They pause, looking at each other.

GLADYS: Yes, of course.

Gladys goes into the house, ostensibly to get some calamine lotion. Piet follows her in.

Scene 2

A short time later, Gladys sits at the dressing table in the bedroom. Piet knocks, asks if he may come in. She hurriedly retrieves her diary from its hiding place, then, clutching it, sits down at the table again and tells Piet he may enter. He does. He has just bathed, and *"in the course of this scene he changes into a safari suit, with short trousers, long socks and brown shoes."*

Noticing how quietly she sits, he asks her whether she's been making an entry in her diary. No, she replies, just looking through her old entries. Opening the book at such an angle that he can't see its contents, she tells him of entries for the past week—nothing much. The most notable was a fellow from the Watch-tower Society who came to the door to say that the Society has worked out the date of the end of the world: "I almost told him there are times when I think it has already happened." She talks further of her sense of isolation, as if she and Piet were the only survivors of some cataclysm.

Piet reminds her they'll have company tonight. Yes, she says, the first real company since she came home almost seven months ago. Doesn't he wonder why, in all of this time, none of their old comrades from the cause has come by or invited them out? There used to be an endless supply of friends. Are they keeping away because of her condition?

Piet denies this. He tells her he believes friends have kept their distance because of the police raids and Steve having been sent to jail. People are frightened. She doesn't accept this explanation. "It's too simple," she says. She asks him if there isn't more to the distance, something of which he hasn't told her. He assures her he has hidden nothing. People are just frightened. He, too, is frightened, even though he may not give that impression as he classifies his aloes and recites poetry: "The aloes give me pleasure, Gladys, not a purpose."

The word "purpose" reminds her of a quotation: "There is a purpose to life, and we will be measured by the extent to which we harness ourselves to it"—Thoreau. She remembers he told her that when they first met, and it had so impressed her she had written it in her diary. She had envied him his purpose. At the time, the terrible focal point of Gladys's life had been her slowly-dying mother. When her mother finally died, Gladys reported to her diary that she hadn't cried and didn't expect to.

Piet changes the subject to distract her. He guesses that this particular diary in her hands must be full now. He will give her another. He gave her the one she now holds almost a year ago. She still has the card that came with it. He had written on it, "Take this sweet soul! We'll start again./They've come and gone all in vain/For we live on"—another quotation, Longfellow this time.

GLADYS *(holding her diary):* I'd be lost without this. It's where I keep all my little secrets. A woman needs them, and as you know, I did lose all of those I once had. You were given a receipt for them, remember? A little piece of paper torn from a grubby notebook.

PIET: Yes, I do. But that is something we must try to forget, Gladys, not remember.

GLADYS: Yes, I realize that. But I can't help myself sometimes. There's so much that keeps reminding me. After all, it was in this very room. He sat down here, opened the first one, and started to read . . .

PIET *(his desperation growing):* I remember it very clearly, my love! I was here! With you! *(He pauses.)* Maybe if we changed the room around . . . rearranged the furniture! That might help. What do you think?

GLADYS: We could try.

PIET: I know what it really needs, though. More light! This is a dark little room. I know what that means. I've had my occasions to sit brooding in them as well. That's the answer, Gladys! As soon as we've got a little something together in the bank again I'm going to put another window in that wall. Light! That's what we need. And we'll change the furniture as well. It will be a different room. I should have thought of it before.

GLADYS *(she hasn't been listening to him):* Yes . . . you led them in and then stood there next to the doorway. I can't remember much about you after that. I was still trying to get into my dressing gown. Then the one in charge saw them on the table, asked you what they were . . . you told them . . . he apologized to me nicely and started to read them . . . page by page. I couldn't believe it was happening. Did I ever get my dressing gown on?

PIET: Please . . .

GLADYS *(violently):* That's an important question, Peter! Did I ever get my dressing gown on?

PIET: No.

GLADYS: So I just stood there . . . ! What did I look like?

PIET: For God's sake, Gladys! What do you want?

GLADYS: An answer to a simple question! What did I look like?

PIET: You had just woken up, you were sleepy, you didn't know what was going on . . .

GLADYS *(she gazes into the dressing-table mirror):* Me.
    Pause.

PIET: They won't visit us again, Gladys.

He tells her there is no reason for them to return. They found nothing. Nothing but her diaries, she retorts. Those they took away and never gave back. Piet says he's trying to get them back. He kept the receipt. She demands he produce it. He does.

GLADYS: Tear it up.
    He hesitates.
Tear it up! Small pieces.
    He does so. She hold out her hand, takes the pieces and puts them down carefully on the dressing table. For a few seconds she lapses into an almost bland normalcy.
There. I've cancelled those years. I'm going to forget I ever lived them. They weren't just laundry lists, you know. There were very intimate and personal things in those diaries, things a woman only talks about to herself. Even then it took me a lot of trust and courage to do that. I knew I never had much of either, but I was learning. *(Her hysteria begins to surface again.)* You were such a persuasive teacher, Peter! "Trust, Gladys. Trust yourself. Trust life." There's nothing left of that. *(She brandishes her diary.)* Must I tell you what I've been trying to do with this all day? Hide it. It's been behind the dressing table . . . under the mattress . . . Can you think of somewhere really safe? Where nobody would find it, including yourself? There isn't, is there? Do you know what I would really like to do with this? Make you eat it and turn it into shit . . . then maybe everybody would leave it alone. Yes, you heard me correctly. Shit! I've learned how to use my dirty words. And just as well, because there's no other adequate vocabulary for this country. Maybe I should do that in case they come again. A page full

of filthy language. Because that is what they were really hoping for when they sat down with my diaries. Filth!

PIET: I don't know what to say.

GLADYS: Thank God! Because if you were to tell me once more that they won't come again . . . ! To start with, I don't believe you, but even if I did, that once was enough. You seem to have difficulty understanding that, Peter. It only needs to happen to a woman once, for her to lose all trust she ever had in anything or anybody. They violated me, Peter. I might just as well have stayed in that bed, lifted up my nightdress and given them each a turn. I've shocked you. Good! Then maybe now you understand. Yes, I can see it. You are frightened.

PIET: That's right.

GLADYS: Of me?

PIET: For you. Please be careful.

GLADYS: You're too late with that advice. You should have given it to the Gladys Adams you conjured with, instead of persuading her that life was to be trusted.. . . . .

In the heat of the moment, she tells Piet that, by so persuading her and by marrying her, he is as responsible for the condition she is in as the police. A second later, she is apologetic. Why didn't he stop her from saying that? "I can't! I've tried," says an anguished Piet. She wonders how they are going to get through the rest of their lives. Trying again to calm her, Piet proposes he head off Steve and Mavis to relieve her of the strain of the visit. No, she says, let them come. She'll be fine. She won't even hide her diary any more. And now, she'd like to change. As he leaves the room, she says, "I am trying, Peter." "I know that," he replies and exits.

Scene 3

A little later, Gladys, now calm, emerges from the house to join Piet in his preparations for their visitors. Gladys begins to fold the serviettes as Piet searches through his book of quotations for something appropriate for a toast. Something about friendship. He settles on a quote from Dickens: "What is the odds so long as the fire of soul is kindled at the taper of conviviality, and the wing of friendship never moults a feather." The image of the taper matches nicely with the candles on the table. He announces his intention to memorize the toast.

Gladys remarks on how much Steve means to him. Piet confirms this. He values Steve second only to her. It was because of meeting Steve that Piet's eyes were opened. Piet was driving a bus in the "Coloured" area during a bus boycott Steve was leading there to protest a hike in the fare. He watched as Steve was arrested, and then as Steve returned a few days later to continue making his speeches. Piet decided he wanted to hear what Steve had to say, so he stopped his bus, which was empty anyway, and went over to where Steve was speaking. Piet was the only white there. When he explained to the crowd that he was there to listen, the warmth of their welcome melted away his bitterness and frustration. "Feelings about life and people, which I thought had withered away like everything else on the farm, were alive again."

Intoxicated by these feelings, Piet had quit his job as bus driver and joined Steve in handling out pamphlets and speaking. The bus company won the boycott shortly, but Steve told Piet that he considered the boycott a success in that it had awakened a new political conscience in many people. Some of them had taken a political stand for the first time. "My first lesson from Steve, and the most important one," Piet recalls. "An evil system isn't a natural disaster. There's nothing you can do, to stop a drought, but bad laws and social injustice are man-made and can be unmade by men. It's as simple as that. We can make this a better world to live in."

Gladys tells Piet that she is glad about what is to happen tonight because she sees it as a sign that Piet and Steve will be able to salvage their friendship. At this, Piet feels compelled to tell her that tonight is the last time he and Steve will see each other. Steve has revealed to Piet that he intends to leave South Africa next week with his wife Mavis and the children and resettle in England for good.

GLADYS: You're joking.

PIET: I'm not.

GLADYS: Well . . . that's a surprise . . . to say the least. Steven leaving. I always thought of him as being like you, hanging on to the bitter end. *(Shaking her head in disbelief.)* I don't know what to say.

PIET: Neither do I.

GLADYS *(her tone hardening):* No. I'm wrong. I do. Good for Steven! And England! From all I've heard, it's a very different world to this one. They are very lucky.

PIET: He's leaving on an exit permit, Gladys.

GLADYS: So?

PIET: He can't come back.

GLADYS: So!

PIET: I don't think it's all that easy for him. This is his home as much as it is ours.

GLADYS: No. I know I was born here, but I will never call it that. Why didn't you tell me earlier?

PIET: I don't know. Maybe because I also find it so hard to believe.

GLADYS: Believe what? That he doesn't love "home" as much as you? It's almost a joke, you know, coming after all you've just been telling me.

PIET: You're being very hard on him, my dear.

GLADYS: Of course. Because I'm jealous. I'd never persuade you to go, would I?

PIET: I haven't had to survive a banning order for three years and then six months in jail.

GLADYS: That's not such a high price to pay for coming to your senses. I still think he's lucky, and I still envy him for getting out.

For the first time, Piet reveals the full truth of his recent encounter with Steve. He hadn't even realized that Steve had been released from jail till he saw his old friend on the street. It was not exactly a warm reunion. Steve had told Piet about his decision to move to England, and the two for the first time had been awkward with each other, embarrassed. Piet had then invited Steve to come by with his family this evening to say goodbye.

Gladys reacts bitterly. Is this how Piet's wonderful cause is to end? With all of his friends disappearing and leaving him alone with his hopeless fight? Where did all the fine slogans and high ideals go? Piet responds that there was nothing wrong with the group's slogans and ideals. It's just that there was a weakness in resolve.

But Gladys won't let him get away with referring to this weakness as an abstraction. The weakness lay in a specific person: whoever it was who had informed against Steve. The group had had a party. Steve, being under banning order and thus legally prohibited from associating with his political friends, was going to break the order and attend the party anyway. One of the people who knew this had obviously informed the police of Steve's intention, and they had arrested Steve and thrown him into jail. She asks Piet if, while she was away, he had figured out who the traitor was. Piet says he hasn't thought about it much because there was no way of knowing for sure, and the suspicion would poison the sense of trust with other members of the group.

Gladys argues that the trust is already gone. Where are all of their friends? She doesn't see any sign of them. Could it be, she asks pointedly, that the others think that Piet was the informer?

PIET: I don't know.

GLADYS: Are you lying to me, or yourself?

She waits.

PIET: Yes. It looks as if . . . they all think . . . I'm the one.

GLADYS: What about Steven?

PIET: No! He wouldn't be coming here if he thought that.

GLADYS: He's not here yet.

PIET: He didn't cross to the other side of the street when he saw me coming.

GLADYS *(outraged):* Who did that?

PIET: It doesn't matter.

GLADYS *(quietly):* My God! I want to scream. Maybe swearing would be better. How long have you known?

PIET: It isn't something I "know" in that way. There's no one day on which a drought starts. But there were meetings to which I wasn't invited and then, as I said, I realized people were avoiding me. There is only one conclusion.

GLADYS: And you didn't tell me because you thought it would aggravate my condition. Didn't you know I'd realize it sooner or later? I haven't been made that insensitive.

PIET: It's not as simple as that, Gladys. Obviously I wanted to avoid upsetting you. But even without that, could we have talked about it? *(He speaks with deep emotion.)* Sat down and discussed over supper the fact that I was considered a traitor? That's the correct word. Could you have made a simple entry to the effect in your diary? God! It's the ugliest thing that has ever happened to me. It makes me feel more ashamed of . . . myself, my fellow men . . . of everything! . . . in a way I never thought possible.

Gladys has been watching him very carefully.

What's the matter?

GLADYS: I'm trying to see you as others do.

PIET: And?

GLADYS: It's not true, is it?

Piet stares back at her for a long time before turning away.

PIET *(vacantly . . . looking at his wrist watch):* They should be here any minute now. I'll . . . I'll light the candles.

GLADYS *(getting up, she goes to the table):* Yes, it looks very good. I'm going inside. Call me . . . if they come.

She walks into the house, leaving Piet alone in the backyard. Curtain.

ACT II

Two hours later, Piet has not given up hope. He still waits for Steve. And finally, out of the darkness of the night, Steve arrives, playing the "Marseillaise" on the harmonica. He is a *"Coloured man"* about the same age as Piet.

He and Piet begin to play a game, Steve playing the role of a member of the Security Branch looking for "a mad Afrikaner who recites English poetry," Piet disclaiming any knowledge of such a subversive type. Putting aside the joking, Piet calls out to Gladys that Steve and his family have arrived. Embarrassed, Steve corrects him. One of the kids is feeling ill, he explains, so Steve has come alone, leaving Mavis to look after the children. Piet expresses his regret that the others couldn't come, but "the two of us were enough for a good time in the past." Steve begins to recite Longfellow's *The Slave's Dream,* a poem about a slave who dies while dreaming of former days of freedom in Africa. *"Steve's delivery is awkward and amateurish and before long he starts floundering for the words. Piet prompts him to start with, but eventually takes over. Steve, one beat behind, struggles to keep up as Piet gets into his stride and then gallops splendidly to the end of the poem. We are obviously watching a little scene that has taken place many times in the past. The effect is both comic and moving. When it is finished, there is a pause as the two men look at each other."* Piet says, quietly, "Welcome, Steve." Steve replies, "Hello, you mad Afrikaner."

Piet goes to the bedroom to fetch Gladys to join them. She promises she will shortly. Returning to the backyard and his guest, Piet joins Steve in some wine Steve has brought. They reminisce about the birth, seven years ago, of Steve's son, Piet's godson; and about the toasts they made that night—first to the new baby, then to this house into which Piet and Gladys had just moved, and then to their comrades in the cause, each comrade toasted separately. They had gotten quite drunk for, as Piet remembers, "Our membership was quite healthy in those days." One would not get drunk toasting the members individually today, Steve notes wryly. He proposes a toast to the old days. "If nothing else, they produced a few revolutionary hangovers." Piet tries to propose a countertoast—the Dickens quotation on friendship—but he has forgotten it. He looks it up in his book and completes it.

Steve asks Piet where this propensity for poetry comes from. Piet explains that it started in the last days of his farm, with one particular incident. He was

Harris Yulin and James Earl Jones in a scene from *A Lesson From Aloes*

attending the funeral of the baby of an African family that had worked for him on the farm. The baby had died of gastroenteritis, a result of the drought. It came time for Piet to say a few words, but he couldn't: "A sense of deep, personal failure overwhelmed me. They waited—I don't know how long—until I just shook my head and walked away." In the few remaining months he'd stayed with the farm, he spent much of his time looking through a book of poetry and stories, trying to find something he could have said. He never did find the right words; but, in the meantime he learned a lot of poetry.

Piet asks Steve if he has seen much of the old gang since he's been out. "Only Solly," Steve replies, explaining that Solly was the one who helped sort things out so that Steve could take his family to England, even paying their fares. Piet remarks that things have been quiet in the cause, but Steve cuts him off, saying that—quiet or busy—he doesn't really want to get into the subject. "It's just that I've had enough, Piet." Piet says he understands.

Gladys appears, breaking the awkward moment between the two men. While Piet goes to bring out the snacks she's made, Steve and Gladys try to break the ice. Gladys tells of Piet's new hobby of collecting aloes, a hobby to fill the void politics left. She congratulates Steve on his forthcoming move. Steve is not so certain how well he'll take transplanting after 42 years. He's not looking forward to the boat, as he gets seasick and doesn't swim. He asks Gladys what England will be like. "Why do you ask me?" she says. Well, Steve has always assumed, from the way she spoke and acted . . . She replies with a curious smile saying that she supposes in a sense that she *is* from England. Steve asks if it's cold there. Gladys responds that in the England in her memories it is always summer.

Piet returns with candles, snacks and sherry and gives a toast to Steve's "new pastures." He asks Steve if he is ready for the move. Steve talks of the trouble trying to put a lifetime into some luggage.

STEVE:. . . . .I've packed and unpacked those bloody suitcases I don't know how many times already, trying to fit in all the damned things. Excuse the language, Gladys, but that is how I feel about it. When I left the house to come here tonight I put my foot in my own face—our wedding photo! . . . so that started Mavis crying . . . you know, bad luck!—and then I stood on that table lamp covered with seashells. You know the one, Piet, with all the mother-of-pearl. My dad made it. It was going to be my special souvenir of this place in our home over there.

GLADYS: I'm sure you'll be able to fix it, Steven.

STEVE: Maybe. I didn't even look to see how broken it was, I was so the hell-in, Gladys. Just slammed the door on the lot . . . wife, children, suitcases, broken glass . . .

Piet laughs.

It's no joke, man. It's a life lying around on that lounge floor like a pile of rubbish. That's what I'm trying to squeeze into a few old suitcases. And the worst part is that you start to hate it. Sometimes I think we should just chuck the whole lot away. Get onto that boat with a pair of pajamas each and a toothbrush. Start over there with nothing. But there's no winning. Because just when you're feeling like that, out of a box or a cupboard drawer comes something you'd forgotten about . . . and before you know it, you're sitting there on the floor smiling at a memory.

From his pocket, Steve takes an old photograph of himself with his father and the large fish they caught one day. He tells the story of how his father caught the fish in the surf not far from Fairview, where they'd lived—30 pounds. His dad had hauled it back to Fairview intact to show their friends. Piet raises his glass to salute the old man, but Steve won't drink the toast. He doesn't want to get sentimental. He doesn't think Piet would be inclined to sentiment if he had seen the old man at his end. Fairview was suddenly declared an area for whites only. Steve's father exhausted what money he had trying to fight the eviction, but he ended up, broke and broken, resettled far away from the sea he loved.

STEVE:. . . . .I'll never forget one day in the backyard there at Salt Lake. I had started to get a bit conscious about things, and I was going on about our rights and what have you. He just listened. When I was finished he shook his head and said: "Ons geslag is verkeerd." Hell, that made me angry! And I told him we have only ourselves to blame if we let them walk over us. He just shook his head and repeated himself: "Ons geslag is verkeerd." Sorry, Gladys. That means . . . how would you say it nice in English, Piet?

PIET: Our generation . . . our race is a mistake.

STEVE: Ja, something like that. And maybe he was right after all.

Gladys tells Steve what a relief it is to have him visit. She and Piet have not had any visitors, and, with Steve going away, she doesn't expect there will be many in the future. Piet might end up talking only to aloes for quite a while. Piet turns the topic of conversation to his plant collection, but Gladys continues to make her point. Piet, she says, is determined to stay in this godforsaken country, much like his precious plants. He is an Afrikaner and this is his home and, good sense and her desires to the contrary, he wouldn't think of leaving South Africa.

Steve tells Piet that, having gotten out of prison, he decided it wasn't worth the pain it would cause for him to stay. Because of his political activities he is prohibited from working, which means, if he were to stay, he and his family would have to survive on the charity of friends. He doesn't have an appetite for martyrdom.

Piet says that Steve owes him no explanations, but Steve continues to defend his decision to leave, to give up the cause. What's more, he believes that Piet would feel the same way were he to have gone through what Steve has gone through. "You're arguing with yourself, Steve," says Piet, "I haven't accused you of anything." Steve continues, however, telling Piet that, "If I had a white skin, I'd also find a lot of reasons for not leaving this country."

After an awkward silence, Steve apologizes. He hasn't been behaving himself since his release. Mavis has told him she thinks his manners were left in his cell. Gladys dryly asks if the party is over. Receiving no answer, she starts to clean away the plates and cutlery.

Piet tries to return to the subject of aloes, but Steve continues. The conclusion he came to in jail was that, for all of their meetings and activities, none of their political work ever made a damn bit of difference in the fight against apartheid. The only way to make a difference, he now believes, is to employ rougher tactics, but such tactics are not for either of them. So another toast—"A lost cause!" Piet declines to drink to this one. Gladys goes into the house with the plates and such.

Steve tells Piet that he has no problem with saying goodbye to the others from the old gang. He figures, if things get hot enough, he'll see them all in England. But he knows that Gladys is right; Piet will not leave. He exhorts Piet to change his mind. Think of the good times they could have together in England! When they felt a political itch, they could scratch it by standing on soap boxes and talking as loudly as they want.

Gladys has returned. She expresses ironic sympathy for Piet. The reunion hasn't gone as well as he'd hoped—too bad. And it will be such a long time before he has any other company. The others don't stop by. At first she thought they wanted to avoid encountering her, because of her condition. But the real reason, she tells Steve, is that they suspect Piet of being the police informer who turned in Steve.

Over Piet's protests, Gladys continues. She asks Steve if that is not the real reason Mavis wouldn't come. And hasn't Steve been trying to figure out for himself if what they say about Piet is true? Well, Gladys will remove all doubt. It *is* true, she says. Piet *did* turn him in.

Steve tells them that Gladys is right about Mavis thinking Piet was the one. He'd had a fight with her about this. The reason he was so late was because he needed a couple of drinks to face Piet. And what has Piet to say?

"Nothing to say," Piet replies. Steve takes this in, shocked at first. Then he laughs. "Nothing to say." That's what he had told the police when they'd questined him. "Nothing to say." They made him talk, finally—not by physical torture, just by putting him into a room, alone, and, every now and then sending someone by to look at and laugh at him. Just laugh. This went on for days, until he broke. His manhood gone, crying, he told them everything he knew.

STEVE:. . . . .Every bloody thing I knew. And if they'd wanted it, I would have told them things I didn't know. But wait . . . the really *big* laugh is still coming. When I had finished and signed my statement, they patted me on the back and said: "Well done, Daniels! But now tell us something we don't know." And they weren't fooling. They knew everything. Somebody had been talking to them for a long time, and about a hell of a lot more than Steve Daniels sneaking out to have a good time. So for Christ's sake, Piet, anything you like . . . a lie if it's necessary . . . but don't tell me you got nothing to say!

PIET: A lie?

STEVE: All right! I'll admit it. I've got doubts. So I'm asking you straight: Is Gladys telling the truth?

PIET: Why me, Steve?

GLADYS: Careful, Steven! He looks like one of them, doesn't he? The same gross certainty in himself! He certainly sounds like them. He speaks English with a dreadful accent. What else, Steven? He's poor enough to do it for money.

STEVE: All right, Gladys!

> *He grabs his jacket, hesitates for a second, then goes over to confront Piet directly.*

Relax, Piet. I've solved our problem. I'm going to hope it was you. I mean it. I'm going to try hard, because, hell, man! . . . will that make it easier going next week . . . if I can throw away our friendship like all the junk on my lounge floor.

> *He turns to go.*

GLADYS *(to Piet):* You're not going to defend yourself and deny it?

PIET: No.

GLADYS: My God, are you that safe? Can nothing threaten you? I'm so jealous, Peter. Aren't you, Steven?

STEVE: Gladys?

GLADYS: Wouldn't you like to be as safe as he is? Because we aren't, you know.

STEVE: Please, Gladys! What's going on? Are you playing games?

GLADYS: You wouldn't be doubting him if you were. I doubt everything now. But not him. When you come to think of it, it's almost stupid. He's lost a farm, his friends . . . you! . . . the great purpose in his life, and he's going to lose a lot more before it's all over, but his faith in himself refuses to be shaken. Of course he didn't do it! What's happened to you, Steven? He isn't an informer. It must have been one of your other trusty comrades. Go back to Mavis and start all over again, because it wasn't him.

STEVE *(angrily):* Then why did you . . . ?

GLADYS *(violently):* That's my business. Yes, mine! My reason for telling you an ugly lie, which you were ready to believe! . . . is *my* business. I accept, Steven, that I am just a white face on the outskirts of your terrible life, but I'm in the middle of mine and yours is just a brown face on the outskirts of that. Do you understand what I am saying? I've got my own story. I don't need yours. I've discovered hell for myself. It might be hard for you to accept, Steven, but you are not the only one who has been hurt. Politics and black skins don't make the only victims in this country.

STEVE: Gladys . . .

PIET: Leave her alone, Steve.

GLADYS *(turning on him with equal violence):* I don't need you! I don't need you to protect me any more! You never did, anyway. When they took away my diaries you did nothing. When the others took away my false teeth and held me down and blew my mind to pieces, you weren't even there! I called for you, Peter, but you weren't there.

PIET *(restraining Gladys physically):* I think you'd better go, Steve!

No, Gladys insists, Steve is not to leave till she finishes telling him about England as she'd promised. She describes a beautiful, peaceful picture of England —green, with a cottage, an old country road and pleasant country folk. And that's what it is—a picture: "Sunset in Dorset." It hangs on the wall where she sat to wait her turn. Waiting, she tried to distract herself from what was to come by imagining herself to be in the pleasant setting of the picture. But it didn't work. Nor did cursing. Nothing helps, she says, "because when your turn does come and they call your name and you sit down on the floor and say 'No,' they pick you up and carry you inside . . . and do it. They've burned my brain as brown as yours, Steven." She hands Steve the present she'd wrapped for Mavis, tells him goodbye and goes inside.

STEVE *(putting on his coat):* What happened?

PIET: Those raids, after your arrest. They took away personal diaries she had been keeping. Then she started to get funny . . . imagining things. Wouldn't go out because people were spying on her. She thought I was one of the Special Branch.

STEVE: Those bastards.

PIET: That's why I couldn't get to your trial. The doctors told me not to leave her alone. Anyway, it got worse, and they took her away to Fort England Clinic.

STEVE *(he makes a half-hearted move to leave):* I don't want to leave this country, Piet. I was born here. It's my home. But they won't give me a chance to live. And they'll do the same to my children. You were prepared to let me go believing that you . . .

PIET: Hell, Steve, you know why. If you could have believed it, there was no point in denying it.

STEVE: Ja. So that's it, then. No quotation for old time's sake?

PIET: No. I'd rather remember this as another occasion when I didn't know what to say.

Steve departs. Piet goes into the bedroom where Gladys is sitting at her dressing table, holding her diary. Piet reassures her that her words didn't hurt the relationship between himself and Steve in any way.

GLADYS *(holding her diary):* I should have wrapped this up as well and given it to him as his farewell present. It would have been appropriate. He's got to start his life again. I know what that means. In some ways that's the worst . . . starting again . . . waking up with nothing left, not even your name, and having to start again. You see, I wasn't able to use it. It's empty. Blank. *(Turning the pages.)* All of them . . . blank . . . blank. It wasn't for want of trying, Peter. I sat down every night, opened it . . . but then nothing. The ink used to clot and dry on the nib while I sat looking at the blank page. I've got no secrets left, except for one which I don't want. I've tried to find others in my life, but all I've got is this one, and I'm frightened of it. There's a little ritual at the end of every meal in Fort England. You sit at your table and wait while the dirty cutlery is taken to the matron, so that she can count the knives. There are none missing tonight, but . . . You're a good man, Peter, and that has become a terrible provocation. I want to destroy that goodness. Ironic, isn't it! That which I most hate and fear about this country is all I seem to have learned.

> *She looks at her diary.*

I'll keep this and try next time. I've got to go back, Peter.

PIET: Are you sure?

GLADYS: Yes. Aren't you?

As she prepares for her return to the hospital in the morning, Piet goes to the backyard, sits and looks at his unidentified aloe. *Curtain.*

ZOOMAN AND THE SIGN

A Play in Two Acts

BY CHARLES FULLER

Cast and credits appear on page 398

CHARLES FULLER was born in Philadelphia March 5, 1939, the son of a printer. He served in the U.S. Army from 1959 to 1962 and was educated at Villanova and LaSalle College, receiving his B.A. in 1967. Between the Army and college he ran the Afro-American Art Theater in Philadelphia. As a playwright, his first New York production was The Perfect Party *off Broadway for 21 performances in 1969. He followed this with* In the Deepest Part of Sleep *at The Negro Ensemble Company for 32 performances in 1974;* Candidate *at New Federal Theater and the musical* Sparrow in Flight *at Amas Repertory Theater, both in 1974; and* The Brownsville Raid, *first offered in a staged reading at the O'Neill Playwrights Conference in 1975 and then produced off Broadway by NEC in 1976 for 112 performances.*

Zooman and the Sign is Fuller's third production at NEC and first Best Play, and it won him a 1981 Obie Award in playwriting. He is the author of film and TV scripts, including an adaptation of Ernest J. Graves's The Sky is Gray *in the American Short Story series. He has been a recipient of Guggenheim, Rockefeller Foundation, National Endowment and CAPS fellowships in playwriting. He is married, with two sons, and lives in Philadelphia.*

Time: The present

Place: Philadelphia, Pa., the home of Rachel and Reuben Tate—the street outside; various locations for Zoo-man

ACT I

SYNOPSIS: A comfortably furnished middle-class living room occupies much of the stage, with porch door, stoop and sidewalk downstage right and access to other rooms upstage left. There is a platform down right, and as the lights come up upon it a young black man is standing there, *"looking at the audience rather contemptuously. He is wearing a mesh and plastic green and white baseball cap tilted to the side. A red T-shirt with the inscription "ME" on it hangs outside a pair of slacks or dungarees designed with two large pockets. He is wearing high top sneaks,"* plus thin gold and silver chains around his neck. He is Zooman, his presence accompanied by low disco background music.

Zooman explains that he is carrying a gun and a 10-in switchblade knife he calls "Magic". He shows the knife to the audience and tells how he knifed a man in the subway the day before.

ZOOMAN *(smiles):*.....*"*Magic" knicked him. "Magic" is sharp as a razor. He ain't even know he was cut 'til he was halfway down the platform, and the blood started runnin' down the ole punk's hand. *(Looks at knife.)* Mothafucka started screamin'—dropped his newspapa'—jumpin' up and down, pleadin' to everybody waitin' on the subway—Ain't nobody do nothin'—ole jive West Indian mothafucka damn near got hit by a train! *(Laughs.)*.....That ole mothafucka yesterday coulda put somebody's eye out. Swingin' his arms around like he owned the whole fuckin' platform. Lotta ole people take advantage of you jes' cause they old. Movin' all slow and shit—mumblin' unda' they breath—shufflin' down the street all bent over and twisted up—skin hangin' all off they faces—makes my stomach turn jes' to look at 'em!.....*(Casually.)* What am I doing here now? I just killed somebody. Little girl, I think. Me and Stockholm turned the corner of this street?—and there's Gustav and them jive mothafuckas from uptown, and this little bitch has to be sittin' on her front steps playin' jacks—or some ole kid shit!

To Zooman, this street is a war zone, and he opened fire on the intruders and hit the little girl by accident: "She was in the wrong place at the wrong time— how am I supposed to feel guilty over somethin' like that? Shiiit, I don't know the little bitch, anyway."

Lights fade on Zooman and come up on the Tates' living room, Reuben, a black man dressed in bus driver's uniform, and his wife Rachel, *"an attractive black woman,"* are seated on the sofa. Uncle Emmett is also present, as is the Tates'

Giancarlo Esposito as Zooman in *Zooman and the Sign*

15-year-old son, Victor, dressed somewhat like Zooman. The parents are mourning death of their little daughter, while Uncle Emmett seethes with the desire to go find the killer and wipe him out, if they have to kill every kid wearing a tilted cap and sneakers.

REUBEN: You can talk, Emmett—but just stop that "killin' " business—we just saw Jinny stretched out on a table dead!

EMMETT: All right—

Slight pause.

I guess y'all the bereaved family, huh? Well, I want you to know, I'm family too!

REUBEN: Nobody said nothin' about you not bein' in the family!

EMMETT: Y'all are not the only people gonna miss her—I was her godfather, too, remember that! I carried her first bassinet down here on the train from New York. You have any idea what losin' Jinny did to us? There ain't that many of us left! Five—and Ash is Rachel's kin! *(He points to Victor.)* That's the last Tate sittin' right there—and I'm not supposed to have something to say? I'll tell you what: If they come back through here again with they little gang war—I got something for 'em!

REUBEN: Come on, Emmett—that's enough, now.

EMMETT: What's wrong with you? I can remember the time I'da had to hold him back—nobody messed with the Tates! Thing like this happen, your father and the rest of us would be on the street until we caught the little sons-a-bitches, and took an eye for an eye!

REUBEN: We're not headhunters. This is not the old days! Emmett—you livin' in the past!

Reuben suggests they cool off with a beer. Emmett goes to fetch one. Victor wants to go out, but Rachel fears he may meet with an accident too and wants to keep her family together here in this room. Gently but firmly, Reuben insists that Victor be allowed to go outside, provided he stays around the front steps. Despite his mother's misgivings, Victor goes outside.

Rachel, in tears, is obsessed with her memories of her beloved Jinny. Emmett returns with the beer. Reuben insists that Rachel get some rest. He guides her upstairs, as Rachel asks him to call Ash (Reuben has already done so, and Ash is on her way).

Outside, Victor is joined by his friend Russell. Russell has heard that someone who goes by the name of Zooman killed Jinny—Zooman who, with his brother, once beat up his own mother. At Victor's request, Russell agrees to procure him a gun.

Victor goes back into the house, where Reuben and Emmett are trying to talk about ordinary things—Reuben about how the new gadgets on his bus never work, Emmett about how his assistants on the Bellevue Hospital cleaning staff don't know their jobs. Finally Emmett explodes: "I wanna do something, Reuben!" Reuben replies, "What, Emmett? Kill somebody? Dammit, let it be! There's nothin' to do! Leave it to the police—them boys ran through here in broad daylight!"

Victor goes upstairs to look in on his mother. Emmett has seen that Reuben and Rachel are having problems with their marriage, but Reuben doesn't want to talk about that.

The doorbell rings—it's Donald Jackson, a neighbor from down the street who used to be a fan of Reuben's when Reuben was a light heavyweight prize fighter. Jackson has come to see if there's anything he can do and to tell them that he and his wife saw nothing of the murder—his wife was in the back of the house, and Jackson was at work. He has a message for Reuben from his wife.

JACKSON: . . . . .Cop told her he went to every house on the block and not one person claim they saw anything.

REUBEN: What!

JACKSON: That's what the cop said.

REUBEN: There's forty—fifty families around here!

JACKSON: It seemed strange to my wife too, 'cause she said when she came outside, everybody in the block was on their porch. About half on your side, and most of them on my side.

REUBEN: You sure that's what the cop said? *(Jackson nods.)* And they covered every house?

EMMETT: They ain't shit, Reub!

REUBEN: That's impossible. Mrs. Smith sits on her porch morning til night. Davis stays at his window—he can't even get upstairs. I don't believe it!

Rachel, on her way downstairs, overhears this conversation and insists that the neighbors are lying—she saw all of them at their front doors or hanging out windows when she went outside. She continues to insist that the neighbors are lying if they say they didn't see anything. She yields to angry tears as Reuben tries to comfort her, and the lights fade indoors and come up outdoors on Zooman playing with his knife.

ZOOMAN: When you got nothin' to do, come to the zoo! *(Quieter.)* First couple hours are the worse. The big, blue fools are probably sweeping the neighborhood by now, picking up everybody in sight. So there ain't that many mothafuckin' places to hide—except maybe in a junkie-hole—or out here in the mothafuckin' park—

Pause.

I got someplace to go. I just don't wanna git nobody in trouble, that's all! You stay away from your people as long as you can—besides, my Mom neva could take pressure, no way! She'd just sit there and cry—plus, it's the first damn place the mothafuckin' Man is gonna look! I ain't that dumb!

Sudden mood swing.

I shot the little bitch 'cause I felt like it! Zoo-man felt like shooting somebody!. . . .

Zooman complains that he was picked up 21 times last year, sometimes for something he didn't do, like a gang rape of a teacher at his school. He remembers that tomorrow is the tenth birthday of his little half-sister, who lives in Birmingham. He has relatives everywhere, "Plus I got friends in town! PJ—Mooky, Christine—so I got plenty of places to go if I want to! Plenty. *(Pause.)* I just don't want to."

Lights fade on Zooman and come up on the Tate household, where it is after midnight and Ash Boswell, Rachel's cousin, has arrived. Ash is *"a smallish woman in her late 50s,"* dressed in a robe but *"stylish and for her age a good-looking woman."* Reuben is telling Ash and Rachel how it was when he went through the neighborhood asking questions. Everyone claims to have seen or heard nothing, but the Tates know their neighbors are lying. Reuben fears that if they catch the person who killed his daughter, he may go free if everyone refuses to identify him. "Black people don't like to deal with the police," Ash comments, and then goes on: "I blame a lot of this on them food stamps. . . . .When the 'Negro' was hungrier, we treated each other better. Nowadays everybody's got their bellies full and we sit up belchin', watching those damn soap operas and game shows all day—hot dog in one hand, the phone in the other, a beer or a

Pepsi on the floor beside us—the baby crawlin' around dirty, the whole house filthy. . . . .When we knew we might have to borrow a cup of flour—or a pair of pants—or a white shirt from the people across the street, we were a lot more concerned about them, and a lot more conscientious about ourselves."

If they don't care about how they look, or their health, why should they care about their neighbors? Ash continues. Reuben insists the problem is more personal, as Ash goes out to the kitchen to do the dishes. Alone, Rachel picks a quarrel with Reuben over an infidelity which Reuben swears is now over and done with—but their grief over Jinny's death soon drives away all other emotions.

Rachel suggests that they move out of this neighborhood, where the neighbors didn't even call the police after the shots were fired. They can't afford to move just now, Reuben insists; besides, they have to stay here until they find a witness.

Ash comes in to say that she's making potato salad for anybody who happens to call to pay their respects. Rachel is on the verge of tears, as Reuben tries to comfort her.

Lights fade on the Tates and come up on Zooman, who says, "You know, I damn near got caught? Yeah. I go snatch this ole bitch's pocketbook, and she started yellin'—wig came off, and shit! I had to knock her down! Then this hero mothafucka chases my ass five blocks before I could duck into an all night movie," where the police searched the auditorium but failed to identify Zooman. "I'm glad I got rid of that gun. 'Magic' is all I need anyway. You shoulda seen that bitch when I stuck it in her face—she was lucky her pocketbook was all I took. You ain't expect me to eat out no garbage can, did you?"

The lights fade on Zooman and come up on Reuben dressed in his bus driver's uniform and cap and carrying a rolled-up sign. "Losing Jinny was like waking up and discovering the sun had a hole in it," he declares. He wants to beat somebody up, but instead, "I went downtown this morning and had this sign made to hang over our porch. Get these folks off their asses. It sure can't hurt nobody. Not the way I could. But maybe it'll make somebody come forward."

Reuben exits as a sign unrolls above the stage: THE KILLERS OF OUR DAUGHTER JINNY ARE FREE ON THE STREETS BECAUSE OUR NEIGHBORS WILL NOT IDENTIFY THEM! Light is concentrated on the sign and then goes to black, to the faint accompaniment of Zooman music. *Curtain.*

ACT II

There is a wreath on the Tate door now, and a broken window has been covered with cardboard. Rachel, alone onstage, remembers how it was when Reuben quit the prize ring, before he landed a job with the bus company, and they bought this house with borrowed money and moved in without a stick of furniture. "This neighborhood was already black then," Rachel tells the audience, "and we never turned on ourselves—we kept the block clean, swept the sidewalks, gave our little block parties and watched out for each otha's kids. I could run to the store and leave my front door open. *(Pause.)* The only stranger would be somebody who didn't live around here. *(Pause.)* But I can remember the day, and the hour, that

Ray Aranha as Reuben Tate, Frances Foster as Ash Boswell and
Mary Alice as Rachel Tate in a scene from *Zooman and the Sign*

fool down at the end of the street, Julius Williams, began fixing used cars in the
middle of the damn sidewalk, and the oil stains and dirt tracked their way through
the entire block. And outside of Reuben and Mr. Neal up at the corner nobody
around here said or did anything! Couple months later they shot Scherr in the
grocery store—the Armistead family across the street staged a gun-battle with the
cops, then the riots closed all the stores on the Avenue, and gave the nighttime
to the thieves! It's been like livin' on a burning fuse! *(Quietly.)* Reuben can hang
up all the signs he wants to—you can't bring the dead back to life. Not them—
not Jinny. I just want to move."

Lights up in the living room, where Victor and Russell are listening to music
and watching TV with the sound turned off. Victor is determined to go after
Zooman, but Russell warns him to leave those killers to the police. Many of the
neighbors resent Reuben's sign, as Russell says: "Half these niggahs 'round here
can't even read that sign, and those that can, it just pisses them off, 'cause it brings
the whole neighborhood down—'n' somebody's always claimin' our people ain't
no good." Victor resents Russell's criticism of his father. Anyway, Russell won't
supply Victor with bullets for his gun.

Rachel and Ash appear, as Grace Georges, about Rachel's age, hair in curlers
and dressed in dungarees and a T-shirt, comes to the door. After glancing at the
sign and shaking her head. Grace enters. Ash introduces herself and offers some
potato salad, but Grace has come over for only a brief visit to pay her respects
and express her sympathy to Rachel. Grace's girl Denise and Jinny used to play
together. Grace has to get home to get her husband Mike's dinner, but she has
time for a question before she leaves.

GRACE: Why did you let Reuben hang that sign up, Rachel? He's got these people around here climbing the walls! Don't none of them appreciate it—in fact, Cortez and Williams told Mike they were planning to hold a block meeting about it.

Pause.

And the truth is, I kinda think it makes the whole street look bad myself. You know what I mean? Like, what if you didn't see it? Thing like that lumps the good with the bad—and every time you turn around black folks are saying something terrible about each other! "We can't get together—our men ain't no good—we're triflin', everywhere we live is a slum!" I get tired of it myself—and Reuben's sign makes this look like the worst place in the world.

ASH: But then you didn't lose your little Denise, did you honey?

GRACE: If we had, I wouldn't let Mike advertise about it! That's y'all's private business!

ASH: Seems like a killing on the block would be everybody's business.

GRACE: The Tates ain't no better than nobody else! Rachel and Reuben didn't come to Myrtle Coleman's layout—or to Mr. Stewart's funeral either! I didn't see the Tates get excited when those hoodlums raped Lou Jefferson's little girl—or robbed my place! Why should anybody go out of their way for them? I didn't hang up no sign!

RACHEL: Did you see it, Grace?

GRACE *(stiffens defensively):* What? No! Don't you accuse me!

A brick and a bottle crash against the screen door. Victor goes outside, and Ash sees that he has a gun. He insists that the family needs it for protection, but Rachel will not permit him to carry it. She takes it away from him, and he exits. Rachel gives the gun to Ash to throw away and orders Grace out of the house.

Grace departs, Rachel admits she thinks the sign is "disrespectful." Victor brings in a broom and dustpan to clean up the mess. Rachel is explaining that she didn't take part in those neighborhood events Grace mentioned because Reuben was away, and she didn't want to go alone.

Reuben and Emmett come in—they have obviously been in a fight and are hurt. It was a bar fight, Reuben explains: "We were drinking two beers, and this fella from Croskey Street—I've seen him before. He walks up in *my* face and tells me HE didn't want us in there—unless I took my sign down!" It is giving the black community a bad name, the man insisted, and they soon came to blows.

Rachel tells Reuben about Victor's gun, and Reuben reacts as expected: "You want me to let loose on you, boy?!" The phone rings, and Reuben answers it—it's a hostile caller. "Say that to my face, punk!" is Reuben's reply. The next call is from TV Channel 22 wanting to come over and talk to Reuben about the sign. He tells them he'll think about it and hangs up.

REUBEN: They heard about the sign and want to interview me.

RACHEL: I'm sick of that sign!

REUBEN: What's wrong with the sign?

RACHEL: We're supposed to be in mourning—We lost Jinny three days ago—why are you doing this now?

REUBEN: Rachel, that sign hasn't hurt anybody unless they feel guilty—it doesn't fire bullets—punch out people—

RACHEL: It is making people hate us, Reuben!

REUBEN *(angrily):* That's because there's not *enough* signs! I'ma put up more of 'em—saturate the whole neighborhood! Telephone poles—store windows—buses—let everybody know! They want to be nasty?

RACHEL: You're making this a side-show!

REUBEN: The side-show was the day they ran through here, shot up the street, killed our daughter, and nobody on this block did anything about it! I'm not gonna let them forget Jinny's life!

Jinny was gentle and shy, Rachel points out—violence and anger have nothing to do with her. Emmett comes in, helped by Ash and Victor; his arm is broken, he must be taken to the hospital. All exit except Rachel, who comments, "Somebody needs to pay more attention to Jinny . . ."

Lights down on the Tate house and up on Zooman, who comments, "It's no fun being on the run. But I happen to know, if a black kills a black, and they don't catch you right away, they liable to forget about it—" He remembers a time when he and a friend hid out successfully for ten days, with his girl friend Christine bringing them food.

ZOOMAN: I ain't really worried yet. But that niggah with them signs? Ain't nobody ever pulled that kinda shit before! Killings, rapes, drugs—all kinds of shit be goin' on every day and nobody says nothin'! That section was always run down and dangerous—vacant "junkie-holes" everywhea, trash on the streets—*(Shakes head.)* Always some mothafucka wanna be a hero! Wasn' neva no stores on the Avenue! You have to go halfway around the world to get to the Chinese laundry —get your clothes cleaned or your shoes fixed! Ain't nothin' in there but barber shops and junkie corner groceries—and every now and then a drug store where the Man sells you your pills and cough syrup behind a bullet-proof glass! Shiiiittt! The first junkie I ever met was a mothafucka lived 'cross the street—and I know every mothafucka that's stealin', muggin', hustlin' and procurin'—grew up with all of 'em! Everybody I know buys hot clothes! Curtis's mother? Walkin' around passin' out all that Let-Jesus-Save-You shit? Buys truckloads of hot dresses and be sellin' them to her Holy-Moly congregation. And I've seen Greenie's fatha stealin' cookies out the supermarket—puttin' tuna fish and shit under his coat! Now he's gonna make that zoo a neighborhood puttin' everybody on me? The little bitch was in the way, that's all! Who the fuck he think he is? Sendin' people afta me, like I'm some animal! If he wants to blame somebody—you don't leave no little girl sittin' on her steps by herself nowadays! I don't let my sista go out by herself! He shoulda known better—what kinda fatha is he? *(Slight pause.)* But I'll tell you what—if somebody don't git his ass straight soon, I'ma show him just what a killer is—Niggahs can't be heroes, don't he know nothin'?

The light fades on Zooman and comes up at the Tates where, dressed in black (and Emmett with his arm in a sling), they have just attended Jinny's wake, which Rachel found somewhat ugly. Ash—who didn't go—reports that Jackson has been over a couple of times and seems to want to talk to Reuben and Rachel.

Some people at the wake told Reuben they were happy about the sign; others wrote slighting remarks in the register. One loudmouth out on the sidewalk even threatened to burn down the Tates' house.

Jackson comes in carrying loaves of bread as a present. He has come to say how much he and his wife like the Tates, and "I'm glad you put up that sign, but we didn't see nothin'—my wife or me. We ain't them kinda people, Reuben!" A group of neighbors means to pull down or burn the sign, but the Jacksons refused to join them.

Jackson departs. Reuben is determined—"The sign stays up"—even though Rachel would like to have it removed.

The phone rings: Police Sergeant Harrison informs Reuben that they've caught one 15-year-old involved in the shooting. The sergeant remembers Reuben from his boxing days. He'll have a patrol car swing by the house from time to time during the night. The lad the police caught, named Stockholm, has informed on his accomplice Zooman.

Victor goes to sit outside, as Rachel once again urges Reuben to take down the sign and Reuben once again refuses. He isn't afraid of reprisals (though the rest of the family is): "You can't live across the street from me, see my daughter get killed, and not do nothin'!" Rachel orders Reuben to take the sign down or leave the house. Reuben declares he will do neither.

The lights fade inside and come up outside, where Victor is reflecting, "They always tell me that I've got a better education than they had—that I know more —should do great things, but they never let me say anything. I don't have a voice in nothin'—no opinions, no pros—cons—and most of the time they talk over me like I'm not even there. And I know a whole lot more than they know." Victor believes he is the one who misses Jinny the most. They were close, sharing little secrets. She confided to Victor how angry it made her when her mother wouldn't let her father stay in the house: "She told me once that sometimes, when she missed him a lot, she would show off just to get on my Mom's nerves so bad she would have to call my father over, just to punish her. At least she would see him."

Victor moves across the stage as Zooman enters, crossing from the other side. Each is wary of the other as they come nearer, Zooman taking his knife from his pocket, flicking it open and holding it out of sight. They cross without incident, though, Victor going into the house and Zooman, putting his knife away, to his platform.

Zooman assumes that the police have forced Stockholm to talk, and Stockholm is probably putting all the blame for the killing on Zooman—that's what Zooman would have done in Stockholm's place. Zooman was accosted in his hiding place by a homosexual last night, and knifed him.

ZOOMAN:. . . . .shiiittt! And y'all got the nerve to hunt me? Y'all let anything walk the streets—and you mothafuckas never showed me no mercy!
    Pause.

I'll be off your streets soon, don't worry—I just got one more thing to do.

> *Zooman steps from the platform and starts across the stage boldly toward the Tate house. Before he reaches the steps he is hollering, his knife in his hand.*

Hey mothafucka! This is Zooman out here!

> *He reaches up and begins to rip and tear at the sign.*

Don't nobody do this shit! You don't send people after me! You hear that, mothfucka!? This is Zooman you fuckin' with!

> *Lights come on inside the house and Emmett, half frightened, half asleep, emerges from the dining room with a gun in his hand.*

EMMETT: Reuben?

ZOOMAN *(at once):* Come on out!

> *Emmett fires immediately through the window. The shot hits Zooman and knocks him down, and he pulls down the sign with him. He is in surprised agony for a few moments as he begins to die.*

EMMETT: Reuben! They're outside! Reuben!

> *He fires again.*

Go 'way!

> *Reuben bursts onto the stage upstairs.*

REUBEN: Emmett—what the hell are you doin'? *(He starts down.)*

EMMETT: They're outside! They were pullin' on the sign! I heard 'em—it woke me up! They were tryin' to come in!

REUBEN *(starts toward the front door):* That sounded like some kid—

EMMETT: That wasn' no kid I heard! Them people were comin' in! I heard 'em on the porch! I heard 'em!

> *Rachel and Victor and Ash emerge as Reuben opens the door and steps out onto the porch. Reuben bends over the body.*

REUBEN: Be still.

ZOOMAN: Fuck you! I'm Zooman.

Reuben orders the others to call the police. Rachel, realizing that this is the person who killed Jinny, feels the urge to kill him—but he's already dead. Releasing the anguish of recent events, Rachel reaches out, weeping, to Reuben, who takes her back into the house. The lights fade, as another sign slowly appears over the porch. "*It reads: HERE, LESTER JOHNSON WAS KILLED. HE WILL BE MISSED BY FAMILY AND FRIENDS. HE WAS KNOWN AS ZOOMAN. A spotlight builds to brilliance on this new sign, then slowly fades out. The stage goes to black, but Zooman's music lingers in the air, mixed with the sound of a distant siren. Curtain.*"

Louis Turenne (van Swieten), Paul Harding (von Strack), Tim Curry (bowing, Mozart), Nicholas Kepros (Emperor Joseph), Ian McKellen (Salieri) and Patrick Hines (Rosenberg) in a court scene from *Amadeus*

AMADEUS

A Play in Two Acts

BY PETER SHAFFER

Cast and credits appear on page 360

PETER SHAFFER was born in England, at Liverpool, in 1926 (Anthony Shaffer, author of Sleuth, *is his twin). He attended St. Paul's School in London and spent three years at Trinity College, Cambridge, and three more working in the coal mines as a "Bevin Boy" in World War II. In 1951, aged 25, he came to the United States, where for still another three years he worked in New York City at Doubleday Book Shop and as an assistant in the Acquisitions Department of the New York Public Library. He also worked as an editor in the Symphonic Department of a distinguished London firm of music publishers, all the while pursuing a writing career which began to take shape with the production of his* The Salt Land, The Prodigal Father *and* Balance of Terror *on British television. In 1958 his play* Five Finger Exercise *was a success in London, winning the Standard award for drama. In December 1959 it was produced in New York at the Music Box and was named a Best Play of its season and won the New York Drama Critics Circle award for best foreign play. A pair of Peter Shaffer one-acters,* The Private Ear *and* The Public Eye, *were produced in 1963 at the Morosco on Broadway after a London production that ran 18 months.*

Shaffer's next play, The Royal Hunt of the Sun *(1964), was the first work by a contemporary playwright to be done at England's National Theater. The following season, in 1965, it was presented on Broadway for 261 performances and was named a Best Play of 1965–66. His next play,* Black Comedy, *was commissioned by the National Theater, which produced it in 1965. It came to Broadway in 1967 for 337 performances on a program with* White Lies *(written by Shaffer especially for this tandem production) and was also named a Best Play of its season.*

Shaffer followed this with The Battle of Shrivings *under the direction of Peter Hall in the 1970 London season for 73 performances. He returned to the National Theater in July, 1973 with his famed* Equus, *brought to Broadway in October 1974 for a phenomenal run of 1,209 performances (and later made into a motion picture), a Best Play of its year and the winner of the Drama Critics, Tony and other awards as the season's best-of-bests.*

Shaffer's Amadeus *appeared at the National Theater on Nov. 2, 1979 (its author now being the contemporary playwright most frequently presented by the National Theater). Its Broadway incarnation, in which it now becomes Shaffer's fifth Best Play, took place on Dec. 17, 1980.*

Among his other activities, Shaffer served as a music critic, in 1961–62, for the magazine Time and Tide. *Trans-Atlantically active as he is both professionally and personally, he now resides in New York City.*

Time: November 1823 and, in recall, the decade 1781–1791

Place: Vienna

ACT I

SYNOPSIS: A wooden rectangle set into the floor is to delineate many interiors and now holds a small table bearing a cake stand at right, a wheelchair with its back turned at center, a fortepiano at left and a chandelier above. The general decor is rococo, and there is an added space behind an archway upstage. Changes of time and place within the fluidly continuous movement will take place by means of liveried servants moving and arranging the necessary props (*"Through a pleasant paradox of theater their constant coming and going, bearing tables, chairs or cloaks, should render them virtually invisible, and certainly unremarkable"*).

In the darkness, gossipy whispers are heard, among which can be barely distinguished the words "Salieri" and "assassin." As the lights come up to reveal an old man sitting in the wheelchair, the hisses intensify, seemingly emanating from shadowy silhouettes of fashionably attired Viennese thrown onto the wall of the upstage space.

The Venticelli—two middle-aged gentlemen—enter. They are to be *"purveyors of fact, rumor and gossip throughout the play,"* and here they seethe with the latest rumor that old Antonio Salieri, the famous court musician, is beating his breast and crying aloud for Mozart's forgiveness. Salieri's valet and cook come onstage as if to verify the report of Salieri's supposed confession. The Venticelli continue their excited exchange.

VENTICELLO 1: There was talk once before, you know.
VENTICELLO 2: Thirty-two years ago.
VENTICELLO 1: When Mozart was dying.
VENTICELLO 2: He claimed he'd been poisoned.
VENTICELLO 1: Some said he accused a man.
VENTICELLO 2: Some said that man was Salieri.
VENTICELLO 1: But no one believed it.
VENTICELLO 2: They *knew* what he died of!
VENTICELLO 1: Syphilis, surely.
VENTICELLO 2: Like everybody else.
    Pause.
VENTICELLO 1 *(slyly):* But what if Mozart was right?
VENTICELLO 2: If he really *was* murdered?
VENTICELLO 1: And by him. Our First Kapellmeister!
VENTICELLO 2: Antonio Salieri!
VENTICELLO 1: It can't possibly be true.
VENTICELLO 2: It's not actually credible.
VENTICELLO 1: Because *why?*
VENTICELLO 2: Because why?
VENTICELLI 1 & 2: *Why on earth would he do it?*
VENTICELLO 1: And why confess *now?*
VENTICELLO 2: After thirty-two years!
WHISPERERS: SALIERI!
SALIERI: Mozart! Mozart! *Perdonami!* . . . *Il tuo assassino ti chiede perdono!*

The Venticelli look at each other and depart wondering what the truth may be. The cook and valet remain, and Salieri swivels his wheelchair around to face the audience. He is a man of 70 in old dressing gown and shawl. It is 3 o'clock of a November morning in 1823, and Salieri asks the audience—"ghosts of the future"—to keep him company, as he means to stay awake till dawn. He orders his two servants to return at 6 o'clock, and they exit.

Salieri confesses that he is in final hour of his life. He goes to the piano, playing and singing in a cracked voice to invoke the "ghosts of the future" as the lights come up on the audience and he can now "see" the specters he has raised. He goes to the cake stand to refresh himself with a sweetmeat, while chattering about his birth in the North of Italy in 1750 and his early years there; his growing thirst for success and fame in his chosen world of music ("Absolute music! A note of music is either right or wrong—*absolutely!* Not even time can alter that: music is God's art"). By the age of 12 he set his sights on being a composer, and at 16 he knelt to bargain with God: "Signore, let me be a composer! Grant me sufficient fame to enjoy it. In return I will live with virtue. I will be chaste. I will strive to better the lot of my fellows. And I will honor you with much music all the days of my life!" It seemed to Salieri that he sensed God agreeing to this bargain. The next day a family friend sent him to Vienna to study music, and it was not long before he gained the favor of the Emperor of Austria.

The year he left Italy, Salieri notes, "A young prodigy was touring Europe. A miraculous virtuoso aged ten years. Wolfgang Amadeus Mozart." He informs the audience that he is going to present to them his last work, entitled "The Death of Mozart—or, Did I Do It?" He rises, bows and doffs his ragged old clothes, transforming himself into a young man in the prime of life, elegantly attired.

The scene is transformed into the Court of Vienna in the year 1781. The Emperor Joseph II and his Court are revealed upstage before a golden fireplace listening to music, with old Kapellmeister Bonno at the keyboard. Salieri prepares to don a powdered wig.

SALIERI:. . . . .I am thirty-one. Already a prolific composer to the Hapsburg Court. I own a respectable house and a respectable wife—Teresa.
> *Enter Teresa, a padded, placid lady who seats herself upright in the upstage chair.*
I do not mock her, I assure you. I required only one quality in a domestic companion—lack of fire. And in that omission Teresa was conspicuous.
> *Ceremoniously, he puts on his powdered wig.*
I also had a prize pupil: Katherina Cavalieri.
> *Katherina swirls on from the opposite side: a beautiful girl of 20. The music becomes vocal: faintly, we hear a soprano singing a concert aria. Like Teresa's, Katherina's part is mute—but as she stands by the fortepiano, she energetically mimes her rapturous singing. At the keyboard old Bonno accompanies her appreciatively.*
She was a bubbling student with merry eyes and a sweet, eatable mouth. I was very much in love with Katherina—or at least in lust. But because of my vow to God, I had never laid a finger upon the girl. . . . .

Salieri's ambition was still burning brightly, however, and he coveted old Bonno's post of First Royal Kapellmeister. The action on the stage freezes while Salieri explains that court musicians of his era were in large part mere servants of the well-to-do but managed to make a great impact on their patrons through the music which enhanced every aspect of their patrons' lives and immortalized their memory after their deeds were forgotton.

The Emperor drifts offstage after handing a rolled-up paper to one of three stiffly-standing courtiers, who remain while the Venticelli enter to inform Salieri that Mozart is on his way to Vienna and means to establish himself here permanently. Mozart wrote his first symphony at five years of age and now, at 25, he is a composer renowned throughout Europe.

The lights come up on the trio of courtiers at the Palace of Schonbrunn: Von Strack *("stiff and proper, aged 55")*, Orsini-Rosenberg *("plump, supercilious, aged 60")* and Van Swieten *("cultivated and serious, aged 50")*. Strack hands the Emperor's rolled-up piece of paper to Rosenberg.

STRACK *(to Rosenberg):* You are required to commission a comic opera in German from Herr Mozart.

SALIERI *(to audience):* Johann Von Strack. Royal Chamberlain. A Court official to his collar bone.

ROSENBERG *(loftily):* Why in German? Italian is the only possible language for opera!

SALIERI: Count Orsini-Rosenberg. Director of the Opera. Benevolent to all things Italian—especially myself.

STRACK *(stiffly):* The idea of a National Opera is dear to His Majesty's heart. He desires to hear pieces in good plain German.

VAN SWIETEN: Yes, but why comic? It is not the function of music to be funny.

SALIERI: Baron Van Swieten. Prefect of the Imperial Library. Ardent Freemason. Yet to find anything funny. Known for his enthusiasm for old-fashioned music as "Lord Fugue."

VAN SWIETEN: I heard last week a remarkable *serious* opera from Mozart: *Idomeneo, King of Crete.*

ROSENBERG: I heard that too. A young fellow trying to impress beyond his abilities. Too much spice. Too many notes.

STRACK *(firmly, to Rosenberg):* Nevertheless, kindly convey the commission to him today.

ROSENBERG *(taking the paper reluctantly):* I believe we are going to have trouble with this young man.

Rosenberg and Strack depart, while Van Swieten confers with Salieri on the subject of Freemasonry, inviting an exceedingly deferential Salieri to join his lodge, then taking his leave. Salieri admits to the audience that he is somewhat alarmed at the prodigy Mozart's arrival in Vienna.

The Venticelli come in to inform Salieri that Mozart is settled in lodgings and is to appear at the Baroness Waldstadten's the next evening, where some of his music will be played.

The following evening, in the Baroness's library, Salieri helps himself to a sweet and settles into a large wing chair, where he happens to be invisible to anyone else who may enter the room. Someone does: Constanze, *"a pretty girl in her early 20s, full of high spirits,"* playfully acting the part of a mouse and hiding under the piano. Enter Wolfgang Amadeus Mozart, *"a small, pallid, large-eyed man in a showy wig and a showy set of clothes. . . . .as we get to know him through his next scenes, we discover several things about him: he is an extremely restless man, his hands and feet in almost continuous motion; his voice is light and high; and he is possessed of an unforgettable giggle—piercing and infantile."* His behavior at this moment is also infantile, as he pretends to be a cat chasing his pretty, fleeing mouse on all fours crying "Miaouw!", as well as extremely vulgar as he leaps upon her, ignorant of Salieri's presence in the room.

MOZART: I'm going to bite you in half with my fangs-wangs! My little Stanzerl-wanzerl-banzerl!

She giggles delightedly, lying prone beneath him.

You're trembling! . . . I think you're frightened of puss-wuss! . . . I think you're scared to death! *(Intimately.)* I think you're going to shit yourself!

She squeals but is not really shocked.

In a moment it's going to be on the floor!

CONSTANZE: Ssh! Someone'll hear you!

He imitates the noise of a fart.

Stop it, Wolferl! Ssh!

Salieri sits in appalled silence, undiscovered, as the two continue their byplay and then approach the subject of marriage: Mozart's father will never consent to such a match, Constanze declares, but Mozart proposes to her anyway. They are interrupted by the entrance of the Major Domo, come to announce that the Baroness is ready for the concert to begin. The couple exit with the Major Domo, never having discovered Salieri's presence in the room.

The concert is heard offstage, as Salieri speaks about the music, pulsing serenely "like a rusty squeezebox" in the low registers, then suddenly invaded by a high note on the oboe, which is heard as Salieri speaks of it.

SALIERI:. . . . .It hung there unwavering—piercing me through—till breath could hold it no longer, and a clarinet withdrew it out of me, and sweetened it into a phrase of such delight it had me trembling. The light flickered in the room. My eyes clouded! *(With ever-increasing emotion and vigor.)* The squeezebox groaned louder, and over it the higher instruments wailed and warbled, throwing lines of sound around me—long lines of pain around and through me—Ah, the pain! Pain as I had never known it. I called up to the sharp old God, *"What is this? . . . What?!"* But the squeezebox went on and on, and the pain cut deeper into my shaking head until I suddenly was running—

> *He bolts out of the chair and runs across the stage in a fever. The music continues, fainter, underneath.*

—dashing through the side-door, stumbling downstairs into the street, into the cold night gasping for life. *(Calling up in agony.)* *"What?! What is this? Tell me, Signore.* What is this *pain?* What is this *need* in the sound? Forever unfulfillable yet fulfilling him who hears it, utterly. Is it *Your* need? Can it be Yours? . . ."

> *Pause.*

Dimly the music sounded from the salon above. Dimly the stars shone on the empty street. I was suddenly frightened. It seemed to me I had heard a voice of God—and that it issued from a creature whose own voice I had also heard—and it was the voice of an obscene child!

Following this occurrence, Salieri busies himself in his work, ignores Mozart's presence in the city and begs God, "Let your voice enter *me.*" The Venticelli visit Salieri in his apartments with manuscripts of a volume of precocious, clever but rather conventional music Mozart had been composing before his arrival in Vienna. Salieri decides the glorious serenade he heard at the Baroness's must have been a fluke. He decides to seek out Mozart and welcome the young man to Vienna.

At the Palace of Schonbrunn, the Emperor Joseph *("a dapper, cheerful figure, aged 40, largely pleased with himself and the world")* is accompanied by Strack, Van Swieten and Rosenberg as they prepare to receive and meet Mozart for the first time. Salieri moves to the piano; and when Mozart enters, Salieri strikes up a March of Welcome *("an extremely banal piece")* which he has written for the occasion. The Emperor pronouces it "charming". He gives Mozart his hand to kiss, which Mozart does extravagantly. The Emperor tells an anecdote of Mozart's childhood and then introduces the two composers, who make elaborate acknowledgements of each other. Salieri presents Mozart with the written music for the march.

Emperor Joseph inquires after the opera he has commissioned for the National Theater, and Mozart, giggling, reveals that he's found a libretto, set in a seraglio but—Mozart hastens to assure the court—in no way offensive to the most decorous morals, but a celebration of love in its most genuine form. Mozart, eager to please his new patron, heaps flattery upon the Emperor, partly in French which the Emperor does not understand. Joseph employs his favorite expression—"Ah. Well, there it is"—to break off the conversation and exit, followed by the members of his Court.

Alone with Salieri, Mozart confides that he has found a singer for his new opera: Katherina Cavalieri, Salieri's prize pupil. Salieri can hardly bear the thought of Mozart's getting his hands on her upon whom he has so determinedly kept hands off.

MOZART: You're a good fellow, Salieri! And that's a jolly little thing you wrote for me.

SALIERI: It was my pleasure.

MOZART: Let's see if I can remember it. May I?

SALIERI: By all means. It's yours.

MOZART: *Grazie, Signore.*

> *Mozart tosses the manuscript on to the lid of the fortepiano where he cannot see it, sits at the instrument and plays Salieri's March of Welcome perfectly from memory—at first slowly, recalling it—but on the reprise of the tune, very much faster.*

The rest is just the same, isn't it?

> *He finishes it with insolent speed.*

SALIERI: You have a remarkable memory.

MOZART *(delighted with himself)*: Grazie ancora, Signore!

> *He plays the opening seven bars again, but this time stops at the interval of the fourth, and sounds it again with displeasure.*

It doesn't really *work,* that fourth—does it? . . . Let's try the third above . . .

> *He does so—and smiles happily.*

Ah yes! . . . Good! . . .

More and more happily, Mozart explores his own, improved version of Salieri's march (under his fingers it becomes "Non piu andrai" from *The Marriage of Figaro*). Salieri freezes the smile on his face as the sheer virtuosity of Mozart becomes more and more evident as he plays— *"The whole time he himself remains totally oblivious to the offense he is giving."*

Mozart finishes the piece and departs, leaving Salieri to to express his resentment to the audience, his resolve to compose "a huge tragic opera" to make the world sit up and take notice.

In a theater setting, the Emperor, his Court and citizens of Vienna have come to hear the first performance of *The Abduction From the Seraglio,* "The German expression of manly love." Listening to the soprano's (Katherina's) aria, Salieri knows at once that Mozart has had his way with her: "The creature had had my darling girl."

Emperor Joseph joins the applause which follows the opera. Mozart introduces the flamboyant Constanze as his fiancee. Prompted by Rosenberg, the Emperor observes that the opera is "a good effort" which nevertheless contains "too many notes." He forces his Court Composer, Salieri, to echo this opinion. Stung, Mozart replies that "There are just as many notes, Majesty, neither more nor less, as are required." The Emperor takes refuge in his "Ah . . . Well, there it is" and leads his Court off.

MOZART *(nervous):* Is he angry?

SALIERI: Not at all. He respects you for your views.

MOZART *(nervously):* I hope so . . . What did you think yourself, sir? Did you care for the piece at all?

SALIERI: Yes, of course, Mozart—at its best it is truly charming.

MOZART: And at other times?

SALIERI *(smoothly):* Well, just occasionally at other times—in Katherina's aria for example—it was a little excessive.

MOZART: Katherina is an excessive girl. In fact she's insatiable.

SALIERI: All the same, as my revered teacher the Chevalier Gluck used to say to me—one must avoid music that smells of music.

MOSART: What does that mean?

SALIERI: Music which makes one aware too much of the virtuosity of the composer.

MOZART: Gluck is absurd.

SALIERI: What do you say?

MOZART: He's talked all his life about modernizing opera, but creates people so lofty they sound as though they shit marble.

Constanze gives a little scream of shock.

CONSTANZE: Oh, 'scuse me! . . .

MOZART *(breaking out):* No but it's too much! Gluck says! Gluck says! Chevalier Gluck! . . . What's Chevalier? I'm a Chevalier. The Pope made me a Chevalier when I was still wetting my bed.

CONSTANZE: Wolferl!

MOZART: Anyway it's ridiculous. Only stupid farts use titles.

SALIERI *(blandly):* Such as Court Composer?

MOZART: What? . . . *(Realizing.)* Ah. Oh. Ha. Ha. Well! . . . My father's right again. He always tells me I should padlock my mouth. . . . .

Mozart introduces Constanze to Salieri and explains that they are waiting for his father's consent to get married. Salieri advises the 26-year-old young man to go ahead with his wedding soon, regardless of parental approval. Mozart and Constanze depart, happy to have received this advice, leaving Salieri with thoughts of dallying with Constanze in revenge for Mozart's dalliance with Katherina.

The Venticelli enter with the news that Mozart and Constanze are married and living beyond their limited means. Mozart seems to have a knack (the Venticelli observe) of offending those whom he most desires to cultivate.

At Kapellmeister Bonno's house, Mozart has consumed too much wine and is telling Strack that his host is a "worthless Wop" and Salieri is a "musical idiot" whose last opera is "dried dogshit."

Rosenberg joins them. Joking drunkenly, Mozart tells him he resembles a toad. In a sudden change of mood, Mozart kisses Rosenberg's hand and begs to be appointed to the Court post of instructor to the Princess Elizabeth—but this appointment is in the hands of Salieri, who (Salieri tells the audience) is now resolved to take revenge on his rival.

A month later at a party at the Baroness Waldstadten's, Salieri is once again positioned in his concealing chair, while Constanze plays at forfeits with the Venticelli, who are measuring her legs. Mozart enters, interrupts the game and —after the Venticelli leave the room—accuses her of shaming him. On the contrary, Constanze declares, Mozart has shamed *her* with every one of his female pupils, even Katherina Cavalieri: *"She* wasn't even your pupil—she was Salieri's. Which actually, my dear, may be why he has hundreds and you have none! He doesn't drag them into bed!"

Mozart replies, "Of course he doesn't! He can't get it up, that's why! . . . Have you heard his music? That's the sound of someone who *can't get it up!"*

Constanze bursts into tears, and Mozart is at once contrite. He hands her a ruler, cajoling her, urging her to beat him in punishment. She does so, becoming more and more sportive. Finally Salieri in his hiding place cannot help uttering an exclamation of disgust. His presence now discovered at this awkward moment, he yawns and stretches, pretending he's just awakened from a nap and has overheard nothing.

Mozart is sent off to fetch sorbets for the three of them. Constanze seizes the opportunity to tell Salieri of Mozart's desperate need for some sort of emploment, preferably as tutor to the Princess.

CONSTANZE: Please . . . please, Excellency. You can't imagine what a difference it would make.
SALIERI: We can't speak of it now.
CONSTANZE: When then? Oh, please!
SALIERI: Can you come and see me tomorrow? Alone?
CONSTANZE: I can't do that.
SALIERI: I'm a married man.
CONSTANZE: All the same.
SALIERI: When does he work?
CONSTANZE: Afternoons.
SALIERI: Then come at three.
CONSTANZE: I can't possibly!
SALIERI: Yes or no? In his interests?
  A pause. She hesitates—opens her mouth—then smiles and abruptly runs off.
(To audience.) So I'd done it. Spoken aloud. Invited her! What of that vow made in church? Virtue . . . chastity, all of that? I couldn't think of that now!

In Salieri's salon the next afternoon, Constanze arrives on the dot of three o'clock. She has brought a collection of Mozart's manuscripts for Salieri to peruse (they are the originals, which Constanze must return; Mozart doesn't make copies of his work).

Salieri offers Constanze an especially delicious sweetmeat—"Nipples of Venus," chestnuts in brandied sugar. He decides he is going to call Constanze "La Generosa" in honor of what he expects from her. She asks after Salieri's wife and learns that Teresa is visiting her mother in Verona. This information startles Constanze, but Salieri reminds her that he's dining with the Emperor the following evening and could easily drop a word about an appointment for Mozart in exchange for the generous favors of Constanze. She yields him a small kiss, then a longer one, but that is as far as she will permit his clumsy advances to progress. Salieri sinks so low as to beg for tenderness, but Costanze merely chides him for playing the fool: "Ah—you are sulking? *Are* you? . . . When Mozart sulks I smack his botty. He rather likes it. Do you want me to scold you a bit and smack your botty too?"

Infuriated, Salieri calls her a "silly, common girl," then icily takes up the subject of her husband: "He is a brilliant keyboard player, no question. However, the Princess Elizabeth also requires a tutor in vocal music. I am not convinced he is the man for that." Coldly, Salieri lays it on the line: he will study Mozart's manuscripts overnight, while she thinks over his proposal—quid pro quo, her services rendered in exchange for his services rendered. He turns his back upon her, dismissing her.

Alone, Salieri rants in disgust at himself for this fiasco, but blames Mozart for the fact that everything in his life seems to be going wrong. He cannot resist looking over the music manuscripts, however, and as he looks at the page, the music of Mozart's Twenty-Ninth Symphony in A Major is heard. Salieri notices that there are no corrections of any kind in the manuscript. As he looks up at the audience, the music stops; as he looks at the scores again, other Mozart compositions are heard. To his amazement, Salieri sees that Mozart is simply transcribing music which pours out of his head complete, perfect, unalterable.

SALIERI *(to the audience):.* . . . . Here again—only now in abundance—were the same sounds I'd heard in the library. The same crushed harmonies—glancing collisions—agonizing delights.

    And he looks up. Again the music stops.
The truth was clear. That Serenade had been no accident.

    Very low, in the theater, a faint thundery sound is heard accumulating, like a distant sea.
I was staring through the cage of those meticulous ink strokes at an Absolute Beauty!

    And out of the thundery roar writhes and rises the clear sound of a soprano singing the Kyrie from the C Minor Mass. The accretion of noise around her voice falls away—it is suddenly clear and bright— then clearer and brighter. The light grows bright—too bright—burning white, then scalding white! Salieri rises in the downpour of it, and in the flood of the music which is growing ever louder—filling the theater —as the soprano yields to the full chorus, fortissimo, singing its massive counterpoint.

    This is by far the loudest sound the audience has yet heard. Salieri staggers towards us, holding the manuscripts in his hand, like a man caught in a tumbling and violent sea. . . . .

Salieri lets the manuscripts fall, and there is a crash of music, followed by silence and a dimming of the lights to normal. Salieri addresses God

SALIERI:. . . . .Tonight at an inn somewhere in this city stands a giggling child who can put on paper, without actually setting down his billiard cue, casual notes which turn my most considered ones into lifeless scratches. *Grazie, Signore!* You gave me the desire to serve You—which most men do not have—then saw to it the service was shameful in the ears of the server. *Grazie!* You gave me the desire to praise You—which most men do not feel—then made me mute. *Grazie tanti!* You put into me perception of the Incomparable—which most men never know! —then ensured that I would know myself forever mediocre. *(His voice gains power.) Why?. . . What is my fault?* . . . Until this day I have pursued virtue with rigor. I have labored long hours to relieve my fellow men. I have worked and worked the talent You allowed me. *(Calling up.) You know how hard I've worked!* Solely that in the end, in the practice of the art which alone makes the world comprehensible to me, I might hear Your voice! And now I do hear it—and it says only one name: MOZART! . . . Spiteful, sniggering, conceited, infantine Mozart—who has never worked one minute to help another man! Shit-talking Mozart, with his botty-smacking wife! *Him* You have chosen to be Your sole conduct! And *my* only reward—my sublime privilege—is to be the sole man alive in this time who shall clearly recognize Your incarnation! *(Savagely.) Grazie e grazie ancora!*
     Pause.
So be it! From this time we are enemies, You and I! I'll not accept it from You —*do you hear?* They say God is not mocked. I tell You, *Man* is not mocked! . . . *I* am not mocked! . . . They say the spirit bloweth where it listeth: I tell you NO! It must list to virtue or not blow at all! *(Yelling.) Dio ingiusto*—You are the Enemy! I name Thee now—*Nemico Eterno!* And this I swear: To my last breath I shall *block* You on earth as far as I am able!. . . . .

Salieri dons his old dressing gown and shawl, returning time to 1823, and promising to tell the audience about "the war I fought with God through Mozart, named *Amadeus.* In the waging of which, of course, the Creature had to be destroyed." He snatches a bonbon and goes, as the curtain falls.

ACT II

Salieri enters his salon in gown and shawl, reminding the audience that this is the last hour of his life. He wants to be understood, not forgiven. Taking off gown and shawl and putting on powdered wig, he admits that his whole purpose in life became the opposing of God Himself on the battlefield of Mozart.

Constanze returns (her husband is at a concert) to let Salieri have his way with her. He now refuses her favors, infuriating her, and sends her away with Mozart's

Ian McKellen and Tim Curry in a scene from *Amadeus*

manuscripts. He confesses, "I would have liked her—oh yes, just then more than ever! But now I wanted nothing petty! . . . My quarrel wasn't with Mozart—it was through him! Through him to God who loved him so. *(Scornfully.) Amadeus!*"

The next day when Katherina Cavalieri comes for her lesson, Salieri easily manages to persuade her into his bed. There is no longer any reason for him to keep his vow and remain virtuous. He resigns from all his committees in aid of needy musicians and recommends "a man of no talent whatever to instruct the Princess Elizabeth."

At the palace, Emperor Joseph hears from Salieri that he didn't recommend Mozart because "one hears too many stories" about him. The Emperor accepts Salieri's advice, to Mozart's great chagrin.

The Venticelli come onstage discussing Mozart's growing indigence. He now has an infant to support as well as a wife. Meanwhile, Salieri is prospering.

SALIERI:. . . . .If I had expected anger from God—none came. None! . . . Instead —incredibly—in Eighty-four and Eighty-five I came to be regarded as infinitely the superior composer. And this despite the fact that those were the two years in which Mozart wrote his best keyboard concerti and his string quartets.

> *The Venticelli stand on either side of Salieri. Mozart sits at the fortepiano.*

VENTICELLO 1: Haydn calls the quartets unsurpassed.

SALIERI: They were—but no one heard them.

VENTICELLO 2: Van Swieten calls the concerti sublime.

SALIERI: They were, but no one noticed.

> *Mozart plays and conducts from the keyboard. Faintly we hear the*
> *rondo from the Piano Concerto in A Major.*

(Over this.) The Viennese greeted each unique concerto with the squeals of pleasure they usually reserved for a new style of bonnet. Each was played once —then totally forgotten! . . . By contrast, my operas were played everywhere and saluted by everyone! I composed my *Semiramide* for Munich.

VENTICELLO 1: Rapturously received!

VENTICELLO 2: People *faint* with pleasure!

Salieri's work is celebrated throughout Europe, "Almost as if I were being pushed deliberately from triumph to triumph!" With his fame comes fortune, and Salieri fills his house with gilt furniture and covers himself with a gold satin frock coat.

Salieri hears that Mozart has slighted a new comedy of his, and that the upstart is further invading his terrain by planning to write an Italian opera based on Beaumarchais' *The Marriage of Figaro*. Van Swieten joins Salieri, calls Mozart's idea "rubbish." Mozart himself enters with Strack and argues for his new project.

MOZART:. . . . .I want to do a piece about real people, Baron! And I want to set it in a real place! A *boudoir!*—because that to me is the most exciting place on earth! Underclothes on the floor! Sheets still warm from a woman's body! Even a pisspot brimming under the bed!

VAN SWIETEN *(outraged):* Mozart!

MOZARR: I want life, Baron. Not boring legends!

STRACK: Herr Salieri's recent *Danaius* was a legend that did not bore the French.

MOZART: It is impossible to bore the French—except with real life!

VAN SWIETEN: I had assumed, now that you have joined our Brotherhood of Masons, you would choose more elevated themes.

MOZART *(impatiently):* Oh, elevated! Elevated! . . . The only thing a man should elevate is his doodle.

VAN SWIETEN: You are provoking, sir! Has everything to be a joke with you?

MOZART *(desperate):* Excuse language, Baron, but really! . . . How go on forever with these gods and heroes?

The figures of legend represent the eternal, the best of human nature, Van Swieten argues, but Mozart declares them all boring, his own *King of Crete* as well as Salieri's *Danaius*. All stare at Mozart in disapproval, and he imagines what each of them must be thinking. He uses their separate but simultaneous attitudes to illustrate his point: "That's why opera is important, Baron. Because it's realer than any play! A dramatic poet would have to put all those thoughts down one after another to represent this second of time. The composer can put them all down at once—and still make us hear each one of them. Astonishing device: a vocal quartet! *(More and more excited.)* . . . I tell you I want to write a finale lasting half an hour. A quartet becoming a quintet becoming a sextet. On and on, wider and wider—all sounds multiplying and rising together—and the together making a sound entirely new! . . . I bet you that's how God hears the world. Millions of sounds ascending at once and mixing in His ear to become an unending music, unimaginable to us! (To *Salieri.*) That's our job! That's our job, we composers: combining the inner minds of him and him and him, and her and her—the thoughts of chambermaids and Court Composers—and turn the audience into God."

Mozart further informs them that the opera is finished in his head—all that remains is for him to write the notes down. He exits, pleased with himself, leaving the others astonished and resentful. Salieri schemes to prevent Mozart from having a success with the new opera.

In an unlit theater, Rosenberg orders Mozart to let him peruse the score of *Figaro,* then reminds Mozart that the Emperor has forbidden ballet in his operas. Mozart has included one in this new work. It is not a ballet but a wedding dance, Mozart contends, and as such is an integral part of the story. Nevertheless, Rosenberg tears the dance pages out of the score, infuriating Mozart, who feels that his perfect work has been mutilated. Instinctively, Mozart senses that there is a conspiracy against him, with Salieri as its prime mover. He thinks of appealing to the Emperor by holding a special rehearsal, but Rosenberg is adamant: the Emperor doesn't attend rehearsals; Mozart must rewrite or withdraw the work.

To Mozart's surprise, Salieri approaches him and offers to ask the Emperor to come to a rehearsal. Salieri does not keep this promise, but to everyone's surprise the Emperor actually appears in the middle of the last rehearsal of *Figaro.*

In the theater, the Emperor seats himself in one of the gilt chairs, excitedly anticipating his first encounter with a new opera. Mozart is abjectly grateful to Salieri, who in his turn wonders now whether God is finally acting to defend his Amadeus.

The Emperor is intently listening to the third act, when the music stops and the performers are apparently resorting to an interval of pantomime. The Emperor is puzzled and disturbed by this. Rosenberg explains that the dance music was excised in accordance with the Emperor's own regulation against ballet in opera.

JOSEPH:. . . . .I can't say that I like it.
MOZART: Nor do I, Majesty.
JOSEPH: Do you like it, Rosenberg?
ROSENBERG: It's not a question of liking, Majesty. Your own law decrees it.
JOSEPH: Yes. All the same, this is nonsense. Look at them: they're like waxworks up there.
ROSENBERG: Well, not exactly, Majesty.
JOSEPH: I don't like waxworks.
MOZART: Nor do I, Majesty.
JOSEPH: Well, who would? What do you say, Salieri?

SALIERI: Italians are fond of waxworks, Majesty. *(Pause.)* Our religion is largely based upon them.

JOSEPH: You are *cattivo* again, Court Composer.

STRACK *(intervening creamily):* Your Majesty, Count Rosenberg is very worried that if this music is put back it will create the most unfortunate precedent. One will have thereafter to endure hours of dancing in opera.

JOSEPH: I think we can guard against that, you know, Chamberlain. I really think we can guard against hours of dancing. *(To Rosenberg.)* Please restore Herr Mozart's music.

ROSENBERG: But Majesty, I must insist—

JOSEPH *(with a touch of anger):* You will oblige me, Rosenberg! I wish to hear Mozart's music. Do you understand me?

ROSENBERG: Yes, Majesty.

> *Mozart explodes with joy, jumps over a chair and throws himself at Joseph's feet.*

MOZART: Oh God, I thank your Majesty!

> *He kisses the Emperor's hand extravagantly, as at their first meeting.*

Oh thank you—thank you—thank you Sire, forever!

JOSEPH *(withdrawing hand):* Yes, yes—very good. A little less enthusiasm. I beg you!

MOZART *(abashed):* Excuse me.

> *The Emperor rises. All follow suit.*

JOSEPH: Well. *There it is!*

The Emperor, the Court, the public are present at the opening performance of *Figaro.* In the tune of "Non piu andrai" Salieri recognizes his little March of Welcome enchantingly transformed.

SALIERI *(raptly and quietly, to audience):* Trembling, I hear the second act. *(Pause.)* The restored third act. *(Pause.)* The astounding fourth. What shall I say to you who will one day hear this last act for yourselves? You will—because whatever else shall pass away, this must remain.

> *Faintly we hear the solemn closing ensemble from Act IV of "Figaro," "Ah! Tutti contenti. Saremo cosi."*

(Over this.) The scene was night in a summer garden. Pinprick stars gleamed down on shaking summerhouses. Plotters glided behind pasteboard hedges. I saw a woman, dressed in her maid's clothes, hear her husband utter the first tender words he has offered her in years, only because he thinks she is someone else. Could one catch a realer moment? And how, except in a net of pure artifice? The disguises of opera had been invented for Mozart. *(He can barely look out at the "stage".)* The final reconciliation melted sight. *(Pause.)* Theough my tears I saw the Emperor . . . yawn.

> *Joseph yawns. The music fades. There is scant applause. Joseph rises and the Courtiers follow suit. Mozart bows.*

JOSEPH *(coolly):* Most ingenious, Mozart. You are coming along nicely . . . *(To Rosenberg.)* I do think we must omit encores in future. It really makes things far too long. Make a note, Rosenberg.

ROSENBERG: Majesty.
Mozart lowers his head, crushed.
JOSEPH: Gentlemen, good night to you. . . . .

The Emperor exits with his Court, after which the others go out, leaving Salieri alone with Mozart. Salieri is forced to admit that the opera is "marvellous." The best ever written, Mozart agrees, insulting Salieri by adding that no one else in the world would be capable of writing such a work.

Mozart departs, and as the lights change the Venticelli come on telling of Rosenberg's anger at Mozart for having the Emperor restore the dance. Aided by this anger, Salieri manages to manupulate the schedule so that *Figaro* is performed only nine times that season. He pretends to commiserate with Mozart when the opera is withdrawn from production with no plans for revival. Salieri determines to see more of Mozart in future, to study his weaknesses.

In the Waldstadten library, Mozart tells Salieri that he can't go back to London to try to make a fresh start there because he can't afford to take his wife and child with him. His father won't help by taking the child off Mozart's hands because, Mozart is convinced, down deep his father is jealous of his son's celebrity. Mozart says that he detests his father—but then when he receives the news of his father's death he feels remorse for not having been a more dutiful son. Salieri tries to offer himself as a bulwark in the father's place, but instead Mozart sublimates his emotions by creating the ghost father of *Don Giovanni*. The black specter in cloak and tricorne hat appears menacingly before kneeling Mozart, while Salieri describes him: "A father more accusing than any in opera. So rose the figure of a guilty libertine cast into hell! . . . I looked on astounded as from his ordinary life he made his art. We were both ordinary men, he and I. Yet he from the ordinary created legends—and I from legends created only the ordinary."

If God had pitied Salieri (he continues), perhaps Salieri might have pitied Mozart. This did not occur, and Salieri is now determined to destroy his rival by starving him.

At the Palace of Schonbrunn, the Emperor is aware of Mozart's plight and threatens to undo Salieri's schemes by offering Mozart a post—the late Gluck's post of Chamber Composer. Salieri can't prevent the appointment but persuades the Emperor to pay Mozart only 200 florins a year instead of the 2,000 Gluck received. Salieri pretends to Mozart that he has done him a favor by obtaining him this appointment. Though Mozart is aware of its inadequacy, he is perforce grateful to Salieri for such help as he has obtained.

Salieri expects that God will punish him for this stroke, but instead he is granted his dearest wish. Kappellmeister Bonno dies, and Salieri is appointed to fill his place. Meanwhile, Mozart is suffering from stomach cramps and is dosing himself with medicines, while his wife is expecting another child.

Mozart and Constanze, shabby-looking and pregnant, meet Salieri and the Venticelli in the Prater. Mozart congratulates Salieri, complains of his pains and of bad dreams in which a faceless cloaked figure beckons him.

Constanze hints that Mozart needs employment. Mozart leads her away, embarrassed, while the Venticelli reveal that the Mozarts have moved into a slum neighborhood and are living partly by begging from brother Masons. Salieri realizes that if he is to bring Mozart to destitution he must somehow prevent the Masons from giving him assistance.

At the Masonic lodge, under a Masonic emblem, Van Swieten is chiding Mozart for begging from the members and advises him to improve his prospects by writing the kind of music that will please, not offend, his listeners. Van Swieten gives Mozart a small commission for some Bach arrangements and exits, as Salieri comes in.

Mozart tells Salieri that a fellow lodge member, an actor named Schickaneder, has offered him the opportunity of writing a popular vaudeville, promising Mozart half the box office receipts when the show opens. Salieri suggests that Mozart put his brother Masons and their rituals into his new work, demonstrating his brotherly love by celebrating them in this fashion. Mozart thinks it an excellent idea. He will keep it a secret, a surprise for his Masonic brothers when the show is put on.

Music from *The Magic Flute* is heard, as the stage is set with two contrasting living quarters: gilded chairs and table with gold cake-stand at Salieri's, a wooden table covered with bottles and manuscripts (and the presence of an obviously very pregnant Constanze) at Mozart's. Salieri helps himself to a bonbon, while gloating over Mozart self-destructing by exposing the secret Masonic rituals out on the stage. Mozart, wrapped in a blanket for warmth, is writing music while Constanze declares that Mozart's father arrested his son's emotional development with too much babying. Constanze confesses that she hated the elder Mozart and burned all his letters in the fire the night before.

CONSTANZE (savagely): At least it kept us warm! What else will do that? Perhaps we should dance! You love to dance, Wolferl—let's dance! Dance to keep warm! *(Grandly.)* Write me a contredanze, Mozart! It's your job to write dances, isn't it?
> *Hysterical, she starts dancing roughly around the room like a demented peasant to the tune of "Non piu andrai."*
(Singing wildly):
> *Non piu andrai, farfallone amoroso—*
> *Notte e giorno d'itorno girando!*
MOZART *(shrieking):* Stop it! Stop it!
> *He siezes her.*
Stanzi-marini! Marini-bini! Don't, please. Please, please, please I beg you . . . Look there's a kiss! Where's it coming from? Right out of that corner! There's another one—all wet, all sloppy wet coming straight to you!
> *She pushes him away. Constanze dances. Mozart catches her. She pushes him away.*
CONSTANZE: Get off!
> *Pause.*
MOZART: I'm frightened, Stanzi. Something awful's happening to me.
CONSTANZE: I can't bear it. I can't bear much more of this.
MOZART: And the Figure's like this now—*(Beckoning faster.)* "Here! Come here! Here!" Its face still masked—invisible!

CONSTANZE: Stop it, for God's sake! . . . Stop! . . . It's me who's frightened . . . Me! . . . You frighten me . . . If you go on like this I'll leave you. I swear it.

MOZART *(shocked):* Stanzi!

CONSTANZE: I mean it . . . I do . . .

> *She puts her hand to her stomach, as if in pain.*

MOZART: I'm sorry . . . Oh God, I'm sorry . . . I'm sorry, I'm sorry, I'm sorry! . . . Come here to me, little wife of my heart! Come . . . Come . . .

> *He kneels and coaxes her to him. She comes half-reluctantly, half-willingly.*

Who am I? . . . Quick: tell me. Hold me and tell me who I am.

CONSTANZE: Pussy-wussy.

They are exchanging childish endearments in their fashion, when suddenly Constanze cries out in pain. She is delivered of a boy (the Venticelli explain while Constanze slowly exits).

Mozart crosses to Salieri's room and tells Salieri that Constanze has taken the baby and gone off to a spa, which will cost them the last cent they own. Constanze thinks Mozart has lost his mind, and—Mozart confesses to Salieri—maybe he has. The mysterious Figure of his dreams has ordered him to write a Requiem Mass; whether the apparition is real or imagined Mozart is no longer able to judge.

Mozart has finished his vaudeville, and Salieri offers to attend the performance (the Court is not expected to attend a music hall) in company with Katherina to cheer Mozart up in Constanze's absence; a Mozart, as Salieri puts it, "demented and drunk on the cheap wine which was now his constant habit."

At the vaudeville in the Theater by the Weiden, the audience is eating sausage and exploding with mirth at the jokes, while Salieri is seized in spite of himself with admiration for the work itself: ". . . . .I alone in their midst heard *The Magic Flute.* . . . . He had put the Masons into it right enough. Oh, yes—but how? He had turned them into an Order of Eternal Priests. I heard voices calling out of ancient temples. I saw a vast sun rise on a timeless land, where animals danced and children floated: and by its rays all the poisons we feed each other drawn up and burnt away!"

Furthermore, the father figure was no longer threatening but had become a high priest of love—Mozart had at last come to terms with the memory of his father. Listening to the wild applause and realizing that Mozart is the very personification of a magic musical instrument, Salieri feels something very near to pity for this fragile and talented creature.

Van Swieten appears, having also attended this performance—at Salieri's suggestion. Van Swieten declares Mozart a traitor to the Masonic order for having exposed their rituals onstage. He orders Mozart never to speak to him again. Mozart is stunned, knowing all is now lost, as Salieri remarks to the audience, "Now he was ruined. Broken and shunned by all men of influence. And for good measure, he did not even get his half receipts from the opera."

In the Mozart apartment, Mozart is huddled in his blanket as the Venticelli explain that Schickaneder gives the composer only enough out of the box office receipts to keep him in drink. Mozart is busy writing the Requiem Mass, and Salieri decides to make still another move to destroy him. He acquires a grey hat, cloak and mask and appears as the ghost outside Mozart's window at midnight, holding up seven fingers to indicate the number of days Mozart has left, then one less each night for seven nights; then, all fingers counted, beckoning to Mozart like the dream figure. But instead of obeying, Mozart beckons to the ghost, inviting him with the same words addressed to the statue in *Don Giovanni.*

SALIERI: For a long moment one terrified man looked at another. Then—unbelievably—I found myself nodding, just as in the opera. Starting to move across the street!
> *The rising and falling scale passage from the overture to Don Giovanni sounds darkly, looped in sinister repetition. To this hollow music Salieri marches slowly upstage.*

Pushing down the latch of his door—tramping up the stairs with stone feet. There was no stopping it. *I was in his dream!*
> *Mozart stands terrified by his table. Salieri throws open the door. An instant light change. Salieri stands still, staring impassively downstage.*

MOZART *(urgently, and in awe):* It's not finished! . . . Not nearly! . . . Forgive me. Time was I could write a Mass in a week! . . . Give me one month more, and it'll be done: I swear it! . . . He'll grant me that, surely? God can't want it unfinished! . . . Look—look, see what I've done.
> *He snatches up the pages from the table and brings them eagerly to the Figure.*

Here's the Kyrie—that's finished! Take that to Him—He'll see it's not unworthy!. . . . .

The beginning of the Requiem Mass is heard as Salieri looks at the pages. Mozart wonders why he has been brought from his former happy state to this misery—is God punishing him for wickedness? Salieri tears the paper in half and the music stops, but he admits to Mozart that the music is good. In an action paralleling that of religious Communion, Salieri tears off a corner of one of the pages, places it on his tongue and eats it as though though it were a portion of the Host.

SALIERI *(in pain):* I eat what God gives me. Dose after dose. For all of life. His poison. We are both poisoned, Amadeus. I with you: you with me.
> *In horror Mozart moves slowly behind him, placing his hand over Salieri's mouth—then, still from behind, slowly removes the mask and hat. Salieri stares at the audience.*

Eccomi. Antonio Salieri. Ten years of hate have poisoned you to death.
> *Mozart falls to his knees by the table.*

MOZART: Oh God!

SALIERI *(contemptuously): God?!* . . . God will not help you! God *does* not help!

MOZART: Oh God! . . . Oh God! . . . Oh God!

SALIERI: God does not love you, Amadeus! God does not love! He can only *use!* . . . He cares nothing for who He uses: nothing for who He denies! . . . You are no use to Him any more—You're too weak—too sick! He has finished with you! All you can do now is *die!*

MOZART: *Ah!*

> *With a groan Mozart crawls quickly through the trestle of the table, like an animal finding a burrow—or a child a safe place of concealment. Salieri kneels by the table, calling in at his victim in desperation.*

SALIERI: Die, Amadeus! Die, I beg you, die! . . . Leave me alone, *ti imploro!* Leave me alone at last! Leave me alone!

> *He beats on the table in his despair.*

Alone! Alone! Alone! Alone!

MOZART *(crying out at the top of his lungs):* PAPAAAAA!

With this cry, Mozart becomes and acts as a child, possessed by infantile nature. He calls for his father and sings a nursery tune as Salieri exits and Constanze enters, returned from Baden to find her husband reverted to childhood. She takes him in her arms and comforts him, in a vein not so very different from the childish role-playing of their love-making.

Mozart informs Constanze that Salieri has killed him, but she helps him to bed and tucks her shawl around him, assuring him that she will never leave him again and that he will get better.

The music of the Requiem Mass is heard. Mozart is beating his hand in time to the music, composing it, not listening to his wife as she tells him how much she and the children need him. The drumbeats in the music get slower and stop, as Constanze tells him, "Know one thing. It was the best day of my life when you married me. And as long as I live I'll be the most honored woman in the world."

Just as she is finished speaking, she realizes that Mozart has died. She opens her mouth in a silent cry and raises her arm as the "Amen" chord reverberates.

The citizens of Vienna are dressed in black as Mozart's corpse is disposed of in a pauper's mass grave. Salieri comments: "The death certificate said kidney failure, hastened by exposure to cold. . . . .What did I feel? Relief, of course: I confess it. And pity too, for the man I helped to destroy. I felt the pity God can never feel. I weakened God's flute to thinness. God blew—as He must—without cease. The flute split in the mouth of His insatiable need."

Salieri's voice ages as he recalls the years that followed: Constanze married a Danish diplomat, lived happily, and sold off Mozart's manuscripts at so much a note. One Count Walsegg, it seems, had commissioned Mozart to write the Requiem, and Walsegg claimed it as his own work after Mozart's death. Salieri's original desire for fame was now fulsomely and ironically satisfied. He became the most famous musician in Europe, ". . . . .Bricked up in fame! Embalmed in fame! Buried in fame—but for work I knew to be *absolutely worthless!"*

Hardest to bear of all, Salieri lived long enough to outlive this fame. His music was totally forgotten, never played, while Mozart's resounded through the world.

In Salieri's apartment in 1823, the night has passed and dawn is at hand. The old man announces from his wheelchair that he means to be remembered—if not in fame, then in infamy. He has written out a false confession that he poisoned Mozart with arsenic out of envy: "For the rest of of time whenever men say

Mozart with love, they will say Salieri with loathing!. . . *I am going to be immortal after all!* And He is powerless to prevent it. So, Signore—see now if Man is mocked!"

The valet brings in the shaving things and is given the written confession to take out and sign as a witness. Salieri takes up and opens the razor, saying, "Now I go to become a ghost myself. I will stand in the shadows when you come here to this earth in your turns. And when you feel the dreadful bite of your failures —and hear the taunting of the unachievable, uncaring God—I will whisper my name to you: 'Antonio Salieri: Patron Saint of Mediocrities!' And in the depth of your downcastness you can pray to me. And I will forgive you. *Vi saluto.*"

Salieri cuts his throat and falls backward into the wheelchair. The cook and valet come in, distraught, and they are soon followed by the Venticelli discussing the latest news. Old Salieri, it seems, has cut his throat—but is still alive!

> *Venticello 1 hands a newspaper to Venticello 2.*

VENTICELLO 2 *(reading):* "Our worthy Salieri just cannot die. In the frenzy of his imagination he is even said to accuse himself of complicity in Mozart's early death. A rambling of the mind believed in truth by no one but the deluded old man himself."

> *Salieri lowers his head, conceding defeat.*

VENTICELLO 1: I don't believe it.

VENTICELLO 2: I don't believe it.

VENTICELLO 1: I don't believe it.

VENTICELLO 2: I don't believe it.

VENTICELLI 1 & 2: *No one believes it in the world!*

> *They go off. The light dims a little. Salieri stirs—raises his head—and looks out far into the darkness of the theater.*

SALIERI: Mediocrities everywhere—now and to come—I absolve you all! Amen!

> *He extends his arms upwards and outwards to embrace the assembled audience in a wide gesture of benediction—finally folding his arms high across his own breast.*
>
> *The light fades completely. The last four chords of the Masonic Funeral Music of Amadeus Mozart sound throughout the theater. Curtain.*

CRIMES OF THE HEART

A Play in Three Acts

BY BETH HENLEY

Cast and credits appear on page 431

BETH HENLEY was born in Jackson, Miss. in 1952, the daughter of a lawyer. After graduation from high school she attended Southern Methodist University, receiving her B.S.A. in 1974, and the graduate program in acting at the University of Illinois. She had written a play and the book for a musical while still in college. Her first professionally-produced playscript, Crimes of the Heart, *is also her first New York production, winner of the 1981 Pulitizer Prize and New York Drama Critics Circle award as best American play, and her first Best Play. Its world premiere took place in regional theater at the Actors' Theater of Louisville in February, 1979. It was repeated at the California Actors' Theater in Los Gatos in April, 1979; at the Loretto-Hilton Theater in St. Louis in October, 1979; at Center Stage, Baltimore in April, 1980; and in an off-off-Broadway production at Manhattan Theater Club's UpStage Theater December 21, 1980 (the basis for the Critics Award and this Best Play citation).*

Miss Henley is also the author of The Miss Firecracker Contest *produced at the Victory Theater, Burbank, Calif. and* Am I Blue *presented in Circle Repertory's Festival of One-Acts, both in the 1979–80 season. She is single and lives in Los Angeles.*

Time: In the fall; five years after hurricane Camille

Place: The kitchen in the MaGrath sisters' house in Ha-zlehurst, Miss., a small southern town

ACT I

SYNOPSIS: Lenny MaGrath, *"a 30-year-old woman with a round figure and face,"* the oldest of the three MaGrath sisters, enters carrying a saxophone case, a suitcase and another parcel and puts them on the kitchen table. She proceeds to set a candle onto a cookie and light it, just as the voice of her cousin, Chick, is heard outside. Lenny stuffs the arrangement into her dress pocket as Chick, 29, *"a brightly dressed matron with yellow hair and shiny red lips,"* comes in. Chick feels humiliated by an article in this morning's paper. She's also eager to change into some new pantyhose Lenny has brought her. She does so, somewhat grotesquely, right here in the kitchen.

There is obviously a crisis in the family; Lenny has telegraphed her sister Meg to come home. Chick wishes she hadn't, as Meg's local reputation isn't of the best and reflects on them all—once it almost prevented Chick from getting into the Ladies' League, where she is now a committee head.

Ostentatiously, Chick presents Lenny with a box of candy for her birthday (Lenny is not all that enthusiastic about it, especially after Chick complains about the quality of a dress Lenny gave her for one of Chick's children's birthdays).

Doc Porter, 30, *"an attractively worn man with a slight limp,"* comes into the kitchen with a bag of pecans for Lenny. Chick exits, on her way to pick up Babe, the youngest MaGrath sister. Doc has read the bad news in the paper, and he has some more bad news for Lenny on her birthday: her 20-year-old horse Billy Boy, in pasture out at Doc's farm, was struck by lightning and killed the day before. Lenny is moved to tears.

DOC: . . . . . Come on. Hey, hey now. You know I can't stand it when you MaGrath women start to cry. You know it just gets me.
LENNY: Oh-ho! Sure! You mean when Meg cries! Meg's the one you could never stand to watch cry! Not me! I could fill up a pig's trough!
DOC: Now, Lenny . . . stop it. Come on. Jesus!
LENNY: Okay! Okay! I don't know what's wrong with me. I don't mean to make a scene. I've been on this crying jag.
She blows her nose.
All this stuff with Babe, and Old Granddaddy's gotten worse in the hospital, and I can't get in touch with Meg.
DOC: You tried calling Meggy?
LENNY: Yes.
DOC: Is she coming home?
LENNY: Who knows? She hasn't called me. That's what I'm waiting here for —hoping she'll call.

DOC: She still living in California?
LENNY: Yes; in Hollywood.
DOC: Well, give me a call if she gets in. I'd like to see her.
LENNY: Oh, you would, huh?
DOC: Yeah, Lenny, sad to say, but I would.
LENNY: It is sad. It's very sad indeed.

Doc is now married, with two children. He leaves to pick up his son on his first visit to the dentist. After Doc exits, Lenny furtively sets up the cookie-and-candle rig, lights it, sings "Happy Birthday" to herself, blows it out and obviously makes a silent wish. The phone rings. It is someone named Lucille, calling with information about the state of her brother, Zackery. Lenny repeats her message aloud as she writes it down: ". . . . . His liver's saved. Oh, that's good news! . . . Well, of course, when you look at it like that . . . Breathing stabilized. Damage to the spinal column, not yet determined . . . Okay . . . Yes, Lucille, I've got it all down. Uh-huh, I'll give her that message."

As Lenny puts down the phone, a whistle is heard offstage. Meg, 27, the middle MaGrath sister, *"sad, magic eyes and wears a hat,"* comes in carrying a worn suitcase. The sisters fall into each other's arms, then Meg asks about their third sister.

MEG: Now just what's all this business about Babe? How could you send me such a telegram about Babe? And Zackery! You say somebody's shot Zackery?!
LENNY: Yes; they have.
MEG: Well, good Lord! Is he dead?
LENNY: No. But he's in the hospital. He was shot in his stomach.
MEG: In his stomach! How awful! Do they know who shot him?
    Lenny nods.
Well, who? Who was it? Who? Who?!
LENNY: Babe! They're all saying Babe shot him! They took her to jail! And they're all saying she shot him! They're all saying it! It's horrible! It's awful!
MEG *(overlapping):* Jail! Good Lord, jail! Well, who? Who's saying it? Who?!
LENNY: Everyone!! The policemen, the sheriff, Zackery, even Babe's saying it! Even Babe herself!!
MEG: Well, for God's sake. For God's sake.
LENNY *(overlapping as she falls apart):* It's horrible! It's horrible!! It's just horrible!!!
MEG: Now calm down, Lenny. Just calm down. Would you like a Coke? Here, I'll get you some Coke.
    Meg gets a Coke from the refrigerator. She opens it and downs a large swig.
Why? Why would she shoot him? Why?
    Meg hands the Coke bottle to Lenny.
LENNY: I talked to her this morning and I asked her that very question. I said, "Babe, why would you shoot Zackery? He was your own husband. Why would you shoot him?" And do you know what she said? *(Meg shakes her head.)* She said, " 'Cause I didn't like his looks. I just didn't like his looks."

Mia Dillon and Mary Beth Hurt in *Crimes of the Heart*

MEG *(after a pause):* Well, I don't like his looks.

LENNY: But you didn't shoot him! You wouldn't shoot a person 'cause you didn't like their looks! You wouldn't do that! Oh, I hate to say this—I do hate to say this—but I believe Babe is ill. I mean in-her-head ill.

MEG: Oh, now, Lenny, don't you say that! There're plenty of good sane reasons to shoot another person and I'm sure that Babe had one. Now what we've got to do is get her the best lawyer in town. Do you have any ideas on who's the best lawyer in town?

LENNY: Well, Zackery is, of course; but he's been shot!

Babe already has a lawyer, a young man named Barnette Lloyd, new in town. Lenny reminds Meg that she is 30 today, and Meg agrees that they are all three getting old—Babe is now all of 24.

Meg notices the cot in the kitchen—Lenny put it here to be near Old Grand-daddy when he was in the downstairs bedroom (this is his house, but he's now in the hospital, has been for three months). Lenny wrote Meg all this in her letters, and about how Old Granddaddy was so interested to hear the latest about Meg's singing career—but, Meg confesses, "Sometimes I kinda don't read your letters." It gives her chest pains to be reminded of home, not that she doesn't love her family.

They remember how proud Old Granddaddy was when Babe married Zackery, "the richest and most powerful man in all of Hazlehurst." And now she has shot him and is out on bail and on her way to stay here in the MaGrath house.

Meg would appreciate a bourbon, but there is no liquor in the house. She reveals that her singing career in Los Angeles seems to have come to a halt, and she is now working as a clerk in a dog food company. Meg reaches for a pecan, which reminds Lenny to tell her (to Meg's surprise) that her friend Doc Porter is now married to a Yankee named Joan and they have two children, a boy and a girl.

The sound of Chick's car is heard, and then the voice of Babe crying, "I'm home! I'm free!" Babe *("24, an angelic face and fierce, volatile eyes")* enters, sees Meg and runs to hug her. Chick greets Meg coolly; Chick is preoccupied with the wrong that Babe has done and its possible consequences. Chick demands to know how Babe (whom she calls by her real name, Rebecca) is going to explain her action to her lawyer. Babe replies, glaring, "I didn't like his looks! I just didn't like his stinking looks!! And I don't like yours much either, Chick-the-Stick! So, just leave me alone!" Babe makes her escape upstairs.

Meg is also hostile to Chick, and Lenny is trying to smooth the situation, when the phone rings. It's Chick's baby sitter, reporting that the children have eaten some paint. Lenny accompanies Chick off, and seeing Chick has gone, Babe comes back downstairs.

BABE: You know, Chick's hated us ever since we had to move here from Vicksburg to live with Old Grandmama and Old Granddaddy.

MEG: She's an idiot.

BABE: Yeah. You know what she told me this morning while I was still behind bars and couldn't get away?

MEG: What?

BABE: She told me how embarrassing it was for her all those years ago, you know, when mama—

MEG: Yeah, down in the cellar.

BABE: She said our mama had shamed the entire family, and we were known notoriously all through Hazlehurst. *(About to cry.)* Then she went on to say how I would now be getting just as much bad publicity and humiliating her and the family all over again.

MEG: Ah, forget it, Babe. Just forget it.

BABE: I told her, "Mama got national coverage! National!" And if Zackery wasn't a senator from Copiah County, I probably wouldn't even be getting state-wide.

MEG: Of course you wouldn't.

BABE *(after a pause):* Gosh, sometimes I wonder . . .

MEG: What?

BABE: Why she did it. Why Mama hung herself.

MEG: I don't know. She had a bad day. A real bad day. You know how it feels on a real bad day.

BABE: And that old yellow cat. It was sad about that old cat.

MEG: Yeah.

BABE: I bet if Daddy hadn't of left us, they'd still be alive.

MEG: Oh, I don't know.

BABE: 'Cause it was after he left that she started spending whole days just sitting there and smoking on the back porch steps. She'd sling her ashes down onto the different bugs and ants that'd be passing by.

MEG: Yeah. Well, I'm glad he left.

BABE: That old yellow cat'd stay back there with her.

MEG: God, he was a bastard.

BABE: I thought if she felt something for anyone it woulda been that old cat. Guess I musta been mistaken.

MEG: Really, with his white teeth, Daddy was such a bastard.

BABE: Was he? I don't remember.

Babe makes lemonade, while Meg asks her about the shooting. Babe says she had a good reason and was protecting someone—but she admits she did it: "I shot him all right. I meant to kill him. I was aiming for his heart, but I guess my hands were shaking and I—just got him in the stomach." It will be a relief for Babe to go to jail, getting away from Zackery and his sister Lucille, learning to play her new saxophone (which Lenny has brought here for her).

Lenny runs in and out to tell her sisters Chick's children are all right but she's driving them to the doctor's just to make sure. Meg and Babe agree that Lenny needs some affection in her love-starved life (Lenny's affliction—a shrunken ovary—has made her painfully shy with men). They speculate on whether Lenny is a virgin—Babe thinks not and remembers a time when Old Granddaddy went into the hospital and Lenny wrote to a Lonely Hearts club and met a Charlie Hill from Memphis. After he visited her in Hazlehurst a few times, Lenny spent a weekend with him in Memphis, where—Babe is convinced—they had a love affair. Charlie was "a nice man, too—kinda chubby with red hair and freckles, always telling these funny jokes." Lenny took him to meet Old Granddaddy in the hospital, but then (Lenny once told Babe) they decided not to marry because of Lenny's defective ovary.

"Something about that doesn't seem exactly right," Meg comments, pacing the kitchen and coming upon the box of candy Chick gave Lenny—reminding both Meg and Babe that today is Lenny's birthday. They note that the candy box is decorated with poinsettias—probably a leftover from Christmas. They decide to get Lenny the biggest birthday cake the bakery will make.

They are interrupted by the arrival of Babe's lawyer, Barnette Lloyd, *"26, a slender, intelligent young man with an almost fanatical intensity that he subdues by sheer will."* Babe doesn't want to see him and runs off, leaving Meg to talk to him. It turns out that Barnette was a great fan of Meg's when she used to sing in a local night club. He tells her his qualifications for defending Babe: first in his class at Ole Miss Law School, plus special studies in criminal law at Harvard, plus an unrelenting personal vendetta against Zackery F. Botrelle.

BARNETTE: . . . . . I not only intend to keep that sorry s.o.b. from ever being re-elected to the state senate by exposing his shady, criminal dealings; but I also intend to decimate his personal credibility by exposing him as a bully, a brute and a red-neck thug!

MEG: Well; I can see that you're—fanatical about this.

BARNETT: Yes; I am. I'm sorry if I seem outspoken. But, for some reason, I feel I can talk to you . . . those songs you sang. Excuse me; I feel like a jackass.

MEG: It's all right. Relax. Relax, Barnette. Let me think this out a minute.

She takes out a cigarette. He lights it for her.

Now just exactly how do you intend to get Babe off? You know, keep her out of jail.

BARNETTE: It seems to me we can get her off with a plea of self-defense, or possibly we could go with innocent by reason of temporary insanity. But basically, I intend to prove that Zackery Botrelle brutalized and tormented this poor woman to such an extent that she had no recourse but to defend herself in the only way she knew how!

MEG: I like that!

BARNETTE: Then, of course, I'm hoping this will break the ice and we'll be able to go on to prove that the man's a total criminal, as well as an abusive bully and contemptible slob!

MEG: That sounds good! To me that sounds very good!

BARNETTE: It's just our basic game plan.

To Meg's astonishment and then anger, a photostatic copy of Babe's medical history for the past four years indicates that this may be no less than the truth. Looking at the chart, Meg has an impulse to kill Zackery herself. But Barnette needs to know "what was accidental and what was not." Meg promises to help him after she's had a talk with Babe. As he leaves, Barnette admits that he has Babe's interests at heart: "She sold me a pound cake at a bazaar once. And I'm fond of her."

Babe comes downstairs, having called the bakery and found they can't have the cake ready for today. Under Meg's questioning, Babe admits that Zackery was rough with her: "He started hating me because I couldn't laugh at his jokes. I just started finding it impossible to laugh at his jokes the way I used to. And then the sound of his voice got to where it tired me out awful bad to hear it. I'd fall asleep just listening to him at the dinner table." As Meg takes a nibble out of each piece of candy in Lenny's birthday box, Babe tells her how the son of one of her domestics, little Willie Jay, had to give up his dog because they couldn't afford to feed it. Babe decided to keep Willie Jay's dog and invited the boy to come over and visit his pet any time he felt like it.

BABE: . . . . .Anyhow, time goes on and Willie Jay keeps coming over and over. And we talk about Dog and how fat he's getting and then, well, you know, things start up.

MEG: No, I don't know. What things start up?

BABE: Well, things start up. Like sex. Like that.

MEG: Babe, wait a minute—Willie Jay's a boy. A small boy, about this tall. He's about this tall!

BABE: No! Oh, no! He's taller now! He's fifteen now. When you knew him he was only about seven or eight.

MEG: But, even so—fifteen. And he's a black boy; a colored boy; a Negro.

BABE (flustered): Well, I realize that, Meg. Why do you think I'm so worried about his getting public exposure? I don't want to ruin his reputation!

MEG: I'm amazed, Babe. I'm really, completely amazed. I didn't even know you were a liberal.

BABE: Well, I'm not! I'm not a liberal! I'm a democratic! I was just lonely! I was so lonely. And he was good. Oh, he was so, so good. I never had it that good. We'd always go out into the garage, and—

MEG: It's okay. I've got the picture; I've got the picture!

One day when Willie Jay was visiting her (Babe continues), they were on the back porch playing with Dog, when Zackery came home unexpectedly. Zackery ordered Willie Jay off the place, knocked him down the porch steps, hurting him, and warned him never to come back. Willie Jay departed in tears, followed by the dog.

BABE: . . . . .After that, I don't remember much too clearly; let's see . . . I went on into the living room, and I went right up to the davenport and opened the drawer where we keep the burglar gun . . . I took it out. Then I—I brought it up to my ear. That's right. I put it right inside my ear. Why, I was gonna shoot off my own head! That's what I was gonna do. Then I heard the back door slamming and suddenly, for some reason, I thought about Mama . . . how she'd hung herself. And here I was about ready to shoot myself. Then I realized—that's right, I realized how I didn't want to kill myself! And she—she probably didn't want to kill herself. She wanted to kill him, and I wanted to kill him, too. I wanted to kill Zackery, not myself. 'Cause I—I wanted to live! So I waited for him to come on into the living room. Then I held out the gun, and I pulled the trigger, aiming for his heart, but getting him in the stomach. (After a pause.) It's funny that I really did that.

MEG: It's a good thing that you did. It's a damn good thing that you did.

BABE: It was.

Meg advises Babe to tell the lawyer everything—he'll understand, and Willie Jay will be all right. But Babe can't bear the thought of telling all these personal details to a virtual stranger, and she prevents Meg from phoning Barnette. She's much more concerned about Lenny's birthday cake—it will be delivered tomorrow with the inscription, "Happy Birthday, Lenny—A Day Late," a chocolate cake with white icing and red trim, the biggest they have. Meg, now finally dialling the phone, is sure Lenny will like it. *Blackout; curtain.*

ACT II

Later that evening in the kitchen, Barnette is taking notes on what Babe is telling him. He assures her it's in their interests to keep Willie Jay all the way out of it. After she shot Zackery (Babe tells Barnette) she made a pitcher of lemonade, then realized that Zackery was lying wounded and she'd better call the hospital—which she did. Babe made the lemonade because her mouth was dry: "I was afraid they would see that I had tried to shoot Zackery, in fact, that I had shot him, and they would accuse me of possible murder and send me away to jail."

Barnette urges her to fill in all the details of her medical reports and assures her that he will have "a solid defense." Barnette looks familiar to Babe, and Barnette reminds her about the cake sale.

The phone rings—it's Zackery, calling to demand that Babe come over to the hospital. Babe hands the phone to Barnette, with the comment, "He says he's got some blackening evidence that's gonna convict me of attempting to murder him in the first degree." On the phone, Barnette tells Zackery he will come to see him and tells Babe that all communication between her and Zackery should be done only through him from now on. Babe asks Barnette about his vendetta. It concerns the ruin of his father, but he will give her no further details, as he goes off to see Zackery.

Lenny comes in—she's angry because Meg lied to Old Granddaddy on her visit to his hospital room, delighting the old man by telling him that her Hollywood singing career is going well. Lenny is angered further when she sees that Meg has taken a bite out of each of piece of her birthday candy, looking in vain for nuts among the creams: "It gets me upset! Why, Meg's always run wild—she started smoking and drinking when she was fourteen years old, she never made good grades—never made her own bed! But somehow she always seemed to get what she wanted. She's the one who got singing and dancing lessons; and a store-bought dress to wear to her senior prom. Why, do you remember how Meg always got to wear twelve jingle bells on her petticoats, while we were only allowed to wear three apiece?"

Babe argues that Meg has had it especially hard because it was she who found their mother dead, and her odd behavior dates from that incident. She put herself through various kinds of horrible experiences to prove to herself how strong she was.

LENNY: Well, I suppose you'd have to be a pretty hard person to be able to do what she did to Doc Porter.

BABE *(exasperated):* Oh, shoot! It wasn't Meg's fault that hurricane wiped Biloxi away. I never understood why people were blaming all that on Meg—just because the roof fell in and crunched Doc's leg. It wasn't her fault.

LENNY: Well, it was Meg who refused to evacuate. Jim Craig and some of Doc's other friends were all down there, and they kept trying to get everyone to evacuate. But Meg refused. She wanted to stay on because she thought a hurricane would be—oh, I don't know—a lot of fun. Then everyone says she baited Doc into staying there with her. She said she'd marry him if he'd stay.

BABE *(taken aback by this new information):* Well, he has a mind of his own. He could have gone.

LENNY: But he didn't. 'Cause . . . 'cause he loved her. And then after the roof caved, and they got Doc to the high school gym, Meg just left. She just left him there to leave for California—'cause of her career, she says. I think it was a shameful thing to do. It took almost a year for his leg to heal, and after that he gave up his medical career altogether. He said he was tired of hospitals. It's such a sad thing. Everyone always knew he was gonna be a doctor. We've called him Doc for years.

BABE: I don't know. I guess, I don't have any room to talk; 'cause I just don't know.

Meg comes in with a bottle of bourbon she's purchased and a newspaper with the story about Babe on the front page. She defends her lie about her career to Old Granddaddy: "All I wanted was to see him smiling and happy."

Babe cuts the article out of the paper and finds her photo album among the things Lenny packed and brought here for her. The sisters turn the pages, evoking the past, which makes Meg weep. They find a picture of their father ("Jimmy—clowning at the beach—1952"), with his white teeth; then a picture of their mother with the old yellow cat (Babe comments, "I bet if she hadn't of hung that old cat along with her, she wouldn't have gotten all that national coverage"). The shared memories, even the repugnant ones, make the sisters feel closer to one another. They decide to lighten the atmosphere by popping some corn and playing a game of Hearts—but the phone rings, to inform them that Doc Porter is just down the street and on his way to call on them.

Lenny reminds Meg, pointedly, that Doc is married now. She is still angry over Meg's assault on the candies, and Meg promises to get her another box—but that's not the point, Lenny tells her: "You have no respect for other people's property! You just take whatever you want. You just take it!" She reminds Meg of the bells on the petticoats.

MEG: Oh, God! She's starting up about those stupid jingle bells!

LENNY: Well, it's an example! A specific example of how you always get what you want!

MEG: Oh, come on, Lenny, you're just upset because Doc called.

LENNY: Who said anything about Doc? Do you think I'm upset about Doc? Why, I've long since given up worrying about you and all your men.

MEG *(turning in anger):* Look, I know I've had too many men. Believe me, I've had way too many men. But it's not my fault you haven't had any—or maybe just that one from Memphis.

LENNY *(stopping):* What one from Memphis?

MEG *(slowly):* The one Babe told me about. From the—club.

LENNY: Babe!!!

BABE: Meg!!!

LENNY: How could you?!! I asked you not to tell anyone! I'm so ashamed! How could you?! Who else have you told? Did you tell anyone else?

BABE *(overlapping, to Meg):* Why'd you have to open your big mouth?!

MEG *(overlapping):* How am I supposed to know? You never said not to tell!

Meg tries to explain that they only want Lenny to break loose from her bondage as nursemaid to Old Granddaddy and find happiness, but Lenny doesn't believe that any man would love a woman afflicted as she is. Lenny admits, however, that she never mentioned the problem to her Memphis lover, she just assumed he'd reject her when he found out. Lenny runs upstairs in obvious distress, and Babe follows to comfort her, leaving Meg alone to entertain Doc. Meg gives him a drink of bourbon and asks after his wife and children. Then in good time she fixes another drink for them both.

DOC: Well, it's been a long time.

MEG: It has been a long time.

DOC: Let's see—when was the last time we saw each other?

MEG: I can't quite recall.

DOC: Wasn't it in Biloxi?

MEG: Ah, Biloxi. I believe so.

DOC: And wasn't there a—a hurricane going on at the time?

MEG: Was there?

DOC: Yes there was, one hell of a hurricane. Camille, I believe they called it. Hurricane Camille.

MEG: Yes, now I remember. It was a beautiful hurricane.

DOC: We had a time down there. We had quite a time. Drinking vodka, eating oysters on the half shell, dancing all night long. And the wind was blowing.

MEG: Oh, God, was it blowing.

DOC: Goddamn, was it blowing.

MEG: There never has been such a wind blowing.

DOC: Oh, God, Meggy. Oh, God.

MEG: I know, Doc. It was my fault to leave you. I was crazy. I thought I was choking. I felt choked.

DOC: I felt like a fool.

MEG: No.

DOC: I just kept on wondering why.

MEG: I don't know why . . . 'Cause I didn't want to care. I don't know. I did care, though. I did.

DOC *(after a pause):* Ah, hell—

After that, Meg's career went from bad to worse until finally she couldn't sing any more. She confides to Doc that she wound up in a psychiatric ward in Los Angeles after losing her job and after a long siege alone inside her apartment. Doc invites her to take a ride in his truck to look at the moon—they both agree that they don't want to "start up," they just want to spend an evening together with the moon and a bottle of bourbon.

After they've gone, Babe comes downstairs and plays a few notes on her

Mary Beth Hurt and Peter MacNicol in *Crimes of the Heart*

saxophone. She's interrupted by the arrival of Barnette, who reports that Zackery's sister Lucille, suspicious of Babe, had her followed and has obtained photos of Babe in the garage with Willie Jay. (The phone rings but Babe ignores it, and it stops.) Barnette has a set of copies, which he hands over. Babe is stunned as she looks through them and is horrified that Barnette has seen them too. Realizing that she can't destroy them because Lucille has the negatives, she lapses into acute despair, banging herself against the kitchen furniture.

> *Lenny comes down the stairs. She is wearing a coat and wiping white night cream off her face with a washrag.*
LENNY: What's the matter? What's going on down here?
BABE: Nothing!
> *She begins dancing ballet-style around the room.*
We're—we're just dancing. We were just dancing around down here.
> *Signaling to Barnette to dance.*
LENNY: Well, you'd better get your shoes on, 'cause we've got—
BABE: All right, I will! That's a good idea!
> *As she goes to get her shoes, she hides the pictures.*
Now, you go on back to bed. It's pretty late and—
LENNY: Babe, will you listen a minute—
BABE *(holding up her shoes):* I'm putting 'em on—

LENNY: That was the hospital that just called. We've got to get over there. Old Granddaddy's had himself another stroke.

BABE: Oh. All right. My shoes are on.

She stands. They all look at each other as the lights black out. Curtain.

ACT III

The following morning, Babe is lying on the cot and a weary Lenny is telling Chick that Old Granddaddy probably won't survive the coma into which he has sunk. Chick wants to start calling people to tell them the bad news; Lenny doesn't feel like it, but she promises to do it anyway. Chick complains that she's doing more than her share because she took the trouble to make the list, and she's only one-fourth of Old Granddaddy's grandchildren.

Chick departs, and Lenny confides to Babe that she feels partly guilty for Old Granddaddy's condition, because yesterday she wished on a birthday candle that her grandfather would be relieved of his pain. Babe assures her wishes don't count unless you have a real cake.

LENNY: Gosh, I wonder when Meg's coming home.

BABE: Should be soon.

LENNY: I just wish we wouldn't fight all the time. I don't like it when we do.

BABE: Me, neither.

LENNY: I guess it hurts my feelings a little, the way Old Granddaddy's always put so much stock in Meg and all her singing talent. I think I've been, well, envious of her 'cause I can't seem to do too much.

BABE: Why, sure you can.

LENNY: I can?

BABE: Sure. You just have to put your mind to it; that's all. It's like how I went out and bought that saxophone, just hoping I'd be able to attend music school and start up my own career. I just went out and did it. Just on hope. Of course, now it looks like . . . Well, it just doesn't look like things are gonna work out for me. But I know they would for you.

LENNY: Well, they'll work out for you, too.

BABE: I doubt it.

LENNY: Listen, I heard up at the hospital that Zackery's already in fair condition. They say soon he'll probably be able to walk and everything.

BABE: Really. And life sure can be miserable.

LENNY: Well, I know, 'cause—day before yesterday, Billy Boy was struck down by lightning.

BABE: He was?

LENNY *(nearing sobs):* Yeah. He was struck dead.

BABE *(crushed):* Life sure can be miserable.

In the midst of this melancholia, Meg enters, exuberant, her hair a mess and a heel broken, but singing a happy song. Meg looks at her downcast sisters and thinks she's the cause of their mood because she stayed out all night. She explains to them that Doc didn't suggest anything improper like running away with him—"He didn't ask me. He didn't even want to ask me." Doc is obviously devoted to his wife and children. Curiously, this did not make Meg feel rejected or humiliated. Instead, it made her very happy, because it was "just such fun. I'm happy. I realized I could care about someone. . . . .I sang right up into the trees!"

Meg has even decided to tell Old Granddaddy the awful truth about her failed career, "and if it sends him into a coma, that's just too damn bad!" In their present state, Lenny and Babe take this remark as a morbid joke. It sends them into gales of laughter, much to Meg's astonishment. By the time they've explained, and stopped laughing, Meg too, is feeling depressed.

Lenny is not looking forward to living alone after Old Granddaddy is gone (and Babe doesn't think she'll be moving in here now). Meg suggests that Lenny get ahold of her onetime friend Charlie and see if they can't get back together. Babe also encourages her to give this a try, and Lenny is finally determined: "I will!" She starts upstairs to call in privacy, when the phone rings. Meg answers it, then puts it down, telling Lenny it was a wrong number. When Lenny goes upstairs, Meg tells Babe it was the bakery—Lenny's cake is ready. She will go down to the corner to get it, but she has noticed that Babe becoming is more and more depressed.

MEG: You okay?
> *Babe shakes her head.*
What is it?
BABE: It's just—
MEG: What?
> *Babe gets up and goes to her suitcase. She opens it and removes the envelope containing the photographs.*
BABE: Here. Take a look.
MEG *(taking the envelope):* What is it?
BABE: It's some evidence Zackery's collected against me. Looks like my goose is cooked.
> *Meg opens the envelope and looks at the photographs.*
MEG: My God, it's—it's you and . . . is *that* Willie Jay?
BABE: Yeh.
MEG: Well, he certainly *has* grown. You were right about that. My, oh, my.
BABE: Please don't tell Lenny. She'd hate me.
MEG: I won't. I won't tell Lenny.
> *Putting the pictures back into the envelope.*
What are you gonna do?
BABE: What can I do?

There is a knock on the door—it's Barnette, come to see how Babe is bearing up, to ask after their grandfather and to pick up the envelope of pictures to be stored in his office safe. Meg discloses that she's seen the photos, and she wants to know what they'll mean for Babe's case. Barnette has enough evidence against Botrelle—"papers that pending word from three varied and unbiased experts could prove graft, fraud, forgery as well as a history of unethical behavior"—to force him to settle on their terms. But it will have to be out of court, now, because the photos must not be shown to a jury or otherwise made public.

Meg, satisfied, goes upstairs as Barnette tells Babe he is giving up his vendetta for the time being in order to strike a deal with Zackery on her behalf. Willie Jay, he tells her, will be heading north on the midnight bus. Babe's comment is, "I guess I'm not making anybody here a bit too happy."

Meg returns and hitches a ride with Barnette to go and get Lenny's cake. Lenny comes downstairs, embarrassed, ashamed that she found herself unable to make the phone call to Charlie. Chick comes in, pretending to sympathize with the two sisters over the degrading behavior of the third: Chick saw Meg "stumbling out of Doc Porter's pickup truck . . . . . looking such a disgusting mess." When Chick calls Meg "cheap Christmas trash" and "a low-class tramp," Lenny orders her out of the house. When Chick reminds Lenny it's *her* grandfather's house too, Lenny picks up a broom and drives her out of the door.

The sound of the phone is heard above the screaming of Lenny and Chick. Babe answers it; it's Zackery, who brings up the subject of the photos and then terrifies Babe by threatening to have her committed to an insane asylum. Frantic, Babe puts down the phone and searches the ribbon drawer for a piece of rope, which she quickly puts back when Lenny enters, swinging her broom and laughing delightedly that she has finally given Chick her comeuppance. Hysterically, Babe joins her in the laughter.

Lenny is in such a euphoric state that she is determined to phone Charlie right now. She dials the number, her hands not even shaking, while Babe takes the length of rope out of the drawer and disappears upstairs.

LENNY: Hello? . . . Hello, Charlie. This is Lenny MaGrath . . . Well, I'm fine. I'm just fine.
An awkward pause.
I was, ah, just calling to see—how you're getting on . . . Well, good. Good . . . Yes, I know I said that. Now I wish I didn't say it . . . Well, the reason I said that before, about not seeing each other again, was 'cause of me, not you . . . Well, it's just I—I can't have any children. I—have this ovary problem . . . Why, Charlie, what a thing to say! . . . Well, they're not all little snot-nosed pigs! . . . You think they are! . . . Oh, Charlie, stop, stop! You're making me laugh . . . Yes, I guess I was. I can see now that I was . . . You are? . . . Well, I'm dying to see you, too . . . Well, I don't know when, Charlie . . . soon. How about, well, how about tonight? . . . You will? . . . Oh, you will! . . . All right, I'll be here. I'll be right here . . . Goodbye, then, Charlie. Goodbye for now.
She hangs up the phone in a daze.
Babe. Oh, Babe! He's coming. He's coming! Babe! Oh, Babe, where are you? Meg! Oh . . . out back—picking up paw paws.
She exits through the back door.
And those paw paws are just ripe for picking up!
There is a moment of silence, then a loud, horrible thud is heard coming from upstairs. The telephone begins ringing immediately. It rings five times before Babe comes hurrying down the stairs with a

broken piece of rope hanging around her neck. The phone continues to ring.

BABE *(to the phone):* Will you shut up!

She is jerking the rope from around her neck. She grabs a knife to cut it off.

Cheap! Miserable! I hate you! I hate you!

She throws the rope violently around the room. The phone stops ringing.

Thank God.

Babe tries putting her head in the oven and turning on the gas, but this proves too slow a means. Before the gas can begin to take effect, Meg comes in with the cake and interrupts the process, obviously distressed at her sister's desperate action. Babe tries to explain, "I'm having a bad day. It's been a real bad day," the worst of it being Zackery's threat to have her put away. Meg reassures Babe that he can't do that; Babe is obviously not insane. He was just trying to scare her.

"Babe, we've just got to learn how to get through these real bad days here," Meg tells her sister, reminding Babe what a pleasure it will be to watch Lenny enjoy her birthday cake. Babe agrees—she wants to be around for that, wouldn't want to miss it. They take the cake out of the box and light the candles, while Babe confides, "I know why Mama hung that cat along with her." She was afraid of dying alone, was afraid to face what was coming, even angels, all alone. Babe realizes that unlike her mother, she is *not* alone.

Lenny comes in just as Babe finishes lighting the candles. Lenny loves the cake and its inscription: "Happy Birthday, Lenny—A Day Late." Lenny is somewhat awed by the large number of candles but is assured that the greater the number of candles, the more likely the wish is to come true. Lenny manages to blow out all the candles, and the others want to know what she wished for.

LENNY: Well, I guess it wasn't really a specific wish. This—this vision just sort of came into my mind.

BABE: A vision? What was it of?

LENNY: I don't know exactly. It was something about the three of us smiling and laughing together.

BABE: Well, when was it? Was it far away or near?

LENNY: I'm not sure; but it wasn't forever; it wasn't for every minute. Just this one moment and we were all laughing.

BABE: What were we laughing about?

LENNY: I don't know. Just nothing I guess.

MEG: Well, that's a nice wish to make.

Lenny and Meg look at each other a moment.

Here, now, I'll get a knife so we can go ahead and cut the cake in celebration of Lenny being born!

BABE: Oh, yes! And give each of us a rose! A whole rose apiece!

LENNY *(cutting the cake nervously):* Well, I'll try—I'll try!

MEG *(licking the icing off of a candle):* Mmmm—this icing is delicious! Here, try some!

BABE: Mmmm! It's wonderful! Here, Lenny!

LENNY *(laughing joyously as she licks icing from her fingers and cuts huge pieces of cake that her sisters bite into ravenously):* Oh, how I do love having birthday cake for breakfast! How I do!

> *The sisters freeze for a moment laughing and eating cake; the lights change and frame them in a magical, golden, sparkling glimmer; saxophone music is heard. The lights dim to black and the saxophone continues to play. Curtain.*

TRANSLATIONS

A Play in Three Acts

BY **BRIAN FRIEL**

Cast and credits appear on page 407

BRIAN FRIEL was born in 1929 in Derry City, Northern Ireland. He became a school teacher but since 1960 has devoted himself to writing. His short stories have appeared in The New Yorker *and have been collected in volumes entitled* The Saucer of Larks *and* The Gold in the Sea.

In more recent years Friel has concentrated on writing plays. His This Doubtful Paradise, The Enemy Within *and* The Blind Mice *were produced in Dublin, Belfast and London. His first far-flung international hit was* Philadelphia, Here I Come!, *produced in Dublin in September 1964 and on Broadway Feb. 16, 1966 for 326 performances (when it was named a Best Play of its season) and since then in every major theater center in Europe and America. His* The Loves of Cass McGuire *had its world premiere on Broadway Oct. 6, 1966. A program of two Friel one-acters,* Lovers, *was named a Best Play at the time of its Broadway engagement at Lincoln Center July 25, 1968 for 148 performances.*

The succession of Friel plays produced in Europe has included Crystal and Fox *(produced in Los Angeles in 1970 and off Broadway in 1973),* The Mundy Scheme *(produced on Broadway Dec. 13, 1969 for 4 performances),* The Gentle Island, The Freedom of the City *(which premiered simultaneously at the Royal Court and Abbey Theaters and was produced by the Goodman Theater Center in Chicago and on Broadway Feb. 17, 1974 for 9 performances),* Aristocrats *and now* Translations, *Friel's third Best Play, produced this season off Broadway by Manhattan Theater Club after its premiere at the Field Day Theater Company in Derry, of which Friel is co-director with Stephen Rea.*

Still another Friel playscript, Faith Healer, *had its world premiere on Broadway for 20 performances beginning April 5, 1979. His next at this writing is scheduled to be a new translation of Chekhov's* Three Sisters *in Derry. He was the recipient of the Irish-American Cultural Institute's 1980 award for his work on the Irish stage, an honor awarded annually, but seldom to a dramatist. Friel is married, with four daughters.*

Time: Late August, 1833

Place: *A hedge-school in the townland of Baile Beag/Ballybeg, an Irish-speaking community in County Donegal*

ACT I

SYNOPSIS: A large, barnlike room is cluttered with the paraphernalia of both the rustic outdoor life and the schoolroom, as though it served as a combination of living quarters, shed and learning institution, which in fact it does. It is a so-called "hedge-school" where Latin, Greek, mathematics and other basics are taught, somewhat informally, in the Irish language. The entrance is at left and the steps leading upward to the living quarters above are at right.

One August afternoon in 1833, Manus *("late 20s-early 30s, the schoolmaster's older son, pale-faced, lightly-built, intense, works as an unpaid assistant—a monitor—to his father. His clothes are shabby, and when he moves we see that he is lame")* is helping a pupil, Sarah, overcome her speech impediment. *"She has a waif-like appearance and could be any age from 17 to 35."* In a corner. Jimmy Jack Cassie, once a child prodigy and now in his 60s, is smiling, reading Homer in Greek. His clothes *"are filthy and he lives in them summer and winter."* Sarah is making inarticulate noises, and Manus is trying to get her to say words. It is a great victory when she manages to get out "My name is Sarah." In the meantime, Jimmy is amused by an exploit of Athene's, turning Ulysses into an old man with a touch of her wand. "Athene of the flashing eyes" is Jimmy's favorite goddess, he declares.

Manus wonders where his father the schoolmaster can be. Sarah—who is now sweeping up the place—mimes the business of attending a christening and then going to the pub to celebrate. Manus decides he'll probably have to take this evening's class, and he starts distributing books and slates, etc. Sarah takes a bunch of flowers from a hiding place and presents them to Manus, who appreciates both the gesture and the fact that Sarah can say "flowers" to him as she presents them.

Manus kisses the top of Sarah's head, as Maire *("a strong-minded, strong-bodied woman in her 20s with a head of curly hair")* enters, bringing a can of milk. Maire has come for the evening lesson. She drops into a chair beside Jimmy.

Stephen Burleigh as Owen, Barnard Hughes as Hugh and
Daniel Gerroll as Lieutenant Yolland in *Translations*

Maire and the other characters throughout this play are presumed to be speaking
in the Irish language (though the play is actually in English) unless otherwise
stated.

MAIRE: Ooooooh. The best harvest in living memory, they say; but I don't want
to see another like it. *(Showing Jimmy her hands.)* Look at the blisters.
JIMMY: *Esne fatigata?*
MAIRE: *Sum fatigatissima.*
JIMMY: *Bene! Optime!*
MAIRE: That's the height of my Latin. Fit me better if I had even that much
English.
JIMMY: I thought you had some English?
MAIRE: Three words. Wait—there was a spake I used to have off by heart.
What's this it was?
> *Her accent is strange because she is speaking a foreign language and
> because she does not understand what she is saying.*
"*In Norfolk we besport ourselves around the May-poll.*" What about that?

MANUS: *May-pole.*

MAIRE *(ignores him):* God have mercy on my Aunt Mary—she taught me that when I was about four, whatever it means. Do you know what it means, Jimmy?

JIMMY: Sure you know I have only Irish like yourself.

MAIRE: And Latin. And Greek.

JIMMY: I'm telling you a lie. I know one English word.

MAIRE: What?

JIMMY: *Boss-om.*

MAIRE: What's a *bossom?*

JIMMY: You know. *(He illustrates with his hands.)* Boss-om—boss-om—you know—Diana, the huntress, she has two powerful *boss-om.*

MAIRE: You may be sure that's the one English word you would know.

Manus tells the others about writing a letter for one of the villagers who became so engrossed in her gossipy communication that she forgot to whom she was dictating and said, "The aul drunken schoolmaster and that lame son of his are still footering about in the hedge-school, wasting people's good time and money." The letter writer also noted that one of the new national schools is now being built nearby.

Maire tells them that a group of English soldiers "below in the tents, them sapper fellas" has volunteered to help with the harvest tomorrow, though there can be no verbal communication between them because they speak different languages. Doalty *("an open-minded, open-hearted, generous and slightly thick young man")* and Bridget *("a plump, fresh young girl, ready to laugh, vain, and with a countrywoman's instinctive cunning")* come into the schoolroom, reporting that the schoolmaster is on his way, having imbibed perhaps more than is good for him. Doalty is carrying a surveyor's pole and explains to the group that the British are working each day with these poles and a theodolite. Doalty amuses himself and perplexes the British by covertly moving their poles and making them believe that something may be wrong with their calculations or their instrument. Bridget speaks in gibberish as an imitation of two confused and agitated British soldiers. Manus compliments Doalty on his obstructive gesture. Bridget warns him to be careful, or he'll be arrested.

They discuss the day's christening and the suitability of black soil for growing corn. Manus calls the class to order (noticing that the Donnelly twins are absent for some unknown reason) and begins to tutor his pupils in literature or mathematics, whatever each happens to be studying. The others talk quietly among themselves as Manus attends to Maire.

MANUS: Can I help you? What are you at?

MAIRE: Map of America. *(Pause.)* The passage money came last Friday.

MANUS: You never told me that.

MAIRE: Because I haven't seen you since, have I?

MANUS: You don't want to go. You said that yourself.

MAIRE: There's ten below me to be raised and no man in the house. What do you suggest?

MANUS: Do you want to go?

MAIRE: Did you apply for that job in the new national school?

MANUS: No.

MAIRE: You said you would.

MANUS: I said I might.

MAIRE: When it opens, this is finished: nobody's going to pay to go to a hedge-school.

MANUS: I know that and I—

> *He breaks off because he sees Sarah, obviously listening, at his shoulder. She moves away again.*

I was thinking that maybe I could—

MAIRE: It's fifty-six pounds a year you're throwing away.

MANUS: I can't apply for it.

MAIRE: You *promised* me you would.

MANUS: My father has applied for it.

MAIRE: He has not!

MANUS: Day before yesterday.

MAIRE: For God's sake, sure you know he's never—

MANUS: I couldn't—I can't go in against him.

MAIRE *(looks at him for a second, then):* Suit yourself.

They hear a report that there is a sweet smell in the fields near where the British are surveying, a possible sign of potato blight. But Maire states emphatically that there's never been blight here in Baile Beg, though they're always sniffing for it and fearing the worst about this, as about everything. Doalty agrees with Maire, then shows off his prowess at mathematics with the seven-times table. They are discussing the new national school, its regulations and its language which is to be exclusively English, when Sarah signals them that the schoolmaster is approaching. The schoolmaster—Hugh—enters in good humor and with Latin words scattered through his greeting. He is *"a large man, with residual dignity, shabbily dressed, carrying a stick, He has, as always, a large quantity of drink taken, but he is by no means drunk. He is in his early 60s."*

Grandly, Hugh hands his hat, coat and stick to Manus, while mentioning the christening. Bridget is curious to know the baby's name, as it will give her a clue to the identity of its unnamed father.

BRIDGET *(innocently):* What name did she put on it, Master?

HUGH: Was it Eamon? Yes, it was Eamon.

BRIDGET: Eamon Donal from Tor! Cripes!

HUGH: And after the *caeremonia nominationis*—Maire?

MAIRE: The ritual of naming.

HUGH: Indeed—we then had a few libations to mark the occasion. Altogether very pleasant. The derivation of the word "baptise"?—where are my Greek scholars? Doalty?

DOALTY: Would it be—ah—ah—

HUGH: Too slow, James?

JIMMY: *"Baptizein"*—to dip or immerse.

HUGH: Indeed—our friend Pliny Minor speaks of *"baptisterium"*—the cold bath.

DOALTY: Master.

HUGH: Doalty?

DOALTY: I suppose you could talk then about baptising a sheep at sheep-dipping, could you?

Laughter; comments.

HUGH: Indeed—the precedent is there—the day you were appropriately named Doalty—seven nines?

DOALTY: What's that, Master?

HUGH: Seven times nine?

DOALTY: Seven nines—seven nines—seven times nine—seven nines are—Cripes, it's on the tip of my tongue, Master—I knew it for sure this morning—funny that the only one that foxes me—

BRIDGET *(prompt):* Sixty-three.

DOALTY: What's wrong with me: sure seven nines are fifty-three, Master.

HUGH: Sophocles from Colonus would agree with Doalty Dan Doalty from Tulach Alainn: To know nothing is the sweetest life.

Hugh notices that there are some absentees including the Donnelly twins, Hugh sends Manus upstairs to fetch strong tea and a slice of soda bread, then brings up a complaint by Capt. Lancey of the Royal Engineers that his equipment has sometimes been tampered with; but the English officer cannot discuss this problem locally because he speaks no Irish. At this, Maire rises and declares that she agrees with the politician Dan O'Connell, called the Liberator: " 'The old language is a barrier to modern progress.' He said that last month. And he's right. I don't want Greek. I don't want Latin. I want English. *(Manus reappears on the platform above.)* I want to be able to speak English because I'm going to America as soon as the harvest's all saved."

Hugh takes a drink from his flask and tells them he's been asked to take charge of the new school. He's had enough for today and is intending to go upstairs and leave the class to Manus, when Owen enters, Hugh's younger son and Manus's brother, *"a handsome, attractive young man in his 20s. He is dressed smartly—a city man. His manner is easy and charming; everything he does is invested with consideration and enthusiasm."* Owen greets each of the others and embraces his father warmly. He has just arrived from Dublin (where, they have heard, Owen is a man of parts) in company with a British lieutenant named Yolland who is attached to the typonymic department ("He gives names to places," Hugh elucidates).

Lt. Yolland is outside with the chief cartographer Capt. Lancey, and Owen asks permission to bring them inside—cheerfully granted. Owen reveals he's on their payroll as "a part-time, underpaid civilian interpreter. My job is to translate the quaint, archaic tongue you people persist in speaking into the King's good English."

As Owen goes out to get his English friends, Hugh tries hurriedly to straighten the place up, and Maire and Manus have a brief exchange over future plans, each disappointed in the other: he that she has finally decided to go to America, she that he cannot now head the new school, as his father has been given the job.

Owen comes back in with Capt. Lancey *("middle-aged; a small, crisp officer, expert in his field as cartographer but uneasy with people")* and Lt. George Yolland *("in his late 20s-early 30s, tall, thin and gangling; blond hair; a shy, awkward manner. A soldier by accident")*. Hugh greets them in English and offers them a libation, which they decline. Lancey has something to say, and he tries to communicate it in English by speaking as if to children, enunciating carefully. He tells them he is making a map, explaining that a map is "a paper picture" of the countryside. They obviously don't understand the English words (appearing in *italics* in the script excerpts in this synopsis), so Owen suggests that Lancey speak naturally while Owen translates simultaneously.

LANCEY: . . . . .*His Majesty's government has ordered the first-ever comprehensive survey of this entire country—a general triangulation which will embrace detailed hydrographic and topographic information and which will be executed to a scale of six inches to the English mile.*

HUGH *(pouring a drink):* Excellent—excellent.

Lancey looks at Owen.

OWEN: A new map is being made of the whole country.

LANCEY *(looks to Owen): Is that all? (Owen smiles reassuringly and indicates to proceed.) This enormous task has been embarked on so that the military authorities will be equipped with up-to-date and accurate information on every corner of this part of the Empire . . .*

OWEN: The job is being done by soldiers because they are skilled in this work.

LANCEY: *And also so that the entire basis of land valuation can be reassessed for purposes of more equitable taxation.*

OWEN: This new map will take the place of the estate-agent's map so that from now on you will know exactly what is yours in law.

Lancey reads some quotations from his charter, and Owen explains that "The Captain hopes that the public will cooperate with the sappers and that the new map will mean that taxes are reduced." Owen tells them England offers this project as proof of its concern for the interests of Ireland.

Yolland has nothing to add to what Lancey has told the group. It is Yolland's job (Owen explains) to see that the place-names on the map are correct. Yolland tells Owen that he means to learn Irish and adds, *"I think your countryside is—is—is—is very beautiful: I've fallen in love with it already. I hope we're not too—too crude an intrusion on your lives. And I know that I'm going to be happy, very happy here."* Owen translates this as "He is already a committed Hibernophile . . . . .he loves Baile Beg; and he loves you all." Hugh, in his drunken way, offers the Englishmen friendship and hospitality, and the formalities are ended.

Manus, who can speak English, meets Owen downstage and accuses him of not translating truly what Lancey was saying.

MANUS:. . . . .It's a bloody military operation, Owen! And what's Yolland's function? What's "incorrect" about the place-names we have here?

OWEN: Nothing at all. They're just going to be standardized.

MANUS: You mean changed into English?

OWEN: Where there's ambiguity, they'll be Anglicized.

MANUS: And they call you Roland! They both call you Roland!

OWEN: Shhhhh. Isn't it ridiculous? They seemed to get it wrong from the very beginning—or else they can't pronounce Owen. I was afraid some of you bastards would laugh.

MANUS: Aren't you going to tell them?

OWEN: Yes—yes—soon—soon.

MANUS: But they—

OWEN: Easy, man, easy. Owen—Roland—what the hell. It's only a name. It's the smae me, isn't it? Well, isn't it?

MANUS: Indeed it is. It's the same Owen.

OWEN: And the same Manus. And in a way we complement each other.
        He punches Manus lightly, playfully and turns to the others.
(As he goes.) All right—who has met whom? Isn't this a job for the go-between?
        Manus watches him move confidently across the floor, taking Maire by the hand and introducing her to Yolland. Hugh is trying to negotiate the steps. Jimmy is lost in a text. Doalty and Bridget are giggling. Sarah is staring at Manus. Curtain.

ACT II

Scene 1

A few days later, this area has now been mapped and Yolland is busy doing his job of Anglicizing each place-name either phonetically or by translating the meaning of the words. He is sitting on the floor, eyes closed as though dreaming of something else while Owen is pronouncing and then translating place-names off a large map. They are speaking English, as they try to name a little beach where a stream meets the sea. Owen speaks its Irish name.

OWEN: Bun na hAbhann.

YOLLAND: Bun na hAbhann.

OWEN: That's terrible, George.

YOLLAND: I know. I'm sorry. Say it again.

OWEN: Bun na hAbhann.

YOLLAND: Bun na hAbhann.

OWEN: That's better. Bun is the Irish name for bottom. And Abha means river. So it's literally the mouth of the river.

YOLLAND: Let's leave it alone. There's no English equivalent for a sound like that.

OWEN: What is it called in the church registry?
        Only now does Yolland open his eyes.

YOLLAND: Let's see . . . Banowen.

OWEN: That's wrong. *(Consults text.)* The list of freeholders calls it Owenmore —that's completely wrong: Owenmore's the big river at the west end of the parish. *(Another text.)* And in the grand jury lists it's called—God!—Binhone!—

Stephen Burleigh and Ellen Parker (as Maire) in a scene from *Translations*

wherever they got that. I suppose we could Anglicize it to Bunowen; but somehow that's neither fish nor flesh.

   Yolland closes his eyes again.

YOLLAND: I give up.

OWEN *(at map):* Back to first principles. What are we trying to do?

YOLLAND: Good question.

OWEN: We are trying to denominate and at the same time describe that tiny area of soggy, rocky, sandy ground where that little stream enters the sea, an area known locally as Bun na hAbhann . . . Burnfoot! What about Burnfoot?

YOLLAND *(indifferently):* Good, Roland. Burnfoot's good.

OWEN: George, my name isn't—

YOLLAND: B-u-r-n-f-o-o-t.

They enter the name on the map, as Yolland comments that they aren't going fast enough to suit Capt. Lancey—the maps can't be printed until the names are all established. Manus comes in and observes the goings-on but insists on speaking Irish to Yolland (Yolland wants to learn the language, but at this point he cannot understand anything Manus says).

OWEN: Can't you speak English before George?

MANUS: Why?

OWEN: Out of courtesy.

MANUS: Doesn't he want to learn Irish? *(to Yolland.)* Don't you want to learn Irish?

YOLLAND: *Sorry—sorry? I—I—*

MANUS: I understand the Lanceys perfectly, but people like you puzzle me.

OWEN: Manus, for God's sake!

MANUS *(still to Yolland):* How's the work going?

YOLLAND: *The work?—the work? Oh, it's it's staggering along—I think— (To Owen.) —isn't it? But we'd be lost without Roland.*

MANUS *(leaving):* I'm sure. But there are always the Rolands, aren't there?

YOLLAND: *What was that he said? Something about Lancey, wasn't it?*

But Owen does not translate. Instead, he tries to explain Manus to George: Manus was crippled in babyhood when his father fell across his cradle. He hasn't married because he has no income except the odd shilling his father gives him.

Owen tries to get on with the names, but Yolland is preoccupied with other thoughts: the occasional hostility of a villager; the mysterious whereabouts of the Donnelly twins, whom Lancey wants for questioning in the disappearance of some equipment; the music that comes from Maire's house almost every night. The Irish place names also seem to have a music of their own. Yolland speculates on whether he could settle down and find a life here. Owen's opinion is, "You wouldn't survive a mild winter here."

Doalty comes in and calls for Manus, who comes downstairs. A couple of strangers down the road want a word with Manus, who accompanies Doalty outside. Yolland tells Owen that Doalty passed his tent that morning with a scythe across his shoulder, "and he came up to me and pointed to the long grass and then cut a pathway round my tent and from the tent down to the road—so that my feet won't get wet with the dew. Wasn't that kind of him? And I have no words to thank him . . ."

Yolland tells Owen something of himself. He was destined by his family for East India Company service but missed the boat—literally—and joined the Army as his only alternative to going back home and facing an irate father. Yolland's exposure to Ireland made him feel as though he were crossing a frontier into a new kind of consciousness that greatly attracts him. He realizes, however, that though he may learn the language he'll never be permitted to penetrate the closed circle of the tribe.

Hugh comes downstairs, jaunty and alert but reaching for the bottle of poteen to fortify himself for a journey to the parish priest's to obtain a testimonial for his prospective employers, also to check with the builders of the new school about his living quarters there. Conversing with Hugh in English, Yolland imparts to the old man some of his feeling of exclusion from this society, whose very language he admires from his little contact with it. Hugh replies in his customarily flowery manner, but in English.

HUGH: Indeed, Lieutenant, a rich language. A rich literature. You'll find, sir, that certain cultures expend on their vocabularies and syntax acquisitive energies and ostentations entirely lacking in their material lives. I suppose you could call us a spiritual people.

OWEN *(not unkindly, more out of embarrassment before Yolland):* Will you stop that nonsense, Father.

HUGH: Nonsense? What nonsense?

OWEN: Do you know where the priest lives?

HUGH: At Lis na Muc, over near—

OWEN: No, he doesn't. Lis na Muc, the Fort of the Pigs, has become Swinefort.

Now turning the pages of the Name-book—a page per name.

And to get to Swinefort you pass through Greencastle and Fair Head and Stranhill and Gort and Whiteplains. And the new school isn't at Poll na gCaorach—it's at Sheepsrock. Will you be able to find your way?

Hugh pours himself another drink.

HUGH: Yes, it is a rich language, Lieutenant, full of the mythologies of fantasy and hope and self-deception—a syntax opulent with tomorrows. It is our response to mud cabins and a diet of potatoes; our only method of replying to . . . inevitabilities. . . . .

He goes to the door and stops there.

To return briefly to that other matter, Lieutenant. I understand your sense of exclusion, of being cut off from a life here; and I trust you will find access to us with my son's help. But remember that words are signals, counters. They are not immortal. And it can happen—to use an image you'll understand—it can happen that a civilization can be imprisoned in a linguistic contour which no longer matches the landscape of . . . fact. Gentlemen. *(He goes.)*

Yolland believes Hugh is an astute man for all his verbal posturing, and he senses that their mapping and re-naming project is eroding something that is probably of value. Owen scoffs at this romantic notion and cites the example of a crossroads, "Tobair Vree," named for a no-longer-existent well whose waters were deemed to have magical powers by a long-dead sufferer. Still conversing in English, Owen puts a question to Yolland.

OWEN: . . . . .What do we do with a name like that? Do we scrap Tobair Vree altogether and call it—what?—the Cross? Crossroads? Or do we keep piety with a man long dead, long forgotten, his name "eroded" beyond recognition, whose trivial little story nobody in the parish remembers?

YOLLAND: Except you.

OWEN: I've left here.

YOLLAND: You remember it.

OWEN: I'm asking you: what do we write in the Name-book?

YOLLAND: Tobair Vree.

OWEN: Even though the well is a hundred yards from the actual crossroads—and there's no well anyway—and what the hell does "Vree" mean?

YOLLAND: Tobair Vree.

OWEN: That's what you want?

YOLLAND: Yes.

OWEN: You're certain?

YOLLAND: Yes.
OWEN: Fine. Fine. That's what you'll get.
YOLLAND: That's what you want, too, Roland.
    Pause.
OWEN *(exploded):* George! For God's sake! *My name is not Roland!*
YOLLAND: What?
OWEN *(softly):* My name is Owen.
    Pause.
YOLLAND: Not Roland?
OWEN: Owen.
YOLLAND: You mean to say—?
OWEN: Owen.
YOLLAND: But I've been—
OWEN: O-w-e-n.
YOLLAND: Where did Roland come from?
OWEN: I don't know.
YOLLAND: It was never Roland?
OWEN: Never.
YOLLAND: Oh my God!
    *Pause. They stare at one another. Then the absurdity of the situation
    strikes them suddenly. They explode with laughter.*

Another drink of poteen sweetens the joke as they conjure with names. Manus enters in the midst of their hilarity, bearing good news. The two men were a delegation from an island village 50 miles to the south offering Manus a salary of 42 pounds a year to found a hedge-school in their area. Owen figures the mapping expedition will have reached there by December, so they can all spend Christmas together. Manus joins them in a celebratory drink and is going out to tell Maire the good news, when Maire comes in bringing her usual can of milk. She takes Manus's news with equanimity and hands him the can, which Manus carries upstairs. In the meantime, Maire—who cannot communicate directly with Yolland—asks Owen to tell the lieutenant there's to be a dance the next night. Yolland asks if he can come and promises to do so.

Manus is in a hurry to walk Maire home and speak to her mother, but Maire hangs back to join the others in a drink. Intoxicated with more than liquor, Yolland raises his glass and shouts all the Irish words he knows—a few place names and the word "poteen." With his exclamation, *"Bloody marvellous!"* there is heard the music of the reel. *Curtain.*

Scene 2

The following night, outdoors, there is music in the distant background, as Maire and Yolland enter at a run, laughing, holding hands. They are awkward with each other; they enjoy the sound of each other's voices, though they can't understand the words. Maire even tries, *"Tu es centurio in exercitu Britannico et in castris,"* but to no avail. She repeats the only English words she knows: *"George . . . water . . . fire . . . earth,"* and Yolland thinks her wonderful.

Finally Maire tries her one English sentence: *"George, in Norfolk we besport ourselves around the May-poll."* Yolland is so enthusiastic that Maire asks herself, "Mother of God, my Aunt Mary wouldn't have taught me something dirty, would she?"

Yolland holds out his hand, but Maire moves away, Yolland speaks her name. Again she moves away. As a last resort, he tries repeating the Irish place names.

YOLLAND: Bun na hAbhann?
>*He says the name softly, almost privately, very tentatively, as if he were searching for a sound she might respond to. He tries again.*

Druim Dubh?
>*She stops. She is listening. He is encouraged.*

Poll na gCaorach. Lis Maol.
>*She turns toward him.*

Lis na nGall.

MAIRE: Lis na nGradh.
>*They are now facing each other and begin moving—almost imperceptibly—towards one another.*

Carraig an Phoill.

YOLLAND: Carraig na Ri. Loch na nEan.

MAIRE: Loch an Iubhair. Machaire Buidhe.

YOLLAND: Machaire Nor. Cnoc na Mona.

MAIRE: Cnoc na nGabhar.

YOLLAND: Mullach.

MAIRE: Port.

YOLLAND: Tor.

MAIRE: Lag.
>*She holds out her hands to him. He takes them. each now speaks almost to himself/herself.*

YOLLAND: *I wish to God you could understand me.*

MAIRE: Soft hands; a gentleman's hands.

YOLLAND: *Because if you could understand me I could tell you how I spend my days, either thinking of you or gazing up at your house in the hope that you'll appear even for a second.*

MAIRE: Every evening you walk by yourself along the Tra Bhan and every morning you wash yourself in front of your tent.

YOLLAND: *I would tell you how beautiful you are, curly-headed Maire. I would so like to tell you how beautiful you are.*

MAIRE: Your arms are long and thin and the skin on your shoulders is very white.

They are long past the need for words now, though Maire picks out one English word—*always*—from Yolland's strange articulations. They understand very well what lies beneath the sound of each other's voices. Maire takes Yolland's face in her hand and asks, "Take me away with you, George." They kiss, as Sarah enters and sees them. Shocked, Sarah runs off crying "Manus!" *Music to crescendo. Curtain.*

ACT III

In the schoolroom the following evening, Owen is working on his names and Sarah on her reading, but they are conscious that Manus is gathering things together, getting ready to leave. Manus's bag falls apart, and Owen gives him his. Owen is staying for awhile—he hasn't made up his mind whether to continue with the Army on this project. No doubt Manus's prospective hedge-school employers will come back looking for him, and Owen will be here to tell them Manus wants the job but may not be able to start it for three or four months.

Owen warns Manus that if he leaves now Lancey will assume he is somehow involved in the disappearance of Lieutenant Yolland, who hasn't been seen since the night before. Owen supposes the search party will find Yolland lying somewhere drunk. Close to tears, Manus remembers that he went looking for Yolland last night with a stone in his hand, "But when I saw him standing there at the side of the road—smiling—and her face buried in his shoulder—I couldn't even go close to them. I just shouted something stupid—something like, 'You're a bastard, Yolland.' " And Manus forgot to say it in English, so Yolland probably didn't even understand.

Manus leaves a few last-minute messages for their father and instructs Owen on how to take care of the old man. As he leaves, Manus puts Sarah once more through her questions and answers. Though in tears, she replies clearly, Manus kisses her goodbye on top of her head, assuring her she did no harm and that "There's nothing to stop you now—nothing in the wide world." Then Manus strides off.

Bridget and Doalty come in, bubbling over with excitement.

DOALTY: You're missing the crack, boys! Cripes, you're missing the crack! Fifty more soldiers arrived an hour ago!

BRIDGET: And they're spread out in a big line from Sean Neal's over to Lag and they're moving straight across the fields towards Cnoc na nGabhar!

DOALTY: Prodding every inch of ground in front of them with their bayonets and scattering animals and hens in all directions!

BRIDGET: And tumbling everything before them—fences, ditches, haystacks, turf-stacks!

DOALTY: They came to Barney Petey's field of corn—straight through it be God as if it was heather!

BRIDGET: Not a blade of it left standing!

DOALTY: And Barney Petey just out of his bed and running after them in his drawers: "You hoors you! Get out of my corn, you hoors you!"

Hugh joined the protest—they report—crying "Visigoths! Huns! Vandals!", as did Jimmy Jack crying "Thermopylae!" Owen questions Bridget about the night before; Bridget saw George and Maire leave the dance, then Manus follow them out. Manus returned, but George and Maire never did. Bridget saw them on a back road going in the direction of Maire's house.

DOALTY: We know nothing. What are you asking us for?

OWEN: Because Lancey'll question me when he hears Manus's gone. *(To*

Bridget.) That's the way George went home? By the back road? That's where you saw him?

BRIDGET: Leave me alone, Owen. I know nothing about Yolland. If you want to know about Yolland, ask the Donnelly twins.

> *Silence. Doalty moves over to the window. . . . .Owen goes to Doalty, who looks resolutely out the window.*

OWEN: What's this about the Donnellys?

> *Pause.*

Were they about last night?

DOALTY: Didn't see them if they were. *(Begins whistling through his teeth.)*

OWEN: George is a friend of mine.

DOALTY: So.

OWEN: I want to know what's happened to him.

DOALTY: Couldn't tell you.

OWEN: What have the Donnelly twins to do with it?

> *Pause.*

Doalty!

DOALTY: I know nothing, Owen—nothing at all—I swear to God. All I know is this: on my way to the dance I saw their boat beached at Port. It wasn't there on my way home, after I left Bridget. And that's all I know, as God's my judge. The half-dozen times I met him I didn't know a word he said to me; but he seemed a right enough sort . . .

Maire enters in obvious distress, her hair disheveled and wet from the rain outside, carring an empty milk can. Maire wants to know if they've heard anything. Yolland left her last night trying to speak Irish but getting it wrong, saying "I'll see you yesterday."

Maire drops to the floor where Owen has spread his map and locates Yolland's home in England with its strange place names that are meaningless to her. She compliments Sarah on the dress she wore the night before, then turns to Owen: "Something very bad's happened to him, Owen. I know. He wouldn't go away without telling me. Where is he, Owen?"

Distraught, Maire sits as though for the evening's lesson, then rises and starts for home. She stops long enough to tell the others that the baby born a few days ago has died in the night. Then she goes out into the rain.

Doalty fears that Manus has drawn suspicion on himself by leaving, and that the soldiers will easily catch him as he limps along.

Lancey comes in purposefully, ordering Owen to translate what he is about to say so that it may be repeated to every family in the area.

OWEN: The Captain has an announcement to make.

LANCEY: *Lieutenant Yolland is missing. We are searching for him. If we don't find him, or if we receive no information as to where he is to be found, I will pursue the following course of action. (He indicates to Owen to translate.)*

OWEN: They are searching for George. If they don't find him—

LANCEY: *Commencing twenty-four hours from now we will shoot all livestock in Ballybeg. (Owen stares at him.) At once.*

OWEN: Beginning this time tomorrow they'll kill every animal in Baile Beg—unless they're told where George is.

LANCEY: *If that doesn't bear results, commencing forty-eight hours from now we will embark on a series of eviction and levelling of every abode in the following selected areas—*

OWEN: You're not—!

LANCEY: *Do your job. Translate.*

Owen does, giving the equivalent Irish names as Lancey reads his Anglicized list of towns. If Lieutenant Yolland is still missing, Lancey adds, he'll lay waste the entire parish. Lancey notices Sarah and demands that she state her name and place of residence—which of course she cannot under these forced circumstances. Owen answers for her, and Lancey is reminded that he wants to have a talk with Owen's brother Manus (Owen says Manus has gone to a wake). Doalty, looking out the window, remarks that the English camp is now on fire. Lancey looks out, sees that it is, and goes off.

Bridget goes to hide livestock, soon followed by Sarah. Almost dreamily, Doalty considers their plight; perhaps the answer is to stick together, the Donnelly twins included, and put up a fight even against the trained army. Doalty goes out to think this over, and Owen goes upstairs.

Hugh and Jimmy Jack enter drunkenly, saturated inside and out. Hugh is complaining loudly that the local Justice of the Peace has informed him that another man is to receive the national school appointment, a schoolmaster from Cork. Hugh shouts for Manus to bring him strong tea, while Jimmy confides loudly that he has finally made up his mind to marry Pallas Athene—he is lonely and he craves companionship. Weeping, he slides to the floor and is immediately asleep.

Hugh takes up the Name-book, opens it and, as Owen comes down with two bowls of tea, recites the new names from it: "Ballybeg. Burnfoot. Kings Head. Whiteplains. Fair Hill. Dunboy. Green Bank." Owen takes the book from him and wakes Jimmy to drink his tea, but Hugh persists, "We must learn where we live. We must learn to make them our own. We must make them our new home . . . . .It is not the literal past, the 'facts' of history that shape us, but images of the past embodied in language. James has ceased to make that distinction."

Owen admonishes Hugh to change out of his wet clothes and goes out in search of Doalty. Meanwhile Hugh is remembering a day when he and Jimmy Jack were young men carrying pikes, marching along on the road to Sligo.

HUGH: . . . . .Striding across the fresh, green land. The rhythms of perception heightened. The whole enterprise of consciousness accelerated. We were gods that morning, James; and I had recently married *my* goddess, Caitlin Dubh Nic Reactainn, may she rest in peace. And to leave her and my infant son in his cradle —that was heroic, too. By God, sir, we were magnificent. We marched as far as —where was it?—Glenties? All of twenty-three miles in one day. And it was there, in Phelan's pub, that we got homesick for Athens, just like Ulysses. The *desiderium nostrorum*—the need for our own. Our *pietas,* James, was for older, quieter things. And that was the longest twenty-three miles back I ever made. *(Toasts Jimmy.)* My friend, confusion is not an ignoble condition.

Maire enters.

MAIRE: I'm back again. I set out for somewhere but I couldn't remember where. So I came back here.

HUGH: Yes, I will teach you English, Maire Chatach.

MAIRE: Will you, Master? I must learn it. I need to learn it.

HUGH: Indeed you may well be my only pupil.

He goes toward the steps and begins to ascend.

MAIRE: When can we start?

HUGH: Not today. Tomorrow, perhaps. After the funeral. We'll begin tomorrow. *(Ascending.)* But don't expect too much. I will provide you with the available words and the available grammar. But will that help you to interpret between privacies? I have no idea. But it's all we have. I have no idea at all. *(He is now at the top.)*

MAIRE: Master, what does the English word *"always"* mean?

HUGH: *Semper—per omnia saecula.* The Greeks called it *aei.* It's not a word I'd start with. It's a silly word, girl.

He goes off. Jimmy is awake. He gets to his feet. Maire sees the Name-book, picks it up and sits with it on her knee.

MAIRE: When he comes back, this is where he'll come to. He told me this is where he was happiest.

Jimmy sits beside her.

JIMMY: Do you know the Greek word *"endogamein?"* It means to marry within the tribe. And the word *"exogamein"* means to marry outside the tribe. And you don't cross those borders casually—both sides get very angry. Now, the problem is this: Is Athene sufficiently mortal or am I sufficiently god-like for the marriage to be acceptable to her people and to my people? You think about that.

He sees Hugh's flask on the table and goes toward it. As he goes, Hugh reappears.

HUGH: *Urbs antiqua fuit*—there was an ancient city which, 'tis said, Juno loved above all the lands. And it was the goddess's aim and cherished hope that here should be the capital of all nations—should the fates perchance allow that. Yet in truth she discovered that a race was springing from Trojan blood to overthrow some day these Tyrian towers—a people *late regum belloque superbum*—kings of broad realms and proud in war who would come forth for Lybia's downfall —such was—such was the course—such was the course ordained—ordained by fate. What the hell's wrong with me? Sure I know it backways. I'll begin again. *Urbs antiqua fuit*— there was an ancient city which, 'tis said, Juno loved above all the lands.

The lights begin to come down.

And it was the goddess's aim and cherished hope that here should be the capital of all nations—should the fates perchance allow that. Yet in truth she discovered that a race was springing from Trojan blood to overthrow some day these Tyrian towers—a people kings of broad realms and proud in war who would come forth for Lybia's downfall . . .

Black. Curtain.

THE FLOATING LIGHT BULB

A Play in Two Acts

BY WOODY ALLEN

Cast and credits appear on page 356

WOODY ALLEN was born in New York City Dec. 1, 1935. After graduating from high school and attending N.Y.U. and City College, the gagwriting he started to develop at age 17 began to pay off in contributions to the Sid Caesar, Art Carney and Herb Shriner TV shows, plus sketches for Broadway revues and night club acts. In 1961 he began performing his own material in New York clubs. His career came into full flower in 1965, as he was asked to write and appear in his first movie, What's New Pussycat? *He has won his principal renown as a movie writer, director and star with such subsequent films as* Take the Money and Run *(1969),* Bananas *(1971),* Sleeper *(1973),* Annie Hall *(1977, winner of the New York Film Critics Award),* Interiors *(1978),* Manhattan *(1979) and* Stardust Memories *(1980).*

Allen's first full-length play for the stage was Don't Drink the Water, *produced by David Merrick on Broadway Nov. 17, 1966 for 598 performances. His second was* Play It Again, Sam *which Merrick also produced on Broadway Feb. 12, 1969 for 453 performances (and Allen wrote the screen versions of both plays). After a hiatus of more than a decade, his third stage script (and first Best Play),* The Floating Light Bulb, *appeared at the reopened Vivian Beaumont Theater in Lincoln Center April 27, 1981 punctuating its new season with success.*

*Allen is also the author of three books—*Getting Even, Without Feathers *and* Side Effects—*and of numerous articles for* The New Yorker, Playboy, New Republic *and other magazines. He is divorced from his former wife, the actress Louise Lasser, and lives in New York City.*

Brian Backer as Paul Pollack and Beatrice Arthur as
Enid Pollack in a scene from *The Floating Light Bulb*

The following synopsis of The Floating Light Bulb *was prepared by Jeffrey Sweet, with the emphasis on quotation from the script in the second act.*

Time: 1945

Place: The Canarsie section of Brooklyn

ACT I

Scene 1

SYNOPSIS: Sixteen-year-old Paul Pollack is practising a magic trick in the bedroom he shares with his 13-year-old brother Steve. It is a trick in which an illuminated light bulb appears to be suspended in midair without support. *"Paul is about 16, awkward, gawky, with thick-lensed glasses. He is painfully shy, problematically so, always looking down, always keeping to his room to practise."*

The lights fade on the bedroom and gradually come up on the Pollacks' apartment, a cheerless place in a poor section of Brooklyn. We see the living room with kitchenette, Paul and Steve's bedroom, the entrance to their parents' room, and, when the front door is open, a bit of the hallway outside.

While Paul continues to practise magic tricks in his room, Enid, his mother, tries to deal simultaneously with a bag of groceries and Steve. Steve is failing most of his classes, eating junk food, shooting craps, setting fires and generally getting in about as much trouble as is possible for a boy his age. She tells Steve that his problem is not stupidity but laziness, and she tries to encourage him to do better. Steve responds with smart-ass comments.

Enid is not too happy with Paul either. An IQ test taken some years back had pegged Paul as an incipient genius, but he has not given any practical expression of his potential, choosing instead to seclude himself with his magic.

Enid pulls Paul into the main room for some food and a lecture. As Paul and Steve eat, she tells them to apply themselves or they'll end up like their father, Max. Max had potential, she insists as she pours herself one of her too-frequent drinks. But Max refused to apply himself. What is he now? Little better than a bum, living on tips as a waiter and flirting with the far fringes of petty crime.

The devil being spoken of enters. Max is a boyish 51, dressed in a self-conscious attempt to look stylish. He throws four dollars on the table, telling Enid that's all he made in tips the night before. She doesn't believe him. She's sure he's holding out on her. They argue. He threatens to walk out. She tells him to be her guest. She is angry at his refusal to meet his responsibilities as a husband and a father, nor does she like the gun he carries around for self-protection. He wouldn't need a gun if he weren't trying to impress the gangsters he pals around with. Max fends off her complaints sullenly.

Enid doesn't let up. She also objects to Max's playing favorites with Steve. What about paying some attention to Paul? Max defensively replies he likes both boys equally, but that it's time Paul found some kind of work and brought in some money. It's obvious that he'll never amount to much scholastically, despite his supposed IQ.

Max and Enid are still fighting when the phone rings. Enid answers. The party on the other end hangs up. She tells Max that she knows this sort of phone call is a signal for him to go out and do something of a questionable nature. Max grins, says, "I have to see a man about a horse," puts on his coat and goes out the front door.

Paul drifts back to his room to practise some more, and Steve bundles up and goes outside, undoubtedly to get into more trouble. Left alone in the room. Enid bitterly reflects on the failure that is her family. "And don't think I don't know where you go off to, Max. Don't think you're fooling me. Believe me, I know." She is drinking again as the scene ends.

Scene 2

In an area suggestive of a cheap hotel room, Max is playing the big man *"with his much younger, cute little mistress, Betty,"* giving her an expensive watch and assuring her that, as soon as he makes his big score, he will ditch Enid and the boys and take her to a life of renewed hope elsewhere. When? As soon as he can pay off the loan sharks. They can be vicious if not satisfied. He carries the gun to give himself an edge against them.

Betty begins to cry. She doesn't believe he'll ever be able to get away. He insists his freedom is just around the corner. All he has to do is hit his number. He's bound to. He's due for a change in his luck. She wonders if it will really be possible for him to walk out on his family when the time comes. "Maybe you're more involved with your family than you think. It's been a long time, Max—and you got two sons." He insists that the kids won't hold him back. Besides, they have to learn to fend for themselves, don't they? He shifts the conversation from his family. He's sure he's going to hit a number soon, he tells her; he's playing her birthday now.

Scene 3

Back in the apartment, Enid is on the phone to her sister Lena, trying to persuade her to help finance a new money-making scheme to export bagels, lox and cream cheese in dry ice to Jews in the South. Lena doesn't seem to be interested. The phone call over, Enid leaves for work muttering, "The woman has never forgiven me to this day for her physical appearance. Like it's my fault."

Scene 4

Steve is listening to a radio serial while Paul practises magic. Paul wants Steve to turn down the volume. Steve tells him he doesn't own the room and, irritated, starts tossing around Paul's magic apparatus and making fun of his brother's stutter.

Enid enters and stops their fighting. She pulls Paul aside. She has just had a meeting with Mr. Parver, the dean of his high school, who told her that Paul has been cutting classes and is not going to make passing grades. She also did not take kindly to Parver's questions about Paul's home life.

Paul tells her he feels lost and confused in the school and that he won't go back. She asks him where he has been going if not to school? To the magic shop, mostly. He loves the equipment there—Chinese boxes, silk handkerchiefs, rings, "and the vanishing bird cage." "I wish I could vanish," says Enid ruefully. Paul apologizes. She tells him that he's got to start living in the real world. The world is not magic. Paul says he'll try again. He'll go to summer school to make up lost credits and graduate. Until then, says Enid, he should get some work to make money to contribute to the family.

But Paul hasn't been very successful at work either. A job as a rug salesman didn't work out very well, for instance. Enid asks him if there's anything he *wants* to do? Well, he replies, maybe he'd like to do magic professionally.

Enid responds sarcastically. A magician. That's really a job to bring in the money, isn't it? And money is what they're going to need, especially if, as Enid suspects, Max is about to run off with his girl.

Paul suggests that, if Max does run off, she could remarry. And whom, she wonders, would she marry? She isn't exactly surrounded by beaux. Besides which, she tells him candidly, she still has deep feelings for Max. She turned down another guy to marry Max. That other guy is now rich, and Max is just . . . Max.

Paul says that maybe things would be better if she didn't always fight with him. "I don't fight," she says. "I reason." If only he would give up his girl, that would be a start. Then maybe things would improve.

Paul promises to look for a job. Enid tells him that show business is a nice dream but nothing to count on for a living. He should have something practical to fall back on. Paul retreats to his room to practise some more.

Scene 5

Max returns from work late. Steve joins him. He tells his father of the marked deck Paul has for his magic tricks. Max tells him he's seen plenty of marked decks. Steve asks to see Max's gun. Max refuses to show it and tells Steve he is never to touch it. Steve asks Max if he carries it to protect himself from gangsters. No, Max insists. He likes to even the odds walking alone in the middle of the night in this neighborhood. Steve tells him Eddie Lynch left a message that Max better pay what he owes.

Enid enters. Max tells her tips were lousy again. Enid grills him about how much he owes Eddie Lynch. Max tells her that he'll take care of whatever it is as soon as he hits his number. "Our whole life we're waiting to hit your number," Enid replies. He bridles when she suggests that a man his age should take it a little easier. He has not reconciled himself to the idea that he is "his age." He tells her that if she hadn't pressured him to get out of the rackets when he was younger, they would be well off today.

Enid tells him about her conversation with Mr. Parver regarding Paul. Max insists there's nothing wrong with Paul that an acquaintance with reality wouldn't take care of. Enid says that what particularly frightens her is the possibility that Paul will never connect, that he will for the rest of his life be dependent on others. For Paul's sake—for the sake of them all—Enid appeals to Max to make a fresh try at meeting his responsibilities as father and husband. If he would start by giving up the girl friend she knows he has been seeing . . .

Enid's awkward attempt at a reconciliation explodes into a shouting match. Max insists his life is his own to do with as he pleases. Enid asks what he expects will happen to her and the boys if he disappears with Betty. "You'll figure out something, Enid," he replies. "Your sons'll shape up. And grow up. You won't starve."

Enid says she'll get a lawyer. Max says that she and her lawyer will need a lot of luck to find him once he hits his number, and so on—until Steve returns to the room and yells, "Can you shut up! Will you both shut up!"

Scene 6

Paul is showing Steve one of his magic tricks and, for once, the younger boy seems to be impressed. Max enters from his bedroom *"all duded up,"* and Steve encourages Paul to show him the necktie trick. Shyly Paul does the trick, which involves cutting Max's fancy tie in half and making it whole again with his magic bag. *"Max is genuinely impressed."*

Max now tries to have an earnest father-son talk with Paul. Paul has got to shape up. He's got to work. He should take an interest in sports. He should make something of himself. "You wanna wind up like me? Always having to hustle?"

In the middle of this, the phone rings. Paul answers. No one is on the other end. It's Max's signal to go, and Paul knows it. Guiltily, Max gives Paul a dollar. "Here," he says, "better shape up. Act a little normal once in awhile." And he's gone.

Steve enters and tries to engage Paul in a conversation about his magic tricks. Steve's chief interest seems to be in skills and equipment that could give him an advantage with girls or gambling. Paul hardly responds. He has come to the grim conclusion that his father hates him. He is about to retreat to his room to practise some more when Enid enters.

Enid has exciting news. The brother of a woman in the building is a Mr. Jerry Wexler, a big-time talent agent, she believes. He knows celebrities like Jack Benny and Cesar Romero. Anyway, she ran into him during one of his visits to his crippled sister, and the conversation turned to Paul and his magic. The upshot of it all is that next Tuesday, when Mr. Wexler again comes to visit his sister, he is going to stop by to see Paul's act. Maybe he'll be able to find work for Paul. Enid projects a vivid picture of the life ahead—making $150 a night in resorts, travelling all over the world, etc.

Paul is hesitant. He doesn't have any act really, and he doens't feel that he can do magic in front of a bunch of people. He doesn't want the audition. But Enid is firm. He's not going to blow this chance. "D'you know the difference this could make in our lives? The doors it could open? The security we'd have—the opportunity to do things—to live! To get out of here!"

She begins to make plans for the Tuesday audition. She'll get him a costume, he can choose his best tricks . . . The prospect terrifies Paul. He feels sick. How can he audition when he can't talk without stuttering? Enid advises him to work a little joke about the stutter into the act. Paul still resists. Enid asks him if he didn't tell her before he wanted to be a magician. "Later! Someday! When I'm r-ready!" says Paul. "Someday is a luxury! We can't wait!" Enid insists. Paul is still reticent.

Enid explodes. She calls him a freak and tells him she'll call off the audition. Fine. And they'll continue to live together after Max and Steve have disappeared. And they will grow old together in this prison of an apartment and end up facing death—"an old woman and her freak son!" She is crying now.

Paul reluctantly agrees to take a crack at the audition. Enid presses Steve into assisting Paul. As Paul begins practising, Enid is feeling hopeful. She sees Paul's floating light bulb, and the light it shines seems to hold a promise of better times ahead.

ACT II

Scene 1

Paul is practising in his room. Some of the tricks go well, but, because of nervousness, he makes a botch of others. Meanwhile, Enid is on the phone trying to get her sister to spring a little cash to help finance the clothes for Paul's audition.

Scene 2

Max is out with Betty again. He has new plans—he's going to go to Nevada and work in a motel that a cousin of a friend owns. The loan sharks would never follow him that far. He'd be able to make a new life for both of them. Betty says she'd be willing. He continues to talk, rationalizing abandoning his family, saying that "just once in a while a person has to put himself first." The kids will have to learn how to take care of themselves. Besides, Max insists, when he gets set up he'll send an occasional check back to help out. Betty wants to go out to celebrate the decision. Max shamefacedly tells her he's too broke to take them anywhere. That's OK, she says, she'll pick this one up. "You're tops, Betty," he replies.

Scene 3

With Steve's help, Enid is readying the house for Mr. Wexler's arrival, arranging flowers, putting out food, etc. She goes to the bedroom to inspect Paul's appearance. He's dressed in a blue suit, and he's very scared. Enid places the turban she bought for the occasion onto his head. Paul hates it, but she thinks it makes him look mysterious. She dashes off to ready her own appearance.

Paul reminds Steve of the part he is to play in the egg trick, i.e. to accuse Paul of holding a "disappeared" egg under his arm. Paul will then raise his arm to show it's not there and miraculously materialize the egg from elsewhere. As he goes over this, he has an attack of dizziness. He hasn't eaten all day because of tension.

"Enid enters with two dresses and a strand of pearls." She asks the boys' opinions of which she should wear. Paul tells her he prefers the blue dress. She agrees. Taking healthy nips of brandy, she launches into (for what must be the umpteenth time) a story about a night many years ago when she wore that dress. She and a friend named Carol Chasen were invited out for a drive by two young men who seemed "sweet and sensitive." In the middle of the drive, they ran into a police roadblock. Her date pulled a loaded gun and told the girls to hit the deck in case shooting started. Nothing, in fact, happened, but the girls demanded to be taken straight home. Before leaving, Enid's date had leaned over and kissed her. The memory still has its romance. "Kissed by an outlaw before he rode off into the night . . . the kissing bandit." Steve is skeptical. It seems to him she embellishes the story more every time she tells it.

Paul's stomach is still upset. Enid tries to reassure him, but her remarks don't help. The doorbell rings. While Steve dresses and Paul tries to pull himself together, Enid answers the door. *"Mr. Jerry Wexler enters. He is a bespectacled, ordinary little man with a bad toupee and Ripley clothes."*

Jerry has just finished dinner at his sister's and is ready to audition Paul. Enid asks him if he wants something to drink. He asks for milk. Enid jokingly asks if he has an ulcer. As a matter of a fact, he says, a small one. Enid says she didn't mean to offend. He assures her it's OK.

Jerry awkwardly compliments Enid on the decoration of the apartment. She confesses she always hoped to be involved in something artistic. "I'm one of those people who has a natural sense of placement and proportion," she says. Her real wish was to be a Rockette, but she never pursued it. Jerry tells her he can tell she would have been fine. Enid is pleased. She calls for Steve to come in and get Jerry a glass of milk while she tends to Paul in the bedroom.

Paul is definitely not feeling well. He wants to cancel. With tears in her eyes, Enid implores him. He relents. He'll be out in a minute. Enid returns to Jerry. She tells him how bright Paul is and about the IQ test. Steve also has aptitudes,

Beatrice Arthur and Jack Weston (as Jerry Wexler) in *The Floating Light Bulb*

she tells him. Steve hears himself described as showing "signs of having a deep feeling for medicine." "Me?" he says.

Jerry says that medicine is a much better way of life than show business—not that he has any complaints. He had offers to do other things, but he knew show business was where his heart was. "Where else, I ask you, can a man be a nobody one day and overnight a millionaire?"

Now on a first-name basis, Enid and Jerry talk about the glamorous life. She asks him if Jack Benny is a client. No, he says, though he's met him. She asks him the names of some of the people he *does* handle. Well, there's Bernie Carter, the comedian. Works in the mountains. And Bobby Drake. Another comedian. Jerry thinks he'll be a big star. He "wears clothes well, he's got the height." Steve asks if Jerry manages anyone famous. Enid sends Steve to fetch Paul. Jerry tells Enid he doesn't manage any big stars. Mostly a bunch of talented youngsters with potential. Enid is disappointed. No real greats? Cesar Romero maybe? "Cesar's an acquaintance," says Jerry. "I didn't more or less handle him . . ."

Enid sets the stage for Paul's entrance, turning down the lights. Steve puts "In a Persian Market" on the phonograph, for atmosphere.

ENID:. . . . .Ladies and gentlemen, the Amazing Pollack!
>*She claps and Steve claps, and Jerry gets the idea and joins. Paul enters, bows, shows a piece of newspaper on both sides, his hands shaking visibly. The paper is empty. He forms it into a cone. Then, he elaborately pours a full pitcher of milk into into the cone. He puts down the pitcher with little stolen flourishes and suddenly crumples the cone up, the milk having vanished miraculously.*

JERRY: Very good!
ENID: Bravo!
>*Paul picks up a rope and a large shears, still trembling. He drops the shears, which clang on the floor like a cymbal.*

PAUL: S-s-sorry . . .
ENID: Just relax, son.
PAUL: I h-h-have h-here th-this p-piece of ordinary r-r-rope . . .
JERRY: Right.
PAUL: A-and th-this s-scissors—
>*He drops them again.*

I c-c-can't—c-c-can't—
ENID *(tensely):* It looks good out here.
JERRY: Don't be nervous. The best of them get the jitters once in a while.
PAUL: I c-cut th-this r-rope in t-two—
>*He does.*

ENID *(helping speech):* Cut it in two.
PAUL: And I t-take th-the two c-cut ends th-thusly—m-m-
ENID *(again helping the stutter):* Make!
PAUL: Make the m-magic p-pass and p-presto!
>*The rope is restored. Enid claps and pushes Steve who claps along with Jerry.*

Incidentally I h-hope you'll f-forgive m-my st-stuttering—
JERRY *(embarrassed):* Of course!
ENID *(correcting Jerry, who doesn't realize Paul's on the way to a gag about it):* No—he kids it!
JERRY: Sure . . .
PAUL: M-my tongue g-got i-in the w-way of m-my eye t-teeth and I c-c-c-can't see wh-what I'm s-saying . . .
ENID: Ha, ha . . . See, he kids it.

Paul proceeds to the egg trick. Steve is a little late picking up his cue to accuse Paul of hiding the egg under his arm—but, with prodding, he does chime in as planned, and Paul finishes the trick.

Paul's nervousness and stuttering have made Jerry feel increasingly uncomfortable and awkward. Sensing this, Paul gets more nervous, shaking so much that he drops and breaks a piece of apparatus, then knocks over another.

PAUL: I c-can't go on—m-my hands are shaking!
ENID: Paul!
PAUL: I c-can't! I'm s-sorry!

ENID: Paul, you're doing wonderfully. Isn't he, Jerry?
JERRY: Er—look, suppose we take a break . . .
PAUL: I d-don't want to g-go on! I d-don't f-feel well.
ENID: Paul, what are you saying!?
PAUL: I'm th-through! I c-can't do it!
ENID: You're doing fine! *(To Jerry.)* Tell him he's doing fine.
PAUL: No!
ENID: Paul—continue!
PAUL: No!
ENID: Paul, finish your routine!
PAUL: Leave m-me alone!
JERRY: Mrs. Pollack—
ENID: Paul, you're embarrassing everyone!
PAUL: T-too bad—
　　He's gathering his stuff to go to the bedroom.
ENID: Paul, come back here!
PAUL *(as he slams bedroom door and locks it):* Leave m-me alone, will you!?
You c-can go to hell!

Steve has disappeared from the room. Jerry starts to gather his things to go.
Desperately, Enid apologizes for the boy's behavior and makes excuses. Jerry
inches his way to the door. Enid pleads for Jerry not to close his mind to the boy.
Jerry says frankly that he doesn't think Paul has a future in show business.

Angrily, Enid sails into him. What would Jerry know? He's obviously small-
time. For all of his name-dropping, all of his clients are nobodies. How dare he
pass judgment? "Maybe we were both laboring under false impressions," says
Jerry. He turns to go.

Enid stops him, crying. She apologizes. She's behaved badly. Jerry says that
it's OK. She explains she was just trying to give Paul a boost. The kid desperately
needs help. She apologizes to Paul through the closed door. Paul says he's sorry,
too. He peeps out to apologize to Jerry. Jerry says he understands. Stage fright.
A disease common to artists. Paul retreats to his room to practise. "See what I
mean?" says Enid. "He's practising and practising for an event that is never going
to come off."

Again she apologizes for insulting Jerry. Jerry says he understands the strain
she's under. His sister has told him all about the situation with her and Max. Enid
is embarrassed to learn her private miseries are common knowledge in the building. She cries. Jerry comforts her.

JERRY *(arm around her shoulder):* Enid, stop crying . . . Enid . . . now come
on . . . you're spoiling the way you look.
ENID: I look awful.
JERRY: You look pretty.
ENID: No.
JERRY: Very pretty. I must say I was pleasantly surprised when I came to the
door. . . . . .
ENID: You really are in a generous mood tonight.

JERRY: Look, my job is working with temperamental people. You're temperamental. It only means that you're sensitive. Passionate. And what's good is, you let it come out. I wish I could. Maybe I wouldn't have an ulcer.

ENID: Which means only that you're a feeling person. But too shy to show it.

JERRY: We're all shy, Enid. You just got like a little girl when I told you you looked pretty.

ENID: Well all anyone has to do is compliment me on my looks. I become like jelly.

JERRY: Well, don't you see, each of us has an area where we're most vulnerable. Yours may be the way you look. And that's natural for a woman.

ENID: Not still at my age, it's not.

JERRY: Now that's not true at all.

ENID *(sips her brandy):* It isn't? Tell me more.

JERRY: I deal with women very frequently. Singers, dancers, acrobats, and what makes them beautiful has nothing to do with how old they are or what they look like.

ENID: But Jerry, I *feel* old.

JERRY: Being a beautiful woman is an art as wonderful as this trick of Paul's.
 Picking up one of Paul's left-over colored boxes.

ENID: Are you saying it's all deception?

JERRY: Look at this box. What is it? A cheap piece of plywood with some fake Chinese letters and a few rhinestones glued on—

ENID: What are you telling me about myself?

JERRY: Don't misunderstand. In the hands of an artist—with the proper flair, the proper presentation and mystery—it becomes a thrilling effect.

ENID: You're talking about fooling people, Jerry.

JERRY: Enid, there's a whole world of people out there who are dying to be fooled. Nothing delights a magician's audience more than when he mystifies them. That's what they pay for. Fool them and they love you for it. What do we have but this silly little novelty—not worth two dollars—but give this gimmick to Blackstone or Houdini—and it becomes a marvel. I'm saying we're all only ordinary people but certain special ones have the ability to project the possibility of the extraordinary.

ENID: You're a very perceptive person, Jerry. And I might add, a master psychologist. You almost had me believing you.

JERRY *(proudly):* Psychology is part of the manager's job. Not that I didn't mean every word. But so much of my time is spent trying to get that message across to young acts. Trying to build their confidence.

ENID: One's confidence takes a beating when a husband of many years trades you in like a car for a newer model.

JERRY: Yes—well—I only meant to get across that you project this sense of excitement—you have in your own way, what we call—star quality.

ENID: No.

JERRY *(solemnly):* Don't contradict me, Enid. You are a theatrical lady.

ENID: And you're what the girls used to call a honeydripper.

JERRY: I know what I see.

ENID: Is your wife in show business?

JERRY: I'm not married.

ENID *(very surprised):* You're not?

JERRY: No.

ENID: Why did I think—your sister mentioned her sister-in-law—

JERRY: That's my brother Cliff's wife. . . . . .

ENID: Well for goodness sake—you see how muddled I am. I just naturally assumed . . . Well what do you know.

> *Music: Steve has turned on radio.*

JERRY: That I was married? No. If you don't count my mother, there are no single women in my life . . .

Jerry explains that the life of a manager is so erratic that he didn't feel it fair to ask a woman to share it with him. Or maybe the real reason was that he never found the right woman. Certainly stable, sensible women are rare in the circles in which he runs.

There was one woman he got involved with: a young singer he handled named Rain Summers. He would have married her if she'd been willing to quit the business. She wasn't. That was the end of that. She ended up marrying a vaudevillian named Professor Backwards. The last he'd heard of them, they were working together and fighting over billing.

Enid shows Jerry a picture of Max. They had had fun until, under pressure from her family, she tried reforming him. "Now he waits tables for tips and plans to leave me with his mistress." She shows him more photos, including pictures of herself when younger. She was a hot number then. She thought she'd live the high life. Jerry confesses he too had dreams of the high life. Instead his days are spent hustling little deals, waiting for a big act to come along and make his fortune. Many of his acts are "ingrates" who leave him for someone else after he's put a lot of work into launching them.

ENID: But there must be some joy in it. Otherwise you wouldn't continue. I mean you said there was always the hope of striking it rich overnight.

JERRY: You hit it on the head. I've taken that abuse and squandered my days and nights in saloons and cheap hotel rooms playing nursemaid to frightened entertainers because of the thought that around the next corner waits that million dollar act. That Jack Benny or Bing Crosby that will justify my life—but I've grown old searching, and lately I begin to think I might not recognize one if he were under my nose.

ENID: Oh don't say that. You're a very perceptive man.

JERRY: No, Enid. Something's wrong. All these years . . . other men, no smarter than me, I tell myself—they somehow have managed to latch on to someone— maybe not a big star—but some performer whose ten percent and whose loyalty they can count on. I could never seem to do that. I've always wasted my time with the small potatoes.

ENID: Probably because your taste is superior. You won't settle for less than that one Judy Garland or Cary Grant.

JERRY: I like to think that—but, I think it's something else—I think the truth is that I never had what it took to go all the way—that I never had the foresight to spot a real winner—or that maybe I've been afraid—that I've lacked the confidence to get myself involved with a big timer. Afraid I would make a fool out of myself if I had to run in real fast company. Say all the wrong things and behave like a real Ignatz.

ENID: Oh, you're being hard on yourself.

JERRY: I'm being truthful. I feel I can talk to you.

ENID: You do?

JERRY: Yes I do. There's something about you I like very much. You have the same openness as my mom and my sister, Ann. And I don't have to pretend everything's all right like I did for my father, may he rest in peace, or put up a front to impress my brother who I've always so been jealous of, I can't sleep nights. The truth is, I've gone nowhere.

ENID: Hardly nowhere.

JERRY: It's not what I'd hoped for. My dream from the beginning was not to grab ten percent of peanuts from a lot of little vaudevillians—because that's what they are—troubled, frightened actors, jugglers, who are consumed with envy and frustration—just as I am.

ENID: If you're a man consumed, you certainly hide it well.

JERRY: That's what I do best. Hide.

ENID: Jerry, you're selling yourself so short.

JERRY: How can you tell? You don't know me.

ENID: I know you're a fine man. In need of a little confidence too. You think only the performers are frightened people?

JERRY: I've always needed half a dozen clients to keep my head above water. But the trick is to have one—to find the one big one so you needn't run yourself ragged servicing the needs of six—to find that young superstar when he himself doesn't even realize his potential—to work with him—then to guide his career to the top. After that, it's easy street—sure there's work to be done, but it's a different world—that world of success. You sit back and take orders.

ENID: But you still have every chance.

JERRY: No—the boat has sailed. And I've followed every lead. Like coming here tonight. You think I was doing you a favor? The truth is, Enid, I've spent my whole life searching—I've played every hunch.

ENID: Well now you *are* describing a lonely man.

JERRY: What have I really got to show after all these many years? My only real steady source of income is Monty Burns and Jason.

ENID: Should I know them?

JERRY: Jason's a dog. He sings "Little Sir Echo."

ENID: The dog?

JERRY: I'm still astonished by it. When Monty, the trainer, holds his throat, the dog can actually say a few words—like hamburger—and mother—I mean it's not like you or I speak—it's *(imitating dog's low, muffled voice)* hamburger—mother . . . like that—So Monty'll sing: "Little Sir Echo/How do you do/Hello?" And the dog goes: "Hello."

ENID: It's bizarre.

JERRY: Strictly club dates. Schools. But it's clean fun. My age, and I'm supported by a German Shepherd. Am I crazy or am I crazy?

They are getting along wonderfully well. He likes her. She's not a self-centered phony. She likes him. He has interesting stories to tell.

He tells her of another unusual act. She laughs at the details. He tells her that she really should have pursued dancing. He can tell she would have done well. "You got the height—you got the bearing—and that certain something." That something that attracts people. Yes, despite her protestations to the contrary, she still has it.

He tells her he once was a performer himself, a comedian. He was not a success at it, so he quit to become a manager. Maybe if he had had a good manager like himself to encourage him, he would have kept at it and made it—a good manager or the right woman.

JERRY: Of course I never felt adequate enough to take on the responsibilities of a wife and a home.

ENID: A wife doesn't demand unrealistic standards of success—not if the husband is decent and loving and honest.

JERRY: You probably think it's funny to imagine that I ever had aspirations for the stage.

ENID: Not at all. In your own way you're quite—charismatic.

JERRY: Y'know Enid, before I talked about fooling the world—turning the everyday into something special. Well the truth is, I try to do that too.

ENID: Well tonight does seem special. In fact they predicted rain but there's a full moon. Not that it's easy to see from this lowly vantage point.
   Straining to see moon and sipping brandy.
Moon over Canarsie . . . or—that old Canarsie moon.

JERRY: Take my looks for instance. You were saying you like compliments before. I'm going to let you in on a secret now—because I know you'll understand although it may stun you.

ENID: I can't imagine.

JERRY: Ready?

ENID: Yes.

JERRY: I'm wearing a hairpiece.

ENID: No!

JERRY: As God is my witness. See—if you look closely you can almost detect the barest rim of cheesecloth. I keep it down with spirit gum.

ENID: Well I'm speechless. It's a perfect little work of art.

JERRY: Because I'm worried about getting older.

ENID: Well welcome to the club.

JERRY: And I fret over how I look.

ENID: And well you should. I mean it's nothing to be alarmed over. You're a handsome individual.

JERRY *(shy demurral):* Not handsome.

ENID: Yes.

JERRY *(a tad vain):* Not handsome—cute maybe—I mean I don't despise my physical appearance.

ENID: You have a strong face.

JERRY: An ulcer and a detached retina. Apart from that I'm a hundred percent. Oh, and I've had two heart attacks—but minor—it's stress—I'm a worrier.

ENID: I do believe that all you've ever really needed is probably just the right woman behind you. Someone who believes in you. To supply you with that little extra confidence, that little added oomph just to get you over the top.

JERRY: God Enid, you do have a winning way. Dare I have one brandy? No. I'll scream with pain later. Oh what the hell—

    Begins pouring.

ENID: Should you?

JERRY: Come on—

    Drinks.

ENID: You certainly fly right into the eye of the storm, don't you? Even with your tiny little ulcer.

JERRY *(likes the drink):* Umm—one more.

    Belts another.

Long time. Yeah—so much depends on luck. Hitting it right. Timing is so important.

ENID: Yes—timing—and luck—but one has to be willing to take a risk.

JERRY: You took a risk. You married your husband. You had some gay times. OK, so it curdled.

ENID: Max cannot be tamed. I know that now.

JERRY: But you had some memories that money can't buy.

    He drinks again.

ENID *(drinking away):* Max knew Legs Diamond—before Legs was killed— well naturally, not after—but who needed that?

JERRY: What's fetching at twenty can be obnoxious at fifty.

ENID: Shouldn't you go easy on that? Especially if it's been awhile since you indulged.

    She takes drink from him.

JERRY: The truth is, what good's life unless you can share it.

ENID: Right. Because misery loves company.

JERRY: Right.

ENID: And each of us deserves to be loved.

JERRY: My mother's words exactly.

ENID: I get the impression you care very deeply about your mother.

JERRY: The way I see it, you only have one mom. Better be nice to her while she's here 'cause she won't be around forever.

ENID: This is true. Although I never got along with mine.

JERRY *(drinks):* Um—I like talking to you, Enid. I like it.

ENID: You do?

JERRY: Shake.

    They shake.

Jerry confesses he's been depressed. One of his clients—a boy singer—is dumping him after three years. His faith in human nature has been upset again. The chance to unburden himself with Enid has been a tonic. She tells him that talking to him has been good for her, too.

He tells her again that she's beautiful and that her husband is a fool for behaving as he does.

JERRY: . . . . . Why you've got that quality we talked about—you project the possibility of the extraordinary.

ENID: You're so discerning to recognize that—even though I haven't shown you anything but the grimmest side of me.

JERRY: But it's there, you see, buried. Under years of struggling and heartache. Am I right?

ENID: Yes. Yes. You constantly impress me with the way you see beneath the surface of a person. Surely someone with your insight could move mountains in a field where human perception counts for everything.

JERRY: I'll tell you, your husband doesn't know what he has—what a jewel.

ENID: Max only sees beauty that's right out on the surface. *(With malicious glee.)* I hear his lover is practically in her teens!

JERRY *(Chuckling):* Robbing the cradle.

ENID: Exactly. *(Drinks.)* Was her name Rain Backwards?

JERRY: What?

ENID: Your old flame—Rain—who married Dr. Backwards . . .

JERRY: Rain Backwards? Well I never thought of it—Rain Backwards, Fall Behind . . . I don't know what I mean by that . . . I just know I'm having a very nice time. I'm glad I drank.

ENID: You make me feel like a young flirt again.

JERRY: You are a young flirt—and a lovely one—and in addition to being every bit as beautiful now as in that photograph you showed me, you're also a hell of a woman—You have ripened superbly. Like a magnificent apple.

In his room Paul is once again floating the light bulb.

ENID *(moved):* It's funny—you're upsetting me.

JERRY: I have to say what I believe. Amidst the peeling paint and falling plaster you shine like a diamond.

ENID: In addition to all else you're a poet.

JERRY: An apple and a diamond. Shake.

They do and he kisses her hand gallantly.

This has turned out to be an evening of magic in its own way.

ENID: I think there's always something magical when strangers meet and suddenly there's feeling.

He continues to hold her hand.

JERRY: If I had known you twenty years ago my life would have been different.

ENID *(staring him in the eyes, pleasantly high):* I'm here now.

JERRY: Fifteen years ago even. Ten . . . five . . .

ENID *(picking up a stub pencil, she scrawls something on a scratch pad that is right there and deposits it in his breast pocket coquettishly):* This is my phone number.

JERRY: Moon over Canarsie. With a hit song like that I could retire twice over.

ENID: I feel like I'm floating in space.

JERRY: Your face has a glow.

ENID: It's meeting you.
JERRY: It's the brandy.
ENID: It's meeting you.
   She brings his hand up to face and presses it to her cheek.
JERRY *(warmly):* Enid—
ENID: Would you hold me for a minute? Just for a minute?
   He does warmly.
Um—I'm now forced to agree—the brandy has gone to my head—and the smile
on my lips is because they're playing my favorite song, "Dream."
   JERRY *(agonizing):* Oh God, Enid—if only I wasn't moving to Phoenix.
ENID: Pardon me?
   In Paul's room, the light bulb suddenly falls and shatters.
JERRY: What was that?
ENID *(still not with it):* What do you mean?
JERRY: My mother's lungs. My poor mother's lousy lungs.

He explains that the doctors have advised him to move his mother to Arizona
on account of terrible asthma. He's going to give up the business and live with
her there. He won't really miss the business much, what with the disappointments
and betrayals.

So why, Enid asks, did he come to audition Paul? Well, Jerry replies, it's the
old instinct. He had to come and see just to make sure that he wasn't missing
getting in on that superstar act that could put him through the top. But Paul
wasn't that act. And now Jerry will go off with his mother to Arizona and read
and fish.

Enid is stunned by this development. "I had hoped to see you again," she says
to him *"slowly and directly."* "Yes—but—it's not—possible," Jerry replies.

Max returns. Still dazed, she makes the introductions. Max asks if the kid did
well. Jerry is noncommittal. Enid tells him that the audition was called off. Max
says that's too bad—the kid needs something to help him over his inferiority
complex, maybe "a good personality course." He disappears into the bedroom to
change, leaving Enid and Jerry alone again.

JERRY: I'll carry this evening with me for a long time, Enid. Instead of having
to go off with the bitter taste of yet another betrayal in my mouth—the boy singer
who left me high and dry after I gave him my life's blood—I can look back, feeling
that my last professional experience—coming here to see your son—enabled me
to make a deep contact with a very special person. Been a long time since a
beautiful woman gave me her phone number. Can I give you a goodbye kiss?
(Pause.) A tiny peck?
   He takes the liberty of doing that.
I can't wait to tell my mother about you. Far as Paul goes—show business is not
for him. Trust my instinct. But he'll realize that when he hits college. I'm sure
he'll latch onto something a lot more substantial. And with his IQ—look out.
Well—goodbye, Enid.
   He goes, leaving her still dazed.

Max, Paul and Steve return to the main room. Steve tells Max that Eddie Lynch called again. Paul voices doubts that his magic will ever be more than a hobby. Enid, almost in a trance, begins to clean up. Paul has a private moment with his mother.

PAUL: I l-liked Mr. Wexler—once you got to know him, he wasn't so scary. You think he might come back some time?

ENID: I don't know. No . . . it's not very likely. Open a window, I feel warm . . .
>   *Paul opens window, peers out.*

PAUL: The m-moon's gone. It's s-starting to rain.

MAX *(to Paul):* What about you? You OK?

PAUL: Huh?

MAX: If something doesn't work, you gotta try again . . . you can't let it get you down . . . Y'hear what I'm saying?

PAUL: Uh-huh . . .

MAX: When I was in the Navy—they always used to pick on me because I was from New York. Try and get my goat. I used to say, c'mon, this is one Jew who's not afraid . . . we'd put on the boxing gloves . . . right on the ship . . . I'd knock 'em for a loop . . . 'Cause I had confidence . . . if I got hit once or twice, didn't bother me . . . Y'see what I'm telling you? The important thing is to stay with it . . .

PAUL: Yeah . . .
>   *Phone rings, Enid starts, goes to it.*

ENID: Hello? . . . Hello? . . .
>   *She hangs up.*

MAX *(grinning):* Well, I gott ago see a man about a horse.
>   *Unable to bear her frustration any longer, Enid flies off the handle at*
>   *Max and runs to him, beating on him in rage.*

ENID: Get out of here! Get out and stay out! Get out! Get out! I'll kill you!

MAX *(defending himself in surprised tussle):* What the hell are you doing!? Get away from me! You crazy!?

ENID: Get out, you bum! Get out of here!
>   *Enid picks up an elegant cane from the table, part of Paul's magic act,*
>   *and goes to hit Max with it. En route, as she brings it downward to*
>   *strike him, it turns into a huge bouquet of paper or feather flowers—*
>   *a standard piece of apparatus. Ludicrously, she is striking him with the*
>   *bouquet.*

PAUL: What are you doing?

ENID: Get out! I'll kill you!

MAX: I'm getting out of here for good, Enid! Soon! You're crazy! You know that? You're crazy!
>   *Slams door, exits. Steve turns on radio to lose himself. Music. Paul*
>   *protectively gathers up certain pieces of apparatus to take to his room.*
>   *Enid, a spent fury, bouquet in hand, winds up alone in room, a comic*
>   *figure. Panting, she sits. The music plays. The flowers are in her hand.*

She looks at them, reflects on life. Soon, she tosses them aside and, with a sigh of resignation, rises and begins straightening up, a figure of dignity that has no choice but to go on with life.

Gradually we dim down and down, the music plays, perhaps her son gets the new light bulb he's fashioned to glow as it did when the play started, and, as she clatters about the kitchen, having resumed the struggle, the curtain falls.

CLOUD 9

A Play in Two Acts

BY CARYL CHURCHILL

Cast and credits appear on page 422

CARYL CHURCHILL is a veteran British playwright who now joins the platoon of British authors whose works enhance season after season on the New York stage. Her first major work for the theater was Owners, *produced at the Royal Court Theater Upstairs in London in 1972 and the following year off Broadway for 2 performances. Her other produced work for the stage includes* Objections to Sex and Violence *at the Royal Court in 1974;* Vinegar Tom *written in 1976 for the Monstrous Regiment, a touring feminist theater group;* Light Shining in Bucking-hamshire, *written in 1976 for the Joint Stock Theater Group and performed at Theater Upstairs, as was* Traps *written in 1977; and* Three More Sleepless Nights, *produced at Soho Poly Theater and Theater Upstairs in 1980. Her first trans-Atlantic hit and first Best Play,* Cloud 9, *was written for Joint Stock and performed on tour and at the Royal Court in 1979 and 1980. Miss Churchill is also the author of numerous plays for BBC radio and television.*

Our method of representing Cloud 9 *in these pages differs somewhat from that of the other Best Plays.* Cloud 9's *sequence of events, unlike that of most playscripts, is no more the quintessential element of its structure than the sequence of events in the impromptu antics of a court jester. Synopsizing it with short excerpts would convey little of its essence as a satire, lampoon or what-you-will (depending on how it might be directed) on human sexuality, expressed in s-curves not only of deviant behavior but also with reverse twists of transsexual casting. Its script is full of nuance but sparing in specific stage direction, leaving it to the director's and actors' imagination to provide the style and point of view—and comedic taste—which is*

its essence, in place of a purposeful sequence of events. Therefore we exemplify
Cloud 9 here with longer sequences from the script within a less-than-skeletal
outline of the rest of the play, and with photos picturing the characters in the
absurdist farce which emerged from this script so irresistably in the 1981 off-
Broadway production under Tommy Tune's direction.

Time: 1880 and 1980

Place: A British colony in Africa, and London

ACT I

A flagpole flying the Union Jack beside a spacious verandah signifies an outpost
of empire in Africa in the reign of Queen Victoria. Manning this outpost are Clive
and his wife Betty; their son Edward, age 9, and daughter Victoria, age 2 (represented by a life-sized doll); their native servant Joshua, governess Ellen and
mother-in-law Maud; and, in the course of events, their visitors Harry Bagley,
an explorer, and Mrs. Saunders, a widow and horsewoman.

Clive is very much the man in charge, a pillar of respectability (but a good deal
of a woman-chaser on the side). His wife Betty (played by a male performer) is
selflessly devoted to husband and home in willing thrall to the Victorian ideal.
Their black servant Joshua (played by a white performer) is slavishly subservient
to Clive but impertinent to Betty (asked to fetch something, he replies to her,
"You have legs under that skirt"). Their daughter Victoria is a model of obedi-
ence; being merely a doll, she is easily manipulated by everyone. Their son
Edward (played by a female performer) loves to play with Victoria's doll, a habit
of which his parents are endeavoring to break him. Ellen the governess is bored
and outspoken, Maud the mother-in-law interfering but dependent.

They have been hearing drums—apparently the natives are restless. A handsome neighbor widow, Caroline Saunders, rides in and takes refuge with them.
Coming in from the wild to visit them is Harry Bagley, explorer and longtime
friend of the family, who enters holding hands with young Edward. Betty is
obviously taken with Harry, though at first she scarcely dares admit this even to
herself. She entices him but runs away when he reaches for her. Harry, in his turn,
takes the first opportunity to go behind the barn with an immediately willing
Joshua.

Left alone with Mrs. Saunders, Clive loses no time in making advances to her, at
first somewhat formally but at last ardently, his head beneath her long riding skirt.

It is Christmas time, and the family organizes itself into a picnic. In the midst
of their games, Clive criticizes his awkward son for his clumsiness in playing with
a ball, uncharacteristic of an active young British male.

CLIVE: You're too silly and you can't catch. You'll be no good at cricket.
MAUD: Why don't we play hide and seek?

ALL ON *CLOUD 9*—In the front row *above* are pictured the play's progenitors: director Tommy Tune, playwright Caryl Churchill (holding the doll which represents the child Victoria) and producer Michel Stuart. Behind them is the cast costumed for the Victorian segment, *left to right:* E. Katherine Kerr as Mrs. Saunders, Don Amendolia as Joshua, Nicolas Surovy (with mustache) as Harry Bagley, Veronica Castang as Maud, Zeljko Ivanek as Betty, Jeffrey Jones as Clive and Concetta Tomei as Edward

EDWARD: Because it's a baby game.
BETTY: You've hurt Edward's feelings.
CLIVE: A boy has no business having feelings.
HARRY: Hide and seek. I'll be it. Everybody must hide. This is base, you have to get home to base.
EDWARD: Hide and seek, yes.
HARRY: Can we persuade the ladies to join us?
MAUD: I'm playing. I love games.
BETTY: I always get found straight away.
ELLEN: Come on, Betty, do. Vicky wants to play.
EDWARD: You won't find me ever.
    They all go except Clive, Harry and Joshua.

HARRY: It is safe, I suppose?

CLIVE: They won't go far. This is very much my territory, and it's broad daylight. Joshua will keep an open eye.

HARRY: Well, I must give them a hundred. You don't know what this means to me, Clive. A chap can only go on so long alone. I can climb mountains and go down rivers, but what's it for? For Christmas and England and children and women singing. This is the empire, Clive. It's not me putting a flag in new lands. It's you. The empire is one big family, I'm one of its black sheep, Clive, and I know you think my life is rather dashing, but I want you to know I admire you. This is the empire, Clive, and I serve it. With all my heart.

CLIVE: I think that's about a hundred.

HARRY: Ready or not, here I come!

He goes.

CLIVE: Harry Bagley is a fine man, Joshua. You should be proud to know him. He will be in history books.

JOSHUA: Sir, while we are alone.

CLIVE: Joshua, of course, what is it? You always have my ear. Any time.

JOSHUA: Sir, I have some information. The stable boys are not to be trusted. They whisper. They go out at night. They visit their people. Their people are not my people. I do not visit my people.

CLIVE: Thank you, Joshua. They certainly look after Beauty. I'll be sorry to have to replace them.

JOSHUA: They carry knives.

CLIVE: Thank you, Joshua.

JOSHUA: And. sir.

CLIVE: I appreciate this, Joshua, very much.

JOSHUA: Your wife.

CLIVE: Ah, yes?

JOSHUA: She also thinks Harry Bagley is a fine man.

CLIVE: Thank you, Joshua.

JOSHUA: Are you going to hide?

CLIVE: Yes, yes I am. Thank you. Keep your eyes open, Joshua.

JOSHUA: I do, sir.

Clive goes. Joshua goes. Harry and Betty race back to base.

BETTY: I can't run. I can't run at all.

HARRY: There, I've caught you.

BETTY: Harry, what are we going to do?

HARRY: It's impossible, Betty.

BETTY: Shall we run away together?

Maud comes.

MAUD: I give up. Don't catch me. I have been stung.

HARRY: Nothing serious, I hope.

MAUD: I have ointment in my bag. I always carry ointment. I shall just sit down and rest. I'm too old for all this fun. Hadn't you better be seeking, Harry?

Harry goes. Maud and Betty are alone for some time. They don't speak.
Harry and Edward race back.

EDWARD: I won, I won, you didn't catch me.

HARRY: Yes I did.

EDWARD: Mama, who was first?

BETTY: I wasn't watching. I think it was Harry.

EDWARD: It wasn't Harry. You're no good at judging. I won, didn't I, Grandma?

MAUD: I expect so, since it's Christmas.

EDWARD: I won, Uncle Harry, I'm better than you.

BETTY: Why don't you help Uncle Harry look for the others.

EDWARD: Shall I?

HARRY: Yes, of course.

BETTY: Run along then. He's just coming.

> *Edward goes.*

Harry, I shall scream.

HARRY: Ready or not, here I come.

> *Harry runs off.*

BETTY: Why don't you go back to the house, Mother, and rest your insect bite?

MAUD: Betty, my duty is here. I don't like what I see. Clive wouldn't like it, Betty. I am your mother.

BETTY: Clive gives you a home because you are my mother.

> *Harry comes back.*

HARRY: I can't find anyone else. I'm getting quite hot.

BETTY: Sit down a minute.

HARRY: I can't do that. I'm it. How's your sting?

MAUD: It seems to be swelling up.

BETTY: Why don't you go home and rest? Joshua will go with you. Joshua!

HARRY: I could take you back.

MAUD: That would be charming.

BETTY: You can't go. You're it.

> *Joshua comes.*

Joshua, my mother wants to go back to the house. Will you go with her, please?

JOSHUA: Sir told me I have to keep an eye.

BETTY: I am telling you to go back to the house. Then you can come back here and keep an eye.

MAUD: Thank you, Betty. I know we have our little differences, but I always want what is best for you.

> *Joshua and Maud go.*

HARRY: Don't give way. Keep calm.

BETTY: I shall kill myself.

HARRY: Betty, you are a star in my sky. Without you I would have no sense of direction. I need you, and I need you where you are. I need you to be Clive's wife. I need to go up rivers and know you are sitting here thinking of me.

BETTY: I want more than that. Is that wicked of me?

HARRY: Not wicked, Betty. Silly.

EDWARD (*calls in the distance*): Uncle Harry, where are you?

BETTY: Can't we ever be alone?

HARRY: You are a mother. And a daughter. And a wife.

BETTY: I think I shall go and hide again.

> *Betty goes. Harry goes. Clive chases Mrs. Saunders across the stage.*
> *Edward and Harry call in the distance.*

EDWARD: Uncle Harry!

HARRY: Edward!

> *Edward comes.*

EDWARD: Uncle Harry!

> *Harry comes.*

There you are. I haven't found anyone, have you?

HARRY: I wonder where they all are.

EDWARD: Perhaps they're lost forever. Perhaps they're dead. There's trouble going on, isn't there, and nobody says because of not frightening the women and children.

HARRY: Yes, that's right.

EDWARD: Do you think we'll all be killed in our beds?

HARRY: Not very likely.

EDWARD: I can't sleep at night. Can you?

HARRY: I'm not used to sleeping in a house.

EDWARD: If I'm awake at night, can I come and see you? I won't wake you up. I'll only come if you're awake.

HARRY: You should try to sleep.

EDWARD: I don't mind being awake, because I make up adventures. Once we were on a raft going down to the rapids. We've lost the paddles because we used them to fight off the crocodiles. A crocodile comes at me and I stab it again and again and the blood is everywhere and it tips up the raft and it has you by the leg and it's biting your leg right off and I take my knife and stab it in the throat and rip open its stomach and it lets go of you but it bites my hand but it's dead. And I drag you onto the river bank and I'm almost fainting with pain and we lie there in each other's arms.

HARRY: Have I lost my leg?

EDWARD: I forgot about the leg by then.

HARRY: Hadn't we better look for the others?

EDWARD: Wait, I've got something for you. It was in Mama's box but she never wears it.

> *Edward gives Harry beads.*

You don't have to wear it either but you might like to look at it.

HARRY: It's beautiful. But you'll have to put it back.

EDWARD: I wanted to give it to you.

HARRY: You did. It can go back in the box. You still gave it to me. Come on now, we have to find the others.

EDWARD: Harry, I love you.

HARRY: Yes I know. I love you too.

EDWARD: You know what we did when you were here before? I want to do it again. I think about it all the time. I try to do it to myself but it's not as good. Don't you want to any more?

HARRY: I do, but it's a sin and a crime and it's also wrong.

Zeljko Ivanek, Veronica Castang (standing) and E. Katherine Kerr (in the Ellen role) as Victorians in *Cloud 9*

EDWARD: But we'll do it anyway, won't we?

HARRY: Yes of course.

EDWARD: I wish the others would all be killed. Take it out now and let me see it.

HARRY: No.

EDWARD: Is it big now?

HARRY: Yes.

EDWARD: Let me touch it.

HARRY: No.

EDWARD: Harry, just hold me.

HARRY: When you can't sleep.

EDWARD: We'd better find the others then. Come on.

HARRY: Ready or not, here we come.

> *They go out with whoops and shouts. Betty and Ellen come.*

BETTY: Ellen, I don't want to play any more.

ELLEN: Nor do I, Betty.

BETTY: Come and sit here with me. Oh Ellen, what will become of me?

ELLEN: Betty, are you crying? Are you laughing?

BETTY: Tell me what you think of Harry Bagley.

ELLEN: He's a very fine man.

BETTY: No, Ellen, what you really think.

ELLEN: I think you think he's very handsome.

BETTY: And don't you think he is? Oh Ellen, you're so good and I'm so wicked.

ELLEN: I'm not as good as you think.

> *Edward comes.*

EDWARD: I've found you.

ELLEN: We're not hiding, Edward.

EDWARD: But I found you.

ELLEN: We're not playing, Edward, now run along.

EDWARD: Come on, Ellen, do play. Come on, Mama.

ELLEN: Edward, don't pull your Mama like that.

BETTY: Edward, you must do what your governess says. Go and play with Uncle Harry.

EDWARD: Uncle Harry!

> *Edward goes.*

BETTY: Ellen, can you keep a secret?

ELLEN: Oh yes, yes please.

BETTY: I love Harry Bagley. I want to go away with him. There, I've said it, it's true.

ELLEN: How do you know you love him?

BETTY: I kissed him.

ELLEN: Betty.

BETTY: He held my hand like this. Oh, I want him to do it again. I want him to stroke my hair.

ELLEN: Your lovely hair. Like this, Betty?

BETTY: I want him to put his arm around my waist.

ELLEN: Like this, Betty?

BETTY: Yes, oh I want him to kiss me again.

ELLEN: Like this, Betty?

> *Ellen kisses Betty.*

BETTY: Ellen, whatever are you doing? It's not a joke.

ELLEN: I'm sorry, Betty. You're so pretty. Harry Bagley doesn't deserve you. You wouldn't really go away with him?

BETTY: Oh, Ellen, you don't know what I suffer. You don't know what love is. Everyone will hate me, but it's worth it for Harry's love.

ELLEN: I don't hate you, Betty, I love you.

BETTY: Harry says we shouldn't go away. But he says he worships me.

ELLEN: I worship you, Betty.

BETTY: Oh, Ellen, you are my only friend.

EDWARD (*calls*): Olly, olly, otsin free.

> *Betty and Ellen embrace. Betty cries. Ellen comforts and kisses her.*
> *The others have all gathered together. Maud has rejoined the party, and*
> *Joshua.*

CLIVE: Come along, everyone, you mustn't miss Harry's conjuring trick.

MAUD: Come along, Betty.
Betty and Ellen go to join the others.
HARRY: What is it that flies all over the world and is up my sleeve?
Harry produces a Union Jack from up his sleeve. General acclaim.
CLIVE: I think we should have some singing now. Ladies, I rely on you to lead the way.
All sing "Good King Wenceslaus."

Offstage, the unruly servants are being punished, while onstage Edward insists on playing with Victoria's doll. Edward joins Uncle Harry in the gazebo.

Clive states very clearly to Betty that she and Harry would break his heart if he ever discovered that they violated his trust. Clive forgives her for whatever Joshua reported she was doing with Harry. After Clive has gone, Edward and Joshua return. Betty gives Joshua an order, to which Joshua replies with an insult. Edward reprimands Joshua firmly and sends him on the required errand, to his mother's admiration.

There has been open hostility between the British and the villagers, but Clive believes everything is now under control—and an Army detachment is on its way. Edward is behaving in an unruly fashion, so that his mother and Ellen can barely control him (he wants to go away with Harry when Harry leaves).

Clive assures Harry that their friendship is so strong it could not be broken by anything the weaker sex might do. Clive feels threatened, though, by some mysterious quality in women, as opposed to the open comradeship of men. Harry misunderstands the implications of Clive's remarks and makes advances to Clive, shocking him utterly. Clive views Harry's aberration with contempt and alarm, seeing it as a betrayal of the cause of empire and the Queen. Clive suggests a kind of expiation: Harry must marry Mrs. Saunders. Limited to a choice between this marriage and suicide, Harry agrees; but, as it turns out, Mrs. Saunders will have none of him.

Clive hears that Joshua's parents were killed in last night's skirmish. He apologizes deeply, but Joshua assures his master he bears no hard feelings. Clive decides to make a match between Harry and Ellen (who seems to be willing). Joshua angers Clive by informing him that Ellen has been making advances to Betty.

On the eve of her wedding to Harry, Ellen confesses to Betty that she doesn't know what to do with a man. Betty advises her to do nothing and let the man have his way.

Betty misses her beads, which she wants to wear at the wedding. Edward tries to blame Joshua for taking them, but Harry informs on Edward.

Mrs. Saunders has sold her farm and is on her way back to England. Clive, overcome with her spirit, kisses her, and Betty immediately assaults her. The men separate the brawling women, and Clive accuses Mrs. Saunders of attacking his wife, bidding her leave at once.

Edward brings back the necklace, claiming he was taking care of it for his mother during the troubles. Clive is giving a speech at the wedding, when *"Joshua raises his gun to shoot Clive. Only Edward sees. He does nothing to warn the others. He puts his hands over his ears. Blackout. Curtain."*

ACT II

The scene moves forward a hundred years to 1980, with the action taking place in various parts of a London park where Edward is employed as a gardener. Three of the characters from the previous act—Edward, Victoria and Betty—are still going strong (by some unexplained and irrelevant alchemy, they are only 25 years older than they were in 1880) in the liberated era of a century later.

Victoria is now married to Martin, a writer, and they have a son Tommy (who never appears onstage). Victoria's friend Lin is the mother of a 4-year-old daughter, Cathy (played by a man). Edward has been living for two years with a companion, Gerry.

Lin rather envies Victoria because Tommy seems more self-sufficient than Cathy, who is very demanding of her mother's attention. Lin has a brother in the army, stationed in Belfast. She left her husband a couple of years ago, while Victoria gets along fairly well with her husband, Martin.

In the park, Edward comes to inform Victoria that their mother Betty is wandering around by herself. When Victoria goes to find Betty, Lin confides to Edward, whom she senses is gay, that she fancies his sister.

Victoria brings Betty in long enough to introduce her to Lin and to hear that Betty means to leave *her* husband. When they have a moment alone, Lin asks Victoria point-blank to have sex. Victoria wonders whether sex with a woman counts as a marital infidelity.

In another part of the park, Edward bickers with his friend Gerry, who launches into an intimate description of a sexual encounter with another man in a train compartment.

Victoria and her husband Martin are walking with Betty. Tommy is playing with the ducks offstage. Betty sits on a bench while the others continue on. Lin joins Betty on the bench.

Victoria and Martin are discussing a crisis in their life: Victoria has been offered a job in Manchester which would cause them to be separated for a while. The decision whether or not to take the job is Victoria's, Martin tells her.

MARTIN: Do you think you're well enough to do this job? You don't have to do it. No one's going to think any the less of you if you stay here with me. There's no point being so liberated you make yourself cry all the time. You stay and we'll get everything sorted out. What it is about sex, when we talk while it's happening I get to feel it's like a driving lesson. Left, right, a little faster, carry on, slow down . . . . . So, I lost my erection last night not because I'm not prepared to talk, it's just that taking in technical information is a different part of the brain and also I don't like to feel that you do it better to yourself. I have read the Hite report. I do know that women have to learn to get their pleasure despite our clumsy attempts at expressing undying devotion and ecstasy, and that what we spent our adolescence thinking was an animal urge we had to suppress is in fact a fine art we have to acquire. I'm not like whatever percentage of American men have become impotent as a direct result of women's liberation, which I am totally in favor of, more, I sometimes think, that you are yourself. Nor am I one of your villains who sticks it in, bangs away and falls asleep. My one aim is to give you pleasure. My one aim is to give you rolling orgasms like I do other women. So why the hell don't you have them? My analysis, for what it's worth, is that despite all my efforts you still feel dominated by me. I in fact think it's very sad that you don't feel able to take that job. It makes me feel very guilty. I don't want you to do it just because I encourage you to do it. But don't you think you'd feel better if you did take the job? You're the one who's talked about freedom. You're the one who's experimenting with bisexuality, and I don't stop you, I think women have something to give each other. You seem to need the mutual support. You find me too overwhelming. So follow it through, go away, leave me and Tommy alone for a bit, we can manage perfectly well without you. I'm not putting any pressure on you, but I don't think you're being a whole person. God knows I do everything I can to make you stand on your own two feet. Just be yourself. You don't seem to realize how insulting it is to me that you can't get yourself together.

    Martin and Vic go.

BETTY: You must be very lonely yourself with no husband. You don't miss him?

LIN: Not really, no.

BETTY: Maybe you like being on your own.

LIN: I'm seeing quite a lot of Vicky. I don't live alone. I live with Cathy.

BETTY: I would have been frightened when I was your age. I thought, the poor children, their mother all alone.

LIN: I've got a lot of friends.

BETTY: I find when I'm making tea I put out two cups. It's strange not having a man in the house. You don't know who to do things for.

LIN: Yourself.

BETTY: Oh, that's very selfish.

LIN: Have you any women friends?

BETTY: I've never been so short of men's company that I've had to bother with women.

LIN: Don't you like women?

BETTY: They don't have such interesting conversations as men. There never has been a woman composer of genius. They don't have a sense of humor. They spoil things for themselves with their emotions. I can't say I do like women very much, no.

LIN: But you're a woman.

BETTY: There's nothing says you have to like yourself.

LIN: Do you like me?

BETTY: There's no need to take it personally, Lin.

    Martin and Vic come back.

MARTIN: Did you know if you put cocaine on your prick you can keep it up all night? The only thing is, of course, it goes numb so you don't feel anything. But you would, that's the main thing. I just want to make you happy.

BETTY: Vicky, I'd like to go home.

VIC: Yes, Mummy, of course.

BETTY: I'm sorry, dear.

VIC: I think Tommy would like to stay out a bit longer.

LIN: Hello, Martin. We do keep out of each other's way.

Pairs meet in these photos who never meet in the play: *above,* Zeljko Ivanek as Gerry in the 1980 segment with Nicolas Surovy as Harry Bagley the Victorian; *below,* Don Amendolia as Cathy in the 1980 segment with Concetta Tomei as young Victorian Edward

MARTIN: I think that's the best thing to do.

BETTY: Perhaps you'd walk home with me, Martin. I do feel safer with a man. The park is so large the grass seems to tilt.

MARTIN: Yes, I'd like to go home and do some work. I'm writing a novel about women from the women's point of view.

Martin and Betty go. Lin and Vic are alone. They embrace.

VIC: Why the hell can't he just be a wife and come with me? Why does Martin make me tie myself in knots? No wonder we can't just have a simple fuck. No, not Martin, why do I make myself tie myself in knots? It's got to stop, Lin. I'm not like that with you. Would you love me if I went to Manchester?

LIN: Yes.

VIC: Would you love me if I went on a climbing expedition in the Andes Mountains?

LIN: Yes.

VIC: Would you love me if my teeth fell out?

LIN: Yes.

VIC: Would you love me if I loved ten other people?

LIN: And me?

VIC: Yes.

LIN: Yes.

VIC: And I feel apologetic for not being quite so subordinate as I was. I am more intelligent than him. I am brilliant.

LIN: Leave him, Vic, and come and live with me.

VIC: Don't be silly.

LIN: Silly. Christ, don't then. I'm not asking because I need to live with someone. I would enjoy it, that's all, we'd both enjoy it. Cathy, for fuck's sake stop throwing stones at the ducks. The man's going to get you.

VIC: What man? Do you need a man to frighten your child with?

LIN: My mother said it.

VIC: You're so inconsistent, Lin.

LIN: I've changed who I sleep with. I can't change everything.

VIC: Like when I had to stop getting a job in a boutique and collaborating with sexist consumerism.

LIN: I should have got that job. Cathy would have liked it. Why shouldn't I have some decent clothes? I'm sick of dressing like a boy, why can't I look sexy, wouldn't you love me?

VIC: Lin, you've no analysis.

LIN: No, but I'm good at kissing, aren't I? I give Cathy guns, my mum didn't give me guns. I dress her in jeans, she wants to wear dresses, maybe she should wear dresses. I don't know. I can't work it out. I don't want to. You read too many books, you get at me all the time, you're worse to me than Martin is to you, you piss me off, my brother's been killed, I'm sorry to win the argument that way but there it is.

VIC: What do you mean, win the argument?

LIN: I mean be nice to me.

VIC: In Belfast?

LIN: I heard this morning. Don't, don't start. I've hardly seen him for two years. I rung my father. You'd think I'd shot him myself. He doesn't want me to go to the funeral.

VIC: What will you do?

LIN: Go, of course.

Lin disciplines Cathy, hitting her. Victoria and the others go off to find and collect Tommy. Edward and Gerry come on. Edward has some fish for dinner, but Gerry doesn't think he'll be home.

GERRY: You're getting like a wife.

EDWARD: I don't mind that.

GERRY: Why don't I do the cooking sometime?

EDWARD: You can if you like. You're just not so good at it, that's all. Do it tonight.

GERRY: I won't be in tonight.

EDWARD: Do it tomorrow. If we can't eat it we can always go to a restaurant.

GERRY: Stop it.

EDWARD: Stop what?

GERRY: Just be yourself.

EDWARD: I don't know what you mean. Everyone's always tried to stop me being feminine, and now you are too.

GERRY: You're putting it on.

EDWARD: I like doing the cooking. I like being fucked. You do like me like this really.

GERRY: I'm bored, Eddy.

EDWARD: Go to the sauna.

GERRY: And you'll stay home and wait up for me.

EDWARD: No, I'll go to bed and read a book.

GERRY: Or knit. You can knit me a pair of socks—

EDWARD: I might knit. I like knitting.

GERRY: I don't mind if you knit. I don't want to be married.

EDWARD: I do.

GERRY: Well, I'm divorcing you.

EDWARD: I wouldn't want to keep a man who wants his freedom.

GERRY: Eddy, do stop playing the injured wife, it's not funny.

EDWARD: I'm not playing. It's true.

GERRY: I'm not the husband, so you can't be the wife.

EDWARD: I'll always be here, Gerry, if you want to come back. I know you men like to go off by yourselves. I don't think I could love deeply more than once. But I don't think I can face life on my own, so don't leave it too long or it may be too late.

GERRY: What are you trying to turn me into?

EDWARD: A monster, darling, which is what you are.

GERRY: I'll collect my stuff from the flat in the morning.

Gerry goes. Edward sits on the bench. It gets darker. Victoria comes.

VIC: Martin's reading Tommy a story. Isn't it quiet.

They sit on the bench, holding hands.

EDWARD: I like women.

VIC: That should please Mother.

EDWARD: No, listen, Vicky. I'd rather be a woman. I wish I had breasts like that, I think they're beautiful. Can I touch them?

VIC: What, pretending they're yours?

EDWARD: No, I know it's you.

VIC: I think I should warn you I'm enjoying this.

EDWARD: I'm sick of men.

VIC: I'm sick of men.

EDWARD: I think I'm a lesbian.

In the park on a summer night, Victoria, Lin and Edward are summoning up an ancient goddess who seems to have specialized in female sexuality (they blame Edward's presence for the fact that she doesn't appear). Their aim is to stimulate an orgy, and when Martin appears they all three leap on him and have sex with him. They do manage to summon up the ghost of Lin's dead brother, starved for sex beyond the grave as he starved for it in the army, and the voice of Harry Bagley crying "Edward!" in the night.

Later, one afternoon, Betty comes in to show Edward and Martin some actual money she has made by holding down a job. Gerry comes in and makes it up with Edward. Betty suggests maybe they could pool their resources and all live together in a big house, but the general reaction isn't enthusiastic.

Betty remains after the others depart and is soon joined by Gerry, who tries to persuade her that living alone is fun. Betty is not so sure. Gerry explains that he's probably going to set up housekeeping with Edward again.

BETTY: . . . . . What I'm being told now is that Edward is "gay," is right? And you are too. And I've been making rather a fool of myself. But Edward does also sleep with women.

GERRY: He does, yes, I don't.

BETTY: Well, people always say it's the mother's fault but I don't intend to start blaming myself. He seems perfectly happy.

GERRY: I could still come and see you.

BETTY: So you could, yes. I'd like that. I've never tried to pick up a man before.

GERRY: Not everyone's gay.

BETTY: No, that's lucky, isn't it.

Gerry goes.

I used to think Clive was the one who liked sex. But then I found I missed it. I used to touch myself when I was very little, I thought I'd invented something wonderful. I used to do it to go to sleep with or to cheer myself up, and one day it was raining and I was under the kitchen table, and my mother saw me with my hand under my dress rubbing away, and she dragged me out so quickly I hit my head and it bled and I was sick, and nothing was said, and I never did it again till this year. I thought if Clive wasn't looking at me there wasn't a person there. And one night in bed in my flat I was so frightened I started touching myself. I thought my hand might go through into space. I touched my face, it was there, my arm, my breast, and my hand went down where I thought it shouldn't, and

I thought well there is somebody there. It felt very sweet, it was a feeling from very long ago, it was very soft, just barely touching and I felt myself gathering together more and more and I felt angry with Clive and angry with my mother and I went on and on defying them, and there was this vast feeling growing in me and all round me and they couldn't stop me and no one could stop me and I was there and coming and coming. Afterwards I thought I'd betrayed Clive. My mother would kill me. But I felt triumphant because I was a separate person from them. And I cried because I didn't want to be. But I don't cry about it any more. Sometimes I do it three times in one night, and it really is great fun.

Joshua comes.

JOSHUA: Did madam hear me wrong? I said you've got legs under that skirt, and more than legs.

Clive comes.

CLIVE: You are not that sort of woman, Betty. I can't believe you are. I can't feel the same about you as I did. And Africa is to be communist, I suppose. I used to be proud to be British. There was a high ideal. I came out onto the verandah and looked at the stars.

Clive goes. Betty from Act I comes. Betty and Betty embrace. Curtain.

A GRAPHIC GLANCE

Ellen March, Danny Aiello, Beatrice Arthur, Eric Gurry, Brian Backer and Jack Weston in *The Floating Light Bulb*

Giancarlo Esposito in *Zooman and the Sign*

Irene Worth, E. G. Marshall and Rosemary Murphy in *John Gabriel Borkman*

Christine Baranski in *Coming Attractions*

Gilda Radner and Sam Waterston in *Lunch Hour*

Catherine Cox in *Shakespeare's Cabaret*

Constance Towers in the revival of
The Sound of Music at Jones Beach

Elizabeth Taylor, Anthony Zerbe, Joe Ponazecki, Maureen Stapleton and Tom Aldredge in the revival of *The Little Foxes*

Hilton Battle in *Sophisticated Ladies*

William Atherton, Joan Copeland and John Randolph in *The American Clock*

Glenda Jackson and Jessica Tandy in *Rose*

Zoë Wanamaker and Jane Lapotaire in *Piaf*

Carolyn Mignini in *Tintypes*

Jerry Zaks in *Tintypes*

Jerry Orbach in *42nd Street*

Clive Revill, Blanche Baker, Donald Sutherland and Ian Richardson in *Lolita*

Aideen O'Kelly, Helen Stenborg, Pat
Hingle and Roy Dotrice in *A Life*

John Heffernan in *The Suicide*

Eva Le Gallienne in *To Grandmother's House We Go*

Richard Thomas in *Fifth of July*

Swoosie Kurtz in *Fifth of July*

Patricia Routledge, Kevin Kline, Linda Ronstadt, George Rose and Rex Smith in the New York Shakespeare Festival's Central Park production of *The Pirates of Penzance*

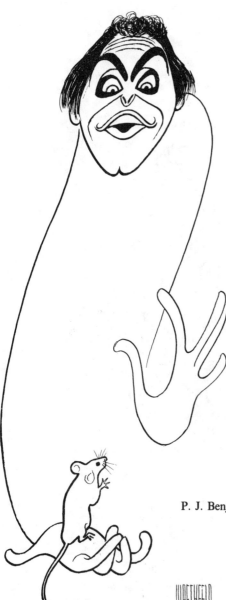

P. J. Benjamin and Algernon in *Charlie and Algernon*

Marilyn Cooper, Harry Guardino and Lauren Bacall in *Woman of the Year*

Jane Seymour, Ian McKellen and Tim Curry in *Amadeus*

Virginia Sandifur in *Perfectly Frank*

Peter Weller in *The Woolgatherer*

Philip Anglim and Maureen Anderman in *Macbeth*

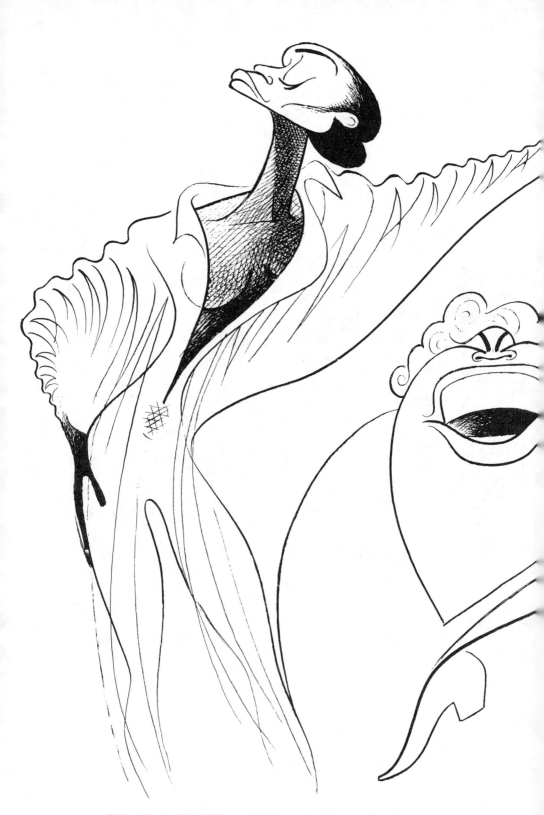

Vivian Reed, Mabel King and Obba Babatunde in *It's So Nice to Be Civilized*

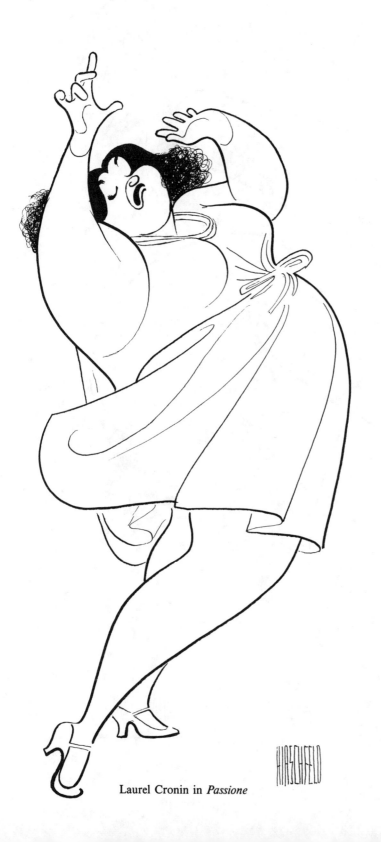

Laurel Cronin in *Passione*

Blythe Danner and Frank Converse in the revival of *The Philadelphia Story*

Harris Yulin in *A Lesson From Aloes*

Maria Tucci in *A Lesson From Aloes*

Anita Dangler, Ellis Rabb and Carrie Nye in the revival of *The Man Who Came to Dinner*

PLAYS PRODUCED
IN NEW YORK

PLAYS PRODUCED ON BROADWAY

Figures in parentheses following a play's title give number of performances. These figures are acquired directly from the production offices and do not include previews or extra non-profit performances. In the case of a transfer, the off-Broadway run is noted but not added to the figure in parentheses.

Plays marked with an asterisk (*) were still running on June 1, 1981. Their number of performances is figured through May 31, 1981.

In a listing of a show's numbers—dances, sketches, musical scenes, etc.—the titles of songs are identified wherever possible by their appearance in quotation marks (").

HOLDOVERS FROM PREVIOUS SEASONS

Plays which were running on June 1, 1980 are listed below. More detailed information about them appears in previous *Best Plays* volumes of appropriate years. Important cast changes since opening night are recorded in the Cast Replacements section of this volume.

*A Chorus Line (2,408). Musical conceived by Michael Bennett; book by James Kirkwood and Nicholas Dante; music by Marvin Hamlisch; lyrics by Edward Kleban. Opened April 15, 1975 off Broadway where it played 101 performances through July 13, 1975; transferred to Broadway July 25, 1975.

*Oh! Calcutta! (1,966). Revival of the musical devised by Kenneth Tynan; with contributions (in this version) by Jules Feiffer, Dan Greenberg, Lenore Kandel, John Lennon, Jacques Levy, Leonard Melfi, David Newman and Robert Benton, Sam Shepard, Clovis Trouille, Kenneth Tynan and Sherman Yellen; music and lyrics (in this version) by Robert Dennis, Peter Schickele and Stanley Walden; additional music by Stanley Walden and Jacques Levy. Opened September 24, 1976 in alternating performances with *Me and Bessie* through December 7, 1976, continuing alone thereafter.

*Annie (1,717). Musical based on the Harold Gray comic strip *Little Orphan Annie*; book by Thomas Meehan; music by Charles Strouse; lyrics by Martin Charnin. Opened April 21, 1977.

*Gemini (1,700). By Albert Innaurato. Opened March 13, 1977 off Broadway where it played 63 performances through May 1, 1977; transferred to Broadway May 21, 1977.

*Deathtrap (1,361). By Ira Levin. Opened February 26, 1978.

*Dancin' (1,327). Musical with music and lyrics by Johann Sebastian Bach, Ralph Burns, George M. Cohan, Neil Diamond, Bob Haggart, Ray Bauduc, Gil Rodin and Bob Crosby, Jerry Leiber and Mike Stoller, Johnny Mercer and Harry Warren, Louis Prima, John Philip Sousa, Carole Bayer Sager and Melissa Manchester, Barry Mann and Cynthia Weil, Felix Powell and George Asaf, Cat Stevens, Edgar Varèse and Jerry Jeff Walker. Opened March 27, 1978.

*Ain't Misbehavin' (1,299). Musical revue with music by Fats Waller; based on an idea by Murray Horwitz and Richard Maltby Jr. Opened May 9, 1978.

*The Best Little Whorehouse in Texas (1,230). Musical with book by Larry L. King and Peter Masterson; music and lyrics by Carol Hall. Opened April 17, 1978 off Broadway where it played 64 performances through June 11, 1978; transferred to Broadway June 19, 1978.

*They're Playing Our Song (971). Musical with book by Neil Simon; music by Marvin Hamlisch; lyrics by Carole Bayer Sager. Opened February 11, 1979.

Sweeney Todd, the Demon Barber of Fleet Street (557). Musical based on a version of *Sweeney Todd* by Christopher Bond; book by Hugh Wheeler; music and lyrics by Stephen Sondheim. Opened March 1, 1979. (Closed June 29, 1980)

*The Elephant Man (875). By Bernard Pomerance. Opened January 14, 1979 off Broadway where it played 73 performances through March 18, 1979; transferred to Broadway April 19, 1979.

Peter Pan, or The Boy Who Wouldn't Grow Up (551). Revival of the musical version of the play by James M. Barrie; music by Mark Charlap; lyrics by Carolyn Leigh; additional music by Jule Styne; additional lyrics by Betty Comden and Adolph Green; original production conceived, directed and choreographed by Jerome Robbins. Opened September 6, 1979. (Closed January 4, 1981)

*Evita (704). Musical with music by Andrew Lloyd Webber; lyrics by Tim Rice. Opened September 25, 1979.

*Sugar Babies (670). Burlesque musical conceived by Ralph G. Allen and Harry Rigby; sketches by Ralph G. Allen based on traditional material. Opened October 8, 1979.

Romantic Comedy (396). By Bernard Slade. Opened November 8, 1979. (Closed October 18, 1980)

Bent (240). By Martin Sherman. Opened December 2, 1979. (Closed June 28, 1980)

Oklahoma! (293). Revival of the musical based on Lynn Riggs's *Green Grow the Lilacs;* book and lyrics by Oscar Hammerstein II; music by Richard Rodgers. Opened December 13, 1979. (Closed August 24, 1980)

West Side Story (333). Revival of the musical based on a Jerome Robbins conception; book by Arthur Laurents; music by Leonard Bernstein; lyrics by Stephen Sondheim. Opened February 14, 1980. (Closed November 30, 1980)

Talley's Folly (277). By Lanford Wilson. Opened May 1, 1979 off Broadway where it played 44 performances through June 3, 1980; transferred to Broadway February 20, 1980. (Closed October 18, 1980)

*Children of a Lesser God (491). By Mark Medoff. Opened March 30, 1980.

I Ought To Be in Pictures (324). By Neil Simon. Opened April 3, 1980. (Closed January 11, 1981 matinee)

*Morning's at Seven (478). Revival of the play by Paul Osborn. Opened April 10, 1980.

Nuts (96). By Tom Topor. Opened April 28, 1980. (Closed July 19, 1980)

*Barnum (454). Musical with book by Mark Bramble; music by Cy Coleman; lyrics by Michael Stewart. Opened April 30, 1980.

*A Day in Hollywood/A Night in the Ukraine (453). Two-part musical with book by Dick Vosburgh; music by Frank Lazarus and others; lyrics by Dick Vosburgh and others. Opened May 1, 1980.

Radio City Music Hall Entertainment Center. 1979–80 schedule ended with **A Rockette Spectacular** (89). Dialogue by Stan Hart; original music and lyrics by Donald Pippin and Sammy Cahn. Opened May 4, 1980. (Closed June 22, 1980)

Home (279). By Samm-Art Williams. Opened December 14, 1979 off Broadway where it played 82 performances through April 13, 1980; transferred to Broadway May 7, 1980. (Closed January 4, 1981)

Blackstone (104). Musical magic show with magic by Harry Blackstone. Opened May 19, 1980. (Closed August 17, 1980)

Billy Bishop Goes to War (12). Written and composed by John Gray in collaboration with Eric Peterson. Opened May 29, 1980. (Closed June 7, 1980 and transferred to off Broadway; see its entry in the Plays Produced off Broadway section of this volume)

PLAYS PRODUCED JUNE 1, 1980–MAY 31, 1981

Your Arms Too Short to Box With God (149). Return engagement of the musical conceived from the Book of St. Matthew by Vinnette Carroll; music and lyrics by Alex Bradford; additional music and lyrics by Micki Grant. Produced by Tom Mallow in association with James Janek at the Ambassador Theater. Opened June 2, 1980. (Closed October 12, 1980)

Adrian Bailey	Linda Morton
Julius Richard Brown	Dwayne Phelps
Cleavant Derricks	Jai Oscar St. John
Sheila Ellis	Kiki Shepard
Ralph Farrington	Leslie Hardesty Sisson
Jamil K. Garland	Ray Stephens
Elijah Gill	Quincella Swyningan
William-Keebler Hardy Jr.	Faruma S. Williams
Jennifer-Yvette Holliday	Marilynn Winbush
Linda James	Linda E. Young
Garry Q. Lewis	

Musicians: Michael Powell conductor, piano; Howard Grate drums; Robert E. Wooten Jr. organ, organ synthesizer, associate conductor; Juan J. Gutierrez percussionist; Henry Grate guitar, guitar synthesizer; Jerry Beckles bass; David Schneck trumpet, flugelhorn; Pat Perrone saxophone, flute; Jimmy Owens trumpet, flugelhorn.

Swing Dancers—Adrian Bailey, Linda James.

Directed by Vinnette Carroll; choreography, Talley Beatty; musical direction, Michael Powell; scenery and costumes, William Schroder; lighting, Richard Winkler; sound, Abe Jacob; orchestrations and dance music, H.B. Barnum; production supervisors, Jerry R. Moore, Richard Martini; artistic production coordinator, Ralph Farrington; production stage manager, Robert Borod; stage manager, Robert Charles; press, Max Eisen, Irene Gandy, Barbara Glenn, Francine L. Trevens.

Your Arms Too Short to Box With God was produced on Broadway 12/22/76 for 429 performances.

The list of musical numbers in *Your Arms Too Short to Box With God* (including authorship of individual song numbers) appears on page 299 of *The Best Plays of 1976–77.*

It's So Nice To Be Civilized (8). Musical with book, music and lyrics by Micki Grant. Produced by Jay Julien, Arnon Milchan and Larry Kalish at the Martin Beck Theater. Opened June 3, 1980. (Closed June 8, 1980)

Sharky	Obba Babatunde	Mr. Anderson	Stephen Pender
Mollie	Vivian Reed	Blade	Dan Strayhorn
Larry	Larry Stewart	Rev. Williams	Eugene Edwards
Sissy	Vickie D. Chappell	Mother	Deborah Burrell
LuAnne	Carol Lynn Maillard	Dancing Bag Lady	Juanita Grace Tyler
Grandma	Mabel King		

Ensemble: Daria Atanian, Paul Binotto, Sharon K. Brooks, P.L. Brown, Jean Cheek, Vondie Curtis-Hall, Paul Harman, Esther Marrow, Wellington Perkins, Dwayne Phelps, Juanita Grace Tyler.

Understudies: Miss King—Jean Cheek; Miss Reed—Esther Marrow; Messrs. Babatunde, Stewart, Strayhorn—Vondie Curtis-Hall; Miss Maillard—Deborah Burrell; Mr. Edwards—P.L. Brown; Mr. Anderson—Paul Harman; Miss Tyler—Allison Renee Manson; Misses Burrell, Chappell—Sharon K. Brooks; Dance Alternates—Allison Renee Manson, Steiv Semien.

Directed by Frank Corsaro; choreography, Mabel Robinson; musical direction, Coleridge-Taylor Perkinson; scenery and visuals, Charles E. Hoefler; costumes, Ruth Morley; lighting, Charles E. Hoefler, Ralph Madero; orchestrations, Danny Holgate, Neal Tate; choral arrangements, Tasha Thomas; dance arrangements, Carl Maultsby; sound, Palmer Shannon; assistant conductor, William Gregg Hunter; associate producer, Danny Holgate; production stage manager, Jack Gianino; stage manager, Carolyn Greer; press, The Merlin Group, Ltd., Cheryl Sue Dolby, Sandra Manley, Marguerite Wolfe, Eileen McMahon, Glen Gary.

Time: A weekend in late summer. Place: Sweetbitter Street.

Lives and loves of the folks in a city neighborhood.

ACT I

"Step Into My World"	Ensemble
"Keep Your Eye on the Red"	Sharky
"Wake-up, Sun"	Sharky, Mollie
"Subway Rider"	Ensemble
"God Help Us"	Larry, Luanne
"Who's Going to Teach the Children?"	Grandma
"Out on the Street"	Ensemble
"Welcome, Mr. Anderson"	Blade, Hawks
"Why Can't Me and You?"	Mr. Anderson
"Why Can't Me and You?" (Reprise)	Sissy, Mr. Anderson
"Out on the Street" (Reprise)	Ensemble
"When I Rise"	Rev. Williams
"World Keeps Going Round"	Mollie, Ensemble

ACT II

"Antiquity"	Ensemble
"I've Still Got My Bite"	Grandma
"Look At Us"	Larry, Luanne
"Keep Your Eye on the Red" (Reprise)	Sharky
"The American Dream"	Mr. Anderson
"Bright Lights"	Mollie
"Step Into My World" (Reprise)	Sharky, Mollie
"It's So Nice To Be Civilized"	Mr. Anderson, Sissy, Hawks
"Like a Lady"	Mollie
"Pass a Little Love Around"	Ensemble

The Music Man (21). Musical revival with book by Meredith Willson and Franklin Lacey; music and lyrics by Meredith Willson. Produced by James M. Nederlander, Raymond Lussa and Fred Walker at the City Center-55th Street Theater. Opened June 5, 1980. (Closed June 22, 1980)

Constable Locke	Dennis Holland	Marian Paroo	Meg Bussert
Jacey Squires	Lee Winston	Mrs. Paroo	Carol Arthur
Oliver Hix	Randy Morgan	Amaryllis	Lara Jill Miller
Olin Britt	Ralph Braun	Winthrop Paroo	Christian Slater
Ewart Dunlop	Larry Cahn	Eulalie MacKechnie Shinn	Jen Jones
Charlie Cowell	Jay Stuart	Zeneeta Shinn	Christina Saffran
Conductor	Peter Wandel	Alma Hix	Marcia Brushingham
Harold Hill	Dick Van Dyke	Maude Dunlop	Mary Gaebler
Mayor Shinn	Iggie Wolfington	Ethel Toffelmier	P.J. Nelson
Marcellus Washburn	Richard Warren Pugh	Mrs. Squires	Mary Roche
Tommy Djilas	Calvin McRae		

Traveling Salesmen: Dennis Holland, Lee Winston, Michael J. Rockne, Tom Garrett, Andy Hostettler, Dennis Batutis, Randy Morgan, Ralph Braun, Larry Cahn.

River City Townspeople, Kids: Victoria Ally, Carol Ann Basch, Dennis Batutis, David Beckett, Mark A. Esposito, Tom Garrett, Liza Gennaro, Dennis Holland, Andy Hostettler, Tony Jaeger, Wendy Kimball, Ara Marx, Darleigh Miller, Gail Pennington, Rosemary Rado, Michael J. Rockne, Coley Sohn, Peter Wandel.

Directed and choreographed by Michael Kidd; musical and vocal direction, Milton Rosenstock; scenery, Peter Wolf; costumes, Stanley Simmons; lighting, Marcia Madeira; sound, Barry Rimler; orchestrations, Don Walker; assistant to Mr. Kidd, Bonnie Evans; production stage manager, Conwell S. Worthington II; press, Solters, Roskin & Friedman, Inc., Milly Schoenbaum, Anne Obert Weinberg, Kevin Patterson.

The Music Man was first produced on Broadway 12/19/57 for 1,375 performances. It was revived by New York City Center Light Opera Company 6/16/65 for 15 performances.

The list of musical numbers in *The Music Man* appears on pages 307–8 of *The Best Plays of 1957–58.*

Fearless Frank (12). Musical with book and lyrics by Andrew Davies; music by Dave Brown. Produced by David Black and Robert Fabian in association with Oscar Lewenstein and Theodore P. Donahue Jr. at the Princess Theater. Opened June 15, 1980. (Closed June 25, 1980)

Cast: Frank Harris—Niall Toibin; French Waiter, Headmaster, Kendrick, Lord Folkenstone, Whistler—Alex Wipf; Secretary, Schoolgirl, Jessie, Lilly—Valerie Mahaffey; Nellie, Kate, Laura—Kristen Meadows; Tobin, Whitehouse, Smith, Chapman, Oscar Wilde—Steve Burney; Nursemaid, Actress, Bootblack, Topsy, Newsboy, Enid—Ann Hodapp; Cowboy, Carlyle, Mr. Clapton, de Maupassant, Dowson—Olivier Pierre; Mrs. Mayhew, Mrs. Clapton, Mrs. Clayton—Evalyn Baron; Schoolboys, New Yorkers, Hotel Guests, Cowboys, Cows, Indians, Crowd, Newsboys, Strollers, Opera Chorus, Harris Detractors, Harris Praisers—Company.

Understudies: Messrs. Wipf, Burney—Ralph Bruneau; Misses Mahaffey, Hodapp—Valerie Beaman; Misses Meadows, Baron—Susan Elizabeth Scott.

Directed by Robert Gillespie; musical staging, Michael Vernon; musical direction, Michael Rose; scenery, Martin Tilley; costumes, Carrie F. Robbins; lighting, Ruth Roberts; orchestrations, Michael Reed; production stage manager, Larry Forde; stage manager, Steven Becker; press, Hunt/Pucci Associates, Betty Lee Hunt, Maria Cristina Pucci, James Sapp.

Time: 1921. Place: Nice and in the mind of Frank Harris.

The literary life and many loves of Frank Harris in the form of a musical. A foreign play previously presented in London.

MUSICAL NUMBERS—ACT I: "The Man Who Made His Life Into a Work of Art"—Niall Toibin, Girls; "Nora, the Nursemaid's Door"—Valerie Mahaffey; "The Examination Song, or Get Me on That Boat"—Alex Wipf, Steve Burney, Toibin; "Halted at the Very Gates of Paradise—a Song of Frustration"—Toibin, Girls; "Come and Help Yourself to America, or Frank in the Melting Pot"

Radio City Music Hall Rockettes in the New York scene of *America*

—Company; "Dandy Night Clerk, or How to Get On in the Hotel Trade"—Company; "Riding the Range—a Song of the Old West"—Company; "Oh, Catch Me, Mr. Harris, Cause I'm Falling for You!"—Kristen Meadows, Ann Hodapp, Mahaffey, Evalyn Baron, Toibin; "The Greatest Man of All"—Toibin, Company.

ACT II: "My Poor Wee Lassie—A Scottish Lament"—Olivier Pierre; "My Own, or True Love at Last"—Toibin, Meadows, Baron, Pierre; "Evening News—a Song of Success"—Company; "Le Maitre de la Conte, or Maupassant Tells All"—Pierre; "Oh, Mr. Harris, You're a Naughty Naughty Man!"—Toibin, Baron; "Great Men, Great Days, or the King of the Cafe Royal"—Toibin; "Free Speech, Free Thought, Free Love"—Hodapp, Toibin, Company; "Mr. Harris, It's All Over Now!"—Toibin, Company; "Fearless Frank"—Company.

Circle in the Square. 1979–80 schedule ended with **The Man Who Came to Dinner** (85). Revival of the play by Moss Hart and George S. Kaufman. Produced by Circle in the Square, Theodore Mann artistic director, Paul Libin managing director, at Circle in the Square. Opened June 26, 1980. (Closed September 7, 1980)

Mrs. Ernest W. Stanley	Patricia O'Connell	Bert Jefferson	Peter Coffield
Miss Preen	Anita Dangler	Prof. Metz; Westcott	Nicholas Martin
Richard Stanley	Jim Dratfield	Mr. Baker; Deputy	Robert O'Rourke
June Stanley	Amanda Carlin	Expressman	John Hallow
John	Bill McCutcheon	Expressman;	
Sarah	Yolanda Childress	Radio Technician	Jeffrey Rodman
Mrs. McCutcheon	Dorothy Stinnette	Lorraine Sheldon	Carrie Nye
Mr. Stanley	Richard Woods	Sandy	Jamey Sheridan
Maggie Cutler	Maureen Anderman	Beverly Carlton	Roderick Cook
Dr. Bradley	Robert Nichols	Banjo	Leonard Frey
Sheridan Whiteside	Ellis Rabb	Deputy	George Spelvin
Harriet Stanley	Kate Wilkinson	Plainclothesman	Charles Hardin

Luncheon Guests: Jason Jerrold, Jeffrey Rodman, George Spelvin. Choir: Dorothy Stinnette, Lilli Syng, Kate Wilkinson.

Standbys: Mr. Rabb—James Cahill; Miss Anderman—Amanda Carlin; Miss Nye—Gwyn Gilliss; Mr. Cook—Bill McCutcheon; Messrs. Nichols, Woods—John Hallow. Understudies: Miss Dangler—Yolanda Childress; Misses O'Connell, Childress, Wilkinson—Dorothy Stinnette; Messrs. Frey, Sheridan; Dratfield, Martin—Jeffrey Rodman; Messrs. Jerrold, Rodman, Hallow—Robert O'Rourke; Mr. Coffield—Jamey Sheridan.

Directed by Stephen Porter; scenery and costumes, Zack Brown; lighting, Jeff Davis; song "What Am I to Do" by Cole Porter; stage managers, Randall Brooks, Nicholas Russiyan; press, Merle Debuskey, Leo Stern.

Time: 1938. Place: The home of Mr. and Mrs. Stanley in a small town in Ohio. Act I, Scene 1: A December morning. Scene 2: About a week later. Act II: Another week has passed; Christmas Eve. Act III: Christmas morning.

The Man Who Came to Dinner was first produced on Broadway 10/16/39 and was named a Best Play of its season. It was revived on Broadway in a musical version entitled *Sherry!* 3/27/67 for 72 performances.

*Radio City Music Hall Entertainment Center. Schedule of two new productions. **Manhattan Showboat** (191). Musical conceived by Robert F. Jani; dialogue script writer, Stan Hart; special material by Nan Mason; original music and lyrics by Don Pippin, Sammy Cahn and Nan Mason. Opened June 30, 1980. (Closed October 15, 1980) ***America** (122). Musical spectacle conceived by Robert F. Jani. Opened March 13, 1981. Produced by Radio City Music Hall Productions, Inc., Robert F. Jani producer, Donald Pippin executive musical director, John J. Moore production executive, at Radio City Music Hall.

MANHATTAN SHOWBOAT

Belle	Karen Anders	Tree	Steven Williford
Edgar	Louis Carry	Daisy	Daisy
Hiram Boggs	Thomas Ruisinger		

And P.T. Barnum—Tony Moore; Buffalo Bill—Buddy Crutchfield; Annie Oakley—Lou Ann Csaszar; Annie—Laurie Stephenson; "Pretty Girl" Solo—Buddy Crutchfield; "Love Is a Simple Thing/Income Tax" Solo—Cleo Price.

Rockettes: Pauline Achillas, Carol Beatty, Catherine Beatty, Dottie Belle, Karen Berman, Susan Boron, Deniene Bruck, Barbara Ann Cittadino, Eileen Collins, Brie Daniels, Susan DiGilio, Susanne Doris, Jacqueline Fancy, Alexis Ficks, Mary Ann Fiordalisi, Prudence Gray, Carol Harbich, Ginny Hounsell, Cynthia Hughes, Pam Kelleher, Dee Dee Knapp, Judy Little, Leslie Gryszko McCarthy, Barbara Moore, Ann Murphy, Lynn Newton, Pam Stacey Pasqualino, Joan Peer, Cindy Peiffer, Geraldine Presky, Sheila Rodriguez, Maryellen Scilla, Terry Spano, Lynn Sullivan, Sunny Summers, Susan Theobald, Carol Toman, Darlene Wendy, Rose Anne Woolsey, Phyllis Wujko.

New Yorkers: Pam Cecil, Joanna Coggins, Lou Ann Csaszar, Buddy Crutchfield, Alvin Davis, Rick Emery, Dale Furry, Bobby Grayson, Phil Hall, Nina Hennessey, Stephen Hope, Deirdre Kane, Dale Kristien, Andrea Lyman, James Mahady, Tony Moore, Sylvia Nolan, Denise O'Neill, Susan Powers, Cleo Price, Jeffory Robinson, Laurie Stephenson, Bob Teterick, Kay Walbye, Scott Whiteleather, Bob Wrenn.

Dancers: Dennis Angulo, Phillip Bond, Ron Chisholm, Angie Daye, Danute Debney, John Michael Doyle, Glenn Ferrugiari, Doug Fogel, Neisha Folkes, Linda Kay Hamil, Kristie Hannum, Edward Henkel, Olgalyn Jolly, Elisa Lenhart, Kim Leslie, Gail Lohla, Cary Lowenstein, Margaret McGee, Terry McLemore, Ron Meier, Lorena Palacios, James Parker, Debra Pigliavento, Michele Pigliavento, Sam Singhaus, Cassie Stein, Alan Stuart, Karen Toto, Barry Weiss.

Organists: Timothy Stella, David Messineo.

Principals staged by Frank Wagner; choreography, Linda Lemac, Howard Parker, Debra Pigliavento, Frank Wagner; Rockette choreography, Violet Holmes; conductor, Elman Anderson; musical routining, Stan Lebowsky; scenery, Robert Guerra; costumes, Frank Spencer, Michael Casey; lighting, David F. Segal; orchestrations, Elman Anderson, Michael Gibson, Arthur Harris, Philip J. Lang; production stage manager, Neil Miller; stage managers, Peter Rosenberg, Ray Chandler, Peter Aaronson; press, Gifford/Wallace Inc., Keith Sherman.

Scenes: I. The Opening, II. The Circus, III. Nightclubs and Floorshows, IV. Vaudeville, V. The Sing-a-long, VI. The Musical Theater, VII. The Great Revues, VIII. The Rockettes, IX. Belle's Turn, X. The Grand Finale.

Original music and lyrics for "Manhattan Showboat" and "There Are No Girls Quite Like Show Girls" by Donald Pippin and Sammy Cahn; original music and lyrics for "Right Here" by Donald Pippin and Nan Mason; bridge lyrics for Vaudeville Medley by Nan Mason.

Compendium of major developments in American musical entertainment.

AMERICA

CAST—Americans: Wendy Edmead, Jeff Johnson, Mark Morales, Reed Jones, Iris Revson. Rockettes: Pauline Achillas, Carol Beatty, Catherine Beatty, Dottie Belle, Susan Boron, Barbara Ann Cittadino, Eileen Collins, Brie Daniels, Susanne Doris, Jacqueline Fancy, Deniene Fenn, Alexis Ficks, Prudence Gray, Jennifer Hammond, Carol Harbich, Terry Spano Higgins, Ginny Hounsell, Cynthia Hughes, Pam Kelleher, Dee Dee Knapp, Judy Little, Kris Mooney, Barbara Moore, Lynn Newton, Pam Stacey Pasqualino, Kerri Pearsall, Joan Peer, Cindy Peiffer, Gerri Presky, Ann Murphy St. John, Lynn Sullivan, Sunny Summers, Susan Theobald, Carol Toman, Patricia Tully, Darlene Wendy, Rose Anne Woolsey, Phyllis Wujko, Joyce Dwyer (Captain).

New Yorkers: Michael Booker, Andrew Charles, Buddy Crutchfield, Lou Ann Csaszar, Johnny Driscoll, Catherine Fries, Dale Furry, David Holland, David Michael Johnson, Rena Phillips, Kitty Preston, Cleo Price, Edward Prostak, Lance Roberts, Danny Robins, Lisa Sherman, Marc Villa, Andrea Wright.

Dancers: Blake Atherton, David Beckett, Ron Chisholm, Rick Conant, Lloyd Bulbreath, Renee DuLaney, Byron Easley, Glenn Ferrugiari, Karen Fraction, Michael Graham, Tony Jaeger, David Lee, Kim Leslie, Bronna Lipton, David Roman, Sam Singhaus, Thomas Stanton, Maureen Stevens, Jamie Torcellini, Kim Woollen.

Organists: Robert Maidhof, George Wesner.

Directed by Robert F. Jani; musical direction and routines, Tom Bahler; choreography, Violet Holmes, Linda Lemac, Frank Wagner; principals staged by Frank Wagner; scenery, Robert Guerra; costumes, Michael Casey; lighting, Ken Billington; special materials and dialogue, Harvey Jacobs; synthesizer program and performance, Don Dorsey; orchestrations, Mitch Farber, Robert M. Freedman, Jay Kennedy, Billy May; original music and lyrics, Tom Bahler, Mark Vieha; production stage manager, Donald Christy; stage managers, Ray Chandler, Peter Aaronson, Jack Horner.

PROGRAM—I. The Opening; II. The Story of America; III. Fifty Great Places All in one Place (words and music by Tom Bahler and Mark Vieha); IV. The Spirit of America (words and music by Tom Bahler and Mark Vieha); V. A Tour de Force of America; VI. Hawaii Is the 50th Star; VII. The Electro-Live-Synthomagnetic Radio City Music Hall Orchestra (Kevin Farrell conductor, Paul Bogaev assistant conductor); VIII. Freedom; IX: A New American Spirit Is Alive; X. On Parade; XI. The Finale—"America the Beautiful".

Multimedia revue of Americana, with spectacular cast and effects, with all 50 states represented.

Radio City Music Hall also presented a return engagement of *The Magnificent Christmas Spectacular* for 86 performances 11/21/80-1/4/81.

Camelot (56). Revival of the musical based on *The Once and Future King* by T.H. White; book and lyrics by Alan Jay Lerner; music by Frederick Loewe. Produced by Mike Merrick and Don Gregory by arrangement with James M. Nederlander at the New York State Theater. Opened July 8, 1980. (Closed August 23, 1980)

Arthur	Richard Burton	Mordred	Robert Fox
Sir Sagramore	Andy McAvin	Dap	Robert Molnar
Merlyn; Friar	James Valentine	Lady Anne	Nora Brennan
Guenevere	Christine Ebersole	Lady Sybil	Deborah Magid
Sir Dinidan	William Parry	Sir Lionel	William James
Nimue	Jeanne Caryl	King Pellinore	Paxton Whitehead
Lancelot Du Lac	Richard Muenz	Horrid	Bob

Sir Lionel's Squire............ Davis Gaines   Sir Dinidan's Squire .... Herndon Lackey
Sir Sagramore's Squire .... Steve Osborn   Tom .... Thor Fields

Knights of the Investiture: Ken Henley, Gary Jaketic, Jack Starkey, Ronald Bennett Stratton.

Knights, Lords, Ladies of the Court: Nora Brennan, Jeanne Caryl, Melanie Clements, Stephanie Conlow, Van Craig, John Deyle, Debra Dickinson, Richard Dodd, Cecil Fulfer, Davis Gaines, Lisa Ann Grant, Ken Henley, John Herrera, Gary Jaketic, William James, Kelby Kirk, Herndon Lackey, Deborah Magid, Andy McAvin, Laura McCarthy, Robert Molnar, Steve Osborn, Patrice Pickering, Janelle Price, Nancy Rieth, Patrick Rogers, Deborah Roshe, D. Paul Shannon, Jack Starkey, Ronald Bennett Stratton, Sally Ann Swarm, Sally Williams. Alternates: Lynn Keeton, Richard Maxon.

Understudies: Mr. Burton—William Parry; Miss Ebersole—Janelle Price; Mr. Muenz—Gary Jaketic; Mr. Whitehead—James Valentine; Mr. Fox—Andy McAvin; Mr. Valentine—Robert Molnar; Miss Caryl—Deborah Magid; Mr. Parry—D. Paul Shannon, Herndon Lackey; Mr. James —John Deyle; Mr. McAvin—Herndon Lackey; Mr. Molnar—John Herrera.

Directed by Frank Dunlop; original New York production staged by Moss Hart; choreography, Buddy Schwab; musical direction, Franz Allers; scenery and costumes, Desmond Heeley; lighting, Thomas Skelton; orchestra conductor, James Martin; sound design, John McClure; orchestrations, Robert Russell Bennett, Phil Lang; musical coordinator, Robert Kreis; production supervisor, Jerry Adler; artistic consultant, Stone Widney; a Dome/Cutler-Herman production; stage manager, Jonathan Weiss; press, Seymour Krawitz, Patricia McLean Krawitz.

Camelot was produced on Broadway 12/3/60 for 873 performances.

ACT I

Prologue: A battlefield near Joyous Gard—a long time ago
"Guenevere" .... Ensemble
Scene 1: A hilltop near Camelot—eight years earlier
"I Wonder What the King Is Doing Tonight?" .... Arthur
"The Simple Joys of Maidenhood".. Guenevere
"Camelot" .... Arthur, Guenevere
"Follow Me"... Nimue
Scene 2: Arthur's study—five years later
"Camelot" (Reprise).. Arthur, Guenevere
Scene 3: A roadside near Camelot—a few months later
"C'Est Moi" .... Lancelot
Scene 4: A park near the castle—immediately following
"The Lusty Month of May" .... Guenevere, Ensemble
Scene 5: A terrace of the castle—two months later
"How to Handle a Woman" .... Arthur
Scene 6: The jousting fields—the next day
"The Jousts" .... Arthur, Guenevere, Ensemble
Scene 7: The terrace—early evening of that day
"Before I Gaze at You Again"... Guenevere
Scene 8: The great hall—immediately following

ACT II

Prologue: The castle garden—a few years later
Scene 1: A cloister on the castle grounds—immediately following
"If Ever I Would Leave You" .... Lancelot
"The Seven Deadly Virtues" .... Mordred
Scene 2: The terrace—a few weeks later
"What Do Simple Folk Do?" .... Guenevere, Arthur
"Fie on Goodness"... Mordred, Knights
Scene 3: The forest—the following day
Scene 4: The Queen's bedchamber—immediately following
"I Loved You Once in Silence" .... Guenevere
Scene 5: Camelot—a month later
"Guenevere" (Reprise)... Ensemble

Scene 6: A battlefield near Joyous Gard—a few weeks later
"Camelot" (Reprise)... Arthur

*42nd Street (320). Musical based on the novel by Bradford Ropes; book by Michael Stewart and Mark Bramble; music and lyrics by Harry Warren and Al Dubin; other lyrics by Johnny Mercer and Mort Dixon. Produced by David Merrick at the Winter Garden. Opened August 25, 1980.

Andy Lee.................	Danny Carroll	Lorraine....................	Ginny King
Oscar	Robert Colston	Phyllis.......................	Jeri Kansas
Mac; Thug; Doctor..............	Stan Page	Julian Marsh	Jerry Orbach
Annie	Karen Prunczik	Dorothy Brock	Tammy Grimes
Maggie Jones.................	Carole Cook	Abner Dillon	Don Crabtree
Bert Barry	Joseph Bova	Pat Denning...............	James Congdon
Billy Lawlor..............	Lee Roy Reams	Thug.....................	Ron Schwinn
Peggy Sawyer..............	Wanda Richert		

Ensemble: Carole Banninger, Steve Belin, Robin Black, Joel Blum, Mary Cadorette, Ronny DeVito, Denise DiRenzo, Mark Dovey, Rob Draper, Brandt Edwards, Jon Engstrom, Sharon Ferrol, Cathy Greco, Dawn Herbert, Christine Jacobsen, Jeri Kansas, Ginny King, Terri Ann Kundrat, Shan Martin, Beth McVey, Maureen Mellon, Sandra Menhart, Bill Nabel, Tony Parise, Don Percassi, Jean Preece, Vicki Regan, Lars Rosager, Linda Sabatelli, Nikki Sahagen, Ron Schwinn, Yveline Semeria, Alison Sherve, Robin Stephens, David Storey, Karen Tamburrelli.

Understudies: Misses Grimes, Cook—Leila Martin; Mr. Orbach—James Congdon; Miss Richert —Nancy Sinclair, Mary Cadorette; Mr. Reams—Joel Blum; Messrs. Bova, Page—Bill Nabel; Mr. Carroll—Don Percassi; Messrs. Crabtree, Congdon—Stan Page; Miss Prunczik—Karen Tamburrelli; Mr. Colston—Donald Johnston; Ensemble—Lorraine Person, Rick Pessagno.

Directed and choreographed by Gower Champion; musical direction and vocal arrangements, John Lesko; scenery, Robin Wagner; costumes, Theoni V. Aldredge; lighting, Tharon Musser; orchestrations, Philip J. Lang; dance arrangements, Donald Johnston; sound, Richard Fitzgerald; dance assistants, Karin Baker, Randy Skinner; production stage manager, Steve Sweigbaum; stage manager, Arturo E. Porazzi; press, Fred Nathan, Louise Weiner Ment, also Josh Ellis, Milly Schoenbaum.

Time: 1933. Place: New York City and Philadelphia.

Musical stage version of the understudy-to-star fable presented in the 1933s movie *42nd Street*, with the score augmented.

Nancy Sinclair replaced Wanda Richert 10/15/80. Karen Prunczik replaced Nancy Sinclair 10/20/80. Wanda Richert replaced Karen Prunczik 10/25/80.

A Best Play; see page 129.

ACT I

Scene 1: 42nd Street Theater, New York City
"Audition" .... Andy Lee, Ensemble
"Young and Healthy" .... Billy Lawlor, Peggy Sawyer
"Shadow Waltz"................................... Maggie Jones, Dorothy Brock, Girls
"Shadow Waltz" (Reprise) .... Dorothy
Scene 2: Gypsy Tea Kettle
"Go Into Your Dance" .... Maggie, Peggy, Annie, Andy, Lorraine, Phyllis
Scene 3: On stage
"You're Getting to Be a Habit With Me"................ Dorothy, Billy, Peggy, Ensemble
Scene 4: Dorothy Brock's dressing room
Scene 5: On stage
"Getting Out of Town" .... Pat Denning, Bert Barry, Maggie, Annie, Dorothy, Ensemble
Scene 6: Arch Street Theater, Philadelphia
"Dames" .... Billy, Ensemble
Scene 7: Regency Club and Dorothy Brock's suite at Hotel Stratford
"I Know Now"... Dorothy
Scene 8: Opening night, Arch Street Theater, Philadelphia

"I Know Now" (Reprise) .... Billy, Girls
"We're in the Money" .... Annie, Peggy, Lorraine, Phyllis, Billy, Ensemble
Act I Finale.. Dorothy, Peggy, Company

ACT II

Scene 1: Outside Dorothy Brock's dressing room, ten minutes later
Scene 2: Dressing rooms at the Arch Street Theater
  "Sunny Side to Every Situation".................................... Annie, Ensemble
Scene 3: Stage of the Arch Street Theater
Scene 4: Broad Street Station, Philadelphia
  "Lullaby of Broadway" .... Julian, Company
Scene 5: 42nd Street Theater, New York City
Scene 6: Peggy's dressing room
  "About a Quarter to Nine".. Dorothy, Peggy
Scene 7: Opening night of *Pretty Lady,* 42nd Street Theater, New York City
  Overture.. Orchestra
  "Shuffle Off to Buffalo" .... Annie, Bert, Maggie, Girls
  "42nd Street" .... Peggy, Billy, Ensemble
Scene 8: Backstage
  "42nd Street" (Reprise).. Julian

Charlie and Algernon (17). Musical based on *Flowers for Algernon* by Daniel Keyes; book and lyrics by David Rogers; music by Charles Strouse. Produced by the John F. Kennedy Center for the Performing Arts, Isobel Robins Konecky, The Fisher Theater Foundation and the Folger Theater Group at the Helen Hayes Theater. Opened September 14, 1980. (Closed September 28, 1980)

Charlie	P.J. Benjamin	Lita	Loida Santos
Alice Kinnian	Sandy Faison	Frank	Patrick Jude
Dr. Strauss	Edward Earle	Charlie's Mother	Julienne Marie
Dr. Nemur	Robert Sevra	Little Charlie	Matthew Duda
Mrs. Donner	Nancy Franklin	Charlie's Father	Michael Vita

Directed by Louis W. Scheeder; choreography, Virginia Freeman; musical direction and conductor, Liza Redfield; scenery, Kate Edmunds; costumes, Jess Goldstein; lighting, Hugh Lester; orchestrations, Philip J. Lang; sound, William H. Clements; producers, Michael Sheehan, Louis W. Scheeder; stage managers, Martha Knight, Peter Dowling, P'nenah Goldstein; press, Michael Alpert, Marilynn LeVine, Mark Goldstaub.

Based on the novel which also was the source for the 1968 movie *Charly,* the story of a medical experiment to turn a brain-damaged mental invalid into a genius. The play was presented without intermission. Previously produced in Edmonton, Alberta, in London and in Washington, D.C.

MUSICAL NUMBERS: "Have I the Right?", "I Got a Friend," "I Got a Friend" (Reprise), "Some Bright Morning," "Jelly Donuts and Chocolate Cake," "Hey Look at Me," "Reading," "No Surprises," "Midnight Riding," "Dream Safe With Me," "Not Another Day Like This," "Somebody New," "I Can't Tell You," "Now," "Charlie and Algernon," "The Maze," "Whatever Time There Is," "Everything Was Perfect," "Charlie," "I Really Loved You," "Whatever Time There Is" (Reprise).

Passione (16). By Albert Innaurato. Produced by John Wulp, Roger Berlind, Richard Horner and Hinks Shimberg at the Morosco Theater. Opened September 23, 1980. (Closed October 5, 1980 matinee)

Little Tom	Richard Zavaglia	Aggy	Angela Paton
Oreste	Daniel Keyes	Renzo	Dick Latessa
Berto	Jerry Stiller	Francine	Laurel Cronin
Sarah	Sloane Shelton		

Directed by Frank Langella; scenery, David Gropman; costumes, William Ivey Long; lighting, Paul Gallo; production stage manager, Jay Adler; press, Bob Ullman.

Prodigal wife returns to an Italian-American family in South Philadelphia. The play was presented in two parts. Previously produced off off Broadway at Playwrights Horizons.

Circle in the Square. 30th Anniversary Season schedule of three revivals followed by one new play. **The Bacchae** (61). By Euripides; translated by Michael Cacoyannis. Opened October 2, 1980. (Closed November 23, 1980) **John Gabriel Borkman** (61). By Henrik Ibsen; translated by Rolf Fjelde. Opened December 18, 1980. (Closed February 8, 1981) **The Father** (29). By August Strindberg; translated by Harry G. Carlson. Opened April 2, 1981. (Closed April 26, 1981) And *Scenes and Revelations* by Elan Garonzik scheduled to open June 25, 1981. Produced by Circle in the Square, Theodore Mann artistic director, Paul Libin managing director, at Circle in the Square.

THE BACCHAE

Dionysus (Bacchus, Brommus) .... Christopher Rich	Guards .... Peter Efthymiou, Alfred Karl, Gary Tacon
Tiresias..................... Tom Klunis	Herdsman................. David Schramm
Cadmus .... Philip Bosco	Messenger...................... Paul Perri
Pentheus.............. John Noah Hertzler	Agave .... Irene Papas

Chorus of Bacchae: Sheila Dabney, Elain Graham, Ernestine Jackson, Jodi Long, Karen Ludwig, Valois Mickens, Socorro Santiago, Catherine Lee Smith, Michele-Denise Woods.

Standby: Miss Papas—Karen Ludwig. Understudies: Messrs. Rich, Schramm, Efthymiou—Gary Tacon; Messrs. Bosco, Klunis, Schramm—Alfred Karl; Mr. Hertzler—Peter Efthymiou.

Directed by Michael Cacoyannis; scenery and costumes, John Conklin; lighting, Pat Collins; music, Theodore Antoniou; stage manager, Randall Brooks; press, Merle Debuskey, Leo Stern.

The play was presented without intermission. The only previous New York productions of record of *The Bacchae* were off off Broadway by The Performance Group as *Dionysus in '69* in the 1968–69 season and as part of a special summer series at Roundabout 8/15/72.

JOHN GABRIEL BORKMAN

Mrs. Gunhild Borkman ... Rosemary Murphy	Erhart Borkman .... Freddie Lehne
Malene .... Brittain McGowin	John Gabriel Borkman........ E.G. Marshall
Miss Ella Rentheim........... Irene Worth	Frida Foldal................. Viveca Parker
Mrs. Fanny Wilton...... Patricia Cray Lloyd	Vilhelm Foldal.............. Richard Kuss

Standbys: Mr. Marshall—George Morfogen; Misses Worth, Murphy—Elizabeth Hubbard; Miss Parker—Brittain McGowin; Mr. Lehne—Joseph Adams.

Directed by Austin Pendleton; scenery, Andrew Jackness; costumes, Jennifer Von Mayrhauser; lighting, Paul Gallo; production stage manager, Randall Brooks; stage manager, Rick Ralston.

Time: A winter evening, late 1890s. Place: The Rentheim family mansion outside the Norwegian capital. Act I: Mrs. Borkman's sitting room. Act II: Upstairs in the great drawing room. Act III, Scene 1: Mrs. Borkman's sitting room. Scene 2: Outside the house.

John Gabriel Borkman was first produced on Broadway 11/22/97 for 1 matinee performance and 4/1/15 for 4 performances. Its Broadway production 1/29/26 entered Civic Repertory 11/9/26 for 15 performances. Its repertory revival 11/12/46 for 20 performances was its most recent New York professional production of record.

THE FATHER

Captain..................... Ralph Waite	Pastor..................... Richard Woods
Laura .... Frances Sternhagen	Noyd...................... Peter Crombie
Bertha...................... Kate Purwin	Emma....................... Jessica Allen
Margaret................. Pauline Flanagan	Svaird.................... David Faulkner
Dr. Ostermark............... W.B. Brydon	Laura's Mother .... Molly Adams

John Lithgow in Steve Tesich's *Division Street*

Directed by Goran Graffman; scenery, Marjorie Kellogg; costumes, Jennifer Von Mayrhauser; lighting, Arden Fingerhut; music, Kirk Nurock.

The last professional New York revival of *The Father* was by the Roundabout off Broadway 9/11/73 for 97 performances.

Insideoutsideandallaround Shelley Berman (28). One-man performance by Shelley Berman. Produced by Arthur Shafman International Ltd. at the Bijou Theater. Opened October 2, 1980. (Closed October 25, 1980)

Production supervisor, Kitzi Becker; press, Jeffrey Richards Associates, Robert Ganshaw, C. George Willard, Ben Morse, Ted Killmer, Helen Stern.

The show was presented in two parts. Comedy routines with and by Mr. Berman.

Division Street (21). By Steve Tesich. Produced by Emanuel Azenberg, The Shubert Organization, The Mark Taper Forum and Gordon Davidson at the Ambassador Theater. Opened October 8, 1980. (Closed October 25, 1980)

Chris	John Lithgow	Nadja	Murphy Cross
Mrs. Bruchinski	Theresa Merritt	Roger	Joe Regalbuto
Yovan	Keene Curtis	Dianah	Christine Lahti
Betty	Justin Lord	Sal	Anthony Holland

Understudies: Mr. Lithgow—Raymond Baker; Miss Merritt—Barbara Meek; Mr. Lord—Stephen Burks; Mr. Curtis—George Touliatos; Messrs. Regalbuto, Holland—Stephen Van Benschoten; Misses Lahti, Cross—Joy Rinaldi.

Directed by Tom Moore; scenery, Ralph Funicello; costumes, Robert Blackman; lighting, Martin Aronstein; associate producers, William P. Wingate, Kenneth Brecher; production stage manager, Franklin Keysar; stage manager, Mary Michele Miner; press, Bill Evans, Howard Atlee, Bruce Cohen.

Time: The present. Place: Chicago. The play was presented in two parts.

The 1960s radicals now grown up, presented in a context directed to be played in a tempo of "allegro con sentimento." Previously produced at the Mark Taper Forum, Los Angeles.

The Suicide (60). By Nikolai Erdman; translated by George Genereux, Jr. and Jacob Volkov; adapted by Trinity Square Repertory Company, Adrian Hall director, and Jonas Jurasas. Produced by The Aurora StageWing Inc. at the ANTA Theater. Opened October 9, 1980. (Closed November 29, 1980)

Semyon Semyonovich		Victor Victorovich.............. Chip Zien
Podsekalnikov .... Derek Jacobi		Father Yelpidy.............. William Myers
Maria Lukyanovna		Cleopatra Maximovna....... Laura Esterman
Podsekalnikova .... Angela Pietropinto		Raisa Filippovna .... Mary Lou Rosato
Serafima Ilyinishna .... Grayson Hall		Pervaya (Balalaika); Woman .... Leda Siskind
Alexander Petrovich		Vtoraya (Violin) .... Susan Edwards
Kalabushkin.............. Clarence Felder		Tretya (Tambourine)........ Cheryl Giannini
Margarita Ivanovna...... Carol Mayo Jenkins		Pervy (Mandolin);
Aristarkh Dominikovich		Young Boy........... David Patrick Kelly
Grand-Skubik .... John Heffernan		Vtoroy (Violin) .... Derek Meader
Yegor Timofeevich ... John Christopher Jones		Trety (Guitar) .... Jeff Zinn
Waldemar Arsenyevich		
Pugachov .... David Sabin		

Offstage Musicians: Bill Moersch, Andy Seligson.

Standby: Mr. Jacobi—Russell Horton. Understudies: Misses Hall, Esterman—Cheryl Giannini; Miss Pietropinto—Leda Siskind; Messrs. Felder, Sabin, Myers—Chrisopher Loomis; Miss Rosato—Susan Edwards; Mr. Zien—Derek Meader; Misses Siskind, Edwards, Giannini—Polly Pen; Messrs. Jones, Kelly, Meader—John Seeman.

Directed by Jonas Jurasas; scenery and costumes, Santo Loquasto; lighting, F. Mitchell Dana; sound, Jack Shearing; music composed by Richard Weinstock; movement, Ara Fitzgerald; producers, Bill Dyer, Dick De Benedictis; executive producers, James L. Stewart, Rich Irvine; associate producers, R. Tyler Gatchell Jr., Peter Neufeld; production stage manager, Peter Lawrence; stage manager, Jim Woolley; press, Jeffrey Richards Associates, C. George Willard, Robert Ganshaw, Ben Morse, Helen Stern, Ted Killmer.

Time: The 1920s. Place: A Moscow tenement. The play was presented in two parts.

Comedy about an unemployed worker hassled by family, friends and "the system," finally getting their attention and respect by promising to commit suicide. A foreign (Russian) play written in the 1920s but never performed or published in Russia; previously produced by the Royal Shakespeare Company in England and at Trinity Square Repertory Company, Providence, R.I. (and subsequently at the Goodman Theater, Chicago; Yale University, New Haven; and the Arena Stage, Washington, D.C.).

Brigadoon (133). Revival of the musical with book and lyrics by Alan Jay Lerner; music by Frederick Loewe. Produced by Zev Bufman and The Shubert Organization in the Wolf Trap production at the Majestic Theater. Opened October 16, 1980. (Closed February 8, 1981 matinee)

Tommy Albright .... Martin Vidnovic		Meg Brockie .... Elaine Hausman
Jeff Douglas............. Mark Zimmerman		Harry Beaton................... John Curry
Angus McGuffie .... Kenneth Kantor		Andrew MacLaren .... Jack Dabdoub
Archie Beaton .... Casper Roos		Fiona MacLaren .... Meg Bussert
Sandy Dean .... Michael Cone		Jean MacLaren .... Mollie Smith
Maggie Anderson .... Marina Eglevsky		Charlie Dalrymple.......... Stephen Lehew

Mr. Lundie............... Frank Hamilton   Jane Ashton.................. Betsy Craig
Frank .... Mark Herrier

Singers: Michael Cone, Betsy Craig, Larry French, Larry Hansen, Linda Hohenfeld, Michael Hayward-Jones, Diane Pennington, Cheryl Russell, Linda Wonneberger.

Dancers: Bill Badolato, Cherie Bower, Amy Danis, Tom Fowler, John Giffin, Mickey Gunnersen, Jennifer Henson, David Hughes, Phil LaDuca, Elena Malfitano, Susi McCarter, Jerry Mitchell, Eric Nesbitt, Holly Reeve, Dale Robbins, Harry Williams.

Swing Dancers, Singers: Randal Harris, Suzi Winson. Bagpiper: Larry Cole.

Standbys: Miss Bussert—Linda Wonneberger; Mr. Hamilton—Jack Dabdoub; Mr. Curry—Eric Nesbitt. Understudies: Mr. Vidnovic—Mark Zimmerman; Mr. Zimmerman—Mark Herrier; Miss Hausman—Diane Pennington; Mr. Hamilton—Casper Roos; Misses Bussert, Craig—Linda Hohenfeld; Mr. Lehew—Larry Hansen; Messrs. Kantor, Cone—Michael Hayward-Jones; Messrs. Roos, Dabdoub—Kenneth Kantor; Mr. Herrier—Larry French; Miss Smith—Holly Reeve; Mr. Curry—Tom Fowler; Miss Eglevsky—Amy Danis.

Directed by Vivian Matalon; choreography and musical staging, Agnes de Mille; musical direction and vocal arrangements, Wally Harper; scenery, Michael J. Hotopp, Paul de Pass; costumes, Stanley Simmons; lighting, Thomas Skelton; assistant to Miss de Mille, David Evans; conductor, Tom Helm; orchestrations, Mack Schlefer, Bill Brohn; sound, T. Richard Fitzerald; Wolf Trap executive producer, Craig Hankenson; Miss de Mille's choreography recreated by James Jamieson; production stage manager, Joe Lorden; stage manager, Jack Gianino; press, Fred Nathan, Louise Weiner Ment.

Brigadoon was originally produced on Broadway 3/13/47 for 581 performances and was named a Best Play of its season and won the Critics Award for best musical. It was revived six times at New York City Center, the most recent being 12/13/67 for 23 performances. This production was previously presented in New Orleans, Vienna, Va. (Wolf Trap) and Washington, D.C.

ACT I

Scene 1: A hillside in Scotland
"Once in the Highlands"... Ensemble
"Brigadoon" .... Ensemble
Scene 2: MacConnachy Square
"Down on MacConnachy Square"............ Sandy, Meg, Men and Women of Brigadoon
"Waitin' for My Dearie".. Fiona, Girls
"I'll Go Home With Bonnie Jean".................................... Charlie, Men
(Bonnie Jean danced by Harry, Maggie and Men and Women of Brigadoon)
Scene 3: A Hillside in Brigadoon
"Heather on the Hill" .... Tommy, Fiona
"Rain Exorcism" .... Men and Women of Brigadoon
Scene 4: The Brockie Shed
"The Love of My Life" .... Meg
Scene 5: Outside the MacLaren house
(Jeannie's Packing Up danced by Girls)
"Come to Me, Bend to Me"... Charlie
(Come to Me, Bend to Me danced by Jean and Girls)
"Almost Like Being in Love"....................................... Tommy, Fiona

ACT II

Scene 1: Outside Mr. Lundie's house
Scene 2: The glen
(Wedding Dance led by Jean and Charlie, danced by Men and
Women of Brigadoon)
(Sword Dance led by Harry, danced by Company)
Scene 3: The forest
"The Chase" .... Harry, Men of Brigadoon
"There But for You Go I" .... Tommy, Fiona
Scene 4: Outside the MacLaren house
(Steps Stately danced by Men and Women of Brigadoon)
(Drunken Reel danced by Men and Women of Brigadoon)

(Funeral Dance danced by Maggie)
Scene 5: A hillside in Scotland
   "From This Day On" .... Tommy, Fiona
   "Brigadoon" .... Ensemble
Scene 6: A cocktail bar in New York City
   "Come to Me, Bend to Me," "Heather on the Hill" (Reprise)..................... Fiona
Scene 7: A hillside in Scotland
   "From This Day On" (Reprise) .... Tommy
   "Brigadoon" (Reprise) .... Ensemble

Banjo Dancing (38). One-man performance by Stephen Wade; devised by Stephen Wade with Milton Kramer. Produced by Stuart Oken and Jason Brett and The Klezmer Corp. at the Century Theater. Opened October 21, 1980. (Closed November 30, 1980)

Directed by Milton Kramer; scenery, David Emmons; lighting, Dennis Parichy; an Apollo Group Production in association with Jeffrey Wachtel; production stage manager, Annette Jops; press, Jeffrey Richards Associates, Robert Ganshaw, Ben Morse, Helen Stern, C. George Willard, Ted Killmer.

Subtitled "The 48th Annual Squitters Mountain Song Dance Folklore Convention and Banjo Contest . . . and How I Lost," a banjo concert by Stephen Wade, together with songs, jokes, monologues, etc. The show was presented in two parts. Previously produced at the Apollo Theater, Chicago.

Tintypes (93). Transfer from off Broadway of the musical revue conceived by Mary Kyte with Mel Marvin and Gary Pearle. Produced by Richmond Crinkley and Royal Pardon Productions, Ivan Bloch, Larry J. Silva, Eve Skina in association with Joan F. Tobin in the American National Theater and Academy production at the John Golden Theater. Opened October 23, 1980. (Closed January 11, 1981 matinee)

Mel Marvin (piano)	Trey Wilson
Carolyn Mignini	Mary Catherine Wright
Lynne Thigpen	Jerry Zaks

Understudies: Misses Mignini, Wright—Marie King; Messrs. Wilson, Zaks—Wayne Bryan; Miss Thigpen—S. Epatha Merkerson.

Directed by Gary Pearle; musical staging, Mary Kyte; scenery, Tom Lynch; costumes, Jess Goldstein; lighting, Paul Gallo; sound, Jack Mann; musical and vocal arrangements, Mel Marvin; orchestrations and vocal arrangements, John McKinney; production stage manager, Steve Beckler; stage manager, Bonnie Panson; press, Betty Lee Hunt, Maria Cristina Pucci, James Sapp.

This revue of musical numbers from the Gay Nineties to World War I was first produced in New York by the American National Theater and Academy off Broadway 4/17/79 for 134 performances through 8/10/79 (see its entry in the Plays Produced Off Broadway section of *The Best Plays of 1979–80*). Previously produced at the Arena Stage, Washington, D.C., and the Asolo Theater, Sarasota.

MUSICAL NUMBERS—ACT I. Arrivals: "Ragtime Nightingale" by Joseph F. Lamb, 1915), "The Yankee Doodle Boy" (by George M. Cohan, 1904), "Ta-Ra-Ra Boom-De-Ay!" (by Henry J. Sayers, 1891), "I Don't Care" (by Jean Lenox and Harry C. Sutton, 1905), "Come Take a Trip in My Airship" (by George Evans and Ren Shields, 1904), "Kentucky Babe" (by Richard H. Buck and Adam Geibel, 1896), "A Hot Time in the Old Town Tonight" (by Joe Hayden and Theo A. Metz, 1896), "Stars and Stripes Forever" (by John Philip Sousa, 1897).

Ingenuity and Inventions: "Electricity" (by Harry B. Smith and Karl Hoschna, 1905).

TR: "El Capitan" (by John Philip Sousa, 1896).

Wheels: "Pastime Rag" (by Artie Matthews, 1920), "Meet Me in St. Louis" (by Andrew Sterling and Kerry Mills, 1904), "Solace" (by Scott Joplin, 1909), "Waltz Me Around Again, Willie" (by Will D. Cobb and Ren Shields, 1906), "Wabash Cannonball" (traditional), "In My Merry Oldsmobile" (by Gus Edwards and Vincent P. Bryan, 1905).

Jerry Zaks in the revue *Tintypes*

The Factory: "Wayfaring Stranger" (traditional), "Sometimes I Feel Like a Motherless Child" (traditional), "Aye, Lye, Lyu, Lye" (traditional), "I'll Take You Home Again, Kathleen" (by Thomas P. Westendorf, 1876), "America the Beautiful" (by Katherine Lee Bates and Samuel Ward, 1910), "Wait for the Wagon" (traditional), "What It Takes to Make Me Love You—You've Got It" (by J.W. Johnson and James Reese Europe, 1914).

Anna Held: "The Maiden With the Dreamy Eyes" (by J.W. Johnson and Bob Cole, 1901), "If I Were on the Stage (Kiss Me Again)" (by Henry Blossom and Victor Herbert, 1905).

Outside Looking In: "Shortnin' Bread" (traditional), "Nobody" (by Alex Rogers and Bert Williams, 1905).

Fitting In: "Elite Syncopations" (by Scott Joplin, 1902), "I'm Goin' to Live Anyhow, 'Til I Die" (by Shepard N. Edmonds, 1900).

ACT II. "The Ragtime Dance" (by Scott Joplin, 1902).

Panama: "I Want What I Want When I Want It" (by Henry Blossom and Victor Herbert, 1905).

The Ladies: "It's Delightful To Be Married!" (by Anna Held and V. Scotto, 1907), "Fifty-Fifty" (by Jim Burris and Chris Smith, 1914), "American Beauty" (by Joseph F. Lamb, 1913).

Rich and Poor: "Then I'd Be Satisfied With Life" (George M. Cohan, 1902), "Narcissus" (by Ethelbert Nevin, 1891), "Jonah Man" (by Alex Rogers, 1903), "When It's All Goin' Out and Nothin' Comin' In" (by Bert Williams and George Walker, 1902), "We Shall Not Be Moved" (traditional).

Vaudeville: "Hello, Ma Baby" (by Joseph E. Howard and Ida Emerson, 1899), "Teddy Da Roose" (by Ed Moran and J. Fred Helf, 1910), "A Bird in a Gilded Cage" (by Arthur J. Lamb and Harry Von Tilzer, 1900), "Bill Bailey, Won't You Please Come Home?" (by Hughie Cannon, 1902), "She's Gettin' More Like the White Folks Every Day" (by Bert Williams and George Walker, 1901), "You're a Grand Old Flag" (by George M. Cohan, 1906), "The Yankee Doodle Boy" (Reprise).

Finale: "Toyland" (by Glen McDonough and Victor Herbert, 1903), "Smiles" (by J. Will Callahan and Lee S. Roberts, 1918).

Quick Change (5). One-man performance by Michael McGiveney; written by Bruce Belland, Roy M. Rogosin and Michael McGiveney. Produced by Arthur Shafman International, Ltd. at the Bijou Theater. Opened October 30, 1980. (Closed November 2, 1980)

Directed by Roy M. Rogosin; costumes, Mary Wills; lyrics, Bruce Belland; stage manager, Ernie Guderjahn; press, Jeffrey Richards Associates, Robert Ganshaw, C. George Willard, Ben Morse, Ted Killmer, Helen Stern.

Act I: Carnival, The Triumph of Arthur, The Lady Recites, Bill Sikes (from Dickens's *Oliver Twist*). Act II: Pitchman & The Cop, Quicker Than the Eye, A Misunderstood Minority, Shoot-Out at Belle's Saloon.

Performing tour de force of 30 different characters with 75 costume changes.

A Life (72). By Hugh Leonard. Produced by Lester Osterman, Richard Horner, Hinks Shimberg and Freydberg-Cutler Diamond Productions at the Morosco Theater. Opened November 2, 1980. (Closed January 3, 1981)

Drumm.....................	Roy Dotrice	Desmond (Young Drumm) ...	Adam Redfield
Dolly.....................	Helen Stenborg	Lar (Young Kearns)..........	David Ferry
Mary.....................	Aideen O'Kelly	Kearns	Pat Hingle
Mibs (Young Mary)	Lauren Thompson	Dorothy (Young Dolly)	Dana Delany

Understudies: Mr. Dotrice—Edward Earle; Mr. Hingle—Vince O'Brien; Misses O'Kelly, Stenborg—Sylvia Short; Misses Thompson, Delany—Terry Finn; Messrs. Redfield, Ferry—Chris Hagan.

Directed by Peter Coe; scenery and costumes, Robert Fletcher; lighting, Marc. B. Weiss; associate producers, Lynne Stuart, Spencer Berlin; production stage manager, Elliott Woodruff; stage manager, Eileen Haring; press, Seymour Krawitz, Patricia McLean Krawitz, Warren Knowlton.

Time: The present. Place: A small town just south of Dublin. The play was presented in two parts. A foreign play previously produced at the 1979 Dublin Theater Festival and at Edmonton, Alberta.

The life and times of the Irish civil servant Drumm introduced as a character in the author's 1978 Best Play *"Da"*. A foreign play previously produced at the 1979 Dublin Theater Festival and Citadel Theater, Edmonton, Canada.

A Best Play; see page 139.

*Fifth of July (239). Return engagement of the play by Lanford Wilson. Produced by Jerry Arrow, Robert Lussier and Warner Theater Productions, Inc. at the New Apollo Theater. Opened November 5, 1980.

Kenneth Talley Jr.	Christopher Reeve	June Talley................	Joyce Reehling
Jed Jenkins...................	Jeff Daniels	Shirley Talley................	Amy Wright
John Landis...............	Jonathan Hogan	Sally Friedman	Mary Carver
Gwen Landis...............	Swoosie Kurtz	Weston Hurley..............	Danton Stone

Understudies: Misses Kurtz, Reehling—Tanya Berezin; Messrs. Reeve, Daniels, Hogan—Phil Clark; Miss Wright—Jane Fleiss; Mary Carver—Edith Larkin.

Directed by Marshall W. Mason; scenery, John Lee Beatty; costumes, Laura Crow; lighting, Dennis Parichy; sound, Chuck London; song "Your Loving Eyes" by Jonathan Hogan; production stage manager, Fred Reinglas; press, Max Eisen, Barbara Glenn, Francine L. Trevens.

Time: 1977. Place: The Talley Place, a farm near Lebanon, Mo. Act I: Early evening, Independence Day. Act II: The following morning, outside.

New Broadway production of the Lanford Wilson play originally produced off Broadway 4/27/78 for 158 performances under the title *The 5th of July* and named a Best Play of its season (the director, designers and two performers in this production served the off-Broadway version in the same capacity). This was the first of its author's Talley Family plays to appear in production (though the last in time sequence).

Phillip Clark replaced Christopher Reeve 3/24/81. Richard Thomas replaced Phillip Clark 3/27/81.

Tricks of the Trade (1). By Sidney Michaels. Produced by Gilbert Cates in association with Matthew Alexander at the Brooks Atkinson Theater. Opened and closed at the evening performance, November 6, 1980.

Dr. August Browning.......	George C. Scott	Howard	Lee Richardson
Diana Woods............	Trish Van Devere	Paul	Geoffrey Pierson

Directed by Gilbert Cates; scenery and lighting, Peter Dohanos; costumes, Albert Wolsky; incidental music, Charles Fox; sound, Peter Berger; production associate, Tom Folino; production stage manager, Martin Gold; stage manager, Carlos Gorbea; press, Merle Debuskey, Leo Stern.

Time: The present. Place: The office of Dr. August Browning, New York City. Act I, Scene 1: October, early morning. Scene 2: November, 5 o'clock. Scene 3: December, 5 o'clock. Scene 4: February, 5 o'clock. Scene 5: April, early morning. Act II, Scene 1: June, early morning. Scene 2: July 3, early afternoon. Scene 3: August 14, night. Scene 4: August 15, afternoon. Scene 5: That night, 11 o'clock.

Self-styled "a romantic mystery" with psychiatrist and patient playing a C.I.A. cat-and-mouse game.

*Lunch Hour (231). By Jean Kerr. Produced by Robert Whitehead and Roger L. Stevens at the Ethel Barrymore Theater. Opened November 12, 1980.

Oliver	Sam Waterston	Leo	Max Wright
Nora	Susan Kellermann	Peter.....................	David Rasche
Carrie	Gilda Radner		

Standby: Messrs. Waterston, Wright, Rasche—Jack Gilpin.

Directed by Mike Nichols; scenery, Oliver Smith; costumes, Ann Roth; lighting, Jennifer Tipton; production stage manager, Nina Seely; stage manager, Wayne Carson; press, Seymour Krawitz, Patricia McLean Krawitz, Warren Knowlton.

Time: Summertime. Place: A house in the Hamptons, Long Island.

Comedy, the pitfalls of wife-swapping.

A Best Play; see page 161.

*The Lincoln Center Theater Company. Schedule of three programs. **The Philadelphia Story** (60). Revival of the play by Philip Barry. Opened November 14, 1980. (Closed January 4, 1981) **Macbeth** (53). Revival of the play by William Shakespeare. Opened January 22, 1981. (Closed March 8, 1981 matinee) ***The Floating Light Bulb** (41). By Woody Allen. Opened April 27, 1981. Produced by The Lincoln Center Theater Company, Richmond Crinkley producer, at the Vivian Beaumont Theater.

ALL PLAYS: Members of the artistic directorate, Edward Albee, Woody Allen, Sarah Caldwell, Liviu Ciulei, Robin Phillips, Ellis Rabb; press, Betty Lee Hunt, Maria Cristina Pucci, James Sapp.

THE PHILADELPHIA STORY

Edward...................	Edward Fabry	William Tracy	George Ede
Elsie	Anne Sargent	Macaulay Connor	Edward Herrmann
May	Kim Beaty	Elizabeth Imbrie	Mary Louise Wilson
Thomas....................	Robert Burr	George Kittredge..........	Richard Council
Dinah Lord	Cynthia Nixon	C.K. Dexter Haven........	Frank Converse
Tracy Samantha Lord.......	Blythe Danner	Seth Lord...............	Douglass Watson
Margaret Lord..............	Meg Mundy	Mac......................	Count Stovall
Alexander Lord............	Michael Gross		

Standbys: Miss Danner—Kim Beaty; Messrs. Converse, Herrmann, Council—J. Kenneth Campbell; Messrs. Watson, Ede—Robert Burr; Miss Mundy—Anne Sargent; Miss Wilson—Kim Beaty; Messrs. Gross, Burr—Edward Fabry; Misses Nixon, Sargent, Beaty—Tiffany Bogart; Messrs. Fabry, Burr—Count Stovall.

Directed by Ellis Rabb; scenery, John Conklin; costumes, Nancy Potts; lighting, John Gleason; sound, Richard Fitzgerald; incidental music, Claibe Richardson, played by the Roslyn Artists String Quartet; production supervisor, Helaine Head; stage manager, Peter Glazer.

Time: A period of 24 hours in the late 1930s. Place: In the summer room and garden of the Lords' home in the country outside of Philadelphia. Part I, Scene 1: Late morning, Friday. Scene 2: Early evening, Friday. Part II, Scene 1: Before dawn, Saturday. Scene 2: Late morning, Saturday.

The Philadelphia Story was originally produced on Broadway 3/28/39 for 417 performances and was named a Best Play of its season. This is its first major New York revival of record.

MACBETH

Lady Macbeth	Maureen Anderman	Lady Macduff	Kaiulani Lee
Macbeth	Philip Anglim	Angus	Kevin McClarnon
Caithness; Murderer	Ivar Brogger	Fleance; Son of Macduff	William Morrison
Young Siward; Rosse Aide	Robert Burns	Duncan Attendant;	
Macduff	J. Kenneth Campbell	Shield Bearer	Conal O'Brien
Seyton; Captain	Jarlath Conroy	Donalbain; Menteith	Eugene Pressman
Witch	Michael Dash	Witch; Lady	Judith Roberts
Lennox	Kelsey Grammer	Banquo	Norman Snow
Witch	Ellen Gould	Porter	Roy K. Stevens
Witch; Lady	Cordis Heard	Bishop; Old Siward	Sam Stoneburner
Rosse	James Hurdle	Doctor; Old Man;	
Gentlewoman; Witch; Lady	Dana Ivey	Murderer	Peter Van Norden
Sewer; English Soldier	Esquire Jauchem	Malcolm	John Vickery
English Soldier;		Duncan	Neil Vipond
Duncan Attendant	Randy Kovitz	Acolyte; Macduff Child	Jonathan Ward

Musicians: Edward Barnes conductor; Jessica Murrow oboe; Andrew Schwartz bassoon; Justin Cohen trumpet; William Barnewitz French horn; Richard Fitz percussion; Steven Machamer percussion.

Directed by Sarah Caldwell; scenery, Herbert Senn, Helen Pond; costumes and apparitions, Carrie F. Robbins; lighting, John Gleason; sound, Richard Fitzgerald; fight coordinator, B.H. Barry; music, Edward Barnes; production stage manager, Robert Bennett; stage manager, Nancy Finn.

Place: Scotland, and at the end of Act IV, England. The play was presented in two parts.

The last professional New York production of *Macbeth* took place off Broadway 1/4/71 for 132 performances.

THE FLOATING LIGHT BULB

Paul Pollack	Brian Backer	Max Pollack	Danny Aiello
Steve Pollack	Eric Gurry	Betty	Ellen March
Enid Pollack	Beatrice Arthur	Jerry Wexler	Jack Weston

Standby: Miss Arthur—Tresa Hughes.

Directed by Ulu Grosbard; scenery and costumes, Santo Loquasto; lighting, Pat Collins; sound, Richard Fitzgerald; production stage manager, Franklin Keysar; stage manager, Wendy Chapin.

Time: 1945. Place: The Canarsie section of Brooklyn. The play was presented in two parts.

A mother dominates her family, including a diffident son who aspires to be a stage magician.

A Best Play; see page 260.

A Lesson From Aloes (96). By Athol Fugard. Produced by Jay J. Cohen, Richard Press and Louis Busch Hager in association with Yale Repertory Theater, Lloyd Richards artistic director, at the Playhouse Theater. Opened November 17, 1980. (Closed February 8, 1981 matinee)

Piet Bezuidenhout	Harris Yulin	Steve Daniels	James Earl Jones
Gladys Bezuidenhout	Maria Tucci		

Understudies: Miss Tucci—Linda McGuire; Mr. Yulin—Baxter Harris; Mr. Jones—Zakes Mokae.

Directed by Athol Fugard; scenery, Michael H. Yeargan; costumes, Susan Hilferty; lighting, William Armstrong; executive producer, Ashton Springer; production stage manager, Laurence Rothenberg; stage manager, Neal Ann Stephens; press, Max Eisen, Irene Gandy.

Time: 1963. Place: Two areas representing the backyard and the bedroom of a small house in Algoa Park, Port Elizabeth, South Africa.

The desert-blooming aloe as a metaphor for human endurance and survival in the forbidding sociopolitical environment of South Africa. A foreign (South African) play previously produced at Yale Repertory Theater.

Zakes Mokae replaced James Earl Jones 1/20/81.

A Best Play; see page 175.

The American Clock (12). By Arthur Miller; inspired by Studs Terkel's *Hard Times.* Produced by Jack Garfein, Warner Theater Productions, Inc. and Herbert Wasserman in the Harold Clurman Theater production at the Biltmore Theater. Opened November 20, 1980. (Closed November 30, 1980 matinee)

Lee Baum................	William Atherton	Durant; Sheriff; Piano	
Moe Baum.................	John Randolph	Mover; Toland................	Alan North
Clarence; Waiter; Isaac; Jerome;		Tony; Taylor; Dugan	Edward Seamon
Piano Mover	Donny Burks	Waiter; Bicycle Thief; Rudy; Piano	
Rose Baum.................	Joan Copeland	Mover; Ryan	Bill Smitrovich
Frank; Livermore; Man in Welfare		Joe; Bush	David Chandler
Office; Stanislaus	Ralph Drischell	Doris; Isabel; Grace	Marilyn Caskey
Grandpa; Kapush	Salem Ludwig	Irene.....................	Rosanna Carter
Fanny Margolies; Myrna	Francine Beers	Jeanette Ramsey; Edie; Lucille;	
Clayton; Sidney Margolies;		Attendant................	Susan Sharkey
Ralph	Robert Harper		

Standby; Miss Copeland—Tresa Hughes. Understudies: Misses Caskey, Sharkey—Suzanne Reichard; Misses Carter, Beers—Lil Henderson; Messrs. Burks, Simtrovich, North, Drischell—Peter Francis-James.

Directed by Vivian Matalon; scenery, Karl Eigsti; lighting, Neil Peter Jampolis; costumes, Robert Wojewodski; incidental music, Robert Dennis; production stage manager, Robert LoBianco; stage manager, Jane Neufeld; press, Joe Wolhandler Associates, Steven Wolhandler, Kathryn Kempf.

Self-styled "mural for the theater," a panorama of the Great Depression and its specific effects upon one family. Previously produced off off Broadway at the Harold Clurman Theater and at the Spoleto Festival, Charleston, S.C. The play was presented in two parts.

Perfectly Frank (17). Musical conceived and written by Kenny Solms; music and lyrics by Frank Loesser. Produced by Gladys Rackmil and Fred Levinson in association with Emhan, Inc. at the Helen Hayes Theater. Opened November 30, 1980. (Closed December 13, 1980)

Andra Akers	David Ruprecht
Wayne Cilento	Virginia Sandifur
Jill Cook	Debbie Shapiro
Don Correia	Jo Sullivan
David Holliday	Jim Walton

Understudies: Messrs. Cilento, Correia—Robert Brubach; Messrs. Holliday, Ruprecht, Walton—Michael Byers; Misses Akers, Shapiro, Sandifur, Sullivan—Emily Greenspan; Miss Cook—Barbara Hanks.

Directed by Fritz Holt; choreography, Tony Stevens; musical direction, Yolanda Segovia; scenery and costumes, John Falabella; lighting, Ken Billington; music consultant, Larry Grossman; orchestrations, Bill Byers; dance arrangements, Ronald Melrose; sound, Larry Spurgeon; associate producer,

William Atherton and Joan Copeland in Arthur Miller's *The American Clock*

Vivian Serota; production stage manager, A. Robert Altshuler; stage manager, T.L. Boston; press, Shirley Herz, Jan Greenberg, Sam Rudy.

Act I: Prologue; Screen Test; USO Show; Dressing Room; Understudy Rehearsal; Manhattan. Act II: Entre'acte; Rumble, Rumble; Marriage; Rosabella; Dressing Room; Blues; Finale.

In a framework of reminiscences by Mrs. Loesser (Jo Sullivan), a revue of more than 60 Frank Loesser numbers including "Sit Down You're Rockin' the Boat," "I Don't Want to Walk Without You," "The Lady's in Love With You," "Junk Man," "My Darling, My Darling," "They're Either Too Young or Too Old," "Once in Love With Amy," "Baby, It's Cold Outside," "I Like Everybody," "Some Like It Hot," "Can't Get Out of This Mood," "My Heart Is So Full of You," "Somebody, Somewhere," plus other selections from *Guys and Dolls, The Most Happy Fella, Where's Charley?* and *How to Succeed in Business Without Really Trying.*

Onward Victoria (1). Musical with book and lyrics by Charlotte Anker and Irene Rosenberg; music by Keith Herrmann. Produced by John N. Hart Jr. in association with Hugh J. Hubbard and Robert M. Browne at the Martin Beck Theater. Opened and closed at the evening performance December 14, 1980

Little Girl;	Fleming . . . . Gordon Stanley
Mrs. Randolph . . . . . . Lora Jeanne Martens	Baxter . . . . John Kildahl
Victoria Woodhull . . . . Jill Eikenberry	Woman Investor #1 . . . . Carol Lurie
Tennie Claflin . . . . Beth Austin	Johnson . . . . Scott Fless
Telegraph Boy;	Perkins . . . . Ian Michael Towers
Randolph . . . . Marty McDonough	William Evarts . . . . Rex Hays
Jim . . . . Dan Cronin	Woman Investor #2 . . . . . . Dru Alexandrine
Cornelius Vanderbilt . . . . Ted Thurston	Beth Tilton . . . . Martha Jean Sterner
Mrs. Fleming . . . . Carrie Wilder	Theodore Tilton . . . . Edmond Genest
Mrs. Baxter . . . . Karen Gibson	Elizabeth Cady Stanton . . . . Laura Waterbury

Jim's Girlfriend . . . . Lauren Goler
Congressman Butler . . . . Ken Waller
Henry Ward Beecher . . . . Michael Zaslow
Susan B. Anthony . . . . Dorothy Holland

Grant Speaker; Maginnes;
  Judge . . . . Kenneth H. Waller
Eunice Beecher . . . . Linda Poser
Charlie Delmonico; Fullerton . . Lenny Wolpe
Anthony Comstock . . . . Jim Jansen

Directed by Julianne Boyd; musical numbers staged by Michael Shawn; musical direction, Larry Blank; scenery, William Ritman; costumes, Theoni V. Aldredge; lighting, Richard Nelson; orchestrations, Michael Gibson; dance arrangements, Donald Johnston; vocal arrangements, Keith Herrmann, Larry Blank; sound, Lewis Mead; production stage manager, Ed Aldridge; stage manager, Joseph Corby; press, Shirley Herz, Jan Greenberg, Sam Rudy.

Musical episodes about the noted feminist, the first woman to run for President (in 1872), previously produced off off Broadway at Manhattan Theater Club and the Joseph Jefferson Theater.

ACT I

Scene 1: Opening—New York City, 1871
  "The Age of Brass" . . . . Victoria, Tennie, Henry Beecher, Anthony Comstock,
        Theodore and Beth Tilton, Elizabeth Cady Stanton, Susan B. Anthony, Ensemble
Scene 2: Commodore Cornelius Vanderbilt's office
  "Magnetic Healing" . . . . Victoria, Tennie, Cornelius Vanderbilt
Scene 3: Victoria's salon, six months later
  "Curiosity" . . . . William Evarts, Beth and Theodore Tilton,
        Elizabeth Cady Stanton, Vanderbilt, Ensemble
Scene 4: Plymouth Curch, Brooklyn Heights
  "Beecher's Processional" . . . . Beecher, Congregation
Scene 5: Woodhull and Claflin's brokerage
  "I Depend on You" . . . . Victoria, Tennie
Scene 6: Washington, D.C., Congress, May 24, 1871
Scene 7: Victoria's campaign tour
  "Victoria's Banner" . Victoria, Tennie, Elizabeth Cady Stanton, Susan B. Anthony, Ensemble
  "Changes" . . . . Victoria
Scene 8: Beecher's study, the next day
Scene 9: Victoria's brokerage/Beecher's study, three months later
  "A Taste of Forever" . . . . Victoria, Theodore Tilton
Scene 10: Delmonico's Restaurant, two hours later
  "Unescorted Women" . . . . Charlie Delmonico, Tennie, Victoria, Ensemble

ACT II

Scene 1: Victoria brokerage, the next day
  "Love and Joy" . . . . Victoria, Beecher
Scene 2: Beecher's study, two months later
  "Everyday I Do a Little Something for the Lord" . . . . Comstock
  "It's Easy for Her" . . . . Beecher
Scene 3: Victoria's brokerage, early evening
Scene 4: Steinway Hall
  "You Cannot Drown the Dreamer" . . . . Victoria, Elizabeth
Scene 5: Victoria's brokerage, two days later
  "Respectable" . . . . Tennie
  "Another Life" . . . . Victoria
Scene 6: Brokerage/street/jail
  "Read It in the Weekly" . . . . Victoria, Beecher, Theodore Tilton, Tennie,
        Comstock, Newsboys, Readers
Scene 7: Exterior and interior of courtroom, six months later
  "A Valentine for Beecher" . . . . Ensemble
  "Beecher's Defense" . . . . Victoria
  "Another Life" (Reprise) . . . . Victoria, Beecher
  "You Cannot Drown the Dreamer" (Reprise) . . . . Victoria, Tennie

*Amadeus (189). By Peter Shaffer. Produced by The Shubert Organization, Elizabeth I. McCann, Nelle Nugent and Roger S. Berlind at the Broadhurst Theater. Opened December 17, 1981.

Antonio Salieri.	Ian McKellen	Baron van Swieten	Louis Turenne
The "Venticelli"	Gordon Gould,	Priest	Michael McCarty
	Edward Zang	Giuseppe Bonno	Russell Gold
Salieri's Valet.	Victor Griffin	Teresa Salieri	Linda Robbins
Salieri's Cook.	Haskell Gordon	Katherina Cavalieri.	Caris Corfman
Joseph II	Nicholas Kepros	Constanze Weber.	Jane Seymour
Johann Kilian von Strack.	Paul Harding	Wolfgang Amadeus Mozart	Tim Curry
Count Orsini-Rosenberg.	Patrick Hines	Major Domo	Philip Pleasants

Citizens of Vienna: Caris Corfman, Michele Farr, Russell Gold, Haskell Gordon, Victor Griffin, Martin LaPlatney, Warren Manzi, Michael McCarty, Philip Pleasants, Linda Robbins. Valets: Ronald Bagden, Rick Hamilton, Richard Jay-Alexander, Peter Kingsley, Mark Nelson, Mark Torres.

Standby: Mr. McKellen—Jeremiah Sullivan. Understudies: Messrs. Curry, Gould, Zang—Warren Manzi; Miss Seymour—Caris Corfman; Messrs. Kepros, Gould, Zang—Philip Pleasants; Messrs. Harding, Turenne, Griffin—Russell Gold; Messrs. Hines, Gordon—Michael McCarty; Misses Robbins, Corfman—Michele Farr; Mr. Pleasants and Valets—Martin La Platney. 2d Understudy: Mr. Curry—Mark Nelson.

Directed by Peter Hall; design, John Bury; associate scene designer, Ursula Belden; associate costume designer, John David Ridge; associate lighting designer, Beverly Emmons; music directed and arranged by Harrison Birtwistle; production stage manager, Robert L. Borod; stage manager, Robert Charles; press, Merle Debuskey, William Schelble.

Time: November 1823, and, in recall, the decade 1781–1791. Place: Vienna. The play was presented in two parts.

Moderately gifted but politically influential composer Salieri envies Mozart his musical genius and makes him suffer for it. A foreign play previously produced by the National Theater in London.

Caris Corfman replaced Jane Seymour and Michele Farr replaced Caris Corfman 5/26/81.

A Best Play; see page 205.

Mixed Couples (9). By James Prideaux. Produced by Frederick Brisson in association with the John F. Kennedy Center for the Performing Arts at the Brooks Atkinson Theater. Opened December 28, 1980. (Closed January 3, 1981)

Pilot	John Stewart	Don.	Rip Torn
Alden	Michael Higgins	Clarice	Julie Harris
Elberta	Geraldine Page		

Standbys: Misses Harris, Page—M'el Dowd; Messrs. Torn, Higgins, Stewart—Peter McRobbie.

Directed by George Schaefer; scenery, Oliver Smith; costumes, Noel Taylor; lighting, Martin Aronstein; production supervisor, Stone Widney; assistant to producer, Dwight Frye; production stage manager, Robert Townsend; stage manager, Charles Kindl; press, Jeffrey Richards Associates, C. George Willard, Robert Ganshaw, Ben Morse, Helen Stern.

Time: September, 1927. Place: A workshop hangar at an airfield in New Jersey. The play was presented in two parts.

Married couples who have switched partners meet again 25 years later, by chance.

Frankenstein (1). By Victor Gialanella. Produced by Terry Allen Kramer, Joseph Kipness, James M. Nederlander and Stewart F. Lane in association with 20th Century-Fox Productions at the Palace Theater. Opened and closed at the evening performance, January 4, 1981.

Victor Frankenstein.	David Dukes	Peter Schmidt	Dennis Bacigalupi
Hans Metz.	John Seitz	Henry Clerval	John Glover

Elizabeth Lavenza	Dianne Wiest	Frau Mueller	Kate Wilkinson
William Frankenstein	Scott Schwartz	Alphonse Frankenstein	Douglas Seale
Justine Moritz	Jill P. Rose	The Creature	Keith Jochim
Lionel Mueller	Richard Kneeland	DeLacey	John Carradine

Directed by Tom Moore; scenery, Douglas W. Schmidt; costumes and puppets, Carrie F. Robbins; lighting, Jules Fisher, Robby Monk; special effects and sound, Bran Ferren; music, Richard Peaslee; fight coordinator, N.H. Barry; associate producer, Marvin A. Krauss; production stage manager, Michael Martorella; stage manager, John Fennessy; press, Merle Debuskey, Leo Stern.

Time: The mid-1800s. Place: In and around the Frankenstein estate, Geneva, Switzerland.

Act I, Scene 1: A graveyard, evening. Scene 2: A sitting room of the chateau, later that evening. Scene 3: The tower laboratory, that night. Scene 4: A cottage, one week later. Scene 5: Outside the cottage, three months later.

Act II, Scene 1: The grounds of the chateau, two months later. Scene 2: The sitting room, two hours later. Scene 3: The laboratory, one week later. Scene 4: Elizabeth's bedroom, one year later. Scene 5: The laboratory, immediately following.

Another dramatization of Mary Shelley's tale of Frankenstein and his monster. Previously produced at the Loretto-Hilton Repertory Theater, St. Louis.

*The Pirates of Penzance (165). Transfer from off Broadway of the operetta revival with book and lyrics by W.S. Gilbert; music by Arthur Sullivan. Produced by Joseph Papp in the New York Shakespeare Festival production at the Uris Theater. Opened January 8, 1981.

Pirate King	Kevin Kline	Kate	Marcie Shaw
Samuel	Stephen Hanan	Isabel	Wendy Wolfe
Frederic	Rex Smith	Mabel	Linda Ronstadt
Ruth	Estelle Parsons	Maj.-Gen. Stanley	George Rose
Edith	Alexandra Korey	Sergeant	Tony Azito

Maj.-Gen. Stanley's Daughters: Robin Boudreau, Maria Guida, Nancy Heikin, Bonnie Simmons.

Pirates and Police: Dean Badolato, Mark Beudert, Brian Bullard, Scott Burkholder, Walter Caldwell, Tim Flavin, Ray Gill, George Kmeck, Daniel Marcus, G. Eugene Moose, Joseph Neal, Walter Niehenke, Joe Pichette, Ellis Skeeter Williams, Michael Edwin Willson.

Orchestra: Dan Berlinghoff associate conductor; Richard Cohen, Simeon Westbrooke winds; Keith Underwood, Sheryl Henze flutes; Lauren Draper, Ron Stinson trumpets; Keith Greene trombones; Dan Berlinghoff, Allen Shawn, Susan Anderson, Ada Janik keyboards; William Moersch, William Ruyle, Larry Spivack percussion; Dennis Masuzzo, Michael Tomasulo bass; Steven Hartman clarinet.

Understudies: Mr. Kline—Ray Gill; Mr. Hanan—G. Eugene Moose; Miss Parsons—Wendy Wolfe; Mr. Smith—Scott Burkholder; Miss Korey—Nancy Heikin; Mr. Rose—Joe Pichette; Mr. Azito—Daniel Marcus; Miss Ronstadt—Karla De Vito; Miss Shaw—Bonnie Simmons; Miss Wolfe—Maria Guida; Swings—Laurie Beechman, Roy Alan.

Directed by Wilford Leach; choreography, Graciela Daniele; conductor, William Elliott; scenery, Bob Shaw, Wilford Leach; scenery supervision, Paul Eads; costumes, Patricia McGourty; lighting, Jennifer Tipton; music adapted by William Elliott; sound, Don Ketteler; production supervisor, Jason Steven Cohen; production stage manager, Zane Weiner; stage manager, Frank Di Filia; press, Merle Debuskey, Richard Kornberg, John Howlett.

This New York Shakespeare Festival production was previously produced at the Delacorte Theater in Central Park 7/15/80–8/31/80 for 42 performances; see its entry in the Plays Produced off Broadway section of this volume.

Karla De Vito replaced Linda Ronstadt 6/2/81.

ACT I

"Pour, O Pour the Pirate Sherry"	Pirate King, Samuel, Frederic, Pirates
"When Frederic Was a Little Lad"	Ruth
"Oh, Better Far to Live and Die"	Pirate King, Pirates

"Oh, False One, You Have Deceived Me!"................................ Ruth, Frederic
"Climbing Over Rocky Mountain"............................... Edith, Kate, Daughters
"Stop, Ladies, Pray!".. Frederic, Daughters
"Oh, Is There Not One Maiden Breast" .... Frederic, Daughters
"Poor Wandering One"... Mabel, Daughters
"What Ought We to Do?" .... Edith, Kate, Daughters
"How Beautifully Blue the Sky"........................... Mabel, Frederic, Daughters
"Stay, We Must Not Lose Our Senses"........................ Frederic, Daughters, Pirates
"Hold, Monsters!" .... Mabel, Samuel, Major-General, Daughters, Pirates
"I Am the Very Model of a Modern Major-General".............. Major-General, Ensemble
"Oh, Men of Dark and Dismal Fate" .... Ensemble

ACT II

"Oh, Dry the Glistening Tear"...................................... Mabel, Daughters
"Then Frederic"... Major-General, Frederic
"When the Foemen Bares His Steel".................... Sergeant, Mable, Police, Daughters
"Now for the Pirates' Lair!".................................. Frederic, Pirate King, Ruth
"When You Had Left Our Pirate Fold" .... Ruth, Frederic, Pirate King
"My Eyes Are Fully Open" (from *Ruddigore*).................. Frederic, Ruth, Pirate King
"Away, Away! My Heart's on Fire" .... Ruth, Pirate King, Frederic
"All Is Prepared".. Mabel, Frederic
"Stay, Frederic, Stay!"... Mabel, Frederic
"Sorry Her Lot" (from *H.M.S. Pinafore*) .... Mabel
"No, I Am Brave".. Mabel, Sergeant, Police
"When a Felon's Not Engaged in His Employment"...................... Sergeant, Police
"A Rollicking Band of Pirates We"............................. Pirates, Sergeant, Police
"With Cat-Like Tread, Upon Our Prey We Steal".................... Pirates, Police, Samuel
"Hush, Hush! Not a Word" .... Frederic, Pirates, Police, Major-General
"Sighing Softly to the River" .... Major-General, Ensemble
Finale (restoration of part of 1879 New York finale by Richard Traubner) .... Ensemble

Emlyn Williams as Charles Dickens (22). Return engagement of the one-man performance by Emlyn Williams in scenes from the novels and stories by Charles Dickens. Produced by Arthur Cantor at the Century Theater. Opened January 14, 1981. (Closed February 1, 1981)

Production supervisor, Robert Crawley; press, Arthur Solomon, Marguerite Wolfe.

Act I: Moving in Society (from *Our Mutual Friend*); A Call Upon a Strange Man *(The Black Veil,* a story from *Sketches by Boz); Mrs. Gamp (from *Martin Chuzzlewit*); Paul (from *Dombey and Son*).

Act II: Mr. Chops *(The Tale of a Little Person,* from *Christmas Stories); Once Upon a Time (from *The Battle of Life*); Moving Higher in Society (from *Little Dorrit*); The Fancy Ball (from *A Tale of Two Cities*); A Bedtime Story for a Good Child (a nurse's story from *The Uncommercial Traveller*).

Emlyn Williams previously presented his one-man show as Charles Dickens in New York 2/4/52 for 48 performances, 4/20/53 for 24 performances and 11/7/70 for 5 performances.

To Grandmother's House We Go (61). By Joanna M. Glass. Produced by Doris Cole Abrahams and Burry Fredrik in association with Leon Becker at the Biltmore Theater. Opened January 15, 1981. (Closed March 8, 1981 matinee)

Grandie	Eva Le Gallienne	Jared.................	Shepperd Strudwick
Harriet	Kim Hunter	Beatrice	Anne Twomey
Muffy	Pamela Brook	Paul	David Snell
Clementine..................	Ruth Nelson	Twyla	Leslie Denniston

Understudies: Miss Le Gallienne—Ruth Nelson; Misses Nelson, Hunter—Betty Low; Mr. Strudwick—Edward Earle; Mr. Snell—Alex Wipf; Misses Brook, Hilboldt, Twomey—Harriet Harris.

Shepperd Strudwick, David Snell, Pamela Brook (seated on floor), Leslie Denniston, Ruth Nelson, Anne Twomey, Kim Hunter and Eva Le Gallienne are the family circle in *To Grandmother's House We Go* by Joanna M. Glass

Directed by Clifford Williams; scenery, Ben Edwards; costumes, Jane Greenwood; lighting, Marc B. Weiss; production stage manager, Robert Corpora; stage manager, Audrey Koran; press, Shirley Herz, Jan Greenberg.

Time: The present. Place: A small town outside Hartford, Conn. Act I, Scene 1: Late afternoon, the day before Thanksgiving. Scene 2: Later that evening. Act II, Scene 1: Early Thanksgiving Day. Scene 2: Four days later.

A family gathers for the holidays, creating inevitable conflicts and emotional disclosures. Previously produced at the Alley Theater, Houston, Tex.

Lisa Hilboldt replaced Leslie Denniston 2/17/81.

Shakespeare's Cabaret (54). Musical with words by William Shakespeare; concept and music by Lance Mulcahy. Produced by Arthur Shafman at the Bijou Theater. Opened January 21, 1981. (Closed March 8, 1981 matinee)

Alan Brasington	Patti Perkins
Catherine Cox	Larry Riley
Pauletta Pearson	Michael Rupert

Directed by John Driver; choreography, Lynne Taylor-Corbett; musical direction, Don Jones; scenery and costumes, Frank J. Boros; lighting, Marc B. Weiss; orchestrations and vocal arrangements, Don Jones; production stage manager, Kitzi Becker; stage manager, John Handy; press, Jeffrey Richards Associates, Robert Ganshaw, C. George Willard, Ben Morse, Ted Killmer, Helen Stern.

Revue with lyrics from Shakespeare's works, particularly the songs and poems. Previously produced off Broadway by Colonnades Theater Lab 2/1/80 for 40 performances; see its entry in the Plays

Produced off Broadway section of *The Best Plays of 1979–80.* The show was presented without intermission.

MUSICAL NUMBERS: "If Music and Sweet Poetry Agree" (from *The Passionate Pilgrim*)— Ensemble; "What Thou See'st When Thou Dost Awake" (from *A Midsummer Night's Dream*)— Ensemble; "All That Glisters" (from *The Merchant of Venice*)—Catherine Cox, Patti Perkins, Pauletta Pearson; "Why Should This a Desert Be?" (from *As You Like It*)—Michael Rupert; "Crabbed Age and Youth" (from *The Passionate Pilgrim*)—Alan Brasington, Perkins; "Orpheus With His Lute" (from *Henry VIII*)—Pearson; "Music With Her Silver Sound" (from *Romeo and Juliet*)—Cox, Rupert, Perkins, Brasington; "Come Live With Me and Be My Love" (attributed to Christopher Marlowe)—Larry Riley; "Have More Than Thou Showest" (from *King Lear*)—Rupert, Brasington; *Venus and Adonis* Suite—Ensemble; "Tell Me Where Is Fancy Bred?" (from *The Merchant of Venice*)—Ensemble; "If Music Be the Food of Love" (from *Twelfth Night*)—Brasington, Pearson; "Epitaph for Marina" (from *Pericles*)—Rupert, Cox; "The Phoenix and the Turtle"—Brasington, Perkins, Pearson, Cox, Rupert.

Also "Now" (from *A Midsummer Night's Dream*)—Riley; "The Willow Song" (from *Othello*)— Cox; "Immortal Gods" (from *Timon of Athens*)—Brasington; "Tomorrow Is St. Valentine's Day" (from *Hamlet*)—Perkins; "Fathers That Wear Rags" (from *King Lear*)—Pearson; "The Grave Digger's Song" (from *Hamlet*)—Riley; "Now" (Reprise)—Riley, Perkins, Pearson, Cox, Brasington; "Come Unto These Yellow Sands" (from *The Tempest*)—Ensemble; "Shall I Compare Thee to a Summer's Day?" (from Sonnet 18)—Cox, Brasington; "Lawn as White as Driven Snow" (from *The Winter's Tale*)—Ensemble; "Rosalynde" (from *As You Like It*)—Riley, Brasington; "Let Me the Canakin Clink" (from *Othello*)—Ensemble; "Shakespeare's Epitaph"—Ensemble; "Fear No More the Heat of the Sun" (from *Cymbeline*)—Ensemble; "Shakespeare's Epitaph" (Reprise)— Ensemble.

The Five O'Clock Girl (14). Revival of the musical with book by Guy Bolton and Fred Thompson; music and lyrics by Bert Kalmar and Harry Ruby. Produced by Rodger H. Hess at the Helen Hayes Theater. Opened January 28, 1981. (Closed February 8, 1981 matinee)

Madame Irene	Sheila Smith	Rodney	Richard Ruth
Hudgins	Ted Pugh	Sam	Rodney Pridgen
Susan Snow	Pat Stanley	Ethel; Molly	Annette Michelle
Patricia Brown	Lisby Larson	Elsie	Lora Jeanne Martens
Gerald Brooks	Roger Rathburn	Bunnie	Jean McLaughlin
Ronnie Webb	Barry Preston	Polly	Debra Grimm
Cora Wainwright	Dee Hoty	Maisie	Carla Farnsworth-Webb
Jasper Cobb	Timothy Wallace	Jules	Jonathan Aronson
Jeanie	Teri Corcoran	Detective	G. Brandon Allen
Pete	James Homan	Bobby	Gary Kirsch

Understudies: Miss Stanley—Jean McLaughlin; Miss Larson—Lora Jeanne Martens; Miss Hoty —Carla Farnsworth-Webb; Mr. Rathburn—Richard Ruth; Mr. Preston—Jonathan Aronson; Miss Smith—Teri Corcoran; Mr. Pugh—Timothy Wallace; Mr. Wallace—G. Brandon Allen; Swings— Danute Debney, Robert Rabin.

Directed by Sue Lawless; musical staging and choreography, Dan Siretta; musical direction, Lynn Crigler; scenery, John Lee Beatty; costumes, Nanzi Adzima; lighting, Craig Miller; sound, Richard Fitzgerald; orchestrations and dance arrangements, Russell Warner; assistant choreographer, Larry McMillian; production consultant, Warren Pincus; assistant producer, Jamey Cohan; music research consultant, Alfred Simon; production assistant, Sheila Tronn Cooper; production stage manager, John J. Bonanni; stage manager, Peter Weicker; press, Shirley Herz, Jan Greenberg.

The Five O'Clock Girl (5 O'clock Girl) was originally produced on Broadway 10/10/27 for 280 performances. This revival, originally produced in 1979 and in 1980 at Goodspeed Opera House, East Haddam, Conn., has dropped some of the original songs and added the Bert Kalmar-Harry Ruby songs indicated in the list below by an asterisk (*), with any additional collaborators listed in parentheses.

ACT I

Overture. . . . . Orchestra
Scene 1: A block party near Beekman Place, New York City
  "In the Old Neighborhood" . . . . Madame Irene, Ensemble
Scene 2: On the telephone
  "Keep Romance Alive"* . . . . Telephone Girls
  "Thinking of You". . . . . Pat, Gerry
Scene 3: Gerry's apartment
  "I'm One Little Party" . . . . Ronnie, Female Ensemble
  "Up in the Clouds" . . . . Pat, Gerry, Ensemble
  "My Sunny Tennessee"* (Herman Ruby) . . . . Jasper, Female Ensemble
  "Any Little Thing" . . . . Sue, Hudgins
Scene 4: The Snowflake Cleaners
Scene 5: The Kit Kat Club
  "Manhattan Walk"* (Herbert Stothart). . . . . Madame Irene, Ronnie, Cora, Jasper, Ensemble

ACT II

Entr'acte . . . . Orchestra
Scene 1: Outside the Field and Stream Hotel, Southhampton, L.I.
  "Long Island Low Down"*. . . . . Madame Irene, Ensemble
  "Who Did? You Did!". . . . . Pat, Gerry
  "Any Little Thing" (Reprise) . . . . Sue
Scene 2: The Snowflake Cleaners
  "Nevertheless"* . . . . Sue, Hudgins
Scene 3: A street in New York
  "All Alone Monday"* . . . . Gerry
Scene 4: Roof garden between the apartments of Gerry and Ronnie
  "Dancing the Devil Away"* (Otto Harbach) . . . . Ronnie, Ensemble
Scene 5: The church
  "Up in the Clouds" (Reprise). . . . . Pat, Gerry
Finale. . . . . Company

Piaf (133). By Pam Gems. Produced by Elizabeth I. McCann, Nelle Nugent, The Shubert Organization and Ray Larsen in association with Warner Theater Productions, Inc. at the Plymouth Theater. Opened February 5, 1981.

Emcee/Manager (Henri). . . . . . . David Leary	Little Louis; German Soldier #2;
Piaf. Jane Lapotaire	Lucien; Dope Pusher . . . . Michael Ayr
Piaf (Wed. matinees). . . . . Judith Ivey	Police Inspector; Georges;
Papa Leplee;	Physiotherapist . . . . Kenneth Welsh
American Sailor #2. . . . . . Peter Friedman	Paul; American Sailor #1;
Toine . . . . Zoë Wanamaker	Theo . . . . David Purdham
Emil; Jacko . . . . Nicholas Woodeson	Marlene . . . . Jean Smart
Legionnaire; Pierre; Agent . . . . Stephen Davies	Madeleine. . . . . Judith Ivey
Jacques; German Soldier #1;	Madeleine (Wed. matinees) . . . . Sherry Steiner
Angelo . . . . Lewis Arlt	Nurse . . . . Sherry Steiner
Eddie; Butcher;	Nurse (Wed. matinees). . . . . . . Cynthia Carle
Marcel; Barman. . . . . Robert Christian	

The Band: Michael Dansicker music director, piano; Charles Sauss accordion; Ray Kilday bass.
Understudies: Lewis Arlt, Cynthia Carle, Robert Christian, Stephen Davies, Peter Friedman, Michael Hammond, Christopher McHale, David Purdham, Sherry Steiner, Robert Thaler, Kenneth Welsh, Nicholas Woodeson.
Directed by Howard Davies; scenery, David Jenkins; costumes, Julie Weiss; lighting, Beverly Emmons; musical direction and arrangements, Michael Dansicker; assistant director, Helaine Head; production stage manager, Helaine Head; stage manager, William Gammon; press, Solters/Roskin/Friedman, Inc., Josh Ellis, David LeShay.

Time: The late 1920s through 1963. The play was presented in two parts.

Self-described as "A celebration of the life of Edith Piaf" in episodes of the life and career of the French singer. A foreign play previously produced by the Royal Shakespeare Company and in two succeeding London productions.

Jacques Brel Is Alive and Well and Living in Paris (21). Revival of the musical conceived by Eric Blau and Mort Shuman; music by Jacques Brel; English lyrics and additional material by Eric Blau and Mort Shuman, based on Jacques Brel's lyrics and commentary. Produced by Lily Turner Attractions at Town Hall. Opened February 19, 1981. (Closed March 8, 1981 matinee)

Sally Cooke	Joe Masiell
Shawn Elliott	Betty Rhodes

Bertha Melnik conductor-pianist, Bobby Grillo guitar, Ron Raffio bass, Vince Chiurazzi percussion.

Original direction by Moni Yakim; production stage manager, Steve Helliker; press, M.J. Boyer, Rosemary Carey.

This revue celebrating the songs of the late French artist Jacques Brel was first produced off Broadway 1/22/68 for 1,847 performances, off Broadway's fourth longest-running production, finally moving to Broadway 9/15/72 for 51 performances. It was revived off Broadway 5/17/74 for 125 performances.

MUSICAL NUMBERS—ACT I: "Marathon"—Company; "Alone"—Shawn Elliott; "Madeleine"—Company; "I Loved"—Sally Cooke; "Mathilde"—Joe Masiell; "Bachelor's Dance"—Elliott; "Timid Frieda"—Cooke; "My Death"—Betty Rhodes; "Girls and Dog"—Masiell, Elliott; "Jackie"—Masiell; "The Statue"—Elliott; "Desperate Ones"—Company; "Sons Of"—Rhodes; "Amsterdam"—Masiell.

ACT II: "The Bulls"—Elliott; "Old Folks"—Rhodes; "Marieke"—Rhodes; "Brussels"—Cooke; "Fannette"—Elliott; "Funeral Tango"—Masiell; "Middle Class"—Masiell, Elliott; "You're Not Alone"—Rhodes; "Next"—Masiell; "Carousel"—Rhodes; "If We Only Have Love"—Company.

Heartland (24). By Kevin Heelan. Produced by Gretl Productions, Inc. and Ned Davis in association with Ken Cotthoff and Boyd Ralph at the Century Theater. Opened February 23, 1981. (Closed March 15, 1981 matinee)

Earl	Larry Nicks	Cotton	Keith Jochim
Skeet	J.C. Quinn	Pauline	Martyn St. David
James	Sean Penn		

Directed by Art Wolff; scenery and lighting, Bill Ballou; costumes, Kiki Smith; special visual and audio effects, Tom Brumberger; production stage manager, Christine Devereux; press, Jacksina and Freedman, Angela Wilson, Dolph Browning.

Time: The present, late spring. Place: A small town in the Midwest. Act I: Early evening, Act II: One half-hour later.

Melodrama, a homicidal maniac terrorizes a small town.

*Sophisticated Ladies (106). Musical revue conceived by Donald McKayle; based on the music of Duke Ellington. Produced by Roger S. Berlind, Manheim Fox, Sondra Gilman, Burton L. Litwin and Louise Westergaard in association with Belwin Mills Publishing Corp. and Norzar Productions, Inc. at the Lunt-Fontanne Theater. Opened March 1, 1981.

Priscilla Baskerville	Gregory Hines
Hinton Battle	Phyllis Hyman
P.J. Benjamin	Judith Jamison
Gregg Burge	Terri Klausner
Mercedes Ellington	

Sophisticated Ladies: Claudia Asbury, Mercedes Ellington, Paula Lynn, Wynonna Smith. Gentlemen: Adrian Bailey, Michael Lichtefeld, Michael Scott Gregory, T.A. Stephens.

Band soloists: Lloyd Mayers piano; Richard Pratt drums; Barry Lee Hall, Jon Longo trumpets.

Standbys: Miss Hyman—Anita Moore; Miss Baskerville—Naomi Moody. Understudies: Mr. Hines —Hinton Battle, Gregg Burge; Miss Jamison—Wynonna Smith; Mr. Burge—Michael Scott Gregory; Miss Klausner—Paula Lynn; Mr. Benjamin—Michael Lichtefeld; Mr. Battle—T.A. Stephens; Sophisticated Ladies—Valerie Pettiford; Sophisticated Gentlemen—Faruma S. Williams.

Directed by Michael Smuin; choreography and musical staging, Donald McKayle, Michael Smuin; special tap choreography, Henry LeTang; musical direction, Mercer Ellington; scenery, Tony Walton; costumes, Willa Kim; lighting, Jennifer Tipton; sound, Otts Munderloh; orchestrations, Al Cohn; musical and dance arrangements, Lloyd Mayers; vocal arrangements, Malcolm Dodds, Lloyd Mayers; associate choreographer, Bruce Heath; assistant choreographer, Mercedes Ellington; production stage manager, Martin Gold; stage manager, Carlos Gorbea; press, Fred Nathan, Eileen McMahon.

Tribute to Duke Ellington in a volatile presentation of his songs, as listed below; music and lyrics by Duke Ellington unless otherwise noted.

MUSICAL NUMBERS: ACT I, Overture—Mercer Ellington and Band; "I've Got To Be a Rug Cutter"—Hinton Battle, Gregg Burge, Michael Scott Gregory, Michael Lichtefeld; "Music Is a Woman" (based on "Jubilee Stomp", lyrics by John Guare)—Gregory Hines, Judith Jamison. "The Mooche" (music by Duke Ellington and Irving Mills)—Burge, Claudia Asbury, Mercedes Ellington, Paula Lynn, Wynonna Smith; "Hit Me With a Hot Note and Watch Me Bounce" (lyrics by Don George)—Terri Klausner; "I Love You Madly"/"Perdido"—Jamison, Burge, Battle; "Fat and Forty" (music and lyrics by Al Hibbler and Duke Ellington)—P.J. Benjamin; "It Don't Mean a Thing"—Phyllis Hyman, Burge, Hines, Adrian Bailey, Lichtefeld, Gregory, T.A. Stephens; "Bli-Blip" (lyrics by Duke Ellington and Sid Kuller)—Benjamin, Klausner.

Also in Act I, "Cotton Tail"—Benjamin, Klausner, Ensemble; "Take the A Train" (music by Billy Strayhorn)—Hyman, Hines; "Solitude"—Jamison, Priscilla Baskerville; "Don't Get Around Much Anymore" (lyrics by Bob Russell)—Hines; "I Let a Song Go Out of My Heart" (lyrics by Irving Mills and John Redmond)—Jamison; "Caravan" (music by Duke Ellington and Juan Tizol, lyrics by Irving Mills)—Burge, Mercedes Ellington, Ensemble; "Something to Live For" (music and lyrics by Duke Ellington and Billy Strayhorn)—Hines; "Old Man Blues" (music and lyrics by Duke Ellington and Irving Mills)—Jamison, Battle; "Drop Me Off in Harlem" (lyrics by Nick Kenny)— Battle, Benjamin, Burge, Hines, Baskerville, Ensemble; "Rockin' in Rhythm" (music by Duke Ellington, Irving Mills and Harry Carney)—Company.

ACT II, "Duke's Place" (lyrics by Bill Katz and R. Thiele)—Hines; "In a Sentimental Mood" (lyrics by Danny Kurtz and Irving Mills)—Hyman; "I'm Beginning to See the Light" (music and lyrics by Duke Ellington, Don George, Johnnie Hodges and Harry James)—Jamison, Hines; "My Love"—Baskerville; "Satin Doll" (lyrics by Billy Strayhorn and Johnny Mercer)—Benjamin; "Just Squeeze Me" (lyrics by Lee Gaines)—Klausner; "Dancers in Love"—Burge, Battle, Mercedes Ellington; "Echoes of Harlem"—Burge, Battle, Ladies "I'm Just a Lucky So-and-So" (lyrics by Mack David)—Hines, Gentlemen.

Also in Act II, "Hey Baby"—Benjamin, Mercedes Ellington; "Imagine My Frustration" (music and lyrics by Duke Ellington, Billy Strayhorn and Gerald Wilson)—Klausner, Burge; "Kinda Dukish"—Hines; "Ko-Ko"—Hines, Bailey, Lichtefeld, Gregory, Stephens; "I'm Checking Out Goombye" (music and lyrics by Duke Ellington and Billy Strayhorn)—Hyman; "Do Nothing 'Til You Hear From Me" (lyrics by Bob Russell)—Hines; "I Got It Bad and That Ain't Good" (lyrics by Paul Francis Webster)—Hyman; "Mood Indigo" (music by Duke Ellington, Irving Mills and Albany Bigard)—Hyman, Klausner; "Sophisticated Lady" (lyrics by Mitchell Parish and Irving Mills)— Hines, Jamison, Company; "It Don't Mean a Thing" (reprise)—Hines, Company.

The Survivor (8). By Susan Nanus; based on the book by Jack Eisner; music by Gary William Friedman. Produced by Craig Anderson and Stafford Productions at the Morosco Theater. Opened March 3, 1981. (Closed March 8, 1981 matinee)

Jacek	David Marshall Grant	Rudy's Mother	Ruth S. Klinger
Zlatke	Joanna Merlin	Lutek's Mother	Rochelle Parker

Sevek's Mother	Nada Rowand	Grandma Masha	Lilia Skala
Hela	Loren Brown	Polish Blackmailer; Rudy's	
Rudy	Lonny Price	Father; Jewish Collaborator	Ralph Drischell
Lutek	Joseph Adams	Aron	Len Gochman
Sevek	Mark Bendo	Lutek's Father; Stash;	
Yankele	Zeljko Ivanek	Escapee	Richard M. Davidson
Halina	Ann Lange	Markowsky	Richard Greene

Understudies: Mr. Grant—Joseph Adams; Mr. Gochman—Richard M. Davidson; Misses Klinger, Parker, Rowand—Joan de Marrais; Mr. Greene—Ralph Drischell; Mr. Price—Zeljko Ivanek; Miss Skala—Ruth S. Klinger; Misses Brown, Lange—Wendy Rosenberg; Miss Merlin—Nada Rowand; Messrs. Adams, Bendo, Ivanek—Jeff Marcus; Messrs. Davidson, Drischell—Hal Sherman.

Directed by Craig Anderson; scenery, Steven Rubin; costumes, Bill Walker; lighting, John Gleason; sound, Jan Nebozenko; associate producer, Buddy Bloom; production stage manager, Louis D. Pietig; stage manager, Shari Genser; press, Howard Atlee, Bill Evans.

Time: November 1940 to April 1943. Place: In and around the Warsaw ghetto. The play was presented in two parts.

The horrors of Nazi persecution in the Warsaw ghetto, based on the memoirs of a survivor.

Bring Back Birdie (4). Musical with book by Michael Stewart; music by Charles Strouse; lyrics by Lee Adams. Produced by Lee Guber, Shelly Gross, Slade Brown and Jim Milford at the Martin Beck Theater. Opened March 5, 1981. (Closed March 7, 1981)

Storyteller; Reporter #2	Donna Monroe	Tourist; Reporter #1	Bill Bateman
Albert	Donald O'Connor	Tourist's Wife; Effie	Zoya Leporska
Rose	Chita Rivera	Shopping Bag Lady	Rebecca Renfroe
Mtobe	Maurice Hines	Indian Squaw	Janet Wong
Hogan; Guard; Marshall	Howard Parker	Indian Brave; Reporter #3	Larry Hyman
Albert Jr.	Evan Seplow	Mae Peterson	Maria Karnilova
Jenny	Robin Morse	Mayor C.B. Townsend	Marcel Forestieri
Gary	Jeb Brown	House Manager	Peter Oliver Norman
Porter; Rev. Sun;		Rose II	Lynnda Ferguson
Street Cleaner; Reporter #3	Frank DeSal	Cameraman	Michael Blevins
Sunnie	Betsy Friday	Walter	Kevin Petitt

Girl Friends: Barbara Dare Thomas, Vanessa Bell, Julie Cohen, Christine Langner. "Filth" Group: Evan Seplow, Jeb Brown, Cleve Asbury, Leon Evans, Mark Frawley. Birdettes; Chorus Girls: Betsy Friday, Rebecca Renfroe, Vanessa Bell. Stage Door Johnnies: Bill Bateman, Peter Oliver Norman, Cleve Asbury, Frank DeSal.

Standbys: Mr. O'Connor—Howard Parker; Miss Rivera—Michon Peacock. Understudies: Miss Karnilova—Zoya Leporska; Mr. Hines—Peter Oliver Norman; Mr. Seplow—Michael Blevins; Mr. Brown—Cleve Asbury; Miss Ferguson—Betsy Friday; Swings—Donna Ritchie, Porter Hudson.

Production conceived and directed by Joe Layton; musical direction and vocal arrangements, Mark Hummel; scenery, David Mitchell; costumes, Fred Voelpel; lighting, David Hays; sound, Otts Munderloh; video sequences, Wakefield Poole, Frank O'Dowd; still photographs, Barbara J. Rossi; dance music arrangements, Daniel Troob; orchestral arrangers, Ralph Burns, Stanley Applebaum, Daniel Troob, Philip J. Lang, Jim Tyler, Gary Anderson, Gerald Alters, Scott Kuney, Coleridge-Taylor Perkinson, Charles Strouse; production stage manager, Nicholas Russiyan; stage manager, Tony Manzi; press, Solters/Roskin/Friedman, Inc., Milly Schoenbaum, Josh Ellis, Kevin Patterson.

The *Bye Bye Birdie* characters 20 years after the events of that musical, which was produced on Broadway 4/14/60 for 607 performances.

ACT I

Scene 1: A darkened office
"Twenty Happy Years" .... Rose, Albert
Scene 2: Forest Hills and environs
"Movin' Out" .... Jerry, Gary, Kids

Donald O'Connor (*center,* arm raised) and company in *Bring Back Birdie*

Broadway Follies (1). Vaudeville conceived by Donald Driver; music and lyrics by Walter Marks. Produced by Edgar Lansbury, Joseph Beruh and James M. Nederlander at the Nederlander Theater. Opened and closed at the evening performance March 15, 1981.

Cast: Robert Shields, Lorene Yarnell, Michael Davis, Tessie O'Shea, Milo & Roger, Scott's Royal Boxers, Los Malambos, Gaylord Maynard & Chief Bearpaw.

Chorus: Stephen Bourneuf, Kitty Kuhn, Mark Martino, Nancy Meadows, Brad Miskell, Alice Anne Oakes, Aurelio Padron, R.J. Peters, D'Arcy Phifer, Mark Ruhala, Karen Teti, Suzanne Walker.

Directed by Donald Driver; choreography, Arthur Faria; musical direction and vocal and dance arrangements, Marvin Laird; scenery, Peter Larkin; costumes, Alvin Colt; lighting, Robert Morgan; sound, Abe Jacob; orchestrations, Bill Byers; production stage manager, Robert V. Straus; stage manager, John Actman; press, Gifford/Wallace, Inc., Gerald Vitagliano, Keith Sherman, Valerie Warner.

Vaudeville show of acts recruited internationally.

ACT I: "Broadway Follies"—Follies Ensemble; Vaudeville—Robert Shields and Lorene Yarnell; Wonderful U—Scott's Royal Boxers and Follies Ensemble; "Piccadilly"—Tessie O'Shea; The Oasis —Milo & Roger; The Pampas—Los Malambos; The Toyshop—Shields and Yarnell; "The Paper Bag Rag"—Tessie O'Shea, Bud's Paper Bag Band.

ACT II: At Home With the Clinkers—Shields and Yarnell; "The Barnyard"—Tessie O'Shea, Chicks; Specialty—Shields; The Saloon—Gaylord Maynard and Chief Bearpaw; Tap My Way to the Stars—Yarnell, Follies Ensemble; The Rest of Michael Davis—Michael Davis; Grand Parade— Company.

Lolita (12). By Edward Albee; adapted from the novel by Vladimir Nabokov. Produced by Jerry Sherlock at the Brooks Atkinson Theater. Opened March 19, 1981. (Closed March 28, 1981)

A Certain Gentleman........	Ian Richardson	Constance....................	Bella Jarrett
Humbert Humbert	Donald Sutherland	Head Nurse	Yvette Hawkins
Lolita	Blanche Baker	Nurse #1................	Colette Alexander
Charlotte	Shirley Stoler	Nurse #2..................	Barbara Ware
Annabel	Alaina Wojek	Dick	Kevin Conroy
Louise...................	Marcella Lowery	Bill	Joe Pagano
Clare Quilty.................	Clive Revill	Doctor	Norman Abrams

Standby: Miss Stoler—Tresa Hughes. Understudies: Messrs. Sutherland, Richardson, Revill— William Mooney; Misses Baker, Wojek—Barbara Ware; Miss Lowery—Yvette Hawkins; Mr. Conroy —Joe Pagano; Mr. Pagano—Norman Abrams.

Directed by Frank Dunlop; scenery, William Ritman; costumes, Nancy Potts; lighting, David F. Segal; executive producer, Robert Hartman; associate producer, Kee Young; production stage manager, Jon R. Hand; stage manager, Sally Hassenfelt; press, Henry Luhrman Associates, Bill Miller, Terry M. Lilly, Kevin P. McAnarney.

The play was presented in two parts.

Dramatization of the 1958 novel about a middle-aged professor's passion for a 12-year-old "nymphet."

Rose (68). By Andrew Davies. Produced by Elizabeth I. McCann, Nelle Nugent and The Shubert Organization in association with Colin Brough for The Luton Theater Company, Ltd. and Warner Theater Productions, Inc. at the Cort Theater. Opened March 26, 1981. (Closed May 23, 1981)

Rose	Glenda Jackson	Jim Beam	J.T. Walsh
Mother	Jessica Tandy	Sally	Jo Henderson
Smale	Beverly May	Jake	Guy Boyd
Malpass	Margaret Hilton	Geoffrey	John Cunningham

School Caretaker, Teachers: Don McAllen Leslie, Cynthia Crumlish, Lori Cardille.

Standbys: Misses May, Tandy—Myvanwy Jenn; Messrs. Cunningham, Walsh—Guy Boyd; Miss Jackson—Jo Henderson; Mr. Boyd—McAllen Leslie.

Directed by Alan Dossor; scenery, John Gunter; costumes, Linda Fisher; lighting, Andy Phillips; set supervision, Tom Lynch; production stage manager, Steven Beckler; stage manager, Arlene Grayson; press, Joshua Ellis, Solters/Roskin/Friedman, Inc., Becky Flora.

Place: In and around a Midlands town. The play was presented in two parts.

A school teacher in professional crisis with her colleagues and personal emotional crisis with her husband and family. A foreign play previously produced in London.

*Woman of the Year (73). Musical based on the M-G-M film by Ring Lardner Jr. and Michael Kanin; book by Peter Stone; music by John Kander; lyrics by Fred Ebb. Produced by Lawrence Kasha, David S. Landay, James M. Nederlander, Warner Theater Productions, Inc./Claire Nichtern, Carole J. Shorenstein and Stewart F. Lane at the Palace Theater. Opened March 29, 1981.

Chairperson; Cleaning Woman	Helon Blount	Ellis McMaster	Rex Hays
Tess Harding	Lauren Bacall	Abbott Canfield	Lawrence Raiken
Floor Manager	Michael O'Gorman	Maury	Rex Everhart
Chip Salisbury	Daren Kelly	Helga	Grace Keagy
Gerald	Roderick Cook	Alexi Petrikov	Eivind Harum
Pinky Peters	Gerry Vichi	Cleaning Woman	Marian Haraldson
Phil Whitaker	Tom Avera	Jan Donovan	Marilyn Cooper
Sam Craig	Harry Guardino	Larry Donovan	Jamie Ross

Chorus: DeWright Baxter, Joan Bell, Helon Blount, Sergio Cal, Donna Drake, Richard Glendon-Larson, Marian Haraldson, Michael Kubala, Paige Massman, Gene Montoya, Michael O'-Gorman, Susan Powers, Daniel Quinn, Robert Warners. Swings: Ed Nolfi, Karen Giombetti.

Standby: Mr. Guardino—Jamie Ross. Understudies: Miss Keagy—Marian Haraldson; Mr. Harum—Robert Warners; Mr. Kelly—Richard Glendon-Larson; Messrs. Avera, Hays, Ross—Ralston Hill; Messrs. Raiken, Vichi, Everhart—Michael Davis; Miss Cooper—Paige Massman.

Directed by Robert Moore; musical numbers staged by Tony Charmoli; musical direction and vocal arrangements, Donald Pippin; scenery, Tony Walton; costumes, Theoni V. Aldredge; lighting, Marilyn Rennagel; sound, Abe Jacob; orchestrations, Michael Gibson; dance arrangements, Ronald Melrose; animations, Michael Sporn; assistant to Mr. Charmoli, Ed Nolfi; production stage manager, David Taylor; stage managers, Robert LoBianco, T.L. Boston; press, Merle Debuskey, Leo Stern, Diane Judge.

Musical stage version of the 1942 Katharine Hepburn-Spencer Tracy film about the sports writer (in this case a cartoonist) and the intellectual (in this case a TV morning show hostess).

ACT I

Scene 1: Backstage at a hotel ballroom

"Woman of the Year" .... Tess, Women

Scene 2: A TV studio and Sam's studio
"A Poker Game" .... Sam, Cartoonists
"See You in the Funny Papers" .... Sam
Scene 3: Tess's office
"When You're Right, You're Right!".................................... Tess, Gerald
Scene 4: Sam's studio
"Shut Up, Gerald".. Tess, Sam, Gerald
"So What Else Is New?" .... Sam, Katz
Scene 5: The Inkpot
"One of the Boys" .... Tess, Cartoonists, Maury, Men
"Table Talk".. Tess, Sam
Scene 6: Tess's apartment
"The Two of Us" .... Tess, Sam
Scene 7: Around New York
"It Isn't Working" .... Cartoonists, Chip, Helga, Gerald, New Yorkers
Scene 8: Tess's apartment
"I Told You So".. Gerald, Helga
Scene 9: Tess's apartment and a hotel ballroom
"Woman of the Year" (Reprise)... Tess

ACT II

Scene 1: The street
"So What Else Is New?" (Reprise)... Sam, Katz
Scene 2: The Inkpot
"I Wrote the Book"... Tess, Cleaning Women
Scene 3: A ballet rehearsal room
"Happy in the Morning"..................................... Alexi, Tess, Dancers
Scene 4: Sam's studio
"Sometimes a Day Goes By" .... Sam
Scene 5: Larry's house
"The Grass Is Always Greener"... Tess, Jan
Scene 6: The TV studio
"We're Gonna Work It Out" .... Tess, Sam

Fools (40). By Neil Simon. Produced by Emanuel Azenberg at the Eugene O'Neill Theater. Opened April 6, 1981. (Closed May 9, 1981)

Leon Tolchinsky	John Rubinstein	Yenchna	Florence Stanley
Snetsky	Gerald Hiken	Doctor Zubritsky	Harold Gould
Magistrate	Fred Stuthman	Lenya Zubritsky	Mary Louise Wilson
Slovitch	David Lipman	Sophia Zubritsky	Pamela Reed
Mishkin	Joseph Leon	Gregor Yousekevitch	Richard B. Shull

Standbys: Messrs. Rubinstein, Hiken—Jeff Abbott; Misses Wilson, Stanley—Diaan Ainslee; Miss Reed—Deborah Allison.

Directed by Mike Nichols; scenery, John Lee Beatty; costumes, Patricia Zipprodt; lighting, Tharon Musser; music, John Rubinstein; production stage manager, Martin Herzer; stage manager, Cathy B. Biaser; press, Bill Evans & Associates, Howard Atlee, Sandra Manley, Leslie Anderson, Jim Baldassare.

Time: Long ago. Place: The village of Kulyenchikov. The play was presented in two parts.

Farcical fantasy, a school teacher labors to lift an ancient curse of stupidity from a Russian village.

Aaah Oui Genty! (29). Marionette revue by and with the Compagnie Philippe Genty. Produced by Arthur Shafman International, Ltd. at the Bijou Theater. Opened April 9, 1981. (Closed May 3, 1981)

In Neil Simon's *Fools,* John Rubinstein and Pamela Reed kneel for the wedding ceremony, observed by *(left to right)* David Lipman, Gerald Hiken, Richard B. Shull, Fred Stuthman, Harold Gould, Mary Louise Wilson, Joseph Leon and Florence Stanley

The Compagnie Philippe Genty: Mary Genty, Philippe Genty, Michel Gillaume, Jean-Louis Heckel.

Production supervisor, Christopher Dunlop; production stage manager, Remi Jullien; press, Jeffrey Richards Associates, Bob Ganshaw.

French company's *"théâtre d'animation"* of marionettes, marottes, hand puppets, black light figures and other such effects.

Copperfield (13). Musical based on *David Copperfield* by Charles Dickens; book, music and lyrics by Al Kasha and Joel Hirschhorn. Produced by Don Gregory and Mike Merrick at the ANTA Theater. Opened April 13, 1981. (Closed April 26, 1981 matinee)

David Copperfield	Brian Matthews	Mealy Potatoes	Brian Quinn
Dr. Chilip; Baker	Richard Warren Pugh	Billy Mowcher	Christian Slater
Peggoty	Mary Stout	Bootmaker	David Horwitz
Nurse; Julia Mills	Katharine Buffaloe	Butcher	Bruce Sherman
Aunt Betsey Trotwood	Carmen Mathews	Mrs. Micawber	Linda Poser
Young David	Evan Richards	Mr. Micawber	George S. Irving
Clara Copperfield	Pamela McLernon	Victoria	Spence Ford
Mr. Murdstone	Michael Connolly	Vanessa	Dana Moore
Jane Murdstone	Maris Clement	Constable	Michael Danek
Mr. Quinion	Ralph Braun	Janet	Darleigh Miller
Mick Walker	Gary Munch	Mr. Dick	Lenny Wolpe

Uriah Heep .... Barrie Ingham   Agnes Wickfield .... Leslie Denniston
Mrs. Heep .... Beulah Garrick   Dora Spenlow .... Mary Mastrantonio
Mr. Wickfield .... Keith Perry   Ticket Taker .... Michael Gorman

Ensemble: Cleve Asbury, Ralph Braun, Katharine Buffaloe, Maris Clement, Michael Danek, Spence Ford, Michael Gorman, David Horwitz, Pamela McLernon, Darleigh Miller, Dana Moore, Gary Munch, Keith Perry, Linda Poser, Richard Warren Pugh, Brian Quinn, Lynne Savage, Bruce Sherman, Claude Tessier, Missy Whitchurch.

Swing Dancers: Heather Lea Gerdes, Daniel Dee.

Understudies: Mr. Richards—Christian Slater; Miss Mathews—Linda Poser; Mr. Connolly—Ralph Braun; Miss Stout—Missy Whitchurch; Mr. Ingham—Keith Perry; Mr. Irving—Lenny Wolpe; Mr. Wolpe—Richard Warren Pugh; Miss Garrick—Katharine Buffaloe; Miss Mastrantonio—Pamela McLernon; Mr. Matthews—David Horowitz; Miss Denniston—Darleigh Miller.

Directed and choreographed by Rob Iscove; musical direction and vocal arrangements, Larry Blank; scenery, Tony Straiges; costumes, John David Ridge; lighting, Ken Billington; orchestrations, Irwin Kostal; dance arrangements and incidental music, Donald Johnston; sound, John McClure; production stage manager, Peter Lawrence; stage manager, Jim Woolley; press, Seymour Krawitz, Patricia McLean Krawitz, Warren Knowlton.

Musicalization of Dickens's novel about a young man growing up in the Victorian era.

ACT I

Scene 1: A stormy December night, 1812; the drawing room of the Copperfield cottage in Blunderstone, Suffolk

"I Don't Want a Boy" .... Aunt Betsey, Peggoty, Ensemble

Scene 2: An afternoon in autumn, 1822; the garden of the Copperfield cottage

"Mama, Don't Get Married" .... Young David, Clara, Peggoty

Scene 3: The following spring; the drawing room of the Copperfield cottage

Scene 4: The Murdstone and Grimby warehouse

"Copperfield" .... Young David, Mr. Quinion, Mealy Potatoes, Billy Mowcher, Mick Walker, Ensemble

Scene 5: The following summer; a London street near the Micawber home and inside the Micawber home

"Something Will Turn Up" .... Mr. Micawber, Young David, Creditors, Ensemble

Scene 6: Immediately following; on the road to Dover

"Anyone" .... Young David

Scene 7: A few days later; Aunt Betsey Trotwood's country house in Dover; and ten years later

"Here's a Book" .... Aunt Betsey, Mr. Dick, Young David

"Here's a Book" (Reprise) .... Aunt Betsey, Mr. Dick, David

Scene 8: A week later; Mr. Wickfield's sitting room in London

" 'Umble" .... Uriah, Mrs. Heep

Scene 9: The following Sunday; Soutwark Fair

"The Circle Waltz" .... David, Dora, Agnes, Ensemble

ACT II

Scene 1: Several months later; Mr. Wickfield's office

"Up the Ladder" .... Uriah Heep, Mr. Micawber

"I Wish He Knew" .... Agnes

Scene 2: Outside the church

"The Lights of London" .... David, Dora, Company

Scene 3: Several months later; Mr. Wickfield's sitting room

" 'Umble" (Reprise) .... Uriah Heep

Scene 4: Several weeks later; the home of David and Dora Copperfield

"Something Will Turn Up" (Reprise) .... Mr. Micawber, David

Scene 5: The office of Wickfield and Heep

"Villainy Is the Matter" .... David, Uriah Heep, Micawber, Agnes, Aunt Betsey, Mr. Dick, Mrs. Heep, Peggoty, Mrs. Micawber

Scene 6: The home of David and Dora Copperfield

"With the One I Love" .... David

Scene 7: One year later; the London docks
"Something Will Turn Up" (Reprise) .... Mr. Micawber, Ensemble
"Anyone" (Reprise) .... David, Agnes

Animals (1). Program of three one-act comedies by Eddie Lawrence: *The Beautiful Mariposa, Louie and the Elephant* and *Sort of an Adventure.* Produced by Steve Salvatore and Michael Jordan in association with Joel B. Leff at the Princess Theater. Opened and closed at the evening performance, April 22, 1981.

The Beautiful Mariposa
Maria Rios................. Cecilia Flores
Juan Ribera................. Lazaro Perez
Maid.............. Cara Duff-MacCormick
Manuelo Ribera............ Demo DiMartile
1st State Trooper............... Ben Kapen
2d State Trooper........... Dino Laudicina
Scene 1: A motel room in Kansas, 12:30 A.M.
Scene 2: The motel room, early next morning.
Scene 3: The motel room, that night.

Louie and the Elephant
Louie Bengal................. Dan Frazer
Thaddeus................. Dino Laudicina

Elephant.................... Joel Kramer
Lulu Hopper .... Barbara Erwin
Scene 1: A San Francisco night club, the Tusk, 5 A.M. Scene 2: The Tusk, six years later.

Sort of an Adventure
Harriet Greshaw........... Jeanne Wechsler
Hester Cable .... Barbara Erwin
Eddie Greshaw .... Ben Kapen
Hedda Webb-Winters . Cara Duff-MacCormick
Scene 1: The dining-living area of an apartment in West Greenwich Village, 11 P.M. Scene 2: The same, five days later. Scene 3: The same, three weeks later.

Directed by Eddie Lawrence; scenery, John Wright Stevens; costumes, Marilyn Bligh-White; lighting, Marc B. Weiss; associate producers, Steven Kent Goldberg, Anthony Mazzarella; elephant head and duck bill, Jane Stein; sound, Christopher J. Chambers; production stage manager, Jack Timmers; stage manager, Margaret Peckham; press, Solters/Roskin/Freidman, Inc., Maurice Turet, Kevin Patterson.

In *The Beautiful Mariposa,* a Spanish matador plans to kill a bull in each of the 50 United States. In *Louie and the Elephant,* an elephant wishes he were a human being. In *Sort of an Adventure* a freakish creature is transformed into a woman.

Can-Can (5). Revival of the musical with book by Abe Burrows; music and lyrics by Cole Porter. Produced by James M. Nederlander, Arthur Rubin, Jerome Minskoff, Stewart F. Lane, Carole J. Shorenstein and Charles D. Kelman at the Minskoff Theater. Opened April 30, 1981. (Closed May 5, 1981)

Bailiff; Tabac Waiter;
Chief Justice .... Joseph Cusanelli
Judge Paul Barriere........... David Brooks
Court President;
Monarchist; Prosecutor....... Tom Batten
Judge Aristide Forestier...... Ron Husmann
Claudine; Eve.............. Pamela Sousa
Hilaire Jussac.............. Swen Swenson
Boris Adzinidzinadze .... Avery Schreiber
Waiter; Jail Guard .... John Remme

La Mome Pistache .... Zizi Jeanmaire
Hercule................. Michael Dantuono
Theophile............... Mitchell Greenberg
Etienne.................... Tommy Breslin
Photographer................ James Dunne
Model................... Deborah Carlson
Adam .... Darrell Barnett
Mimi....................... Donna King
Apache Leader .... Luigi Bonino
Patrons....... Nealey Gilbert, Dennis Batutis

Policemen: Tommy Breslin, John Remme, John Dolf, Dennis Batutis, Kevin McCready. The Snake: Zizi Jeanmaire, Dennis Batutis, James Horvath, Steven LaChance, Kevin McCready.

Ensemble: Deborah Carlson, Pam Cecil, Edyie Fleming, Nealey Gilbert, Linda Haberman, Nancy Hess, Brenda Holmes, Donna King, Manette LaChance, Meredith McIver, Gail Pennington, Rosemary Rado, Daryl Richardson, Linda Von Germer, Darrell Barnett, Dennis Batutis, John Dolf, James Dunne, James Horvath, Steven LaChance, Kevin McCready, Gregory Schanuel. Swings: Kim Noor, Bob Renny.

Understudies: Mr. Husmann—Michael Dantuono; Mr. Schreiber—Mitchell Greenberg; Miss

Sousa—Donna King; Mr. Brooks—Tom Batten; Mr. Dantuono—Joseph Cusanelli; Mr. Greenberg —John Remme.

Directed by Abe Burrows; entire production staged and choreographed by Roland Petit; musical direction and vocal arrangements, Stanley Lebowsky; scenery, David Mitchell; costumes, Franca Squarciapino; lighting, Thomas Skelton; orchestrations, Philip J. Lang; dance arrangements and new dance music, Donald York; sound, Larry Spurgeon; production stage manager, Mortimer Halpern; stage manager, Nate Barnett; press, The Merlin Group, Ltd., Cheryl Sue Dolby, Merle Frimark.

Place: Paris. Time: 1893.

New version, revised by Abe Burrows, of the musical first produced on Broadway May 7, 1953 for 892 performances. It was revived on Broadway by New York City Center Light Opera Company 5/16/62 for 16 performances.

ACT I

Prologue . . . . Policemen, Girls
Scene 1: Police Correctional Court
  "Maidens Typical of France" . . . . Girls
  "Maidens Typical of France" (Reprise) . . . . Girls, Court Personnel
Scene 2: Montmartre—Exterior of Bal du Paradis
Scene 3: Montmartre—Interior of Bal du Paradis
  "Never Give Anything Away" . . . . Pistache, Girls
Scene 4: Pistache's office
  "C'Est Magnifique" . . . . Pistache, Aristide
Scene 5: Interior—Bal du Paradis
  Quadrille Dance . . . . Girls, Men
Scene 6: Exterior—Bal du Paradis
  "Come Along With Me" . . . . Hilaire, Claudine
  "Come Along With Me" (Reprise) . . . . Boris
Scene 7: A jail
  "Live and Let Live" . . . . Pistache
  "I Am in Love" . . . . Aristide
Scene 8: The artist's studio
Scene 9: Exterior—Bal du Paradis
Scene 10: Interior—Bal du Paradis
  "Montmartre" . . . . Company
  Garden of Eden Ballet . . . . Pistache, Girls, Men
  "Allez-Vous En" . . . . Pistache

ACT II

Scene 1: The artist's studio
  "Never, Never Be an Artist" . . . . Artists, Boris, Aristide
Scene 2: Tabac exterior
  "It's All Right With Me" . . . . Aristide, Mimi, Girls
Scene 3: La Blanchisserie
  Apache Dance . . . . Girls, Men
Scene 4: A Paris street
Scene 5: Rooftop of La Blanchisserie
  "I Love Paris" . . . . Pistache
  "C'Est Magnifique" (Reprise) . . . . Aristide, Pistache
Scene 6: A jail
Scene 7: Court D'Assizes
  "Can-Can" . . . . Pistache, Girls, Men
Finale . . . . Company

The Moony Shapiro Songbook (1). Musical with book by Monty Norman and Julian More; music by Monty Norman; lyrics by Julian More. Produced by Stuart Ostrow in association with T.A.T. Communications Company at the Morosco Theater. Opened and closed at the evening performance, May 3, 1981.

Gary Beach   Judy Kaye
Jeff Goldblum   Annie McGreevey
Timothy Jerome

Back-Up Singers: Philip Hoffman, Audrey Lavine, Brenda Pressley. March of Time Announcer: Philip Hoffman.

Directed by Jonathan Lynn; musical numbers staged by George Faison; musical direction, Elman Anderson; scenery, Saul Radomsky; costumes, Franne Lee; lighting, Tharon Musser; production stage manager, Phil Friedman; stage manager, Perry Cline; press, John Springer Associates, Meg Gordean, Suzanne Salter, Jeffrey Wise.

Satirical view of the life and work of a writer of popular songs, portrayed revue-style by five performers playing about 100 characters, mostly show-business types. A foreign play previously produced in London.

MUSICAL NUMBERS—ACT I: "Songbook"—Company; "East River Rhapsody"—Gary Beach, Company; "Talking Picture Show"—Jeff Goldblum, Judy Kaye, Annie McGreevey, Beach; "Meg"—Timothy Jerome; "Mister Destiny"—Kaye; "Your Time Is Different to Mine"—Kaye; "Pretty Face"—Beach, McGreevey, Kaye; "Je Vous Aime, Milady"—Goldblum; "Les Halles"— McGreevey; "Olympics '36"—Company; "Nazi Party Pooper"—Jerome; "I'm Gonna Take Her Home to Momma"—McGreevey, Kaye, Goldblum, Beach; "Bumpity-Bump"—McGreevey; "The Girl in the Window"—Kaye; "Victory"—Company; "April in Wisconsin," "It's Only a Show," "Bring Back Tomorrow"—Beach; "Songbook" (Reprise)—Company.

ACT II: "Happy Hickory"—McGreevey; "When a Brother Is a Mother to His Sister"—Jerome; "Climbin' "—McGreevey; "Don't Play That Lovesong Any More"—Jerome; "Happy Hickory" (Reprise)—Company; "Lovely Sunday Mornin' "—McGreevey, Beach; "Rusty's Dream Ballet"— Kaye, Goldblum; "A Storm in My Heart"—Beach, McGreevey, Goldblum, Kaye; "The Pokenhatchit Public Protest Committee"—Company; "Happy Hickory" (Reprise)—Company; "Happy Hickory" (Reprise)—Beach, McGreevey, Kaye, Goldblum; "I Accuse"—McGreevey, Kaye; "Messages I"—Goldblum; "Messages II"—Beach; "I Found Love"—McGreevey, Kaye, Goldblum, Beach; "Don't Play That Lovesong Any More" (Reprise)—Kaye; "Golden Oldie"—Jerome; "Climbin' " (Reprise)—McGreevey, Beach, Goldblum, Kaye, Jerome; "Nostalgia"—Goldblum; Finale—Company.

Passionate Ladies (8). One-woman performance by and with Barbara Perry. Produced by Arthur Shafman and Shelly Maibaum at the Bijou Theater. Opened May 5, 1981. (Closed May 10, 1981)

Directed by Edmund Balin; introductions, Regis Cordie; incidental music and recording consultant, Leonora Shildkraut; associate producer, Andrea Shapiro. Press, Jeffrey Richards Associates, Robert Ganshaw, Ben Morse, Helen Stern, C. George Willard, Ted Killmer.

Act I: The Stripper; My Friend Shakespeare. Act II: Modern Acting (by Josephine Dillon Gable); Con Amore; Betty Bruce Is Dead.

Character portrayals of five women, in monologue: a stripper, a teacher of Shakespeare; an acting teacher (Clark Gable's first wife), a ballet teacher and a tap-dancer.

Inacent Black (14). By A. Marcus Hemphill; original music and lyrics by McFadden & Whitehead & Moore. Produced by Gloria Hope Sher, Marjorie Moon and Jay J. Cohen in association with Zaida Coles Edley and Spirit Will Productions, Inc. at the Biltmore Theater. Opened May 6, 1981. (Closed May 17, 1981)

Helwin Rydell	Gregory Miller	Charles Rydell	Count Stovall
Mama Essie Rydell	Barbara Montgomery	Percy Rydell	Bruce Strickland
Marv Rydell	Reginald Vel Johnson	Waitress	Rosanna Carter

Inacent Black	Melba Moore	Sally-Baby Washington	Lorey Hayes
Pretty Pete	Ronald Stevens	Voice of Hamilton Rydell	Ed Cambridge
Carmen Casteel	Joyce Sylvester		

Musicians: Neal Tate synthesizer, Petro Bass percussion, Kelvin Jones drums, Ron Miller guitar, Wayne Braithwaite bass.

Understudies: Messrs. Stovall, Miller, Strickland—Skip Waters; Miss Moore—Elain Graham; Misses Hayes, Sylvester—Nora Cole.

Directed by Mikell Pinkney; executive producer, Ashton Springer; scenery, Felix E. Cochren; costumes, Marty Pakledinaz; lighting, Tim Phillips; sound, Joseph Donohue; conductor, Barry Eastmond; production stage manager, Ed Cambridge; stage manager, David Blackwell; press, Jacksina & Freedman, Dolph Browning, Angela Wilson.

Time: Spring, 1980. Place: The Rydell Estate mansion in Old Westbury, L.I. and New York City. Act I, Scene 1: Friday, 10:15 A.M., study of the Rydell mansion. Scene 2: Friday, 1 P.M., Coffee Shop at N.Y. Port Authority. Scene 3: Friday, 4 P.M., Rydell mansion. Scene 4: Saturday, 9 A.M., Rydell mansion. Scene 5: Saturday, noon, Rydell mansion. Act II, Scene 1: Saturday, 2:30 P.M., near an outside phone booth, N.Y.C. Scene 2: Saturday, 3 P.M., Central Park. Scene 3: Saturday, 6 P.M., Rydell mansion. Scene 4: Sunday, 8:15 P.M., Rydell mansion.

Comic fantasy, an angel helps with the affairs of an upper middle class black family. Previously produced at the Billie Holiday Theater, Brooklyn.

*The Little Foxes (17). Revival of the play by Lillian Hellman. produced by Zev Bufman with Donald C. Carter and Jon Cutler at the Martin Beck Theater. Opened May 7, 1981.

Addie	Novella Nelson	Regina Giddens	Elizabeth Taylor
Cal	Joe Seneca	William Marshall	Humbert Allen Astredo
Birdie Hubbard	Maureen Stapleton	Benjamin Hubbard	Anthony Zerbe
Oscar Hubbard	Joe Ponazecki	Alexandra Giddens	Ann Talman
Leo Hubbard	Dennis Christopher	Horace Giddens	Tom Aldredge

Standbys: Misses Taylor, Stapleton—Carol Teitel; Messrs. Aldredge, Ponazecki, Astredo—Conrad L. Osborne; Mr. Christopher—William Youmans; Miss Nelson—Louise Stubbs; Mr. Seneca—Hugh L. Hurd.

Directed by Austin Pendleton; scenery, Andrew Jackness; costumes, Florence Klotz; lighting, Paul Gallo; music adapted by Stanley Silverman; production stage manager, Patrick Horrigan; stage manager, Brian Meister; press, Fred Nathan & Associates, Patt Dale, Eileen McMahon.

Place: A living room in the Giddens house in a small town in the South. Act I: The spring of 1900, evening. Act II: A week later, early morning. Act III: Two weeks later, late afternoon.

The Little Foxes was first produced on Broadway 2/15/39 for 410 performances and was named a Best Play of its season. It was previously revived on Broadway in the form of the musical *Regina* 10/31/49 for 56 performances and by the Repertory Theater of Lincoln Center 10/26/67 for 100 performance.

I Won't Dance (1). By Oliver Hailey. Produced by David Merrick at the Helen Hayes Theater. Opened and closed at the matinee performance, May 10, 1981.

Dom	David Selby	Kay	Arlene Golonka
Lil	Gail Strickland		

Directed by Tom O'Horgan; stage movement, Wesley Fata; incidental music, Tom O'Horgan; scenery, Bill Stabile; costumes, Marty Pakledinaz; lighting, Craig Miller; associate producer, Neal Du Brock; production stage manager, Alan Hall; stage manager, Ruth E. Rinklin; press, Solters/Roskin/Friedman, Inc., Joshua Ellis, Louise Ment.

Time: The present. Place: Los Angeles. The play was presented in two parts.

Black comedy of family frictions, sex and violence, focussing on a central character who is confined to a wheelchair.

Renée Taylor and Joseph Bologna in
their *It Had To Be You*

*It Had To Be You (25). By Renée Taylor and Joseph Bologna. Produced by Allen Klein and Julian Schlossberg with Isobel Robins at the John Golden Theater. Opened May 10, 1981.

Theda Blau . . . . Renée Taylor
Vito Pignoli . . . . Joseph Bologna

Offstage voice: Robert Alto.
Directed by Robert Drivas; scenery, Lawrence King and Michael Yeargan; costumes, Carrie F. Robbins; lighting, Roger Morgan; sound, Richard Fitzgerald; associate producer, Iris W. Keitel; production stage manager, Larry Forde; stage manager, Barbara Schneider; press, Solters/Roskin/-Friedman, Inc., Milly Schoenbaum, Kevin Patterson.
Time: The present, Christmas Eve. Place: New York City. The play was presented in two parts.
Comedy, the strange wooing of an aspiring actress and a TV producer.

*Lena Horne: The Lady and Her Music (21). Musical revue designed as a concert by Lena Horne. Produced by James M. Nederlander, Michael Frazier and Fred Walker in association with Sherman Sneed and Jack Lawrence at the Nederlander Theater. Opened May 12, 1981.

Cast: Lena Horne, Clare Bathé, Tyra Ferrell, Vondie Curtis-Hall, Deborah Lynn Bridges (alternate), Peter Oliver-Norman (alternate).

Lena's Trio: Grady Tate drums, Steve Bargonetti guitar, Bob Cranshaw bass.

Musicians: Cecil Bridgewater, Glenn Drewes, Frank Gordon, Peter Gordon, Craig S. Harris, Jack Jeffers, J.D. Parran Jr., Roger Rosenberg, Mort Silver, Warren Smith, Linda Twine (assistant conductor), Harold Vick.

Directed by Arthur Faria; musical conductor, Coleridge T. Perkinson; musical consultant, Luther Henderson; scenery, David Gropman; costumes, Stanley Simmons; Miss Horne's wardrobe, Giorgio Sant'Angelo; lighting, Thomas Skelton; production stage manager, Joe Lorden; stage manager, Jack Gianino; press, Solters/Roskin/Friedman, Inc., Joshua Ellis, Louise Ment, Cindy Valk.

Collection of song numbers dating from Cotton Club, Big Band and Hollywood days to the present, a showcase for Miss Horne's illustrious career and talents. The play was presented in two parts.

MUSICAL NUMBERS: "Life Goes On" by Paul Williams and Craig Doerge, "I'm Going to Sit Right Down and Write Myself a Letter" by Fred Ahlert and Joe Young, "Stormy Weather," "As Long as I Live" and "Raisin' the Rent" by Ted Koehler and Harold Arlen, "Push De Button" and "Lady With a Fan" by E.Y. Harburg and Harold Arlen, "Fly" by Martin Charnin, "I'm Glad There Is You" by Paul Madeira and Jimmy Dorsey, "That's What Miracles Are All About" and "If You Believe" by Charlie Smalls.

Also "From This Moment On" and "Just One of Those Things" by Cole Porter, "Love" by Ralph Blane and Hugh Martin, "A Lady Must Live," "Where or When," "The Lady Is a Tramp" and "Bewitched, Bothered and Bewildered" by Richard Rodgers and Lorenz Hart, "The Surrey With the Fringe on Top" by Richard Rodgers and Oscar Hammerstein II, "Can't Help Loving Dat Man of Mine" by Jerome Kern and Oscar Hammerstein II.

Also "Copper Colored Gal of Mine" by B. Davis and J. Fred Coots, "Deed I Do" by W. Hirsch and Fred Rose, "I Got a Name" by Norman Gimbel and Charles Fox, "Watch What Happens" by Norman Gimbel and Michel LeGrand, "I Want To Be Happy" by Vincent Youmans and Irving Caesar, "Better Than Anything" by D. Wheat and William Loughborough.

St. Mark's Gospel (20). Return engagement of the one-man performance by Alec McCowen of the Gospel According to St. Mark. Produced by Arthur Cantor and Greer Garson at the Playhouse Theater. Opened May 13, 1981. (Closed May 31, 1981)

Lighting, Leo B. Meyer; production stage manager, Larry Bussard; press, Arthur Cantor Associates.

McCowen's rendition of the Gospel was first produced off Broadway 9/7/78 for 16 performances and transferred to Broadway 10/24/78 for 18 performances.

PLAYS WHICH CLOSED
PRIOR TO BROADWAY OPENING

Productions which were organized by New York producers for Broadway presentation but which closed during their tryout performances are listed below.

One Night Stand. Musical with book and lyrics by Herb Gardner; music by Jule Styne. Produced by Joseph Kipness, Lester Osterman, Joan Culman, James M. Nederlander and Alfred Taubman in previews at the Nederlander Theater. Opened October 20, 1980. (Closed October 25, 1980)

Charlie	Charles Kimbrough	Nat; Sol's Voice	Brandon Maggart
Stage Manager	Thomas Barbour	Eddie	Jack Weston
Sid	Charles Levin	Young Eddie	Steven Boockvor
Gerry	Paul Binotto	Amanda	Catherine Cox

Assistant Stage Manager....... Michael Petro
Margie .... Kate Mostel
Young Charlie
(evening perfs.) .... William Morrison

Young Charlie (matinees). Christopher Balcom
Molly .... Terri Treas
Leo; Barclay................... John Mineo

Suzies: Kerry Casserly, Cheryl Clark, Ida Gilliams, Sonja Stuart, Terri Treas, Kathrynann Wright.

Directed by John Dexter; choreography, Peter Gennaro; musical direction, Eric Stern; scenery, Robin Wagner; costumes, Patricia Zipprodt; lighting, Andy Phillips; orchestrations, Philip J. Lang; dance arrangements, Marvin Laird; production stage manager, Nicholas Russiyan; stage manager, Robert O'Rourke; press, Seymour Krawitz, Patricia McLean Krawitz, Martin Shwartz.

Time: The present, 8 to 10:30 P.M. Place: The bare stage of the Nederlander Theater between bookings.

A once-successful song writer attempts to put on a new show.

ACT I

"Everybody Loves Me"...	Charlie
"There Was a Time" (Part I)..	Charlie
"A Little Travellin' Music Please".......................................	Charlie, Suzies
"Go Out Big"...	Eddie
"Someday Soon"..	Young Charlie
"For You"..	Eddie, Young Charlie
"I Am Writing a Love Song"...	Young Charlie

ACT II

"Gettin' Some"..	Charlie, Sid, Gerry
"Somebody Stole My Kazoo"..	Charlie, Sid, Gerry
"I Am Writing a Love Song" (Reprise).....................................	Charlie
"We Used to Talk Once"	Margie, Eddie
"The 'Now' Dance"..	The 'Now' Company
"Long Way From Home"..	Amanda
"Too Old To Be So Young"..	Charlie
"Everybody Loves Me" (Reprise)..	Charlie
"There Was a Time" (Part II)	Charlie, Amanda
"Here Comes Never"..	Eddie

The Stitch in Time. By Marc Connelly. Produced by M.C. Productions, Leonard Finger associate producer, in rehearsals for an opening at the ANTA Theater February 3, 1981. (Closed in rehearsal January 6, 1981)

Cast: John Hammond, Wesley Addy, Stephen Bradbury, Ray Dooley, Polly Draper, George Hall, Kurt Johnson, Thomas Ruisinger, Amanda Plummer, Carol Teitel.

Directed by Larry Forde; scenery, Bob Guerra; costumes, Carrie F. Robbins; lighting, John Gleason; music arrangements, Marian McPartland; press, Henry Luhrman, Terry M. Lilly.

About a college student with a remarkable psychic gift.

Sarah in America. By Ruth Wolff. Produced by John F. Kennedy Center for the Performing Arts, Roger L. Stevens chairman, Marta Istomin, artistic director, in a pre-Broadway tour. Opened January 23, 1981 at the American Shakespeare Theater, Stratford, Conn. (Closed March 7, 1981 at the Eisenhower Theater of the Kennedy Center, Washington, D.C.)

Sarah Bernhardt...	Lilli Palmer
Marianne..	Georgia Southcotte

Directed by Robert Helpmann; scenery, William Ritman; costumes, Theoni V. Aldredge; lighting, Richard Nelson; special effects, Chic Silber; visuals, Lucie Grosvenor; musical direction, John

Lilli Palmer as Sarah Bernhardt in *Sarah in America*

Lanchbery; production stage manager, Mitchell Erickson; press, Jeffrey Richards Associates, C. George Willard, Robert Ganshaw, Ben Morse, Helen Stern, Ted Killmer.

Act I: The first American tour, 1880–81. Act II: The sixth American tour (first farewell tour), 1905–6; the eighth American tour (third farewell tour), 1913–14; the ninth American tour, (final farewell tour), 1916–18.

Sarah Bernhardt on her American tours aged 36 to 74; virtually a one-woman show, with the other role, that of a maid, non-speaking.

Jitters. By David French. Produced by Arthur Cantor and Greer Garson in a pre-Broadway tryout at the Walnut Street Theater, Philadelphia. Opened March 18, 1981. (Closed March 29, 1981)

Jessica Logan	June Havoc	Nick	William Carden
Philip Mastorakis	George Sperdakos	Susi	Mary Pat Gleason
Tom Kent	Joel Polis	Peggy	Helena Power
George Ellsworth	Jim Jansen	Robert Ross	Dennis Boutsikaris
Patrick Flanagan	Jack Aranson		

Directed by Bill Glassco; scenery, John Lee Beatty; costumes, Robert Wojewodski; lighting, Jamie Gallagher; press, Karen Gromis.

Show business comedy, a theater company tests a play for possible Broadway production. The play was presented in three parts. Previously produced at the Tarragon Theater, Toronto and the long Wharf Theater, New Haven, Conn.

A Reel American Hero. Musical with book by Judith GeBauer and Burt Vinocur; music by Gordon Kent and Stephanie Peters; lyrics by Gerald Paul Hillman and Stephanie Peters. Produced by Gerald Paul Hillman at the Rialto Theater. Opened March 25, 1981; closed in previews March 29, 1981.

Cast: Hillary Bailey, Vidya Kaur, Peter Newman, Jess Richards, Roxanne White.
Directed by Nancy Tribush Hillman; choreography, George Bunt; musical direction and dance arrangements, Roger Neil; scenery and lighting supervision, Harry Silverglat Darrow; costumes, Carol Wenz; lighting, Giles Hogya; orchestrations and vocal arrangements, Gordon Kent; press, Bruce Cohen.
Musical about the influence of the music of the 1930s and 1940s on the America of today. Previously produced off off Broadway by Chareeva.

PLAYS PRODUCED OFF BROADWAY

Some distinctions between off-Broadway and Broadway productions at one end of the scale and off-off-Broadway productions at the other were blurred in the New York theater of the 1970s and 1980s. For the purposes of this *Best Plays* listing the term "off Broadway" is used to distinguish a professional from a showcase (off-off-Broadway) production and signifies a show which opened for general audiences in a mid-Manhattan theater seating 499 or fewer and 1) employed an Equity cast, 2) planned a regular schedule of 7 or 8 performances a week and 3) offered itself to public comment by critics at a designated opening performance.

Occasional exceptions of inclusion (never of exclusion) are made to take in selected Brooklyn productions, visiting troupes, borderline cases and a few non-qualifying productions which readers might expect to find in this list because they appear under an off-Broadway heading in other major sources of record.

Figures in parentheses following a play's title give number of performances. These figures do not include previews or extra non-profit performances.

Plays marked with an asterisk (*) were still running on June 1, 1981. Their number of performances is figured from opening night through May 31, 1981.

Certain programs of off-Broadway companies are exceptions to our rule of counting the number of performances from the date of the press coverage. When the official opening takes place late in the run of a play's regularly-priced public or subscription performances (after previews) we count the first performance of record, not the press date, as opening night—and in each such case in the listing we note the variance and give the press date.

In a listing of a show's numbers—dances, sketches, musical scenes, etc.—the titles of songs are identified wherever possible by their appearance in quotation marks (").

Most entries of off-Broadway productions which ran fewer than 20 performances or scheduled fewer than 8 performances a week are somewhat abbreviated, as are entries on running repertory programs repeated from previous years.

HOLDOVERS FROM PREVIOUS SEASONS

Plays which were running on June 1, 1980 are listed below. More detailed information about them appears in previous *Best Plays* volumes of appropriate date. Important cast changes since opening night are recorded in a section of this volume.

*The Fantasticks (8,768; longest continuous run of record in the American theater). Musical suggested by the play *Les Romantiques* by Edmond Rostand; book and lyrics by Tom Jones; music by Harvey Schmidt. Opened May 30, 1960.

Vanities (1,785). By Jack Heifner. Opened March 2, 1976; suspended May 27, 1979 after 1,313 performances; resumed June 19, 1979. (Closed August 3, 1980)

I'm Getting My Act Together and Taking It on the Road (1,165). Musical with book and lyrics by Gretchen Cryer; music by Nancy Ford. Opened May 16, 1978. (Closed March 15, 1981)

*****Scrambled Feet** (823). Musical revue by John Driver and Jeffrey Haddow. Opened June 11, 1979.

Gertrude Stein Gertrude Stein Gertrude Stein (373). One-character play by Marty Martin with Pat Carroll. Opened June 24, 1979. (Closed August 3, 1980)

*****One Mo' Time** (670). Vaudeville show conceived by Vernel Bagneris. Opened October 22, 1979.

Table Settings (264). By James Lapine. Opened January 14, 1980. (Closed August 31, 1980)

American National Theater and Academy (ANTA). 1979–80 schedule ended with **Tintypes** (134). Musical revue conceived by Mary Kyte with Mel Marvin and Gary Pearle. Opened April 17, 1979. (Closed August 10, 1980 and transferred to Broadway; see its entry in the Plays Produced on Broadway section of this volume)

Manhattan Theater Club. 1979–80 schedule ended with **Mass Appeal** (104). Opened April 22, 1980. (Closed July 20, 1980)

Fourtune (241). Musical with book and lyrics by Bill Russell; music by Ronald Melrose. Opened April 27, 1980. (Closed November 23, 1980)

A Coupla White Chicks Sitting Around Talking (432). By John Ford Noonan. Opened April 28, 1980. (Closed May 17, 1981)

New York Shakespeare Festival Public Theater. 1979–80 schedule included **Mother Courage and Her Children** (40). Revival of the play by Bertolt Brecht; adapted by Ntozake Shangé; music by William Elliott; lyrics adapted by Louisa Rose. Opened May 13, 1980. (Closed June 15, 1980)

BAM Theater Company. 1979–80 repertory of revivals ended with **He & She** (27). By Rachel Crothers. Opened May 22, 1980. (Closed June 15, 1980 matinee). **The Marriage Dance, An Evening of Farce** (27). Program of two one-act plays: *The Wedding* by Bertolt Brecht, translated by Helga Ciulei from the original German; and *The Purging* by Georges Feydeau, adapted by Peter Barnes. Opened May 22, 1980. (Closed June 15, 1980)

PLAYS PRODUCED JUNE 1, 1980–MAY 31, 1981

The American Place Theater. 1979–80 schedule ended with **Killings on the Last Line** (21). By Lavonne Mueller. Produced by The American Place Theater, Wynn Handman director, Julia Miles associate director, at the American Place Theater. Opened May 29, 1980; see note. (Closed June 15, 1980)

Directed by Dorothy Silver; scenery, Henry Millman; costumes, Mimi Maxmen; lighting, Annie Wrightson; music for "Trucker's Sweetheart," Dennis Bacigalupi; stage managers, W. Scott Allison, Mary Lockhart; press, Jeffrey Richards Associates. With Ellen Barkin, Sandy Martin, Verona

Barnes, Rosanna Carter, Joan MacIntosh, Alice Drummond, Marilyn Hamlin, Marian Primont, Pat McNamara, Kathleen Chalfant.
Women workers in a factory making parts for nuclear reactors.
Note: Press date for *Killings on the Last Line* was 6/5/80.

Knitters in the Sun (6). By George Bemberg. Produced by New World Theater at Theater de Lys. Opened June 4, 1980. (Closed June 8, 1980 matinee)

Directed by Jane Stanton; scenery, Bob Phillips; lighting, Mal Sturchio; costumes, Kim Walker; production stage manager, Mark Keller; press, Max Eisen, Francine L. Trevens. With Alexandra O'Karma, Joan Shepard, Evan Thompson, Kelly Fitzpatrick, Will Jeffries.
Problems of a troubled family in a New England college town.

Circle Repertory Company. 1979–80 schedule included **The Woolgatherer** (92). By William Mastrosimone. Opened June 5, 1980. (Closed in repertory September 14, 1980 matinee). **Macready!** (34). One-man performance by and with Frank Barrie; based on the diaries of William Charles Macready. Opened July 29, 1980 in repertory with *The Woolgatherer*. (Closed in repertory September 14, 1980) Produced by Circle Repertory, Marshall W. Mason artistic director, at the Circle Theater.

BOTH PLAYS: Producing director, Porter Van Zandt; dramaturg, Milan Stitt; production manager, Alice Galloway; press, Richard Frankel, Glenna L. Clay.

THE WOOLGATHERER

Rose . . . . Patricia Wettig
Cliff . . . . Peter Weller

Directed by John Bettenbender; scenery, Karl Eigsti; costumes, Joan E. Weiss; lighting, Dennis Parichy; stage manager, Jody Boese.
Time: Now. Place: South Philadelphia, an efficiency apartment. The play was presented in two parts.
An aggressive truck driver is determined to spend the night with the sales girl with whom he has just struck up an acquaintance.

MACREADY!

Directed by Donald MacKechnie; produced by arrangement with Globe Enterprises.
The play was presented in two parts.
Subtitled "A Celebration of the Actor," a portrayal by Frank Barrie of the British actor William Charles Macready (1793–1873), based on his diaries. A foreign play previously produced in England.

New York Shakespeare Festival Public Theater. 1979–80 schedule ended with **FOB** (42). By David Henry Hwang. Produced by New York Shakespeare Festival, Joseph Papp producer, at the Public Theater (Martinson Hall). Opened June 8, 1980 matinee. (Closed July 13, 1980)

Onstage Stage Manager #1;	Dale . . . . Calvin Jung
Percussion . . . . Tzi Ma	Grace . . . . Ginny Yang
Onstage Stage Manager #2;	Steve . . . . John Lone
Percussion . . . . Willy Corpus	Musician; Voice of Radio DJ . . . Lucia Hwong

Directed by Mako; musical direction, Lucia Hwong; scenery, Akira Yoshimura, James E. Mayo; costumes, Susan Hum; lighting, Victor En Yu Tan; battle sequence choreography, John Lone; assistant director, David Oyama; production supervisor, Jason Steven Cohen; production stage manager, Greg Fauss; stage manager, Ruth Kreshka; press, Merle Debuskey, Bob Ullman, Richard Kornberg.

Time: The present. Place: The back room of a small Chinese restaurant in Torrance, Calif. The play was presented in two parts.

Conflict between traditions and Americanization among Chinese immigrants. Previously produced by the Eugene O'Neill Memorial Center National Playwrights Conference, Waterford, Conn.

The Cocktail Party (8). Revival of the play by T.S. Eliot. Produced by The Guardian Company at the Orpheum Theater. Opened June 10, 1980. (Closed June 15, 1980)

Directed by Christopher Cade; scenery, Evelyn Sakash; costumes, Carol Oditz; lighting, Tony Quintavella; incidental music, George David Weiss; dialect coach, Binnie Ravich; press, Shirley Herz, Jan Greenberg. With Alexander Scourby, Jay Bond, Elizabeth Brigulio, Kathryn Callaghan, Richard Lockwood, Joan Matthiessen, Edward Morehouse, Naomi Riordan, James Umphlett.

The Cocktail Party was first produced on Broadway 1/21/50 for 409 performances. It was revived off Broadway in APA-Phoenix repertory 10/7/68 for 44 performances.

Chase a Rainbow (6). Musical with book, music and lyrics by Harry Stone. Produced by Joan Dunham and Segue Productions at Theater Four. Opened June 12, 1980. (Closed June 15, 1980)

Directed by Sue Lawless; choreography, Bick Goss; musical direction, John Franceschina; scenery, Michael Rizzo; costumes, Rita Watson; lighting, Patrika Brown; sound, Martin Feldman; press, Seymour Krawitz. With Ted Pugh, Virginia Sandifur, Suzanne Dawson, Chuck Karel, Stephen McNaughton, Jan Neuberger.

Writer trying to make up his mind between the muse and the money.

Billy Bishop Goes to War (78). Transfer from Broadway of the musical written and composed by John Gray in collaboration with Eric Peterson. Produced by Mike Nichols and Lewis Allen at the Theater de Lys. Opened June 17, 1980. (Closed August 24, 1980)

Cast: Billy Bishop, Upperclassman, Adjutant Perrault, Officer, Sir Hugh Cecil, Lady St. Helier, Cedric, Doctor, Gen. John Higgins, Tommy, Lovely Helene, Albert Ball, Walter Bourne, Officer, Gen. Hugh M. Trenchard, Servant, King George V—Eric Peterson; Narrator, Pianist—John Gray.

Directed by John Gray; scenery, David Gropman; lighting, Jennifer Tipton; sound, Robert Kerzman; co-produced by Vancouver East Cultural Center, Christopher Wootten executive director; associate producers, Stephen Graham, Ventures West Capital, Inc.; production stage manager, George Gracey; press, David Powers, Barbara Carroll.

Billy Bishop Goes to War was produced on Broadway for 12 performances 5/29/80–6/7/80, after which it transferred to off Broadway in the same production; see its entry in the Plays Produced on Broadway section of *The Best Plays of 1979–80*.

Cedric Smith replaced Eric Peterson and Ross Douglas replaced John Gray 8/12/80.

Roundabout Theater Company. 1979–80 schedule of revivals included **Look Back in Anger** (147) by John Osborne. Opened June 6, 1980, press date June 19, 1980. (Closed October 12, 1980) **Fallen Angels** (13). By Noel Coward. Opened July 10, 1980. (Closed July 20, 1980) Produced by Roundabout Theater Company, Gene Feist and Michael Fried producing directors, at the Roundabout Theater (*Look Back in Anger* at Stage One, *Fallen Angels* at Stage Two).

LOOK BACK IN ANGER

Jimmy Porter	Malcolm McDowell	Helena Charles	Fran Brill
Cliff Lewis	Raymond Hardie	Colonel Redfern	Robert Burr
Allison Porter	Lisa Banes		

Carol Teitel and Valerie French in Noel Coward's *Fallen Angels*

Directed by Ted Craig; scenery, Roger Mooney; lighting, Dennis Parichy; costumes, A. Christina Giannini; musical supervision, Philip Campanella; production stage manager, M.R. Jacobs.

Look Back in Anger was first produced on Broadway 10/1/57 for 407 performances and was named a Best Play of its season and received the Critics Award for best foreign play. It was revived off Broadway in the 1958–59 season, immediately after closing on Broadway.

FALLEN ANGELS

Julia Sterroll	Valerie French	Willy Banbury	Don Perkins
Fred Sterroll	John Clarkson	Jane Banbury	Carol Teitel
Saunders	Beulah Garrick	Maurice Duclos	Stephen Schnetzer

Directed by Stephen Hollis; scenery, Roger Mooney; costumes, Andrew B. Marlay; lighting, Norman Coates; sound, Philip Campanella; production stage manager, Michael S. Mantel; press, Susan Bloch & Co.

Place: The dining-drawing room of the Sterrolls' flat in London. Act I: Morning. Act II: Evening. Act III: The next morning.

Fallen Angels was first produced on Broadway 1/12/27 for 36 performances. It was revived on Broadway 1/17/56 for 239 performances.

To Bury a Cousin (54). Revival of the play by Gus Weill. Produced by Shelly Beychok and Tom Nolan at the Cherry Lane Theater. Opened June 25, 1980. (Closed August 10, 1980)

Ben	Robert Bloodworth	Papa	Harvey Pierce
Bert	Harry Goz	Sister	Annie Deutsch Abbott
Mama	Virginia Daly	W.A. Simpson	Walter Williamson

Rabbi . . . . Reuben Schafer   Hilda. Diane Tarleton
Lita. . . . . Lauren Craig

Directed by Philip Oesterman; scenery, Douglas W. Schmidt; costumes, Robert Wojewodski; lighting, David F. Segal; incidental music, Hayden Wayne; production stage manager, Tom Capps; press, Milly Schoenbaum, Kevin Patterson.

To Bury a Cousin was previously produced off Broadway 5/16/67 for 5 performances. The play was presented in two parts.

Cassatt (5). By Dorothy Louise. Produced by Howard Burnett by arrangement with the Philadelphia Company at Playhouse 46. Opened June 26, 1980. (Closed June 29, 1980)

Directed by Robert Hedley; scenery, John Jensen; costumes, Gerry Leahy; lighting, Ronald Wallace; assistant producer, Maggi Burnett; stage manager, Kender Jones; press, Susan L. Schulman. With Tony Musante, Esther Benson, Carlin Glynn, Barbara Spiegel, Jeanne Ruskin, Marcia Mahon, Elek Hartman.

The romance of the painters Mary Cassatt and Degas.

Light Opera of Manhattan (LOOM). Repertory of two new revival productions and 11 running operetta revivals. **Trial by Jury** book and lyrics by W.S. Gilbert, music by Arthur Sullivan; **The Zoo** book and lyrics by B.C. Stephenson ("Bolton Rowe"), music by Arthur Sullivan; **Cox & Box** book and lyrics by F.C. Burnand, music by Arthur Sullivan (21). Program of three one-act operettas. Opened July 23, 1980 and March 18, 1981. (Closed March 29, 1981) **The Desert Song** (35). Book and lyrics by Otto Harbach, Oscar Hammerstein II and Frank Mandel; music by Sigmund Romberg. Opened October 22, 1980. (Closed November 23, 1980) Produced by The Light Opera of Manhattan, William Mount-Burke producer-director, at Eastside Playhouse.

ALL PLAYS—Directed by William Mount-Burke; musical director, William Mount-Burke; associate director, Raymond Allen; choreography, Jerry Gotham. Assistant musical director and pianist, Brian Molloy; assistant conductor and organist, J. Michael Bart; stage manager, Jerry Gotham; press, Jean Dalrymple, Peggy Friedman.

TRIAL BY JURY

Learned Judge . . . . Raymond Allen	Counsel for the Plaintiff . . . . . Craig Schulman
Plaintiff (Angelina) . . . . Joyce Bolton	(Richard Perry)
(Cheryl Savitt)	Usher . . . . Vashek Pazdera (J.J. Weber)
Defendant (Edwin) . . . . Gary Pitts	Foreman of the Jury . . . . Clem Egan
	(Bruce Gould)

THE ZOO

Cesculapius Carboy . . . . Gary Pitts	Letitia . . . . . Kathleen Cuvelier (Cheryl Savitt)
Thomas Brown . . Clem Egan (Robert Barker)	Eliza Smith . . . . Karen Hartman
Mr. Grinder . . . . Raymond Allen (J.J. Weber)	

COX & BOX

Cox . . . . Stephen O'Mara (Robert Barker)	Bouncer . . . . Vashek Pazdera (J.J. Weber)
Box . . . . . . Craig Schulman (Stephen O'Mara)	

Parentheses indicate new casting in the 3/18/81 presentation, after the original presentation 7/23/80.

7/23/80 Ensemble: Kaye Avara, Cathy Cosgrove, Kathleen Cuvelier, Clem Egan, Linda Forrester, Karen Hartman, Joanne Jamieson, Catherine Lankford, Jonathan Levy, Lucille Mascia, Barbara McCullam, Bruce McKillip, Stephen O'Mara, Samuel Silvers, Rhanda Elizabeth Spotton, David Stix, Evan Willis.

3/18/81 Ensemble: Joyce Bolton, Jon Brothers, Cathy Cosgrove, Nancy Crumpler, Bruce Gould, Anna Jessica, Joanne Jamieson, Ann Kirschner, Reneé Kramer, Cole Mobley, Richard Perry, Elizabeth Ramsey, Rhanda Elizabeth Spotton, Michael Wainstein, Clem Egan, Constance Hutchinson, Anthony Michalik.

Trial by Jury and *The Zoo* directed by William Mount-Burke; *Cox & Box* directed by Raymond Allen; scenery, Elouise Meyer; assistant conductor and organist, Stanley German.

Trial by Jury was last revived in LOOM repertory last season. *The Zoo* is a romance set in London's zoological gardens, written in 1875 and never before professionally produced in America. *Cox & Box* was last revived on Broadway by the D'Oyly Carte Company 2/19/51 for 8 performances.

THE DESERT SONG

Sid El Kar	Stephen O'Mara	Lt. La Vergne	Richard Perry
Mindar	Bruce Gould	Gen. Birabeau	Raymond Allen
Hassi	Bruce McKillip	Ali Ben Ali	J.J. Weber
Pierre Birabeau	Gary Ridley	Azuri	Kathleen Cuvelier
Benjamin Kidd	James Nadeaux	Susan	Karen Hartman
Capt. Paul Fontaine	Aaron Wood	Margot Bonvalet	Mary Jennings

Ensemble: Joe Chvala, Cathy Cosgrove, Kathleen Cuvelier, Chandler Evans, Bruce Gould, Anna Jessica, Catherine Lankford, Cole Mobley, Richard Perry, Rhanda Elizabeth Spotton, Don Stewart, Patricia Welch, Evan Willis, Joyce Bolton, Wagne Smith, Ann Kirshner, Eileen Butler, Celeste Mancinelli, Jon Brothers, Michael Wainstein.

Scenery, Elouise Meyer; costumes, James Nadeaux; lighting, Peggy Clark; special book director, Philip Mathias; special music coaching, Stan German; special consultant, Alfred Simon.

Time: The 1920s. Place: Northern Africa. Act I, Scene 1: The retreat of the Red Shadow in the Riff Mountains, evening. Scene 2: A room in General Birabeau's house, the same evening. Act II, Scene 1: The harem of Ali Ben Ali, afternoon of the following day. Scene 2: A corridor, a few minutes later. Scene 3: The Room of the Silken Couch, a few minutes later. Scene 4: Edge of the desert, the following morning half an hour before dawn. Scene 5: Courtyard of General Birabeau's house, two days later.

The Desert Song was last revived on Broadway 9/5/73 for 15 performances, in a version differing somewhat from this one.

ACT I

Prelude and opening chorus: "Feasting Song" .... Riffs
"The Riff Song" .... Red Shadow, Riffs, Sid
"Feasting Song" (Reprise)... Riffs
"The Riff Song" (Reprise)... Red Shadow, Sid
"Margot".. Paul, Soldiers
Scene 1 Finale
Scene 2 opening chorus: "Why Did We Marry Soldiers" .... Soldiers' Wives, Ensemble
"Oh, Girls, Girls, Girls" .... Margot, Ensemble
"Romance" .... Margot, Girls
Duet: "Then You Will Know"... Margot, Pierre
Trio & Chorus: "I Want a Kiss" .... Margot, Paul, Pierre, Ensemble
Duet: "It" .... Susan, Bennie, Girls
Duet: "The Desert Song" .... Margot, Red Shadow
Act I Finale: "Won't You Wish Us Luck" .... Margot, Paul, Pierre, Ensemble

ACT II

Entr'Acte
Eastern & Western Love
    "Let Love Go," "One Flower in
        Your Garden," "One Alone" .... Red Shadow, Sid, Ali, Men

"The Sabre Song".. Margot, Red Shadow
Scene 3 Finaletto: "You Love Me" .... Margot, Red Shadow
"Farewell"... Red Shadow, Men
Scene 5 opening: "All Hail to the General" .... Margot, Paul, Birabeau, Girls
"It" (Reprise) .... Susan, Bennie
Finale: "One Alone" (Reprise) .... Margot, Red Shadow

LOOM's 1980–81 repertory included eleven running productions mounted in previous seasons and presented on the following schedule (operettas have book and lyrics by W.S. Gilbert and music by Arthur Sullivan unless otherwise noted): *The Mikado* (42), opened June 4, July 2, August 20, 1980 and Jan. 21, Feb. 25 and April 1, 1981; *Iolanthe* (21), opened June 11, July 9 and August 27, 1980; *H.M.S. Pinafore* (42), opened June 18, July 16 and September 3, 1980 and February 4, March 11 and April 29, 1981; *The Pirates of Penzance* (35), opened June 25 and August 13, 1980 and January 28, March 4 and April 8, 1981.

Also *Naughty Marietta* (14). book and lyrics by Rida Johnson Young, music by Victor Herbert, opened July 30, 1980; *The Merry Widow* (35), based on the book by Victor Leon and Leo Stein, music by Franz Lehar, English lyrics by Alice Hammerstein Mathias, opened September 10, 1980 and January 7, 1981; *The Vagabond King* (21), book and lyrics by W.H. Post and Brian Hooker, music by Rudolf Friml, opened October 1, 1980; *Babes in Toyland* (49), book by William Mount-Burke and Alice Hammerstein Mathias, music by Victor Herbert, lyrics by Alice Hammerstein Mathias, opened November 26, 1980.

Also *The Gondoliers* (14), opened February 11, 1981; *Patience* (14), opened April 15, 1981; *The Student Prince* (28), book and lyrics by Dorothy Donnelly, music by Sigmund Romberg, opened May 6, 1981. (Repertory closed May 31, 1981)

Performers in LOOM repertory during the 1980–81 season included James Weber, Craig Schulman, Raymond Allen, Tom Olmstead, Gary Pitts, Karen Hartman, Ethelmae Mason, Dennis English, Bruce McKillip, Cheryl Savitt, Mary Lee Rubens, Cathy Cosgrove, Vashek Pazdera, Joyce Bolton, Lucille Mascia, Penny Orloff, Catherine Lankford, Patricia Ernest, Kathleen Cuvelier, Linda Forrester, Stephen O'Mara, Gregg Fischer, Clem Egan, Nancy Temple, Rhanda Elizabeth Spotton, Heather Ross, Edward J. Crafts, Mary Jennings, G. Michael Harvey, James Nadeaux, Ed Harrison, Jean Stroup Miller, Richard Perry, Aaron Wood, Ann Kirschner, Robert Barker, Bruce Gould, Jeff Severson, Claudia O'Neill, Kevin Usher, Dino DiMario, Susanna Organek, Irma Rogers, Georgia McEver, Jon Brothers, Elizabeth Burgess-Harr, Nancy Temple, Julia Davidson, Gary Ridley, Richard Smithies, Lloyd Harris, Anthony Michalik, Eleanore Knapp.

The Pirates of Penzance (30). Revival of the operetta with book and lyrics by W.S. Gilbert; music by Arthur Sullivan. Produced by the New York Shakespeare Festival, Joseph Papp producer, at the Delacorte Theater in Central Park. Opened August 5, 1980. (Closed August 31, 1980)

Pirate King	Kevin Kline	Kate	Marcie Shaw
Samuel	Stephen Hanan	Isabel	Wendy Wolfe
Frederic	Rex Smith	Mabel	Linda Ronstadt
Ruth	Patricia Routledge	Maj.-Gen Stanley.............	George Rose
Edith..................	Alexandra Korey	Sergeant	Tony Azito

Maj.-Gen. Stanley's Daughters: Robin Boudreau, Maria Guida, Nancy Heikin, Bonnie Simmons.

Pirates, Police: Dean Badolato, Mark Beudert, Brian Bullard, Walter Caldwell, Keith David, Tim Flavin, G. Eugene Moose, Joseph Neal, Walter Niehenke, Joe Pichette, Barry Tarallo, Michael Edwin Willson.

Musicians: Richard Cohen, Simeon Westbrooke winds; Keith Underwood flutes; Lauren Draper, Ron Stinson trumpets; Keith Draper trombone; Dan Berlinghoff, Allen Shawn keyboards; William Moersch, William Ruyle percussion; Dennis Masuzzo bass.

Understudies: Mr. Kline—Keith David; Mr. Hanan—G. Eugene Moose; Mr. Smith—Barry Tarallo; Mr. Azito—Tim Flavin; Mr. Rose—Walter Niehenke; Miss Routledge—Wendy Wolfe; Miss Ronstadt—Nancy Heikin; Misses Korey, Shaw, Wolfe—Maria Guida.

Directed by Wilford Leach; choreography, Graciela Daniele; musical direction, William Elliott; scenery, Bob Shaw, Jack Chandler, Wilford Leach; costumes, Patricia McGourty; lighting, Jennifer Tipton; sound, Don Ketteler; orchestrations, arrangements, vocal preparation, William Elliott; assistant choreographer, Adam Grammis; production supervisor, Jason Steven Cohen; production stage manager, Zane Weiner; stage manager, Frank Difilia; press, Merle Debuskey, Bob Ullman, Richard Kornberg, Ed Bullins.

In this production, "Sorry Her Lot" from *H.M.S. Pinafore* and "My Eyes Are Fully Open" from *Ruddigore* were added to the score. This production transferred to Broadway 1/8/81, and its list of musical numbers appears in its entry in the Plays Produced on Broadway section of this volume.

A Sleepless Night With an Honest Man (6). By Lee Schneider. Produced by Scott Goldstein, Lee Schneider and Property Productions at the Orpheum Theater. Opened August 14, 1980. (Closed August 17, 1980)

Directed by Scott Goldstein; scenery, Charles Powell; costumes, Johnetta Lever; lighting, D. Schweppe; art direction, Ditto; dialogue direction, Van Hinman; stage manager, William Ickes; press, Max Eisen, Francine L. Trevens. With Edmond Collins, Robin Harvey, Gisele Richardson.

Benedict Arnold during his London years.

An Act of Kindness (13). By Joseph Julian. Produced by Charlotte Bunin and Marvin Gutin with Joyce Beauvais at the Harold Clurman Theater. Opened September 11, 1980. (Closed September 21, 1980)

Directed by Mark Gordon; scenery, Gregory William Bolton; costumes, Steven Birnbaum; lighting, Carol B. Sealey; stage manager, Priscilla Guastavino; press, David Lipsky. With Scotty Bloch, Eddie Jones.

Loneliness acting upon two strangers, a male writer and a female diarist.

Transcendental Love (14). By Daryl Boylan. Produced by Frank and Mark Gero in association with the Provincetown Playhouse in the Asolo State Theater production at the Provincetown Playhouse. Opened September 25, 1980. (Closed October 5, 1980)

Directed by Robert Strane; scenery, Bennet Averyt; costumes, Catherine King; lighting, Martin Petlock; music, John Franceschina; Press, Shirley Herz, Jan Greenberg. With Robert Murch, Deborah Fezelle, Monique Morgan, Tom Brennan.

Comedy, Ralph Waldo Emerson encounters the transcendental movement in the person of a lady editor. Previously produced at the Asolo Theater, Sarasota, Fla.

A Matter of Opinion (8). Musical with book and lyrics by Mary Elizabeth Hauer; music by Harold Danko and John Jacobson. Produced by Miracle Expressions Inc. at the Players Theater. Opened September 30, 1980. (Closed October 5, 1980)

Directed and choreographed by Shari Upbin; musical supervision, Harold Danko; musical direction, John Jacobson; scenery and costumes, John Arnone; lighting, Joanna Schielke; production supervisor, David S. Rosenak; stage manager, Michael Spellman; press, Solters/Roskin/Friedman Inc., Milly Schoenbaum, Kevin Patterson. With Suzanne Smart, Charles Randolph Wright, Vickie D. Chappell, Janet Bliss, Ralph Braun, Leigh Finner, Kate Klugman, Seymour Penzner, David Anchel, Andy Bey.

Trial of realists vs. fantasists, with rhymed dialogue. The play was presented in two parts.

*New York Shakespeare Festival Public Theater. Schedule of nine programs. **Girls, Girls, Girls** (6). Musical with book and lyrics by Marilyn Suzanne Miller; music by Cheryl Hardwick. Opened September 30, 1980. (Closed October 4, 1980) **The Sea Gull** (40). Revival of the play by Anton Chekhov; adapted by Jean-Claude Van Itallie. Opened November 11, 1980. (Closed December 14, 1980) **Dead End Kids** (97). Conceived by JoAnne Akalaitis in a Mabou Mines production. Opened November 18, 1980. (Closed

March 1, 1981) **True West** (24). By Sam Shepard. Opened December 23, 1980. (Closed January 11, 1981) **Alice in Concert** (32). Musical with book, music and lyrics by Elizabeth Swados; based on Lewis Carroll's *Alice in Wonderland* and *Through the Looking Glass.* Opened December 29, 1980. (Closed January 25, 1981) **Penguin Touquet** (26). Written and musically scored by Richard Foreman. Co-produced by the Ontological-Hysteric Theater. Opened February 1, 1981. (Closed February 22, 1981)

Also **Mary Stuart** (41). By Wolfgang Hildesheimer; translated by Christopher Holmes. A Dodger Theater production, Michael David, Des McAnuff, Edward Strong and Sherman Warner associate directors. Opened February 15, 1981. (Closed March 22, 1981) **Long Day's Journey Into Night** (87). Revival of the play by Eugene O'Neill in the Richard Allen Center for Culture and Art production. Opened March 18, 1981. (Closed May 31, 1981)*The Haggadah, a Passover Cantata** (56). Return engagement of the musical by Elizabeth Swados; adapted from texts by Elie Wiesel. Opened April 14, 1981. Produced by New York Shakespeare Festival, Joseph Papp producer, at the Public Theater (see note).

ALL PLAYS: Production supervisor, Jason Steven Cohen; press, Merle Debuskey, Richard Kornberg, Ed Bullins, John Howlett.

GIRLS, GIRLS, GIRLS

Cast: Valri Bromfield, Frances Conroy, Anne DeSalvo, Judith Ivey, Jay O. Sanders.
Directed by Bob Balaban; musical direction, Cheryl Hardwick; choreography, Graciela Daniele; scenery, Akira Yoshimura; costumes, Karen Roston; lighting, Arden Fingerhut; associate set designer, James E. Mayo.
Self-styled "A collection of different kinds of pieces about different kinds of women."

THE SEA GULL

Owners of the Estate:		Visitors & Guests:	
Arkadina	Rosemary Harris	Trigorin	Christopher Walken
Sorin	George Hall	Nina	Kathryn Dowling
Treplev	Brent Spiner	Dorn	F. Murray Abraham
Managers of the Estate:		Medvedenko	Richard Russell Ramos
Shamraev	Michael Egan	Workers on the Estate:	
Paulina	Joyce Van Patten	Yakov	Michael Butler
Masha	Pamela Payton-Wright	Cook	Janni Brenn
		Maid	Gayle Harbor
		Watchman	Fritz Sperberg

Understudies: Miss Harris—Annette Hunt; Mr. Spiner—Michael Butler; Messrs. Hall, Abraham —John Straub; Miss Dowling—Gayle Harbor; Mr. Egan—Ken Costigan; Misses Payton-Wright, Van Patten—Janni Brenn; Messrs. Walken, Ramos, Butler—Fritz Sperberg.
Directed by Andrei Serban; music, Elizbath Swados; arranged by Elizabeth Swados and Lee Curreri; scenery, Michael H. Yeargan; costumes, Jane Greenwood; lighting, Jennifer Tipton; production stage manager, Richard Jakiel; stage manager, Susan Green.
Place: Sorin's country estate. The play was presented in three parts with intermissions following Acts I and III (between Acts III and IV, two years pass).
This often-revived Chekhov play was first produced on Broadway 5/5/16 for 11 performances. Its most recent New York professional revival of record was by New York Shakespeare Festival 1/8/75 for 42 performances.

DEAD END KIDS

Cast: Scientists, Alchemists, Citizens, Observers—David Brisbin, Scotty Snyder, John Fistos, Michael Kuhling, Greg Mehrten, Terry O'Reilly, Juliet Glass, Zachary Glass; Head Alchemist— Michael Kuhling; Lecturer—B-St. John Schofield; Alchemy Announcer—Chas Cowing; Magician

Mark Linn-Baker, Richard Cox, Meryl Streep (as Alice) and
Michael Jeter in Elizabeth Swados's musical *Alice in Concert*

—Terry O'Reilly; Mary, Prophetess, Gretchen, Secretary, Tracy Henson—Ellen McElduff; Madame Curie—Ruth Maleczech; Faust, L.R. Groves—George Bartenieff; Mephistopheles—Greg Mehrten, Michael Kuhling, B-St. John Schofield, John Fistos, David Brisbin, Terry O'Reilly; Gossip Columnist—Greg Mehrten; Taped Voices—Hilary Granson, Juliet Glass, William Raymond.

Directed by JoAnne Akalaitis; scenery, Robert Israel, JoAnne Akalaitis; costumes, Sally Rosen; lighting, Beverly Emmons; chreography, Mary Overlie, Gail Conrad, Michael Smith; film, David Hardy; music, Philip Glass, Hector Berlioz, Ronnie and the Pomonas, The Four Sargents, Ramsey Lewis.

Mabou Mines theater collaborative members: JoAnne Akalaitis, Lee Breuer, L.B. Dallas, Ruth Maleczech, Frederick Neumann, Terry O'Reilly, Bill Raymond.

Text sources: *The Hermetical and Alchemical Writings of Paracelsus; Madame Curie* by Eve Curie; *Pierre Curie* by Marie Curie; *Faust* by Goethe; Gen. L.R. Groves's report on Alamogordo to the Secretary of War; *The Aleph* by Jorge Luis Borges; *Mammalian Radiation Lethality* (Columbia University); *Effects of Radioactive Fallout on Livestock in the Event of Nuclear War* (National Academy of Science); *Nuclear Terms* (Dept. of Energy); Rasmussen report on Nuclear reactor safety (Nuclear Regulatory Commission).

Dramatized concerns over the perils of radiation, subtitled "A History of Nuclear Power."

TRUE WEST

Lee	Peter Boyle	Saul Kimmer	Louis Zorich
Austin	Tommy Lee Jones	Mom	Georgine Hall

Understudies: Messrs. Jones, Zorich—Dan Moran; Mr. Boyle—William Andrews; Miss Hall—Regina David.

Directed by Robert Woodruff; scenery, David Gropman; costumes, William Ivey Long; lighting, Beverly Emmons; production stage manager, Ruth Kreshka; stage manager, Jane Hubbard.

Love-hate relationship of two brothers, one a screen writer and the other a drifter. The play was presented in two parts.

ALICE IN CONCERT

Cast: Meryl Streep (Alice), Betty Aberlin, Stuart Baker-Bergen, Richard Cox, Sheila Dabney, Rodney Hudson, Michael Jeter, Charles Lanyer, Mark Linn-Baker, Kathryn Morath, Amanda Plummer, Deborah Rush.

Musicians: David Conrad, Carolyn Dutton, Judith Fleisher, Robert J. Magnuson, David Sawyer, William Uttley, Tony Viscardo.

Understudies: Miss Streep—Deborah Rush; Women—Kathryn Morath; Men—David Patrick Kelly, Pi Douglass; Back-Up Singer—David Patrick Kelly.

Directed by Joseph Papp; choreography, Graciela Daniele; conductor, Elizabeth Swados; scenery, Michael H. Yeargan; costumes, Theoni V. Aldredge; lighting, Arden Fingerhut; vocal arrangements, Carolyn Dutton; production stage manager, Richard Jakiel; stage manager, Susan Green.

The adventures of Carroll's Alice, previously produced in a concert version entitled *Wonderland in Concert.*

MUSICAL NUMBERS—ACT I: "What There Is" (based on the poem by Kenneth Patchen)— Meryl Streep; "The Rabbit's Excuse"—Mark Linn-Baker, Company; "Down Down Down"—Streep, Betty Aberlin, Company; "Drink Me"—Deborah Rush, Rodney Hudson, Michael Jeter, Stuart Baker-Bergen, Company; "Good-By Feet"—Streep, Company; "The Rabbit's House"—Jeter, Amanda Plummer, Company; "Bill's Lament"—Jeter, Men; "Caterpillar's Advice"—Richard Cox, Company; "Beautiful Soup"—Streep; "Wow Wow Wow"—Sheila Dabney, Company; "Pretty Piggy"—Streep, Company; "Cheshire Puss"—Hudson, Company; "If You Knew Time"—Aberlin, Company; "No Room No Room"—Cox, Linn-Baker, Jeter, Streep, Company; "Starting Out Again" —Streep, Company; "White Roses Red"—Baker-Bergen, Jeter, Hudson, Rush; "Alphabet"—Company; "Red Queen"—Rush, Company; "Never Play Croquet"—Streep, Company; "Mock Turtle Lament"—Linn-Baker, Rush, Streep; "The Lobster Quadrille"—Cox, Aberlin, Company; "Eating Mushrooms"—Streep, Company.

ACT II: "Child of Pure Unclouded Brow"—Rush, Baker-Bergen; "Jabberwocky"—Cox, Company; "The Bird Song"—Rush, Linn-Baker, Jeter; "Humpty Dumpty"—Streep, Company; "Tweedledum & Tweedledee"—Jeter, Baker-Bergen; "The Walrus & The Carpenter"—Charles Lanyer, Plummer, Company; "The White Queen"—Streep; "The White Knight"—Linn-Baker, Streep; "An Aged, Aged Man"—Streep, Linn-Baker; "The Examination"—Kathryn Morath, Aberlin, Rush, Dabney; "The Lion & The Unicorn"—Dabney; "What There Is" (Reprise)—Hudson, Streep, Cox; "Queen Alice"—Company; "What Is a Letter"—Streep, Aberlin, Company.

PENGUIN TOUQUET

Agatha	Kate Manheim	Waiter in Turban	Shelly Desai
Psychiatrist	David Warrilow	Waiter Who Plays Cymbals	Eric Loeb
Other (Same) Woman	Diana Venora	Tumbling Waiter	Robert Schlee
Grand Dame	Gretel Cummings	Waiter Who Drops	
Tourist	Brenda Currin	Tray	Jeffrey Alan Chandler
Dangerous Man	Raymond J. Barry		

Directed by Richard Foreman; scenery, Heidi Landesman, Richard Foreman; costumes, Carol Oditz; lighting, Pat Collins; sound, Daniel M. Schreier; production stage manager, Michael Chambers; stage manager, Loretta Robertson.

Described by its creator as "a sort of intellectual *Hellzapoppin*," a fantastic kaleidoscope of stage images in the Foreman manner. The show was presented without intermission.

MARY STUART

Executioner	Roy Cooper	Mary Stuart	Roberta Maxwell
Mate	Donald Vanhorn	Didier	George Lloyd

Guard.....................	Todd Waring	Andrew.....................	Brad O'Hare
Gervais...................	Stephen Markle	John	Philip Casnoff
Raoul	John Bottom	Paulet	Herb Foster
Symmons	Ron Faber	Kent	George Hall
Jane......................	Rebecca Schull	Dean of Peterborough.....	Wyman Pendleton
Anne......................	Cecile Callan		

Understudies: Miss Maxwell—Rebecca Schull; Misses Schull, Callan—Johanna Leister; Messrs. Cooper, Lloyd, Faber, Foster, Hall, Pendleton—Jack R. Marks; Messrs. Bottom, Casnoff, Vanhorn, Markle, O'Hare—Todd Waring.

Directed by Des McAnuff; scenery, Jim Clayburgh; costumes, Patricia McGourty; lighting, Fred Buchholz; production stage manager, Bill McComb; stage manager, Wendy Chapin.

Absurdist treatment of the execution of Mary Queen of Scots, a foreign (German) play in its American premiere. The play was presented without intermission.

LONG DAY'S JOURNEY INTO NIGHT

James Tyrone................	Earle Hyman	Edmund Tyrone	Peter Francis-James
Mary Tyrone	Gloria Foster	Cathleen................	Samantha McKoy
Jamie Tyrone..............	Al Freeman Jr.		

Directed by Geraldine Fitzgerald; produced by Hazel J. Bryant; scenery, John Scheffler; costumes, Myrna Colley-Lee; lighting, Paul Mathiesen; production stage manager, William Dolive.

Time: A day in August 1912. Place: The living room of the Tyrones' summer home. Act I: 8:30 A.M. Act II, Scene 1: Around 12:45. Scene 2: About a half hour later. Act III: About 6:30 that evening. Act IV: Around midnight. The play was presented in two parts with the intermission following Act II.

Transfer of an off-off-Broadway production of O'Neill's play with an all-black cast. The last professional New York revival of this play took place off Broadway 1/28/76 for 11 performances.

THE HAGGADAH

Richard Allen	Esther Levy
Anthony B. Asbury	Larry Marshall
Shami Chaikin	Steven Memel
Craig Chang	Martin Robinson
Victor Cook	David Schechter
Sheila Dabney	Peter Schlosser
Jossie de Guzman	Zvee Scooler
Michael Edward-Stevens	Ira Siff
Onni Johnson	Louise Smith
Sally Kate	Kerry Stubbs

Understudies: Joanna Peled, Martha Wingate, Sol Frieder, Kristen Palmieri, Aramis Estevez, Robert Stillman, Steven Memel, Shami Chaikin, Richard Allen.

Musicians: Carolyn Dutton violin; Judith Fleisher keyboards; Leopoldo F. Fleming, David Sawyer percussion; Robert J. Magnuson reeds.

Directed by Elizabeth Swados; scenery, costumes, puppetry and masks, Julie Taymor; lighting, Arden Fingerhut; production stage manager, Richard Jakiel; stage manager, Gretchen Green.

This story of Exodus, performed without intermission, was first produced 3/31/80 for 64 performances.

The list of song and narrative sequences in *The Haggadah* appears on pages 417–8 of *The Best Plays of 1979–80.*

Other 1980–81 programs produced at the Public Theater included *Presenting All of David Langston Smyrl (Or Is It?),* a one-man cabaret show by and with David Langston Smyrl, for 26 performances 11/7/80–12/7/80; *Texts for Nothing,* one-man show with Joseph Chaikin, adapted by Joseph Chaikin and Steven Kent from *Texts for Nothing* and *How It Is,* for 18 performances 3/3/81–3/22/81; The Acting Company productions of *Il Campiello* and *Waiting for Godot* (see entries elsewhere in the Plays Produced Off Broadway section of this volume); plus various experimental and guest productions—see entries in the Plays Produced Off Off Broadway section of this volume.

Note: In Joseph Papp's Public Theater there are many auditoria. *Girls, Girls Girls* and *Dead End Kids* played The Other Stage, *The Sea Gull* and *Penguin Touquet* played the Estelle R. Newman Theater, *True West* played Martinson Hall, *Alice in Concert* and *Long Day's Journey Into Night* played the Anspacher Theater, *Mary Stuart* and *The Haggadah* played LuEsther Hall.

Album (254). By David Rimmer. Produced by Gene Persson, Richard S. Bright, John Loesser in association with 20th Century-Fox Productions and by special arrangement with the WPA Theater at the Cherry Lane Theater. Opened October 1, 1980. (Closed May 10, 1981)

| Peggy | Jenny Wright | Billy | Kevin Bacon |
| Trish | Jan Leslie Harding | Boo | Keith Gordon |

Understudies: Misses Wright, Harding—Jennifer Grey; Messrs. Bacon, Gordon—Bruce Mac-Vittie.

Directed by Joan Micklin Silver; scenery, David Potts; costumes, Susan Denison; lighting, Jeff Davis; sound, Alex McIntyre; production stage manager, Bethe Ward; press, Jeffrey Richards Associates, Ben Morse, C. George Willard, Robert Ganshaw, Helen Stern, Ted Killmer.

Act I: Girls in bedrooms, boys in dormitories. Scene 1: In my room—October 1963, Trish's bedroom and the hallway outside, night (Peggy, Trish, Billy and Boo are 14). Scene 2: The letter—June 1964, Billy's camp, night (Billy is 15). Scene 3: Ticket to ride—September 1965, Trish's bedroom, dusk (Peggy and Trish are 16). Scene 4: Ain't it just like the night—November 1965, Boo's room at school, twilight (Billy and Boo are 16).

Act II: The night before graduation, June 1967. Scene 1: Things we said today—The high school; the corridors and the teachers' room, 10 P.M. (Peggy, Billy, Boo and Trish are 18. Scene 2: Big girls don't cry—The quarry, midnight (Peggy and Billy). Scene 3: Runaway—A room at the Paradise Motel, 2 A.M. (Trish and Boo). Scene 4: Graduation day—The quarry, dawn (Peggy and Billy, Trish and Boo).

Four adolescents growing up. Previously produced off off Broadway at WPA Theater.

Sam Robards replaced Keith Gordon, Ralph Davies replaced Kevin Bacon and Tracy Pollan replaced Jenny Wright 2/10/81.

*The Negro Ensemble Company. Schedule of five programs. **The Sixteenth Round** (40). By Samm-Art Williams. Opened October 7, 1980; see note. (Closed November 9, 1980) **Zooman and the Sign** (33). By Charles Fuller. Opened December 7, 1980. (Closed January 4, 1981) **Weep Not for Me** (48). By Gus Edwards. Opened January 27, 1981; see note. (Closed March 8, 1981). **In an Upstate Motel** (36). Opened April 4, 1981; see note. (Closed May 3, 1981) ***Home** (29). Return engagement of the play by Samm-Art Williams. Opened May 8, 1981. Produced by The Negro Ensemble Company, Douglas Turner Ward artistic director, Gerald S. Krone managing director, Leon B. Denmark managing director as of 5/7/81, at Theater Four.

THE SIXTEENTH ROUND

| Jesse Taft | Paul Benjamin | Lemar Jefferson | Roscoe Orman |
| Marsha Lacewell | Rosalind Cash | | |

Directed by Horacena J. Taylor; scenery, Felix E. Cochren; costumes, Judy Dearing; lighting, Shirley Prendergast; production stage manager, Clinton Turner Davis; stage manager, Femi Sarah Heggie; press, Howard Atlee, Tom Trenkle.

Time: The present, August to October. Place: North Philadelphia, Pa., the apartment of Marsha Lacewell and Jesse Taft. Act I, Scene 1: Middle of August. Scene 2: The next day. Act II, Scene 1: Middle of September. Scene 2: Early October, Sunday morning. Scene 3: Early October, Sunday night.

Dishonest, has-been prize fighter hiding out from the retribution of gangsters.

ZOOMAN AND THE SIGN

Zooman	Giancarlo Esposito	Russell Odoms	Terrance Terry Ellis
Rachel Tate	Mary Alice	Donald Jackson	Steven A. Jones
Emmett Tate	Carl Gordon	Ash Boswell	Frances Foster
Reuben Tate	Ray Aranha	Grace Georges	Carol Lynn Maillard
Victor Tate	Alvin Alexis		

Understudy: Misses Alice, Maillard—Phylicia Ayers-Allen.

Directed by Douglas Turner Ward; scenery, Rodney J. Lucas; costumes, Judy Dearing; lighting, Shirley Prendergast; production stage manager, Clinton Turner Davis; stage manager, Femi Sarah Heggie.

Time: The present. Place: Philadelphia, Pa; the home of Rachel and Reuben Tate; the street outside; various locations for Zooman. The play was presented in two parts.

Father presses for punishment of a punk who caused the death of his daughter in a black city neighborhood.

A Best Play; see page 193.

WEEP NOT FOR ME

Lillian Hendricks	Ethel Ayler	Janet Adams	Phylicia Ayers-Allen
Jake Hendricks	Bill Cobbs	Melvin Walker	Robert Gossett
Crissie Adams	Seret Scott	Henry George	Brian Evaret Chandler
Deanie Adams	Elain Graham	Sylvia George	Sarallen
Wilbur Adams	Chuck Patterson		

Directed by Douglas Turner Ward; scenery, Wynn Thomas; costumes, Judy Dearing; lighting, William H. Grant III; production stage manager, Clinton Turner Davis; stage manager, Femi Sarah Heggie.

Time: Summer, now or in the very near future. Place: An apartment in the South Bronx section of New York City. Act I, Scene 1: Evening. Scene 2: The following evening. Scene 3: The same night, hours later. Scene 4: The same night, about 3 A.M. Act II, Scene 1: 6 o'clock the following morning. Scene 2: 9 o'clock that evening. Scene 3: Later that night.

IN AN UPSTATE MOTEL

Female Shadow	Phylicia Ayers-Allen	Queenie	Donna Bailey
Male Shadow	Carl Gordon	Duke	Charles Henry Patterson

Directed by Paul Carter Harrison; scenery, Edward Burbridge; costumes, Judy Dearing; lighting, Shirley Prendergast; sound, Regge Life; production stage manager, Femi Sarah Heggie; stage manager, Wayne Elbert.

Place: An upstate motel. Act I: Now/and then. Act II: Now/and then.

Criminals on the run, trying to escape the consequences of big city violence—their own as well as that of others.

HOME

Cephus Miles	Samuel L. Jackson	Woman Two	Michele Shay
Woman One/Pattie			
Mae Wells	L. Scott Caldwell		

Understudy: Mr. Jackson—Eugene Lee.

Directed by Douglas Turner Ward; scenery, Felix E. Cochren; costumes, Alvin B. Perry; lighting, William H. Grant III; production stage manager, Clinton Turner Davis; stage manager, Femi Sarah Heggie.

Time: Late 1950s to the present. Place: Cross Roads, North Carolina; a prison in Raleigh, N.C.; a very, very large American City. The play was performed without intermission.

Home was first produced 12/14/79 by NEC for 82 performances and was named a Best Play of its season. It transferred to Broadway 5/7/80 for an additional 279 performances.

Juanita Mahone replaced L. Scott Caldwell and Carol Lynn Maillard replaced Michele Shay 5/26/81.

Note: Press date for *The Sixteenth Round* was 10/19/80, for *Weep Not for Me* 2/8/81, for *In an Upstate Motel* 4/14/81.

The Phoenix Theater. Schedule of five programs. **Bonjour, Là, Bonjour** (30). By Michel Tremblay; translated by John van Burek and Bill Glassco. Opened October 9, 1980; see note. (Closed November 2, 1980) **Beyond Therapy** (30). By Christopher Durang. Opened January 1, 1981; see note. (Closed January 25, 1981) **The Captivity of Pixie Shedman** (29). By Romulus Linney. Opened January 29, 1981; see note. (Closed February 22, 1981) **Meetings** (30). By Mustapha Matura. Opened March 26, 1981; see note. (Closed April 19, 1981) And *Isn't It Romantic* by Wendy Wasserstein scheduled to open June 13, 1981. Produced by The Phoenix Theater, T. Edward Hambleton managing director, Steven Robman artistic director, at Marymount Manhattan Theater.

BONJOUR, LÀ, BONJOUR

Gabriel	Fred Stuthman	Lucienne	Veronica Castang
Albertine	Beverly May	Monique	Cara Duff-MacCormick
Charlotte	Mary Fogarty	Denise	Judith Drake
Serge	William Katt	Nicole	Dianne Wiest

Directed by Steven Robman; scenery, Marjorie Kellogg; costumes, Jennifer Von Mayrhauser; lighting, Ronald M. Bundt; production stage manager, J. Thomas Vivian; press, Susan L. Schulman, Winnie Sampson, Sandi Kimmel.

Place: Montreal. The play was performed without intermission.

Son returns from a trip to find his family relationships severely disturbed. A foreign play previously produced in Canada and at the Tyrone Guthrie Theater, Minneapolis and the Huntington Hartford Theater in Los Angeles.

BEYOND THERAPY

Prudence	Sigourney Weaver	Mrs. Charlotte Wallace	Kate McGregor-Stewart
Bruce	Stephen Collins		
Dr. Stuart Framingham	Jim Borrelli	Bob	Jack Gilpin
Paul	Nick Stannard	Andrew	Conan McCarty

Directed by Jerry Zaks; scenery, Karen Schulz; costumes, Jennifer Von Mayrhauser; lighting, Richard Nelson; sound, David Rapkin.

Sex and psychiatry among a couple and their respective therapists.

THE CAPTIVITY OF PIXIE SHEDMAN

Bertram Shedman	William Carden	Doc Bertram Shedman	Jon DeVries
Pixie Shedman	Penelope Allen	Doc Bertram Shedman Jr.	Leon Russom
Col. Bertram Shedman	Ron Randell	Sandy Shedman	Sarah Nevin

Directed by John Pasquin; scenery, Robert Blackman; costumes, Linda Fisher; lighting, Jennifer Tipton; sound, David Rapkin; dialect consultant, Timothy Monich.

Southern playwright evokes characters and events from his family's past when he tries to dramatize his grandmother's diary.

MEETINGS

Hugh	Carl Lumbly	Elsa	Seret Scott
Jean	Michele Shay		

Directed by Gerald Gutierrez; scenery, John Kasarda; costumes, Karen Miller; lighting Spencer Mosse; sound, David Rapkin; dialect consultant, Beverly Wideman.

Upward-mobile Trinidadian couple caught in the middle of the conflict between old and new values, in a series of encounters in a modern but foodless kitchen setting. A foreign play in its world premiere production.

Note: Press date for *Bonjour, Là, Bonjour* was 10/13/80, for *Beyond Therapy* was 1/5/81, for *The Captivity of Pixie Shedman* was 2/2/81, for *Meetings* was 3/30/81.

Richie (8). By Robert Somerfeld. Produced by Lorin E. Price in association with Roberta Weissman at the Orpheum Theater. Opened October 13, 1980. (Closed October 19, 1980)

Directed by Sherwood Arthur; scenery, Rene D'Auriac; costumes, Margo LaZaro; lighting, Eric Gertner; production stage manager, Bill McComb; press, Cheryl Sue Dolby, Eileen McMahon. With Eric Brown, Stephen Pearlman, Delphi Harrington, George Bamford, Lisa Michaelis, Bea Tendler.

Child of 15 must decide which divorced parent he prefers. The play was presented in three acts.

*Really Rosie (282). Musical with book and lyrics by Maurice Sendak; music by Carole King. Produced by John H.P. Davis and Sheldon Riss in association with Alexander S. Bowers and The Chelsea Theater Center at the Chelsea Theater Center Upstairs Theater; see note. Opened October 14, 1980.

Rosie	Tisha Campbell	Pierre	B.J. Barie
Kathy	April Lerman	Chicken Soup	Jermaine Campbell
Alligator	Joe LaBenz IV	Lion	Matthew Kolmes
Johnny	Wade Raley		

Neighborhood Kids: Lara Berk, Ruben Cuevas, Matthew Kolmes. Mothers: Alison Price, Bibi Humes.

Understudies: Tisha Campbell—April Lerman; Jermaine Campbell—Ruben Cuevas; General Understudies—Lara Berk, Ruben Cuevas, Matthew Kolmes.

Directed and choreographed by Patricia Birch; design, Maurice Sendak; musical arrangements and direction, Joel Silberman; scenery supervision, Douglas W. Schmidt; costume supervision, Carrie F. Robbins; lighting supervision, John Gleason; production stage manager, Janet Friedman; press, Shirley Herz, Jan Greenberg, Sam Rudy.

The play was presented without intermission.

Rosie of Sendak's *The Sign on Rosie's Door* entertains her friends the Nutshell Kids (from Sendak's *Nutshell Library*) by making believe she is collecting material for a Hollywood movie in which she is to star. Previously produced in an animated cartoon version and at the Musical Theater Lab, Washington, D.C.

Note: *Really Rosie* transferred to American Place Theater 11/26/80, following its final performance at Chelsea Theater Center 11/23/80.

MUSICAL NUMBERS

Overture
"Really Rosie" .... Rosie
"Simple Humble Neighborhood" .... Rosie
"Alligators All Around" .... Alligator, Company
"One Was Johnny" .... Johnny
"Pierre" .... Pierre, Company
"Screaming and Yelling" .... Rosie, Company
"The Awful Truth" .... Kathy, Johnny, Alligator, Pierre
"Very Far Away" .... Company
"Avenue P" .... Rosie
"Chicken Soup With Rice" .... Company

William Hurt and Lindsay Crouse in a scene from the Circle
Repertory production of Romulus Linney's *Childe Byron*

Circle Repertory Company. Schedule of six programs. **The Diviners** (41). By Jim Leonard
Jr. Opened October 16, 1980. (Closed November 20, 1980) **Twelfth Night** (27) by William
Shakespeare, December 12, 1980; and **The Beaver Coat** (17) by Gerhart Hauptmann,
translated by Michael Feingold, opened January 11, 1981. Repertory of two revivals.
(Repertory closed February 1, 1981) **Childe Byron** (53). By Romulus Linney. Opened
February 26, 1981. (Closed April 12, 1981) **In Connecticut** (30). By Roy London. Opened
April 30, 1981. (Closed May 24, 1981). And *A Tale Told* by Lanford Wilson scheduled
to open June 11, 1981. Produced by Circle Repertory, Marshall W. Mason artistic director,
at the Circle Theater.

ALL PLAYS: Producing director, Porter Van Zandt; production manager, Alice Galloway; resident stage managers, Jody Boese, Fred Reinglas; press, Richard Frankel, Jane Brandmeir.

THE DIVINERS

Basil Bennett . . . . Jack Davidson	C.C. Showers . . . . Timothy Shelton
Dewey Maples . . . . John Dossett	Ferris Layman . . . . Jimmie Ray Weeks
Buddy Layman . . . . Robert MacNaughton	Norma Henshaw . . . . Jacqueline Brookes
Melvin Wilder . . . . Ben Siegler	Goldie Short . . . . Mollie Collison
Luella Bennett . . . . Elizabeth Sturges	Darlene Henshaw . . . . Laura Hughes
Jennie Mae Layman . . . . Lisa Pelikan	

Directed by Tom Evans; scenery, John Lee Beatty; costumes, Jennifer Von Mayrhauser; lighting,
Arden Fingerhut; stage manager, James M. Arnemann.

Time: The early 1930s. Place: In the homes, fields and public gathering places of the mythical southern Indiana town of Zion, population 40. The play was presented in two parts.

Retarded child with a gift for dowsing, a retired preacher and others in the compression chamber of a very small town. Previously produced at the American College Theater Festival (first prize winner), Washington, D.C.

TWELFTH NIGHT

Orsino	Jay O. Sanders	Feste	Colin Stinton
Curio	Rob Gomes	Malvolio	Marshall W. Mason
Valentine	David Pillard	Olivia	Trish Hawkins
Viola	Lindsay Crouse	Antonio	Robert LuPone
Sea Captain; Priest	Burke Pearson	Sebastian	W.H. Macy
Sir Toby Belch	Michael Lerner	Fabian	Charles T. Harper
Maria	Marcell Rosenblatt	Officer	Ken Kliban
Sir Andrew Aguecheek	Jake Dengel		

Musicians: Lydia Chemelar flute, Lindsay Crouse flute, Charles T. Harper percussion, Robert LuPone oboe, W.H. Macy guitar.

Place: A city in Illyria and the nearby seacoast. The play was presented in two parts.

THE BEAVER COAT

Frau Wolf	Tanya Berezin	Mitteldorf	Burke Pearson
Leontine Wolf	Carol Wade	Judge Wehrhahn	Michael Ayr
Julius Wolf	Ken Kliban	Glasenapp	Colin Stinton
Adelaide Wolf	Jane Fleiss	Krueger	Jake Dengel
Volkov	Tom Brennan	Dr. Fleischer	W.H. Macy
Motes	Charles T. Harper	Philip	Eben Davidson
Frau Motes	Marcell Rosenblatt		

Time: About 1890. Place: Outskirts of Berlin. The play was presented in two parts.

BOTH PLAYS—Scenery, Fred Kolouch; costumes, Clifford Capone; lighting, Dennis Parichy; musical direction, Sara Sugihara; fight director, Peter Nels; production stage manager, Daniel Morris.

TWELFTH NIGHT—Directed by David Mamet; assistant director, Judy Dennis.

The last professional New York production of *Twelfth Night* (other than in musical version) was 3/2/72 at Lincoln Center for 44 performances.

THE BEAVER COAT—Directed by John Bishop; assistant director, Geoffrey Schlaes; cultural consultant, Fay Howard; stage manager, Andrea Naier.

1893 German comedy of thievery and bureaucratic bumbling. This is its first New York production of record under this title.

CHILDE BYRON

Ada	Lindsay Crouse	Young Woman	Stephanie Musnick
Byron	William Hurt	Young Man	Timothy Shelton
Boy	John Dossett	Girl	Patricia Wettig
Man	Richard Seff	Woman	Stephanie Gordon

Directed by Marshall W. Mason; scenery, David Potts; costumes, Michael Warren Powell; lighting, Dennis Parichy; fight director, Peter Nels; sound, Bruce Kaiser, Chuck London; visuals, Daniel Irvine; movement, Mardi Philips; production stage manager, Alice Galloway.

Time: Nov. 27, 1852. Place: London, the bedroom of Augusta Ada, Countess of Lovelace. The play was presented in two parts.

The relationship between Byron and his daughter viewed from the perspective of her deathbed, with quotes from his works. The play was presented in two parts. Previously produced at the Virginia Museum Theater and the Actors' Theater of Louisville.

Debra Mooney replaced Lindsay Crouse 4/2/81.

IN CONNECTICUT

Candy Schull	Rosemary Prinz	Giannina DiPinto	Henrietta Bagley
Irene Call	Lisa Emery	Andrew Call	Robert LuPone
Louis	Jeff McCracken	Valerie Call	Sharon Madden
Federico DiPinto	Shelby Buford Jr.	Maxie	Rob Gomes

Directed by Daniel Irvine and Marshall W. Mason; scenery, David Potts; costumes, Joan E. Weiss; lighting, Dennis Parichy; sound, Chuck London; original music by Michael Valenti; stage manager, M.S. Howard.

Place: A house in New Preston, Conn. Act I: Nearly noon on the Wednesday before Memorial Day. Act II: About seven hours later.

A family's problems in moving from the suburbs to New York City. Previously produced in workshop at Circle Repertory (under the title *In Vienna*) and at the GeVa Theater, Rochester, N.Y.

Circle Repertory also presented Rita Gardner's one-woman show *Say It With Music—Theater Songs of the Twenties* for 3 performances 2/21, 2/23 and 3/1.

Classic Stage Company (CSC). Repertory of five programs. **Oedipus Rex** (58). Revival of the play by Sophocles; translated by Paul Roche. Opened October 16, 1981. **Oedipus at Colonus** (39). Revival of the play by Sophocles; translated by Paul Roche. Opened October 23, 1981. **Antigone** (57). Revival of the play by Sophocles; translated by Paul Roche. Opened October 30, 1981. **Gilles de Rais (Bluebeard)** (32). By Roger Planchon; English version by John Burgess. Opened January 23, 1981. **Woyzeck** and **Leonce and Lena** (30). By George Büchner; English versions by Christopher Martin. Opened April 23, 1981. (Repertory closed May 17, 1981) Produced by CSC Repertory, Christopher Martin artistic director, Dennis Turner executive director, at the Abbey Theater.

ALL PLAYS: Directed by Christopher Martin; music composition and direction, Noble Shropshire; press, Stephen J. Holland.

PERFORMER	"OEDIPUS REX"	"OEDIPUS AT COLONUS"	"ANTIGONE"
Timothy Barrett	Chorus	Chorus	Chorus
Jonathan Bolt	Chorus; Messenger	Chorus; Messenger;	Chorus; Messenger Last Messenger
Julie Krasnow	Antigone		
John Mackay	Chorus Leader	Chorus Leader	Chorus Leader
Christopher Martin	Tiresias		Tiresias
Mary Eileen O'Donnell		Ismene	Ismene
Catherine Rust	Manto		Manto; Euridice
Noble Shropshire	Shepherd	Chorus	Haemon
David Snizek	Chorus	Polyneices	Chorus
Tom Spiller	Corinthian	Chorus	Sentry
Robert Stattel	Oedipus	Oedipus	
Susan Stern	Ismene		
Karen Sunde	Jocasta	Antigone	Antigone
Eric Tavaris	Creon	Creon	Creon
Randall Wheatley	Chorus	Chorus	Chorus
Walter Williamson	Chorus	Theseus	Chorus

Design, Terry A. Bennett; technical direction and lighting, Seth Price; production stage manager, Ryan Kelly.

The last professional New York productions of these Sophocles plays took place as follows: *Oedipus Rex* off Broadway by Roundabout in the 1969–70 season; *Oedipus at Colonus* on Broadway by the National Theater of Greece 11/10/76 for 3 performances; *Antigone* off Broadway by CSC in another

Christopher Martin in the title role of *Gilles de Rais*

translation 12/9/75 for 40 performances. The plays were performed without intermission, and on 11/9/80, 11/29/80, 12/31/80 and 4/18/81 they were presented in marathon performances of the three-play cycle.

PERFORMER	"GILLES DE RAIS"	"WOYZECK"	"LEONCE AND LENA"
Timothy Barrett	Poitou	Monkeyman; 1st Worker; Pawnbroker	Councillor; Policeman
Jonathan Bolt	Captain	Drum Major	Councillor; Inspector
Masha Buell		Katy	Worker; Chambermaid
Michael L.R. Devine	Jean Le Ferron; Gabriel	Mouthorgan; Soldier	Worker; 1st Valet
Paul Eickelberg	Child		
John Mackay	Bishop	Captain	King
Christopher Martin	Gilles de Rais		
Mary Eileen O'Donnell	La Meffraye	Margaret	Governess
Blake Morgan Pitchford	Child		
Catherine Rust	Girl	Grandmother	Lena
Noble Shropshire	Francois Prelati	Karl	Leonce
David Snizek	Roger	Sergeant	Councillor; Chaplain
Tom Spiller	Abbe Blanchet	Andres	Councillor; Schoolmaster
Robert Stattel	Jean the Good	Woyzeck	

PERFORMER	"GILLES DE RAIS"	"WOYZECK"	"LEONCE AND LENA"
Karen Sunde	Wandering Soldier	Marie	Rosetta
Eric Tavaris	Jean Blouyn		Valero
Peter Tulipan	Michael	Canaryman; Soldier	2d Valet; Worker
Randall Wheatley	Henriet	Horseman; 2d Worker	1st Policeman; Councillor
Walter Williamson	Stranger	Doctor	Lord Chamberlain

GILLES DE RAIS—Design, Pamela Howard; lighting, Christopher Martin; dramaturg, Karen Sunde; production stage manager, Ryan Kelly.

Study of a monstrous 15th century murderer, a Bluebeard. A foreign play previously produced in Paris. The play was presented in two parts.

WOYZECK and LEONCE AND LENA—Design, Terry A. Bennett; choreography, Carol Flemming; lighting, Christopher Martin; production stage manager, K.R. Williams.

The last professional New York revival of *Woyzeck* was at the Public Theater off Broadway 3/24/76 for 22 performances. *Leonce and Lena* has received several experimental stagings, one of them last season by CSC for 6 performances.

The American Place Theater. Schedule of four programs. **The Impossible H.L. Mencken** (25). By John Rothman. Opened October 19, 1980. (Closed November 9, 1980) **Memory of Whiteness** (16) By Richard Hamburger. Opened January 13, 1981. (Closed January 25, 1981) **The Amazin' Casey Stengel, or Can't Anybody Here Speak This Game?** (13). By Michael Zettler and Shelly Altman. Opened April 21, 1981. (Closed May 3, 1981) and *The Fuehrer Bunker,* a musical by W.D. Snodgrass and Richard Peaslee, scheduled to open June 2, 1981. Produced by The American Place Theater, Wynn Handman director, Julia Miles associate director, at the American Place Theater.

THE IMPOSSIBLE H.L. MENCKEN

H.L. Mencken	John Rothman
Bartender	Jack Gremli

Directed by Scott Redman; musical direction, Michael Minard; scenery, Michael Molly; costumes, William Ivey Long, lighting, James F. Ingalls; music, Michael Minard; dance movement, Art Bridgeman; press, Jeffrey Richards Associates.

Rothman as Mencken in virtually a one-man show adapted from Mencken's life and works and taking place in a barroom setting.

MEMORY OF WHITENESS

Ben	Bernard Duffy	Leon	David Brooks
Grandma	Katherine Squire	Sherry	Donna Davis
Agnes	Lois Markle	Boy	Rusty Jacobs

Directed by Robert Gainer; scenery, costumes and lighting, Fred Kolouch; associate costume design, Erica Hollmann; sound, Michael Canick; production stage manager, W. Scott Allison; press, Jeffrey Richards Associates, Virginia Snow, Helen Stern, Ted Killmer.

A drama of family conflicts. The play was presented without intermission.

THE AMAZIN' CASEY STENGEL

Casey Stengel	Paul Dooley	Voices	Stephen Zettler
Organist	Marcy Stein		

Directed by Stephen Zuckerman; scenery, Tom Schwinn; costumes, Christina Weppner; lighting, Robby Monk; stage manager, W. Scott Allison.

Virtually a one-man show, with Dooley as the noted Yankees and Mets manager who spoke his own colorful form of the English language. The play was presented in two parts.

Manhattan Theater Club. Schedule of five programs. **Vikings** (48). By Steve Metcalfe. Opened October 21, 1980; see note. (Closed November 30, 1980) **American Days** (48). By Stephen Poliakoff. Opened December 16, 1980; see note. (Closed January 25, 1981) **Close of Play** (48). By Simon Gray. Opened February 10, 1981; see note. (Closed March 22, 1981) **Translations** (48). By Brian Friel. Opened April 7, 1981; see note. (Closed May 17, 1981) And *Hunting Scenes From Lower Bavaria* by Martin Sperr scheduled to open June 14, 1981. Produced by Manhattan Theater Club, Lynne Meadow artistic director, Barry Grove managing director, at Manhattan Theater Club Downstage.

VIKINGS

Peter Larsen	Tom Atkins	Gunnar Larsen	Boyd Gaines
Yens Larsen	William Swetland	Betsy Simmons	Sheila Allen

Standby: Mr. Gaines—Richard Patrick-Warner.

Directed by Lynne Meadow; associate director, George Mead; scenery, Tom Straiges; costumes, Linda Fisher; lighting, F. Mitchell Dana; production stage manager, Virginia Hunter; press, Susan L. Schulman, Winnie Sampson, Sandi Kimmel.

Place: In and around the home of the Larsen family. The play was presented in two parts.

A family of skilled Danish-American construction craftsmen suffers the present poured-concrete era.

AMERICAN DAYS

Tallulah	Anna Levine	Lorraine	Pippa Pearthree
Gary	John Snyder	Don Sherman	John Shea
Ian	Alexander Spencer	Murray	David Blue

Voice of Conroy Anderson—Ed Setrakian.

Standbys: Misses Pearthree, Levine—Jane Hickey; Messrs. Snyder, Spencer—Todd Waring.

Directed by Jacques Levy; scenery, Andrew Jackness; costumes, Kenneth M. Yount; lighting, Dennis Parichy; music, Urban Blight; musical supervisor, Stanley Walden; production stage manager, Edward R. Fitzgerald; stage manager, Wendy Chapin.

Time: The present. Place: An international record company in London. Act I: The listening room in the London office, early afternoon. Act II: The same, evening (*sic,* although in Act II the scene shifted to a subterranean recording area).

Aspiring British rock singers are put to merciless tests by a record company executive. A foreign play previously produced in London.

CLOSE OF PLAY

Jasper	William Roerick	Benedict	John Christopher Jones
Daisy	Pauline Flanagan	Henry	John Horton
Jenny	Lynn Milgrim	Marianne	Veronica Castang
Margaret	Caroline Lagerfelt	Matthew	Alexander Winter

Standbys: Mr. Winter—Michael J. Miller; Miss Flanagan—Kate Wilkinson; Messrs. Jones, Horton—Barry Cullison; Mr. Roerick—Leslie Barrett; Misses Lagerfelt, Milgrim, Castang—Marian Clarke.

Directed by Lynne Meadow; scenery, John Lee Beatty; costumes, Jennifer Von Mayrhauser; lighting, Dennis Parichy; production stage manager, Edward R. Fitzgerald.

Place: The home of Professor Jasper Spencer. Act I: After lunch. Act II: Before tea.

Members of a family one by one air their grievances to each other and to a patriarch who remains only a silent, non-participating symbol of their kinship. A foreign play previously produced at the National Theater in London.

TRANSLATIONS

Manus.	Jarlath Conroy	Bridget	Lauren Thompson
Sarah.	Valerie Mahaffey	Hugh.	Barnard Hughes
Jimmy Jack	Jake Dengel	Owen	Stephen Burleigh
Maire	Ellen Parker	Capt. Lancey	George Taylor
Doalty.	Sam McMurray	Lt. Yolland	Daniel Gerroll

Standbys: Messrs. Dengel, Hughes, Taylor—John Bennes; Messrs. Conroy, Gerroll—Pope Brock; Misses Mahaffey, Thompson, Parker—Bairbre Dowling; Messrs. Burleigh, McMurray—Larkin Malloy.

Directed by Joe Dowling; scenery, Kate Edmunds; costumes, David Murin; lighting, David F. Segal; production stage manager, Loretta Robertson.

Place: A hedge-school in the townland of Baile Beag/Ballybeg, an Irish-speaking community in County Donegal. Act I: An afternoon in late August, 1833. Act II: A few days later. Act III: The evening of the following day.

Irish country folk and English soldiers in conflict as ever, in this case partly over usages of the Gaelic and English languages.

A Best Play; see page 243.

Note: Press date for *Vikings* was 11/9/80, for *American Days* was 1/1/81, for *Close of Play* was 2/24/81, for *Translations* was 4/14/81.

*Roundabout Theater Company. 15th Anniversary Festival schedule of five revivals. **The Winslow Boy** (104). By Terence Rattigan. Opened October 28, 1980. (Closed January 25, 1981) **Don Juan in Hell** (48). By George Bernard Shaw. Opened December 16, 1980. (Closed January 25, 1981) **Inadmissible Evidence** (49). By John Osborne. Opened February 23, 1981. (Closed April 5, 1981) ***A Taste of Honey** (39). By Shelagh Delaney. Opened April 28, 1981. ***Hedda Gabler** (35). By Henrik Ibsen; adapted by Christopher Hampton. Opened May 5, 1981. Produced by Roundabout Theater Company, Gene Feist and Michael Fried producing directors, at the Roundabout Theater, (*Don Juan in Hell, Inadmissible Evidence* and *Hedda Gabler* at Stage One, *The Winslow Boy* and *A Taste of Honey* at Stage Two).

THE WINSLOW BOY

Ronnie Winslow	David Haller	Catherine Winslow	Giulia Pagano
Violet	Barbara Colton	John Wetherstone	Michael Tylo
Arthur Winslow	Ralph Clanton	Desmond Curry	James Higgins
Grace Winslow	Elizabeth Owens	Sir Robert Morton	Remak Ramsay
Dickie Winslow	Lee Toombs		

Directed by Douglas Seale; scenery, Roger Mooney; costumes, A. Christina Giannini; lighting, Norman Coates; sound, Philip Campanella; production stage manager, Michael S. Mantel; press, Susan Bloch.

The Winslow Boy was first produced on Broadway 10/29/47 for 215 performances and was named a Best Play of its season and won the Critics Prize for best foreign play. This is its first New York professional revival of record.

In the course of a national tour, this production of *The Winslow Boy* played off Broadway at the Theater de Lys 3/24/81–4/5/81 for 18 performances.

DON JUAN IN HELL

Dona Ana	Arlene Francis	Commandant	Ronald Drake
Don Juan	Paul Sparer	The Devil	Philip Bosco

Directed by George Keathley; scenery, Roger Mooney; costumes coordinated by A. Christina Giannini; lighting, Robert F. Strohmeier; musical supervision, Philip Campanella; production stage manager, M.R. Jacobs.

The last professional New York production of *Don Juan in Hell* (the third act of *Man and Superman*) was on Broadway 1/15/73 for 24 performances (see its production record in *The Best Plays of 1972–73*).

INADMISSIBLE EVIDENCE

Jones...................	Anthony Heald	Joy	Christine Estabrook
Bill Maitland	Nicol Williamson	Mrs. Garnsey.............	Barbara Caruso
Hudson....................	Philip Bosco	Jane Maitland	Andrea Weber
Shirley	Elaine Bromka	Liz	Jeanne Ruskin

Directed by Anthony Page; scenery, Roger Mooney; costumes, Mimi Maxmen; lighting, Arden Fingerhut; musical supervision, Philip Campanella; production stage manager, M.R. Jacobs; stage manager, Morton Milder.

Time: Early 1960s. Place: Bill Maitland's legal office, London. The play was presented in two acts.

Inadmissible Evidence was first produced on Broadway 11/30/65 for 166 performances and was named a Best Play of its season.

A TASTE OF HONEY

Helen	Valerie French	The Boy	Tom Wright
Jo	Amanda Plummer	Geoffrey	Keith Reddin
Peter......................	John Carroll		

Directed by Tony Tanner; scenery, Roger Moore; costumes, A. Christina Giannini; lighting, Robert W. Mogel; sound, Philip Campanella; production stage manager, Howard Kolins.

A Taste of Honey was first produced on Broadway 10/4/60 for 376 performances and was named a Best Play of its season and was cited as best foreign play by the New York Drama Critics Circle. This is its first professional New York revival of record.

HEDDA GABLER

Aunt Julia	Katherine Squire	Mrs. Elvsted.................	Roxanne Hart
Berte....................	Barbara Lester	Judge Brack.................	Philip Bosco
George Tesman	Harris Yulin	Eilert Lovborg...............	Paul Shenar
Hedda Gabler	Susannah York		

Directed by Michael Kahn; scenery, Lawrence King, Michael Yeargan; costumes, Jane Greenwood; lighting, Dennis Parichy; sound, Eric Rissler Thayer; production stage manager, M.R. Jacobs; stage manager, Morton Milder.

Place: Tesman's villa in the fashionable quarter of town. Act I, Scene 1: Morning. Scene 2: Afternoon. Act II, Scene 1: The next day at dawn. Scene 2: Evening.

The last professional New York production of *Hedda Gabler* took place off Broadway by CSC 9/20/75 for 48 performances.

Jeanne Ruskin replaced Suzannah York 6/9/81.

Roundabout Theater Company also presented special engagements of *Streetsongs,* a one-woman show performed by Geraldine Fitzgerald, 10/14/80–10/26–80 for 16 performances; *Here Are Ladies,* a one-woman show from the works of Irish writers, performed by Siobhan McKenna, 10/28/80–11/23/80 for 32 performances; and *Faces of Love,* a one-woman show of 16 characterizations, performed by Carol Teitel, 1/27/81–2/22/81 for 32 performances.

The Chekhov Sketchbook (106). Translated and adapted by Luba Kadison and Joseph Buloff from the Anton Chekhov short stories *The Vagabond, The Witch* and *In a Music Shop.* Produced by The Harold Clurman Theater, Jack Garfein artistic director, at the Harold Clurman Theater. Opened November 9, 1980. (Closed January 18, 1981)

The Vagabond		Time: Circa 1870. Place: On a road in Russia.	
Vagabond....................	John Heard	*The Witch*	
Ptakh	Frank Bara	Raisa.....................	Penelope Allen
Nik	Jack O'Connell	Savely......................	John Heard

Valerie French *(above)* and Amanda Plummer in a scene from *A Taste of Honey*

<table>
<tr><td>Postman .... Stephen D. Newman</td><td>*In a Music Shop*</td></tr>
<tr><td> Time: Circa 1870. Place: Behind a Russian</td><td>Shopkeeper.................... Frank Bara</td></tr>
<tr><td>country church.</td><td>Ivan .... Joseph Buloff</td></tr>
<tr><td></td><td> Time: Circa 1900. Place: In a Russian village.</td></tr>
</table>

Directed by Tony Giordano; scenery, Hugh Landwehr; costumes, David Murin; lighting, Frances Aronson; sound, George Hansen; stage manager, Johnna Murray; press, Joe Wolhandler Associates, Steven Wolhandler, Douglas Urbanski.

In *The Vagabond,* a chained prisoner regales his guards with tales of his youth. *The Witch* is a triangular marital farce. In *In a Music Shop,* a customer has difficulty identifying a song he wishes to purchase.

Jeffrey De Munn replaced John Heard 12/16/80.

Frimbo (1). Musical conceived and adapted by John L. Haber; music by Howard Harris; lyrics by Jim Wann; based on *All Aboard With E.M. Frimbo* by Rogers E.M. Whitaker and Anthony Hiss. Produced by Dodger Productions, John L. Haber and Louis Busch Hager at Grand Central Terminal Tracks 39 to 42. Opened and closed at the evening performance, November 9, 1980.

Directed by John L. Haber; musical arrangements and direction, Howard Harris; scenery, Karl Eigsti with Fred Buchholz; costumes, Patricia McGourty; lighting, Fred Buchholz; associate musical director, Bill Komalko; sound, Roscoe Harring; production stage manager, Herb Vogler; press, Jeffrey Richards Associates, Ted Killmer. With Richard B. Shull, Larry Riley, Deborah May, Patty D'Arcy, Cass Morgan, Pauletta Pearson; also Peter Piacquadio, Peter Ecklund, Britt Woodman, Ralph Olsen, Art Bressier, Lenny Klinger, Matt Glaser, Stephen Roane, Bill Ward, Edwin Rodrigues, Howard Harris.

A revue of railroad lore staged in a train platform area of Grand Central. The show was presented without intermission.

MUSICAL NUMBERS: "The Frimbo Special," "The Ballad of Frimbo," "The Train," "Train Walking," "Trains or Me," "Going Home," "Lady by Choice," "On a Train at Night," "I Hate Trains," "Mama Frimbo," "The Mileage Millionaire," "Gone Everywhere But Home," "Siberia," "Ode to Steam," "That's the Way to Make It Move," "Names of Trains," "Ballad of Frimbo" (Reprise).

Judgement (11). By Barry Collins. Produced by ANTA, Richmond Crinkley producer, at the Common, St. Peter's Church. Opened November 19, 1980. (Closed November 23, 1980) Reopened December 9, 1980. (Closed December 14, 1980)

Directed by Ellen Burstyn; scenery, Raymond C. Recht; costumes, Jane Greenwood; lighting, Jeff Davis; press, Hunt/Pucci Associates. With Philip Anglim.

One-character treatment of cannibalism, a German soldier is trapped in the basement of a monastery.

Ka-Boom! (71). Musical with book and lyrics by Bruce Kluger; music by Joe Ercole. Produced by Jim Payne in association with Sherie Seff and Bruce Kluger at the Carter Theater. Opened November 20, 1980. (Closed January 19, 1981)

Matt	Ken Ward	June	Andrea Wright
Hattie	Fannie Whitehead	Jasmine	Judith Bro
Tony	John Hall	Avery	Terry Barnes

Musicians: Curtis McKonly piano, conductor; Jamie Bell bass; Jim Furino drums.

Directed by John-Michael Tebelak; choreography, Lynne Gannaway; musical direction and vocal arrangements, John Lehman; scenery, Ken Holamon; costumes, Erica Hollmann; lighting, Kirk Bookman; associate director, Nina Faso; musical arrangements, Joe Ercole; stage manager, Matthew Causey; press, Herb Streisfield.

Musical comedy aftermath of a nuclear holocaust, with survivors putting on a show entitled *Creation, Part II.*

ACT I

Overture/Prologue	Musicians
"Now We Pray"	Ensemble
"Oh, Lord"	Ensemble
"A Little Bit O' Glitter"	Tony
"Maybe for Instance"	Jasmine
"With a World to Conquer"	Hattie
"Smile"	June
"Let Me Believe in Me"	Matt
"Believe Us/Receive Us"	Avery, Ensemble
"A Few Get Through"	Jasmine
"Ballad of Adam & Eve"	Tony, Hattie
"Gimme a 'G' "	June
Finale	Ensemble
"Maybe for Instance" (Reprise)	Jasmine
"The Soft Spot"	Tony, Jasmine
"You Are You"	Ensemble
"The Light Around the Corner"	Ensemble

ACT II

"Believe Us/Receive Us" (Reprise)	Ensemble
"Those ABCs"	June, Ensemble
"Judgement Day"	Tony, Ensemble
"Bump & Grind for God"	Hattie, Ensemble
"Let Me Believe in Me" (Reprise)	Matt, Ensemble
"Let the Show Go On!"	Avery, Ensemble

Bohemian Heaven (3). By Jan Novak. Produced by Bohemian Productions, Inc. at the Provincetown Playhouse. Opened November 24, 1980. (Closed November 27, 1980)

Directed by Gerald Mast; scenery, Bob Phillips; costumes, Sydney Brooks; lighting, Gerald Klug; sound, Chris Anderson; press, Valerie Warner. With Peter Burnell, Shelley Wyant, Dave Florek, Douglas Parvin, Peter Noel-Duhamel.

Economics as comedy.

Moma (11). By Tom Coble. Produced by M.W.A.J. at the 3 Muses Theater. Opened November 25, 1980. (Closed December 7, 1980)

Moma	Lorraine Spritzer	Jean Duckworth	Mary Anisi
Johnny Gamble	Pat Legere		

Directed by Joe Nikola; scenery and lighting, Steve M. Curt; costumes, Joan Harris; stage manager, Don Buschmann; press, Max Eisen.

Time: The present, with a flashback in Act II, Scene 1 to the day President Carter granted amnesty to the war resisters, four years previously. Prelude: Moma (Pacific Grove, Calif.) Act I, Scene 1: Johnny (New York City). Scene 2: Moma and Jean (Pacific Grove). Prelude: Johnny (New York City). Act II, Scene 1: Moma, Jean and Johnny (Pacific Grove). Scene 2: Johnny (New York City). Scene 3: Moma and Jean (Pacific Grove).

The impact of Vietnam and its aftermath on an American family.

Naomi Court (16). Revival of the play by Michael Sawyer. Produced by David Matthew at the Players Theater. Opened November 25, 1980. (Closed December 7, 1980)

Sally Dugan	B. Constance Barry	Bunny Berry	John A. Coe
Lenny Santini	Bruno Ragnacci	Harper	David Bostick
Florence	Joanne Jacobson		

Directed by Ted Weiant; scenery, Bob Phillips; costumes, George Potts; lighting, Ned Hallick; original score, David McHugh; production stage manager, Michael Spellman; press, Fred Nathan.

Time: The last days of August. Place: A tenement house in the Yorkville section of New York City. Act I: Apartment 2-B, Wednesday. Act II: Apartment 5-C, Thursday night.

Revision of cat-and-mouse melodrama previously produced off off Broadway at Manhattan Theater Club in 1974 and Wonderhorse in 1980.

Coming Attractions (145). By Ted Tally. Produced by Michael Frazier and Susan Madden Samson in the Playwrights Horizons production at Playwrights Horizons. Opened December 3, 1980. (Closed April 12, 1981)

Cast: Hostage, 1st TV Reporter, Secretary, Miss America, Backup Girl, Gofer—Christine Baranski; Manny Alter—Larry Block; Hostage, Newswoman, Bystander, Teri Sterling, Lab Coat #2, Backup Girl, Sunflower, Stenographer, Script Girl—Randy Graff; Lonnie Wayne Burke—Jonathan Hadary; Hostage, 2d TV Reporter, Cop, Publisher, TV Interviewer, M.C., Lab Coat #3, Announcer, Interpreter, Private Eye #2, Prosecutor, Chaplain—Stephen Mellor; Hostage, 2d Newsman, Detective, Cameraman, Mister X, Lab Coat #1, Sammy Dazzle, Private Eye #1, Defense Attorney,

Director—Fred Sanders; Cop's Voice, 1st Newsman, Biff Braddock, Witness, Victim's Father, Tweed Jacket, Khaled El Hashish, Judge, Warden—Allan Wasserman.

Understudy: Mr. Block, ensemble roles—John Lefkowitz.

Directed by Andre Ernotte; music by Jack Feldman; lyrics by Bruce Sussman and Jack Feldman; scenery, Andrew Jackness; costumes, Ann Emonts; lighting, Paul Gallo; sound, Alex McIntyre; orchestrations, Arnold Gross; musical staging Theodore Pappas; production stage manager, Fredric H. Orner; press, Betty Lee Hunt, Maria Cristina Pucci, James Sapp.

Black comedy (with four songs) about a small-time hoodlum who acquires a sort of celebrity in the media by means of multiple murders.

Trixie True, Teen Detective (86). Musical with book, music and lyrics by Kelly Hamilton. Produced by Doug Cole, Joe Novak, Spencer Tandy and Joseph Butt at the Theater de Lys. Opened December 4, 1980. (Closed February 15, 1981)

Joe	Gene Lindsey	Dick Dickerson	Keith Rice
Al; Wilhelm	Jay Lowman	LaVerne	Alison Bevan
Miss Snood; Mme. Olga	Marilyn Sokol	Maxine	Marianna Allen
Trixie True	Kathy Andrini	Bobby	Keith Caldwell

Understudies: Miss Sokol—Alison Bevan; Miss Andrini—Marianna Allen; Mr. Rice—Keith Caldwell; Messrs. Lindsey, Lowman, Caldwell—Tim Cassidy; Misses Bevan, Allen—Christina Saffran.

Directed by Bill Gile; musical staging, Arthur Faria; musical direction and vocal arrangements, Robert Fisher; scenery, Michael J. Hotopp, Paul De Pass; costumes, David Toser; lighting, Craig Miller; orchestrations, Eddie Sauter; associate producer, Peter Alsop; dance arrangements, Jimmy Roberts; technical consultant, Dale E. Ward; production stage manager, John Brigleb; press, Jeffrey Richards Associates, Ben Morse, C. George Willard, Robert Ganshaw, Helen Stern, Ted Killmer.

Time: The mid-1940s. Place: The New York offices of Snood Publishing and in the mythical town of Cherry Hill, N.J.

The teen-aged pulp-fiction heroine as detective.

ACT I

"Trixie's on the Case!"	Al, Joe, Miss Snood, Trixie, Crooks
"This Is Indeed My Lucky Day"	Trixie
"Most Popular and Most Likely to Succeed"	Dick, Bobby, Maxine, LaVerne
"Mr. and Mrs. Dick Dickerson"	Dick, Trixie
"Juvenile Fiction"	Miss Snood
"Trixie's on the Case!" (Reprise)	Trixie, Maxine, LaVerne
"A Katzenjammer Kinda Song"	Olga, Wilhelm
"You Haven't Got Time for Love"	Dick, Trixie
Act I Finaletto	

ACT II

Entr'acte	
"In Cahoots"	Joe, Olga
"The Mystery of the Moon"	Trixie
"The Secret of the Tapping Shoes"	Trixie, Maxine, LaVerne, Bobby
"This Is Indeed My Lucky Day" (Reprise)	Joe, Bobby, Maxine, LaVerne
"In Cahoots" (Reprise)	Joe
"Rita From Argentina"	Miss Snood, Joe
"Trixie True, Teen Detective"	Maxine, LaVerne, Bobby, Joe, Dick
Finale	Ensemble

The Lincoln Center Theater Company. Schedule of two programs. **Truman Capote at Lincoln Center** (11). One-man performance by and with Truman Capote. Opened Decem-

William Newman, Marilyn Rockafellow, Kathleen Widdoes and Graham Beckel in *Stops Along the Way* by Jeffrey Sweet at Lincoln Center

ber 16, 1980. (Closed December 28, 1980) **The One Act Play Festival** (37). Program of three one-act plays: *Stops Along the Way* by Jeffrey Sweet, *In Fireworks Lie Secret Codes* by John Guare and *Vivien* by Percy Granger. Edward Albee, artistic director. Opened March 5, 1981. (Closed April 5, 1981) Produced by The Lincoln Center Theater Company, Richmond Crinkley producer, at the Mitzi E. Newhouse Theater.

TRUMAN CAPOTE AT LINCOLN CENTER

Jointly produced with Lester Persky and United Artists; lighting, John Gleason; stage manager, T. Schuyler Smith; press, Betty Lee Hunt, Maria Cristina Pucci, James Sapp.

Readings by Truman Capote from his works in two programs, the first comprising *Music for Chameleons, A Day's Work, Mr. Jones* and *A Christmas Memory,* and the second from *Handcarved Coffins.*

THE ONE ACT PLAY FESTIVAL

Stops Along the Way
Donna.................. Kathleen Widdoes
Larry .... Graham Beckel
Ray..................... William Newman
Waiter; Clerk................ Michael Egan
Gas Station Attendant;
    Bartender........... Marilyn Rockafellow
    Understudies: Miss Widdoes—Barbara An-
dres; Mr. Beckel—James Woods; Mr. Newman, Miss Rockafellow—Michael Egan; Mr. Egan—William Newman, Robin Miller.

In Fireworks Lie Secret Codes
#1 .... William Newman
#2 .... Kathleen Widdoes
#3 .... James Woods
#4 .... Barbara Andres

#5 . . . . Graham Beckel
Understudies: Misses Widdoes, Andres—
Marilyn Rockafellow; Messrs. Newman, Woods,
Beckel—Robin Miller.
Vivien
Vivien . . . . Michael Egan

Paul . . . . James Woods
Mrs. Tendesco . . . . Barbara Andres
Understudies: Mr. Egan—William New-
man; Mr. Woods—Graham Beckel; Miss Andres
—Marilyn Rockafellow.

Stops Along the Way and *Vivien* directed by Kevin Conway; *In Fireworks Lie Secret Codes* directed by John Guare; scenery, John Wright Stevens; costumes, David Murin; lighting, Marc B. Weiss; sound, Richard Fitzgerald; production stage manager, Rita Calabro; stage manager, Robin Miller.

In *Stops Along the Way,* a married woman and her onetime lover reflect various sexual attitudes on a journey back home together. In *In Fireworks Lie Secret Codes,* a Fourth of July celebration stimulates those watching it to conversational activity and antics. In *Vivien,* a father and son explore each other's natures while journeying to see a stage production the son has directed; previously produced by the Peterborough, N.H. Players.

We Won't Pay! We Won't Pay! (120). By Dario Fo; North American translation by R.G. Davis. Produced by Leavin/Davis Productions in association with Chris Silva and Chelsea Theater Center at Chelsea Theater Center Downstairs Theater. Opened December 16, 1980. (Closed March 29, 1981)

Antonia . . . . Karen Shallo
Margherita . . . . Bonnie Braelow
Giovanni . . . . Harris Laskawy

Sergeant; Carabineri;
Undertaker; Old Man . . . . W.T. Martin
Luigi . . . . Robert DeFrank

Directed by R.G. Davis; scenery, Wolfgang Roth; costumes, Denise Romano; lighting and sound, Terry Alan Smith; production stage manager, William Hare; press, Edward T. Callaghan, Jacqueline Burnham.

Time: 1974. Place: Working class apartment, Milan. Act I: 5:30 P.M. Act II: 5:30 A.M.

Comedy about coping with inflation. A foreign play previously produced in Italy and in Vancouver, Canada.

Hijinks! (39). Musical adapted by Robert Kalfin, Steve Brown and John McKinney from *Captain Jinks of the Horse Marines* by Clyde Fitch. Produced by Chelsea Theater Center, Robert Kalfin producing director, A. Harrison Cromer managing director, The Fisher Theater Foundation and Roger L. Stevens at the Chelsea Theater Center Cheryl Crawford Theater. Opened December 17, 1980. (Closed January 18, 1981)

Mme. Trentoni;
  Aurelia Johnson . . . . Jeannine Taylor
Captain Jinks . . . . Joseph Kolinski
Clyde Fitch; *Times* Reporter;
  Papa Belliarti . . . . Michael Connolly
Policeman; *Sun* Reporter . . . . Sal Basile
Charlie; *Herald*
  Reporter . . . . Randall Easterbrook
Gussie; *Tribune* Reporter . . . . Scott Ellis
Peter . . . . Christopher Ellis

Sailor; Fraulein Hochspits . . . . . Evalyn Baron
Sailor; Mrs. Maggitt . . . . Elizabeth Devine
Sailor; Mrs. Pettitoes . . . . Elaine Petricoff
Piano Player; Detective . . . Michael O'Flaherty
Mrs. Greenborough;
  Mrs. Jinks . . . . Marian Primont
Sailor . . . . Bruce Conner
Monkey . . . . Elyot Chase
Jenny . . . . Sarah Lowman

Directed by Robert Kalfin; dances and musical staging, Larry Hayden; musical direction, Michael O'Flaherty; scenery, Sandro La Ferla; costumes, Elizabeth P. Palmer; lighting, Paul Everett; musical arrangements, John McKinney; based on an idea by William Bolcom, David Brooks, Robert Kalfin and Arnold Weinstein; production stage manager, Tony Melchior; stage manager, Allison Sommers; press, Edward T. Callaghan.

Time: 1872. Act I: The landing dock of the Cunard Steamship Company in New York, end of October. Act II: At Madame Trentoni's in the Brevoort House, a fortnight later. Act III: The same night.

Music of the period added to the Fitch play about an opera singer's arrival and adventures in the U.S. *Captain Jinks of the Horse Marines* was first produced on Broadway 2/4/01 for 168 performances (Ethel Barrymore made her Broadway debut in this production) for 168 performances. It has been revived 2/18/07 for 33 performances; in a musical version entitled *Captain Jinks* 9/8/25; in WPA Theater for 2 performances in 1938; and off Broadway in the 1948–49 season.

AUTHORS OF MUSICAL NUMBERS: Music by M.W. Balfe, Ernest R. Ball, Frank Campbell, Robert Cooms, H.P. Danks, Barney Fagan, Harry von Tilzer, Friedrich von Flotow, Stephen C. Foster, S. Glover, Joseph E. Howard, Alfred Lee, William Lingard, J.L. Molloy, John Howard Payne, Charles E. Pratt, J.P. Skelly, Giuseppi Verdi, W.V. Wallace, Septimus Winner, Henry Clay Work.

Lyrics by G. Clifton Bingham, Steve Brown, Robert Burns, Alfred Bunn, J.E. Carpenter, Robert Cooms, George Cooper, Barney Fagan, Stephen C. Foster, Mrs. Mary E. Hewitt, Joseph E. Howard, Francis Scott Key, George Leybourne, William Kingard, Harry Miller, John Howard Payne, Billy Reeves, Eben E. Rexford, Andrew B. Sterling, J.J. Walker, Septimus Winner, Henry Clay Work.

Last Summer at Bluefish Cove (80). By Jane Chambers. Produced by John Glines and Lawrence Lane in The Glines production at the Actors Playhouse. Opened December 22, 1980. (Closed March 1, 1981)

Lil	Jean Smart	Rae	Lauren Craig
Eva	Susan Slavin	Rita	Dulcie Arnold
Kitty	Janet Sarno	Sue	Celia Howard
Annie	Holly Barron	Donna	Robin Mary Paris

Directed by Nyla Lyon; scenery, Reagan Cook; costumes, Giva R. Taylor; lighting, Jeffrey Schissler; sculpture, Dorothy Abbott; associate producers, Bill Blackwell, Peter Pope; production stage manager, Paula Ellen Cohen; press, Max Eisen, Francine L. Trevens.

Time: The present, early summer through late fall. The play was presented in two parts.

Summer romances within a lesbian clique. Previously produced off off Broadway at The Glines.

Holly Barron replaced Jean Smart and Susan Bloomaert replaced Holly Barron 12/25/80.

BAM Theater Company. Repertory of five revivals. **A Midsummer Night's Dream** (26). By William Shakespeare. Opened January 4, 1981; see note. (Closed March 29, 1981) **The Recruiting Officer** (26). By George Farquhar. Opened January 15, 1981; see note. (Closed February 26, 1981) **The Wild Duck** (26) By Henrik Ibsen; new version by Thomas Babe from a translation by Erik J. Friis. Opened March 5, 1981; see note. (Closed April 5, 1981 matinee) **Jungle of Cities** (26). By Bertolt Brecht; version by Richard Nelson. Opened April 9, 1981; see note. (Closed May 3, 1981 matinee) **Oedipus the King** (28). By Sophocles; version by Stephen Berg and Diskin Clay. Opened April 16, 1981; see note. (Closed May 10, 1981) Produced by the BAM Theater Company, David Jones artistic director, Arthur Penn associate director, Charles Dillingham managing director, at the Brooklyn Academy of Music (*Oedipus the King* at the Leperq Space, other programs at the Helen Carey Playhouse).

PERFORMER	"A MIDSUMMER NIGHT'S DREAM"	"THE RECRUITING OFFICER"	"THE WILD DUCK"	"JUNGLE OF CITIES"
Seth Allen			Kasperson	Shlink
Sheila Allen	Titania		Mrs. Sorby	
C.B. Anderson	Philostrate	Mr. Scruple; Citizen		C. Maynes

PERFORMER	"A MIDSUMMER NIGHT'S DREAM"	"THE RECRUITING OFFICER"	"THE WILD DUCK"	"JUNGLE OF CITIES"
Gerry Bamman	Nick Bottom	Thomas	Dr. Relling	
Dominic Chianese	Egeus	Mr. Scale; Citizen	Old Ekdal	
Jerome Dempsey	Peter Quince	Mr. Balance	Bergman	
Laura Esterman	Helena	Melinda		
Sam Gray		Birdewell; Citizen	Werle	John Garga
Tracy Griswold	Attendant	Steward; Citizen		Drummer; 1st Man
Michael Gross			Gregers Werle	
Ben Halley Jr.	Attendant	Pluck	Molvik	
James Harper	Theseus	Harvester; 1st Recruit; Citizen	Jensen	Collie Couch
Olivia Virgil Harper	1st Fairy	Citizen		Salvation Army Girl
Richard Jamieson		Capt. Brazen	Petterson	
Cheryl Yvonne Jones	Hippolyta	Lucy		
Laurie Kennedy		Silvia		
Frank Maraden	Francis Flute	Mr. Worthy	Hjalmar Ekdal	J. Finnay
Beth McDonald	Hermia	Rose		Mary Garga
Michael John McGann	Robin Starveling	Bullock		Pat Manky
William L. McMullen		Watch	Waiter	
Randle Mell	Snug	Costar Pearmain	Graberg	
Keith Moore	Cobweb	Cartwheel; Watch; Citizen	Waiter	Salvation Army Officer
Joe Morton	Lysander	Kite	Naval Officer	
Brian Murray	Oberon	Capt. Plume		
Joan Pape			Gina Ekdal	Mae Garga
Vic Polizos				Skinny
Scott Richards	Mustardseed	Melinda Servant; Citizen		Waiter; 2nd Man
Kristin Rudrud	Peaseblossom	Wife of 2d Recruit; Citizen		Secretary; Salvation Army Girl
Robert Rutland	Attendant	2d Recruit; Citizen	Flor	Chuck
Don Scardino	Demetrius	Thomas Appletree		George Garga
Priscilla Shanks	Moth	Wife of 1st Recruit; Citizen		Jane Larry
Ted Sod	Puck	Tycho		Snub-Nosed Man
Tenney Walsh			Hedvig Ekdal	

A MIDSUMMER NIGHT'S DREAM—Directed by David Jones; scenery and costumes, Santo Loquasto; lighting, F. Mitchell Dana; assistant director, Emily Mann; music, Bruce Coughlin; choreography, Cheryl McFadden; production stage manager, Susie Cordon; press, Rima Corben.

The last professional New York production of *A Midsummer Night's Dream* was off Broadway in CSC repertory 11/10/77 for 32 performances.

THE RECRUITING OFFICER—Children of Shrewsbury: Timaree Larson, Jason Lillard, Lynn Robinson, David Smith.

Directed by Laird Williamson; scenery, Robert Blackman; costumes, Dunya Ramicova; lighting, F. Mitchell Dana; music, John McKinney; stage manager, Ray Gin.

The only New York revival of record in this century of this Restoration (1706) comedy of military and sexual antics was by the Cubiculo off off Broadway 2/24/77.

THE WILD DUCK—Directed by Arthur Penn; scenery, John Lee Beatty; costumes, Carol Oditz; lighting, F. Mitchell Dana; stage manager, Susie Cordon.

The last professional New York production of *The Wild Duck* was by the Association of Producing Artists (APA) on Broadway 1/11/67 for 41 performances.

JUNGLE OF CITIES—Directed by David Jones; scenery, John Jensen; costumes, Susan Hilferty; lighting, F. Mitchell Dana; composer, Norman L. Berman; literal translation, Douglas Arthur; stage manager, Ray Gin; press, Ellen Lampert.

Brecht's 1923 play set in an imaginary Chicago in 1912 and dealing with multiple social ills including gangsterism has not had a previous professional New York production of record.

OEDIPUS THE KING

Oedipus	Joe Morton	Teiresias	Michael Gross
Priest	Ben Halley Jr.	Boy	Jonathan Manzo
Kreon	Richard Jamieson	Jocasta	Sheila Allen
Chorus:		Servant	Randle Mell
Peasant Woman	Laura Esterman	Messenger	Jerome Dempsey
Young Woman	Cheryl Yvonne Jones	Shepherd	Dominic Chianese
Young Man	Gedde Watanabe	Antigone	Erika Larson
Leader	Gerry Bamman	Ismene	Timaree Larson

Directed by Emily Mann; scenery, Ming Cho Lee; costumes, Jennifer Von Mayrhauser; lighting, Arden Fingerhut; composer and musician, Bill Vanaver; stage manager, Susie Cordon.

Sophocles' *Oedipus* was last revived in New York off Broadway by Roundabout in the 1969–70 season. The play was presented without intermission.

Note: Press date for *A Midsummer Night's Dream* was 1/10/81, for *The Recruiting Officer* was 1/22/81, for *The Wild Duck* was 3/12/81, for *Jungle of Cities* was 4/16/81, for *Oedipus the King* was 4/22/81.

An Evening With Joan Crawford (15). Musical conceived by Julian Neil, based on the original characterization by Lee Sparks; music by Joseph Church and Nick Branch. Produced by Joe Bianco in association with Monroe Arnold at the Orpheum Theater. Opened January 28, 1981. (Closed February 8, 1981)

Directed by Julian Neil; choreography and musical staging, Sydney Smith; musical direction and vocal arrangements, Joseph Church; scenery, J. Patrick Mann; costumes, Barbara Gerard; lighting, Paul Everett; instrumental arrangements, Joseph Church; associate producer, Philip S. Kaufman; production stage manager, Tom W. Picard; press, Susan L. Schulman, Glenna Freedman, Sandi Kimmel. With Kristine Zbornik, Frances Robertson, Lee Sparks (as Joan Crawford), Joyce Fullerton, Michael J. Hume, Fracaswell Hyman, Michael Kemmerling.

A characterization of the movie star, with dialogue arrived at partly through improvisational techniques. Previously produced off off Broadway at New York Theater Ensemble.

MUSICAL NUMBERS—ACT I: "Blame It All on Me" (music by Joseph Church, lyrics by Joseph Church and Richard Schill); "The Devil's Song" (music and lyrics by Nick Branch); "Hollywood Lullaby" (music and lyrics by Joseph Church), "Give Em Hell (music by Joseph Church, lyrics by Kristine Zbornik).

ACT II: "Too Much Money Blues" (music and lyrics by Julian Neil and Lee Sparks); "You Are One of a Kind" (music and lyrics by Joseph Church); "Ain't No Place Like Home" (music and lyrics by Nick Branch); "Take a Vacation" (music and lyrics by Nick Branch); "What It's Like To Be a Legend" (music and lyrics by Nick Branch).

The Legendary Stardust Boys (12). By D.B. Gilles. Produced by Andrew Unangst and Elizabeth Baker at the South Street Theater. Opened February 12, 1981. (Closed February 22, 1981)

John Milligan and Georgine Hall in Ira Levin's *Veronica's Room*

Directed by Rudy Caringi; scenery and lighting, Robert Fox; stage manager, Randy Etheredge; press, Shirley Herz, Jan Greenberg. With Robert Mont, Nick Ferrari, Nick Cosco, Marvin Beck. Four working class men moonlight as members of a touring band.

Marching to Georgia (9). By Barbara Daniel. Produced by International Media Studies Foundation, Inc., William O'Boyle executive producer, at the Players Theater. Opened March 8, 1981. (Closed March 15, 1981)

Directed by Milton Moss; scenery, Kenneth E. Lewis; costumes, Gail Cooper-Hecht; lighting, Robby Monk; assistant producer, Dennis Luzak; production stage manager, Richard W. Van Wyk; press, Howard Atlee, Bill Evans. With Janice Fuller, Kristin Griffith, Moultrie Patten, Jack Davidson, Joseph Daly, Lois Diane Hicks, John Corey.

Time: The present. Place: A small house on a side street in South Boston, Va. War between husband and wife (whose name is Georgia).

Veronica's Room (97). Revival of the play by Ira Levin. Produced by Veronica Productions Company in association with the Provincetown Playhouse at the Provincetown Playhouse. Opened March 8, 1981. (Closed May 17, 1981)

The Woman...............	Georgine Hall	The Girl............	Innes-Fergus McDade
The Man	John Milligan	The Young Man	Claude-Albert Saucier

Directed by Arthur Savage; scenery, M. Cabot McMullen; costumes, Timothy Dunleavy; lighting, Fred Jason Hancock; technical director, Sam Buccio; executive producer, Barbara Savage; associate producers, Wendy Borow, Kenneth Borow; production stage manager, Judeth Erwin; press, Shirley Herz, Jan Greenberg, Sam Rudy.

Time: An evening in spring. Place: A room in a house about half an hour's drive from Boston. Act I: Susan. Act II: Veronica.

This thriller was first produced on Broadway 12/29/73 for 75 performances. This is its first New York revival of record.

Black Elk Lives (6). By Christopher Sergel; based on *Black Elk Speaks* by John G. Neihardt. Produced by Victor Lurie and Alex Van Lerberg at the Entermedia Theater. Opened March 12, 1981. (Closed March 15, 1981)

Directed by Tom Brennan; design, masks and puppets, Julie Taymor; costumes, David Murin; lighting, William Armstrong; additional staging, Jane Lind; production stage manager, Ed Preston; press, Cheryl Sue Dolby, Gary S. James. With Manu Tupou, Sal Anthony, Clayton Corbin, Tino Juarez, Jane Lind, Christina Moncarz, Carl Battaglia, Carlo Grasso, Michael Lamont, W.T. Martin, Edward O'Ross, Lee Rozie.

Indian history from 1492 to 1890 as viewed by a Sioux spiritual leader. Previously produced at the Folger Theater, Washington, D.C.

Marry Me a Little (96). Musical with songs by Stephen Sondheim; conceived and developed by Craig Lucas and Norman René. Produced by Diane de Mailly in association with William B. Young at the Actors' Playhouse. Opened March 12, 1981. (Closed May 31, 1981)

Suzanne Henry   Craig Lucas

Standbys: Miss Henry—Carole Doscher; Mr. Lucas—Michael Pace. Standbys assumed roles at extra Friday performances 4/10/81–5/29/81.

Directed by Norman René; choreography, Don Johanson; musical direction, E. Martin Perry; scenery, Jane Thurn; costumes, Oleksa; lighting, Debra J. Kletter; production stage manager, David L. Nathans; press, Solters/Roskin/Friedman, Inc., Milly Schoenbaum, Kevin Patterson.

Time: The present. Place: An apartment house in New York City. The show was performed without intermission.

Collection of Sondheim numbers written for Broadway but never included in his Broadway shows, in a context about two young people dreaming alone and finally meeting.

MUSICAL NUMBERS: "Two Fairy Tales," "Saturday Night," "Can That Boy Foxtrot!", "All Things Bright and Beautiful," "Bang!" "All Things Bright and Beautiful" (Part II), "The Girls of Summer," "Uptown, Downtown," "Who Could Be Blue?", "Little White House," "So Many People," "Your Eyes Are Blue," "A Moment With You," "Marry Me a Little," "Happily Ever After," "Pour le Sport," "Silly People," "There Won't Be Trumpets," "It Wasn't Meant to Happen."

Glasshouse (9). By Fatima Dike. Produced by Lucille Lortel and Haila Stoddard in association with the Common, in the White Barn Theater production, at St. Peter's Church. Opened March 22, 1981. (Closed March 29, 1981)

Directed by Rina Yerushalmi; scenery, Wynn P. Thomas; costumes, Susan Hilferty; lighting, Robby Monk; original music, Don Elliott; musician, Jack Scavella; assistant director, Meyer Baron; press, John Springer Associates, Meg Gordean. With Mary Alice, Maggie Soboil.

Childhood friends living in Cape Town, one black and one white, are forced apart by government racial policies. A foreign (South African) play previously produced in Westport, Conn.

The Buddy System (8). By Jonathan Feldman. Produced by Mark R. Gordon at Circle in the Square Downtown. Opened April 13, 1981. (Closed April 19, 1981)

Directed by Edward Berkeley; scenery, Dan Leigh; costumes, Hilary Rosenfeld; lighting, Fred Buchholz; sound, Paul Garrity; production stage manager, Julia Gillett; press, Solters/Roskin/Friedman, Inc., Becky Flora. With Ron Fassier, David Wohl, Christopher Gartin, John Rothman, Keith Gordon, Victor Bevine, Ralph Bruneau.

Reunion of onetime summer-camp friends, now grown up. Previously produced at Cincinnati Playhouse in the Park.

It's Me, Sylvia (9). One-woman performance by Sylvia Miles of a musical with book and lyrics by Sylvia Miles; music by Galt MacDermot. Produced by Steven A. Greenberg at the Playhouse Theater. Opened April 13, 1981. (Closed April 19, 1981)

Directed by Arthur Sherman; scenery, Eugene Lee; costumes, Clifford Capone; lighting, Roger Morgan; musical direction, Galt MacDermont; production stage manager, Carmine R. Pontilena; press, Shirley Herz, Jan Greenberg.

Miss Miles's picture of her own life, drawn from autobiographical newspaper articles.

The Acting Company. Schedule of three revivals. **Il Campiello, a Venetian Comedy** (5). By Carlo Goldoni; literal translation by Erica Gastelli; adapted by Richard Nelson. Opened April 15, 1981. (Closed April 18, 1981). **Waiting for Godot** (3). By Samuel Beckett. Opened April 22, 1981. (Closed April 24, 1981). **A Midsummer Night's Dream** (2). By William Shakespeare. Opened April 25, 1981. (Closed April 26, 1981) Produced by Joseph Papp in The Acting Company productions, John Houseman producing artistic director, Michael Kahn and Alan Schneider artistic directors, Margot Harley executive producer, at the Public (Estelle R. Newman) Theater.

PERFORMER	"IL CAMPIELLO"	"WAITING FOR GODOT"	"A MIDSUMMER NIGHT'S DREAM"
Casey Biggs	Fabrizio		Lysander
Becky Borczon	Townsperson; Musician		Mustardseed
Johann Carlo	Gnese	Boy	1st Fairy; Peaseblossom
Lynn Chausow	Donna Pasqua		Hermia
Keith David		Pozzo	Theseus; Oberon
Richard Howard	Count	Vladimir	Philostrate; Puck
Richard S. Iglewski	Townsperson; Musician	Estragon	Bottom
Robert Lovitz	Anzoletto		Demetrius
Kevin McGuire	Townsperson; Musician		Starveling
Pamela Nyberg	Gasparina		Helena
Lori Putnam	Lucietta		Cobweb
Brian Reddy	Zorzetto		Snug
Jeffrey M. Rubin	Sansuga		Snout; Egeus
Alan Silver	Townsperson; Musician		Peter Quince
Laura Smyth	Orsola		
Paul Walker	Urchin	Lucky	Flute
Michele-Denise Woods	Donna Katherina		Hippolita; Titania

ALL PLAYS—Lighting, Dennis Parichy; production stage manager, Don Judge; stage manager, Kathleen B. Boyette; press, Merle Debuskey, Richard Kornberg, John Howlett, Ed Bullins.

IL CAMPIELLO, A VENETIAN COMEDY—Directed by Liviu Ciulei; scenery, Radu Boruzescu; costumes, Miruna Boruzescu; musical direction, Bruce Adolphe; choreography, Anna Sokolow; assistant director, Christopher J. Markle.

Place: Venice. The play was presented in two parts.

Il Campiello was first performed in Venice in 1756.

WAITING FOR GODOT—Directed by Alan Schneider; scenery, Radu Boruzescu; costumes, Miruna Boruzescu; assistant director, Randolph Foerster.

Waiting for Godot was first performed in Paris in 1952, following which it was produced on Broadway 4/19/56 for 59 performances and was named a Best Play of its season. Its last professional New York revival took place off Broadway 5/11/78 for 23 performances.

Craig Lucas and Suzanne Henry in the Stephen Sondheim musical *Marry Me a Little*

A MIDSUMMER NIGHT'S DREAM—Directed by David Chambers; assistant director, Christopher J. Markle; scenery, Heidi Landesman; costumes, Carol Oditz; music composed and directed by Ken Guilmartin; electronic music design composed by Pril Smiley; movement, Kathryn Posin; assistant set designer, Tom Bynum; assistant costume designer, Debra Stein.

The last professional New York revival of this Shakespeare comedy took place off Broadway 11/10/77 for 32 performances.

Ah, Men (14). Musical revue by Paul Shyre; music and lyrics by Will Holt. Produced by Jay Garon at the South Street Theater. Opened May 11, 1981. (Closed May 24, 1981)

Jack Betts	Stephen Lang
Curt Dawson	Jane White

Standbys: Miss White—Jane Bergère; Men—Wayne Maxwell.

Directed by Paul Shyre; scenery and costumes, Eldon Elder; Lighting, John Gisondi; production stage manager, Peter Jablonski; press, Max Eisen, Francine L. Trevens.

Musical treatment of "the male experience," with reference to the views of Groucho Marx, George Bernard Shaw, Henry Miller, Lucky Luciano, Rudolph Valentino, Bertrand Russell, Clifford Irving, Tommy Trantino, Sean O'Casey, Ned Rorem, Art Buchwald, D.H. Lawrence, Frank Harris, George Burns, Sherwood Anderson, Arthur Schopenhauer, Jean-Jacques Rousseau, August Strindberg, Eugene O'Neill, Lenny Bruce, Malcolm Muggeridge, Ayatollah Khomeini, George Jean Nathan. The show was presented without intermission.

MUSICAL NUMBERS: "Ah, Men"—Company; "Man Is for the Woman Made"—Curt Dawson; "When After You Pass My Door"—Jane White; "My First"—Steven Lang; "The Last Minute Waltz"—Jack Betts; "Truck Stop"—White; "Illusions"—White; "Daddy Blues"—Men; "Ah Men" (Reprise)—Company.

*I Can't Keep Running in Place (21). Musical with book, music and lyrics by Barbara Schottenfeld. Produced by Ray Gaspard in association with Chris Silva, Stephen Dailey and Will Dailey at the Westside Arts Theater. Opened May 14, 1981.

Michelle	Marcia Rodd	Gwen	Jennie Ventriss
Beth	Helen Gallagher	Sherry	Bev Larson
Mandy	Mary Donnet	Alice	Evalyn Baron
Eileen	Joy Franz		

Understudies: Misses Rodd, Gallagher—Sally Stark; Misses Franz, Larson, Donnet—Christine Anderson.

Directed by Susan Einhorn; choreography, Baayork Lee; musical direction, Robert Hirschhorn; scenery, Ursula Belden; costumes, Christina Weppner; lighting, Victor En Yu Tan; musical supervision, John McKinney; assistant choreographer, Dennis Grimaldi; orchestrations, Barbara Schottenfeld; production stage manager, Meryl Schaffer; press, Jeffrey Richards Associates, Robert Ganshaw, Ben Morse, C. George Willard, Helen Stern.

Time: Six Wednesday night workshop sessions from late winter to early spring. Place: A loft somewhere in Soho. Act I, Scene 1: The first session. Scene 2: The third session; later that evening. Act II, Scene 1: The fifth session. Scene 2: The last session.

Six women in sessions with their psychiatrist, with overtones of feminism.

ACT I

"I'm Glad I'm Here" .... Company
"Don't Say Yes If You Want to Say No" .... Michelle, Company
"I Can't Keep Running in Place" .... Eileen
"More of Me to Love" .... Gwen, Alice
  (orchestrated by Robert Hirschhorn)
"I Live Alone" .... Beth
"I Can Count on You" .... Alice, Company
"I'm on My Own" .... Michelle

ACT II

"Penis Envy" .... Michelle, Company
"Get the Answer Now" .... Sherry, Company
  (orchestrated by Robert Hirschhorn)
"What If We . . ." .... Michelle
"Almosts, Maybes and Perhapses" .... Beth
"Where Will I Be Next Wednesday
  Night?" .... Company

*Cloud 9 (16). By Caryl Churchill. Produced by Michel Stuart and Harvey J. Klaris in association with Michel Kleinman Productions at the Theater de Lys. Opened May 18, 1981.

PERFORMER	ACT I	ACT II
Don Amendolia	Joshua	Cathy
Veronica Castang	Maud	Lin
Victoria	Herself	
Zeljko Ivanek	Betty	Gerry
Jeffrey Jones	Clive	Edward
E. Katherine Kerr	Ellen; Mrs. Saunders	Betty

Nicolas Surovy   Harry Bagley   Martin
Concetta Tomei   Edward   Victoria

Understudies: Men—Michael Morris, Martin Shakar; Women—Barbara Berg.

Directed by Tommy Tune; scenery, Lawrence Miller; costumes, Michel Stuart, Gene London; lighting, Marcia Madeira; title song and incidental music, Maury Yeston; sound, Warren Hogan; associate producer, Mark Begelman; production stage manager, Murray Gitlin; press, Jacksina and Freedman, Angela Wilson, Dolph Browning.

Act I: Africa, 1880. Act II: London, 1980 (but for the characters it is only 25 years later).

Sexual confusions of a repressed (1880) era and a liberated (1980) era, with transsexual casting. A foreign play produced at the Royal Court Theater in London and elsewhere.

A Best Play; see page 279.

*March of the Falsettos (13). Musical by William Finn. Produced by Playwrights Horizons, Andre Bishop artistic director, Robert Moss producing director, at Playwrights Horizons. Opened May 20, 1981.

Marvin .... Michael Rupert   Whizzer Brown .... Stephen Bogardus
Trina..................... Alison Fraser   Mendel .... Chip Zien
Jason.................... James Kushner

Understudies: Messrs. Zien, Rupert, Bogardus—Ralph Bruneau; Miss Fraser—Emily Grinspan; Mr. Kushner—Jonathan Ward.

Directed by James Lapine; musical direction, Michael Lee Stockler; scenery, Douglas Stein; costumes, Maureen Connor; lighting, Frances Aronson; orchestrations, Michael Starobin; production stage manager, Johnna Murray; press, Bob Ullman.

Emotional stresses of a broken family whose husband and father has taken a homosexual lover and divorced his wife, with the heavy presence of the family psychiatrist, all expressed entirely in song. Previously produced as an off-off-Broadway presentation by Playwrights Horizons 4/9/81. The play was presented without intermission.

MUSICAL NUMBERS

"Four Jews in a Room Bitching".. Company
"A Tight-Knit Family" .... Marvin
"Love Is Blind" .... Trina, Mendel, Company
"The Thrill of First Love" .... Marvin, Whizzer
"Marvin at the Psychiatrist" (a
    three-part mini-opera) .... Marvin, Mendel, Jason
"My Father's a Homo" .... Jason
"Everyone Tells Jason to See
    a Psychiatrist".. Company
"This Had Better Come to a Stop" .... Company
"Please Come to My House" .... Trina, Mendel, Jason
"Jason's Therapy" .... Jason, Mendel, Company
"A Marriage Proposal" .... Mendel
"A Tight-Knit Family" (Reprise)....................................... Marvin, Mendel
"Trina's Song" .... Trina
"March of the Falsettos"... Men
"The Chess Game" .... Marvin, Whizzer
"Making a Home" .... Trina, Mendel, Whizzer
"The Games I Play" .... Whizzer
"Marvin Hits Trina" .... Company
"I Never Wanted to Love You".. Company
"Father to Son" .... Marvin, Jason

PLAYS PRODUCED
OFF OFF BROADWAY

AND ADDITIONAL PRODUCTIONS

Here is a comprehensive sampling of off-off-Broadway and other experimental or peripheral 1980–81 productions in New York, compiled by Camille Croce. There is no definitive "off-off-Broadway" area or qualification. To try to define or regiment it would be untrue to its fluid, exploratory purpose. The listing below of hundreds of works produced by 63 OOB groups and others is as inclusive as reliable sources will allow, however, and takes in all leading Manhattan-based, new-play-producing, English-language organizations.

The more active and established producing groups are identified in **bold face type,** in alphabetical order, with artistic policies and the name of the managing director(s) given whenever these are a matter of record. Each group's 1980–81 schedule is listed with play titles in CAPITAL LETTERS. Often these are works-in-progress with changing scripts, casts and directors, sometimes without an engagement of record (but an opening or early performance date is included when available).

Many of these off-off-Broadway groups have long since outgrown a merely experimental status and are offering programs which are the equal in professionalism and quality (and in some cases the superior) of anything in the New York theater, with special contractual arrangements like the showcase code, letters of agreement (allowing for longer runs and higher admission prices than usual) and, closer to the edge of the commercial theater, a so-called "mini-contract." In the list below, all available data on opening dates, performance numbers and major production and acting credits (almost all of them Equity members) is included in the entries of these special-arrangement offerings.

A large selection of lesser-known groups and other shows that made appearances off off Broadway during the season appears under the "Miscellaneous" heading at the end of this listing.

The Actors Studio. Workshop for professional actors, directors and playwrights. Lee Strasberg, artistic director.

ANDROMEDA II (12). By Ronald Ranieri Whyte. July 16, 1980. Director, Edward Cornell; scenery, Allan Trumpler; lighting, F. Mitchell Dana; costumes, Nicole Klagsbrun; sound, Frank Vince. With Ellen Burstyn, Randy Rocca.

THE SECRET THIGHS OF NEW ENGLAND WOMEN (16). By Jan Paetow. May 21, 1981. Director, Patrick Brafford. With Robert Fitch, Gayle Greene, Denise Lute, Rusti Moon, Rory O'Moore, Sam Schacht, Madeleine Thornton-Sherwood.

In-process workshops

THE SECRET THIGHS OF NEW ENGLAND WOMEN by Jan Paetow. November 12, 1980. Directed by Patrick Brafford.

IT'S ME MARIE! by and with Marcia Haufrecht. January 2, 1981. Directed by Robert Lu-Pone, Myra Turley.
JOEY "NO-TALK" by Richard Vetere. January 27, 1981. Directed by John Camera.
ON BLISS STREET IN SUNNYSIDE written and directed by Marcia Haufrecht. April 24, 1981. With Jacqueline Knapp, Eulalie Noble.
SECOND-STORY SUNLIGHT by Bruce Serlen. April 10, 1981. Directed by June Rovenger; with Ann Hennessey, Martin Shakar.

Amas Repertory Theater. Creative arts as a powerful instrument of peaceful change, towards healthier individuals. Rosetta LeNoire, founder and artistic director.

THE PEANUT MAN, GEORGE WASHINGTON CARVER (15). By Melvin Hasman. October 15, 1980. Director, Regge Life; choreographer, Andy Torres; scenery, Bob Phillips; lighting, Mark Diquinzio; costumes, Amanda Klein. With Mel Johnson Jr., Lance Roberts, Sharon K. Brooks, Christopher Stewart, Leon Summers, Jr.

MAMA, I WANT TO SING (13). Book and lyrics, Vy Higginsen; lyrics and additional story consultation, Ken Wydro; music, Richard Tee. December 3, 1980. Director, Duane L. Jones; choreographer, Joseph Cohen; musical director, Frederic Gripper; scenery, Felix E. Cochren; lighting, Sandra L. Ross; costumes, Georgia Collins-Langhorne. With Steve Bland, Ursuline Kairson, Andrew Friarson, Ann Duquesnay, Crystal Johnson.

MO' TEA, MISS ANN? (15). Book and lyrics, Bebe Coker; music, Leander Morris. February 18, 1981. Director and choreographer, Denny Shearer; musical director, Ernie Scott; scenery, Lisa Cameron; lighting, Mark Diquinzio; costumes, Vickie McLaughlin. With Zoe Walker, Juanita Walsh, Jimmy Almistad, Alonzo G. Reid, Herb Quebec.

THE CRYSTAL TREE (15). Book and lyrics, Doris Julian; music, Luther Henderson. April 19, 1981. Director, Billie Allen; choreographer, Walter Raines; musical director, J. Leonard Oxley; scenery, William R. Waithe; lighting, Mark Diquinzio; costumes, Bernard Johnson. With T. Reneé Crutcher, Jean Du Shon, Val Eley, Ira Hawkins, Norman Matlock, Christine Spencer.

American Place Theater. In addition to the regular off-Broadway subscription season, cabaret and other special projects are presented. Wynn Handman, director, Julia Miles, associate director.

The Women's Project
AFTER THE REVOLUTION (12). By Nadja Tesich. November 16, 1980. Director, Joyce Aaron; scenery, Christina Weppner; lighting, Frances Aronson; costumes, Sally J. Lesser, Kathleen Smith. With Lily Knight, Karen Ludwig, John Nesci, Will Patton, Joe Ponazecki, Ebbe Roe Smith, Lydia Stryk.

American Humorists Series
SIM: ONE NIGHT WITH A LADY UNDERTAKER FROM TEXAS (10). Written and directed by William Osborn. June 2, 1980. With Mary Bozeman. (Reopened October 20, 1980 for 8 performances.)

Circle Repertory Projects in Progress. Developmental programs for new plays. Marshall W. Mason, artistic director.

4 performances each
THE DIVINERS by Jim Leonard Jr. June 22, 1980. Directed by Tom Evans; with Richard Seff, Jeff Daniels, Timothy Shelton, James Ray Weeks, Tanya Berezin.
DIARY OF A SHADOW WALKER by Shelby Buford Jr. October 26, 1980. Directed by Daniel Irvine; with Robert LuPone, Lisa Emery.
THE SNOW ORCHID by Joseph Pintauro. January 4, 1981. Directed by Tony Giordano; with Robert LuPone, Ben Siegler, Antonio Rey, John Braden.

THE GREAT GRANDSON OF JEDEDIAH KOHLER by John Bishop. March 8, 1981. Directed by Geoffrey Shlaes; with Jake Dengel, Edward Seamon, Beryl Towbin, Timothy Shelton, Jimmie Ray Weeks, Janice Kay Young.

CHARLIE McCARTHY'S MONOCLE by Maxine Fleischman. May 4, 1981. Directed by Stephen Zuckerman; with Stephanie Gordon, Jack Davidson, William Mooney, Debra Mooney.

Encompass Theater. Dedicated to exploring the American spirit by presenting adventurous, vital productions of American opera and contemporary music theater; also provides a forum for the development of new composers, librettists, and playwrights. Nancy Rhodes, artistic director, Roger Cunningham, producer.

VAMPYR (24) (opera). Libretto, Wilhelm August Wohlbruck, translated by Michael Feingold; music and lyrics, Heinrich Marschner. September 24, 1980. Director, Nancy Rhodes; choreographer, Holly Harbinger; musical director, Paulette Haupt-Nolen; scenery, Holmes Easley; lighting, Larry Johnson; costumes, A. Christina Giannini. With David Evitts, Richard Gratton, Gerard Boyd, Edwin Cardona, Marshall Cooper, Raymond Murcell, James Stith, Sheila Wormer, Sheryl King-Lazzarotti, Patricia Ernest, Michael Burgess, Dean Shoff, Jane Vernon.

HEADSHOTS: SONGS FROM A ROMANCE (15) (musical cabaret). By Gene Paul Rickard. May 14, 1981. Director, Nick Deutsch; choreographer, Rodney Griffin; musical director, Christopher Berg; scenery, Loy Arcenas; lighting, Larry Johnson; costumes, Bud Santora. With Jim Lyness, Kenny Morris.

Ensemble Studio Theater. Nucleus of playwrights-in-residence dedicated to supporting individual theater artists and developing new works for the stage. 60–80 projects each season, initiated by E.S.T. members. Curt Dempster, artistic director.

EL HERMANO by Romulus Linney, TWO PART HARMONY by Katharine Long, and LANDSCAPE WITH WAITRESS by Robert Pine (one-act plays). January 21, 1981. With Richmond Hoxie, Wende Dasteel.

FATHER DREAMS. By Mary Gallagher. March 18, 1981. Director, Charles Karchmer; scenery, Brian Martin; lighting, Richard Lund; costumes, Karen Miller; sound, Rick Segal. With Christine Jansen, Chris Lutkin, Bernie McInerney, Lenka Peterson.

THE SCENTED GARDEN. By Tim Kelly. April 29, 1981. With Biff McGuire, Jeannie Carson.

MARATHON 1981 (one-act play festival): A PUBLIC STREET MARRIAGE by Edward Allen Baker, directed by Jack Caputo; STUCK IN THE PICTURES ON A SUNDAY AFTERNOON by Bill Bozzone, directed by Bill Cwikowski; A SERMON written and directed by David Mamet; THE LADY OR THE TIGER by Shel Silverstein, directed by Art Wolff; with Richard Dreyfuss; APRIL OFFERING by Elizabeth Karp, directed by John Schwab; DOWN THE TUBES by Brian McConnachie, directed by Risa Bramon; IN CAHOOTS by James Ryan, directed by Kent Lantaff; THE SMASH by Neil Cuthbert; DUMPING GROUND by Elizabeth Diggs; THE RODEO STAYS IN TOWN FOR AT LEAST A WEEK by Jerry Stubblefield; GOOD HELP IS HARD TO FIND by Arthur Kopit; OPEN ADMISSIONS by Shirley Lauro; AMERICAN GARAGE by Peter Maloney. May 26-June 9, 1981.

GEOGRAPHY OF A HORSE DREAMER by Sam Shepard. April 14, 1981. Directed by Risa Bramon.

Equity Library Theater. Actors' Equity sponsors a series of revivals each season as showcases for the work of its actor-members and an "informal series" of original, unproduced material. George Wojtasik, managing director.

THE DEVIL'S DESCIPLE by George Bernard Shaw. September 25, 1980. Directed by Robert Barton; with Richard Leighton, Barry Ford, Herbert Du Val, Carol Potter, Maxine Taylor-Morris.

A FUNNY THING HAPPENED ON THE WAY TO THE FORUM (musical) book by Larry Gelbart and Burt Shevelove, music and lyrics by Stephen Sondheim. October 30, 1980. Directed by Cash Baxter; with Connie Colt, Jonathan Kestly, Geoffrey Webb, Art Ostrin, Scott Bylund.

KIND LADY by Edward Chodorov, from a story by Hugh Walpole. December 4, 1980. Directed by Carol Thompson.

GODSPELL (musical) conceived by John-Michael Tebelak, music and lyrics by Stephen Schwartz. January 8, 1981. Directed by William Koch; with Alynne Amkraut, Scott Bakula, Andy Roth, Elizabeth Bruzzese, Liz Callaway, Michael J. Duran, Jason Graae, Bev Larson, Kevin Rogers, Laurine Towler.

DEATH TAKES A HOLIDAY by Alberto Casella, rewritten for the American stage by Walter Ferris. February 12, 1981. Directed by Michael Diamond; with Mary Portser, John Bergstrom, Ron Johnston.

ANYTHING GOES (musical) book by Guy Bolton, P.G. Wodehouse, Howard Lindsay, and Russel Crouse, music and lyrics by Cole Porter. March 12, 1981. Directed by Rich Michaels; with Jan Neuberger, Clayton Berry, Cynthia Meryl, John Remme.

THE MISER (musical) by Molière, translated and directed by Earl McCarroll, music and lyrics by Robert Johanson. April 16, 1981. With Martha Danielle, Daniel Stewart, Lola Powers, Alan Kass, Robert Yacko, Claudine Cassan, Lyle Kanouse, Carol Trigg, Valerie Toth, Joel Frederickson, Stockman Barner.

RAISIN (musical) book by Robert Nemiroff and Charlotte Zaltzberg, based on Lorraine Hansberry's *A Raisin in the Sun,* music by Judd Woldin, lyrics by Robert Brittan. May 14, 1981. Directed by Helaine Head; with Claudia McNeil, Rhetta Hughes, Robert Jason, Deborah Lynn Sharpe, Nate Barnett, Saundra McClain, Ronald E. Richardson.

Informal Series: 3 performances each
SAVE THAT SONG FOR ME music and lyrics by Dennis Andreopoulos. September 15, 1980. With Helena Andreyko, Michael Crouch, Liza Gennaro, William Daniel Grey, Cass Morgan, E.G. Roberts, Zoe Walker.
A MAN BETWEEN TWILIGHTS: THE LIFE AND WRITINGS OF JAMES AGEE conceived by Kevin Edward Kennedy, music by Christopher Kennedy. October 20, 1980. Directed by Kathlyn Chambers; with Suzanne Ford, Douglas Jones, Deborah Strang.
SARA by Michael Brady. November 17, 1980. Directed by Richard Bruno; with Catherine Bruno, Ellen Kaplan, Olivia Virgil Harper, Jennifer Johanos, Gregory Johnson, James McDonnell, Cindy Rosenthal, Russell Bonanno.
ACTORS by Geoffry Brown. December 8, 1980. Directed by Elowyn Castle; with Thomas Wagner, Geoffrey Wade, Bob McDonald, David Anthony, David Garwood, John Fanning, James Bartz, Don Hampton, Regina O'Malley, Wendy Nute, Elaine Hyman.
A BIT OF OLD IRELAND (one-act plays): THE MEADOW GATE, MICHELIN, THE BOGIE MEN by Lady Gregory, THE TINKER'S WEDDING by John Millington Synge. January 19, 1981. Directed by Elowyn Castle and John Fanning; with Conan Carroll, Mary Reid Horan, Lori Lynott, Michael Meyerson, J. Patrick O'Sullivan.
MOLNAR IN THE AFTERNOON, STILL LIFE and AN ACTOR FROM VIENNA (one-act plays) by Ferenc Molnar. February 2, 1981. Directed by Phillip B. Epstein; with Thomas H. Costello, Bob J. Mitchell, Albert Owens, Tee Scatuorchio, Carrie Zivetz.
BUT SHIRLEY FAIRWEATHER! (musical) book by Deidre Barber, music by Stephen Brown, lyrics by Paul Gaston. March 16, 1981. Directed by Peg Zitko; with Dennis Bateman, Kate Ingram, Susan Glaze, Diane Maggio, Ronald Owen, Kevin Paul.
STARRY NIGHT by Monte Merrick. April 27, 1981. Directed by John Henry Davis; with Toby Parker, Allan Carlsen, Jill Eikenberry.
I STAND HERE IRONING by Tillie Olsen and THE AUTUMN DOG by Paul Theroux. May 11, 1981. Directed by Lee Beltzer; with Lee Croghan, Kevin Kelly, Kathleen Morrison, Victoria Rauch.

NEW FEDERAL THEATER—Franz Jones, Victoria Howard, Lucy Holland and Hy Mencher in *Things of the Heart: Marian Anderson's Story* by Shauneille Perry

Gene Frankel Theater Development of new works and revivals for the theater. Gene Frankel, artistic director.

GAY COMPANY REVISITED (satirical revue). Music and lyrics, Fred Silver. August 8, 1980. Director and choreographer, Miriam Fond; musical director, Wes McAfee; scenery, Vittorio Capecce; lighting, Andrea Wilson; costumes, Van Ramsey. With Hal Davis, Arne Gundersen, Michael McAssey, James Scopeletis, Susan Elizabeth Scott.

SISTER AIMEE (13). Book, music, and lyrics by Worth Gardner. April 17, 1981. Director, David Holdgreiwe; musical director, Fred Barton; scenery, J.R. Modereger; lighting, Dan Farley; costumes, Van Ramsey. With Deb G. Girdler, Jennifer Lewis, Willi Kirkham, David Adamson, Donna Sontag, Jack Kyrieleison.

Hudson Guild Theater. Presents plays in their New York, American, or world premieres. David Kerry Heefner, producing director, Judson Barteaux, managing director.

35 performances each

SUMMER. By Hugh Leonard. September 17, 1980. Director, Brian Murray; scenery, Steven Rubin; lighting, Dennis Parichy; costumes, Jane Greenwood. With David Canary, Swoosie Kurtz, Victor Bevine, Thomas A. Carlin, Charlotte Moore, Mia Dillon, James Greene, Pauline Flanagan.

THE SLAB BOYS. By John Byrne. November 19, 1980. Director, Peter Maloney; scenery, James Leonard Joy; lighting, Jeff Davis; costumes, Elizabeth Covey. With Gene O'Neill, John Pankow, Daniel Gerroll, Richmond Hoxie, Bo Smith, Ian Trigger, Helena Carroll, Noreen Tobin.

WAITING FOR THE PARADE. By John Murrell. January 14, 1981. Director, David Kerry Heefner; scenery and costumes, Christina Weppner; lighting, Robby Monk. With Mia Dillon, Roxanne Hart, Jo Henderson, Marti Maraden, Marge Redmond.

KNUCKLE. By David Hare. March 4, 1981. Director, Geoffrey Sherman; scenery and lighting, Paul Wonsek; costumes, Denise Romano. With Fran Brill, Alice Drummond, Gwyllum Evans, Daniel Gerroll, Peter Jolly, Donald R. Klecak.

NED AND JACK. By Sheldon Rosen. May 13, 1981. Director, Colleen Dewhurst; scenery, James Leonard Joy; lighting, Robby Monk; costumes, David Murin. With Barbara Caruso, Peter Michael Goetz, Dwight Schultz.

INTAR. Innovative culture center for the Hispanic American community of New York City focusing on the art of theater. Max Ferrá, artistic director.

LIFE IS DREAM (24). By Pedro Calderon de la Barca, adapted and directed by Maria Irene Fornes. May 28, 1981. Music, George Quincy; scenery, Christina Weppner; lighting, Joe Ray; costumes, Molly Maginnis. With Margaret Harrington, Manuel Martinez, Dain Chandler, Shirley Lemmon, Abe Wald, Christofer De Oni, Ellen Black, Cliff Seidman.

Intar's Hispanic-American Playwrights-in-Residence Laboratory (staged readings): MUNDO by Lynne Alvarez; HUSTLERS WITH WORN-OUT SHOES by Lucky Cienfuegos; A LITTLE HOLY WATER by Ramon Delgado; THE ASH CAN AND THE COBRA by Tee Saralegui; IN ANOTHER PART OF THE CITY by Eduardo Gallardo; INITIATION by Victor Fragoso; YERBA BUENA by Sandra Maria Esteves; ORPHANS by Michael Alasa; BEMPIRES by Shamsul Alam. November 5-December 7, 1980.

Interart Theater. A professional environment primarily for women playwrights, directors, designers and performers to participate in theatrical activity. Margot Lewitin, artistic director, Abigail Franklin, managing director.

ELECTRA SPEAKS (24). By Clare Coss, Sondra Segal, and Roberta Sklar. October 31, 1980. Directors, Sondra Segal and Roberta Sklar; scenery, Beth Kuhn; lighting, Annie Wrightson; costumes, Laura Vogel. With Sharon Dennis, Amy Lerner, Mary Lum, Mary Lyon, Sondra Segal.

REQUEST CONCERT (100+). By Franz Xaver Kroetz, translated by Peter Sander. March 11, 1981. Director, JoAnne Akalaitis; scenery, lighting, costumes, Manuel Lutgenhorst, Douglas E. Ball. With Joan MacIntosh.

The Judson Poets' Theater. The theater arm of Judson Memorial Church and its pastor, Al Carmines, who creates a series of new, unconventional musicals which are sometimes transferred to the commercial theater. Al Carmines, artistic director.

THE AGONY OF PAUL (16). By Al Carmines. October 3, 1980. Director and choreographer, Bob Herget; scenery, Steve Prest; lighting, Andrew Taines; costumes, Jim Corry. With Tony Calabro, Molly Stark, Fiddle Viracola, Ronn Smith, Carol Estey, Essie Borden.

CHRISTMAS RAPPINGS (annual production) by Al Carmines. December 12, 1980.

T.S. ELIOT: MIDWINTER VIGIL(ANTE) (16). Opera-play by Al Carmines. March 20, 1981. Choreographer, Matthew Nash; scenery and costumes, George Deem; lighting, Andrew Taines. With Judith Elaine, Richard Battaglia, Essie Borden, Georgia Creighton, Blaine Brown, Robert Herrig, Tony Calabro.

La Mama Experimental Theater Club (ETC). A busy workshop for experimental theater of all kinds. Ellen Stewart, founder, Wesley Jensby, artistic director.

Schedule included:

MAY I (one-man show). June 3, 1980. With Bob Lloyd.
LOVE AND JUNK by Ruis Woertendyke. June 4, 1980. Directed by Michael Dennis Moore.
DIRECTIONS TO SERVANTS by Shuji Terayama. June 19, 1980. Directed by Shuji Terayama and J.A. Seazer; with Tenjosajiki.

TOURISTS AND REFUGEES (collaborative work) by The Other Theater, music by Harry Mann, Peter Golub, and William Uttley. July 9, 1980. Directed by Joseph Chaikin.

BOY MEETS SWAN by Richard Morrock. July 9, 1980. Directed by Frank Carucci.

THIRD WORLD INSTITUTE OF THEATER ARTS STUDIES (Third World Cultural series to celebrate United Nations Day). October 7-19, 1980.

KATANA (THE SWORD). By Kikue Tashiro. October 17, 1970. Director, lighting, and costumes, Linda Mussman; scenery, Jun Maeda. With Claudia Bruce, Jeannine Haas, Toshi Toda, Kim Miyori, Beth Orr, Gedde Watanabe.

THEATRIKA (festival by The Greek Theater of New York). October 21-November 2, 1980. With Olympia Dukakis.

A DAY IN THE LIFE OF THE CZAR, OR I TOO HAVE LIVED IN ARCADIA. By Frank O'Hara and V.R. Lang. October 23, 1980. Director, Peter Sellars; scenery, Roald Simonson; lighting, James F. Ingalls; costumes, Shay Cunliffe. With Dennis Boutsikaris, Ann Lange, Benn Halley Jr., Ellen Parker.

FROM THE DIARY OF ONE NOT BORN and GIMPEL THE FOOL by Isaac Bashevis Singer. November 12, 1980. Directed by David Schechter; with Steven Reisner, Susan Jurick.

DADDY! DADDY! written and directed by Tad Truesdale. December 3, 1980.

ART WAR written and directed by Rudy Kocevar. December 10, 1980.

NUIT BLANCHE. Written and directed by Ping Chong. January 1, 1981. Art director, Tony Jannetti; lighting, Blu. With John Miglietta, Pablo Vela, Tone Blevins, Louise Smith, David Wolpe, Joel Beard, Ping Chong.

DAYS OF ANTONIO by Dario D'Ambrosi. January 15, 1981. Directed by Osvald Rodriguez.

THE HISTORY OF THE UNIVERSITY ACCORDING TO THOSE WHO'VE HAD TO LIVE IT by Ed Montgomery and Robbie McCauley. February 10, 1981. Directed by Ed Montgomery. With Sedition Ensemble.

TOTAL ECLIPSE by Christopher Hampton. February 19, 1981. Directed by Randy Buck.

T.N.T. (musical revue) by Richard Morrock. February 19, 1981. Directed by Frank Carucci; with Joseph Romagnoli, Joanne Bradley, Christine Campbell.

SOFT TARGETS by Ben Maddow and the Talking Band Company. March 3, 1981. Director, Paul Zimet; music, Alice Eve Cohen and Ellen Maddow; scenery, Jeremy Lebensohn; lighting, Alan Adelman; costumes, Tim Buckley. With Tina Shepard, Raymond Barry, Alice Eve Cohen, Juliet Glass, Sybille Hayn, Ellen Maddow, Arthur Strimling.

GREEN CARD BLUES by Annalita Alexander. March 19, 1981. Directed by John Ferraro; with the Cooper-Keaton Group.

TWISTS AND TURNS by Ulrike Dopfer, Rudi Roth, and Axel Tangerding. April 9, 1981. With Theaterprojekt Werkhaus Moosach.

A PIECE OF MONOLOGUE by Samuel Beckett. April 9, 1981. With David Warrilow.

ROCKABY by Samuel Beckett. April 13, 1981. Directed by Alan Schneider.

ALIEN COMIC (one-man show) written and performed by Tom Murrin. April 16, 1981.

THE RAMAYANA by Sukhendu Dutt. April 17, 1981. Directed by Cecile Guidote; with the Twitas Ensemble.

AFTER STARDRIVE. Book, music, and lyrics by Kathleen Cramer and O-Lan Shepard. May 8, 1981. Director, Bevya Rosten; musical director, John Woelz; scenery and costumes, Linda Hartinian; lighting, Anne Militello. With Deidre O'Connell, John Patrick Hurley, Walter Hadler, Marjorie Hayes, Barbara Eda-Young, Michael French, Tony Pasqualini.

A PRELUDE TO THE TAIN from the Irish epic, *Tain go Cuailinge*. May 14, 1981. Directed by Michael McQuaid and Judy Trupin.

PANTHER written and directed by Manuel Lutgenhorst, music by Philip Glass. May 27, 1981. With The Panther Group.

Lion Theater Company. Actors' company with an electric repertory. Gene Nye, artistic director, Eleanor Meglio, producing director.

DÉCLASSÉE (24). By Zoë Akins. February 25, 1981. Director, Gene Nye; scenery, Linda Skipper; lighting, Frances Aronson; costumes, Molly Maginnis. With Andrew Arnault, Bill Buell, Eileen Burns, Maria Cellario, Helen-Jean Arthur, Ken Costigan, Colin Leslie Fox, Francine

Farrell, Michael Fischetti, Sharon Laughlin, Julia Mackenzie, Allan Manning, Paul Murray, Kevin O'Rourke, Lorraine Totaro.

Manhattan Punch Line. Comedy theater. Steve Kaplan, Mitch McGuire, producing directors.

16 performances each

CLOSE RELATIONS. Written and directed by Leslie Weiner. November 6, 1980. Scenery and costumes, Ernest Allen Smith; lighting, Robert F. Strohmeier. With Henderson Forsythe, Michael Tolan, Laurie Heineman.

THE PREVALENCE OF MRS. SEAL. By Otis Bigelow. February 5, 1981. Director, Jason Buzas; scenery, Bob Phillips; lighting, Mal Sturchio; costumes, Karen Hummel. With Frances Sternhagen, Humphrey Davis, Matthew Lewis, Nancy Donohue, Stephen Ahern, Beth Austin, Richard Council, I.M. Hobson, Tony Cummings.

A PAIR OF HEARTS. By Monte Merrick. May 21, 1981. Director, Steve Kaplan; scenery, Steve Axtell; lighting, Susan A. White; costumes, Gayle Everhart; sound, Robert Armin. With Leslie Frances Williams, Nancy Linehan, Mitch McGuire, Mary Baird, Kathrin King Segal, Richard Woods, Steven Worth.

THE INCOMPARABLE MAX by Jerome Lawrence and Robert E. Lee. June, 1980. Directed by Steve Kaplan; with Michael-Eliot Cooke, Brad Bellamy, Michael Champagne.
WILL SUCCESS SPOIL ROCK HUNTER? by George Axelrod. July 17, 1980.
THE MALE ANIMAL by James Thurber and Elliott Nugent. October 2, 1980. Directed by John Gerstad; with Carole Monferdini, Mitch McGuire.
THE FRONT PAGE by Ben Hecht and Charles MacArthur. December 11, 1980. Directed by Steve Kaplan.
THE COMEDY OF ERRORS by William Shakespeare. March 12, 1981. Directed by Paul Schneider.
ENGAGED by W.S. Gilbert. April 16, 1981. Directed by Jerry Heymann; with Larry Pine, Arthur Erickson, Beth Austin.

Manhattan Theater Club. A producing organization with three stages for fully-mounted off-Broadway productions, readings, workshop activities and cabaret. Lynne Meadow, artistic director, Barry Grove, managing director.

UpStage/Cabaret

ONE TIGER TO A HILL (35). By Sharon Pollock. October 28, 1980. Director, Thomas Bullard; scenery, David Potts; lighting, F. Mitchell Dana; costumes, Judy Dearing. With John Getz, Margaret Whitton, Vic Polizos, Denzel Washington, Sam Gray, Alan Mixon, Michael Tucker, Larry Joshua, Dann Florek, Jane Hoffman.

CRIMES OF THE HEART (35). By Beth Henley. December 9, 1980. Director, Melvin Bernhardt; scenery, John Lee Beatty; lighting, Dennis Parichy; costumes, Patricia McGourty. With Stephen Burleigh, Mia Dillon, Mary Beth Hurt, Lizabeth Mackay, Peter MacNicol, Julie Nesbit. A Best Play; see page 226.

REAL LIFE FUNNIES (35). Adapted and directed by Howard Ashman, from Stan Mack's comic strip; songs by Alan Menken. Choreographer, Douglas Norwick; musical director, Larry Hochman; lighting, Frances Aronson. With Pamela Blair, Gibby Brand, Merwin Goldsmith, Janie Sell, Dale Soules, Chip Zien.

In-the-Works (plays in process, 14 performances each)

AFTER ALL. By Vincent Canby. March 17, 1981. Director, Douglas Hughes; scenery, David Emmons; lighting, Dawn Chiang; costumes, Christa Scholtz. With George Guidall, Lois Smith.

THE CHISOLM TRAIL WENT THROUGH HERE. By Brady Sewell. March 31, 1981. Director, Steven Schachter; scenery, David Emmons; lighting, Dawn Chiang; costumes, Christa Scholtz. With William Converse-Roberts, Jean DeBaer, Robert Desiderio, John Goodman, Shannon John, Kristen Palmieri, William Russ, Helen Stenborg, Ellen Tobie, Paula Trueman, Ed Van Nuys.

A CALL FROM THE EAST. By Ruth Prawer Jhabvala. April 14, 1981. Director, John Tillinger; scenery, David Emmons; lighting, Dawn Chiang; costumes, Christa Scholtz. With Lisa Banes, Dana Ivey, Theodore Sorel, W.H. Macy, Veronica Castang, John Vickery.

SCENES FROM LA VIE DE BOHEME. By Anthony Giardina. April 28, 1981. Director, Douglas Hughes; scenery, David Emmons; lighting, Dawn Chiang; costumes, Christa Scholtz. With Mike Brennan, Al Corley, Mia Dillon, John Christopher Jones, Robin Karfo, Michael Kaufman, Rick Lieberman, Frank Nastasi, Marcell Rosenblatt.

Special Events

AN EVENING WITH SHIFFMAN AND VANCE (12). Material by Tim Grundmann. February 10, 1981. With Fred Shiffman, Dana Vance.

JAKE HOLMES AND FRIENDS (6). March 19, 1981.

The New Dramatists. An organization devoted to playwrights; member writers may use the facilities for anything from private could readings of their material to public script-in-hand readings. David Copelin, literary services director.

Staged readings

THE SADDEST SUMMER OF VAL by Dennis McIntyre. June 21, 1980. Directed by Peter Maloney; with Lloyd Davis, Jr., John Danielle, Gary Bolling, Matthew Cowles, Lisa Wilkinson.

A PLAY ABOUT LOVERS by Robert Wallsten. June 24, 1980. Directed by Kristoffer Tabori; with Rachel Roberts, Pamela Brook, Edward Gero, Kristoffer Tabori.

KETCHUP by John Patrick Shanley. October 15, 1980. Directed by Susan Gregg; with Jeffrey Anderson-Gunter, Joseph Montalbo, Tony Shultz, Jan Buttram, Carol Ann Mansell.

MY SISTER IN THIS HOUSE by Wendy Kesselman. November 20, 1980. Directed by Inverna Lockpez; with Sofia Landon, Patricia Charbonneau, Rebecca Schull, Brenda Currin, Annemarie Hollander.

THESE DAYS THE WATCHMEN SLEEP by Karl Evans. December 17, 1980. Directed by Stephan Maro; with Herbert Rubens, Joseph Giardina, Dan Lauria, Michael Hardstack, George Pollack.

SHIRLEY BASIN by Jack Gilhooley. January 7, 1981. Directed by Robert Siegler; with Theresa Karanik, Erika Petersen, Ken Costigan, Peg Murray, Jane Cronin.

LA VISIONARIA by Renaldo Eugenio Ferradas. January 14, 1981. Directed by John Henry Davis; with Dennis Parker, Dan Lauria, Paul Farin, Valerie von Volz, Rebecca Schull.

GORILLA by John Patrick Shanley. January 21, 1981. Directed by Susan Gregg; with Jim Maxwell, Phyllis Somerville, Bruce Somerville, Tom Bade, Michael Morin.

BRIGITTE BERGER by Stanley Taikeff. March 18, 1981. Directed by Thomas Grunewald; with Anita Keal, Larry Joshua, Jeffrey Anderson-Gunter, Kathy Danzer, Ron Siebert.

THE WAR BRIDES by Terri Wagener. March 25, 1981. Directed by Elaine Kanas; with Frances Fisher, Sarah Jessica Parker, Libby Boone, Catherine Wolf, Sloane Shelton.

EVE OF ALL SAINTS by Syl Jones. April 6, 1981. Directed by Susan Gregg; with Jack R. Marks, Victoria Boothby, Theresa Karanik, Victor Slezak, Ivonne Coll.

ABOUT SPONTANEOUS COMBUSTION by Sherry Kramer. April 22, 1981. Directed by Pat Carmichael; with Susan Merson, Dolores Kenan, Eddie Jones, Cleve Roller, David Strathairn.

SNOW IN THE VIRGIN ISLANDS by Marisha Chamberlain. May 4, 1981. Directed by Richard Dow; with Damien Leake, Theresa Karanik.

QUARTET by Peter Dee. May 20, 1981. Directed by John Henry Davis; with Cynthia Neer, Theresa Karanik, Jonathan Bolt, Eddie Jones.

New Federal Theater. The Henry Street Settlement's training and showcase unit for playwrights, mostly black and Puerto Rican. Woodie King Jr., producer.

12 performances each

BRANCHES FROM THE SAME TREE. By Marjorie Eliot. July 10, 1980. Scenery, Wynn Thomas; lighting, Sandra Ross; costumes, Judy Dearing. With Verona Barnes, Louise

NO SMOKING PLAYHOUSE—Carrick Glenn and Fran
Carlon in a scene from *Sweet/Sour* by Sebastian Stuart

Stubbs, Vickie Thomas, David Downing, Joe Fields, Yolanda Karr, Maxwell Glanville, Clebert
Ford.

THE CONNECTION. By Jack Gelber. October 23, 1980. Director, Carl Lee; music, Gary
Bartz; video, Shirley Clarke; scenery, Robert Edmonds; lighting, Leo Gambacorta; costumes,
Edna Watson. With Morgan Freeman, Lindzee Smith, Sam McMurray, Robert Silver, Greg
DuHart, Michael Auder.

SOMETHING LOST. By Anthony Wisdom. November 20, 1980. Director, Richard Gant; scenery, Robert Edmonds; lighting, Marshall Williams; costumes, Myrna Colley-Lee. With Herbert
Kerr, Kirk Kirksey, Greg DuHart, Herb Rice, Patricia Hayling.

THE TRIAL OF DR. BECK. By Hughes Allison. January 2, 1981. Director, Phillip Lind-
say; scenery, Robert Edmonds; lighting, Larry Johnson; costumes, Carlo Thomas. With Reuben
Green, La Tanya Richardson, Elizabeth Van Dyke, Minnie Gentry, Carl Pistilli, Herb
Downer.

WIDOWS. By Mfundi Vundla. March 26, 1981. Director, Vantile E. Whitfield; scenery, Llewel-
lyn Harrison; lighting, Leo Gambacorta; costumes, Judy Dearing. With Victoria Howard, Pamela
Poitier, Tina Sattin.

NO (15+). By Alexis De Veaux, adapted and directed by Glenda Dickerson. April 24, 1981.
Scenery, Robert Edmonds; lighting, Marshall Williams; costumes, Rise Collins, Glenda Dickerson. With Cheryl Lynn Bruce, Rise Collins, Yvette Erwin, Marilyn Nicole Worrell.

Family Matinee Series

GRAND STREET by Robert Reiser. November 29, 1980. Directed by Elaine Kanas; with Robert
Trebor, Harold Guskin, Olivia Negron, Neil Napolitan.

THINGS OF THE HEART: MARIAN ANDERSON'S STORY by Shauneille Perry. January 10, 1981. Directed by Denise Hamilton; with Victoria Howard, Franz Jones, Hy Mencher, Addison Greene, Celestine Heard, Robert Grossman, Marina Stefan.

LA MORENA (one-act play) by Beth Turner. February 14, 1981. Directed by Raul Davila; with Carlos Carrasco, Lucy Vega, Miluka Rivera.

THE DANCE AND THE RAILROAD by David Henry Hwang. March 21, 1981. Directed by John Lone; with John Lone, Tzi Ma, Glenn Kubota.

New York Shakespeare Festival Public Theater. Schedule of experimental workshop productions and guest residencies, in addition to its regular productions. Joseph Papp, producer.

AN EVENING OF SHOLOM ALEICHEM (1). Translated by Joseph Singer. August 20, 1980. Director, Richard Maltby Jr.; costumes, Pegi Goodman. With Murray Horwitz.

GIRLS, GIRLS, GIRLS (30). By Marilyn Suzanne Miller; music and musical direction, Cheryl Hardwick. September 9, 1980. Director, Bob Balaban; choreographer, Graciela Daniele; scenery, Akira Yoshimura; lighting, Arden Fingerhut; costumes, Karen Roston. With Valri Bromfield, Frances Conroy, Anne DeSalvo, Judith Ivey, Jay O. Sanders.

YOU KNOW AL HE'S A FUNNY GUY (81). Written and performed by Jerry Mayer. September 11, 1980. Director, John Pynchon Holms.

PRESENTING ALL OF DAVID LANGSTON SMYRL (OR IS IT?) (26). Written and performed by David Langston Smyrl. November 7, 1980. Director and arranger, James Milton; lighting, Victor En Yu Tan.

DEAD END KIDS (96). Conceived and directed by JoAnne Akalaitis. November 9, 1980. Assistant director, Chas Cowing; scenery, Robert Israel in collaboration with JoAnne Akalaitis; lighting, Beverly Emmons; costumes, Sally Rosen. With David Brisbin, Scotty Snyder, John Fistos, Michael Kuhling, Greg Mehrten, Terry O'Reilly, Juliet Glass, Zachary Glass, B-St. John Schofield, Chas Cowing, Ellen McElduff, Ruth Maleczech, George Bartenieff, Jerry Mayer, Hilary Granson, William Raymond. (Mabou Mines production)

TEXTS (18). By Samuel Beckett, adapted by Joseph Chaikin and Steven Kent. March 8, 1981. Director, Steven Kent; scenery, Gerald Bloom; lighting, Craig Miller; costumes, Mary Brecht. With Joseph Chaikin.

WRONG GUYS. From *Wrong Guys* by Jim Strahs, created by Ruth Maleczech. April 28, 1981. Scenery, Michael Kuhling; lighting, Julie Archer; costumes, Greg Mehrten; sound, Craig Jones. With Bill Raymond, Terry O'Reilly, Greg Mehrten, B-St. John Schofield, Chas Cowing, Lee Breuer, Julie Archer, Craig Jones, Stephanie Rudolph, Michael Kuhling, Rigel Spencer, Phillip Price, Lydia Schwarz. (Mabou Mines production)

No Smoking Playhouse. Emphasis on new plays and adaptation of classics, stressing the comedic. Norman Thomas Marshall, artistic director.

ENTER MIDSUMMER WITH A FLOURISH (one-act play festival): SHEPHERD'S TALE by Joseph Mathewson, directed by Fay Bright; MIDDLE MAN OUT by Dick Riley, directed by Granville W. Burgess; KITCHEN INTERLUDE by Charles Pulaski, directed by Norman Marshall; CRACKED CANINES by Lucas Myers, directed by Norman Marshall; REMISSION by Richard Dresser, directed by Joe Correa; I TALK TO MYSELF by William Redfield, directed by Adam Redfield; THE DOUBLERS by Betzie Parker White, directed by Phil Davis; LOUISE by Walter Corwin, directed by Ken Buckshi; TIMBERLINES by Jeanine O'Reilly, directed by George Wolf Reily. July 17–August 24, 1980.

DANGEROUS CORNER by J.B. Priestley. January 15, 1981. Directed by Marvin Einhorn; with Alan Bluestone, George Wolf Reily, Maggie Miller, Sue Willis, Marina Posvar.

HAMLET by William Shakespeare. March 19, 1981. Directed by George Wolf Reily; with Adam Redfield, Chet Carlin, Marina Posvar, Eden Lee Murray, Marvin Einhorn, Sylvester Rich, Malcolm Gray.

SWEET/SOUR. By Sebastian Stuart. April 30, 1981. Director, Norman Thomas Marshall; scenery, R. Patrick Sullivan; lighting, Leslie Ann Kilian; costumes, Van Ramsey. With Marina Posvar, Richard Spore, Fran Carlon, Natalie Ross, Tom Matsusaka.

The Open Space Theater Experiment. Emphasis on experimental works. Lynn Michaels, Harry Baum, directors.

THE SANCTUARY LAMP (17). Written and directed by Thomas Murphy. June 5, 1980. Scenery, Gregory William Bolton; lighting, Carol B. Sealey; costumes, Elaine R. Mason; sound, David Nunemaker. With Hazen Gifford, Peter Rogan, Mary Garripoli, Wally Peterson, Sue Sheehy.

WHERE HAVE ALL THE DREAMERS GONE? (16). By Melba Thomas. April 9, 1981. Director, Don Price; scenery, Barry Axtell; lighting, Susan A. White; costumes, Mary Whitehead. With Merle Louise, Yvonne Warden, Ernesto Gonzalez, Ron Johnston, Fred Morsell, Natalie Priest, Marilyn Berry, Robin Thomas, Grace Roberts, Hugh Byrnes.

A COLLIER'S FRIDAY NIGHT (12). By D.H. Lawrence. May 14, 1981. Director, John Beary; scenery, Jack Chandler; lighting, Tom Hennes; costumes, Carol H. Beule. With Robin Howard, Susan Stevens, Cecile Callan, Tom Brennan, Ron Keith, Martin Treat, Ryn Hodes, Maura Ellyn.

A DREAM PLAY by August Strindberg, translated by Elizabeth Sprigge. February 19, 1981. Directed by Susan Einhorn; with Susan Stevens, Martin Treat, Charles Shaw-Robinson, Bruce Somerville, Michael Arkin, Bonnie Brewster, Paul Peeling, Diane Tarleton.

Pan Asian Repertory Theater. Aims to present professional productions which employ Asian American theater artists, to encourage new plays which explore Asian American themes, and to combine traditional elements of Far Eastern theater with Western theatrical techniques. Tisa Chang, artistic director.

MONKEY MUSIC (17). By Margaret Lamb. July 17, 1980. Director, Tisa Chang; choreographer, Sachiyo Ito; music, Simeon Westbrooke; scenery, Bob Phillips; lighting, Linnaea Tillet; costumes, Amanda Klein. With Mel D. Gionson, Henry Yuk, Ron Nakahara, Alvin Lum, Jodi Long, Ernest Abuba, Michael G. Chin, Lilah Kan.

AN AMERICAN STORY (22). By Ernest H. Abuba. November 7, 1980. Director, Tisa Chang; scenery, Jess Adkins; lighting, Chaim Gitter; costumes, Loy Arcenas. With Channing Chase, Raul Aranas, Glenn Cabrera, Jean Anderson, Marlea Evans, George Buck, Frank Girardeau, Al Israel, Mia Katigbak.

FLOWERS AND HOUSEHOLD GODS (18). By Momoko Iko. April 17, 1981. Director, Tisa Chang; scenery, Jess Adkins; lighting, Joseph Chu; costumes, Cynthia Kunishige, Lydia Tnaji. With Kitty Chen, Ron Nakahara, Natsuko Ohama, Alvin Lum, Raul Aranas, Keenan Shimizu.

Playwrights Horizons. Dedicated to the support and development of new American playwrights through a series of readings, workshops and full-scale productions at the off-Broadway level. Robert Moss, producing director, Robin J. Gold, managing director, André Bishop, artistic director.

COMING ATTRACTIONS (67). By Ted Tally; music by Jack Feldman; lyrics by Bruce Sussman and Jack Feldman. November 22, 1981. Directed by Andre Ernotte; musical staging, Theodore Pappas; scenery, Andrew Jackness, costumes, Ann Emonts; lighting, Paul Gallo. With Christine Baranski, Larry Block, Griffin Dunne, June Gable, Jonathan Hadary, Dan Strickler, Allan Wasserman.

MARCH OF THE FALSETTOS (musical) by William Finn. April 7, 1981. Directed by James Lapine; scenery, Douglas Stein; costumes, Maureen Connor; lighting, Frances Aronson; musical direction, Michael Starobin. With Michael Rupert, Alison Fraser, James Kushner, Stephen Bogardus, Chip Zien.

Productions at Queens Theater-in-the-Park included:

THE GENTLE PEOPLE (23). By Irwin Shaw. December 6, 1980. Directed by Robert Moss; scenery, John Kasarda; costumes, Nan Cibula; lighting, David Segal. With Edward O'Neill, Nana Tucker, Lee Wallace, James Carruthers, Marilyn Chris, Richard Frank.

HEAT OF RE-ENTRY (22). By Abraham Tetenbaum. April 11, 1981. Directed by Lev Shekhtman; scenery, Joseph A. Varga; costumes, Karen Miller; lighting, Annie Wrightson; original music, Norman L. Berman. With Ellen Gould, Richard Grusin, Charlotte Jones, Keith McDermott.

Puerto Rican Traveling Theater. Professional company presenting bilingual productions primarily of Puerto Rican and Hispanic playwrights, emphasizing subjects of relevance today. Miriam Colon, founder and producer.

LA ERA LATINA (31). By Dolores Prida and Victor Gragoso. August 9, 1980. Director, Raul Davila; scenery, Ernest Allen Smith; lighting, Marvin Watkins; costumes, Maria F. Contessa. With Cintia Cruz, Felipe Gorostiza, José Maldonado, Hector Mercado, Ray Ramirez, Socorro Santiago.

DEATH SHALL NOT ENTER THE PALACE (26). By Rene Marques, translated by Gregory Rabassa. March 25, 1981. Director, Pablo Cabrera; scenery, Carl Baldasso; lighting, Bill Frein; costumes, Benito Gutierrez Soto. With Sandra Rivera, Norberto Kerner, Miranda Santiago, Manuel Sebastian, Edwin Sanchez, Carmen Gutierrez, David Crommett, John Traviss, Marta Viana, Manuel Juan, Sara Rodriquez.

BETANCES (28). By Jaime Carrero. May 13, 1981. Director, Alba Oms; scenery, Carl Baldasso; costumes, Maria Contessa.

Quaigh Theater. Primarily a playwrights' theater, devoted to the new playwright, the established contemporary playwright and the modern (post-1920) playwright. Will Lieberson, artistic director.

DULCY (19) by Marc Connelly and George S. Kaufman. October 27, 1980. Director, Clinton Atkinson; scenery, Ken Holamon; lighting, John Hickey; costumes, Jacqueline Watts. With Kathy Morath, James Harder, Ben Lemon, Dennis Helfend, George Cavey, Michael Waldron, David Dannenbaum.

THE BUTTERFINGERS ANGEL, MARY AND JOSEPH, HEROD THE NUT AND THE SLAUGHTER OF 12 HIT CAROLS IN A PEAR TREE (20). By William Gibson. November 27, 1980. Director, Francine L. Trevens assisted by James R. Smith; choreographer, Frank Hatchett; musical director, Nathan Hurwitz; scenery, Bob Phillips; lighting, Marie Barrett; costumes, Johnetta Lever; sound, George Jacobs. With Paul Haggard, Keren Liswood, Shamus Murphy, Dori Salois, Melissa Thea, J. Scott Williams.

THE HUMBUG MAN (9). Written and performed by Kricker James. January 8, 1981. Director, Ernest McCarty; assistant director, lighting, Lys Hopper; costumes, Diane Lent.

DARKNESS AT NOON (21). By Sidney Kingsley. March 10, 1981. Director, Will Lieberson; scenery, Stephen Caldwell; lighting, E. St. John Villard; costumes, Elizabeth Lynch. With Frank Biancamano, Frank Dwyer, Carl Trone, Kricker James, Susan Monts, Patrick Egan, Gisli Johnson, Leslie Goldstein, Paul Hart, Richard Dahlia, Mary Beth Pape.

A NICKEL FOR PICASSO (18). By Elliott Caplin. April 10, 1981. Director, Gary Bowen; scenery, John Dollinger; lighting, Jeffrey McRoberts; costumes, Elizabeth Lynch. With Neil Bernstein, Suzanne Toren, John Michalski, Steven Gilborn, Mary Ellen Murphy, Elaine Grollman, Rea Rosno.

Lunchtime Theater

YUK YUK by Will Lieberson; THE LAST OF THE LONG DISTANCE TRAVELLERS by Lawrence Blackmore. October 27, 1980. Directed by Rich Samuelson; with Terence Cartwright.

THE SECOND STAGE—Daniel Stern and Bob Gunton
in a scene from *How I Got That Story* by Amlin Gray

AN HOUR OF CHEKHOV adapted and performed by Carl Don. November 17, 1980.

THE EXCHANGE by Ernest McCarty. January 5, 1981. Directed by Kricker James.

THE BOND by Howard Brown. January 26, 1981. Directed by James Paradise; with Peter Johl, Wendel Meldrum.

THE GOLDEN FLEECE by A.R. Gurney Jr.. February 9, 1981. Directed by Larry Staroff; with Patti Eastep, John MacKane.

THE SILVER YEARS written and performed by Basia McCoy. February 23, 1981. Directed by Margot Dee.

THE WORLD TIPPED OVER AND LAYING ON ITS SIDE by Mary Feldhaus-Weber. March 16, 1981. Directed by David Danenbaum; with Nick Ruggeri, William Pitts, John Q. Bruce, Sara Herrnstadt.

HELLO AND GOODBYE (one-act plays) by Bill Majeski. March 30, 1981. Directed by Peter deMaio; with Merriman Gatch, Daniel Graham, Robert Barend.

AMOURESQUE and ARABESQUE by Victor Gluck. April 13, 1981. Directed by Francine L. Trevens.

THE ILLAUNASPIE TRIANGLE by Sydney Bernard Smith. April 27, 1981. Directed by Kelly Cuba; with Michael McMahon, Katherine Cuba, Richard DeMares.

INSIDE written and directed by Norman Beim. May 11, 1981. With Patricia Mertens, Christopher Nelson.

The Ridiculous Theatrical Company. Charles Ludlam's camp-oriented group devoted to productions of his original scripts and broad adaptations of the classics. Charles Ludlam, artistic director and director of all productions.

REVERSE PSYCHOLOGY. By Charles Ludlam. September 14, 1980. With Black-Eyed Susan, Charles Ludlam, Bill Vehr, Charlotte Forbes.

Richard Morse Mime Theater. Permanent mime repertory theater dedicated to creating a specifically American mime form. Richard Morse, artistic director.

OFF CENTER conceived and directed by Rasa Allan. October 3, 1980.
NOVEMBER 29, 1980 conceived and directed by Richard Morse. November 29, 1980.
THE BLUEBIRD by Anastasia Nicole. December 24, 1980. Directed by Richard Morse.
MAN IN MOTION conceived and directed by Richard Morse. February 6, 1981.

The Second Stage. Committed to producing plays of the last ten years believed to deserve another chance. Robyn Goodman, Carole Rothman, artistic directors.

HOW I GOT THAT STORY (20). By Amlin Gray. November 26, 1980. Director, Carole Rothman; scenery, Patricia Woodbridge; lighting, Victor En Yu Tan; costumes, Susan Denison; sound, Gary Harris. With Bob Gunton, Daniel Stern.

IN TROUSERS (musical) by William Finn. March 22, 1981. Directed by Judith Swift; with Jay O. Sanders, Alaina Reed, Karen Jablons, Kate Dezina.

FISHING by Michael Weller. April 17, 1981. Directed by Amy Saltz; with Richard Cox, Robyn Goodman, Daniel Hugh-Kelly, Penelope Milford, Timothy Phillips, Ralph Roberts, John Spencer.

Shelter West. Aims to bring the community challenging theater based on artistic integrity. Judith Joseph, artistic director.

A CHRISTMAS CAROL. By Charles Dickens, adapted by Shaun Sutton. November 28, 1980. Director, Judith Joseph; scenery, Lilian Engel; lighting, David Landau; costumes, MaryAnn D. Smith. With Robert Hock, Ben Lourie, Kevin Madden, Joaquim de Almeida, Dande Gellis, Sarah Hoffman.

DREAMS. By Thomas Sharkey. February 20, 1981. Director, Judith Joseph; scenery, Lilian Engel; lighting, David Landau; costumes, MaryAnn D. Smith. With Paul Michael, Robert Hock, Sarah Hofman, Ben Lourie, John D. Davis Jr., Kevin Madden, Bill Fisher.

A COMPANY IN PROGRESS (one-act plays): THE ROOMING HOUSE by Conrad Bromberg and THE LOVELIEST AFTERNOON OF THE YEAR by John Guare, directed by Judith Joseph; EMOTIONAL PITCH by Leslie Apinks and IN THE SHADOW OF THE GLEN by John Millington Synge, directed by Eugene Pelfrey; PLAYING WITH FIRE by August Strindberg, directed by Ann Raychel. July 16–August 16, 1980.

THE SIGN IN SIDNEY BRUSTEIN'S WINDOW by Lorraine Hansberry. August 27, 1980. Directed by Alan Harmon.

Soho Rep. Infrequently or never-before-performed plays by the world's greatest authors, with emphasis on language and theatricality. Marlene Swartz, Jerry Engelbach, artistic directors.

FAIRY TALES OF NEW YORK. By J.P. Donleavy. June 6, 1980. Director, Jerry Engelbach; scenery, Valerie Kuehn; lighting, Ron Katz; costumes, Jim Lowe. With W.T. Martin, Pat Freni, Peter Waldren, Karen Jones.

THE IDOL MAKERS. By Stephen Davis Parks. April 23, 1981. Director, Marlene Swartz; scenery, Joseph Varga; lighting, Scott Pinkney; costumes, Melissa Binder; music, Erik Frandsen. With Cynthia Neer, Dustin Evans, George Gerdes, Burt Wherry, John Didrichsen, Christine Mitchell.

LOVE IN THE COUNTRY. Book and lyrics, Michael Alfreds; music and directed by Anthony Bowles. May 21, 1981. Musical director, Barry Koron; scenery, David Harnish; lighting, Scott Pinkney; costumes, Steven L. Birnbaum. With Richard Behren, Erick Devine, Suzanne Ford, Mary Eileen O'Donnell, Terri Beringer, Eileen Schuyler, Steve Sterner.

DESIRE CAUGHT BY THE TAIL by Pablo Picasso. October 16, 1980. Directed by Jonathan Foster; with Shelly Desai, Licia Columbi.
THE STREETS OF NEW YORK by Dion Boucicault. October 30, 1980. Directed by Trueman Kelley; with Mark Brandon, Shelley Rogers.

THE DOCTOR AND THE DEVILS by Dylan Thomas. February 26, 1981. Adapted and directed by Carol Corwen; with Kenneth Gray, Dustin Evans, George Gerdes, Patrick Clear, Allison Brennan.

OLD TIMES by Harold Pinter. March 19, 1981. Directed by Jerry Engelbach; with Jennifer Sternberg, Maggie Burke, George Taylor, John Corey.

Theater at St. Clement's. New American plays presented in New York premieres. Michael Hadge, artistic director, Stephen Berwind, managing director.

SEVENTY SCENES OF HALLOWEEN (16). By Jeffrey M. Jones. September 18, 1980. Director, Matthew Maguire; scenery and lighting, Jim Clayburgh; costumes, Maura Clifford. With Christopher McCann, Caroline McGee, Frederikke Meister, Kevin O'Rourke.

EVERY PLACE IS NEWARK (16). By Ira Lewis. December 4, 1980. Director, Michael Hadge; scenery, Steven Rubin; lighting, Victor En Yu Tan; costumes, Margo LaZaro. With Joseph Ragno, Ben Slack, James Dukas, Bernie Passeltiner, Rutanya Alda, Gerald Gregorio, Mike Starr, Hy Anzell, Nora Elcar, Ira Lewis.

THE CARNIVAL OF GLORIE (16). By Joseph Hindy. February 19, 1981. Director, Anita Khanzadian; scenery and lighting, Terry A. Bennett; costumes, Miriam Nieves; music, Lou Rodgers. With Tom Everett, Janet Ward, James Greene, Mike Houlihan.

ESCOFFIER: KING OF CHEFS (19). Written and performed by Owen S. Rachleff. April 9, 1981. Director, Laurence Carr; scenery and lighting, Peter Harrison; costumes, Linda Vigdor.

Theater for the New City. Developmental theater, incorporating live music and dance into new plays. George Bartenieff, Crystal Field, artistic directors.

Schedule included:

COLD & LAZY & ELAINE (16) (one-act plays). By Stephen Holt. September 9, 1980. Scenery, Bobjack Callejo; lighting, Richard Currie; costumes, Molly Parkin. With Lola Pashalinski.

SUNDAY CHILDHOOD JOURNEYS TO NOBODY AT HOME (20). Collaboration by Arthur Sainer, author, Lee Breuer, director, Alison Yerxa, set designer. September 18, 1980. Music, Sidney Dickler. With Bella Bruno, Murray Goldberg, Sonia Golub, Bernard Goodman, Ted Hoffman, Lucille Paisley.

THE YELLOW WALLPAPER (24). By Charlotte Perkin Gilman, adapted and directed by Florence Falk. December 4, 1980. Music, Linda Smukler; scenery, Jun Maeda; lighting, Beverly Emmons; costumes, Madeline Cohen. With Margot Lee Sherman.

ORPHEUS AND AMERICA (16). Book, lyrics and directed by Robert Patrick; music, Rob Felstein, Robert Patrick. December 12, 1980. Choreographer, Matt Callahan; musical director, Rob Felstein; lighting, Joanna Schielke. With Tino Salas, Matt Callahan, Paul Dorman, Claudia Rose Golde, Bruce Altman.

BUTTERFACES (20). By Leonard Melfi. February 5, 1981. Director, Crystal Field; scenery, Lance Miller; lighting, Joanna Schielke; costumes, Edmund Felix. With Julia Barr, Robin Klauber, Brenda Morgan, John Carroll, Maggie Burke.

A DAY AT HARMENZ (12). By Tadeusz Borowski, adapted and directed by Steven Reisner. February 15, 1981. Scenery, Lise Engle; lighting, Brian MacDevitt; costumes, Lisa Fahrner. With Rob Kenter, Paul Lawrence, Fred Einhorn, Douglas Stone, Raymond Stough.

CHUCKY'S HUNCH (16). By Rochelle Owens. March 19, 1981. Director, Elinor Renfield; scenery, Abe Lubelski; lighting, Peter Kaczorowski; costumes, Carla Kramer; sound, Paul Garrity. With Kevin O'Connor.

SHORT TIMERS (12). By Douglas Anderson. April 9, 1981. Director, John Pynchon Holms; scenery and lighting, Richard Harmon. With Aki Aleong, Neil Harris, Mary Ann Chance, Tom Crawley, Gale Garnett.

A MIDNIGHT MOON AT THE GREASY SPOON (12). By Miguel Piñero. April 16, 1981. Director, Steve Reed; scenery, Reagan Cook; lighting and sound, Terry Alan Smith; costumes, Maura Clifford. With Harvey Pierce, Joan Turetzky, Art Kempf, Clarenze F. Jarmon, Israel Juarbe, Alexis Mylonas.

Theater of the Open Eye. Total theater involving actors, dancers, musicians, and designers working together, each bringing his own talents into a single project. Jean Erdman, artistic director.

DETAILS (OF THE SIXTEENTH FRAME) (20). By Robert Walter. June 5, 1980. Director, Nola Hague; scenery, Campbell Baird; lighting, Michael Orris Watson; sound, Gary Harris. With Courtney Burr, Brian Evers, Rosemary McNamara, Eric Schiff.

DAMIEN (32). By Aldyth Morris. April 7, 1981. Director, Nola Hague; music, William Ha'o; scenery and lighting, Craig Evans; costumes, Bobbie Hodges; sound, Gary Harris. With Eugene Troobnick.

REDEYE (one-act Western) (24). By Steven Tenney. April 22, 1981. Music, David Tenney; director, Amie Brockway; scenery, lighting, costumes, Adrienne J. Brockway. With Anne Barcley, George Dash, Richard Henson, Ed Hyland, Steve Kushner, Leigh Podgorski.

THE SHINING HOUSE (collaborative dance opera) created by Jean Erdman. October 8, 1980.

Theater Off Park. Provides the Murray Hill-Turtle Bay residents with a professional theater, showcasing the talents of new actors, playwrights, designers, and directors. Patricia Flynn Peate, executive director.

16 performances each

RIVERS RETURN. Written and directed by Robert Corpora. April 1, 1981. Scenery, John Kasarda; lighting, Leslie Spohn; costumes, Henri Saavedra. With John Beal, Meg Mundy, Olga Druce.

WOMEN IN TUNE. Conceived and directed by Aubrey Cooke. May 13, 1981. Choreographer, Todd Rinehart; musical director, Betsy Maxwell; scenery, Terry Ariano; lighting, John Senter; costumes, Henri Saavedra. With Rosalyn Rahn, LuAnn Barry, Hal Maxwell, Stuart Zagnit, Alynne Amkraut.

FAITH HEALER by Brian Friel. January 7, 1981. Directed by Jamie Brown; with Mary Fogarty, William Knight, Lium O'Begley.

TO BE YOUNG, GIFTED AND BLACK by Robert Nemiroff. February 11, 1981. Directed by Lynnie Godfrey.

Urban Arts Theater. Dedicated to the development of theater arts and craft skills in the black community. Vinnette Carroll, artistic director, Anita MacShane, managing director.

MOONY'S KID DON'T CRY and TALK TO ME LIKE THE RAIN by Tennessee Williams. September 1, 1980. Directed by Steven Gomer.
NO ROOM AT THE INN conceived by Alberta Bradford. November 13, 1980. Directed by Elmore James.
THE COLLECTION by Harold Pinter. January 20, 1981. Directed by Elmore James.
WHEN THE LIGHTS COME UP (musical) conceived and directed by Steiv Semien. March 7, 1981. With Sheila Ellis, Pat Lundy, Jamil Garland.
AMERICANA by John Shandly. May 21, 1981. Directed by Jeffrey Anderson-Gunter. With Christopher Roosevelt.

WPA Theater. Produces neglected American classics and new American plays in the realistic idiom. Kyle Renick, producing director, Howard Ashman, artistic director, Edward T. Gianfrancesco, resident designer/technical director.

WPA THEATER—Alma Cuervo, Michael Gross and Jean
DeBaer in *Put Them All Together* by Anne Commire

ALBUM (16). By David Rimmer. June 5, 1980. Director, Joan Micklin Silver; scenery, David
Potts; lighting, Craig Evans; costumes, Susan Denison. With Ann Richards, Jan Leslie Harding, Kevin Bacon, Keith Gordon.

PUT THEM ALL TOGETHER (20). By Anne Commire. October 3, 1980. Director, Howard
Ashman; scenery, Edward T. Gianfrancesco; lighting, Craig Evans; costumes, Marcia Cox. With
Alma Cuervo, Jean DeBaer, Michael Gross, Adam Stolarsky, Bonnie Campbell-Britton, Bryan
Clark, Suzanne Collins.

THE FREAK (20). By Granville Wyche Burgess. February 19, 1981. Director, Stephen
Zuckerman; scenery, Edward T. Gianfrancesco; lighting, Richard Winkler; costumes, Susan
Denison. With Dann Florek, Polly Draper, William R. Riker, James Rebhorn, Peter J.
Saputo, David James Forsyth, Richard Patrick-Warner, Rod Houts.

THE TRADING POST (20). By Larry Ketron. April 2, 1981. Director, R. Stuart White; scenery,
Edward T. Gianfrancesco; lighting, Craig Evans; costumes, Susan Denison. With Conrad
McLaren, Jane Cronin, David Morse, Kristin Griffith, Burke Pearson, Betsy Aidem.

MICHAEL GRANDO: BODY MAGIC PANTOMIME (15). April 30, 1981.

The York Players. Each season, productions of classics and contemporary plays are
mounted with professional casts, providing neighborhood residents with professional theater. Janet Hayes Walker, artistic director.

RELATIVELY SPEAKING (12). By Alan Ayckbourn. November 14, 1980. Director, Christopher Murney; scenery, James Morgan; lighting, David Gotwald; costumes, Konnie Kittrell
Berner; sound, Miles White. With Ben Gotlieb, Nancy Nichols, William Cain, Janet Hayes.

FACADE (poems by Edith Sitwell), music by William Walton. January 23, 1981. Directed by
Fran Soeder; with Kermit Brown, Mayla McKeehan, Rosemary McNamara, Kevin Sweeney,
Timothy Wahrer, Sara Wiedt.

A LITTLE NIGHT MUSIC (musical) book by Hugh Wheeler; music and lyrics by Stephen Sondheim. March 20, 1981. Directed by Fran Soeder; with Jay Stuart, Kathryn Morath, Keith Rice, Barbara Broughton, Kenneth Kantor, Mary Lynne Metternich, Helen Lloyd Breed, Jane Krakowski.

THE LADY'S NOT FOR BURNING by Christopher Fry. May 22, 1981. Directed by Janet Hayes Walker; with Carol Mayo Jenkins, Joseph Culliton, Molly Scates, James Duff, Joan Shepard, Joe Aiello, Sam Stoneburner, Frank Lowe, John Rainer, Evan Thompson.

Miscellaneous

In the additional listing of 1980–81 off-off-Broadway productions below, the names of the producing groups or theaters appear in CAPITAL LETTERS and the titles of the works in *italics*. This list consists largely of new or reconstituted works and excludes most revivals, especially of classics. It includes a few productions staged by groups which rented space from the more established organizations listed previously.

ACADEMY ARTS THEATER COMPANY. *Twister* by Pat Staten. May 28, 1981. Directed by June Rovenger; with William Severs, Cullen Johnson, Lenny Von Dohlen, Tacey Phillips.

AMDA STUDIO ONE. *The Story of the Gadsbys* by Rudyard Kipling, adapted and directed by William J. Lentsch. December 5, 1980. With Elizabeth DeBruler, David Silber, Marian Clarke, Stephen C. Bradbury.

AMERICAN JEWISH THEATER. *From the Memoirs of Pontius Pilate* by Eric Bentley. January 17, 1981. Directed by Dan Held; with Con Roche, Zvee Scooler, Albert Sinkys, Terry Christgau, David H. Kieserman.

AMERICAN THEATER LABORATORY. *Dirt Show* (one-man show) by and with Bob Carroll. January, 1981.

AMERICAN THEATER OF ACTORS. *Turns* (musical) adapted and directed by Robert Livingston, music by Gary William Friedman, lyrics by Will Holt. June 8, 1980. With Tiger Haynes, Rita Gardner, Thelma Carpenter, Bobo Lewis, Ted Thurston. *The Incognita* by Steven Braunstein. March 11, 1981. Directed by Frank Cento; with Gayle Greene, Roger Morden, Richie Allan. *As to the Meaning of Words* by Mark Eichman. May 15, 1981. Directed by Ted Snowdon; with Ron Foster, John Bentley.

ARK THEATER COMPANY. *Starmites* (musical) book, music, and lyrics by Barry Keating. October 23, 1980. Directed by Charles Karchmer; with Wendy Jo Belcher, Ron Golding, Perry Arthur. *Trouble* by Marisa Gioffre. May 14, 1981. Directed by Charles Karchmer; with Kay Michaels, Theresa Saldana, Stefano Loverso, Paul Vincent.

BLACK THEATER ALLIANCE. *Time Out of Time* by Clifford Mason. October 17, 1980. Directed by Billie Allen; with Frank Adu, Hazel Medina, Pamela Poitier, Clifford Mason, Vaughn Dwight Morrison, Monica Williams, Donald Lee Taylor, David Connell, Adisa Jahmu.

BREAD AND PUPPET THEATER. *Goya* and *Rising from the Water*. February 25, 1981. *Woyzeck*, based on George Buchner's play, March 11, 1981.

BYRD HOFFMAN FOUNDATION. *Dialog/Curious George*, text by Christopher Knowles. June 24, 1980. Directed by Robert Wilson; with Christopher Knowles, Robert Wilson.

CHELSEA THEATER CABARET. *Sister and Miss Lexie* from the works of Eudora Welty, adapted by David Kaplan and Brenda Currin. June 18, 1980. With Brenda Currin.

THE FAMILY. *The Marriage Proposal* by Anton Chekhov, adapted and directed by Marvin Felix Camillo. December 17, 1980. With Raymond Ruiz, Ellen Cleghorne, Marvin Felix Camillo.

HAROLD CLURMAN THEATER. *The Tantalus* by Ian Cullen and Catherine Arley. March 16, 1981. Directed by Stephen Joyce; with Ron Randell, Kelly Wood, David Knapp, Richard Lupino.

JEAN COCTEAU REPERTORY. *The Roman Actor* by Philip Massinger. July 31, 1980. Directed by Eve Adamson; with Coral S. Potter, Dominique Cieri, Craig Smith. *The Witch of Edmonton* by Thomas Dekker, William Rowley, and John Ford. October 3, 1980. *Pericles* by William Shakespeare. December 5, 1980. Directed by Toby Robertson; with Elton Cormier, Deborah Houston, John Schmerling, Harris Berlinsky, J.D. Eiche, Phyllis Deitschel, Craig Smith.

JEWISH REPERTORY THEATER. *36* by Norman Lessing. June 10, 1980. Directed by Marc Daniels; with Joe Ponazecki, Charles Carshon, Harold Guskin, Richard DeFabees, Sherry Rooney, William Wise. *Me and Molly* by Gertrude Berg. October 15, 1980. Directed by Edward M. Cohen; with Julie Garfield, Herman O. Arbeit, Ira Katz, Sheldon Silver, Ann Spettell, Richard Niles. *Success Story* by John Howard Lawson. December 3, 1980. Directed by Lynn Polan. *The Birthday Party* by Harold Pinter. February, 1981. Directed by Anthony McKay; with Vic Polizos, Loudon Wainwright III, Ruth Miller. *Incident at Vichy* by Arthur Miller. May 16, 1981. Directed by Ran Avni.

JONES BEACH THEATER. *The Sound of Music* (musical) book by Howard Lindsay and Russel Crouse, music by Richard Rodgers, lyrics by Oscar Hammerstein II. June, 1980. Directed by John Fearnley; with Constance Towers, Earl Wrightson, Lois Hunt.

MODERN TIMES THEATER. *The Bread and Roses Play* by Steve Friedman. May 10, 1981. Directed by Denny Partridge; with Peggy Pettit, Joan Rosenfels, Janet Langon, Phil Marsh, Steve Friedman.

MUSIC THEATER PERFORMING GROUP. *Was It Good for You?* written and directed by Susan Rice, suggested by original material by Edward Koren. June, 1980. With Sam Schacht, Alexandra Borrie. *Disrobing the Bride* written and directed by Harry Kondoleon, music by Gary S. Fagin. April, 1981. With Mary Beth Lerner, Ellen Greene, Caroline Kava.

PERFORMING GARAGE. *The Survivor and the Translator* conceived and performed by Leeny Sack. August, 1980. Directed by Stephen Borst. *Point Judith* (collaborative work) by Spalding Gray, Jim Clayburgh, Willem Dafoe, Libby Howes, Elizabeth LeCompte, Ron Vawter, Matthew Hansell, Michael Rivkin, directed by Elizabeth LeCompte; *A Personal History of the American Theater* written and performed by Spalding Gray. December, 1980.

PERRY STREET THEATER. *Practice* by Jack O'Donnell. June 10, 1980. Directed by John Noah Hertzler; with Kevin Fisher, Eric Zengota, Donald Campbell, Stoney Richards, Owen Parmele. *Forty-Deuce* by Alan Bowne. March, 1981. Directed by Sheldon Larry; with John Pankow, Barry Miller, John Seitz, W.M. Hunt.

PRISM THEATER. *Bull Pen* by John Shamsul Alam, Jim Borrelli, Ron Comenzo. June 9, 1980. Directed by Ron Comenzo; with Jim Borrelli, Neil Harris, J.J. Johnson, Jaime Tirelli.

PRIVATE THEATER CORPORATION. *Our Father* by Michael Stephens. November, 1980. Directed by Lloyd Lynford; with Robert Sloan, John Gould Rubin, Lewis Black, Roy Steinberg, William Foeller, Michael Varna.

THE PRODUCTION COMPANY. *Casualties* by Karolyn Nelke. October 2, 1980. Directed by Norman René; with Randy Danson, Monique Fowler, George Hall, Georgine Hall, Stephen McHattie, Brad O'Hare, Lillie Robertson. *Marry Me a Little* (songs by Stephen Sondheim) conceived by Craig Lucas. November, 1980. Directed by Norman René; with Suzanne Henry, Craig Lucas, Martin Perry. *Tied by the Leg* by Georges Feydeau, adapted, translated, and directed by Ted Bank. January, 1981. With Anderson Matthews, Diane Heles. *Missing Persons* by Craig Lucas. May, 1981. Directed by Norman René; with Richard Backus.

RAFT THEATER LTD. *The Traveling Lady* by Horton Foote. July 24, 1980. Directed by William Alderson; with Pamela Moller, Greg Zittel, Phillip Stewart.

RICHARD ALLEN CENTER FOR CULTURE AND ART. *Black Nativity* by Langston Hughes. December 30, 1980. Concept and direction by Esteban Vega, Howard A. Roberts; with Christophe Pierre, Agnes Johnson, Thomas Reid.

RIVERSIDE SHAKESPEARE COMPANY. *Love's Labour's Lost* by William Shakespeare. April, 1981. Directed by John Clingerman; with Madeleine Porter, Timothy Oman, Deanna Deignan, Timothy Doyle, Mike Rogers, George Holmes, James McGuire, Peter Siiteri.

SANCTUARY THEATER. *The Button* by Michael McClure, directed by Phillip Price; *Spider Rabbit* by Michael McClure, directed by Tony Barsha; *Village Wooing* by George Bernard Shaw, directed by Rip Torn (one-act plays). July, 1980. With Amy Wright, Jack Racklis, Taylor Mead, Madeleine le Roux, Adam Moroski.

SEVEN OAKS PRODUCTIONS. *Desperately Yours* by Ruby Wax. September 17, 1980. Directed by Alan Rickman; with Beverly Penberthy, Brenda Currin, Ruby Wax.

78TH STREET THEATER LAB. *Irish Coffee* by Meir Z. Ribalow. February, 1981. Directed by Michael Heaton; with Irina Brook, Tom Kleh, Guy Louthan, Valerie Shaldene.

SOLID PRODUCTIONS. *You Gonna Let Me Take You Out Tonight, Baby?*, *How Do You Do*, and *A Son, Come Home* (one-act plays) by Ed Bullins. December 27, 1980. Directed by Robert Macbeth; with Milton Grier, Mel Davis, Kim Yancey, Martin D. Pinckney, Helen Pearl Ellis.

SPECTRUM THEATER. *Gethsemane Springs* by Harvey Perr. April 30, 1981. Directed by Alan Mokler; with Nada Rowand, Lola Pashalinski, Dean Kyburz.

SQUAT THEATER. *Three Sisters* by Anton Chekhov. October, 1980. With Peter Breznyik, Peter Halasz, Istvan Balint.

THREE MUSES THEATER. *. . . And the Pursuit of Happiness* (musical satire) by Herbert Nelson. September, 1980. With Eva Nelson, Herbert Nelson.

TWIN OAK PRODUCTIONS LTD. *The Glass Menagerie* by Tennessee Williams. November 4, 1980. Directed by Tom Kamm; with Julie Haydon, Anthony Heald, Patricia Angelin, William Anton.

WEST SIDE ARTS THEATER. *Broadway Jukebox* (musical revue) conceived and directed by Ed Linderman. May, 1981. With Helena Grenot, Suzanne Lukather, Lisa Steinman, Joseph Scalzo, Allan Marks, Christopher Welles.

WESTSIDE MAINSTAGE THEATER. *City Sugar* by Stephen Poliakoff. August, 1980. Directed by John Greenwood; with William Vanderber, Paul Bonner, Peter Johl, Cathy Russell. *The Brixton Recovery* by Jack Gilhooley. January 8, 1981. Directed by Mike Houlihan; with Barry Cullison, Hazel Medina. *Entertaining Mr. Sloane* by Joe Orton. May 14, 1981. Directed by John Tillinger; with Joseph Maher, Maxwell Caulfield, Barbara Byrne, Richard Russell Ramos.

WONDERHORSE THEATER. *Naomi Court* by Michael Sawyer. August 5, 1980. Directed by Ted Weiant; with Rica Martens, David Bostick, Joanne Jacobson, Ron Johnston, Bruno Ragnacci. *Oh Me, Oh My, Oh Youmans* (musical revue of Vincent Youmans's work) conceived by Darwin Knight and Tom Taylor. January 14, 1981. Directed by Darwin Knight; with Todd Taylor, Sally Woodson, Jo Ann Cunningham, Ronald Young. *Half-Life* by Julian Mitchell. April 1, 1981. Directed by Jane Stanton; with Evan Thompson, Paul Milikin, Martha Farrar, Anne Burr, Robert Walsh.

CAST REPLACEMENTS AND TOURING COMPANIES

Compiled by Stanley Green

The following is a list of the more important cast replacements in productions which opened in previous years, but were still playing in New York during a substantial part of the 1980–81 season; or were still on a first-class tour in 1980–81, or opened in New York in 1980–81 and went on tour during the season (casts of first-class touring companies of previous seasons which were no longer playing in 1980–81 appear in previous *Best Plays* volumes of appropriate years).

The name of each major role is listed in *italics* beneath the title of the play in the first column. In the second column directly opposite appears the name of the actor who created the role in the original New York production (whose opening date appears in *italics* at the top of the column). Indented immediately beneath the original actor's name are the names of subsequent New York replacements, together with the date of replacement when available.

The third column gives information about first-class touring companies, including London companies (produced under the auspices of their original New York managements). When there is more than one roadshow company, #1, #2, etc., appear before the name of the performer who created the role in each company (and the city and date of each company's first performance appears in *italics* at the top of the column). Their subsequent replacements are also listed beneath their names, with dates when available.

AIN'T MISBEHAVIN'

New York 5/9/78

Nell Carter
  Avery Sommers 5/15/79
  Zoe Walker
  Yvette Freeman 10/79
  Roz Ryan

André DeShields
  Alan Weeks 3/5/79
  Lonnie McNeil 3/81

Armelia McQueen
  Teresa Bowers 10/79

Ken Page
  Ken Prymus 10/79

Charlaine Woodard
  Debbie Allen 3/5/79
  Adriane Lenox 10/79

ANNIE

	New York 4/21/77	#1 Toronto 3/24/78 #2 London 5/3/78 #3 San Francisco 6/22/78 #4 Dallas 10/3/79

Oliver Warbucks	Reid Shelton
	Keene Curtis 2/6/78
	Reid Shelton 2/27/78
	John Schuck 12/25/79
	Harve Presnell 12/17/80
	John Schuck 1/7/81
		#1 Norwood Smith
		#2 Stratford Johns
		#3 Keene Curtis
		   Reid Shelton 12/28/79
		#4 Harve Presnell
		   Jack Collins 12/17/80
		   Harve Presnell 1/7/81

Annie	Andrea McArdle
	Shelley Bruce 3/6/78
	Sarah Jessica Parker 3/6/79
	Allison Smith 1/29/80
		#1 Kathy-Jo Kelly
		   Dara Brown 1/79
		   Kathy-Jo Kelly 2/8/79
		   Mary K. Lombardi 4/79
		   Theda Stemler 9/30/80
		   Louanne 5/20/81
		#2 Andrea McArdle
		   Ann-Marie Gwatkin
		   6/78
		#3 Patricia Ann Patts
		   Louanne
		   Marisa Morell
		   Kristi Coombs 12/29/80
		#4 Rosanne Sorrentino
		   Bridget Walsh 3/27/81

Miss Hannigan	Dorothy Loudon
	Alice Ghostley 8/15/78
	Dolores Wilson 8/21/79
	Alice Ghostley 1/29/80
	Betty Hutton 9/17/80
	Alice Ghostley 10/8/80
	Marcia Lewis 4/29/81
		#1 Jane Connell
		   Ruth Kobart
		#2 Sheila Hancock
		   Maria Charles 7/79
		#3 Jane Connell
		#4 Patricia Drylie
		   Kathleen Freeman
		   3/27/81

Grace Farrell	Sandy Faison
	Lynn Kearney 1/22/79
	Mary Bracken Phillips 8/79
	Kathryn Boulé 7/29/80
	Anne Kerry 4/29/81
		#1 Kathryn Boulé
		   Jan Pessano
		   Ellen Martin
		   Kathleen Marsh
		   Martha Whitehead
		   11/25/80
		#2 Judith Paris
		#3 Kathryn Boulé
		   Lisa Robinson
		   Krista Neumann 1/7/81
		#4 Deborah Jean Templin
		   Lauren Mitchell 3/27/81

Rooster Hannigan	Robert Fitch
	Gary Beach 1/29/80
	Richard Savellico 4/29/81
		#1 Gary Beach
		   Bob Morrisey
		   Michael Calkins 8/26/80
		#2 Kenneth Nelson
		#3 Swen Swenson
		   Tom Offt

		#4 Michael Leeds Dennis Parlato 10/4/80
Lily	Barbara Erwin Annie McGreevey 9/78 Barbara Erwin 5/29/79 Rita Rudner 1/29/80 Dorothy Stanley 2/11/81	#1 Lisa Raggio Dorothy Holland Jacalyn Switzer Pamela Matteson 7/15/80 #2 Clovissa Newcombe #3 Connie Danese Jacalyn Switzer Edie Cowan Maggie Gorrill 11/4/80 #4 Katharine Buffaloe Wendy Kimball 10/4/80
FDR	Raymond Thorne	#1 Sam Stoneburner Stephen Everett Randall Robbins 8/26/80 #2 Damon Sanders #3 Tom Hatten Alan Wikman 12/17/80 #4 Jack Denton

Note: In London, because of British law, two sets of children alternate the role of Annie, and no child is allowed to give more than 40 performances a year.

BARNUM

	New York 4/30/80	*New Orleans 5/16/81*
Phineas Barnum	Jim Dale Tony Orlando 5/5/81 Jim Dale 5/26/81	Stacy Keach
Chairy Barnum	Glenn Close Catherine Cox 3/3/81	Dee Hoty
Jenny Lind	Marianne Tatum	Catherine Gaines
Tom Thumb	Leonard John Crofoot	Bobby Lee
Joyce Heth	Terri White Lillias White 4/14/81	Terri White
Ringmaster	William C. Witter Terrence V. Mann 4/14/81	Gabriel Barrie

THE BEST LITTLE WHOREHOUSE IN TEXAS

	N.Y. Off Bway 4/17/78 *N.Y. Bway 6/19/78*	*London 2/26/81*
Mona Stangley	Carlin Glynn Bobbi Jo Lathan 8/6/79 Carlin Glynn 8/20/79 Fannie Flagg 5/12/80 Candace Tovar 11/24/80	Carlin Glynn
Ed Earl Dowd	Henderson Forsythe Larry L. King 1/15/79	Henderson Forsythe

	Henderson Forsythe 1/29/79	
	Gil Rogers 8/4/80	
Jewel	Delores Hall	Miquel Brown
*Amber**	Pamela Blair	Betsy Brantley
	Gena Ramsel 8/78	
	Tina Johnson	
Doatsey May	Susan Mansur	Sheila Brand
	Carol Hall 1/1/79	
	Susan Mansur 1/8/79	
	Bobbi Jo Lathan	
	Candace Tovar	
	Becky Gelke	
Melvin P. Thorpe	Clinton Allmon	Nigel Pegram
Governor	Jay Garner	Fred Evans
	Tom Avera 8/6/79	
	Jay Garner 8/13/79	
	Patrick Hamilton 5/80	

*Character name changed to Angel during New York run.

BILLY BISHOP GOES TO WAR

	New York 5/29/80
Billy Bishop, etc.	Eric Peterson
	Cedric Smith 8/12/80
Narrator, Pianist	John Gray
	Ross Douglas 8/12/80

CAMELOT

	New York 7/8/80	*Dallas 9/30/80*
Arthur	Richard Burton	Richard Burton
		William Parry 3/17/81
		Richard Harris 4/13/81
Guenevere	Christine Ebersole	Christine Ebersole
		Meg Bussert 6/4/81
Lancelot du Lac	Richard Muenz	Richard Muenz
King Pellinore	Paxton Whitehead	Paxton Whitehead
		Barrie Ingham 6/4/81
Mordred	Robert Fox	Robert Fox
		Albert Insinnia 6/4/81

CHILDREN OF A LESSER GOD

	New York 3/30/80	*Chicago 12/16/80*
James Leeds	John Rubinstein	Peter Evans
	Robert Steinberg 11/13/80	
	John Rubinstein 12/8/80	
	David Ackroyd 12/22/80	
Sarah Norman	Phyllis Frelich	Linda Bove

A CHORUS LINE*

N.Y. Off Bway 4/15/75
N.Y. Bway 7/25/75

Kristine
Renee Baughman
  Cookie Vazquez 4/26/76
  Deborah Geffner 10/76
  P.J. Mann 9/78
  Deborah Geffner 1/79
  Christine Barker 3/79

Sheila
Carole Bishop (name changed to Kelly Bishop 3/76)
  Kathrynann Wright 8/76
  Bebe Neuwirth 6/80
  Susan Danielle 3/81

Val
Pamela Blair
  Barbara Monte-Britton 4/26/76
  Karen Jablons 10/76
  Mitzi Hamilton 3/1/77
  Karen Jablons 12/77
  Mitzi Hamilton 3/78
  Lois Englund 7/78
  Deborah Henry 10/79
  Mitzi Hamilton 10/80

Mike
Wayne Cilento
  Jim Litten 6/77
  Jeff Hyslop 1/79
  Don Correia 6/79
  Buddy Balou' 6/80

Larry
Clive Clerk
  Jeff Weinberg 10/76
  Clive Clerk 1/77
  Adam Grammis 2/77
  Paul Charles 12/77
  R.J. Peters 3/79
  T. Michael Reed 11/79
  Michael-Day Pitts 3/80
  Donn Simione 4/81

Maggie
Kay Cole
  Lauree Berger 4/26/76
  Donna Drake 2/77
  Christina Saffran 7/78
  Betty Lynd 6/5/79
  Marcia Lynn Watkins 8/79

Richie
Ronald Dennis
  Winston DeWitt Hemsley 4/26/76
  Edward Love 6/77
  A. William Perkins 12/77
  (name changed to Wellington
  Perkins 6/78)
  Larry G. Bailey 1/79
  Carleton T. Jones 3/80

*Original casting of the three touring companies of A Chorus Line appears on pages 472–3 of The Best Plays of 1978–79. Changes have become too numerous for a continuing record.

	Ralph Glenmore 6/80 Kevin Chinn 1/81
Judy	Patricia Garland Sandahl Bergman 4/26/76 Murphy Cross 12/77 Victoria Tabaka 11/78 Joanna Zercher 7/79 Angelique Ilo 8/79 Jannet Horsley 9/80 (name changed to Jannet Moranz 2/81)
Don	Ron Kuhlman David Thomé 4/26/76 Dennis Edenfield 3/80
Bebe	Nancy Lane Gillian Scalici 4/26/76 Rene Ceballos 9/77 Karen Meister 1/78 Rene Ceballos 3/81
Connie	Baayork Lee Lauren Kayahara 4/26/76 Janet Wong 2/77 Cynthia Carrillo Onrubia 11/79 Janet Wong 12/79 Lauren Tom 10/80
Diana	Priscilla Lopez Barbara Luna 4/26/76 Carole Schweid 5/7/76 Rebecca York 8/76 Loida Iglesias 12/76 Chris Bocchino 10/78 Diane Fratantoni 9/79 Chris Bocchino 12/79 Gay Marshall 7/80 Chris Bocchino 8/80
Zach	Robert LuPone Joe Bennett 4/26/76 Eivind Harum 10/76 Robert LuPone 1/31/77 Kurt Johnson 5/77 Clive Clerk 7/77 Kurt Johnson 8/77 Anthony Inneo 8/78 Eivind Harum 10/78 Scott Pearson 8/79 Tim Millett 3/81
Mark	Cameron Mason Paul Charles 10/76 Timothy Scott 12/77 R.J. Peters 4/78 Timothy Wahrer 3/79 Dennis Daniels 5/80 Timothy Wahrer 6/80 Gregory Brock 8/80 Danny Herman 5/81

Cassie	Donna McKechnie
	Ann Reinking 4/26/76
	Donna McKechnie 9/27/76
	Ann Reinking 11/29/76
	Vicki Frederick 2/9/77
	Pamela Sousa 11/14/77
	Candace Tovar 1/78
	Pamela Sousa 3/78
	Cheryl Clark 12/78
	Deborah Henry 10/80
Al	Don Percassi
	Bill Nabel 4/26/76
	John Mineo 2/77
	Ben Lokey 4/77
	Don Percassi 7/77
	Jim Corti 1/79
	Donn Simione 9/79
	James Warren 5/80 (name changed to James Young 9/80)
	Jerry Colker 5/81
Greg	Michel Stuart
	Justin Ross 4/26/76
	Danny Weathers 6/78
Bobby	Thomas J. Walsh
	Christopher Chadman 6/77
	Ron Kurowski 1/78
	Tim Cassidy 11/78
	Ronald Stafford 3/79
	Michael Gorman 8/80
	Matt West 9/80
Paul	Sammy Williams
	George Pesaturo 4/26/76
	René Clemente 2/78

A COUPLA WHITE CHICKS SITTING AROUND TALKING

New York 4/28/80

Maude Mix	Susan Sarandon
	Dorothy Lyman 7/15/80
	Louise Lasser 10/14/80
	Susan Tyrrell 1/20/81
	Carrie Snodgress 4/21/81
Hannah Mae Bindler	Eileen Brennan
	Dixie Carter 7/15/80
	JoBeth Williams 10/14/80
	Anne Archer 1/20/81
	Candy Clark 4/21/81

DANCIN'

New York 3/27/78

Lydia Abarca

Joan DeLuca

Lisa Embs

Bill Hastings

Edmund La Fosse

Stephen Moore

MaryAnn Neu

Cynthia Onrubia

Alyson Reed

Adrian Rosario

Beth Shorter

Note: Because replacements do not generally succeed specific performers in *Dancin'*, listed above in alphabetical order are those new members of the company who were in it as of May 31, 1981. The casting from the opening through May 31, 1980 appears in *The Best Plays of 1979–80*.

DEATHTRAP

New York 2/26/78

Sidney Bruhl	John Wood
	  Patrick Horgan 11/27/78
	  John Wood 12/11/78
	  Stacy Keach 1/15/79
	  John Cullum 7/17/79
	  Robert Reed 9/2/80
	  Farley Granger 3/17/81

Myra Bruhl	Marian Seldes
Helga Ten Dorp	Marian Winters Elizabeth Parrish 10/78

Clifford Anderson	Victor Garber
	  Daren Kelly 10/78
	  Steve Bassett 10/79

Porter Milgrim	Richard Woods William LeMassena 11/78

THE ELEPHANT MAN

	N.Y. Off Bway 1/14/79 *N.Y. Bway 4/19/79*	*#1 Washington 2/27/80* *#2 London 7/15/80*
Frederick Treves	Kevin Conway Donal Donnally 10/15/79	#1 Ken Ruta #2 Peter McEnery

John Merrick	Philip Anglim
	  Jack Wetherall 10/29/79
	  Bruce Davison 2/18/80
	  Jeff Hayenga 7/15/80
	  David Bowie 9/23/80
	  Benjamin Hendrickson 1/6/81
	  Mark Hamill 6/9/81
		#1 Philip Anglim
		  David Bowie 7/29/80
		  Jeff Hayenga 9/23/80
		#2 David Schofield

Mrs. Kendal	Carole Shelley
	  Patricia Elliott 10/15/79
	  Carole Shelley 1/6/81
		#1 Penny Fuller
		#2 Jennie Stoller

EVITA

	New York 9/25/79	*#1 Los Angeles 1/13/80* *#2 Chicago 9/30/80*
Eva	Patti LuPone Terri Klausner (matinees) Derin Altay 1/12/81 Nancy Opel (matinees)	#1 Loni Ackerman Derin Altay (matinees) #2 Valerie Perri Joy Lober (matinees)
Juan Peron	Bob Gunton David Cryer 10/20/80	#1 Jon Cypher #2 Robb Alton
Che	Mandy Patinkin James Stein 10/20/80	#1 Scott Holmes #2 John Herrera

THE FANTASTICKS

	New York 5/3/60
El Gallo	Jerry Orbach Gene Rupert Bert Convy John Cunningham Don Stewart 1/63 David Cryer Keith Charles 10/63 John Boni 1/13/65 Jack Metter 9/14/65 George Ogee Keith Charles Tom Urich 8/30/66 John Boni 10/5/66 Jack Crowder 6/13/67 Nils Hedrick 9/19/67 Keith Charles 10/9/67 Robert Goss 11/7/67 Joe Bellomo 3/11/68 Michael Tartel 7/8/69 Donald Billett 6/70 Joe Bellomo 2/15/72 David Rexroad 6/73 David Snell 12/73 Hal Robinson 4/2/74 Chapman Roberts 7/30/74 David Brummel 2/18/75 David Rexroad 8/31/75 Roger Brown 9/30/75 David Rexroad 9/1/76 Joseph Galiano 10/14/76 Douglas Clark 5/2/78 Joseph Galiano 5/23/78 Richard Muenz 10/78 Joseph Galiano 2/20/79 George Lee Andrews 11/27/79 Sal Provenza 5/13/80
Luisa	Rita Gardner Carla Huston

Liza Stuart 12/61
Elieen Fulton
Alice Cannon 9/62
Royce Lennelle
B.J. Ward 12/1/64
Leta Anderson 7/13/65
Carole Demas 11/22/66
Anne Kaye 5/28/68
Carolyn Mignini 7/29/69
Virginia Gregory 7/27/70
Leta Anderson
Marti Morris 3/7/72
Sharon Werner 8/1/72
Leilani Johnson 7/73
Sharon Werner 12/73
Sarah Rice 6/24/74
Cheryl Horne 7/1/75
Sarah Rice 7/29/75
Betsy Joslyn 3/23/76
Kathy Vestuto 7/18/78
Betsy Joslyn 8/8/78
Kathryn Morath 11/28/78
Debbie McLeod 4/17/79
Joan Wiest 10/9/79
Marti Morris 11/6/79
Carol Ann Scott 5/20/80
Beverly Lambert 9/2/80
Judith Blazer 12/1/80

Matt   Kenneth Nelson
Gino Conforti
Jack Blackton 10/63
Paul Giovanni
Ty McConnell
Richard Rothbard
Gary Krawford
Bob Spencer 9/5/64
Erik Howell 6/28/66
Gary Krawford 12/12/67
Steve Skiles 2/6/68
Craig Carnelia 1/69
Samuel D. Ratcliffe 8/5/69
Michael Glenn-Smith 5/26/70
Jimmy Dodge 9/20/70
Geoffrey Taylor 8/31/71
Erik Howell 3/14/72
Phil Killian 7/4/72
Richard Lincoln 9/72
Bruce Cryer 7/24/73
Phil Killian 9/11/73
Michael Glenn-Smith 6/17/74
Ralph Bruneau 10/29/74
Bruce Cryer 9/30/75
Jeff Knight 7/19/77
Michael Glenn-Smith 1/9/79
Christopher Seppe 3/6/79

Note: As of May 31, 1981, 28 actors had played the role of El Gallo, 25 actresses had played Luisa, and 21 actors had played Matt.

GEMINI

	N.Y. Off Bway 3/13/77 *N.Y. Bway 5/21/77*

Fran Geminiani	Danny Aiello
	  Dick Boccelli 10/78
	  Frank Biancamano

*Lucille Grande**	Anne DeSalvo
	  Stephanie Gordon 11/22/77
	  Anne DeSalvo 4/10/78
	  Jennie Ventriss
	  Barbara Coggin
	  Kaye Kingston 1/19/81

Francis Geminiani	Robert Picardo
	  Dennis Bailey 2/27/78
	  Philip Cates
	  S. Edward Singer (name changed to Steve Singer)

*Marshall Lowenstein**	Jonathan Hadary
	  Warren Pincus
	  Wayne Knight

*Character names changed to Lucille Pompi and Herschel Weinberger for Broadway run.

I OUGHT TO BE IN PICTURES

	New York 4/3/80	*St. Petersburg 12/1/80*

Herb	Ron Liebman
	  Bill Macy 9/8/80
	  Dick Latessa 11/17/80
		Bill Macy

Libby	Dinah Manoff Valerie Landsburg 12/15/80	Alexa Kenin
Steffy	Joyce Van Patten Bernice Massie 10/5/80	Patricia Harty

I'M GETTING MY ACT TOGETHER AND TAKING IT ON THE ROAD

	New York 5/16/78	*#1 Chicago 3/12/80* *#2 London 3/31/81*

Heather	Gretchen Cryer
	  Virginia Vestoff 5/29/79
	  Betty Aberlin 11/30/79
	  Gretchen Cryer 1/18/80
	  Carol Hall 2/19/80
	  Betty Buckley 4/1/80
	  Carol Hall 6/10/80
	  Anne Kaye 10/14/80
	  Nancy Ford 10/21/80
	  Phyllis Newman 1/20/81
	  Gretchen Cryer 3/10/81
		#1 Gretchen Cryer
		  Phyllis Newman 8/12/80
		  Betty Aberlin 10/7/80
		  Donna McKechnie
		  10/21/80
		  Nancy Linari 1/27/81
		  Gretchen Cryer 2/8/81
		#2 Diane Langton

Joe	Joel Fabiani
	  Steven Keats 5/29/79
		#1 Mark Hutter
		  Howard Platt 10/7/80

	George Hosmer 9/25/79	Peder Melhuse 1/20/81
	Orson Bean 3/3/81	Orson Bean 2/8/81
		#2 Ben Cross

MASS APPEAL

	New York 4/22/80
Father Tim Farley	Milo O'Shea
Mark Dolson	Eric Roberts
	Bill C. Davis 7/2/80

MORNING'S AT SEVEN

	New York 4/10/80
Esther Crampton	Maureen O'Sullivan
Cora Swanson	Teresa Wright
David Crampton	Gary Merrill
	Shepperd Strudwick 4/28/81
Ida Bolton	Nancy Marchand
	Harriet Rogers 11/17/80
	Kate Reid 12/14/80
Aaronetta Gibbs	Elizabeth Wilson
Homer Bolton	David Rounds

OKLAHOMA!

	New York 12/13/79	*Orlando, Fla., 1/21/81*
Curly McLain	Laurence Guittard	William Mallory
	Joel Higgins 5/12/80	
Laurey Williams	Christine Andreas	Christine Andreas
		Jeannine Taylor 3/17/81
Aunt Eller	Mary Wickes	Mary Boucher
Ado Annie Carnes	Christine Ebersole	Paige O'Hara
	Susan Bigelow 6/10/80	
	Catherine Cox 7/80	
Will Parker	Harry Groener	Lara Teeter
Ali Hakim	Bruce Adler	Bruce Adler
Jud Fry	Martin Vidnovic	Richard Leighton
	David Brummel	

ONE MO' TIME

	New York 10/22/79	*Philadelphia 7/2/80*
Bertha	Sylvia "Kuumba" Williams	Sandra Reaves-Phillips
Ma Reed	Thais Clark	Jackee Harry
Thelma	Topsy Chapman	Deborah Burrell

Papa Du	Vernel Bagneris Bruce Strickland	Vernel Bagneris
Theater Owner	John Stell	James Red Wilcher

PETER PAN

	New York 9/6/79	*Boston 4/15/81*
Peter Pan	Sandy Duncan	Sandy Duncan
Mr. Darling, Capt. Hook	George Rose Christopher Hewett 10/17/79	Christopher Hewett

ROMANTIC COMEDY

	New York 11/8/79	*Toronto 10/20/80*
Jason Carmichael	Anthony Perkins Keith Baxter 9/16/80	Keith Baxter
Phoebe Craddock	Mia Farrow Julia Mackenzie Mia Farrow Karen Valentine 9/16/80	Karen Valentine
Blanche Dailey	Carole Cook Neva Patterson Benay Venuta 9/16/80	Benay Venuta

SUGAR BABIES

	New York 10/8/79	*Boston 9/25/80*
	Ann Miller	Carol Channing
	Mickey Rooney Joey Bishop 2/2/81 Mickey Rooney 3/2/81	Robert Morse
		Chaz Chase
	Ann Jillian Anita Morris 3/8/80 Jane Summerhays 11/80	Sally Benoit
		Maxie Furman
	Jack Fletcher	Carol Ann Basch
	Sid Stone	
	Bob Williams	
	Michael Davis*	

*Mr. Davis was added to the cast 3/2/81.

SWEENEY TODD, THE DEMON BARBER OF FLEET STREET

	New York 3/1/79	#1 *London 7/2/80* #2 *Washington 10/24/80*
Mrs. Lovett	Angela Lansbury Marge Redmond 9/3/79 Angela Lansbury 9/12/79 Dorothy Loudon 3/4/80	#1 Sheila Hancock #2 Angela Lansbury Denise Lor

Sweeney Todd	Len Cariou George Hearn 3/4/80	#1 Dennis Quilley #2 George Hearn
Anthony Hope	Victor Garber Cris Groenendaal 8/79	#1 Andrew C. Wadsworth #2 Cris Groenendaal
Johanna	Sarah Rice Betsy Joslyn	#1 Mandy More #2 Betsy Joslyn
Beadle Bamford	Jack Eric Williams	#1 David Wheldon- Williams #2 Calvin Remsburg
Beggar Woman	Merle Louise	#1 Dilys Watling #2 Angelina Réaux
Tobias Ragg	Ken Jennings	#1 Michael Staniforth #2 Ken Jennings
Judge Turpin	Edmund Lyndeck	#1 Austin Kent #2 Edmund Lyndeck

TALLEY'S FOLLY

	N.Y. Off B'way 5/1/79 *N.Y. B'way 2/20/80*	*Chicago 5/22/81*
Matt Friedman	Judd Hirsch Jordan Charney 6/24/80 Judd Hirsch 9/23/80	Jordan Charney
Sally Talley	Trish Hawkins Debra Mooney 6/24/80	Debra Mooney

THEY'RE PLAYING OUR SONG

		#1 Chicago 12/1/79 *#2 London 9/20/80*
	New York 2/11/79	*#3 Wilmington 1/19/81*
Vernon Gersch	Robert Klein John Hammil 11/27/79 Tony Roberts 12/17/79 John Hammil Ted Wass 4/7/81	#1 Victor Garber #2 Tom Conti #3 John Hammil
Sonia Wolsk	Lucie Arnaz Stockard Channing 3/6/80 Rhonda Farer 6/2/80 Anita Gillette 9/23/80 Diana Canova 4/7/81	#1 Ellen Greene #2 Gemma Craven #3 Lorna Luft

WHOSE LIFE IS IT ANYWAY?

	New York 4/17/79	*Los Angeles 8/18/80*
Ken (Claire) Harrison	Tom Conti Mary Tyler Moore 2/24/80	*Lawrence Luckinbill
Dr. Scott	Jean Marsh James Naughton 2/24/80 Everett McGill 3/20/80	*Lucie Arnaz

*Alternated in the roles of Harrison and Scott.

THE WINSLOW BOY

	New York 10/28/80	Seattle 2/3/81
Sir Robert Morton	Remak Ramsay	Remak Ramsay
Ronnie Winslow	David Haller	David Haller
Arthur Winslow	Ralph Clanton	Ralph Clanton

FACTS AND FIGURES

LONG RUNS ON BROADWAY

The following shows have run 500 or more continuous performances in a single production, usually the first, not including previews or extra non-profit performances, allowing for vacation layoffs and special one-booking engagements, but not including return engagements after a show has gone on tour. In all cases the numbers were obtained directly from the shows' production offices. Where there are title similarities, the production is identified as follows: (p) straight play version, (m) musical version, (r) revival.

THROUGH MAY 31, 1981

(PLAYS MARKED WITH ASTERISK WERE STILL PLAYING JUNE 1, 1981)

Plays	Number Performances	Plays	Number Performances
Grease	3,388	Oh! Calcutta!	1,314
Fiddler on the Roof	3,242	*Ain't Misbehavin'	1,299
Life With Father	3,224	Angel Street	1,295
Tobacco Road	3,182	Lightnin'	1,291
Hello, Dolly	2,844	Promises, Promises	1,281
My Fair Lady	2,717	The King and I	1,246
*A Chorus Line	2,408	Cactus Flower	1,234
Man of La Mancha	2,328	*The Best Little Whorehouse in	
Abie's Irish Rose	2,327	Texas	1,230
Oklahoma!	2,212	Sleuth	1,222
*Oh! Calcutta! (r)	1,966	1776	1,217
Pippin	1,944	Equus	1,209
South Pacific	1,925	Guys and Dolls	1,200
The Magic Show	1,920	Cabaret	1,165
Harvey	1,775	Mister Roberts	1,157
Hair	1,750	Annie Get Your Gun	1,147
*Annie	1,717	The Seven Year Itch	1,141
*Gemini	1,700	Butterflies Are Free	1,128
The Wiz	1,672	Pins and Needles	1,108
Born Yesterday	1,642	Plaza Suite	1,097
Mary, Mary	1,572	Kiss Me, Kate	1,070
The Voice of the Turtle	1,557	Don't Bother Me, I Can't Cope.	1,065
Barefoot in the Park	1,530	The Pajama Game	1,063
Mame (m)	1,508	Shenandoah	1,050
Same Time, Next Year	1,453	The Teahouse of the August	
Arsenic and Old Lace	1,444	Moon	1,027
The Sound of Music	1,443	Damn Yankees	1,019
How To Succeed in Business		Never Too Late	1,007
Without Really Trying	1,417	Any Wednesday	982
Hellzapoppin	1,404	*They're Playing Our Song	971
The Music Man	1,375	A Funny Thing Happened on	
*Deathtrap	1,361	the Way to the Forum	964
Funny Girl	1,348	The Odd Couple	964
*Dancin'	1,327	Anna Lucasta	957
Mummenschanz	1,326	Kiss and Tell	956

Plays	Number Performances	Plays	Number Performances
Dracula (r)	925	West Side Story	732
Bells Are Ringing	924	High Button Shoes	727
The Moon Is Blue	924	Finian's Rainbow	725
Beatlemania	920	Claudia	722
Luv	901	The Gold Diggers	720
Chicago	898	Jesus Christ Superstar	720
Applause	896	Carnival	719
Can-Can	892	The Diary of Anne Frank	717
Carousel	890	I Remember Mama	714
Hats Off to Ice	889	Tea and Sympathy	712
Fanny	888	Junior Miss	710
Follow the Girls	882	Last of the Red Hot Lovers	706
*The Elephant Man	875	Company	705
Camelot	873	*Evita	704
I Love My Wife	872	Seventh Heaven	704
The Bat	867	Gypsy (m)	702
My Sister Eileen	864	The Miracle Worker	700
No, No, Nanette (r)	861	Da	697
Song of Norway	860	The King and I (r)	696
Chapter Two	857	Cat on a Hot Tin Roof	694
A Streetcar Named Desire	855	Li'l Abner	693
Comedy in Music	849	Peg o' My Heart	692
Raisin	847	The Children's Hour	691
That Championship Season	844	Purlie	688
You Can't Take It With You	837	Dead End	687
La Plume de Ma Tante	835	The Lion and the Mouse	686
Three Men on a Horse	835	White Cargo	686
The Subject Was Roses	832	Dear Ruth	683
Inherit the Wind	806	East Is West	680
No Time for Sergeants	796	Come Blow Your Horn	677
Fiorello!	795	The Most Happy Fella	676
Where's Charley?	792	The Doughgirls	671
The Ladder	789	*Sugar Babies	670
Forty Carats	780	The Impossible Years	670
The Prisoner of Second Avenue	780	Irene	670
Oliver	774	Boy Meets Girl	669
Bubbling Brown Sugar	766	Beyond the Fringe	667
State of the Union	765	Who's Afraid of Virginia Woolf?	664
The First Year	760	Blithe Spirit	657
You Know I Can't Hear You When the Water's Running	755	A Trip to Chinatown	657
Two for the Seesaw	750	The Women	657
Death of a Salesman	742	Bloomer Girl	654
For Colored Girls, etc.	742	The Fifth Season	654
Sons o' Fun	742	Rain	648
Candide (mr)	740	Witness for the Prosecution	645
Gentlemen Prefer Blondes	740	Call Me Madam	644
The Man Who Came to Dinner	739	Janie	642
Call Me Mister	734	The Green Pastures	640
		Auntie Mame (p)	639

Plays	*Number Performances*	*Plays*	*Number Performances*
A Man for All Seasons........	637	Sunrise at Campobello.........	556
The Fourposter	632	Jamaica.....................	555
Two Gentlemen of Verona (m) .	627	Stop the World—I Want to Get	
The Tenth Man	623	Off	555
Is Zat So?...................	618	Florodora	553
Anniversary Waltz............	615	Ziegfeld Follies (1943)........	553
The Happy Time (p)..........	614	Dial "M" for Murder	552
Separate Rooms..............	613	Good News	551
Affairs of State..............	610	Peter Pan (r)	551
Star and Garter	609	Let's Face It.................	547
The Student Prince	608	Milk and Honey..............	543
Sweet Charity...............	608	Within the Law	541
Bye Bye Birdie..............	607	The Music Master............	540
Irene (r)	604	Pal Joey (r)..................	540
Broadway	603	What Makes Sammy Run?.....	540
Adonis......................	603	The Sunshine Boys	538
Street Scene (p)	601	What a Life	538
Kiki........................	600	The Unsinkable Molly Brown ..	532
Flower Drum Song	600	The Red Mill (r)	531
A Little Night Music	600	A Raisin in the Sun..........	530
Don't Drink the Water........	598	Godspell	527
Wish You Were Here	598	The Solid Gold Cadillac	526
A Society Circus	596	Irma La Douce	524
Absurd Person Singular	592	The Boomerang	522
Blossom Time................	592	Follies	521
The Me Nobody Knows.......	586	Rosalinda	521
The Two Mrs. Carrolls........	585	The Best Man	520
Kismet	583	Chauve-Souris	520
Detective Story..............	581	Blackbirds of 1928...........	518
Brigadoon...................	581	The Gin Game...............	517
No Strings	580	Sunny	517
Brother Rat	577	Victoria Regina	517
Show Boat	572	Half a Sixpence	511
The Show-Off................	571	The Vagabond King	511
Sally	570	The New Moon	509
Golden Boy (m)..............	568	The World of Suzie Wong	508
One Touch of Venus..........	567	The Rothschilds..............	507
Happy Birthday..............	564	Sugar.......................	505
Look Homeward, Angel	564	Shuffle Along	504
The Glass Menagerie..........	561	Up in Central Park	504
I Do! I Do!.................	560	Carmen Jones................	503
Wonderful Town	559	The Member of the Wedding...	501
Rose Marie..................	557	Panama Hattie...............	501
Strictly Dishonorable..........	557	Personal Appearance..........	501
Sweeney Todd, the Demon		Bird in Hand	500
Barber of Fleet Street.......	557	Room Service................	500
A Majority of One............	556	Sailor, Beware!..............	500
The Great White Hope........	556	Tomorrow the World	500
Toys in the Attic............	556		

LONG RUNS OFF BROADWAY

Plays	Number Performances	Plays	Number Performances
*The Fantasticks	8,768	The Connection	722
The Threepenny Opera	2,611	The Passion of Dracula	714
Godspell	2,124	Adaptation & Next	707
Jacques Brel	1,847	Oh! Calcutta!	704
Vanities	1,785	Scuba Duba	692
You're a Good Man Charlie		The Knack	685
Brown	1,547	The Club	674
The Blacks	1,408	The Balcony	672
Let My People Come	1,327	*One Mo' Time	670
The Hot 1 Baltimore	1,166	America Hurrah	634
I'm Getting My Act Together		Hogan's Goat	607
and Taking It on the Road	1,165	The Trojan Women (r)	600
Little Mary Sunshine	1,143	Krapp's Last Tape & The Zoo	
El Grande de Coca-Cola	1,114	Story	582
One Flew Over the Cuckoo's		The Dumbwaiter & The	
Nest (r)	1,025	Collection	578
The Boys in the Band	1,000	Dames at Sea	575
Your Own Thing	933	The Crucible (r)	571
Curley McDimple	931	The Iceman Cometh (r)	565
Leave It to Jane (r)	928	The Hostage (r)	545
The Mad Show	871	Six Characters in Search of an	
*Scrambled Feet	823	Author (r)	529
The Effect of Gamma Rays on		The Dirtiest Show in Town	509
Man-in-the-Moon Marigolds	819	Happy Ending & Day of	
A View From the Bridge (r)	780	Absence	504
The Boy Friend (r)	763	The Boys From Syracuse (r)	500
The Pocket Watch	725		

NEW YORK CRITICS AWARDS, 1935–36 to 1980–81

Listed below are the New York Drama Critics Circle Awards from 1935–36 through 1980–81 classified as follows: (1) Best American Play, (2) Best Foreign Play, (3) Best Musical, (4) Best, regardless of category (this category was established by new voting rules in 1962–63 and did not exist prior to that year).

1935–36—(1) Winterset
1936–37—(1) High Tor
1937–38—(1) Of Mice and Men, (2) Shadow and Substance
1938–39—(1) No award, (2) The White Steed
1939–40—(1) The Time of Your Life
1940–41—(1) Watch on the Rhine, (2) The Corn Is Green
1941–42—(1) No award, (2) Blithe Spirit

1942–43—(1) The Patriots
1943–44—(2) Jacobowsky and the Colonel
1944–45—(1) The Glass Menagerie
1945–46—(3) Carousel
1946–47—(1) All My Sons, (2) No Exit, (3) Brigadoon
1947–48—(1) A Streetcar Named Desire, (2) The Winslow Boy
1948–49—(1) Death of a Salesman, (2) The Mad-

woman of Chaillot, (3) South Pacific
1949–50—(1) The Member of the Wedding (2) The Cocktail Party, (3) The Consul
1950–51—(1) Darkness at Noon, (2) The Lady's Not for Burning, (3) Guys and Dolls
1951–52—(1) I Am a Camera, (2) Venus Observed, (3) Pal Joey (Special citation to Don Juan in Hell)
1952–53—(1) Picnic, (2) The Love of Four Colonels, (3) Wonderful Town
1953–54—(1) Teahouse of the August Moon, (2) Ondine, (3) The Golden Apple
1954–55—(1) Cat on a Hot Tin Roof, (2) Witness for the Prosecution, (3) The Saint of Bleecker Street
1955–56—(1) The Diary of Anne Frank, (2) Tiger at the Gates, (3) My Fair Lady
1956–57—(1) Long Day's Journey Into Night, (2) The Waltz of the Toreadors, (3) The Most Happy Fella
1957–58—(1) Look Homeward, Angel, (2) Look Back in Anger, (3) The Music Man
1958–59—(1) A Raisin in the Sun, (2) The Visit, (3) La Plume de Ma Tante
1959–60—(1) Toys in the Attic, (2) Five Finger Exercise, (3) Fiorello!
1960–61—(1) All the Way Home, (2) A Taste of Honey, (3) Carnival
1961–62—(1) The Night of the Iguana, (2) A Man for All Seasons, (3) How to Succeed in Business Without Really Trying
1962–63—(4) Who's Afraid of Virginia Woolf? (Special citation to Beyond the Fringe)
1963–64—(4) Luther, (3) Hello, Dolly! (Special citation to The Trojan Women)
1964–65—(4) The Subject Was Roses, (3) Fiddler on the Roof
1965–66—(4) The Persecution and Assassination of Marat as Performed by the In-

mates of the Asylum of Charenton Under the Direction of the Marquis de Sade, (3) Man of La Mancha
1966–67—(4) The Homecoming, (3) Cabaret
1967–68—(4) Rosencrantz and Guildenstern Are Dead, (3) Your Own Thing
1968–69—(4) The Great White Hope, (3) 1776
1969–70—(4) Borstal Boy, (1) The Effect of Gamma Rays on Man-in-the-Moon Marigolds, (3) Company
1970–71—(4) Home, (1) The House of Blue Leaves, (3) Follies
1971–72—(4) That Championship Season, (2) The Screens, (3) Two Gentlemen of Verona (Special citations to Sticks and Bones and Old Times)
1972–73—(4) The Changing Room, (1) The Hot 1 Baltimore, (3) A Little Night Music
1973–74—(4) The Contractor, (1) Short Eyes, (3) Candide
1974–75—(4) Equus, (1) The Taking of Miss Janie, (3) A Chorus Line
1975–76—(4) Travesties, (1) Streamers, (3) Pacific Overtures
1976–77—(4) Otherwise Engaged, (1) American Buffalo, (3) Annie
1977–78—(4) "Da", (3) Ain't Misbehavin'
1978–79—(4) The Elephant Man, (3) Sweeney Todd, the Demon Barber of Fleet Street
1979–80—(4) Talley's Folly, (2) Betrayal, (3) Evita (Special citation to Peter Brook's Le Centre International de Créations Théâtrales for its repertory)
1980–81—(4) A Lesson From Aloes, (1) Crimes of the Heart (Special citations to Lena Horne: The Lady and Her Music and the New York Shakespeare Festival production of The Pirates of Penzance)

NEW YORK DRAMA CRITICS CIRCLE VOTING, 1980–81

The New York Drama Critics Circle voted Athol Fugard's *A Lesson from Aloes* the best play of the season on the second ballot, after no play achieved the necessary majority of first choices of the 21 critics voting, one by proxy. First choices of these critics on the first ballot were as follows: *Amadeus* by Peter Shaffer (8)—Clive Barnes (New York *Post*), John Beaufort *(Christian Science Monitor)*, Glenne Currie (United Press International), Jack Kroll *(Newsweek)*, Norman Nadel (Scripps-Howard), William Raidy (Newhouse), Allan Wallach *(Newsday)*, Edwin Wilson *(Wall Street Journal)*; *A Lesson from Aloes* (4) —Mel Gussow (New York *Times*), Don Nelson (New York *Daily News*), Frank

Rich (New York *Times*) Marilyn Stasio (New York *Post*); *Crimes of the Heart* by Beth Henley (2)—Edith Oliver *(New Yorker)*, John Simon *(New York)*; *A Life* by Hugh Leonard (1)—Brendan Gill *(New Yorker)*; *True West* by Sam Shepard (1)—Michael Feingold *(Village Voice)*; *Coming Attractions* by Ted Tally (1)—Ted Kalem *(Time)*; *The Suicide* by Nikolai Erdman (1)—Jules Novick *(Village Voice)*; *How I Got That Story* by Amlin Gray (1)—Douglas Watt (New York *Daily News*); Abstain (2)—Walter Kerr (New York *Times*), Howard Kissel *(Womens Wear Daily)*. Lanford Wilson's *Fifth of July* was ineligible for this year's critics' voting, it was decided, because it had been previously produced in New York, off Broadway, in 1978.

After no play won the necessary majority of first choices on the first ballot, according to its voting rules the Circle then proceeded to a second, multiple-choice ballot for best play, weighted to produce a point consensus with 3 points given to a critic's first choice, 2 for second and 1 for third. In order to win, a play must receive a point total of three times the number of those voting (20 without the proxy) divided by two, plus 1, i.e. 31 points. *A Lesson from Aloes* won on this ballot with 32 points over *Amadeus* (29), *Crimes of the Heart* (15), *A Life* (15), *Coming Attractions* (5), *The Suicide* (3), *How I Got That Story* (3), *The American Clock* (2), *True West* (2), *Limbo Tales* (1), *Piaf* (1).

Having named a foreign (South African) play best-of-bests, the Circle then named Beth Henley's *Crimes of the Heart* the best American play of the season on the first ballot with a majority of 11 first-choice votes (Barnes, Currie, Kroll, Wallach, Wilson, Gussow, Nelson, Rich, Stasio, Oliver, Simon) over *How I Got That Story* (3—Novick, Raidy, Watt), *The Floating Light Bulb* (1—Beaufort), *True West* (1—Feingold), *Coming Attractions* (1—Kalem) and *The American Clock* (1—Kissel), with Gill, Kerr and Nadel abstaining.

The Circle decided not to vote an award for best musical this year but voted two special awards to musical attractions: *Lena Horne: The Lady and Her Music* and the New York Shakespeare Festival production of *The Pirates of Penzance*.

CHOICES OF SOME OTHER CRITICS

Critic	Best Play	Best Musical
Casper Citron WOXR, WOR-TV	Amadeus	Woman of the Year
Judith Crist *Saturday Review, TV Guide*	Amadeus	Lena Horne: the Lady and Her Music
John Gambling WOR	Amadeus	Lena Horne
Joan Hamburg WOR	Amadeus	Lena Horne
Katie Kelly WNBC-TV	Amadeus	42nd Street
Alvin Klein WNYC	Fifth of July	Lena Horne
Stewart Klein WNEW-TV	Amadeus	Lena Horne

Joanna Langfield WMCA	Amadeus	Woman of the Year
Jeffrey Lyons WCBS, WPIX-TV	To Grandmother's House We Go	Lena Horne
Leida Snow WINS, ABC Radio News	The Suicide	Lena Horne

PULITZER PRIZE WINNERS, 1916–17 to 1980–81

1916–17—No award

1917–18—Why Marry?, by Jesse Lynch Williams

1918–19—No award

1919–20—Beyond the Horizon, by Eugene O'Neill

1920–21—Miss Lulu Bett, by Zona Gale

1921–22—Anna Christie, by Eugene O'Neill

1922–23—Icebound, by Owen Davis

1923–24—Hell-Bent fer Heaven, by Hatcher Hughes

1924–25—They Knew What They Wanted, by Sidney Howard

1925–26—Craig's Wife, by George Kelly

1926–27—In Abraham's Bosom, by Paul Green

1927–28—Strange Interlude, by Eugene O'Neill

1928–29—Street Scene, by Elmer Rice

1929–30—The Green Pastures, by Marc Connelly

1930–31—Alison's House, by Susan Glaspell

1931–32—Of Thee I Sing, by George S. Kaufman, Morrie Ryskind, Ira and George Gershwin

1932–33—Both Your Houses, by Maxwell Anderson

1933–34—Men in White, by Sidney Kingsley

1934–35—The Old Maid, by Zoë Akins

1935–36—Idiot's Delight, by Robert E. Sherwood

1936–37—You Can't Take It With You, by Moss Hart and George S. Kaufman

1937–38—Our Town, by Thornton Wilder

1938–39—Abe Lincoln in Illinois, by Robert E. Sherwood

1939–40—The Time of Your Life, by William Saroyan

1940–41—There Shall Be No Night, by Robert E. Sherwood

1941–42—No award

1942–43—The Skin of Our Teeth, by Thornton Wilder

1943–44—No award

1944–45—Harvey, by Mary Chase

1945–46—State of the Union, by Howard Lindsay and Russel Crouse

1946–47—No award

1947–48—A Streetcar Named Desire, by Tennessee Williams

1948–49—Death of a Salesman, by Arthur Miller

1949–50—South Pacific, by Richard Rodgers, Oscar Hammerstein II and Joshua Logan

1950–51—No award

1951–52—The Shrike, by Joseph Kramm

1952–53—Picnic, by William Inge

1953–54—The Teahouse of the August Moon, by John Patrick

1954–55—Cat on a Hot Tin Roof, by Tennessee Williams

1955–56—The Diary of Anne Frank, by Frances Goodrich and Albert Hackett

1956–57—Long Day's Journey Into Night, by Eugene O'Neill

1957–58—Look Homeward, Angel, by Ketti Frings

1958–59—J. B., by Archibald MacLeish

1959–60—Fiorello!, by Jerome Weidman, George Abbott, Sheldon Harnick and Jerry Bock

1960–61—All the Way Home, by Tad Mosel

1961–62—How to Succeed in Business Without Really Trying, by Abe Burrows, Willie Gilbert, Jack Weinstock and Frank Loesser

1962–63—No award

1963–64—No award

1964–65—The Subject Was Roses, by Frank D. Gilroy

1965–66—No award

1966–67—A Delicate Balance, by Edward Albee

1967–68—No award

1968–69—The Great White Hope, by Howard Sackler

1969–70—No Place To Be Somebody, by Charles Gordone

1970–71—The Effect of Gamma Rays on Man-in-the-Moon Marigolds, by Paul Zindel

1971–72—No award

1972–73—That Championship Season, by Jason Miller

1973-74—No award
1974-75—Seascape, by Edward Albee
1975-76—A Chorus Line, by Michael Bennett, James Kirkwood, Nicholas Dante, Marvin Hamlisch and Edward Kleban

1976-77—The Shadow Box, by Michael Cristofer
1977-78—The Gin Game, by D.L. Coburn
1978-79—Buried Child, by Sam Shepard
1979-80—Talley's Folly, by Lanford Wilson
1980-81—Crimes of the Heart, by Beth Henley

THE TONY AWARDS, 1980-81

The Antoinette Perry (Tony) Awards are voted by members of the League of New York Theaters and Producers, the governing bodies of the Dramatists Guild, Actors Equity, the American Theater Wing, the Society of Stage Directors and Choreographers, the United Scenic Artists Union and members of the first and second night press, from a list of four nominees in each category.

The four nominations (Broadway shows only; off-Broadway excluded) are made by a committee of theater journalists and professionals whose personnel changes annually at the invitation of the abovementioned League, which administers the Tony Awards under an agreement with the American Theatre Wing. The 1980-81 Nominating Committee was composed of Clive Barnes of the New York *Post,* Hazel Bryant of the Black Theater Alliance, Schuyler Chapin of Columbia University, Richard Coe, critic emeritus of the Washington *Post,* Anna Crouse of Theater Development Fund, Brendan Gill of *The New Yorker,* William Glover, former theater critic for Associated Press, Henry Hewes of the American Theater Critics Association, Mary Henderson of the Museum of the City of New York, Kevin Kelly of the Boston *Globe,* Michael Langham, director of the Theater Center of the Juilliard School, Elliot Norton of the Boston *Herald-American,* Seymour Peck of the New York *Times,* Dorothy Rodgers, Joan Rubin, editor-in-chief of *Playbill,* Jay Sharbutt of the Associated Press and Glenna Syse of the Chicago *Sun-Times.*

The list of 1980-81 nominees follows, with winners in each category listed in **bold face type.**

BEST PLAY (award goes to both producer and author). *A Lesson from Aloes* by Athol Fugard, produced by Jay J. Cohen, Richard Press, Louis Busch Hager Associates and the Yale Repertory Theater; *A Life* by Hugh Leonard, produced by Lester Osterman, Richard Horner, Hinks Shimberg and Freydberg-Cutler-Diamond Productions; **Amadeus** by **Peter Shaffer,** produced by **The Shubert Organization, Elizabeth I. McCann, Nelle Nugent** and **Roger S. Berlind**; *Fifth of July* by Lanford Wilson, produced by Jerry Arrow, Robert Lussier and Warner Theater Productions, Inc.

BEST MUSICAL (award to producers). **42nd Street** produced by **David Merrick**; *Sophisticated Ladies* produced by Roger S. Berlind,

Manheim Fox, Sondra Gilman, Burton L. Litwin, Louise Westergaard, Belwin Mills Publishing Corp. and Norzar Productions, Inc.; *Tintypes* produced by Richmond Crinkley, Royal Pardon Productions, Ivan Bloch, Larry J. Silva, Eve Skina and Joan F. Tobin; *Woman of the Year* produced by Lawrence Kasha, David S. Landay, James M. Nederlander, Warner Theater Productions, Inc., Claire Nichtern, Carole J. Shorenstein and Stewart F. Lane.

BEST BOOK OF A MUSICAL. *42nd Street* by Michael Stewart and Mark Bramble; *The Moony Shapiro Songbook* by Monty Norman and Julian More; *Tintypes* by Mary Kyte, Gary Pearle and Mel Marvin; **Woman of the Year** by **Peter Stone**.

1981 TONY AWARD WINNERS—Lauren Bacall, winner as outstanding actress in a musical, appears *above* in a scene from *Woman of the Year* with Marilyn Cooper, winner as outstanding featured actress in a musical.

BEST SCORE OF A MUSICAL. *Charlie and Algernon,* music by Charles Strouse, lyrics by David Rogers; *Copperfield,* music by Al Kasha and Joel Hirschhorn, lyrics by Al Kasha and Joel Hirschhorn; *Shakespeare's Cabaret,* music by Lance Mulcahy; **Woman of the Year**, music by **John Kander**, lyrics by **Fred Ebb**.

OUTSTANDING ACTOR IN A PLAY. Tim Curry in *Amadeus*, Roy Dotrice in *A Life*, **Ian McKellen** in *Amadeus*, Jack Weston in *The Floating Light Bulb*.

OUTSTANDING ACTRESS IN A PLAY. Glenda Jackson in *Rose*, **Jane Lapotaire** in *Piaf*, Eva Le Gallienne in *To Grandmother's House We Go*, Elizabeth Taylor in *The Little Foxes*.

OUTSTANDING ACTOR IN A MUSICAL. Gregory Hines in *Sophisticated Ladies*, **Kevin Kline** in *The Pirates of Penzance*, George Rose in *The Pirates of Penzance*, Martin Vidnovic in *Brigadoon*.

OUTSTANDING ACTRESS IN A MUSICAL. **Lauren Bacall** in *Woman of the Year*, Meg Bussert in *Brigadoon*, Chita Rivera in *Bring Back Birdie*, Linda Ronstadt in *The Pirates of Penzance*.

OUTSTANDING FEATURED ACTOR IN A PLAY. Tom Aldredge in *The Little Foxes*, **Brian Backer** in *The Floating Light Bulb*, Adam Redfield in *A Life*, Shepperd Strudwick in *To Grandmother's House We Go*.

OUTSTANDING FEATURED ACTRESS IN A PLAY. **Swoosie Kurtz** in *Fifth of July*, Maureen Stapleton in *The Little Foxes*, Jessica Tandy in *Rose*, Zoë Wanamaker in *Piaf*.

OUTSTANDING FEATURED ACTOR IN A MUSICAL. Tony Azito in *The Pirates of Penzance*, **Hinton Battle** in *Sophisticated Ladies*, Lee Roy Reams in *42nd Street*, Paxton Whitehead in *Camelot*.

OUTSTANDING FEATURED ACTRESS IN A MUSICAL. **Marilyn Cooper in** *Woman of the Year*, Phyllis Hyman in *Sophisticated Ladies*, Wanda Richert in *42nd Street*, Lynne Thigpen in *Tintypes*.

OUTSTANDING DIRECTION OF A PLAY. Peter Coe for *A Life*, **Peter Hall** for *Amadeus*, Marshall W. Mason for *Fifth of July*, Austin Pendleton for *The Little Foxes*.

OUTSTANDING DIRECTION OF A MUSICAL. Gower Champion for *42nd Street*, **Wilford Leach** for *The Pirates of Penzance*, Robert Moore for *Woman of the Year*, Michael Smuin for *Sophisticated Ladies*.

OUTSTANDING SCENIC DESIGN. John Lee Beatty for *Fifth of July*, **John Bury** for *Amadeus*, Santo Loquasto for *The Suicide*, David Mitchell for *Can-Can*.

OUTSTANDING COSTUME DESIGN. Theoni V. Aldredge for *42nd Street*, John Bury for *Amadeus*, **Willa Kim** for *Sophisticated Ladies*, Franca Squarciapino for *Can-Can*.

OUTSTANDING LIGHTING DESIGN. **John Bury** for *Amadeus*, Tharon Musser for *42nd Street*, Dennis Parichy for *Fifth of July*, Jennifer Tipton for *Sophisticated Ladies*.

OUTSTANDING CHOREOGRAPHY. **Gower Champion** for *42nd Street*, Graciela Daniele for *The Pirates of Penzance*, Henry Le Tang, Donald McKayle, Michael Smuin for *Sophisticated Ladies*, Roland Petit for *Can-Can*.

OUTSTANDING REPRODUCTION OF A PLAY OR MUSICAL. *Brigadoon* produced by Zev Bufman and The Shubert Organization; *Camelot* produced by Mike Merrick and Don Gregory; *The Little Foxes* produced by Zev Bufman, Donald C. Carter and Jon Cutler; **The Pirates of Penzance** produced by **Joseph Papp** and the **New York Shakespeare Festival**.

SPECIAL TONY AWARDS. **Trinity Square Repertory Company**, Providence, Rhode Island; **Lena Horne**.

TONY AWARD WINNERS, 1947–1981

Listed below are the Antoinette Perry (Tony) Award winners in the categories of Best Play and Best Musical from the time these awards were established (1947) until the present.

1947—No play or musical award
1948—Mister Roberts; no musical award
1949—Death of a Salesman; Kiss Me, Kate
1950—The Cocktail Party; South Pacific
1951—The Rose Tattoo; Guys and Dolls
1952—The Fourposter; The King and I
1953—The Crucible; Wonderful Town
1954—The Teahouse of the August Moon; Kismet
1955—The Desperate Hours; The Pajama Game
1956—The Diary of Anne Frank; Damn Yankees

1957—Long Day's Journey Into Night; My Fair Lady
1958—Sunrise at Campobello; The Music Man
1959—J.B.; Redhead
1960—The Miracle Worker; Fiorello! and The Sound of Music (tie)
1961—Becket; Bye Bye Birdie
1962—A Man for All Seasons; How to Succeed in Business Without Really Trying
1963—Who's Afraid of Virginia Woolf?; A Funny Thing Happened on the Way to the Forum

1964—Luther; Hello, Dolly!
1965—The Subject Was Roses; Fiddler on the Roof
1966—The Persecution and Assassination of Marat as Performed by the Inmates of the Asylum of Charenton Under the Direction of the Marquis de Sade; Man of La Mancha
1967—The Homecoming; Cabaret
1968—Rosencrantz and Guildenstern Are Dead; Hallelujah, Baby!
1969—The Great White Hope; 1776
1970—Borstal Boy; Applause
1971—Sleuth; Company

1972—Sticks and Bones; Two Gentlemen of Verona
1973—That Championship Season; A Little Night Music
1974—The River Niger; Raisin
1975—Equus; The Wiz
1976—Travesties; A Chorus Line
1977—The Shadow Box; Annie
1978—Da; Ain't Misbehavin'
1979—The Elephant Man; Sweeney Todd, the Demon Barber of Fleet Street
1980—Children of a Lesser God; Evita
1981—Amadeus; 42nd Street

THE OBIE AWARDS, 1980–81

The *Village Voice* Off-Broadway (Obie) Awards are given each year for excellence in various categories of off-Broadway—and frequently off-off-Broadway—shows, as close distinctions between these two areas are ignored in Obie Award-giving. The Obies are voted by a committee of *Village Voice* critics and others.

SUSTAINED ACHIEVEMENT. **The Negro Ensemble Company**.

BEST PLAY. **FOB** by David Henry Hwang.

BEST PRODUCTION. **Still Life** by Emily Mann.

PLAYWRITING. **Charles Fuller** for *Zooman and the Sign*, **Amlin Gray** for *How I Got That Story*, **Len Jenkins** (script and direction) for *Limbo Tales*.

DIRECTION. **Melvin Bernhardt** for *Crimes of the Heart*, **Wilford Leach** for *The Pirates of Penzance*, **Toby Robertson** for *Pericles*.

PERFORMANCE. **Giancarlo Esposito** in *Zooman and the Sign*, **Bob Gunton** in *How I Got That Story*, **Mary Beth Hurt** in *Crimes of the Heart*, **Kevin Kline** in *The Pirates of Pen-*

zance, **John Lone** in *FOB* and *The Dance and the Railroad*, **Mary McDonnel**, **Timothy Near** and **John Spencer** in *Still Life*, **William Sadler** in *Limbo Tales*, **Michele Shay** in *Meetings*, **Meryl Streep** in *Alice in Concert*, **Christopher Walken** in *The Sea Gull*.

DESIGN. **Bloolips** for *Lust in Space* (costumes), **Manuel Lutgenhorst** and **Douglas Ball** for *Request Concert*, **Jun Maeda** for sustained excellence in set design, **Douglas Parichy** for sustained excellence in lighting design.

SPECIAL CITATIONS. **JoAnne Akalaitis** and the **Mabou Mines Company** for *Dead End Kids*, **Joseph Chaikin** and the **Winter Project** for *Tourists and Refugees*, **Bill Irwin** for inspired clowning, **Bruce Myers** for *A Dybbuk for Two People*, the Spanish-language company **Repertorio Espanol**.

ADDITIONAL PRIZES AND AWARDS, 1980–81

The following is a list of major prizes and awards for achievement in the theater this season. In all cases the names of winners appear in **bold face type.**

MARGO JONES AWARD. For the producer and producing organization whose continuing policy of producing new theater works has made an outstanding contribution to the encouragement of new playwrights. 1980 Award: **John Clark Donahue** and **The Children's Theater Company of Minneapolis**. 1981 Award: **Lynne Meadow** and **Manhattan Theater Club**.

1981 JOSEPH MAHARAM FOUNDATION AWARDS. For distinguished theatrical design for original New York productions. Scenery: **John Lee Beatty** for *Fifth of July*, **Manuel Lutgenhorst** with **Douglas E. Ball** for *Request Concert*. Costumes: **Patricia McGourty** for *The Pirates of Penzance*. Lighting: **Dennis Parichy** for *Fifth of July*. Citations—Scenery: Terry A. Bennett for *The Oedipus Cycle*, Gerald Bloom for *Texts for Nothing*, Ping Chong for *Nuit Blanche*, Edward T. Gianfrancesco for *The Freak* and *Put Them All Together*, David Gropman for *Passione*, David Jenkins for *Piaf*, Wilford Leach and Bob Shaw for *The Pirates of Penzance*, Santo Loquasto for *The Floating Light Bulb*, David Mitchell for *Bring Back Birdie* Douglas W. Schmidt with Bran Ferren for *Frankenstein*, Julie Taymor for *Way of Snow*, Tony Walton for *Sophisticated Ladies*, Paul Wonsek for *Knuckle*, Michael Yeargan for *The Sea Gull*. Citations—costumes: Gabriel Berry for *Tirai*, Mary Brecht for *Tourists and Refugees*, Laura Crow for *Fifth of July*, Willa Kim for *Sophisticated Ladies*, Carrie F. Robbins for *Macbeth*, Bruce D. Schwartz for *The Rat of Huge Proportions and Other Works*, Patricia Zipprodt for *Fools*. Citations—lighting: Pat Collins for *Penguin Touquet*, Beverly Emmons for *Piaf*, Craig Miller for *Bring Back Birdie*, Thomas Skelton for *Lena Horne*, Jennifer Tipton for *Sophisticated Ladies*.

37th ANNUAL THEATER WORLD AWARDS. For outstanding new talent in Broadway and off-Broadway productions during the 1980–81 season. **Brian Backer** in *The Floating Light Bulb*, **Lisa Banes** in *Look Back in Anger*, **Meg Bussert** in *The Music Man* and *Brigadoon*, **Michael Davis** in *Broadway Follies*, **Giancarlo Esposito** in *Zooman and the Sign*, **Daniel Gerroll** in *Slab Boys* and *Knuckle*, **Phyllis Hyman** in *Sophisticated Ladies*, **Cynthia Nixon** in *The Philadelphia Story*, **Amanda Plummer** in *A Taste of Honey*, **Adam Redfield** in *A Life*, **Wanda Richert** in *42nd Street*, **Rex Smith** in *The Pirates of Penzance*.

4th ANNUAL JAMES N. VAUGHAN

AWARD. To a non-profit performing arts institution selected on the basis of an exceptional achievement or contribution to the development or growth of the professional theater. **Circle Repertory Company**.

OUTER CRITICS CIRCLE AWARDS. For distinguished achievement in the New York theater season, voted by critics of foreign and out-of-town periodicals. Play: **Amadeus** by Peter Shaffer. Off-Broadway play: **March of the Falsettos** by William Finn. Performance by an actor: **Ian McKellen** in *Amadeus*. Performance by an actress: **Swoosie Kurtz** in *Fifth of July*. Revival: **The Pirates of Penzance**. Lucille Lortel Award as most noteworthy new director: **Geraldine Fitzgerald** for *Mass Appeal* and *Long Day's Journey Into Night*.

DRAMA DESK AWARDS. For outstanding achievement, voted by an association of New York drama reporters, editors and critics. Play: **Amadeus** by Peter Shaffer. Musical: **The Pirates of Penzance**. Direction: **Peter Hall** for *Amadeus*, **Wilford Leach** for *The Pirates of Penzance*. Choreography: **Gower Champion** for *42nd Street*. Actor in a play: **Ian McKellen** in *Amadeus*. Actress in a play: **Joan Copeland** in *The American Clock*. Actor in a musical: **Kevin Kline** in *The Pirates of Penzance*. Actress in a musical: **Lena Horne** in *Lena Horne: the Lady and Her Music*. Featured actor in a play: **Brian Backer** in *The Floating Light Bulb*. Featured actress in a play: **Swoosie Kurtz** in *Fifth of July*. Featured actor in a musical: **Tony Azito** in *The Pirates of Penzance*. Featured actress in a musical: **Marilyn Cooper** in *Woman of the Year*. Scenery: **John Lee Beatty** for *Fifth of July*. Lighting, **Jules Fisher** and **Bran Ferren** for *Frankenstein*. Costumes (tie): **Theoni V. Aldredge** for *42nd Street* and **Patricia McGourty** for *The Pirates of Penzance*. Unique theatrical experience: **Request Concert**.

JOHN F. WHARTON AWARD. For original contributions to the business practise of the theater. **W. McNeil Lowry**.

GEORGE JEAN NATHAN AWARD. For drama criticism. **Sean Mitchell** of the Dallas *Times-Herald*.

GEORGE OPPENHEIMER-NEWSDAY AWARD. For the best new play produced in New York or on Long Island. **Table Settings** by James Lapine.

ELIZABETH HULL-KATE WARRINER AWARD to the playwright whose work dealt with controversial subjects involving the fields of political, religious or social mores of the time, selected by the Dramatists Guild Council. 1978–79 season: **Hugh Wheeler** and **Stephen Sondheim** for *Sweeney Todd, the Demon Barber of Fleet Street*. 1979–80 season: **Martin Sherman** for *Bent*.

ROSAMUND GILDER AWARD. For creative achievement, voted by the New Drama Forum. **JoAnne Akalaitis** of Mabou Mines.

CLARENCE DERWENT AWARDS. For the most promising female and male actors on the metropolitan scene. **Mia Dillon** in *Crimes of the Heart* and *Summer*; **Bob Gunton** in *How I Got That Story*.

8th ANNUAL JOSEPH JEFFERSON AWARDS. For outstanding work in Chicago theater. Production: **Getting Out** at Wisdom Bridge. Musical: **I'm Getting My Act Together and Taking It On the Road** at Travel Light Director: **Robert Falls** for *Getting Out*. Ensemble: **Say Goodnight, Gracie** Scenery: **John Lee Beatty** for *Talley's Folly*. Lighting: **Michael Merritt** for *Wings*. Costumes: **Christa Scholtz** for *Cyrano De Bergerac*. Choreography: **David H. Bell** for *Cabaret*. Original incidental music: **Edward Zelnis** for *The Dick Gibson Show*. Principal actor: **Frank Galati** in *Travesties*. Principal actor, musical: **Dionisio** in *Latin Chicago*. Principal actress: **Roslyn Alexander** in *Wings*. Principal actress, musical: **Gretchen Cryer** in *I'm Getting My Act Together*, etc. Supporting actor: **Gary Sinese** in *Getting Out*. Supporting actor, musical: **Lawrence McCauley** in *Camelot*. Supporting actress: **Glenne Headly** in *Say Goodnight, Gracie*. Supporting actress, musical: **Patti Wilkus** in *Funny Girl*. Cameo: **Ed Meekin** in *The Play's the Thing*. Special awards: **Victory Gardens** and **Latino Chicago** for adding the Latino idiom to the Chicago theater vocabulary; **The Artaud Project**, Jim Rinnert producer, for mixed media artistry; **Wings** for audio design; **Thomas Guerra** for many years of outstanding stage management in Chicago; Organic Theater's **Warp I, II, III**; **Lee Ditkowsky** for special effects; **Joyce Sloane**, associate producer, Second City.

LOS ANGELES DRAMA CRITICS CIRCLE AWARDS. For distinguished achievement in Los Angeles Theater. Production: **Eden, The Elephant Man, The Grapes of Wrath**. Direction: **Yurek Bogayevicz** for *The Resistible Rise of Arturo Ui*, **Edmund J. Cambridge** for *Eden*. **Jack Hofsiss** for *The Elephant Man*, **Terence Shank** for *The Grapes of Wrath*, **Warner Shook** for *Philadelphia, Here I Come*. Playwriting: **Steve Carter** for *Eden*, **John Gray** and **Eric Peterson** for *Billy Bishop Goes to War*. Performance in a major role: **Philip Anglim** in *The Elephant Man*, **Georgia Brown** in *An Evening with Georgia Brown and Her Friends*, **Julie Harris** in *On Golden Pond*, **Carl Lumbly** in *Eden*, **Eric Peterson** in *Billy Bishop Goes to War*, **Ford Rainey** in *Home*. Performance in a featured role: **Mary Jo Catlett** in *Philadelphia, Here I Come*, **Marilyn Coleman** in *Eden*, **Harold Gary** in *The Price*. Ensemble performance: **Tracers**. Scene design: **John Lee Beatty** for *Holiday*, **Gene Mazzanti** for *The Grapes of Wrath*, **James Riddle** for *The Barretts of Wimpole Street*, **John Wulp** for *The Crucifer of Blood*. Costume design: **Garland Riddle** for *The Barretts of Wimpole Street*. Choreography: **Tommy Tune** for *The Best Little Whorehouse in Texas*. Special visual and sound effects: **Bran Ferren** for *The Crucifer of Blood*. Margaret Harford Award for distinguished achievement in the theater: **Diane White** of Los Angeles Actors Theater. Special awards: **Lehman Engel** for his musical theater workshops, **Cathleen Nesbitt** for a career spanning more than 70 years.

1980–1981 PUBLICATION
OF RECENTLY-PRODUCED PLAYS

Amadeus. Peter Shaffer. Harper & Row (paperback).
American Days. Stephen Poliakoff. Methuen (paperback).
Arch Brown's News Boy. Arch Brown. The JH Press (paperback).
Ashes. David Rudkin. Talonbooks (paperback).
Barbarians. Barrie Keeffe. Methuen (paperback).
Class Enemy. Nigel Williams. Methuen (paperback).
Cloud Nine. Caryl Churchill. Pluto Press (paperback).

Faith Healer. Brian Friel. Faber & Faber (paperback).
Forever After. Doric Wilson. The JH Press (paperback).
I Ought To Be in Pictures. Neil Simon. Random House.
Jitters. David French. Talonbooks (paperback).
Lady From Dubuque, The. Edward Albee. Atheneum.
Lesson From Aloes, A. Athol Fugard. Random House.
Life, A. Hugh Leonard. Atheneum (paperback).
Marie and Bruce. Wallace Shawn. Grove Press (paperback).
Mass Appeal. Bill C. Davis. Avon/Appeal (paperback).
Romans in Britain, The. Howard Brenton. Methuen (paperback).
Strawberry Fields. Stephen Poliakoff. Methuen (paperback).
Suicide, The. Nikolai Erdman. Talonbooks (paperback).
Summer-Party, The. Stephen Poliakoff. Methuen (paperback).
Wild Duck, The. Henrik Ibsen; new translation by Christopher Hampton. Faber & Faber (paperback).

A SELECTED LIST OF OTHER PLAYS PUBLISHED IN 1980–81

Apologia and Two Folk Plays. August Strindberg. University of Washington Press.
Bernard Shaw: Selected Plays. George Bernard Shaw. Dodd, Mead.
Brand. Henrik Ibsen; translated by Michael Meyer. Methuen (paperback).
Brisburial: A Feast. Edward Pomerantz. Magic Circle Press (paperback).
Chamber Plays, The. August Strindberg; translated by Evert Springchorn, Seabury Quinn Jr. and Kenneth Petersen. University of Minnesota Press.
Death of a Salesman: Special Illustrated Edition. Arthur Miller. Viking Press.
Devils, The. John Whiting. Heinemann (paperback).
Drinks Before Dinner. E.L. Doctorow. Bantam (paperback).
Enjoy. Alan Bennett. Faber & Faber (paperback).
Hothouse, The. Harold Pinter. Grove Press (also in paperback).
House of Mirth: The Play of the Novel. Edith Wharton and Clyde Fitch. Fairleigh Dickinson University Press.
Journalists, The: A Triptych. Arnold Wesker. Jonathan Cape.
Lion in Love, The. Shelagh Delaney. Methuen (paperback).
Lute, The: Kao Ming's "P'i-p'a chi." Columbia University Press.
Memorandum, The. Vaclav Havel; translated by Vera Blackwell. Grove Press (paperback).
Narrow Road to the Deep North. Edward Bond. Methuen (paperback).
New Plays by Women. Susan LaTempa, editor. Shameless Hussy Press (paperback).
Orestes and Other Plays. Euripides; translated by Philip Vellacott. Penguin (paperback).
Oresteia of Aeschylus, The. Translated by Robert Lowell. Farrar, Straus, Giroux (paperback).
Peer Gynt. Henrik Ibsen; translated by Michael Meyer. Methuen (paperback).
Peer Gynt. Henrik Ibsen; translated by Rolf Fjelde. University of Minnesota Press.
Plays by American Women: The Early Years. Judith E. Barlow, editor. Avon/Bard (paperback).
Ibsen—Plays: One. Ibsen—Plays: Two. Ibsen—Plays: Three. Ibsen—Plays: Four. Translated by Michael Meyer. Methuen.
Magnificence: Revels Plays Edition. John Skelton. Johns Hopkins University Press.
Mary Stuart. Stephen Spender. Ticknor & Fields (paperback).
Polyeuctus/The Lion/Nicomedes. Pierre Corneille; translated by John Cairncross. Penguin (paperback).
Spring Awakening. Frank Wedekind; translated by Edward Bond. Methuen (paperback).
Stage Struck. Simon Gray. Seaver Books/Grove Press (paperback).
Streetcar Named Desire, A. Tennessee Williams. New Directions (paperback).
Sugar and Spice/Trial Run. Nigel Williams. Methuen (paperback).

Two Tudor Interludes. Editor, Ian Lancashire. Johns Hopkins University Press.
Undiscovered Country. Tom Stoppard; English version of Arthur Schnitzler's play. Faber & Faber (paperback).
Volunteers. Brian Friel. Faber & Faber (paperback).
Word Plays: An Anthology of New American Drama. Editors, Bonnie Marranca and Gautam Dasgupta. Performing Arts Journal Publications.
Worlds With the Activists Papers, The. Edward Bond. Methuen. (paperback).
Woyzeck. George Büchner; translation by John Mackendrick. Methuen (paperback).

MUSICAL AND DRAMATIC RECORDINGS
OF NEW YORK SHOWS

Title and publishing company are listed below. Each record is an original cast album unless otherwise indicated. An asterisk (*) indicates recording is also available on cassettes. Two asterisks (**) indicate it is available on eight-track cartridges.

Barnum. Columbia. (*) (**)
Camelot (London cast). Stet DS. (*)
A Day in Hollywood/A Night in the Ukraine. DRG. (*)
Elephant Man, The (with John Morris). Pacific.
42nd Street. RCA. (*) (**)
Good Old Bad Oklahoma. London OC
Lena Horne: The Lady and Her Music (2 records). Qwest (distributed by Warners)
Make Me an Offer. A.E.
On Your Toes. DS. (*)
One Mo' Time. Warwick. (*) (**)
Pirates of Penzance, The (2 records). Elecktra Asylum
Robert & Elizabeth. London OC. A.E.1.
Rock Justice. EM. (*) (**)
Scrambled Feet. DRG. (*)
Sophisticated Ladies (2 records). RCA
Tintypes (2 records). DRG
Woman of the Year. Arista

NECROLOGY

MAY 1980–MAY 1981

PERFORMERS

Adams, Robert E. (59)—May 15, 1980
Alexander, C.K. (57)—September 2, 1980
Allen, Gharme (89)—October 4, 1980
Armstrong, Jean Abbott (58)—January 17, 1981
Astaire, Adele (83)—January 25, 1981
Baker, Frank (86)—December 30, 1980
Baker, Jack E. (68)—October 5, 1980
Baptiste, Charles (58)—January 23, 1981
Barbee, John (88)—April 20, 1981
Barr, Leonard (77)—November 22, 1980
Barrett, Elaine (58)—October 4, 1980
Barrett, Sheila (71)—August 10, 1980
Barrett, Wilson (80)—Winter 1981
Barry, Donald (69)—July 17, 1980
Barton, Elsie (82)—October 29, 1980
Battista, Miriam (68)—December 24, 1980
Baucom, Earl (70)—March 16, 1981
Beard, Matthew (57)—January 8, 1981
Beauvell, Ria (73)—December 20, 1980
Beeks, Clarence (58)—March 21, 1981
Beir, Fred (53)—June 3, 1980
Berkoff, Louis (78)—March 14, 1981
Biddleman, Christine Fokine (61)—February 18, 1981
Billimoria, Eddie (70's)—February 18, 1981
Bloch, Ruth Anderson (57)—June 22, 1980
Bock, Sybil (mid-70's)—May 28, 1980
Bondi, Beulah (92)—January 11, 1981
Bonelli, Richard (91)—June 7, 1980
Boone, Richard (63)—January 10, 1981
Bowen, Reuben (63)—August 21, 1980
Brazzi, Lydia (late 50's)—April 21, 1981
Breisford, Albert (74)—Summer 1980
Brice, Eugene (67)—October 31, 1980
Brown, Kelly (52)—March 13, 1981
Brunson, Perry (48)—April 30, 1981
Burbig, Henry (83)—December 14, 1980
Burt, Benny (80)—May 27, 1980
Busch, Ernst (80)—June 8, 1980
Bux, Kuda (mid-70's)—February 5, 1981
Cairn, Victor (48)—January 2, 1981
Calahan, William (50)—April 6, 1981
Campbell, Jim P. (67)—September 24, 1980
Carroll, Joe (65)—February 1, 1981
Cavanagh, Peter (66)—February 23, 1981
Chalfant, Frank E. (59)—January 3, 1981

Chambliss, Woodrow (66)—January 8, 1981
Clarke, Everett (68)—September 9, 1980
Cobbey, Marguerite—September 25, 1980
Coggin, Barbara (41)—January 19, 1981
Cookson, Maurine—January 8, 1981
Crawford, Kathryn (72)—December 7, 1980
Cross, James (61)—January 25, 1981
Dahmer, Wayne (40)—September 25, 1980
Dassin, Joe (42)—August 21, 1980
Davenport, Doris (63)—June 18, 1980
Davis, Jim (65)—April 26, 1981
Daykarhanova, Tamara (91)—August 2, 1980
De Banzie, Brenda (66)—March 5, 1981
Delaney, Mary O'Moore (77)—May 27, 1980
Denver, Maryesther (62)—June 3, 1980
Dieudonne, Helene (93)—Autumn 1980
Dime, James (83)—May 11, 1981
Dixon, Jean (85)—February 12, 1981
Dodd, Molly (late 50s)—March 26, 1981
Douglas, Helen Gahagan (79)—June 28, 1980
Eline, Marie—January 3, 1981
Elsom, Isobel (87)—January 12, 1981
Engel, Roy (67)—Winter 1981
Enlow, Grayson Maynard (63)—May 18, 1980
Enserro, Michael T. (62)—March 4, 1981
Ernster, Dezso (82)—February 15, 1981
Erway, Ben (88)—February 6, 1981
Escudero, Vincente (91)—December 4, 1980
Euard, Opal (80s)—May 13, 1980
Evans, Joan Hathaway—February 6, 1981
Evans, Madge (71)—April 26, 1981
Evelyn, Clara (96)—May 22, 1980
Faire, Virginia Brown (75)—June 30, 1980
Fallis, Barbara (56)—September 5, 1980
Farrand, Jan (52)—November 4, 1980
Faye, Herbie (81)—June 28, 1980
Feraldis, Marguerite (65)—November 10, 1980
Fielder, Frank (96)—December 24, 1980
Foran, Mary (61)—April 10, 1981
Fordred, Dorice (77)—August 4, 1980
Francis, Eve (84)—December 6, 1980
Fuller, Frances (73)—December 18, 1980
Gafni, Miklos (59)—March 8, 1981
Gale, Alan (72)—May 26, 1980
Gardiner, Reginald (72)—July 7, 1980
Garner, Alice Keolahou (70)—October 18, 1980
Gilbert, Olive (80s) February 19, 1981

Glass, Mel (60)—September 3, 1980
Godfrey, Freda (91)—September 5, 1980
Gollner, Nana (73)—August 30, 1980
Green, Aileen (59)—July 9, 1980
Hale, Richard (88)—May 18, 1981
Hanneman, Frederick G. (66)—October 3, 1980
Hardin, Tim (40)—December 29, 1980
Harrington, Carolyn T. (87)—December 8, 1980
Harris, Alan L. (78)—June 15, 1980
Hartman, Sylvia Stone (76)—February 26, 1981
Hayes, Gertrude Jr. (76)—December 13, 1980
Hazelton, Lasca Winter—August 8, 1980
Heidt, Joan (67)—January 3, 1981
Helwig, Alphone—April 2, 1981
Hendricks, Colleen J. (25)—May 5, 1981
Hendrix, Wanda (52)—February 1, 1981
Henry, Hank (74)—March 31, 1981
Hilger, Winifred Stockwell (96)—February 8, 1981
Hines, Janear (30)—March 2, 1981
Hite, Wiletta D. (62)—March 20, 1981
Hodgson, Laura (88)—June 1980
Hoerbiger, Paul (87)—Winter 1981
Hoffman, Clarence (62)—March 26, 1981
Hokul, Ron (42)—November 1980
Holtz, Lou (87)—September 22, 1980
Huber, Paul (85)—March 14, 1981
Innes, Edward Gordon (73)—December 29, 1980
Isaacs, Norman Kaleimanuia (55)—December 2, 1980
Jackson, Eddie (84)—July 15, 1980
Jackson, Irene Williams (84)—December 6, 1980
Janney, Leon (63)—October 28, 1980
Jessel, George (83)—May 23, 1981
Johnson, Brad (56)—April 4, 1981
Jones, London B. (79)—January 2, 1981
Jordan, Peggy Knudsen (57)—July 11, 1980
Joslyn, Allyn Morgan (79)—January 21, 1981
Joyce, Yootha (53)—August 24, 1980
Justice, Barry (39)—September 1980
Kelem, Adeline Neece (45)—November 26, 1980
Kent, Arthur (74)—December 3, 1980
Kunze, Alice (65)—March 20, 1981
Laird, Kenneth (50)—May 29, 1980
Latino, Anthony P. (51)—March 17, 1981
Laurie, John (83)—June 23, 1980
Lee, Bernard (73)—January 16, 1981
Lee, Elmer (75)—March 13, 1981
Levene, Sam (75)—December 28, 1980
Levkova, Sonja (66)—August 19, 1980
Lewis, Adah (83)—May 30, 1981

Lindsay, Margaret (70)—May 9, 1981
Loden, Barbara (48)—September 5, 1980
Loeb, Leo Jr. (67)—December 14, 1980
MacAdam, Virginia Root (96)—June 2, 1980
MacCloskey, Ysabel (64)—March 11, 1981
Malis, Fran (mid-50s)—June 22, 1980
Mallory, Dorothy (51)—May 4, 1981
Marsh, Garry (78)—Winter 1981
Marquard, Rube (90)—June 2, 1980
Martin, Strother (61)—August 1, 1980
Matthews, Anne Elstner (82)—January 29, 1981
May, Alyce (mid-60s)—December 31, 1980
McCauley, John B. (79)—June 13, 1980
McConnell, Margaret (54)—March 28, 1981
McCormick, Parker—July 22, 1980
McDade, Wendy (29)—April 6, 1981
McDowell, Norman—July 4, 1980
McGraw, Charles (66)—July 29, 1980
McLean, Grace (Dryborough)—August 22, 1980
McQueen, Steve (50)—November 7, 1980
Michael, Mary (77)—November 6, 1980
Midgley, Walter (66)—September 18, 1980
Milne, Lennon—Summer 1980
Morrow, Mary K.—July 3, 1980
Murdock, Kermit (72)—February 11, 1981
Myers, Carmel (80)—November 9, 1980
Nehrling, W.A. (69)—May 26, 1980
Ney, Marie (86)—April 11, 1981
Nugent, Norma Lee (81)—December 12, 1980
Nye, Hermes (72)—January 25, 1981
O'Connell, Arthur (73)—May 18, 1981
O'Connor, Effie (91)—January 11, 1981
O'Neil, Barbara (70)—September 3, 1980
Ormond, Ron (70)—May 11, 1981
Osbiston, Max (66)—March 12, 1981
Palace, John T. (85)—May 29, 1980
Parker, Donald (42)—January 8, 1981
Paskman, Alma Rosine (87)—December 2, 1980
Passer, Dirch (54)—Summer 1980
Patrick, Gail (69)—July 6, 1980
Paul, Charles (Beulcke) (67)—June 15, 1980
Pavloff, Michel (90)—May 13, 1981
Pearl, Irwin (35)—November 13, 1980
Petroff, Paul (73)—April 27, 1981
Phillpotts, Ambrosine (68)—October 12, 1980
Polen, Nat (66)—May 3, 1981
Ponselle, Rosa (84)—May 25, 1981
Prevost, Jeanne (93)—November 24, 1980
Raft, George (85)—November 24, 1980
Randolph, Lillian (65)—September 12, 1980
Renaldo, Duncan (76)—September 3, 1980
Rhodes, Lila (90)—October 5, 1980
Riker, Lois Long (96)—February 13, 1981

Robbins, Penny (50)—November 4, 1980
Roberts, Rachel (53)—November 27, 1980
Robinson, Cece (57)—January 10, 1981
Rochelle, Claire (70s)—May 23, 1981
Royce, Riza (72)—October 20, 1980
Saad, Francis (50)—November 5, 1980
Sagal, Boris (58)—May 24, 1981
Sands, Dorothy (87)—September 11, 1980
Santorio, Jack (82)—October 23, 1980
Sappington, Harriet R. (83)—June 16, 1980
Savant, Dean Dominick (82)—November 6, 1980
Savian, Nick (56)—November 8, 1980
Schaefer, Lorraine (60)—November 14, 1980
Sellers, Peter (54)—July 24, 1980
Shellhamer, Herbert (84)—January 21, 1981
Sheriff, Ernest J. (83)—May 22, 1981
Sherman, Mary (93)—August 13, 1980
Shimoda, Yuki (59)—May 21, 1981
Shove, Dawna (53)—April 14, 1981
Skibine, George (60)—January 14, 1981
Smith, Joe (97)—February 22, 1981
Spiegel, Maxine Burdette (76)—Winter 1981
Stanbury, Douglas (81)—December 6, 1980
Stark, Jim (47)—April 5, 1981
Steele, Joseph Henry (85)—September 21, 1980
Steiner, Dorothy P. (80)—January 12, 1981
Stempel, Jane Arden (76)—March 21, 1981
Stone, Milburn (75)—June 12, 1980
Stone, Sylvia (76)—July 30, 1980
Stratten, Dorothy (20)—August 14, 1980
Strode, Luukialuana (63)—September 17, 1980
Strong, Michael (mid-50s)—September 17, 1980
Stuart-Fife, John T. (78)—January 11, 1981
Sullivan, Lee (70)—May 29, 1981
Sunada, Mae Utaka (49)—June 6, 1980
Sundarambal, Kodumudi Balambal (72)—Autumn 1980
Swartzkoph, Marie T. Lumley (97)—August 15, 1980
Sweetser, Norman (86)—August 28, 1980
Sylvia, Gaby (60)—June 26, 1980
Szekely, Rudolph R. (81)—January 14, 1981
Tannen, Charles D. (65)—Winter 1981
Tanner, Pearl King (100)—July 16, 1980
Teeman, Eleanor Klein (55)—July 15, 1980
Thatcher, Torin (76)—March 4, 1981
Thomas, Billy (49)—October 10, 1980
Thomas, David (73)—January 27, 1981
Thorn, Pauline Kramer (72)—January 1, 1981
Van, Bobby (51)—July 31, 1980
van Loon, Gerard William (69)—November 11, 1980
Veloz, Frank (70s)—February 27, 1981
Versois, Odile (50)—June 23, 1980

Villard, Frank (63)—September 1980
Walker, Ray (76)—October 6, 1980
Walsh, Sammy (mid-70s)—October 5, 1980
Walton, Florence (90)—January 7, 1981
Ward, Anna M. (83)—Winter 1981
Ward, Edna Northlane (99)—February 2, 1981
Warner, Jack (85)—May 24, 1981
West, Mae (87)—November 22, 1980
Wharton, Betty (69)—October 13, 1980
Wilson, Susan B. (66)—February 27, 1981
Wortman, Don (53)—January 13, 1981
Wright, O.V. (41)—November 16, 1980
Young, Pearl (85)—January 24, 1981
Yung, Sen (65)—November 9, 1980
Zimelman, Samuel (80)—July 5, 1980

PLAYWRIGHTS

Amidei, Sergio (76)—April 14, 1981
Bagnold, Enid (91)—March 31, 1981
Barber, Philip (78)—May 8, 1981
Connell, Vivian (76)—March 24, 1981
Connelly, Marc (90)—December 21, 1980
Cree, Sam (52)—October 25, 1980
Davis, Fitzroy K. (68)—September 30, 1980
Fabbri, Diego (69)—Summer 1980
Frings, Ketti (71)—February 11, 1981
Gilbert, Willie (64)—December 2, 1980
Gray, Nicholas S. (61)—March 17, 1981
Green, Paul (87)—May 4, 1981
Gribble, Harry W. (90)—January 28, 1981
Guillox, Louis (81)—October 14, 1980
Hays, Hoffman Reynolds (76)—October 17, 1980
Levy, Melvin (76)—December 1, 1980
Long, Reginald (80's)—August 12, 1980
Lortz, Richard (63)—November 5, 1980
Mercer, David (52)—August 8, 1980
Norman, Frank (49)—December 23, 1980
Nugent, Elliott (83)—August 9, 1980
Ober, Harry L. (72)—July 26, 1980
Pascal, John Robert (48)—January 7, 1981
Richards, Stanley (62)—July 26, 1980
Robertson, Milton (66)—March 22, 1981
Robinson, Charles Knox (79)—June 4, 1980
Saroyan, William (72)—May 18, 1981
Schary, Dore (74)—July 6, 1980
Simon, Robert (84)—April 27, 1981
Sneider, Vernon J. (64)—May 1, 1981
Stewart, Donald Ogden (85)—August 2, 1980
Stuart, Aimee (95)—April 17, 1981
Thomas, Gwyn (67)—April 13, 1981
Travers, Ben (94)—December 18, 1980
Yablokoff, Herman (77)—April 3, 1981

Zavin, Benjamin R. (61)—February 23, 1981
Zelinka, Sydney (74)—January 17, 1981

COMPOSERS, LYRICISTS

Adamson, Harold (73)—August 17, 1980
Alsop, Mary O'Hara (94)—October 15, 1980
Alter, Louis (78)—November 5, 1980
Barber, Samuel (70)—January 23, 1981
Cassel, Mana Zucca (89)—March 8, 1981
Cesana, Otto (81)—December 9, 1981
de Stefano, Salvatore Mario (94)—May 18, 1981
Edwards, Sherman (61)—March 30, 1981
Forrest, Jimmy (60)—August 1980
Friedhofer, Hugo (79)—May 17, 1981
Grainer, Ron (57)—February 21, 1981
Green, Bud (83)—January 2, 1981
Handy, Charles Eugene (90)—August 5, 1980
Hanson, Howard (84)—February 26, 1981
Harburg, Edgar Y. (84)—March 5, 1981
Heyer, Bill (54)—August 26, 1980
Heyman, Edward (74)—March 30, 1981
Johnson, J.C. (84)—February 27, 1981
Kaempfert, Bert (56)—June 22, 1980
Lawrence, William (85)—March 17, 1981
Lennon, John (40)—December 8, 1980
Liefland, Wilhelm E. (41)—August 25, 1980
Lloyd, Norman (70)—July 31, 1980
Lowe, Ruth (Sandler) (66)—January 3, 1981
Malneck, Matty (78)—February 25, 1981
McPeek, Ben (46)—January 14, 1981
Miller, Jacques (78)—August 30, 1980
Montenegro, Hugo (55)—February 6, 1981
Moore, Thelma Matesky (66)—November 30, 1980
Nohain, Jean (81)—January 25, 1981
Padwa, Vladimir (81)—April 28, 1981
Pearson, Duke (47)—August 4, 1980
Pitot, Genevieve (71)—October 4, 1980
Pysh, Fred S. (75)—April 9, 1981
Ravitz, Shlomo (95)—December 28, 1980
Reggiani, Stephane (37)—July 29, 1980
Rogers, Eric (60)—April 8, 1981
Russell, Gene (49)—May 3, 1981
Sauter, Eddie (66)—April 21, 1981
Schramm, Rudolf (78)—April 6, 1981
Schudson, Hod David (38)—November 17, 1980
Shapiro, Ted (81)—May 26, 1980
Steele, Larry—June 18, 1980
Stern, Jack (66)—September 10, 1980
Valle, Joe (57)—November 13, 1980
Wilder, Alec (73)—December 24, 1980
Williams, Mary Lou (71)—May 28, 1981
Worth, Stan (48)—August 31, 1980

CRITICS

Ager, Cecilia (79)—April 3, 1981
Askinazy, Sam (62)—September 29, 1980
Birdoff, Harry (80)—May 11, 1981
Cheney, Sheldon Warren (94)—October 10, 1980
Clurman, Harold (78)—September 9, 1980
Crowther, Bosley (75)—March 7, 1981
Eisenman, Mort (80)—December 23, 1980
Fallon, Gabriel (81)—June 10, 1980
Golea, Antoine (74)—October 12, 1980
Gormley, Paul (72)—March 12, 1981
Hall, Bob Z. (74)—December 13, 1980
Haskell, Arnold L. (77)—November 16, 1980
Kohler, Roy (58)—January 16, 1981
Lee, Mary Ann (44)—February 12, 1981
McCaslin, Walt (57)—April 17, 1981
McCormick, T. Bidwell (84)—April 27, 1981
Mishkin, Leo (74)—December 27, 1980
Monahan, Kasper (86)—August 24, 1980
Perlov, Yitchok (69)—November 17, 1980
Simon, Robert (84)—April 27, 1981
Tynan, Kenneth (53)—July 29, 1980
Watts, Richard (82)—January 2, 1981
Woodbury, George Mitchell (83)—March 23, 1981

CONDUCTORS

Abas, Nathan (83)—June 1, 1980
Barnet, Charles C. (68)—March 23, 1981
Brown, Bernard R. (82)—February 20, 1981
Bruce, Leslie L. (75)—January 26, 1981
Bryan, Donald P. (80)—Winter 1981
Burgin, Richard (88)—April 29, 1981
Fields, Shep (70)—February 23, 1981
Froeba, Frank (73)—February 18, 1981
Gorodetzer, Bernard (73)—February 16, 1981
Gresh, Charles F. (74)—December 20, 1980
Haley, Bill (55)—February 9, 1981
Harnley, Leslie (62)—November 11, 1980
Harris, Lester E. (89)—December 1, 1980
Kogan, Boris—August 19, 1980
Kondrashin, Kiril (67)—March 7, 1981
Korn, Richard Kaye (72)—April 27, 1981
LaMonaca, Caesar (94)—August 21, 1980
Leonard, Richard (48)—January 19, 1981
Selvin, Ben (82)—July 15, 1980
Sherwood, Bobby Jr. (56)—January 23, 1981
Sinatra, Ray Dominic (76)—Autumn 1980
Singer, Jacques (70)—August 11, 1980
Speck, Jay (82)—October 14, 1980
Stabile, Dick (71)—September 25, 1980
Taylor, Clarence W. (63)—December 8, 1980

Thomas, John Adolph Jr. (93)—November 26, 1980
Turner, Ken (62)—Autumn 1980
Yates, Billy (73)—September 28, 1980

MUSICIANS

Aitken, Webster (72)—May 11, 1981
Alkire, Elbern H. (73)—January 25, 1981
Anderson, William (64)—April 20, 1981
Aronoff, Max (73)—April 11, 1981
Aronson, Ruth (Cove)—March 23, 1981
Astruc, Yvonne (91)—Autumn 1980
Azzaro, Albert W. (60)—July 4, 1980
Barnes, Paul (80)—April 13, 1981
Bartold, Gabriel (61)—October 31, 1980
Bastien, Vincent R. (71)—November 13, 1980
Bigard, Barney (74)—June 27, 1980
Bloomfield, Michael (38)—February 15, 1981
Butler, William H. (77)—March 19, 1981
Castillo, Louis (54)—October 20, 1980
Cavalli, Vincent (47)—April 25, 1981
Cazden, Norman (65)—August 18, 1980
Chamberlain, Willburne (59)—August 31, 1980
Cimber, Alphonse (83)—March 16, 1981
Cole, Cozy (71)—January 29, 1981
Cooke, Gary (24)—July 23, 1980
Coyle, Marion J. (84)—May 23, 1981
Crea, Bobby (52)—October 7, 1980
Crowder, Albert (77)—March 10, 1981
Duprey, Don (77)—May 22, 1980
Elkan, Henri (82)—June 12, 1980
Evans, Bill (51)—September 15, 1980
Ferrante, Joseph J. (51)—June 28, 1980
Fox, Virgil Keen (68)—October 25, 1980
Gerold, Carl (79)—August 9, 1980
Gidney, Bill (62)—May 14, 1981
Gilmore, Loring E. (71)—February 19, 1981
Hagnes, Helen (30)—July 23, 1980
Harms, John (74)—March 30, 1981
Hill, William (59)—January 9, 1981
Howell, John E. (55)—May 17, 1980
Iturbi, Jose (84)—June 28, 1980
Jenks, Harry Jr.—June 2, 1980
Johnson, Winifred (62)—October 15, 1980
Jordan, Arthur (85)—October 15, 1980
Juele, Frank (77)—February 20, 1981
Kaua, Arthur (63)—June 29, 1980
Kaufman, Schima (77)—March 3, 1981
Lais, John (55)—January 5, 1981
Landry, George (63)—August 9, 1980
Lastie, Walter (42)—December 28, 1980
Lougherty, Edward J. (62)—November 25, 1980
Mack, Austin (86)—October 15, 1980

Mastern, Carmen (68)—March 31, 1981
Menuhin, Hephzibah (Hauser) (60)—January 1, 1981
Metcalf, George (87)—June 14, 1980
Mischakoff, Mischa (85)—February 1, 1981
Moffatt, Alfred C. (73)—March 11, 1981
Morehouse, Chauncey (78)—October 31, 1980
Newell, Laura Crockett (80)—January 24, 1981
Pahinui, Gabby (59)—October 13, 1980
Pascuzzi, Wayne (66)—June 6, 1980
Procope, Russell (72)—January 21, 1981
Rafalo, Herman (84)—July 8, 1980
Ragland, Harold W. (77)—July 20, 1980
Rehrig, Howard W. (82)—March 30, 1981
Ricciardi, John Jr. (84)—November 14, 1980
Richter-Haaser (68)—December 17, 1980
Rose, Jean—December 29, 1980
Sadowski, Fryderyk (58)—June 14, 1980
Scharf, Henry (92)—April 23, 1981
Schlatter, Miriam (85)—September 12, 1980
Sebastian, John (65)—August 18, 1980
Shevland, Patrick E. (72)—October 18, 1980
Sullivan, Joseph Benjamin (79)—December 8, 1980
Verrecchia, Joseph (67)—October 14, 1980
Walters, Albert (74)—October 20, 1980
Watts, George J. (34)—Spring 1981
Williams, Helen Hull (77)—April 25, 1981
Xydis, Anna (58)—December 15, 1980

PRODUCERS, DIRECTORS, CHOREOGRAPHERS

Adams, Robert K. (72)—February 13, 1981
Banghart, Charles Kenneth (70)—May 25, 1980
Barstow, Richard (73)—May 2, 1981
Butcher, Blayne R. (77)—October 13, 1980
Cardin, George (68)—Spring 1981
Carroll, Peggy (66)—March 3, 1981
Champion, Gower (60)—August 25, 1980
Clair, Rene (82)—March 15, 1981
Coghill, Nevill (81)—November 8, 1980
Elliot, James S. (54)—January 12, 1981
Elliott, Laura Wilck (84)—May 30, 1980
Fitzpatrick, James (86)—June 12, 1980
Florman, Irving (88)—May 9, 1981
Gingold, Hedwig (79)—February 25, 1981
Henderson, Randall (59)—June 24, 1980
Hobson, Lucille Wagner (77)—January 21, 1981
Irving, Charles (68)—February 15, 1981
Knight, Arthur J. (72)—May 25, 1981
Krimsky, John (74)—October 7, 1980

Lambert, Sammy (72)—September 19, 1980
Lang, Howard M. (72)—March 1, 1981
Lathrop, Welland (75)—February 24, 1981
Lazowski, Yurek (66)—July 6, 1980
Leathem, Ruth Elton (81)—August 6, 1980
Levin, Dan (58)—July 29, 1980
MacOwan, Michael (74)—August 25, 1980
Mathews, Hale (49)—May 22, 1980
Milestone, Lewis (84)—September 25, 1980
Plumb, Edward W. (72)—Summer 1980
Quick, George Rayburn (62)—August 26, 1980
Rawlings, John (51)—December 23, 1980
Reed, Marshall (62)—April 15, 1980
Sanft, Myron (62)—December 31, 1980
Schlissel, Jack (58)—February 10, 1981
Sendar, Saul (68)—August 17, 1980
Snyder, Sam (late 70's)—November 4, 1980
Spector, Arnold (72)—April 12, 1981
Stohn, Carl Jr. (56)—August 21, 1980

DESIGNERS

Anheier, Thomas L. (53)—December 21, 1980
Aronson, Boris (81)—November 16, 1980
Morrison, Paul (74)—December 29, 1980
Shafton, Jack (61)—March 7, 1981
Splittgerber, Lewis David (66)—October 30, 1980

OTHERS

Albach-Retty, Rosa (105)—August 26, 1980
Austrian-Hungarian court actress
Alvin, Joseph (72)—October 9, 1980
Publicist
Bernays, Doris Fleischman (88)—July 10, 1980
Publicist
Bertell, Jack (76)—November 5, 1980
Agent
Bronte, Peter (75)—January 18, 1981
Stage manager
Brooks, Alfred G. (53)—August 30, 1980
Theater arts teacher
Buechler, Gen. Theodore Earl (87)—November 6, 1980
Troop entertainment tours
Butlin, Sir William (80)—June 12, 1980
Philanthropist
Campbell, Patrick (67)—November 9, 1980
Wit, raconteur
Combs, Carl (64)—June 2, 1980
Publicist

Cuneo, Fred (81)—May 25, 1981
Company manager
Davidson, Joseph (77)—April 3, 1981
Speech, theater teacher
Dosse, Philip (55)—September 8, 1980
Publisher-editor
Earnfred, Thomas S. (84)—November 21, 1980
Publicist
Feinstone, Sol (92)—October 17, 1980
Philanthropist
Florian, Louise (54)—March 18, 1981
Artists' manager
Foley, George (62)—Spring 1980
Attorney
Foley, Paul A. (78)—May 4, 1981
Stage manager
Forman, William R. (68)—April 29, 1981
Founder, Pacific Theaters
Frank, Otto (91)—August 19, 1980
Father of Anne Frank
Frank, Rudy (67)—November 3, 1980
Publicist
Galamian, Ivan (78)—April 14, 1981
Violin teacher
Gibbs, Patricia Kook (48)—July 29, 1980
Play reader
Ginsberg, Diane (58)—March 29, 1981
Girls Friday of Showbusiness
Goldreyer, Michael (84)—April 31, 1981
Manager
Goldstone, Jules C. (80)—June 18, 1980
Agent
Gordon, Fran (late 50s)—July 15, 1980
Secretary, AGVA
Graham, Perry (Roger) (87)—November 10, 1980
Reagan aide
Habich, William (71)—July 7, 1980
Louisville Ballet
Haggerty, Helen (77)—March 14, 1981
American Theater Wing
Halsey, Reece (65)—June 16, 1980
Talent agent
Harris, J. Jeff (64)—September 13, 1980
Booking agent
Harris, John P. (63)—January 31, 1981
Theater manager
Herz, Harold W. (97)—August 23, 1980
Investor
Holleb, Lou (90)—September 19, 1980
Vaudeville booker
Jelliffe, Russel (88)—June 7, 1980
Founder, Karamu House
Kahn, Ade (64)—January 16, 1981
Publicist
Kintner, Robert E. (73)—December 20, 1980
President, NBC and ABC

Kipnis, Claude (42)—February 8, 1981
  Founder, Israeli Mime Theater
Kirkus, Virginia (86)—September 10, 1980
  Founder, book review service
Koudriavtzeff, Nicolas (84)—Summer 1980
  Canadian impressario
Larson, Elmer R. (62)—February 27, 1981
  Owner, Marigold Ballroom
Laurent, Jean (74)—October 23, 1980
  Co-founder, Ballet de l'Etoile
Leathem, Barclay (80)—February 1, 1981
  Drama teacher
Lee, Olga (81)—August 22, 1980
  Agent
Lewis, Stephen (33)—January 23, 1981
  Columnist, interviewer
Lindquist, John (90s)—September 1, 1980
  Dance photographer
Lynn, Lowell A. (47)—Spring 1981
  Drama teacher
MacHarg, Eddie (77)—November 29, 1980
  Personal manager
Manning, Knox (76)—August 26, 1980
  Chairman, AFTRA
Mark, Richard (58)—September 10, 1980
  Attorney
Martin, Pete (79)—October 22, 1980
  Editor, writer
Mayer, Arthur L. (94)—April 14, 1981
  Showman, teacher
McCarthy, Martin J.E. (76)—September 15,
  1980
  Charter member, Variety Club
McKay, Louis (72)—March 10, 1981
  Booking agent
Meiklejohn, William (78)—April 26, 1981
  Casting, talent executive
Milgram, David E. (73)—November 23, 1980
  National Ass'n of Theater Owners
Miller, John J. (76)—April 16, 1981
  Showman
Mitchell, Herbert (81)—August 2, 1980
  Still photographer
Morgan, Joe (72)—April 22, 1981
  Publicist
Munsell, Warren P. (90)—June 8, 1980
  Trustee, Actors' Fund
Nelson, Gilbert V. (57)—November 7, 1980
  Agent
Newman, Marcus L. (67)—August 1, 1980
  Agent
Nielsen, Arthur Charles (83)—June 1, 1980
  Founder, A.C. Nielsen Co.

Paranov, Pauline Hart—February 22, 1981
  Music teacher
Propper, Murray (58)—September 1, 1980
  Chief barker, Variety Club
Raines, Halsey (78)—January 22, 1981
  Publicist
Reeves, Roberta (50)—March 3, 1981
  Drama teacher
Richardson, Clair (59)—September 12, 1980
  Skylight Theater
Rikko, Fritz (76)—June 13, 1980
  Julliard professor
Schaff, George (95)—April 23, 1981
  Electrician
Schreiber, Ida (late 70s)—January 15, 1981
  S. California Theater Owners Ass'n
Segal, Ruth (58)—February 17, 1981
  Stage manager
Slaughter, Richard Lewis (73)—March 1,
  1981
  Drama teacher
Solomon, Florence (58)—April 2, 1981
  Writer, show business books
Stein, Jules C. (85)—April 29, 1981
  Founder, MCA
Stern, Edith (85)—September 11, 1980
  Philanthropist
Tamarin, Alfred H. (67)—August 18, 1980
  Publicist
Terracciano, Anthony (82)—August 8, 1980
  Philadelphia opera
Traill, Sinclair (76)—Winter 1981
  Jazz authority
Turner, Jim F. (36)—February 19, 1981
  Talent agent
Veidt, Kitty—November 22, 1980
  Talent agent
Vogel, Larry (84)—June 3, 1980
  Music publisher
Weinberg, Anne Obert (47)—June 21, 1980
  Publicist
Weissberger, L. Arnold (74)—February 27,
  1981
  Attorney
Whitaker, Rogers E.M. (82)—May 11, 1981
  Editor, writer
Williams, Edwina Dakin (95)—June 1, 1980
  Mother of Tennessee Williams
Willner, George (76)—January 17, 1981
  Agent
Yates, Reggie (81)—October 28, 1980
  Theatrical assistant

THE BEST PLAYS, 1894–1980

Listed in alphabetical order below are all those works selected as Best Plays in previous volumes in the *Best Plays* series. Opposite each title is given the volume in which the play appears, its opening date and its total number of performances. Those plays marked with an asterisk (*) were still playing on June 1, 1981 and their number of performances was figured through May 31, 1981. Adaptors and translators are indicated by (ad) and (tr), the symbols (b), (m) and (l) stand for the author of the book, music and lyrics in the cast of musicals and (c) signifies the credit for the show's conception.

NOTE: A season-by-season listing, rather than an alphabetical one, of the 500 Best Plays in the first 50 volumes, starting with the yearbook for the season of 1919–1920, appears in *The Best Plays of 1968–69.*

PLAY	VOLUME	OPENED	PERFS.
ABE LINCOLN IN ILLINOIS—Robert E. Sherwood	38–39.	.Oct. 15, 1938.	. 472
ABRAHAM LINCOLN—John Drinkwater	19–20.	.Dec. 15, 1919.	. 193
ACCENT ON YOUTH—Samson Raphaelson	34–35.	.Dec. 25, 1934.	. 229
ADAM AND EVA—Guy Bolton, George Middleton	19–20.	.Sept. 13, 1919.	. 312
ADAPTATION—Elaine May; and NEXT—Terrence McNally	68–69.	.Feb. 10, 1969.	. 707
AFFAIRS OF STATE—Louis Verneuil	50–51.	.Sept. 25, 1950.	. 610
AFTER THE FALL—Arthur Miller	63–64.	.Jan. 23, 1964.	. 208
AFTER THE RAIN—John Bowen	67–68.	.Oct. 9, 1967.	. 64
AH, WILDERNESS!—Eugene O'Neill	33–34.	.Oct. 2, 1933.	. 289
AIN'T SUPPOSED TO DIE A NATURAL DEATH—(b, m, l) Melvin Van Peebles	71–72.	.Oct. 7, 1971.	. 325
ALIEN CORN—Sidney Howard	32–33.	.Feb. 20, 1933.	. 98
ALISON'S HOUSE—Susan Glaspell	30–31.	.Dec. 1, 1930.	. 41
ALL MY SONS—Arthur Miller	46–47.	.Jan. 29, 1947.	. 328
ALL OVER TOWN—Murray Schisgal	74–75.	.Dec. 12, 1974.	. 233
ALL THE WAY HOME—Tad Mosel, based on James Agee's novel *A Death in the Family*	60–61.	.Nov. 30, 1960.	. 333
ALLEGRO—(b,l) Oscar Hammerstein II, (m) Richard Rodgers	47–48.	.Oct. 10, 1947.	. 315
AMBUSH—Arthur Richman	21–22.	.Oct. 10, 1921.	. 98
AMERICA HURRAH—Jean-Claude van Itallie	66–67.	.Nov. 6, 1966.	. 634
AMERICAN BUFFALO—David Mamet	76–77.	.Feb. 16, 1977.	. 135
AMERICAN WAY, THE—George S. Kaufman, Moss Hart	38–39.	.Jan. 21, 1939.	. 164
AMPHITRYON 38—Jean Giraudoux, (ad) S. N. Behrman	37–38.	.Nov. 1, 1937.	. 153
ANDERSONVILLE TRIAL, THE—Saul Levitt	59–60.	.Dec. 29, 1959.	. 179
ANDORRA—Max Frisch, (ad) George Tabori	62–63.	.Feb. 9, 1963.	. 9
ANGEL STREET—Patrick Hamilton	41–42.	.Dec. 5, 1941.	.1,295
ANIMAL KINGDOM, THE—Philip Barry	31–32.	.Jan. 12, 1932.	. 183
ANNA CHRISTIE—Eugene O'Neill	21–22.	.Nov. 2, 1921.	. 177
ANNA LUCASTA—Philip Yordan	44–45.	.Aug. 30, 1944.	. 957
ANNE OF THE THOUSAND DAYS—Maxwell Anderson	48–49.	.Dec. 8, 1948.	. 286
*ANNIE—(b) Thomas Meehan, (m) Charles Strouse, (l) Martin Charnin, based on Harold Gray's comic strip "Little Orphan Annie"	76–77.	.Apr. 21, 1977.	.1,717
ANOTHER LANGUAGE—Rose Franken	31–32.	.Apr. 25, 1932.	. 344
ANOTHER PART OF THE FOREST—Lillian Hellman	46–47.	.Nov. 20, 1946.	. 182
ANTIGONE—Jean Anouilh, (ad) Lewis Galantière	45–46.	.Feb. 18, 1946.	. 64
APPLAUSE—(b) Betty Comden and Adolph Green, (m) Charles Strouse, (l) Lee Adams, based on the film *All About Eve* and the original story by Mary Orr	69–70.	.Mar. 30, 1970.	. 896

INDEX

Play titles appear in **bold face**. *Bold face italic* page numbers refer to those pages where complete cast and credit listings for New York productions may be found.